If found As
return to
Ramiro Arellano
Dept Anesthesia

Risk Adjustment for Measuring Healthcare Outcomes

Second Edition

Risk Adjustment for Measuring Healthcare Outcomes

Second Edition

Edited by
Lisa I. Iezzoni

Health Administration Press
Chicago, Illinois

01   00   99   98   97   5   4   3   2   1

Library of Congress Cataloging-in-Publication Data

Risk adjustment for measuring healthcare outcomes / edited by Lisa I. Iezzoni. — 2nd ed.
    p.   cm.
   Includes bibliographical references and index.
   ISBN 1-56793-054-9
   1. Health risk assessment.   2. Outcome assessment (Medical care)   I. Iezzoni, Lisa I.
RA427.3.R567   1997
362.1—dc21   97-21
                                                       CIP

The paper used in this publication meets the minimum requirements of American National Standard for Information Sciences—Permanence of Paper for Printed Library Materials, ANSI Z39.48-1984. ∞™

Health Administration Press
A division of the Foundation of the
   American College of Healthcare Executives
One North Franklin Street, Suite 1700
Chicago, IL 60606-3491
312/424-2800

Contents

Tables

Figures and Exhibits

Figures

Exhibits

Preface

Examining healthcare outcomes is the conceptual cornerstone of efforts to rationalize the American healthcare system. Analyzing outcomes, or how patients do, helps to distinguish effective from ineffective treatments and to identify areas needing improvement. Given the major changes reconfiguring America's healthcare landscape—from the growing reach of managed care to tightened constraints on resource use to heightened competition across plans and providers to fundamental restructuring of Medicare and Medicaid—questions about maintaining access and quality abound. Monitoring healthcare outcomes can highlight areas requiring attention or further investigation.

Meaningful comparisons of patients' outcomes—whether across therapeutic options or care providers—requires adjustment for patient risk. Risk adjustment "levels the playing field," accounting for factors that patients bring to healthcare encounters that could affect their outcomes. Risk adjustment facilitates comparisons of "apples to apples," sorting patients by similar characteristics so that like is compared to like. Controlling for patients' risk factors is essential for drawing useful inferences from observed healthcare outcomes about treatment effectiveness, provider performance, or quality of care.

Our book aims to introduce the issues underlying risk adjustment and to suggest important conceptual and methodological considerations in designing and evaluating a risk-adjustment strategy. This second edition builds on the conceptual discussions of the first edition, adding more empirical evidence to underscore important points. Since completing the first edition in 1993, significant studies involving risk adjustment have either concluded or published pertinent findings, including the National Veterans Affairs Surgical Risk Study, the Study to Understand Prognoses and Preferences for Outcomes and Risks of Treatment, the Medical Outcomes

Study, and the various Patient Outcome Research Teams funded by the Agency for Health Care Policy and Research (AHCPR). In addition, we completed a study, "Evaluating Severity Adjustors for Patient Outcome Studies," also supported by AHCPR, which examined a variety of tools for risk adjusting hospital outcomes. While still incomplete, the evidence about risk-adjustment methodologies is thus expanding, and we took advantage of this growing literature in preparing our second edition.

As will become clear, designing a meaningful risk adjustment methodology is inherently a multidisciplinary task. At a minimum, it requires input from diverse clinicians as well as research methodologists and statisticians. This was obvious to us, a multidisciplinary team, as we wrote this book. Although each chapter lists only one to three authors, this book was truly a collaborative undertaking. Most chapters reflect thoughtful and invaluable insight from the other contributors, bringing different knowledge and perspectives than those of the designated authors.

We wrote this book for a multidisciplinary audience, realizing that some readers will concentrate only on certain chapters. Because of this, selected key concepts are repeated throughout the book. In addition, we avoid detailed methodological discussions of techniques used in designing and evaluating risk-adjustment measures (e.g., logistic modeling, multivariable regression, Bayesian analysis, reliability testing). We discuss only aspects of these techniques that are especially relevant for risk-adjustment approaches and refer readers to excellent outside sources for in-depth methodological discussions.

Our initial thanks go to readers of the first edition for their generous support and helpful comments. We sincerely appreciate their input and advice, which has resulted in a better book. At their suggestion, this second edition includes a new chapter on methods for comparing outcomes across providers. In addition, we thank Elinor Walker, our AHCPR project officer, for her unwavering support and enthusiasm throughout our study of severity methodologies. We owe an enormous debt to Don Davies, research assistant, for meticulously orchestrating the technical production of this second edition, with activities ranging from checking facts to producing graphics to learning the equation editor to ordering towering stacks of references. We also thank the following individuals for their essential contributions: Kristin A. Miller, for help researching the literature and obtaining references; Roger B. Davis, Sc.D., for valuable comments on several chapters; Yevgenia D. Mackiernan, for conducting additional analyses using our AHCPR project database; and C. Ronald Bouchard, for secretarial assistance. Developers of selected severity measures cited throughout this book endured numerous queries and requests for information. We appreciate their patience and assistance. However, the final content of this book remains our responsibility alone.

L. I. I.

Chapter 1

Risk and Outcomes

Lisa I. Iezzoni

Risk permeates daily life. As individuals, we constantly confront choices large and small, often making decisions based on our perceptions of the risks posed by different options. In making these choices, we usually strive to achieve the best outcome, or at least one better than the alternatives. In colloquial usage, the word "risk" portends negative consequences: "the possibility of suffering harm or loss; danger" (Morris 1973, 1121). Given the personal stakes, decisions about healthcare especially require weighing risks of good versus bad outcomes, variously defined. Until now, what constituted acceptable risks and good or bad outcomes generally was determined solely by individual patients and their healthcare providers.

Recently, the aggregate impact of these myriad individual decisions has attracted in-depth scrutiny, given the effect on healthcare costs—one virtually guaranteed outcome of every healthcare decision. The staggering escalation in these costs, now consuming almost 14 percent of the nation's gross domestic product, is troubling enough. Equally worrisome are the unanswered questions: What are we buying for these rapidly rising healthcare dollars? What are the benefits, not only to individuals but also to American public health overall?

Persistent reports provide vexing findings of unexplained variations in use of expensive procedures and interventions across groups of ostensibly similar patients (Wennberg and Gittelsohn 1973; Chassin et al. 1986; Perrin et al. 1989; Wennberg et al. 1989; Chassin 1993; Welch et al. 1993; Center for Evaluative Clinical Studies, Dartmouth Medical School 1996). By the late 1980s, these concerns coalesced around calls to investigate the causes and consequences of varying healthcare practices. This initiated the "era of assessment and accountability," dubbed the third revolution in

American healthcare since World War II, following the eras of expansion (late 1940s to 1960s) and cost containment (1970s to early 1980s) (Relman 1988). In this context, outcomes of healthcare are defined broadly (Table 1.1):

> Outcomes are those changes, either favorable or adverse, in the actual or potential health status of persons, groups, or communities that can be attributed to prior or concurrent care. What is included in the category of "outcomes" depends, therefore, on how narrowly or broadly one defines "health" and the corresponding responsibilities of . . . practitioners or the health care system as a whole. (Donabedian 1985, 256)

This era of assessment and accountability emphasizes not only the clinical outcomes of care but also costs. Assessment focuses on outcomes of services delivered by providers in the general community or in usual and customary practice settings—the so-called effectiveness of care. This contrasts with the interest in efficacy typical of controlled clinical trials. In efficacy studies, treatments are administered by experts through tightly specified protocols in closely monitored practice settings.

Given its major role in underwriting health services delivery, the federal government championed this cause. In 1988, leaders of the Health Care Financing Administration (HCFA), the federal organization that administers the giant Medicare and Medicaid healthcare programs, were explicit:

> Federal health programs will no longer focus only on financing services, conducting biomedical research, implementing laws, and administering bureaucratic rules. Federal agencies will also be involved in the collection of data and the distribution of information about health care itself—information on health outcomes that will influence medical practices. (Roper et al. 1988, 1201)

Even leaders of the medical community supported evaluating the relative merits of different practices by examining their effect on patients' outcomes or health. At the 99th annual Shattuck Lecture to the Massachusetts

Table 1.1   Examples of Outcomes

- Longevity, mortality
- Acute physiologic stability
- Chronic disease and morbidity
- Complications, of disease or of medical care
- Physical functional status
- Psychosocial functioning
- Quality of life
- Costs of care
- Use of specified services
- Satisfaction with care, experiences with care

Medical Society, Paul Ellwood (1988) proposed a "technology of patient experience" centered around monitoring outcomes. He described "outcomes management" as a way "to help patients, payors, and providers make rational medical care–related choices based on better insight into the effect of these choices on the patient's life." This technology has four basic components:

1. Development of standards and guidelines
2. Routine, widespread measurement of disease-specific clinical outcomes and patient functioning and well-being
3. Collection of clinical and outcome data "on a massive scale"
4. Analysis and dissemination of findings from a continually expanding database (Ellwood 1988, 1551)

Arnold Relman, editor-in-chief emeritus of the *New England Journal of Medicine*, saw monitoring of outcomes as a way explicitly to direct scarce healthcare dollars:

> To provide a basis for decisions on the future funding and organization of health care, we will have to know more about the variations in performance among institutions and medical practitioners and what these may mean. We also need to know much more about the relative costs, safety, and effectiveness of all the things physicians do or employ in the diagnosis, treatment, and prevention of disease. (Relman 1988, 1221)

Few can argue with the obvious value of measuring and monitoring the outcomes of care. However, as with other concepts, the devil is in the details. Despite almost a decade of intensive research, consensus on methods for producing that technology of patient experience has proven elusive. Meaningful assessment of patients' outcomes generally requires:

- a measure of the outcome itself (Table 1.1)
- a way to adjust for patients' risks for various outcomes

Why is risk adjustment important? Failing to account adequately for patients' risks can have embarrassing consequences, as demonstrated by the furor accompanying the first public release of hospital-level mortality figures by HCFA in March 1986 (Brinkley 1986). According to governmental predictions, 142 hospitals had significantly higher death rates than predicted, while 127 had significantly lower rates. At the facility with the most aberrant death rate, 87.6 percent of Medicare patients died, compared to a predicted 22.5 percent. This facility, however, was a hospice caring for terminally ill patients; HCFA's model had not adequately captured patients' risks of death.

The goal of risk adjustment is to account for pertinent patient characteristics before making inferences about the effectiveness or quality of care based on patient outcomes. As suggested by HCFA's hospice example, comparisons of outcomes can prove misleading without first accounting for patients' risks for these outcomes. Risk adjustment "levels the playing field" and facilitates comparisons of "apples with apples." Risk adjustment is therefore essential to most outcome studies.

In prospective clinical trials testing new treatments (i.e., efficacy studies), investigators attempt to control for patient risk factors by restricting subject enrollment. However, even detailed enrollment protocols cannot identify all clinical characteristics that may affect patients' responses to therapy. Because of this, randomized controlled clinical trials—the "gold standard" test of treatment efficacy—aim to account for various patient attributes that could influence therapeutic performance. Randomization intends to assign patients to treatments using bias-free methods, yielding groups that are similar across patient characteristics potentially linked to therapeutic response (both patient attributes identified *a priori* and those that are unanticipated, unknown, or unmeasurable). However, because of their high costs and daunting logistical impediments, relatively few randomized controlled clinical trials are performed.

Studies of treatment effectiveness and medical outcomes differ from prospective clinical trials in several ways that have important implications for the risk-adjustment strategy. Most importantly, effectiveness studies are often retrospective and population based, evaluating events that occurred in the past to groups of patients outside the control of the investigators. Unlike neatly packaged clinical trials, patients are neither randomly allocated to providers and treatments nor does care follow prescribed protocols. According to Blumberg (1986, 355):

> Risk adjustment is a way to remove or reduce the effects of confounding factors in studies where the cases are not randomly assigned to different treatments. The key confounding factors are those aspects of health status that are causally related to the outcome under study.

Identification of patient risk factors can become ensnared in attempts to disentangle the appropriateness of services provided and assessments of the technical quality of care. In addition, data are often severely limited, particularly information about patients' clinical and psychosocial characteristics. Especially in the health policy context, a spectrum of disparate outcomes must be considered, ranging from resource use to death to quality of life. The factors that affect risk for these different outcomes may vary widely.

Purpose of This Book and the Second Edition

As with its first edition, this book examines conceptual and methodological issues raised in risk adjustment for studies of medical effectiveness and the outcomes of care. We touch upon many general methodological concerns—such as ways to measure reliability and validity, general linear and logistic modeling, and approaches for quantifying the performance of statistical models. We emphasize considerations most relevant to risk adjustment and therefore do not duplicate detailed technical discussions found in standard statistical and methodological textbooks.

Since completing the first edition, the U.S. healthcare delivery system has changed at a dizzying pace, with several major shifts affecting our scope and purpose. First was the 1994 demise of nationwide healthcare reform. References to President Bill Clinton's Health Security Act and its proposals for data systems and performance monitoring (White House Domestic Policy Council 1993) laced the first edition. Had that plan passed, methods for monitoring quality of care, including risk-adjusted outcomes, would have become largely uniform across the country.

The second relevant trend flows from this demise: Without a single, nationwide strategy for healthcare financing and delivery, dramatic changes are occurring within individual localities, regions, and states. Reform has been balkanized:

> There remains a moribund indemnity fee-for-service system (mainly Medicare) that may stay alive for a year or two on political life support. Consumers, especially healthy families, have been remarkably price sensitive, exhibiting surprisingly little loyalty to physicians or health plans . . . The largest and fastest-growing health plans are national or regional for-profit entities over which providers exert little control. The health plan's power is exercised through legal contracts with purchasers, consumers, and providers. (Ellwood and Lundberg 1996, 1084)

In certain regions, fierce competition among hospitals, physician groups, insurers, and newly configured healthcare organizations presents an ironic twist. Although optimal competition demands information, increasingly proprietary and competitive entities closely guard their information strategies (e.g., physician performance profiling methods) as their market edge. When data are shared, organizations producing these data choose their own approaches, leading sometimes to striking methodological differences even within regions. For example, Ohio and three of its cities (Cleveland, Cincinnati, and Dayton) each produce data on outcomes for hospitalized patients, but using totally different risk-adjustment strategies (Chapter 11). Literally hundreds of initiatives across the country involve risk-adjusted outcomes information, and new efforts arise almost daily.

Third, in many health policy settings, the words "risk adjustment" have been co-opted by those focused on capitated payment plans (Giacomini, Luft, and Robinson 1995). Capitation is currently the cornerstone of many efforts to contain healthcare costs. Obviously, when determining capitated payment rates, risk adjustment is important. Sicker patients are more likely to require health services and thus cost more over time; risk adjustment improves fairness of payment and reduces the likelihood that sick persons will be excluded from capitated plans. However, as described further in Chapter 2, the current policy usage of "risk adjustment" makes it especially important to declare the meaning assigned to these words—risk of what?

Finally, as elsewhere in our economy, information technologies within healthcare have developed, diversified, and disseminated exponentially. The clear distinction demarcated in the first edition between administrative and medical record information is blurring fast. Although we are probably further from universal paperless medical records than hoped, electronic transmittal of information in real time is increasingly the norm in other healthcare transactions, such as billing. Some of the severity measures used as examples in this book can accept electronic information into their scoring algorithms, downloaded directly from laboratory or other hospital information systems. New cross-walking nomenclatures and thesauruses are arising so that medical language can speak with a common voice, regardless of where words are generated. Therefore, the nature and scope of information readily available to assess patient risk is changing quickly and dramatically.

The combined consequences of these contextual shifts is that specific methods for risk adjustment—variously defined—are a rapidly moving target. New methods are introduced almost weekly, particularly for designing capitated payment systems or producing physician performance profiles. Risk adjustment for capitation and performance profiling forces the focus out of hospitals—where most traditional severity measures arose—and into outpatient settings. Many of these new approaches are proprietary (e.g., developed by insurers) and withheld from external scrutiny. Others are so new that few, if any, publications are available about them. Especially given the long lead time required to publish a book, we cannot pretend to be up-to-date about specific risk-adjustment methodologies.

Given these latter concerns, as in the first edition, we draw examples throughout the remainder of this book primarily about short-term outcomes of hospitalized patients, a dimension of risk often known as "severity of illness" (see Chapter 2). Measuring severity for hospitalized patients has been studied intensively for 15 years, and numerous relevant publications are easily available for interested readers. Hospital-based severity has persisted as a topic of political debate ever since Medicare implemented its prospective hospital payment system based on diagnosis-related groups (DRGs) in 1983. The general conceptual and methodological concerns raised by hospital-based severity systems also pertain to measures of other dimensions of risk. Nonetheless, we added two measures intended primarily for capitation or examining patients over time—Ambulatory Care

Groups (ACGs) and the Diagnostic Cost Groups–Hierarchical Coexisting Conditions (DCGs–HCCs) method. Both are well-published in the literature and thus accessible to readers.

The remainder of this introduction covers four areas. First, to lend perspective to current efforts, two historical precedents for outcomes studies and risk adjustment are briefly discussed. Second, the severity measures used as examples in remaining chapters are introduced. Third, our study, funded by the Agency for Health Care Policy and Research (AHCPR) involving many of these severity measures that are used for empirical examples throughout this book, is presented. Finally, this introduction closes by describing the book's organization and content of each chapter.

Historical Precedents

We tend to think ourselves unusually enlightened in examining outcomes of care. In fact, there are important historical precedents for this pursuit—noteworthy not only because outcomes data were compiled and compared but also because vigorous efforts were undertaken to discover the causes of variations and to use this knowledge to improve care. Many motivations for these activities, and consequent controversies, uncannily anticipate the debates occurring in our time (Iezzoni 1996).

For centuries, England gathered data on population death rates, primarily to track epidemic illness. Overwhelmed by deaths from plague, royal authorities initiated weekly "Bills of Mortality" in the early 1500s (Walker 1929). Starting late in the eighteenth century, the massive social upheavals of the industrial revolution heightened this interest. As populations shifted from the countryside, massing within congested industrial centers, statistics clearly depicted egregious public health consequences. By the 1830s, statistical societies had formed throughout England, founded by civic and business leaders intent on quantifying effects of these social changes. The archetypal member was "a liberal Whig, Unitarian, reform-minded" (Eyler 1979, 14). These early Victorian statisticians viewed "facts" as the scientific means to prompt political change.

English hospitals had independently accumulated statistics on their patients since the 1600s. Hospitals were primarily charitable institutions serving the poor; in the nineteenth century, even England's Registrar-General had trouble determining which institutions, or parts of institutions, were actually hospitals as opposed to workhouses: In 1861, 81 percent of beds for the physically ill were in workhouses (Pinker 1966). Statistics quantified results of their charity for wealthy benefactors and encouraged new subscribers and donations. As today, those paying for hospitals, even philanthropists, wanted proof they were getting their money's worth. In addition, as noted in an 1863 report for the Medical Officer of the Privy Council, "the public as a rule still look to the death-rates of hospitals as the best indication of their relative healthiness" (Bristowe and Holmes 1864, 512).

In 1863, Florence Nightingale (1820–1910) published the third edition of her *Notes on Hospitals*, recommending fundamental changes in the configuration, location, and operation of hospitals to reduce deaths due to unsanitary conditions (Iezzoni 1996). Seven years earlier, Nightingale had returned from Crimean War service at British military hospitals, perhaps the first wartime celebrity ever created by the news media (Cohen 1984). Crafted by *The Times* correspondent, her image as a lone lady nursing sick soldiers lit by her hand-held lamp earned Nightingale an admiring lifelong audience. This gentle, ministering angel persona, however, belied her tough-minded, focused administrative acumen: In 1855, six months after arriving at Barrack Hospital in Scutari, Turkey, she cut military hospital death rates from 42.7 to 2.2 percent (Cohen 1984).

Upon returning to England, Nightingale continued targeting military installations, but needing statistical help, she turned to William Farr (1807–1883), a physician and prominent social reformer who had conducted analyses for the Registrar-General since 1838. In 1856 they made a pact:

Florence Nightingale   Ernest Amory Codman

Courtesy of the Francis A. Countway Library of Medicine, Harvard University, Boston, Massachusetts.

Farr would assist her with army reforms while Nightingale would aid his efforts to reduce civilian deaths (Eyler 1979). In her 1863 *Notes on Hospitals,* Nightingale concentrated primarily on civilian hospitals.

Farr and Nightingale viewed the dangers posed by urban mid-nineteenth-century hospitals as obvious from their death rates, illustrated by deaths at "106 principal hospitals of England" in 1861 (Table 1.2). Most startling was the 90.84 "mortality per cent on inmates" at 24 London hospitals, taken verbatim from Farr's *24th Annual Report of the Registrar-General.* Based on these figures, Nightingale questioned the value of these inner-city hospitals, stating,

> "Facts such as these (and it is not the first time that they have been placed before the public) have sometimes raised grave doubts as to the advantages to be derived from hospitals at all, and have led many a one to think that in all probability a poor sufferer would have a much better chance of recovery if treated at home." (Nightingale 1863, 4)

Nightingale warned that patients' risks were not adequately captured by such figures, observing that, at a minimum, it was necessary to consider differences across hospitals in patient ages and "state of the cases on admission" (Nightingale 1863, 2). Despite these caveats, she observed that

Table 1.2 Mortality Per Cent. in the Principal Hospitals of England: 1861

	Number of SPECIAL INMATES on the 8th April, 1861.	Average Number of INMATES in each HOSPITAL.	Number of DEATHS registered in the Year 1861.	MORTALITY per Cent. on INMATES.
IN 106 PRINCIPAL HOSPITALS OF ENGLAND	12709	120	7227	56·87
24 London Hospitals	4214	176	3828	90·84
12 Hospitals in Large Towns ...	1870	156	1555 .	83·16
25 County and Important Provincial Hospitals	2248	90	886	39·41
30 Other Hospitals	1136	38	457	40·23
13 Naval and Military Hospitals ...	3000	231	470	15·67
1 Royal Sea Bathing Infirmary (Margate)	133	133	17	12·78
1 Dane Hill Metropolitan Infirmary (Margate)	108	108	14	12·96

Source: Nightingale 1863.

death rates were lower at facilities with better sanitation, less crowding in cramped wards, and locations far from sewage disposal and urban congestion. These observations supported Nightingale's theory about miasmas— noxious, disease-spreading vapors—and led her to propose changes in ward configuration, sanitation, and hospital location that ultimately contributed to reductions in hospital mortality. Nightingale introduced into hospitals fresh air, light, and ample space, and she apportioned patients to separate pavilions.

Nightingale continued to argue that compiling and disseminating outcome statistics for hospitals was critical to understanding and improving care. With an eerily modern ring, she lamented the state of this activity:

> Accurate hospital statistics are much more rare than is generally imagined, and at the best they only give the mortality which has taken place in the hospitals, and take no cognizance of those cases which are discharged in a hopeless condition, to die immediately afterwards, a practice which is followed to a much greater extent by some hospitals than by others. We have known incurable cases discharged from one hospital, to which the deaths ought to have been accounted and received into another hospital, to die there in a day or two after admission, thereby lowering the mortality rate of the first at the expense of the second. (Nightingale 1863, 2)

However, Nightingale emphasized that mortality should not be the only focus, stating, "If the function of a hospital were to kill the sick, statistical comparisons of this nature would be admissible" (Nightingale 1863, 4). She urged that, because health is the ultimate object of hospital care, statistics should concentrate on recovery and its speed. Nevertheless, 130 years after Nightingale's observations, information on patients' health following medical encounters is still rarely available.

The hospital statistics story involving Nightingale and Farr does not end here. Publication of *Notes on Hospitals* unleashed several months of acerbic public debate between Farr and his methodological critics. The testy tone and issues raised are similar to today's controversies surrounding releases of report cards on doctors and hospitals. Therefore, this story resumes as an epilogue to Chapter 11.

The most articulate early American proponent of monitoring outcomes of care was Ernest Amory Codman (1869–1940), a Boston surgeon (Berwick 1989; Donabedian 1989; Mulley 1989; Neuhauser 1990). The story, perhaps apocryphal, of how Codman first became interested in monitoring outcomes offers insight not only into his character but also his future methods. Codman and his Harvard Medical School classmate Harvey Cushing (1869–1939), who became a renowned neurosurgeon, served together as clerks at Massachusetts General Hospital (Neuhauser 1990). The role of the medical students was to provide anesthesia to surgical patients. After being anesthetized, Cushing's first patient vomited and died. Although Cushing was troubled by this event, the senior surgeon was unconcerned, stating that such deaths were fairly common. Cushing and Codman challenged each other to compare their patients' outcomes during the remainder of the clerkship. This challenge led both to maintain intraoperative records on each anesthetized patient; Codman's charts, for example, graphed a patient's pulse and respirations every five minutes. These efforts represent the first intraoperative anesthesia charting, now a standard practice. The winner of this challenge is unclear. In 1920, Cushing remembered that Codman had won, but in 1939 he wrote that Codman had lost (Neuhauser 1990).

This experience initiated Codman's lifelong interest—some might say obsession—with determining the outcomes of surgical care. He was not afraid to compare his results with those of others, although he acknowledged: "Comparisons are odious, but comparison is necessary in science. Until we freely make therapeutic comparisons, we cannot claim that a given hospital is efficient, for efficiency implies that the results have been looked into" (Codman 1934, xxiii). Codman's unique contribution was his effort to link specific interventions with their effects on patients. He labeled this perspective the "end results idea,"

> . . . which was merely the common-sense notion that every hospital should follow *every* patient it treats, long enough to determine whether or not the treatment has been successful, and then to inquire "if not, why not" with a view to preventing similar failures in the future. (Codman 1934, xii)

For surgical patients, this could require monitoring them for years following the operation.

Codman tried putting his end results idea into practice at Massachusetts General Hospital, tracking down as many patients as he could a year after they had left and bringing them back for an examination. These activities were viewed as extreme by some of his surgical colleagues. Nevertheless, Codman argued that this approach was essential for improving the quality of care:

> So I am called eccentric for saying in public: that Hospitals, if they wish to be sure of improvement,
>
> 1. Must find out what their results are.
> 2. Must analyze their results, to find their strong and weak points.
> 3. Must compare their results with those of other hospitals . . .
> 8. Must welcome publicity not only for their successes, but for their errors . . .
>
> Such opinions will not be eccentric a few years hence. (Codman 1917, 137)

Discouraged about the prospects for fully implementing the end results idea at Massachusetts General Hospital, in 1911 Codman opened his own ten-bed hospital on Pinkney Street in Boston's Beacon Hill, where he was assisted by two dozen other surgeons, including Cushing (Neuhauser 1990). He completely installed his end results tracking system, and he paid Thomas Todd Company to print annual volumes documenting the outcomes of each individual case treated during the year. If he believed that an error in treatment or other failure had occurred, he categorized the cause. Examples of types of causes include:

- Errors due to lack of technical knowledge or skill
- Errors possibly due to lack of judgment
- Errors due to lack of care or equipment
- Errors due to incorrect diagnosis
- Cases in which the nature and extent of the disease was the main cause of failure
- Cases who refused to accept treatment. (Codman 1917)

Thus, Codman linked specific outcomes to specific interventions or errors in a way that truly informed—going far beyond the information provided in today's report cards on doctors and hospitals (Chapter 11).

However, Codman continued fighting against what he perceived as laxity in the medical establishment, as suggested by the following dedication of the circa 1917 publication of the end results of Codman's hospital:

> This Volume is Dedicated to
> RICHARD C. CABOT
> because I respect his motives, admire his courage and energy,
> but heartily disapprove of some of his opinions and methods,
> for he seems to want to reform the bottom of the
> profession, while I think the blame
> belongs at the top.

In 1914 Codman resigned from Massachusetts General Hospital to protest the seniority system of promotion, which he viewed as antithetical to the end results idea. The day his resignation was accepted, he reapplied, asking to be appointed surgeon-in-chief on the grounds that the end results of his cases for the last decade were better than those of other surgeons. Of course this request was ignored, but two years later Massachusetts General Hospital had abandoned its seniority system of promotion. Nonetheless, this candor made Codman unpopular, and with few referrals, his hospital closed in 1918.

In his discussions surrounding the end results idea, Codman was clearly aware of the notion of risk. As he stated:

For the man who practices surgery, there are two kinds of mortality—chance and intentional.

Chance mortality is the kind which occurs unexpectedly, and which no amount of foresight can prevent. It is caused by unanticipated Calamities or Catastrophes. Death from pulmonary embolism is a good example . . . Is it not possible to determine what this percentage of danger is, just as easily as it is to compute fire risk? . . .

Intentional mortality is incurred by the chief surgeon when he attempts cases in which the condition is acknowledged to be grave. It is speculative-like gambling against known chances in a game in which skill, judgment, and luck all count. (Codman 1917, 93)

The era in which Codman practiced, however, had a somewhat different perspective than today. Nowadays, a major concern about releasing mortality or other outcome information is that providers will turn away difficult cases, fearing that a poor result will be held against them. In Codman's day,

. . . a certain number of deaths are necessary to the surgeon in his business. A surgeon whose cases always get well, gets no reputation for "nerve." It is said that he will never take a chance when he ought to do so. A surgeon must be "fearless" and "bold," and the only way he can prove that he is, is by a death now and then in his practice. (Codman 1917, 105)

Despite this, Codman's attitude toward compensation for his services is also rare today:

Shall I say in the future?:

1. You are too bad a risk; go to a first-class surgeon.
2. You are a bad risk; I must double my usual fee.
3. You are a bad risk; you need not pay unless you live.

All are logical. I like the last best. (Codman 1917, 106)

Both Nightingale and Codman viewed outcomes information as a means to the end of improving patient outcomes and quality of care. The lesson of much of their work is that it is not sufficient simply to know rates of events. One must know why these events occurred. The purpose of risk adjustment is to isolate one potential cause (i.e., patients' characteristics that inherently increase risk).

Although the remainder of this book concerns measurement of risk, we acknowledge that this is only a first step. In and of itself, risk adjustment is a narrow and arcane concern, albeit a necessary one. Other methods and approaches are required for taking the next step—for understanding how outcomes can be improved.

Severity Measures

As stated above, the following chapters draw examples primarily from the literature concerning "severity of illness" measures—methods that quantify risks of short-term outcomes for hospitalized patients. We focus on severity measures for hospitalized patients because this field is more developed than others and because it has generated considerable interest in health policy circles. Two measures, however, quantify patient risk over longer periods (e.g., a year) and are intended for capitating payment or examining care over time. Our goal throughout this book is to illustrate broad concepts that apply equally to other dimensions of risk.

As described above, new severity measures are continually introduced for a broad range of policy-related purposes, such as reimbursement, practice profiling, and monitoring quality of care (Chapter 11). New publications appear almost weekly. Our goal is therefore not to provide an exhaustive catalog of different methods. Instead, we emphasize approaches well represented in the current clinical and health services research literature so that readers will have easy access to pertinent references (Table 1.3).

Given these important caveats, the following paragraphs and tables provide a brief introduction to the severity measures. The tables are organized around basic concepts rather than individual methods, facilitating comparisons across the different measures.

Definitions of Severity

As suggested throughout the remaining chapters, the utility of a severity measure derives from how it defines severity. The measures considered here define severity by linking it to a specific outcome or clinical state (Table 1.4). Most view the acute care hospitalization as the episode of illness; some look at longer time frames, such as a year. Measures can be broadly split into those that implicitly or explicitly define severity based on resource use (e.g., cost, length of stay) and those that focus on more clinical definitions (e.g., risk of death, treatment difficulty, clinical instability). Many vendors now offer families of severity measures, with different versions designed to predict different outcomes.

Table 1.4 also describes the patient population addressed by the measure. Some patient populations involve all hospitalized patients or all hospitalized adults, variously defined (e.g., Medicare beneficiaries). However, others were developed for specific subgroups of patients (e.g., intensive care unit patients, persons with specified conditions) or for pediatric populations.

Table 1.3   Examples of Severity Measures and Selected Citations

Acronym	Name of System; Vendor or Source*	Selected Citations
ACGs	Ambulatory Care Groups; The Johns Hopkins University, Baltimore, MD (academic users) and CSC Healthcare Systems, Farmington Hills, MI	Starfield et al. 1991; Weiner et al. 1991 and 1996; Salem-Schatz et al. 1994; Fowles et al. 1996.
AIM	Acuity Index Method; Iaméter, San Mateo, CA	Thomas and Ashcraft 1991.
APACHE I II III	Acute Physiology and Chronic Health Evaluation Original version First revision Second revision; APACHE Medical Systems, Inc., McLean, VA	 Knaus et al. 1981. Knaus et al. 1985 and 1986. Knaus et al. 1991 and 1993; Knaus, Wagner and Lynn 1991; Shortell et al. 1994; Becker et al. 1995.
APR-DRGs	All Patient Refined Diagnosis-Related Groups; 3M Health Information Systems, Wallingford, CT	Edwards et al. 1994; Goldfield and Boland 1996.
CSI	Computerized Severity Index; International Severity Information Systems, Salt Lake City, UT	Horn et al. 1991; McGuire 1991; Averill et al. 1992; Iezzoni and Daley 1992; Horn, Sharkey, and Gassaway 1996.
DCGs–HCCs	Diagnostic Cost Groups–Hierarchical Coexisting Conditions; DxCG, Inc., Waltham, MA	Ash et al. 1989; Ellis and Ash 1995; Ellis et al. 1996.
DRGs	Diagnosis-Related Groups; 3M Health Information Systems, Wallingford, CT	Fetter et al. 1980; Vladeck 1984.
DS Clinical Coded Staging Scale	Disease Staging; SysteMetrics/MEDSTAT Group, Ann Arbor, MI Clinical criteria version Computerized version calculating disease categories and stages from discharge abstract data Computerized version calculating patient-level severity scales from discharge abstract data	Gonnella et al. 1990. Gonnella, Hornbrook and Louis 1984; Conklin et al. 1984. Gonnella, Hornbrook and Louis 1984; Conklin et al. 1984; Naessens et al. 1992; Yuen 1995. Markson et al. 1991.

Continued

Table 1.3   Continued

Acronym	Name of System; Vendor or Source*	Selected Citations
MMPS	Medicare Mortality Predictor System	Daley et al. 1988.
MPM	Mortality Probability Model	Lemeshow et al. 1988, 1993, and 1994; Zhu et al. 1996.
MedisGroups	MediQual's Atlas 2.0 (MedisGroups); MediQual Systems, Inc., Westborough, MA	
Original	Original version	Brewster et al. 1985; Iezzoni and Moskowitz 1988.
Empirical	Revised, empirically based version	Steen et al. 1993; Steen 1994.
NY CABG	New York State Cardiac Surgery Reporting System	Hannan et al. 1990, 1992, 1994, and 1995.
PMCs	Patient Management Categories; Pittsburgh Health Research Institute at Duquesne University, Pittsburgh, PA	Young, Swinkola, and Zorn 1982; Young 1984.
Categories	Patient Management Categories	
Paths	Patient Management Paths	
RIS	Relative Intensity Score	Young et al. 1985.
Severity Score	PMC Severity Score	Young, Kohler, and Kowalski 1994.
PRISM	Pediatric Risk of Mortality Score	Pollack, Ruttimann, and Getson 1987 and 1988; Pollack et al. 1994; Ruttimann, Pollack, and Fiser 1996.
RAND	Sickness on Admission Measure; RAND Corporation, Santa Monica, CA	Keeler et al. 1990; Kahn et al. 1992.
RAMI	Risk-Adjusted Mortality Index	DesHarnais et al. 1988; DesHarnais et al. 1990.
RACI	Risk-Adjusted Complication Index	DesHarnais et al. 1990; DesHarnais, McMahon, and Wroblewski 1991.
RARI	Risk-Adjusted Readmission Index	DesHarnais et al. 1990.
R-DRGs	Refined diagnosis-related groups developed by Yale University; different versions available from various vendors.	Health Systems Management Group, School of Organization and Management Yale University 1989; Freeman et al. 1991 and 1995; Edwards et al. 1994.

*If no specific source is listed, complete information is available in the published literature.

Table 1.4   Definitions of Severity and Pertinent Patient Populations

System	Definition of Severity	Pertinent Patient Population
ACGs	Expected resource use (ambulatory and total) over one year	All persons within a general population
AIM	Length of hospital stay within DRGs	All hospitalized patients
APACHE I II III	 In-hospital mortality In-hospital mortality Different versions: in-hospital mortality, length of stay	 Adults in intensive care units Adults in intensive care units Adults in intensive care units
APR-DRGs	Different versions: resource intensity (hospital charges), in-hospital mortality	All hospitalized patients
CSI	Treatment difficulty presented to physicians based on the combination of patients' diagnoses and the level of derangement of disease-specific signs and symptoms	All hospitalized patients
DCGs–HCCs	Total Medicare expenditures over the next year	Medicare beneficiaries; privately insured persons under 65 years of age
DRGs	Total hospital charges or length of stay	All hospitalized patients
DS Clinical Coded Staging Scale	 Complexity, etiology, and extent of organ system involvement Complexity, etiology, and extent of organ system involvement Definition depends on individual scale: total charges/costs, length of stay, readmission, in-hospital mortality, and complications of care	 All patients with one or more of 400+ diseases covering all clinical conditions All patients All hospitalized patients
MMPS	Death within 30 days of admission	Medicare beneficiaries hospitalized for stroke, pneumonia, acute myocardial infarction, or congestive heart failure

Continued

Table 1.4   Continued

System	Definition of Severity	Pertinent Patient Population
MPM	In-hospital mortality	Adults in intensive care units
MedisGroups		
Original	Clinical instability as indicated by in-hospital death	All hospitalized patients
Empirical	Different versions: in-hospital mortality based on Review 1 (admission period); in-hospital mortality based on Review 2 (mid-stay); length of stay; probability of receiving a Cesarean section	All hospitalized patients
NY CABG	In-hospital mortality	Adults undergoing coronary artery bypass graft surgery in New York state hospitals
PMCs		
Categories	Classification based on unique combinations of diagnoses and procedures	All hospitalized patients
Paths	Expected care components required	
RIS	Relative intensity of resources	All hospitalized patients
Severity Score	In-hospital morbidity and mortality	All hospitalized patients
PRISM	In-hospital mortality	Children in intensive care units
RAND	Death at 30 and 180 days following admission	Medicare beneficiaries hospitalized for congestive heart failure, acute myocardial infarction, pneumonia, cerebrovascular accident, or hip fracture
RAMI	In-hospital mortality	All hospitalized patients
RACI	In-hospital complications	All hospitalized patients
RARI	Readmission within 30 days of discharge	All hospitalized patients
R-DRGs	Total hospital charges and length of stay	All hospitalized patients

Role of Diagnosis

Throughout the late 1980s, researchers hotly debated whether severity is a diagnosis-specific construct. The measures included in Table 1.5 can be split into those using diagnosis in rating severity and those independent of diagnosis, or "generic." There are three broad strategies relating to diagnosis. Severity measures that are "independent of diagnosis" calculate patients' risks regardless of their diagnoses: The data used to quantify risk (e.g., values of physiologic variables) are scored identically across all patients. "Diagnosis-specific" methods use only patients within particular diagnoses in computing severity scores or deriving rating algorithms. For example, the empirically derived version of MedisGroups rates severity separately for patients within 67 mutually exclusive disease groups (Steen et al. 1993); the Medicare Mortality Predictor System (MMPS) was derived for only four conditions (stroke, pneumonia, acute myocardial infarction [AMI], and congestive heart failure). Finally, some methods "consider diagnoses" in measuring risk, combining separate ratings of severity for all diagnoses present (principal plus secondary) for an individual patient before producing an overall score. For instance, in calculating its value, the Relative Intensity Score (RIS) considers all Patient Management Categories (PMCs), and thus diagnoses, assigned to a patient; the Computerized Severity Index (CSI) rates severity separately for each disease present, then combines these ratings to compute an overall score.

Role of Major Surgery

Some measures define severity or case types using major surgery, while others do not (Table 1.5). This strategy relates directly to the goal of the classification scheme. If the method aims to predict hospitalization costs, including major surgery as a classification variable is important. For example, research has shown that much of the ability of the DRGs to predict costs derives from their grouping surgical cases with similar, relatively high costs and their differentiating expensive surgical cases from generally cheaper medical cases (Iezzoni et al. 1988).

Some measures do not explicitly classify cases by categories of major surgery, but because they consider case types within DRGs, major surgery is implicitly captured. For example, the Acuity Index Method (AIM) assigns cases to five severity levels nested within DRGs. Importantly, the purpose of AIM is to predict resource consumption, specifically length of stay.

Data Requirements and Method Development

An important attribute of a severity measure involves its data requirements. As shown in Table 1.6, these severity measures either use the

Table 1.5   Role of Diagnosis and Major Surgery in Quantifying Risk

System	Role of Diagnosis	Role of Major Surgery
ACGs	Assignments based on constellation of diagnoses in ambulatory and inpatient settings	Independent of major surgery and other procedures
AIM	Calculations performed within DRGs; therefore, considers diagnosis defined by DRG	Calculations performed within DRGs; therefore, considers major surgery as used by DRGs
APACHE I	Calculates APACHE score independent of diagnosis; calculates probability of death	Independent of major surgery
II	Calculates APACHE score independent of diagnosis; calculates probability of death using 50 disease categories	Distinguishes postoperative patients from others
III	Calculates APACHE score independent of diagnosis; calculates probability of death using 78 disease categories	Distinguishes postoperative patients from others
APR–DRGs	Groups medical cases by diagnosis, with some exceptions	Groups major surgery cases by type of operation
CSI	Calculates diagnosis-specific severity for each disease present; overall scores consider severity of all diagnoses	Independent of major surgery and other treatments
DCGs–HCCs	Predicts costs by summing incremental costs associated with each diagnosis present	Independent of major surgery; one version uses selected, invasive, life-sustaining procedures in addition to diagnoses
DRGs	Groups medical cases by diagnosis	Groups major surgery cases by type of operation
DS Clinical	Diagnosis-specific	Independent of major surgery
Coded Staging	Diagnosis-specific	Generally independent of major surgery
Scale	Depends on individual scale: considers stages of all diagnoses to produce overall scale value	Depends on individual scale: can be surgery-specific

Continued

Table 1.5   Continued

System	Role of Diagnosis	Role of Major Surgery
MMPS	Diagnosis-specific	Independent of major surgery
MPM	Independent of diagnosis	Independent of major surgery
MedisGroups		
Original	Independent of diagnosis	Independent of major surgery
Empirical	Diagnosis-specific	Independent of major surgery
NY CABG	Single condition (surgical revascularization for coronary artery disease)	Single surgery (coronary artery bypass graft)
PMCs		
Categories	Specific combinations of diagnoses and procedures	Procedures used with diagnoses
RIS	Considers all PMCs assigned to patient	Considers major surgery
Severity Score	Considers all PMCs assigned to patient	Considers major surgery
PRISM	Independent of diagnosis	Independent of major surgery
RAND	Diagnosis-specific	Independent of major surgery
RAMI	Considers diagnoses	Considers major surgery
RACI	Considers diagnoses	Considers major surgery
RARI	Considers diagnoses	Considers major surgery
R-DRGs	Groups medical cases by diagnosis	Considers major surgery

computerized discharge abstract that hospitals already employ to assign the DRGs (Chapter 3) or claims submitted in payment for services in outpatient settings (Chapter 3), or they require additional clinical data elements abstracted from the medical record or some other primary source (Chapter 4). The data requirements obviously have significant practical implications for the costliness and feasibility of using the measure. In addition, as described in later chapters, data largely dictate the clinical content, and thus meaningfulness, of a measure. Most measures have some mechanism to address data quality (e.g., cleaning routines in software based on administrative data, range checks in computer-guided data entry from medical record abstraction).

Table 1.6 Data Requirements and Development of Measures

System	Data Requirements	System Development
ACGs	Ambulatory care and hospital claims and encounter data	Clinical judgment to create basic framework, then empirical modeling
AIM	Computerized discharge abstract data	Empirical modeling
APACHE		
I	Values of 34 acute physiologic parameters and limited other clinical information	Clinical judgment
II	Values of 12 acute physiologic parameters and limited other clinical information	Clinical judgment with some empirical modeling
III	Values of 17 acute physiologic parameters and limited other clinical information	Empirical modeling with some clinical judgment
APR-DRGs	Computerized discharge abstract data, birth weight	Clinical judgment to create basic framework, then empirical modeling
CSI	Disease-specific clinical factors	Clinical judgment; final calibration based on data concerning length of stay, cost, and mortality
DCGs–HCCs	Diagnosis codes taken from hospital inpatient, hospital outpatient, and physician claims	Clinical judgment to create basic framework, then empirical modeling
DRGs	Computerized discharge abstract data	Clinical judgment to create basic framework, then empirical modeling
DS		
Clinical	Disease-specific clinical variables	Clinical judgment
Coded Staging	Computerized discharge abstract data	Clinical judgment
Scale	Computerized discharge abstract data	Empirical modeling using stages based on clinical judgment
MMPS	Disease-specific clinical variables	Empirical modeling, following clinical input

Continued

Table 1.6   Continued

System	Data Requirements	System Development
MPM	Clinical variables	Empirical modeling
MedisGroups Original	"Key clinical findings"	Clinical judgment; final calibration based on data concerning in-hospital mortality
Empirical	"Key clinical findings"	Empirical modeling (logistic regression)
NY CABG	Condition-specific clinical variables	Empirical modeling, following clinical input
PMCs Categories	Computerized discharge abstract data	Clinical judgment
RIS	Computerized discharge abstract data	Cost-finding methodology
Severity Score	Computerized discharge abstract data	Clinical judgment followed by empirical modeling
PRISM	Clinical variables	Empirical modeling
RAND	Disease-specific clinical variables	Empirical modeling, following clinical input
RAMI	Computerized discharge abstract data	Empirical modeling
RACI	Computerized discharge abstract data	Empirical modeling
RARI	Computerized discharge abstract data	Empirical modeling
R-DRGs	Computerized discharge abstract data	Clinical judgment to create basic framework, then empirical modeling modified by clinical judgment

Data requirements also influence the strategies used to derive and calibrate the severity measure (Table 1.6). Some methods were based largely on clinical judgment of physicians, with little if any guidance from data. In contrast, measures using large administrative databases are often empirically derived (i.e., statistical modeling techniques were applied to existing databases to produce the risk computation algorithm). Some methods, such as the new MedisGroups and the NY CABG measures are empirically derived using detailed clinical data. The way a measure was developed may have implications for its generalizability to other databases or healthcare settings.

Timing of Reviews and Classification Scheme

Depending on one's research goals, distinguishing severity at different points over the hospital stay might be important, raising questions about the timing of reviews (Table 1.7). Measures based on discharge abstracts are tied to discharge diagnoses, which are, by definition, retrospective. The diagnosis codes represent conditions presumably treated during the hospital stay, without specifying when they occurred over the hospital course. Therefore, severity ratings based on discharge abstract data encompass clinical events over the entire hospital stay. (Theoretically, software using discharge abstract data can compute similar scores if coded variables are available for specific periods, such as the first two days of hospitalization, but this is rarely the case.) In contrast, measures based on clinical data can capture severity information from different points over the hospitalization. Different methods emphasize different timing of severity reviews (Table 1.7).

The measures classify severity of illness differently (Table 1.7). The classification schemes can be broadly classed into those employing interval versus ordinal scales. Some measures (e.g., CSI, Disease Staging) have different versions that use both approaches. In interval scales, the increment in severity reflected by increasing values supposedly has intrinsic meaning based on the actual magnitude of the value. For example, in Disease Staging's resource demand scales, a value of 115 indicates a resource intensity that is 15 percent higher than the average. Interval scales generally represent continuous values over a wide range, such as the RIS weights associated with the PMCs, which vary from below 1.0 to the double digits. Using interval scales, means or average values are intrinsically meaningful.

In contrast, ordinal scales group or order cases into levels of increasing severity, without implying that the absolute value of the level has inherent meaning when compared with that of another level. For example, using the CSI, an overall score of 2 does not indicate twice the severity of an overall score of 1. Values derived from an ordinal scale generally cannot be averaged in a meaningful way.

Revisions and Updates of Methods

Finally, as shown in Table 6.1, many severity measures are frequently revised or updated. These reviews and modifications are motivated by

Table 1.7 Timing of Reviews and Classification Approach

System	Timing of Reviews	Classification Approach
ACGs	Claims over an entire year or other extended time period	Persons categorized into one of over 50 mutually exclusive ACGs based on age, sex, and combinations of types of diagnoses; also up to 34 Ambulatory Diagnosis Groups (morbidity clusters)
AIM	Discharge abstract: entire hospitalization	Scores 1, 2, 3, 4, or 5 within DRGs
APACHE		
I	Admission scores taken from worst value over first 32 hours after ICU admission	Integer scores from 0 to 50
II	Admission scores taken from worst value over first 24 hours after ICU admission	Integer scores from 0 to 71
III	Admission scores taken from worst value over first 24 hours after ICU admission; scores can be computed for any day	Integer scores from 0 to 299
APR–DRGs	Discharge abstract: entire hospitalization	382 base DRGs. All except 2 are divided into 4 complexity subclasses (1 = minor, 2 = moderate, 3 = major, 4 = extreme); 1,528 subclasses
CSI	Admission review first 24 hours (first 8 hours for patients in intensive care units); maximum severity score covers entire hospital stay; scores can be computed at any point	Scores 1, 2, 3, or 4 for each individual disease; scores 1, 2, 3, or 4 for all diseases combined; "continuous scores" (integer ≥ 0) for all diseases combined
DCGs–HCCs	Claims over an entire year	Patients' diagnoses are assigned to 34 diagnostic categories; model predicts a year's cost using age, sex, and categories
DRGs	Discharge abstract: entire hospitalization	Over 495 diagnostic categories; each assigned a relative weight for payment purposes

Continued

Table 1.7 Continued

System	Timing of Reviews	Classification Approach
DS		
Clinical	Determined by user; could encompass any period	Stages 1.0, 2.0, or 3.0, with substages possible; number of substages varies across diseases
Coded Staging	Computerized abstract: entire hospitalization or ambulatory period	Stages 1.0, 2.0, or 3.0, with substages possible; number of substages varies across diseases
Scale	Discharge abstract: entire hospitalization	Relative weight with 100 as an average (e.g., a weight of 115 is 15 percent more than average)
MMPS	First values over first 24 hours after admission	Probability of death within 30 days of admission ranging from 0 to 1
MPM	First values over first 24 hours of ICU care; MPM_{24} uses measurements 24 hours into ICU stay	Probability of in-hospital death
MedisGroups		
Original	Admission review includes worst values over first 48 hours; midstay review generally encompasses days 5 through 7	Admission score 0, 1, 2, 3, or 4; midstay score no morbidity, morbid, major morbidity
Empirical	Data collection daily. Review 1 for days 1–2; Review 2 for days 3–5 in adults. Review 1 for day 1 and Review 2 for days 2–5 in pediatrics. Collects all values of most tests including some preadmission findings.	For mortality prediction version, calculates probability of in-hospital death ranging from 0 to 1; probabilities can be grouped into scores paralleling those of the original version. Empirical modeling performed within 67 disease groups.
NY CABG	Preoperative risk factors	Probability of in-hospital death ranging from 0 to 1
PMCs		
Categories	Discharge abstract: entire hospitalization	One of approximately 831 categories
RIS	Discharge abstract: entire hospitalization	Relative intensity score with 1.0 as an average (e.g., a weight of 1.15 is 15 percent more than average)

Continued

Table 1.7   Continued

System	Timing of Reviews	Classification Approach
Severity Score	Discharge abstract: entire hospitalization	Score of 1, 2, 3, 4, 5, 6, or 7
PRISM	Admission data, ICU outcome	Probability of ICU mortality ranging from a score of 0 through 76
RAND	Based on first values obtained within the first two days of admission	Probability of death 30 and 180 days after admission ranging from 0 to 1
RAMI	Discharge abstract: entire hospitalization	Probability of in-hospital death ranging from 0 to 1
RACI	Discharge abstract: entire hospitalization	Probability of in-hospital complications ranging from 0 to 1
RARI	Discharge abstract: entire hospitalization	Probability of readmission ranging from 0 to 1
R-DRGs	Discharge abstract: entire hospitalization	Within adjacent DRGs assigns four levels for surgical cases (A, B, C, and D) and three levels for medical cases (B, C, and D).

several factors, such as changes in databases (e.g., access to more cases or patients from different settings), improvements in statistical methodologies or computational capabilities, introduction of new medical technologies, and evolution of clinical knowledge. Some reflect a changing emphasis—for example, the CSI now has a version for ambulatory patients. References throughout this book to specific measures may not reflect their current state or content.

Overview of Study of Severity Measures

Throughout this book, we draw examples from our AHCPR-funded study, "Evaluating Severity Adjustors for Patient Outcome Studies" (HS 06742, 9/30/91–9/29/94). This study was motivated by two questions: First, what, precisely, is severity? Second, how should severity be measured? We knew that over a dozen methods had been developed to adjust for severity of hospitalized patients, each with unique conceptual underpinnings and rating methods. These differences suggested that severity-adjusted find-ings could depend substantially upon the specific attributes of the severity adjustment approach. Therefore, our overarching research hypothesis was that risk-adjusted patient or hospital outcomes vary when different sever-ity measures are used to adjust for risk.

This study examined several versions, which appeared in 1992 and 1993, of readily available severity measures (Table 1.8). Current attributes of some of these measures are shown in Tables 1.3 through 1.7; a number have experienced important changes since our study. These severity measures were applied to the same large database for comparative analyses. We also performed 27 in-depth case studies to understand better the way that different methods rate severity, and we interviewed physicians to examine how clinicians think about severity. The empirical study database is described briefly below. Additional detail is available in the study's final report (Iezzoni et al. 1995c) and associated publications (Hughes et al. 1996; Iezzoni et al. 1994, 1995a, 1995b, 1996a, 1996b, 1996c, 1996d, 1996e, 1997; Landon et al. 1996; Shwartz et al. 1996).

As shown in Table 1.8, all severity measures, except the MedisGroups and physiology scores, rated severity using standard data elements from hospital discharge abstracts (Chapter 3), such as patient age, sex, and diagnoses and procedures coded using the *International Classification of Diseases, Ninth Revision, Clinical Modification* (ICD-9-CM). MedisGroups and the physiology scores assess severity using clinical data (e.g., vital signs, laboratory results) abstracted from medical records.

Our analytic file came from the 1992 MedisGroups® Comparative Database. MedisGroups databases have also been used by a number of other researchers (see, for example, Geraci et al. 1993; Heuser, Case, and Ettinger 1992; Silber et al. 1992 and 1995; Bradbury, Golec, and Stearns 1991; Smith et al. 1991; Fine et al. 1995). Briefly, this database contains clin-ical information collected on hospitalized patients during medical record reviews using the MedisGroups severity measure (Steen et al. 1993). The 1992 MedisGroups Comparative Database included all 743,964 calendar year 1991 discharges from 108 acute care hospitals nationwide thought to have good quality data and to represent a range of hospital characteristics. For some analyses, we eliminated institutions with fewer than 30 cases to ensure adequate sample sizes for hospital-level studies. Information on hospital characteristics was taken from the American Hospital Association annual survey.

MedisGroups scores were provided by MediQual Systems, but scores for the other measures had to be assigned. The MedisGroups Comparative Database contains standard discharge abstract information assigned by the hospitals, including ICD-9-CM codes for up to 20 diagnoses and 50 procedures; and values of all key clinical findings (KCFs) abstracted from

Table 1.8   Description of Severity Measures Used in AHCPR-Funded Study[a]

Severity Method	Source	Data Used and Definition of Severity[b]	Classification Approach and Derivation[c]
Clinical Data–Based Methods			
MedisGroups (Atlas)	MediQual Systems, Inc., Westborough, MA	Clinical data	
Original version[1]		Clinical instability indicated by in-hospital death; score independent of diagnosis	Admission score 0, 1, 2, 3, or 4; clinical judgment
Empirical version[2]		In-hospital death; score calculated within 64 disease groups	Probability ranging from 0 to 1; empirical modeling
Physiology Score 1	Patterned after Acute Physiology Score APACHE II[3]	Clinical data; in-hospital mortality for patients in intensive care unit	Integer score starting with 0; APACHE II's Acute Physiology Score ranges from 0 to 60; clinical judgment with empirical guidance
Physiology Score 2	Patterned after Acute Physiology Score, APACHE III[4]	Clinical data; in-hospital mortality for patients in intensive care unit	Integer score starting with 0; APACHE III's Acute Physiology Score ranges from 0 to 252; empirical modeling with clinical guidance
Discharge Abstract–Based Methods			
		Methods with a Clinical Definition of Severity	
Body Systems Count[5]	H.C.I.A., Inc., Ann Arbor, MI	Discharge abstract; number of organ systems involved with disease	Integer count; clinical judgment
Comorbidity Index	Developed by Charlson et al.[6]; coded version patterned after Deyo et al.[7]	Discharge abstract; risk of death within one year of medical hospitalization	Integer from additive scale representing number and severity of comorbidities; clinical judgment with empirical guidance

Continued

Table 1.8 Continued

Severity Method	Source	Data Used and Definition of Severity[b]	Classification Approach and Derivation[c]
Disease Staging[8]	SysteMetrics/MEDSTAT Group, Santa Barbara, CA	Discharge abstract	
Mortality Probability		Probability of in-hospital death	Probability ranging from 0 to 1; empirical modeling
Stage		Stage of disease based on risk of death or functional impairment	Three stages (1.0, 2.0, and 3.0) with substages within each stage; clinical judgment
Comorbidities		Number of comorbidities within each of three major stages	Three separate variables: the integer associated with each of three stages (1, 2, and 3); clinical judgment
PMCs Severity Score[9]	Pittsburgh Research Institute, Pittsburgh, PA	Discharge abstract; in-hospital morbidity and mortality	Score of 1, 2, 3, 4, 5, 6, or 7; empirical modeling
Methods with a Resource-Based Definition of Severity			
AIM[10]	Iaméter, San Mateo, CA	Discharge abstract; length of hospital stay within DRGs	Scores 1, 2, 3, 4, or 5 within DRG[d]; empirical modeling
APR–DRGs[11]	3M Health Information Systems, Wallingford, CT	Discharge abstract; total hospital charges	Four complexity classes (1, 2, 3, 4) within adjacent DRGs[d]; empirical modeling with clinical guidance
Disease Staging Relative Resource Scale (RRS)	SysteMetrics/MEDSTAT Group, Santa Barbara, CA	Discharge abstract; relative total hospital charges	Relative weight with 100 as an average

Severity Method	Source	Data Used and Definition of Severity[b]	Classification Approach and Derivation[c]
PMCs RIS[12]	Pittsburgh Research Institute, Pittsburgh, PA	Discharge abstract; relative resource consumption	Weight compared to an average of 1.0; empirical modeling with clinical guidance
R-DRGs[13]	Yale University refinement of DRGs provided by Karen Schneider, Health Systems Consultants, New Haven, CT	Discharge abstract; length of hospital stay, total hospital charges	Three severity classes (B, C, and D) within adjacent medical DRGs[d]; "early" deaths grouped in lowest severity class; empirical modeling with clinical guidance

[a] Citations in table relate to references listed at the end of Chapter 1.

[b] "Discharge abstract" indicates standard hospital discharge data elements (see Chapter 3). "Clinical data" indicates clinical information abstracted from the medical record (see Chapter 4).

[c] Derivation indicates the principal method used to create the severity scoring method. "Clinical judgments" reflects primarily use of expert physician guidance. "Empirical modeling" indicates primarily use of statistical techniques.

[d] "Adjacent DRGs" are formed by grouping individual DRGs previously split by complications and comorbidities.

1 Brewster et al. 1985; Iezzoni and Moskowitz 1988; Blumberg 1991.
2 Steen et al. 1993.
3 Knaus et al. 1985; Knaus et al. 1986.
4 Knaus et al. 1991; Knaus, Wagner, and Lynn 1991; Knaus et al. 1993.
5 Mendenhall 1984.
6 Charlson et al. 1987.
7 Deyo, Cherkin, and Ciol 1992.
8 Gonnella, Hornbrook, and Louis 1984; Markson et al. 1991; Gonnella et al. 1990; Naessens et al. 1992.
9 Young, Kohler, and Kowalski 1994.
10 Iezzoni et al. 1995c; Thomas and Ashcraft 1991.
11 3M Health Information Systems, 1993; Edwards 1994.
12 Young 1984; Young, Swinkola, and Zorn, 1982.
13 Freeman et al. 1991, 1995.

medical records during admission MedisGroups reviews encompassing the first two hospital days. This KCF information was used to create physiology scores patterned after APACHE II and III. Physiologic findings, such as vital signs and serum chemistry results, were assigned the weights specified by APACHE II or III. For example, a pulse of 145 beats/minute generates 13 points (Knaus et al. 1991). As with APACHE, these weights were summed to produce scores. We could not precisely replicate actual APACHE Acute Physiology Scores because complete values for the required physiologic variables were not available: The 1991 MedisGroups chart abstraction protocol did not require specific values of data elements in broadly defined normal ranges (Iezzoni et al. 1993).

Among the discharge abstract–based severity measures, we assigned only the code-based version of the Charlson comorbidity index (Charlson et al. 1987), using an approach adapted from ICD-9-CM diagnosis codes developed by Deyo, Cherkin, and Ciol (1992). Other severity scoring was performed by the vendors (Table 1.8). Based on their specifications, we prepared computer files containing the necessary discharge abstract data elements extracted from the MedisGroups Comparative Database and sent them to the vendors to score with their software. We used version 9.0 of the Medicare DRGs, assigned by MediQual Systems. Vendors returned scored computer files to us, and these databases were then merged into a single analytic file.

We studied patients 18 years of age and older admitted for five diagnoses: AMI, ischemic heart disease, pneumonia, cerebrovascular disease, or hip fracture. We chose these conditions because of their high volume and clinical importance and because AHCPR-funded Patient Outcome Research Teams (PORTs) were studying them. We used PORT definitions, based on ICD-9-CM codes, to select patients within each of the five study conditions (Iezzoni et al. 1995c). Within ischemic heart disease, we focused mainly on patients undergoing CABG surgery. Table 1.9 provides basic information on the study populations.

Organization of This Book

The remainder of this book draws examples from the severity measures introduced above and from the AHCPR-funded severity study to illustrate major conceptual and methodological considerations in performing risk adjustment for medical outcomes studies. Chapter 2 provides the clinical, conceptual foundation, examining patient attributes reflecting different dimensions of risk—severity of illness being only one dimension. Chapters 3 and 4 discuss the nature and implications of data required to quantify risk, focusing on administrative and medical record information, respectively.

Table 1.9   Characteristics of Study Sample

			Condition		
Characteristics	*AMI*	*CABG*	*Pneumonia*	*Stroke*	*Hip Fracture*
Patient characteristics					
Number of cases	11,880	7,765	18,016	9,407	5,664
Mean (s.d.) age in years	68.3 (13.3)	64.0 (10.2)	69.4 (18.1)	73.8 (11.8)	79.1 (11.5)
Percent female	41.9	27.2	51.6	55.9	77.0
Percent died in-hospital	13.2	3.2	9.6	9.7	3.1
Mean (s.d.) length of stay in days	7.7 (5.5)	12.4 (7.6)	9.1 (7.1)	10.2 (9.9)	11.9 (8.9)
Mean (s.d.) number of ICD-9-CM diagnosis codes	5.8 (3.0)	5.9 (3.1)	5.6 (2.9)	6.0 (2.9)	5.6 (2.9)
Hospital characteristics[a]					
Number	100	38	105	94	80
Percent approved residency training program	39.0	78.9	37.1	41.5	48.8
Percent member of Council of Teaching Hospitals	15.0	36.8	14.3	16.0	18.8
Percent private, not-for-profit ownership	96.0	94.8	95.2	94.6	93.7
Percent less than 100 beds	14.0	0	16.2	12.8	3.8
Percent more than 300 beds	42.0	78.9	40.0	42.6	51.2
Percent located in Pennsylvania	55.0	36.8	56.2	58.5	55.0

[a] Nationwide, the percent of hospitals with each characteristic was as follows: approved residency training program, 18.5; member of Council of Teaching Hospitals, 6.6; private, not-for-profit ownership, 56.1; less than 100 beds, 43.3; more than 300 beds, 18.4; located in Pennsylvania, 4.0.

Chapter 5 offers strategies for developing a risk-adjustment approach. Chapter 6 introduces the concept of validity, suggesting ways to assess whether risk-adjustment approaches are valid.

Chapters 7 through 10 address four specific methodological concerns. Chapter 7 examines the issue of reliability, describing aspects of a risk-adjustment methodology that affect reliability and briefly sketching techniques for assessing reliability. Chapter 8 discusses ways to evaluate how well a risk adjustment method actually accounts for risk, focusing on outcomes measured as continuous values, such as length of stay and hospital charges. Chapter 9 reviews similar concerns for dichotomous outcomes (outcomes that are either present or absent), such as death or development of a complication. Chapter 10 explores methodological considerations in using severity measures to compare or profile performance of healthcare providers. The book concludes with Chapter 11, which describes major initiatives across the country using risk adjustment to monitor quality of care, in this time of swift and radical change throughout the healthcare marketplace.

References

Ash, A., F. Porell, L. Gruenberg, E. Sawitz, and A. Beiser. 1989. "Adjusting Medicare Capitation Payments Using Prior Hospitalization Data." *Health Care Financing Review* 10 (4): 17–29.

Averill, R. F., T. E. McGuire, B. E. Manning, D. A. Fowler, S. D. Horn, P. S. Dickson, M. J. Coye, D. L. Knowlton, and J. A. Bender. 1992. "A Study of the Relationship between Severity of Illness and Hospital Cost in New Jersey Hospitals." *HSR: Health Services Research* 27 (5): 587–606.

Becker, R. B., J. E. Zimmerman, W. A. Knaus, D. P. Wagner, M. G. Seneff, E. A. Draper, T. L. Higgins, F. G. Estafanous, and F. D. Loop. 1995. "The Use of APACHE III to Evaluate ICU Length of Stay, Resource Use, and Mortality After Coronary Artery By-Pass Surgery." *Journal of Cardiovascular Surgery* 36 (1): 1–11.

Berwick, D. M. 1989. "E. A. Codman and the Rhetoric of Battle: A Commentary." *Milbank Quarterly* 67 (2): 262–7.

Blumberg, M. S. 1986. "Risk Adjusting Health Care Outcomes: A Methodologic Review." *Medical Care Review* 43 (2): 351–93.

———. 1991. "Biased Estimates of Expected Acute Myocardial Infarction Mortality Using MedisGroups Admission Severity Groups." *Journal of the American Medical Association* 265 (22): 2965–70.

Bradbury, R. C., J. H. Golec, and F. E. Stearns. 1991. "Comparing Hospital Length of Stay in Independent Practice Association HMOs and Traditional Insurance Programs." *Inquiry* 28 (1): 87–93.

Brewster, A. C., B. G. Karlin, L. A. Hyde, C. M. Jacobs, R. C. Bradbury, and Y. M. Chae. 1985. "MEDISGRPS®: A Clinically Based Approach to Classifying Hospital Patients at Admission." *Inquiry* 22 (4): 377–87.

Brinkley, J. "U.S. Releasing Lists of Hospitals with Abnormal Mortality Rates," *New York Times*, March 12, 1986, p. 1.

Bristowe, J. S., and T. Holmes. 1864. "Report on the Hospitals of the United Kingdom." In *Sixth Report of the Medical Officer of the Privy Council. 1863.* Edited by George E. Eyre and William Spottiswoode. London, England: Her Majesty's Stationery Office.

Center for Evaluative Clinical Studies, Dartmouth Medical School. 1996. *The Dartmouth Atlas of Health Care.* Chicago: American Hospital Association.

Charlson, M. E., P. Pompei, K. L. Ales, and C. R. MacKenzie. 1987. "A New Method of Classifying Prognostic Comorbidity in Longitudinal Studies: Development and Validation." *Journal of Chronic Diseases* 40 (5): 373–83.

Chassin, M. R. 1993. "Explaining Geographic Variations: The Enthusiasm Hypothesis." *Medical Care* 31 (5) supplement: YS37–44.

Chassin, M. R., R. H. Brook, R. E. Park, J. Keesey, A. Fink, J. Kosecoff, K. Kahn, N. Merrick, and D. H. Solomon. 1986. "Variations in the Use of Medical and Surgical Services by the Medicare Population." *New England Journal of Medicine* 314 (5): 285–90.

Codman, E. A. Circa 1917. *A Study in Hospital Efficiency as Demonstrated by the Case Report of the First Five Years of a Private Hospital.* Boston: Thomas Todd Company, Printers.

———. 1934. *The Shoulder: Rupture of the Supraspinatus Tendon and Other Lesions in or about the Subacromial Bursa.* 1934. Boston: Thomas Todd Company.

Cohen, I. B. 1984. "Florence Nightingale." *Scientific American* 250 (3): 128–37.

Conklin, J. E., J. V. Lieberman, C. A. Barnes, and D. Z. Louis. 1984. "Disease Staging: Implications for Hospital Reimbursement and Management." *Health Care Financing Review* Annual Supplement: 13–22.

Daley, J., S. Jencks, D. Draper, G. Lenhart, N. Thomas, and J. Walker. 1988. "Predicting Hospital-Associated Mortality for Medicare Patients: A Method for Patients with Stroke, Pneumonia, Acute Myocardial Infarction, and Congestive Heart Failure." *Journal of the American Medical Association* 260 (24): 3617–24.

DesHarnais, S. I., J. D. Chesney, R. T. Wroblewski, S. T. Fleming, and L. F. McMahon, Jr. 1988. "The Risk-Adjusted Mortality Index: A New Measure of Hospital Performance." *Medical Care* 26 (12): 1129–48.

DesHarnais, S. I., L. F. McMahon, Jr., R. T. Wroblewski, and A. J. Hogan. 1990. "Measuring Hospital Performance: The Development and Validation of Risk-Adjusted Indexes of Mortality, Readmissions, and Complications." *Medical Care* 28 (12): 1127–41.

DesHarnais, S. I., L. F. McMahon, Jr., and R. T. Wroblewski. 1991. "Measuring Outcomes of Hospital Care Using Multiple Risk-Adjusted Indexes." *HSR: Health Services Research* 26 (4): 425–45.

Deyo, R. A., D. C. Cherkin, and M. A. Ciol. 1992. "Adapting a Clinical Comorbidity Index for Use with ICD-9-CM Administrative Databases." *Journal of Clinical Epidemiology* 45 (6): 613–9.

Donabedian, A. 1985. *The Methods and Findings of Quality Assessment and Monitoring: An Illustrated Analysis. Volume 3.* Ann Arbor, MI: Health Administration Press.

———. 1989. "The End Results of Health Care: Ernest Codman's Contribution to Quality Assessment and Beyond." *Milbank Quarterly* 67 (2): 233–56.

Edwards, N., D. Honemann, D. Burley, and M. Navarro. 1994. "Refinement of the Medicare Diagnosis-Related Groups to Incorporate a Measure of Severity." *Health Care Financing Review* 16 (2): 45–64.

Ellis, R. P., and A. Ash. 1995. "Refinements to the Diagnostic Cost Group (DCG) Model." *Inquiry* 32 (4): 418–29.

Ellis, R. P., G. C. Pope, L. I. Iezzoni, J. Z. Ayanian, D. W. Bates, H. Burstin, and

A. S. Ash. 1996. "Diagnosis-Based Risk Adjustment for Medicare Capitation Payments." *Health Care Financing Review* 17 (3): 101–28.

Ellwood, P. 1988. "Shattuck Lecture—Outcomes Management: A Technology of Patient Experience." *New England Journal of Medicine* 318 (23): 1549–56.

Ellwood, P. M., and G. D. Lundberg. 1996. "Managed Care: A Work in Progress." *Journal of the American Medical Association* 276 (13): 1083–6.

Eyler, J. M. 1979. *Victorian Social Medicine. The Ideas and Methods of William Farr.* Baltimore, MD: The Johns Hopkins University Press.

Fetter, R. B., Y. Shin, J. L. Freeman, R. F. Averill, and J. D. Thompson. 1980. "Case Mix Definition by Diagnosis-Related Groups." *Medical Care* 18 (2) Supplement: 1–53.

Fine, M. J., B. H. Hanusa, J. R. Lave, D. E. Singer, R. A. Stone, L. A. Weissfeld, C. M. Coley, T. J. Marrie, and W. N. Kapoor. 1995. "Comparison of a Disease-Specific and a Generic Severity of Illness Measure for Patients with Community-Acquired Pneumonia." *Journal of General Internal Medicine* 10 (7): 359–68.

Fowles, J. B., J. P. Weiner, D. Knutson, E. Fowler, A. M. Tucker, and M. Ireland. 1996. "Taking Health Status into Account When Setting Capitation Rates: A Comparison of Risk-Adjustment Methods." *Journal of the American Medical Association* 276 (16): 1316–21.

Freeman, J. L., R. B. Fetter, H. Park, K. C. Schneider, J. L. Lichtenstein, W. A. Bauman, C. C. Duncan, J. S. Hughes, D. H. Freeman, Jr., and G. R. Palmer. 1991. "Refinement." In *DRGs: Their Design and Development*, edited by R. B. Fetter, D. A. Brand, and D. Gamache. Ann Arbor, MI: Health Administration Press.

Freeman, J. L., R. B. Fetter, H. Park, K. C. Schneider, J. L. Lichtenstein, J. S. Hughes, W. A. Bauman, C. C. Duncan, D. H. Freeman, Jr., and G. R. Palmer. 1995. "Diagnosis-Related Group Refinement with Diagnosis- and Procedure-Specific Comorbidities and Complications." *Medical Care* 33 (8): 806–27.

Geraci, J. M., A. K. Rosen, A. S. Ash, K. J. McNiff, and M. A. Moskowitz. 1993. "Predicting the Occurrence of Adverse Events After Coronary Artery Bypass Surgery." *Annals of Internal Medicine* 118 (1): 18–24.

Giacomini, M., H. S. Luft, and J. C. Robinson. 1995. "Risk Adjusting Community Rated Health Plan Premiums: A Survey of Risk Assessment Literature and Policy Applications." *Annual Review of Public Health* 16: 401–30.

Goldfield, N., and P. Boland, eds. 1996. *Physician Profiling and Risk Adjustment.* Gaithersburg, MD: Aspen Publishers, Inc.

Gonnella, J. S., M. C. Hornbrook, and D. Z. Louis. 1984. "Staging of Disease: A Case-Mix Measurement." *Journal of the American Medical Association* 251 (5): 637–44.

Gonnella, J. S., D. Z. Louis, C. Zeleznik, and B. J. Turner. 1990. "The Problem of Late Hospitalization: A Quality and Cost Issue." *Academic Medicine* 65 (5): 314–9.

Hannan, E. L., H. Kilburn, Jr., J. F. O'Donnell, G. Lukacik, and E. P. Shields. 1990. "Adult Open Heart Surgery in New York State: An Analysis of Risk Factors and Hospital Mortality Rates." *Journal of the American Medical Association* 264 (21): 2768–74.

Hannan, E. L., H. Kilburn, Jr., M. L. Lindsey, and R. Lewis. 1992. "Clinical Versus

Administrative Data Bases for CABG Surgery: Does It Matter?" *Medical Care* 30 (10): 892–907.

Hannan, E. L., H. Kilburn, Jr., M. Racz, E. Shields, and M. R. Chassin. 1994. "Improving the Outcomes of Coronary Artery Bypass Surgery in New York State." *Journal of the American Medical Association* 271 (10): 761–66.

Hannan, E. L., A. L. Siu, D. Kumar, H. Kilburn, Jr., and M. R. Chassin. 1995. "The Decline in Coronary Artery Bypass Graft Surgery Mortality in New York State. The Role of Surgeon Volume." *Journal of the American Medical Association* 273 (3): 209–13.

Health Systems Management Group, School of Organization and Management, Yale University. 1989. *DRG Refinement with Diagnostic Specific Comorbidities and Complications: A Synthesis of Current Approaches to Patient Classification.* Prepared for the Health Care Financing Administration, under Cooperative Agreement No. 15-C-98930/1–01 and 17-C-98930/1–0251. New Haven: Yale University.

Heuser, M. D., L. D. Case, and W. H. Ettinger. 1992. "Mortality in Intensive Care Patients with Respiratory Disease. Is Age Important?" *Archives of Internal Medicine* 152 (8): 1683–88.

Horn, S. D., P. D. Sharkey, J. M. Buckle, J. E. Backofen, R. F. Averill, and R. A. Horn. 1991. "The Relationship between Severity of Illness and Hospital Length of Stay and Mortality." *Medical Care* 29 (4): 305–17.

Horn S. D., P. D. Sharkey, and J. Gassaway. 1996. "Managed Care Outcomes Project: Study Design, Baseline Patient Characteristics, and Outcome Measures." *American Journal of Managed Care* 2 (3): 237–47.

Hughes, J. S., L. I. Iezzoni, J. Daley, and L. Greenberg. 1996. "How Severity Measures Rate Hospitalized Patients." *Journal of General Internal Medicine* 11 (5): 303–11.

Iezzoni, L. I. 1996. "100 Apples Divided by 15 Red Herrings: A Cautionary Tale from the Mid-19th Century on Comparing Hospital Mortality Rates." *Annals of Internal Medicine* 124 (12): 1079–85.

Iezzoni, L. I., and M. A. Moskowitz. 1988. "A Clinical Assessment of MedisGroups." *Journal of the American Medical Association* 260 (21): 3159–63.

Iezzoni, L. I., A. S. Ash, J. L. Cobb, and M. A. Moskowitz. 1988. "Admission MedisGroups Score and the Cost of Hospitalizations." *Medical Care* 26 (11): 1068–80.

Iezzoni, L. I., and J. Daley. 1992. "A Description and Clinical Assessment of the Computerized Severity Index." *Quality Review Bulletin* 18 (2): 44–52.

Iezzoni, L. I., E. K. Hotchkin, A. S. Ash, M. Shwartz, and Y. Mackiernan. 1993. "MedisGroups Data Bases: The Impact of Data Collection Guidelines on Predicting In-Hospital Mortality." *Medical Care* 31 (3): 277–83.

Iezzoni, L. I., M. Shwartz, A. S. Ash, Y. Mackiernan, and E. K. Hotchkin. 1994. "Risk Adjustment Methods Can Affect Perceptions of Outcomes." *American Journal of Medical Quality* 9 (2): 43–48.

Iezzoni, L. I., M. Shwartz, A. S. Ash, J. S. Hughes, J. Daley, and Y. D. Mackiernan. 1995a. "Using Severity-Adjusted Stroke Mortality Rates to Judge Hospitals." *International Journal for Quality in Health Care* 7 (2): 81–94.

Iezzoni, L. I., A. S. Ash, M. Shwartz, J. Daley, J. S. Hughes, and Y. D. Mackiernan.

1995b. "Predicting Who Dies Depends on How Severity is Measured: Implications for Evaluating Patient Outcomes." *Annals of Internal Medicine* 123 (10): 763–70.

Iezzoni, L. I., M. Shwartz, A. S. Ash, J. S. Hughes, J. Daley, Y. D. Mackiernan, and D. Stone. 1995c. *Evaluating Severity Adjustors for Patient Outcome Studies. Final Report.* Prepared for the Agency for Health Care Policy and Research under grant no. RO1-HS06742. Boston: Beth Israel Hospital.

Iezzoni, L. I., M. Shwartz, A. S. Ash, J. S. Hughes, J. Daley, and Y. D. Mackiernan. 1996a. "Severity Measurement Methods and Judging Hospital Death Rates for Pneumonia." *Medical Care* 34 (1): 11–28.

Iezzoni, L. I., M. Shwartz, A. S. Ash, and Y. D. Mackiernan. 1996b. "Using Severity Measures to Predict the Likelihood of Death for Pneumonia Inpatients." *Journal of General Internal Medicine* 11 (1): 23–31.

———. 1996c. "Does Severity Explain Differences in Hospital Length of Stay for Pneumonia Patients?" *Journal of Health Services Research and Policy* 1 (2): 65–76.

———. 1996d. "Predicting In-Hospital Mortality for Stroke Patients: Results Differ Across Severity Measurement Systems." *Medical Decision Making* 16 (4): 348–56.

Iezzoni, L. I., A. S. Ash, M. Shwartz, J. Daley, J. S. Hughes, and Y. D. Mackiernan. 1996e. "Judging Hospitals by Severity-Adjusted Mortality Rates: The Influence of the Severity-Adjustment Method." *American Journal of Public Health* 86 (10): 1379–87.

Iezzoni, L. I., A. S. Ash, M. Shwartz, and Y. D. Mackiernan. 1997. "Differences in Procedure Use, In-Hospital Mortality, and Illness Severity by Gender for Acute Myocardial Infarction Patients. Are Answers Affected by Data Source and Severity Adjustment Method?" *Medical Care* 35 (2): 158–71.

Kahn, K. L., D. Draper, E. B. Keeler, W. H. Rogers, L. V. Rubenstein, J. Kosecoff, M. J. Sherwood, E. J. Reinisch, M. F. Carney, C. J. Kamberg, S. S. Bentow, K. B. Wells, H. Allen, D. Reboussin, C. P. Roth, C. Chew, and R. H. Brook. 1992. *The Effects of the DRG-Based Prospective Payment System on Quality of Care for Hospitalized Medicare Payments.* Publication no. R-3931-HCFA. Santa Monica: RAND.

Keeler, E. B., K. L. Kahn, D. Draper, M. J. Sherwood, L. V. Rubenstein, E. J. Reinisch, J. Kosecoff, and R. H. Brook. 1990. "Changes in Sickness at Admission Following the Introduction of the Prospective Payment System." *Journal of the American Medical Association* 264 (15): 1962–68.

Knaus, W. A., J. E. Zimmerman, D. P. Wagner, E. A. Draper, and D. E. Lawrence. 1981. "APACHE—Acute Physiology and Chronic Health Evaluation: A Physiologically Based Classification System." *Critical Care Medicine* 9 (8): 591–97.

Knaus, W. A., E. A. Draper, D. P. Wagner, and J. E. Zimmerman. 1985. "APACHE II: A Severity of Disease Classification System." *Critical Care Medicine* 13 (10): 818–29.

———. 1986. "An Evaluation of Outcome from Intensive Care in Major Medical Centers." *Annals of Internal Medicine* 104 (3): 410–18.

Knaus, W. A., D. P. Wagner, E. A. Draper, J. E. Zimmerman, M. Bergner, P. G. Bastos, C. A. Sirio, D. J. Murphy, T. Lotring, A. Damiano, and F. E. Harrell, Jr. 1991. "The APACHE III Prognostic System: Risk Prediction of Hospital Mortality for Critically Ill Hospitalized Adults." *Chest* 100 (6): 1619–36.

Knaus, W. A., D. P. Wagner, and J. Lynn. 1991. "Short-Term Mortality Predictions for Critically Ill Hospitalized Adults: Science and Ethics." *Science* 254 (18): 389–94.

Knaus, W. A., D. P. Wagner, J. E. Zimmerman, and E. A. Draper. 1993. "Variations in Mortality and Length of Stay in Intensive Care Units." *Annals of Internal Medicine* 118 (10): 753–61.

Landon, B., L. I. Iezzoni, A. S. Ash, M. Shwartz, J. Daley, J. S. Hughes, and Y. D. Mackiernan. 1996. "Judging Hospitals by Severity-Adjusted Mortality Rates: The Case of CABG Surgery." *Inquiry* 33 (2): 155–66.

Lemeshow, S., D. Teres, J. S. Avrunin, and R. W. Gage. 1988. "Refining Intensive Care Unit Outcome Prediction by Using Changing Probabilities of Mortality." *Critical Care Medicine* 16 (5): 470–77.

Lemeshow, S., D. Teres, J. Klar, J. S. Avrunin, S. H. Gehlbach, and J. Rapoport. 1993. "Mortality Probability Models (MPM II) Based on an International Cohort of Intensive Care Unit Patients." *Journal of the American Medical Association* 270 (20): 2478–86.

Lemeshow, S., J. Klar, D. Teres, J. S. Avrunin, S. H. Gehlbach, J. Rapoport, and M. Rue. 1994. "Mortality Probability Models for Patients in the Intensive Care Unit for 48 or 72 Hours: A Prospective, Multicenter Study." *Critical Care Medicine* 22 (9): 1351–58.

3M Health Information Systems. 1993. *All Patient Refined Diagnosis Related Groups. Definitions Manual.* Wallingford, CT: 3M Health Information Systems.

Markson, L. E., D. B. Nash, D. Z. Louis, and J. S. Gonnella. 1991. "Clinical Outcomes Management and Disease Staging." *Evaluation and the Health Professions* 14 (2): 201–27.

McGuire, T. E. 1991. "An Evaluation of Diagnosis-Related Group Severity and Complexity Refinement." *Health Care Financing Review* 12 (4): 49–60.

Mendenhall, S. 1984. "DRGs Must Be Changed to Take Patient's Illness Severity into Account." *Modern Healthcare* 14 (15 November): 86, 88.

Morris, W., ed. 1973. *The American Heritage Dictionary of the English Language.* New York: American Heritage Publishing Co., Inc., and Houghton Mifflin Company.

Mulley, A. G., Jr. 1989. "E. A. Codman and the End Results Idea: A Commentary." *Milbank Quarterly* 67 (2): 257–61.

Naessens, J. M., C. L. Leibson, I. Krishan, and D. J. Ballard. 1992. "Contribution of a Measure of Disease Complexity (COMPLEX) to Prediction of Outcome and Charges among Hospitalized Patients." *Mayo Clinic Proceedings* 67 (12): 1140–49.

Neuhauser, D. 1990. "Ernest Amory Codman, M.D., and End Results of Medical Care." *International Journal of Technology Assessment in Health Care* 6 (2): 307–25.

Nightingale, F. 1863. *Notes on Hospitals.* 3rd ed. London: Longman, Green, Longman, Roberts, and Green.

Perrin, J. M., C. J. Homer, D. M. Berwick, A. D. Woolf, J. L. Freeman, and J. E. Wennberg. 1989. "Variations in Rates of Hospitalization of Children in Three Urban Communities." *New England Journal of Medicine* 320 (18): 1183–87.

Pinker, R. 1966. *English Hospital Statistics 1861–1938.* London: Heinemann Educational Books Ltd.

Pollack, M. M., U. E. Ruttimann, and P. R. Getson. 1987. "Accurate Prediction of the Outcome of Pediatric Intensive Care: A New Quantitative Method." *New England Journal of Medicine* 316 (3): 134–39.

———. 1988. "Pediatric Risk of Mortality, PRISM Score." *Critical Care Medicine* 16 (11): 1110–16.

Pollack, M. M., T. T. Cuerdon, K. M. Patel, U. E. Ruttimann, P. R. Getson, and M. Levetown. 1994. "Impact of Quality-of-Care Factors on Pediatric Intensive Care Unit Mortality." *Journal of the American Medical Association* 272 (12): 941–46.

Relman, A. S. 1988. "Assessment and Accountability: The Third Revolution in Medical Care." *New England Journal of Medicine* 319 (18): 1220–22.

Roper, W. L., W. Winkenwerder, G. M. Hackbarth, and H. Krakauer. 1988. "Effectiveness in Health Care: An Initiative to Evaluate and Improve Medical Practice." *New England Journal of Medicine* 319 (18): 1197–1202.

Ruttimann, U. E., M. M. Pollack, and D. H. Fiser. 1996. "Prediction of Three Outcome States from Pediatric Intensive Care." *Critical Care Medicine* 24 (1): 78–85.

Salem-Schatz, S., G. Moore, M. Rucker, and S. D. Pearson. 1994. "The Case for Case-Mix Adjustment in Practice Profiling: When Good Apples Look Bad." *Journal of the American Medical Association* 272 (11): 871–74.

Shortell, S. M., J. E. Zimmerman, D. M. Rousseau, R. R. Gillies, D. P. Wagner, E. A. Draper, W. A. Knaus, and J. Duffy. 1994. "The Performance of Intensive Care Units: Does Good Management Make a Difference?" *Medical Care* 32 (5): 508–25.

Shwartz, M., L. I. Iezzoni, A. S. Ash, and Y. D. Mackiernan. 1996. "Do Severity Measures Explain Differences in Length of Hospital Stay? The Case of Hip Fracture." *HSR: Health Services Research* 31 (4): 365–85.

Silber, J. H., S. V. Williams, H. Krakauer, and J. S. Schwartz. 1992. "Hospital and Patient Characteristics Associated with Death After Surgery: A Study of Adverse Occurrence and Failure to Rescue." *Medical Care* 30 (7): 615–29.

Silber, J. H., P. R. Rosenbaum, J. S. Schwartz, R. N. Ross, and S. V. Williams. 1995. "Evaluation of the Complication Rate as a Measure of Quality of Care in Coronary Artery Bypass Graft Surgery." *Journal of the American Medical Association* 274 (4): 317–23.

Smith, D. W., M. Pine, R. C. Bailey, B. Jones, A. Brewster, and H. Krakauer. 1991. "Using Clinical Variables to Estimate the Risk of Patient Mortality." *Medical Care* 29 (11): 1108–29.

Starfield, B., J. Weiner, L. Mumford, and D. Steinwachs. 1991. "Ambulatory Care Groups: A Categorization of Diagnoses for Research and Management." *HSR: Health Services Research* 26 (1): 53–74.

Steen, P. M., A. C. Brewster, R. C. Bradbury, E. Estabrook, and J. A. Young. 1993. "Predicted Probabilities of Hospital Death as a Measure of Admission Severity of Illness." *Inquiry* 30 (2): 128–41.

Steen, P. M. 1994. "Approaches to Predictive Modeling." *Annals of Thoracic Surgery* 58 (6): 1836–40.

Thomas, J. W., and M. L. F. Ashcraft. 1991. "Measuring Severity of Illness: Six Severity Systems and Their Ability to Explain Cost Variations." *Inquiry* 28 (1): 39–55.

Vladeck, B. C. 1984. Medicare Hospital Payment by Diagnosis-Related Groups. *Annals of Internal Medicine* 100 (4): 576–91.

Walker, H. M. 1929. *Studies in the History of Statistical Method*. Baltimore, MD: The Williams & Wilkins Company.

Weiner, J. P., B. H. Starfield, D. M. Steinwachs, and L. M. Mumford. 1991. "Development and Application of a Population-Oriented Measure of Ambulatory Care Case-Mix." *Medical Care* 29 (5): 452–72.

Weiner, J. P., B. H. Starfield, N. R. Powe, M. E. Stuart, and D. M. Steinwachs. 1996. "Ambulatory Care Practice Variation Within a Medicaid Program." *HSR: Health Services Research* 30 (6): 751–70.

Welch, W. P., M. E. Miller, H. G. Welch, E. S. Fisher, and J. E. Wennberg. 1993."Geographic Variation in Expenditures for Physicians' Services in the United States." *New England Journal of Medicine* 328 (9): 621–7.

Wennberg, J., and A. Gittelsohn. 1973. "Small Area Variations in Health Care Delivery." *Science* 182 (117): 1102–8.

Wennberg, J. E., J. L. Freeman, R. M. Shelton, and T. A. Bubolz. 1989. "Hospital Use and Mortality among Medicare Beneficiaries in Boston and New Haven." *New England Journal of Medicine* 321 (17): 1168–73.

White House Domestic Policy Council. 1993. *Health Security: The President's Report to the American People*. Washington, D.C.: The Council.

Young, W. W. 1984. "Incorporating Severity of Illness and Comorbidity in Case-Mix Measurement." *Health Care Financing Review* Annual Supplement: 23–31.

Young, W. W., R. B. Swinkola, and D. M. Zorn. 1982. "The Measurement of Hospital Case Mix." *Medical Care* 20 (5): 501–12.

Young, W. W., D. Z. Joyce, J. L. Schuchert, M. A. Hutton, and D. P. Macioce. 1985. *Measuring the Costs of Care Using Patient Management Categories: Final Report*. Volume I, NTIS No. PB86101979; Volume II, NTIS No. PB86101987. Springfield, VA: National Technical Information Service.

Young, W. W., S. Kohler, and J. Kowalski. 1994. "PMC Patient Severity Scale: Derivation and Validation." *HSR: Health Services Research* 3 (29): 367–90.

Yuen E. J., J. S. Gonnella, D. Z. Louis, K. R. Epstein, S. L. Howell, and L. E. Markson. 1995. "Severity-Adjusted Differences in Hospital Utilization by Gender." *American Journal of Medical Quality* 10 (2): 76–80.

Zhu, B. P., S. Lemeshow, D. W. Hosmer, J. Klar, J. Avrunin, and D. Teres. 1996. "Factors Affecting the Performance of the Models in the Mortality Probability Model II System and Strategies of Customization: A Simulation Study." *Critical Care Medicine* 24 (1): 57–63.

Chapter 2

Dimensions of Risk

Lisa I. Iezzoni

The first step in risk adjustment is defining one's terms. Clinicians have long used words such as "severity" and "risk," assuming their colleagues shared common definitions. In the 1980s, however, various other participants in the healthcare marketplace adopted these terms, spurred initially by Medicare's adoption of prospective hospital payment based on DRGs. "Risk adjustment" joined other poorly defined but oft-used words and phrases—such as "case mix," "severity," "sickness," "intensity," "complexity," "comorbidity," and "health status"—used not only by clinicians and researchers but also by payors, policymakers, financial analysts, quality assessors, regulators, health insurance actuaries, and managers of healthcare organizations.

In the 1980s, "severity" attracted the greatest attention, generated by concerns that DRGs were insensitive to illness severity (see Chapter 11). In his 1982 report proposing Medicare's prospective payment system, U.S. Department of Health and Human Services Secretary Richard S. Schweiker (1982, 74–75) acknowledged this possibility, but argued:

> The DRGs cover a wide range, from very expensive cases (e.g., heart transplant, kidney transplant, coronary by-pass, and severe burn) to very inexpensive kinds of cases. Thus, the DRGs account for the major variations in severity of illness across patients . . . Severity within DRG is primarily a concern if certain hospitals tend to have more severe cases within DRGs compared to other hospitals, and if severity is positively associated with costs.

Given the hospital payment context, Schweiker clearly focused on linking severity with inpatient resource use. Medicare hospital reimbursement mechanisms, such as indirect medical education adjustments paid to teaching hospitals, were instituted partially to compensate for this potential limitation of DRGs. One problem underlying the ensuing lively policy debate was that "severity" had no single, precise definition—it meant different things to different people. According to Gertman and Lowenstein (1984, 85), " 'Severity' is what sociologists term a 'folk wisdom' word like 'satisfaction' or 'happiness,' operationally indefinable in a way that is perfectly acceptable to all parties."

Medical Meaningfulness

"Severity" typifies the concept of "risk"—the higher the severity, the higher patients' risks (or likelihood) of poor outcomes, variously defined. The broader notion of "risk adjustment" also eludes a single meaning, given its inextricable linkage to the question, risk of what? This query generates many replies, ranging from resource consumption to death to iatrogenic complications to physical functioning to patient satisfaction. To be clear, this question generally needs an addendum specifying the time window— risk of what *over how long?*—resource consumption for a single hospitalization or over a year, death imminently or within 30 or 90 days? Hence, it is not surprising that different measures of "severity" use different definitions of "risk" and different windows of observation (see Tables 1.4 and 1.7).

The answer to the question—risk of what over how long?—depends on one's purpose. As Hornbrook (1985, 295) wrote, "The purpose . . . establishes the logical criterion for judging the validity and consistency of alternative measures. Without a clearly defined purpose, measurement becomes arbitrary. For this reason, specification of purpose is the first step. . . ." So delineating one's goals is the first requirement of risk adjustment.

A common goal is using risk adjustment to calculate the so-called "algebra of effectiveness"—the concept that patient outcomes are a complex function not only of the patient's clinical attributes and other factors such as random events but also of the effectiveness and quality of the services provided (Figure 2.1). The specifics of this equation vary depending on the outcome of interest (risk of what?). Given the diversity of these outcomes, a uniform definition of what comprises risk is neither possible nor necessarily desirable. Nonetheless, one can suggest broad sets of patient characteristics that reflect various dimensions or sources of risk (Table 2.1). Depending on the specific goals, one or more of these dimensions should be considered as patient risk factors.

Evaluating potential relationships between these different dimensions and the outcome of interest is essential for assessing the "medical meaningfulness" of a risk-adjustment strategy: "The extent to which knowledge of a patient's case type alone—without other information about the individual patient—conveys clinical expectations and enables clinicians to exchange information about those expectations" (Wood, Ament,

Table 2.1 Dimensions of Risk

- Age
- Sex
- Race and ethnicity
- Acute clinical stability
- Principal diagnosis ("case mix")
- Severity of principal diagnosis
- Extent and severity of comorbidities
- Physical functional status
- Psychological, cognitive, and psychosocial functioning
- Cultural and socioeconomic attributes and behaviors
- Health status and quality of life
- Patient attitudes and preferences for outcomes

and Kobrinski 1981, 249). In many contexts, medical meaningfulness is critical to evaluating the validity of a risk-adjustment approach (see Chapter 6). Medical meaningfulness also influences the acceptance, especially by clinical audiences, of information generated with risk adjustment (see Chapter 11).

Given that the ultimate intent of risk-adjusted outcome information is frequently to affect physician behavior (e.g., through drawing inferences about quality of care), medical meaningfulness is therefore a crucial consideration. However, clinical credibility is important for quantifying risk even within the payment context. For example, New Jersey physicians contributed to the demise of an early version of the DRGs, which contained 383 groups and was used by the state for hospital payment. Although these DRGs grouped patients with similar lengths of stay, the physicians argued that within-DRG diagnoses were too clinically heterogeneous to permit meaningful speculation about patients or their care (Vladeck 1984). In revising the DRGs, Yale University researchers explicitly considered medical meaningfulness, trying to create "medically interpretable" categories that physicians "should be able to relate to" (Fetter et al. 1980).

Systematic consideration of the full range of clinical dimensions is most pressing when making judgments about effectiveness or quality of care. Because of practical impediments (see Chapters 3 and 4), no risk-adjustment strategy can account for all patient attributes. By noting patient characteristics excluded from the risk-adjustment model, one can begin to identify sources of unexplained variations in patient outcomes: Did differences in outcomes result from unmeasured patient factors or from variations in therapeutic effectiveness or quality of care? In addition, depending on the context, it may be inappropriate *to adjust for* certain patient attributes. For example, evidence suggests that African American

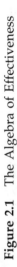

Figure 2.1 The Algebra of Effectiveness

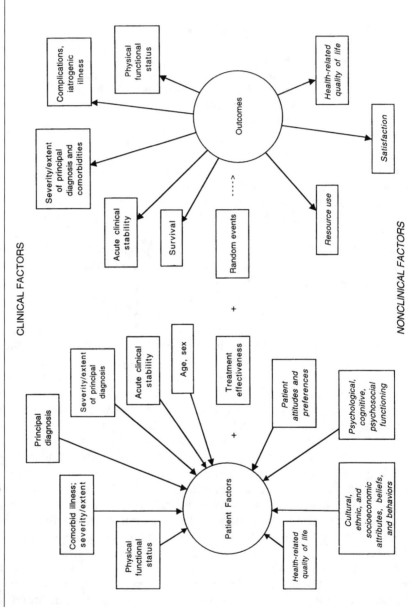

patients may receive worse quality care than white patients (Kahn et al. 1994). If the goal is to use risk-adjusted outcomes information to look specifically at quality, adjusting for race would mask these differences. In this instance, examining patient outcomes separately within racial strata would highlight such inequities.

This chapter describes dimensions of patient characteristics and provides examples of how they relate to risks of different outcomes. The implied distinction among these dimensions in the ensuing presentation is artificial: These concepts often overlap and are seldom clinically separable, especially at the patient level. I discuss these dimensions individually to organize a systematic and thorough review of wide-ranging, intertwined attributes. Different dimensions of risk are more or less important depending on their distribution across patients within the populations of interest. For example, when examining risk-adjusted mortality rates across hospitals, patient characteristics that are distributed evenly across hospitals are less problematic than those that are common in some facilities and rare in others. The following discussion considers each potential dimension of risk listed in Table 2.1, and Table 2.2 presents 11 brief clinical synopses that reflect these dimensions. Cases from this table are cited throughout the chapter.

Age

Age is a fixed patient attribute—it cannot be altered, regardless of the effectiveness or quality of care. Although the physiology of aging remains poorly understood, in most comparable situations, older persons are more likely to have worse clinical outcomes than younger persons. The cost of caring for older persons may also be higher than for younger patients, due, for example, to prolonged recuperative periods or greater incidence of complications.

In assessing overall patient risk, age may have an independent effect regardless of other patient attributes. For example, even for gravely ill patients treated in intensive care units (ICUs), age is often an important independent predictor of imminent death regardless of the extent of organ system failure. APACHE III, a severity measure designed for ICU patients and based primarily on routinely available physiologic parameters, assigns separate points to its score based on patient age, as follows: ≤ 44 years, 0 points; 45–59 years, 5 points; 60–64 years, 11 points; 65–69 years, 13 points; 70–74 years, 16 points; 75–84 years, 17 points; and ≥ 85 years, 24 points (Knaus et al. 1991, 1624).

Depending on the clinical setting, other dimensions of risk should be viewed within the context of patients' ages. The most obvious such

Table 2.2   Ten Clinical Synopses: Adenocarcinoma of the Prostate

Patient	Clinical Synopsis
A	Mild urinary symptoms relating to benign prostatic hypertrophy. A microscopic nidus of well-differentiated adenocarcinoma found in prostate gland chips following a transurethral prostatectomy. Considered a surgical cure. Otherwise in good health.
B	Mild urinary symptoms relating to benign prostatic hypertrophy. A microscopic nidus of well-differentiated adenocarcinoma found in prostate gland chips following a transurethral prostatectomy. Considered a surgical cure. History of stroke one year ago. Paralyzed on right side of body and has difficulty speaking.
C	Mild urinary symptoms relating to benign prostatic hypertrophy. A microscopic nidus of well-differentiated adenocarcinoma found in prostate gland chips following a transurethral prostatectomy. Considered a surgical cure. Patient has refused medication to treat a profound depression; he recently lost his job. No known family or friends.
D	Major urinary symptoms relating to benign prostatic hypertrophy, including urinary obstruction, hydroureter, and acute renal compromise. Patient acutely septic and in shock. A microscopic nidus of well-differentiated adenocarcinoma found in prostate gland chips following prostatectomy. Renal function returns to normal. Considered a surgical cure. Otherwise in good health.
E	Large prostatic adenocarcinoma with invasion into surrounding pelvic structures. No evidence of distant metastases. Otherwise in good health.
F	Large prostatic adenocarcinoma with invasion into surrounding pelvic structures. No evidence of distant metastases. History of poorly controlled essential hypertension, with routine blood pressure readings of 164/94 mm Hg.
G	Large prostatic adenocarcinoma with invasion into surrounding pelvic structures, causing urinary obstruction, hydroureter, and acute renal compromise. No evidence of distant metastases. Patient acutely septic and in shock.
H	Widespread metastatic disease. Patient desires active intervention, including intensive care unit admission and intubation if necessary.
I	Widespread metastatic disease. Patient requests "do not resuscitate" status, desiring "comfort measures only."
J	Patient doing well during admission, but dies unexpectedly.
K	Patient doing poorly during admission, and dies as expected.

distinction is among newborns, children, and adults. For example, the PRISM index uses 14 routinely measured, physiologic variables to predict in-hospital mortality for pediatric ICU patients. In assigning points, PRISM employs different ranges for systolic blood pressure, heart rate, and respiratory rate depending on the patient's age (Pollack, Ruttimann, and Getson 1988). For example, seven points are assigned for systolic blood pressures of <40 mm Hg for infants and <50 mm Hg for children; five points are assigned for respiratory rates of >90 breaths/minute for infants and >70 breaths/minute for children (Pollack, Ruttimann, and Getson 1988, 1113). Calculations of the probability of in-hospital mortality include not only PRISM scores but also patient age in months. Thus, using PRISM, certain physiologic variables receive different weights depending on patient age, and age is also an independent predictor of death.

Standard statistical measures, such as c and R^2 values quantifying the contribution of age in predictive models (Chapters 8 and 9), are typically unimpressive. For example, investigators from RAND Corporation examined 30-day postadmission mortality for persons 65 years of age and older, and they found that age and sex explained only 1 percent of variation in mortality for congestive heart failure and hip fracture, 2 percent for acute myocardial infarction (AMI) and stroke, and 3 percent for pneumonia (Keeler et al. 1990, 1967). In our AHCPR-funded severity study (see Chapter 1), we found that age and sex produced the following c values for predicting in-hospital mortality: 0.69 for AMI (Iezzoni et al. 1996a), 0.67 for pneumonia (Iezzoni et al. 1996b), and 0.60 for stroke (Iezzoni et al. 1995). Because a c of 0.5 indicates the model is no better than random chance, age and sex obviously provide only modest ability to discriminate between patients who lived and died.

Nevertheless, because age is one variable that is almost always available, its effect is generally easy and inexpensive to test. A better understanding of age effects may arise from looking separately within age strata. For instance, the version of DRGs first implemented for Medicare hospital payment in 1983 separated some patients into those older and younger than age 70. Recent revisions of DRGs eliminated this age distinction, because it did not distinguish patients with different hospitalization costs.

The importance of age may, however, depend on the range of ages being studied and the outcome of interest. In studies of wide age ranges (e.g., "adults" defined as 18 years of age and older), separating patients into young and old age strata may be crucial. For example, we compared the severity of illness of about 4,500 adult patients hospitalized at teaching and nonteaching hospitals in metropolitan Boston in 1985 (Iezzoni et al. 1990). DRG-adjusted disease-specific severity levels were higher for patients admitted to teaching compared to nonteaching hospitals for bronchitis/asthma, coronary artery disease, low back disorders, and AMI. However, when severity was compared across hospital types for patients separated into broad age strata, some differences disappeared. Only bronchitis/asthma patients older than 64 years of age had higher severity at teaching than nonteaching institutions. Only younger teaching hospital patients (age 18 to 64 years) had higher severity in coronary artery disease and low back disorders. For acute myocardial infarction, however, severity was higher at teaching hospitals for both younger and older patients. We hypothesized that some of these differences may relate to patient preferences and practice patterns—younger and older patients may differ in their willingness to travel to distant hospitals or to seek intensive, high-technology care.

Blumberg (1991) examined predictions of 30-day mortality by Medis-Groups admission severity scores for 3,037 patients age 65 and older. The version of MedisGroups used in this analysis did not consider age in computing severity. Blumberg divided these cases into five age strata (65–69, 70–74, 75–79, 80–84, and ≥ 85) and found that the MedisGroups score overestimated the risk of death for the youngest age stratum and underestimated it for the oldest. In our AHCPR-funded severity study, we produced similar results using this older version of MedisGroups to predict in-hospital death among 17,577 AMI patients 18 years of age and older (Iezzoni et al. 1994). MedisGroups predicted fewer deaths than occurred among the oldest patients and predicted more deaths than occurred among the youngest patients. In fact, this "bias" affected comparisons of mortality outcomes by payor types that are rough proxies for age (Medicare and Medicaid, Table 2.3). Using MedisGroups, it appeared that Medicare patients did poorly: Their death rates were higher than expected. In contrast, Medicaid patients seemed to do well: Their death rates were lower than expected. The results for Medicaid patients were diametrically opposite, however, using another risk-adjustment model that explicitly considered age. This model predicted fewer Medicaid deaths than actually occurred, suggesting that Medicaid patients died at a higher-than-expected rate. The empirically derived version of MedisGroups that replaced this older version explicitly added age to its model and found that age significantly predicted mortality for many of the 64 disease groups examined (MediQual Systems, Inc., 1993; Steen et al. 1993).

Increasing age not only increases the risk of death but also the risks of complications from many procedures and medical treatments. For example, the Multifactorial Index of Cardiac Risk (MICR), a score of risk for postoperative cardiac complications from major surgery, assigns 5 points to age more than 70 years (in comparison, having the operation emergently rates 4 points, and myocardial infarction within 6 months receives 10 points) (Goldman et al. 1977, 848). A study of 13,625 CABG patients found that advanced age was the most significant predictor of neurologic complications, wound infection, and in-hospital mortality (Weintraub et al. 1991). Nonetheless, older patients are increasingly receiving invasive, inherently risky therapies, especially in the United States. For example, higher rates of CABG surgery among the elderly accounted for 75 percent of differences between California and Canada CABG use; in 1989, rates of bypass surgery per 100,000 persons ≥ 75 years of age were 312.2 in California compared

Table 2.3   Comparison of Actual and Predicted Death Rates by
Payor Source

Payor Source	Number of Cases	Observed % Deaths	Predicted % Deaths	
			Model 1	Model 2
Medicare	10,465	18.6%	15.5%	18.1%
Medicaid	894	8.7	12.2	6.7
Private, nongroup	4,613	5.5	10.1	6.2
Private, group	1,241	6.0	11.4	9.7
Other	363	8.0	10.4	6.3

Adapted from: Iezzoni et al. 1994.
Model 1: original MedisGroups admission severity score (0, 1, 2, 3, or 4).
Model 2: patient age category and 12 chronic conditions defined by *International Classification of Diseases, Ninth Revision, Clinical Modification* codes.

to 50.0 in Ontario (Anderson et al. 1993, 1663). Older patients may have different expectations of the outcomes of healthcare services than younger patients. For example, a study of 372 patients undergoing cholecystectomy found significantly more major complications and longer hospital stays among older ($\geq$ 60 years) patients but found similar satisfaction with the outcomes of their operations as for younger patients (Mort et al. 1994). A study of major elective surgery involving 745 patients found that elderly (> 70 years) patients had similar global health perceptions as younger patients, despite worse role and physical function, energy, and fatigue (Mangione et al. 1993).

A special class of patients is the "oldest old," defined variably as persons above 80 or 85 years of age. Many believe that these patients are physiologically different from younger patients, even holding other factors constant, such as disease severity. These patients have lower "physiologic reserves," or ability to rebound from acute illness. In one study of 907 persons at least 60 years old undergoing percutaneous transluminal coronary angioplasty (PTCA), the 67 patients who were 80 years of age and older were much more likely than younger patients to develop complications—38 percent compared to 22 percent (Forman et al. 1992, 21). Controlling for numerous clinical risk factors, the odds ratio of dying in-hospital from CABG surgery compared to a 50-year-old patient was 5.00 for an 85-year-old and 7.69 for a 90-year-old (Hannan and Burke 1994, 1190). Despite acknowledging well-documented higher complication rates among persons over age 80 who undergo CABG surgery, some clinicians believe that carefully selected patients can benefit significantly, with improved postoperative functional status (Glower et al. 1992).

Finally, when adjusting for age in studying medical effectiveness, one must consider the potential effect of "ageism" in therapeutic choices for elderly patients. Despite the increasing number of elderly patients receiving sophisticated invasive treatments, some older patients are treated less intensively than younger patients with similar clinical presentations. For example, one study examined 242 Stage I and II breast cancer patients with minimal comorbid illness (Greenfield et al. 1987). Of patients 50–69 years of age, 96 percent received appropriate treatment compared to 83 percent of those age 70 and older. Similarly, a study of prostate cancer patients with localized disease found less intensive diagnostic evaluation and treatment for men 75 years of age or older than for younger men (Bennett et al. 1991). These findings extend beyond cancer treatment. One study evaluated 402 patients treated for AMI in 1988 and 1989 (Montague et al. 1991). Drugs established by clinical trials to be beneficial in treating AMI (β blockers, nitrates, acetylsalicylic acid) were administered less frequently to patients over age 69 than to younger patients, while drugs known to have either a detrimental or no effect (calcium antagonists, antiarrhythmics) were given equally to older and younger patients.

Separating ageism from changes in preferences among older patients is, however, important. One study found that average ancillary charges per hospital day in Massachusetts were $540 for persons age 60 to 69, but only $186 for persons 100 years of age and older (Perls and Wood 1996, 757). Because this study used hospital discharge abstract data, it was unable to determine the reason for these differences. But informal discussions with centenarians suggest that their attitudes about intensive, expensive care differs from those of younger patients.

Age is a simple, straightforward variable with good "face validity" as an important clinical risk factor (see Chapter 6). Although it is not always a statistically significant predictor of outcomes, age is generally routinely available in databases and is easy to understand. Therefore, age is an important dimension in designing a risk-adjustment strategy.

Sex

Differentiating patients by sex can be important in assessing patient risk for some outcomes. Women and men differ anatomically, physiologically, and hormonally. For instance, women metabolize certain antihypertensive and cardiovascular medications, such as β blockers, more slowly than men. Men and women also differ in their risks for certain diseases and death by age strata. For example, women have a longer average life expectancy than men. In the United States in 1993, white men had higher age-adjusted death rates than white women for heart disease, cerebrovascular disease, malignant neoplasms, chronic obstructive pulmonary disease, pneumonia and influenza, chronic liver disease and cirrhosis, diabetes mellitus, accidents, suicides, and homicides (National Center for Health Statistics 1996, 110–11). Findings were comparable for African Americans, with the exception that African American women had comparable age-adjusted death rates for diabetes mellitus to African American men.

While gender is thus important in epidemiologic studies of long-term, population outcomes, the statistical performance of gender in predicting shorter-term outcomes is often modest. For example, neither APACHE III (Knaus et al. 1991) nor PRISM (Pollack, Ruttimann, and Getson 1988) includes patient sex in their predictive models; sex was used in MMPS models for stroke and pneumonia but not for myocardial infarction or congestive heart failure (Daley et al. 1988); and DRGs do not split patients by sex. In the RAND study mentioned above, sex was important in predicting 30-day mortality for only one of the five conditions—hip fracture—with males having higher risk of death than females (Keeler et al. 1990). In a study of patients older than 50 years of age admitted to ICUs for lower respiratory tract disease, sex was not a statistically significant predictor of in-hospital mortality (Heuser, Case, and Ettinger 1992).

One problem in creating *a priori* hypotheses about the clinical effect of sex differences is that efficacy trials of new treatments have often either excluded women or included too few women to perform separate analyses by gender. A study by the General Accounting Office found that 60 percent of clinical trials for new drugs underrepresented female subjects (U.S. General Accounting Office 1992). Of 53 drug trials studied, only 25 (47 percent) specifically assessed whether men and women responded differently to the medication being tested. Female representation was particularly poor for trials involving new cardiovascular drugs: For 7 of 13 cardiovascular medication trials examined, the proportion of female subjects was more than 20 percent below the percent of women in the population with the disease in question. Similar underrepresentation of women in federally funded research studies prompted 1990 congressional hearings and the creation of the National Institutes of Health, Office of Research on Women's Health. Nonetheless, extensive evidence from clinical trials concerning gender differences is unlikely anytime soon.

Gender-based differences in treatments and outcomes have gained public notice since the late 1980s, although despite this interest, the cause and nature of discrepancies are not always clear. The RAND study of quality of care for Medicare beneficiaries found slightly worse overall process of care scores for women than men, but the magnitude of the difference (albeit statistically significant) was small (Pearson et al. 1992). Most attention has concentrated on the use and results of invasive technologies for diagnosing and treating coronary artery disease. For example, the clinical literature suggests that women are more likely to die in-hospital following CABG surgery than men. One study of 13,625 CABG patients found that, even after multivariate adjustment for a range of factors (age, left ventricular ejection fraction, angina class, number of vessels involved, comorbid illness, and whether the surgery was emergent), the odds ratio of death for women compared to men was 2.3 (Weintraub et al. 1991, 230). Clinical speculation about the cause of these discrepancies focused on the effect of possible differences in coronary anatomy: Women generally have smaller vessels than men. Another study of only very old CABG patients (80 to 93 years of age), however, found no differences by sex in in-hospital mortality (Glower et al. 1992).

As with concerns about ageism, caution about "gender bias" may complicate efforts to evaluate patient outcomes following adjustment for sex. For example, a retrospective study using 1987 discharge abstract data from Massachusetts and Maryland found that, even after adjusting for age, diagnosis, comorbid illness, race, and insurance status, women were much less likely than men to receive angiography, PTCA, and CABG surgery (Ayanian and Epstein 1991). Given the nature of the database (see Chapter 3), the authors could judge neither the appropriateness of these different rates nor whether the rates represented underuse in women or overuse in men. Similarly, a study of thousands of Medicare beneficiaries, also using hospital discharge abstract data, found lower use of coronary angiography, PTCA, and CABG surgery among women (Udvarhelyi et al. 1992). A recent study of 454 CABG patients collected clinical data from medical records and administered surveys to surviving patients (Ayanian, Guadagnoli, and Cleary 1995). Women were much older and more likely than men to have severe angina, recent myocardial infarction, congestive heart failure, diabetes mellitus, and anemia; women were less likely than men to have left main coronary disease. But among the 96 percent of survivors, women had similar or better functioning, along a variety of dimensions, than men.

As with age, sex is a simple, routinely available, easily measured variable with potential "face validity" as a risk factor in certain settings. In particular, longer-term, epidemiologic studies should consider differences between the sexes in risks for numerous conditions. For shorter-term outcomes, sex may not be a statistically significant predictor. Nonetheless, suspicions about gender bias in patient treatment need further exploration and could confound medical effectiveness studies. Stratifying analyses by gender could clarify this concern.

Race and Ethnicity

Several parallels with gender arise when viewing race and ethnicity as risk factors. As with gender, well-documented differences exist in disease prevalence by race and ethnicity. For example, the two leading causes of death for white, black, and Hispanic males in 1993 were overwhelmingly heart disease and cancer, but the third through seventh leading causes of death varied as follows: among whites—cerebrovascular diseases, chronic obstructive pulmonary diseases, accidents, pneumonia/influenza, and suicide; among blacks—homicide, human immunodeficiency virus (HIV) infection, accidents, cerebrovascular disease, and pneumonia/influenza; and among Hispanics—accidents, HIV infection, homicide, cerebrovascular diseases, and chronic liver disease/cirrhosis (National Center for Health Statistics 1996, 114–15). Even after controlling for many characteristics including stage of disease, African Americans had higher-case fatality rates for certain cancers than other persons (Manton, Patrick, and Johnson 1987). As with gender, generating *a priori* hypotheses about the clinical effect of racial or ethnic differences is hampered by the historical exclusion of minorities from therapeutic trials. One study of clinical efficacy trials from the mid-1980s found that 15 out of 35 studies (43 percent) had no black subjects, and almost two-thirds had a lower proportion of blacks than lived in the surrounding communities (Svensson 1989, 263–64).

However, unlike gender and many other dimensions of risk reviewed in this chapter, race and ethnicity are hard to capture in a clear, consistent, and meaningful fashion. Perhaps "racial, ethnic, and other forms of ancestral identification are not amenable to the standard scientific criteria that apply to characteristics such as age, weight, and sex" (Hahn and Stroup 1994, 13). As LaVeist (1994, 2–4, 6, 11) observed:

> Race is a social category, not a biological concept. It is a concept that has changed over time and is variable across societies . . . Race is a concept that is determined fundamentally by political and social forces without regard to biogenetics or scientific rigor . . . in the United States the finer distinctions of ethnic tribal or national variations within race groups is obscured in favor of physical appearance . . . [In research,] we must acknowledge that what is measured by the race dummy variable is not culture, biology, values, or behavior. What is actually measured by the race variable is skin color.

Although some advocate abandoning collection of racial data because of such ambiguities, others counter that these data are crucial precisely because of the social, economic, and political considerations that are inextricably linked to race by our nation's history and its continuing legacy (McKenney and Bennett 1994). The U.S. Bureau of the Census has collected data by race since the first decennial census in 1790, and it has traditionally viewed race and ethnicity as two distinct concepts. The census bureau generally follows the guidelines of Federal Statistical Policy Directive No. 15, promulgated by the federal Office of Management and Budget in 1978 (McKenney and Bennett 1994; Hahn 1992). Directive No. 15

aimed to establish uniform standards for federal agencies and to increase information on persons of Hispanic origin, as required by Congress. The directive explicitly denies being "scientific or anthropological in nature" (Hahn 1992, 269), offering brief rules for classifying persons into four racial categories—American Indian or Alaskan Native, Asian or Pacific Islander, black, and white—and two ethnic categories—of Hispanic origin and not of Hispanic origin. However, Directive No. 15 does not specify whether race and ethnicity should be determined by persons themselves or some external observer.

Gathering consistent and clear data on race and ethnicity is impeded by several important practical considerations (Hahn 1992; McKenney and Bennett 1994; LaVeist 1994; Hahn and Stroup 1994; Williams 1996). Survey respondents often misunderstand the intended distinction between race and ethnicity or the designated response categories. Respondents frequently feel that a dichotomous response about Hispanic origin ignores important cultural distinctions among ancestral countries (e.g., Cuba, Mexico, Argentina). Answers to questions about race and ethnicity change over time or across surveys due to "fuzzy group boundaries" (ambiguities about what constitutes group membership) and "shifting identity" (changes associated with groups' identity) (Hahn 1992). For example, in reinterviews by the Bureau of the Census in 1980, 41 percent of persons who identified themselves as American Indians had initially categorized themselves as white (Hahn 1992, 270). A huge increase (72 percent) in the American Indian population between the 1970 and 1980 censuses was attributed partially to shifting identification prompted by political and social trends (McKenney and Bennett 1994, 22). Despite Directive No. 15, various survey initiatives (especially regional public health surveillance programs) use different guidelines and response categories, compromising comparisons across data sources.

An especially important factor involves the source of the information—self-reports or external observers (Williams 1996). Race listed in hospital discharge abstracts (see Chapter 3) is either supplied by the patient or noted by someone else (e.g., an intake receptionist or admitting clerk) (LaVeist 1994). Instructions for birth registrations stipulate that personal information be elicited at the time of birth from mothers, fathers, or other knowledgeable persons (Hahn, Mulinare, and Teutsch 1992). In contrast, death certificates typically obtain information from statements by the next of kin to funeral directors; funeral directors, however, sometimes independently assign race, based on their views of the decedent's appearance. One study of infants who died within one year of birth compared the races listed on the birth registrations and death certificates. Discrepancies between the race listed at birth and death were found for 1.2 percent of infants classified at birth as white, 4.3 percent classified as black, and 43.2 percent classified as all other races (Hahn, Mulinare, and Teutsch 1992, 261).

Health services research studies often include race in their models, frequently as a proxy for the unmeasured quantities of socioeconomic status, discrimination, culture, and unspecified but presumed biological differences (LaVeist 1994). Williams (1994) examined 192 studies published between 1966 and 1990 in *HSR: Health Services Research*. He found that 63.0 percent included race and ethnicity; however, 54.5 percent made a black-white distinction only (most including this binary variable as a dummy in regression equations), and only 13.2 defined or justified the use of race in their research. Using racial variables in regression analyses may obscure important relationships, such as those involving education, socioeconomic class, culture, and health beliefs (Schulman et al. 1995). For example, "the growing mortality differentials between whites and blacks cannot be understood by looking only at race; they are part and parcel of larger mortality differentials: class differentials" (Navarro 1991, 233). Observing that African American adults had higher unadjusted mortality rates than did whites, one study separated the causes using information from the National Health and Nutrition Examination Survey/Epidemiologic Follow-up Study (Otten et al. 1990). About 31 percent of the unexplained mortality differential disappeared after adjusting for six risk factors (smoking, systolic blood pressure, cholesterol level, body-mass index, alcohol intake, and diabetes mellitus). Another 38 percent of the difference vanished after adjusting for income, but 31 percent of the higher mortality of African Americans versus whites remained unexplained.

The causes of these discrepancies in health and health outcomes are complex and poorly understood.

> Traditional explanations for health status differences between the races have focused on biological differences between racial populations . . . It assumes that race is a valid biological category . . . The available scientific evidence suggests that race is a social and not a biological category . . . Adjusting racial (black-white) disparities in health for SES [socioeconomic status] sometimes eliminates, but always substantially reduces, these differences. However, a frequent finding is that within each level of SES blacks still have worse health than whites . . . irrespective of race, there are large disparities in health by income and education . . . This pattern of results clearly indicates that, while there is considerable overlap between race and SES, race reflects more than SES and that fully understanding racial differences in health will require researchers to move beyond the traditional approaches. (Williams 1996, 493, 495–97).

Studies have repeatedly found that African Americans use fewer health services than do whites, although analyses rarely control for income, occupation, or education level. One study in Massachusetts found that

African American patients were less likely than others to receive coronary angiography and CABG surgery (Wenneker and Epstein 1989). Another study of 27,485 Medicare beneficiaries found an adjusted odds of 1.78 for whites compared to blacks for obtaining revascularization procedures within 90 days after coronary angiography (Ayanian et al. 1993a, 2645). One study of hundreds of thousands of Medicare beneficiaries found that blacks were much less likely than whites to receive "referral-sensitive" surgeries (McBean and Gornick 1994). A study of 17,440 consecutive admissions to 40 ICUs around the country found that African Americans received less technological monitoring (arterial and pulmonary artery catheters, pulse oximetry), fewer laboratory tests, and less life-sustaining therapy than whites, even controlling for severity of illness (Williams et al. 1995). An analysis of over 9,000 gravely ill patients admitted to five teaching hospitals—the Study to Understand Prognoses and Preferences for Outcomes and Risks of Treatment (SUPPORT)—found that, even after adjusting for sociodemographic characteristics, illness severity, functional status, and study site, African Americans received significantly fewer procedures and tests than patients of other races (Phillips et al. 1996a). In a study of 1,184 elderly patients admitted to two hospitals, African Americans had shorter lengths of stay and generated fewer charges than whites at each CSI severity level (Buckle et al. 1992).

Most studies find that African Americans are more severely ill than whites on hospital admission. In the ICU study described above, the Acute Physiology Score (APS) of APACHE III was significantly higher for blacks than whites during the first day of intensive care (Williams et al. 1995). African Americans were much more likely than whites to have CSI scores greater than 1 on admission (Buckle et al. 1992). The RAND study of Medicare quality grouped together black patients with persons from poor neighborhoods and did not find differences between these and other patients in sickness on admission (Kahn et al. 1994). However, no racial differences were found in mortality after controlling for various patient and hospital characteristics (Williams et al. 1995; Kahn et al. 1994). A study of 88,205 patients in 30 northeastern hospitals using the Cleveland Health Quality Choice severity measure (see Chapter 11) found generally lower predicted risks of death on admission for African American compared to white patients; across all six diagnoses studied, the multivariable odds of in-hospital death of African American compared to white patients was 0.87 (C.I. 0.80–0.94, $P = 0.001$) (Gordon, Harper, and Rosenthal 1996, 1642).

A few studies have raised questions about the implications of racial differences in resource use given the associated minimal impact on mortality. For instance, a study within the Department of Veterans Affairs (VA) found adjusted odds ratios of 0.59 for receiving CABG and 0.69

for PTCA for African American compared to white patients; nonethe-less, 30-day survival was better for blacks, and survival did not differ across races one and two years later (Peterson et al. 1994, 1178). Without mortality differences, the ICU study questioned whether lower resource use by blacks meant that "African American patients are undertreated or white patients are overtreated" (Williams et al. 1995, 632). However, in an editorial accompanying the VA study, Ayanian (1994, 1208) made the understated observation, "Mortality is only a partial measure of the outcomes of care." We do not know, for example, whether quality-of-life limitations related to anginal symptoms were worse for African Americans than for other patients.

The SUPPORT project investigated the possibility of racial differences in desires for heroic interventions for 1,585 patients who answered a question about preferences for cardiopulmonary resuscitation (CPR). In a bivariable analysis, white patients were much more likely than nonwhite patients to answer that they would *not* want CPR: relative risk = 1.62 (95% C.I. 1.3, 2.1) for not wanting CPR for whites compared to nonwhites (Phillips et al. 1996b, 132). However, in multivariable analyses, race became an insignificant ($P = 0.06$) predictor of CPR preferences after controlling for self-pay or Medicaid payor sources (Phillips et al. 1996b, 133).

Although it failed to find mortality differences, the RAND study of Medicare quality did uncover worrisome discrepancies between the experience of blacks and persons from poor neighborhoods and other patients. Controlling for hospital characteristics, 19.0 percent of blacks or persons from poor neighborhoods were discharged in unstable condition, compared to 13.7 percent of other patients ($p < 0.001$) (Kahn et al. 1994, 1172). Overall processes of care were also worse for blacks or persons from poor neighborhoods, adjusting for hospital characteristics.

Findings such as these raise serious questions about adjusting for race or ethnicity in examining outcomes of care: Such adjustment could hide significant racial disparities or confuse interpretation of the results. The MedisGroups database used in our AHCPR-funded study did not collect information on race or ethnicity, rationalizing that they are inappropriate for risk adjustment. A more recent MedisGroups product, Atlas 2.0, in-cludes race as an optional data field, but a MediQual Systems spokesperson acknowledged, "Customers haven't been asking for it" ("Lack of Race Data" 1995). Neither UB-82 nor UB-92 ask for patient race (see Chapter 3), and fewer hospitals are reporting race in the information they provide to the National Hospital Discharge Survey conducted by the Centers for Disease Control and Prevention.

However, as Williams observed (1994), evidence of persisting racial discrimination in the healthcare system demands continued scrutiny. To understand fully the effect of this important patient attribute on outcomes of care, looking explicitly at outcome differences by race and ethnicity is critical. This is best accomplished by examining results separately for patients grouped into strata by race and ethnicity.

Acute Clinical Stability

Acute clinical stability reflects the immediate physiologic functioning of the patient in terms of basic homeostatic measures. This dimension examines the most general and fundamental measures of bodily function, such as vital signs (heart rate, respiratory rate, blood pressure, temperature), serum electrolytes, hematology findings (e.g., hematocrit, white blood cell count, clotting indices), arterial oxygenation, and levels of consciousness or neurologic functioning. The goal is to evaluate whether the patient is at imminent risk of death. For example, although the extent and nature of the prostatic adenocarcinoma is comparable in Patients A and D and Patients E and F (Table 2.2), the immediate risks of Patients D and F are greater due to urosepsis, shock, and acute renal failure.

Assessments of acute clinical stability are crucial to studies of acutely ill patients in short time frames, such as death during an acute care hospitalization or within a short time window (e.g., 30 days from admission). The physiologic variables used are indicators of those basic organ functions required to keep patients alive (e.g., cardiac, respiratory, renal, and neurologic function). Because of this concentration on core physiologic functions, this dimension can be viewed as independent of specific diagnoses, or "generic," assuming that at the level of the "whole person," there is a "final common pathway" of physiological functions that indicate patient risk. This independence is founded on the concept of "homeostasis" expounded by Walter B. Cannon in 1929—that "the body's major physiologic systems interact to maintain internal balance and rapidly correct disturbances" (Wagner, Knaus, and Draper 1986, 1389). In other words, regardless of whether the patient develops shock because of sepsis, heart failure, or hemorrhage, the same measures (e.g., heart rate, blood pressure) will become deranged in similar ways.

Several comments about the indicators of acute clinical stability are pertinent. First, a relatively small set of variables encompasses the most important predictors, across both children and adults (Table 2.4). For example, the first version of APACHE contained information on 34 physiologic parameters (Knaus et al. 1981). In revising this system, APACHE's developers found that acceptable statistical performance was maintained by a core group of 12 physiologic parameters (Knaus et al. 1985). The most recent version, APACHE III, added several variables but is still based on a core group (Knaus et al. 1991). The new Simplified Acute Physiology Score

(SAPS II) uses even fewer variables (Le Gall, Lemeshow, and Saulnier 1993), while the MPM is the most economical (Lemeshow et al. 1993, 1994). PRISM also uses few variables to predict outcomes for pediatric ICU patients (Table 2.4).

Table 2.4   Physiologic Variables Included in Different Measures of Acute Clinical Stability

Clinical Variables	APACHE II[a]	APACHE III[b]	PRISM[c]	Mortality Probability Model II Admission[d]	At 24, 48, and 72 hours[e]	SAPS II[f]
A-a gradient	x	x				
Albumin		x				
Arterial carbon dioxide		x	x			
Arterial oxygenation	x	x	x		x	
Arterial pH	x	x				
Blood pressure	x	x	x	x		x
Blood urea nitrogen (BUN)		x				x
Bicarbonate			x			x
Calcium			x			
Glucose		x	x			
Heart rate	x	x	x	x		x
Hematocrit	x	x				
Level of consciousness, Glasgow Coma Score	x	x	x	x	x	x
PaO_2/FiO_2						x
Prothrombin time/Partial thromboplastin time (PT/PTT)			x		x	
Respiratory rate	x	x	x			
Serum creatinine	x	x			x	
Serum sodium	x	x				x
Serum potassium	x		x			x
Temperature	x	x				x
Total bilirubin		x	x			x
Urine output		x			x	x
Pupillary reactions			x			
White blood cell count	x	x				x

[a] Knaus et al. 1985.
[b] Knaus et al. 1991.
[c] Pollack, Ruttimann, and Getson 1988.
[d] Lemeshow et al. 1993.
[e] Lemeshow et al. 1994.
[f] Le Gall, Lemeshow, and Saulnier 1994.

Second, because these physiologic parameters serve as clinical guideposts for physicians caring for acutely ill patients, most are measured routinely and with minimal technologic intervention (e.g., venipuncture). Acute physiologic measures are attractive for developing models of risk because so few values are missing; how to handle values that are missing is therefore an important question (see Chapter 5).

Third, measures of acute clinical stability are used most commonly to predict risk of imminent death for gravely ill patients, such as those admitted to ICUs (Lemeshow and Le Gall 1994). However, knowledge of acute physiologic status may not—alone—sufficiently predict imminent death. The MPM considers whether chronic diagnoses of metastatic cancer, chronic renal failure, or cirrhosis are present (Lemeshow et al. 1993); SAPS II incorporates age and metastatic cancer, hematologic malignancy (lymphoma, acute leukemia, multiple myeloma), and AIDS (Le Gall, Lemeshow, Saulnier 1993). APACHE III adds age category in its score calculation; points are also assigned for seven comorbid conditions (Knaus et al. 1991).

Nonetheless, one of the most striking findings of our AHCPR-funded severity study (see Chapter 1) was how well measures based on acute physiologic findings alone (physiology scores 1 and 2) were able to predict in-hospital mortality compared to measures using a more complete range of clinical information (the two MedisGroups scores, see Table 1.9). As shown in Table 2.5, the c and R^2 values of the physiology scores were often similar to those of the MedisGroups scores, despite the economy of the former models.

Finally, a question that is as yet unresolved in research circles is whether the weights assigned to acute physiologic variables in predicting outcomes should vary depending on the patient's diagnosis (see Chapter

Table 2.5   Physiology and MedisGroups Scores Predicting In-Hospital Mortality within Four Conditions

Condition	Physiology Score 1		Physiology Score 2		Original MedisGroups		Empirical MedisGroups	
	c	R^2	c	R^2	c	R^2	c	R^2
AMI	0.82	0.18	0.83	0.23	0.80	0.17	0.83	0.23
CABG surgery	0.73	0.04	0.73	0.03	0.73	0.04	0.74	0.04
Pneumonia	0.78	0.10	0.82	0.15	0.81	0.13	0.85	0.19
Stroke	0.80	0.17	0.84	0.24	0.80	0.15	0.87	0.27

Sources: Iezzoni et al. 1995, 1996a, 1996b; Landon et al. 1996.

5). For example, should blood pressure be weighted differently for patients admitted for congestive heart failure versus gastrointestinal hemorrhage? The developers of the MMPS found that they achieved the best predictions of 30-day postadmission mortality by considering the APACHE II score (calculated according to its diagnosis-independent rules) and then adding independent linear forms of selected physiologic variables within each of the four diseases (stroke, pneumonia, myocardial infarction, and congestive heart failure). This process permitted assignment of diagnosis-specific weights for these variables for some conditions (Daley et al. 1988). The newest physiologic severity measures rely almost entirely on empirical modeling to produce their scoring algorithms, and they consider interrelationships with acute diagnoses in various ways (Lemeshow and Le Gall 1994).

In developing their model to predict death within 180 days, Knaus and other SUPPORT investigators found that relationships between some variables and survival varied by disease. For instance, lower serum albumin was particularly predictive for death among lung and colon cancer patients, and modestly predictive for chronic obstructive pulmonary disease and congestive heart failure patients, but it had little prognostic value for other patients. Low leukocyte count was especially important for patients with acute respiratory failure and multiple organ system failure (Knaus et al. 1995, 194). Therefore, some variables were assigned disease-specific scorings.

Although the debate continues about the need for disease-specific weightings, the value of acute physiologic parameters in assessing patient risk for imminent clinical outcomes is undisputed. Acute clinical stability is obviously central to evaluating risk for imminent death and complications, such as respiratory failure or shock. Its utility for predicting resource use is less apparent.

Principal Diagnosis

> The diagnosis is a hypothesis regarding the nature of the patient's illness . . . The physician's goal is to test his diagnostic hypothesis by applying particular treatments and observing the patient's recovery. Because the diagnosis is such a focal point in the physician's interaction with the patient, this concept is fundamental to measurement of hospital output: the diagnosis establishes the relevant technology of care and, hence, the types and levels of resources required to treat the illness. (Hornbrook 1982, 74)

Few argue that risks for outcomes—from resource use to clinical events—differ dramatically by diagnosis. For example, inguinal hernia patients have very different outcomes than patients presenting with left hemi-spheric strokes; in comparing the long-term mortality from colon surgery, one must separate invasive carcinoma from diverticular disease patients.

Older patients, in particular, rarely have single diagnoses. Instead, various chronic illnesses, such as atherosclerotic cardiovascular disease and non-insulin-dependent diabetes mellitus, often accompany acute conditions requiring medical attention. Even with careful clinical inspection, disentangling a primary disease process from coexisting conditions is frequently difficult. For the sake of discussion, however, I focus first on risks associated with the "principal diagnosis" and then consider "comorbid" disease.

Defining and Delineating Diseases and Diagnoses

For hospitalized patients, the principal diagnosis is defined by the National Committee on Vital and Health Statistics as the leading disease that brings the patient into contact with the healthcare system and for which services are sought (see Chapter 3). This definition belies the complexity of designating diagnoses. Defining "diagnosis" has preoccupied medicine since the time of Hippocrates, spawning volumes of nomenclatures and commentary. As Feinstein noted (1967, 73):

> Diagnosis is the focal point of thought in the treatment of a patient. From diagnosis, which gives a name to the patient's ailment, the thinking goes chronologically backward to decide about pathogenesis and etiology of the ailment. From diagnosis also, the thinking goes chronologically forward to predict prognosis and to choose therapy. As the main language of clinical communication, diagnostic labels transmit a rapid understanding of the contents of the package.

Complete specification of diagnoses involves a series of steps as suggested by Gonnella, Hornbrook, and Louis (1984, 638):

> A disease is a well-defined model of a process of disruption in the normal homeostasis of psychological-physiological systems . . . Each disease should be defined in terms of some specific organ or organ system involved . . . Every disease must specify some characteristic pathophysiological change . . . An etiologic factor or set of factors causing the pathophysiological changes must be given.

By these criteria, designating the diagnosis can be straightforward. Examples include infection by *Streptococcus pneumoniae* affecting the lung (pneumococcal pneumonia), nondisplaced intertrochanteric fracture of the hip following a fall, and Stage I adenocarcinoma of the breast. In many other instances, however, specifying diagnoses by etiology, location, and manifestation is not clearcut.

Absolute diagnosis is not always possible. For example, despite fiberoptic studies, angiography, radionuclide scans, and barium enemas, the source and causes of lower gastrointestinal tract bleeding may remain elusive. A "diagnosis" of "gastrointestinal hemorrhage" is assigned, reflecting a sign of underlying disease rather than the disease itself. Sometimes the stress of immediately managing a cataclysmic event precludes attention to exact diagnosis. For example, a patient arriving acutely short of breath may require emergent intubation and receive an admitting "diagnosis" of "respiratory failure." Later, once the patient is stabilized, one may identify the exact cause of the respiratory compromise.

In certain situations, the dividing line between the presence and absence of disease is blurred. For example, dysplasia of the cervix is an abnormal finding on a Papanicolaou test that can presage cervical cancer. The subtlety of morphologic differences between dysplastic and normal cells certainly hampers making this diagnosis. In most instances, the condition vanishes spontaneously, and even while present, the dysplastic cells do not cause pain or disability (Eddy 1984). Similarly, an elevated serum alkaline phosphatase can antedate overt symptoms of related liver or bone disease by months or years or can occur without a cause ever being found (Rubenstein, Ward, and Greenfield 1986). Numerous examples exist of "diseases . . . being defined by an abnormal result on some test, leaving uncertainty about its real meaning to a patient and the appropriate treatment" (Eddy 1984, 76).

Some diagnostic terminology is used because of habit or sloppiness or because specifying an etiologic agent is not always clinically important. "Congestive heart failure"—a common term—is generally caused by long-standing hypertension or coronary artery disease, but occasionally results from other diverse etiologies, such as viruses, alcohol, or disordered iron metabolism. Some causes require specific interventions. Once congestive heart failure is present, however, exacerbations are often treated similarly (e.g., with diuretics) in most patients. Therefore, physicians may find it unimportant to state the cause of the heart failure when describing the patient.

Finally, certain specific diagnoses produce widely varying manifestations, while very different diseases lead to similar problems. For example, diabetic complications range from blinding retinopathy to chronic renal failure; sequelae of syphilis range from aortic aneurysm to general paresis; and the presentation of systemic lupus erythematosus encompasses renal failure and seizures. Because these varying problems require different therapeutic and diagnostic approaches, grouping together all patients with these types of diagnoses (e.g., all diabetes patients) may be inappropriate. Instead, depending on the purpose of the analysis, grouping all patients whose diagnoses result in a serious manifestation treated identically, regardless of etiology, may be suitable. For example, end-stage renal disease results from such diverse entities as long-standing, poorly controlled hypertension; diabetes; lupus; and certain infections. Chronic renal failure from any cause necessitates costly lifelong dialysis or renal transplantation.

Thus, although the criteria of Gonnella and colleagues (1984) yield the most comprehensive specification of disease, satisfying each requirement is often impossible. Nonetheless, even a less rigorous determination of the principal diagnosis is often critical for risk adjustment. This less-rigorous specification frequently reflects the realities of diagnostic and therapeutic technologies and is, as suggested by Hornbrook above, the context within which decisions are made concerning clinical interventions.

Severity or Extent of Principal Diagnosis

Differentiating patients by their principal diagnoses may be only the necessary first step. In many settings, examining the severity or extent of this principal diagnosis is also crucial. For example, persons with prostate cancer isolated to the gland (Patients A–C, Table 2.2) have different prognoses and therapeutic needs related to their principal diagnosis than persons with widely disseminated malignancy (Patients H and I). Many studies of medical effectiveness and patient outcomes focus on a single principal diagnosis, thus obviating the need to separate patients by diagnoses. Nevertheless, differentiating patients by severity levels within a single principal diagnostic category often remains important.

The concept of severity has many layers; which factors dominate depends on the context. A core organizing concept involves prognosis—expectations about patients' clinical outcomes relating to the extent and nature of disease. Prognoses, obviously, vary depending on the time frame: prognosis over the long run (months or years) versus the short run (hours, days, or weeks). Long- and short-run assessments of severity may differ. For example, Patient D (Table 2.2) presents with benign prostatic hyperplasia obstructing his urinary tract, resulting in urosepsis and hydroureter. He has a high fever and appears acutely toxic; he needs immediate, aggressive treatment. His prostate is resected, relieving the obstruction, and a small nidus of tumor is found within the gland—a common clinical scenario. The cancer is focal without apparent metastases. Patient I's prostate cancer has metastasized to bone. He is admitted to palliate bone pain; he appears cachectic but not acutely ill, not at immediate risk. The short- and long-run prognoses of these patients differ. The first has an immediately life-threatening condition; if treated, he could live for years. The second patient's condition is not immediately life-threatening, but portends a very poor long-term prognosis.

Before using prognosis to delineate clinical correlates of severity, one must answer the question: prognosis for what? Death is commonly the focus of outcome studies and provider report cards (see Chapter 11), primarily because information on death is routinely available. Studying death is perhaps most useful for those diagnoses in which it is a relatively common, immediate result regardless of intensive therapeutic intervention. For example, patients with refractory ventricular arrhythmias or cardiogenic shock are more severely ill than other AMI patients because of their greater risk of imminent death. Imminent death is irrelevant for assessing most ambulatory conditions. For instance, the Framingham study and other investigations suggest that the risk of cardiovascular death associated with hypertension doubles as diastolic blood pressure rises into the range of 80 to 89 mm Hg (Working Group on Risk and High Blood Pressure 1985). Does this mean that, all other factors being equal, patients with a diastolic pressure of 90 mm Hg are twice as "sick" as those with a pressure of 80 mm Hg? For example, is Patient F "sicker" than Patient E (Table 2.2)? Because death is often years away, this may make little difference in the immediate assessment of the patient. Another outcome for assessing severity of chronic diseases involves patient functioning or quality of life, but this can become confounded with the effects of the ambulatory treatments. For example, patients with untreated essential hypertension often "feel just fine," but drug therapies may produce side effects that reduce patients' sense of well-being.

For those many diagnoses in which death is not a frequent, imminent event, precisely defining severity becomes more complicated. One common approach in the medical literature is examining the extent of deviation from "normal." This definitional logic is, however, circular: To define "abnormality" one must first define "normality." For clinical laboratory parameters, "normality" is typically a statistical construct correlated with decades of experience in reviewing results of patients who do not appear sick. But for many clinical variables, determining normality is more complex.

In some cases, disease-specific clinical parameters delimiting severity have been studied extensively. For example, oncologists have devised staging methods based on local tumor manifestations and the extent of lymphatic spread and distant metastases; the New York Heart Association devised a classification scheme for the etiology, anatomy, physiologic function, and clinical manifestations of heart disease. As suggested above, diseases with diverse presentations are more complicated. For instance, is a blind diabetic more severely ill than one with debilitating peripheral vascular disease? Quality-of-life considerations must enter this equation, but quality appraisals are subject to individuals' personal values (e.g., one person may adapt to blindness while another may find it intolerable).

The contrasts are further muddied when comparing acute with chronic manifestations of single diseases. For example, is the patient with sickle cell anemia marked by multiple painful crises sicker than the patient whose disease resulted in renal failure?

Comparing severity among diseases is even more treacherous—it often amounts to comparing apples with oranges. For example, in conventional terms, prostate cancer seems more serious than psoriasis, but the accuracy of this perception depends on the extent of each disease. Early prostate cancer (Patient A) is probably less severe (e.g., in terms of imminent death, discomfort, disability) than psoriasis with diffuse erythroderma and infection with antibiotic-resistant bacteria. Even if severity indicators could be identified, the problem of measurement remains:

> Suppose everyone agreed that a particular collection of signs, symptoms, and test results constituted an unequivocal definition of a disease [and its extent or severity]. Would this eliminate the uncertainty? Unfortunately, even when sharp criteria are created, physicians vary widely in their application of these criteria—in their ability to ask about symptoms, observe signs, interpret test results, and record answers. (Eddy 1984, 77)

As a further complication, this measurement may require not just one assessment but observing the patient over time. For example, suppose three patients presented with acute onset of identical, severe neurologic deficits indicating cerebrovascular disease. The first patient's symptoms resolve fully in 24 hours; the deficits of the second slowly improve over a week but never vanish completely; and the third patient's deficits persist without change. The severity of illness clearly differs across these three patients, but focusing on a single point in time—patient presentation—would miss these important distinctions.

One pitfall with longitudinal examination of severity is possible confounding with substandard care. Patients worsen not only because of the natural progression of disease beyond the reach of current therapeutics but also because of inadequate or inappropriate care. For example, delirium is a common problem for hospitalized elderly patients and can result from exacerbation of intrinsic brain disease (e.g., Alzheimer's dementia), but it is also precipitated by inattention to reduced drug dosage requirements in the old and to failures in treating metabolic derangements. After detecting delirium, attributing it to poor care requires specific investigation.

In other situations, one must not only evaluate the patient over time but also quantify the clinical trajectory. For example, within a few days of AMI, cardiac arrhythmias commonly occur. With a few exceptions, serious concern arises only if the arrhythmias are prolonged or frequent. For example, the clinical significance of ventricular tachycardia depends on the frequency of episodes, their rate and duration, and whether other heart ailments are present. Based on these features, ventricular tachycardia is either of modest clinical significance or life-threatening. Thus, a measure that indicates only that the ventricular tachycardia occurred is not adequately medically meaningful. To quantify this longitudinal perspective, however, requires in-depth and potentially expensive data collection.

Disease-Specific Severity Measurement

As shown in Table 1.5, many believe that other dimensions of patient risk should be viewed within the context of the principal diagnosis. With the CSI, developed by Horn and colleagues (Horn et al. 1991; Averill et al. 1992; Iezzoni and Daley 1992), specific diagnoses dictate the importance assigned to various patient characteristics. Horn and colleagues (1991, 302) cite two examples to illustrate their rationale for this strategy:

- The presence of opisthotonos (the extreme extension of the body occurring in a tetanic spasm) is critically important in judging the severity of tetanus but is not relevant in other disorders.
- A temperature of 102° F is a very severe finding for a patient with leukemia, but it is only a moderately severe finding for a patient with pneumonia.

In the empirically derived MedisGroups (Steen et al. 1993), identical clinical findings also contribute differently depending on the principal diagnosis. This version of MedisGroups computes a probability of in-hospital death for each patient based on logistic regression models calculated separately within each of 64 disease groups. For each disease, key clinical findings (KCFs) are included only if they are statistically significant predictors of death, and their coefficients (indicating their statistical contribution to the prediction model) vary from disease to disease. For example, the coefficients associated with low systolic blood pressure are −0.018 for respiratory neoplasms, −0.026 for heart failure, and −0.030 for gastrointestinal neoplasms (Steen et al. 1993, 136–37).

One practical implication of assigning a global or summary severity score is that scores may have different implications across diagnoses. For 23,361 Medicare cases admitted to one of 836 hospitals across the country, we calculated the fraction dying within 30 days of admission (Iezzoni et al. 1991a). We stratified patients by the older version (i.e., not empirically derived) of MedisGroups, which assigned scores of 0 through 4, using a heuristic algorithm. As shown in Table 2.6, 30-day mortality rates varied substantially by condition, even within MedisGroups admission score categories. For example, 67.5 percent of pneumonia or chronic obstructive pulmonary disease patients with admission scores of 4 died within 30 days,

Table 2.6   Percent Dying within 30 Days of Admission by Admission
MedisGroups Score

	Admission MedisGroups Score					
Condition	0	1	2	3	4	All Cases
	Percent of Cases Dying within 30 Days					
Pneumonia or chronic obstructive pulmonary disease (n = 3,552)	1.4	2.9	9.0	28.7	67.5	12.8
Coronary revascularization (n = 3,367)	2.5	4.7	6.9	19.1	36.4	5.8
Acute myocardial infarction (n = 3,312)	6.3	8.2	15.4	40.9	80.3	23.8
Congestive heart failure (n = 3,524)	5.9	7.6	10.3	23.0	55.4	14.9
Cholecystectomy (n = 3,589)	1.2	1.4	2.8	5.4	33.3*	2.2
Prostate surgery (n = 3,641)	0.6	0.8	2.5	7.1	0.0*	1.1

Source: Iezzoni et al. 1991.
* Cell contains fewer than 10 cases.

compared to 36.4 percent of patients admitted for coronary revascularization (Iezzoni et al. 1991a, 75).

Examples from Four Conditions

As suggested by the tables in Chapter 1, different measures use different
approaches for capturing "severity," variously defined. Some start with
disease-specific components that, when aggregated, contribute to overall
ratings. The CSI, for example, rates the severity of each disease experienced by a patient separately, then disease-specific ratings are combined
to produce the overall severity score. Similarly, Disease Staging and PMCs
assign patients to stages of diseases or PMCs based on all diagnoses present
(as well as procedures for PMCs), then use these assignments to generate
overall ratings, for example, of resource intensity. Other measures compute
overall scores for patients using a single algorithm based on the patient's
principal diagnosis, although that score may incorporate clinical variables
representing diverse organ systems. For instance, MediQual's Atlas MQ
(MedisGroups) has separate algorithms for patients sorted into each of
64 disease groups, but these 64 algorithms can include KCFs representing
various organ systems.

Exhibits 2.1 through 2.4 (located at the end of this chapter) display
components of four approaches: the CSI, Disease Staging, MediQual's Atlas MQ 2.0 (MedisGroups), and PMCs. Each measure provided information

relating to four conditions: bacterial pneumonia, AMI, colon cancer, and hip fracture. Depending on the measure, this information about specific diseases can be combined with other information (e.g., about coexisting illnesses) to produce overall ratings or scores. At the outset, it is important to note that the different measures specify "diseases" in different ways. For example, Disease Staging designates a specific "disease category" (DX-CAT) pertaining to fracture of the head or neck of the femur resulting from trauma; in contrast, MedisGroups' diagnosis grouping combines all fractures, regardless of site. In addition, these exhibits display the approaches of these four systems as of early fall 1996. As stated in Chapters 1 and 6, most systems continually undergo scrutiny and revision when necessary; therefore, the specific components pertaining to these four diseases may have changed. A number of additional comments are necessary to guide review of these approaches.

The CSI (Exhibit 2.1) organizes its criteria used to judge severity around matrices. The ICD-9-CM (see Chapter 3) diagnosis codes used to define each disease are listed above the matrices. The rows of each matrix indicate types or categories of clinical information (e.g., arterial blood gas values, neurological findings) that are used to judge severity for the particular disease. The columns labeled 1 through 4 indicate what values of each type of clinical information fall into the four levels of severity, with 1 reflecting normal or mild derangements and 4 representing life-threatening abnormalities. As shown in Exhibit 2.1, the clinical elements contained in each matrix are disease specific. If patients have coexisting illnesses, additional severity matrices would also be completed; ratings from all pertinent matrices would be combined to produce overall severity scores.

The Disease Staging (Exhibit 2.2) approach is also organized in a matrix form. Above the matrix is listed the disease name, its etiology or cause, and the DXCAT number. The rows of the matrix represent different stages or substages of severity for that disease. Disease Staging separates severity into four major stages, represented by the numbers 1 through 4 to the left of the decimal point. However, depending on the disease, substages may be assigned, reflecting increasing severity within the four major stages. The substage is indicated by the number to the right of the decimal point. The left-most column contains the stage number, while the next column provides a brief clinical description of the stage. The subsequent column enumerates the diagnostic findings that must be met to assign the patient to the stage represented by each row. These are the findings that one would abstract from a medical record when using the clinical criteria version of Disease Staging. The right-most column displays the ICD-9-CM codes used to define each stage and substage by the version of Disease Staging that uses administrative data to score severity. The computerized Disease Staging product can then generate various predictive scales, based on patient characteristics including the stage of each of a patient's diseases. These scales were empirically derived and validated using large administrative databases to predict in-hospital mortality, length of stay, and hospital charges.

The organization of the MediQual Atlas MQ 2.0 (MedisGroups) algorithm (Exhibit 2.3) reflects its empirical derivation. The exhibit displays two MedisGroups models using information from Review 1 (generally the first one or two days of hospitalization) to predict either in-hospital mortality or length of stay within each of the four disease groups. MedisGroups' developers applied logistic regression techniques to derive these models, validating them using split-sample approaches (Steen et al. 1993; Steen 1994). They employed a large database including all KCF information from hospitals around the country that collect MedisGroups severity data. Separate models were produced for mortality and length of stay predictions. Exhibit 2.3 basically depicts the output of the validated regression equations, indicating the independent variables that entered the equations and their resultant coefficients. Values for each of the independent variables (KCFs) are collected during review of the medical record, using specific definitions provided in the MedisGroups Glossary.

As shown in Exhibit 2.4, each PMC has a Patient Management Path. Each of the four requested conditions is represented by more than one PMC—for example, there are eight PMCs for AMI. Exhibit 2.4 therefore presents examples of paths pertaining to the four conditions, not the complete set of paths. Paths indicate those diagnostic and therapeutic services necessary to manage effectively a typical patient in that PMC (Young 1993). To specify each path, physician consultants "stated the reason(s) for hospitalization, the services or components of care required to diagnose that patient type, specific diagnoses, and the components of care required to treat that patient type" (Young 1993, 13). Because each PMC has a path reflecting a clinical management strategy, PMCs can group patients based on the expectation that they will use specific resources. The major data elements used to operationalize PMCs are ICD-9-CM diagnosis and procedure codes. Two or more ICD-9-CM diagnosis codes are often necessary to represent a single disease or its manifestation; some PMCs are also defined by procedure codes. "Information from the Path is used to derive the cost-based relative weights for PMCs and the one Relative Intensity Score (PMC-RIS) assigned to each patient" (Young 1993, 15). "The PMC-RIS is based on a patient's particular combination of clinical conditions and complications (multiple PMCs). The PMC-RIS reflects the relative costs of hospital services expected for that patient as specified by physicians on the Patient Management Paths" (Young 1993, 23).

Extent and Severity of Comorbidities

"Comorbidities," or coexisting diagnoses, are diseases unrelated in etiology or causality to the principal diagnosis. Comorbidities differ from "complications"—sequelae of the principal diagnosis. For example, for patients admitted with prostatic disease (Table 2.2), cerebrovascular disease (Patient B) is a comorbidity, whereas urinary obstruction (Patient G) is a complication. The prototypical comorbidity is a chronic condition, such as diabetes mellitus, chronic obstructive pulmonary disease, or chronic ischemic heart disease (Table 2.7). Depending on the context, however, comorbid illnesses could also be acute (e.g., an AMI following admission to treat prostate cancer). Similarly to considering the severity or extent of the principal diagnosis, the severity or extent of comorbid illness is also often important. For example, assessments of Patient F's hypertension (Table 2.2) would vary depending on whether it has caused little end organ damage or has led to renal insufficiency or heart failure.

In most instances, patients with comorbid illnesses differ importantly from patients without these conditions. Patients with comorbidities often have a higher risk of death, increased chance of complications, lower physiologic reserves and consequently impaired recuperative powers; they frequently require additional diagnostic testing and intensive therapeutic management. For these reasons, most prospective randomized clinical trials exclude patients with significant comorbidity, concerned that comorbid disease could confound perceptions of treatment efficacy. Studies of medical effectiveness, however, examine outcomes in the real world, where chronic diseases are increasingly common, especially as patients age. For example, among Americans 65 to 74 years of age, the prevalence of selected diseases per 1,000 persons is 383.8 for hypertension, 231.6 for heart conditions, 89.7 for diabetes, 57.3 for asthma, and 54.2 for chronic bronchitis (U.S. Bureau of the Census 1992). Chronic conditions are associated with major limitations in functional activities, even among younger persons. For instance, the prevalence of activity limitations per 1,000 women 45 to 69 years of age is 83.5 for arthritis, 53.1 for hypertension, and 26.7 for diabetes (Verbrugge and Patrick 1995).

The effect of a comorbidity can depend on the time frame of observation. Comorbidities are crucial for predicting long-term survival. Charlson and colleagues, for instance, examined the one-year survival of 559 patients admitted to the medical service at New York Hospital during a one-month period in 1984 (Charlson et al. 1987). Information on coexisting illnesses, taken from medical records, was used to create a comorbidity index, produced from adjusted relative risks from a Cox proportional hazards analysis. Based on these findings, each comorbidity was assigned a weight, ranging from 1 (adjusted relative risk ≥ 1.2 and < 1.5) to 6 (adjusted relative

Table 2.7   Variables Included in Three Measures of Comorbid Illness

	Points Assigned		
Comorbid Condition	Charlson Index	RAND Index	APACHE III
Myocardial infarct	1		
Congestive heart failure	1	1	
Peripheral vascular disease	1		
Cerebrovascular disease	1	2	
Dementia	1	2	
Chronic pulmonary disease	1		
Connective tissue disease	1		
Ulcer disease	1		
Mild liver disease	1		
Diabetes without end organ damage	1	1	
Hemiplegia	2		
Moderate or severe renal disease	2	3	
Diabetes with end organ damage	2		
Any tumor, cancer	2	3	
Leukemia	2		10
Lymphoma	2		13
Moderate or severe liver disease	3		
Cirrhosis		2	4
Hepatic failure			16
Metastatic solid tumor	6		11
AIDS	6		23
Immunosuppression		2	10
Multiple myeloma		2	10[a]
Valvular disease or angina or myocardial infarction or heart surgery		2	
Arrhythmias		2	
Swallowing disorders (e.g., aspiration, dysphagia)		2	
Use of nasogastric tube		3	
Hospitalization in the last month		2	
Thoracic or abdominal surgery in the last month		2	
Disease of the thorax		3	
Splenectomy		2	
Smoking		2	
Alcoholism		2	
Morbid obesity		2	
Hypoalbuminemia or malnourishment		3	

Note: Definitions of comorbid conditions vary across measures. See Charlson Index, Charlson et al. 1987; RAND Index, Keeler et al. 1990; APACHE III, Knaus et al. 1991.

[a] APACHE III considers leukemia/multiple myeloma as a single comorbid condition.

risk ≥ 6). Simply counting the number of comorbid conditions significantly ($p < 0.05$) predicted death at one year; the largest difference occurred between patients with zero versus one or more comorbid conditions. The weighted index was also significantly predictive of one-year mortality ($p < 0.0001$) (Charlson et al. 1987, 377).

Greenfield and colleagues (1993) developed a measure to quantify risk from comorbid illness—the Index of Coexistent Disease (ICED). ICED aimed to capture quality of life by answering the question, If a patient is rated as "severe," will he or she have poor quality of life or be unable to tolerate rigorous therapy over the next two or so years? (Greenfield et al. 1994, 300). ICED melds physiologic derangements and impairments related to comorbid illness in computing overall levels of risk. The first component of ICED is "physiological," reflecting severity of 14 health conditions; the second component involves the "functional burden," representing physical impairment resulting from both diagnosed and undiagnosed conditions and assessed within ten body systems. Although scores are rated separately along these two dimensions, the total ICED level, representing the overall effect of coexistent illness, combines these two tallies. In a study of 356 hip fracture patients, ICED was a significant predictor of functional status one year after the acute event (Greenfield et al. 1993).

Both the Charlson Index and ICED have some ability to predict even five-year survival. Krousel-Wood, Abdoh, and Re (1996) examined the ability of three comorbidity indices—the Charlson Index, ICED, and the Kaplan-Feinstein Index (Concato et al. 1992)—to predict five-year survival among 253 men undergoing transurethral prostatectomy. Although the three measures had different conceptual foundations and derivations, they produced statistically similar areas under a receiver operating characteristic curve (see Chapter 9): 0.67 for the Charlson Index; 0.68 for ICED; and 0.75 for the Kaplan-Feinstein Index (Krousel-Wood, Abdoh, and Re 1996, 37).

Comorbidities also are important in examining shorter-term outcomes such as hospital mortality rates. For example, a study of 201 ICU patients found that the Charlson comorbidity index was a significant predictor of in-hospital death; the Charlson Index contributed additional important ($P = 0.03$) prognostic information to APACHE II predictions of in-hospital death (Poses et al. 1996, 745). Greenfield and colleagues (1988) studied patients admitted between 1980 and 1982 for treatment of breast, prostate, or colon cancer. Information on comorbid conditions taken from medical records was dichotomized into none/mild versus severe/life-threatening illness. The percent of patients rated as severe varied across the seven study hospitals from 9.3 to 17.9 percent. Most importantly, the three hospitals with the highest rates of severe comorbid disease also had high mortality rates for at least one diagnosis and had been called high-mortality outliers in a California report on hospital mortality rates (Greenfield et al. 1988).

The RAND study of the effect of Medicare's prospective hospital payment system also considered comorbidity (Keeler et al. 1990), using broad definitions of coexisting conditions (Table 2.7)—including smoking and morbid obesity, as well as procedures (use of a nasogastric tube, thoracic or abdominal surgery in the last month, use of home oxygen). Weights were assigned to each of 16 conditions, based on clinical judgment and logistic regression predictions of 30-day mortality. The comorbidity index significantly predicted 30-day mortality for only two of the five study conditions (pneumonia and hip fracture) when added to a model containing acute physiologic variables.

APACHE III's developers explored the influence of comorbid disease for imminent death in ICU patients (Knaus et al. 1991). After investigating 34 candidate chronic conditions, they found that 7 had independent effects on in-hospital mortality (Table 2.7). Total APACHE III scores range from 0 to 299, and the contribution for comorbid illness varies from 4 points for cirrhosis to 23 for AIDS (Knaus et al. 1991, 1624). Among elective postoperative ICU admissions, however, these conditions were uncommon and did not enhance predictive power of the model. Therefore, points for chronic disease are not included for elective postoperative ICU cases.

Comorbidities affect patients' ability to tolerate treatments and respond to therapy. For example, patients with chronic obstructive pulmonary disease (COPD) are at risk of postoperative complications because their disease compromises air flow and the ability of coughing to clear airways and limit atelectasis (thus reducing the risk of pneumonia and prolonged ventilator support) (Kroenke 1987). Patients with chronic liver or renal disease metabolize certain drugs differently than patients without these conditions, producing different responses to standard drug dosages. Patients with significant multiple organ system diseases are less able to tolerate rigorous medical treatments, such as chemotherapy. In particular, comorbidities are often the crucial determinants of operative risk. Goldman and colleagues (1977) found that preexisting heart conditions and other comorbid diseases were important predictors of postoperative cardiac complications for patients receiving noncardiac surgery. Their MICR for noncardiac surgery patients assigns points for conditions such as myocardial infarction within six months, aortic stenosis, chronic liver disease, chronic pulmonary disease, and renal failure (Goldman et al. 1977).

Comorbidities are even important predictors of outcomes for patients with spinal cord injury. Rochon and colleagues (1996, 1096) examined comorbid illness among 362 persons discharged from a spinal cord injury service (54.2 percent paraplegic and 45.5 percent quadriplegic). They followed patients for 18 months after discharge and looked at both deaths and total hospital days during this period. Comorbid illness, measured in several ways, significantly predicted deaths. One method, the Cumulative Illness Rating Scale, also significantly predicted hospital stays.

As suggested above, "acute comorbidities" may represent iatrogenic events, raising questions about quality of care. The exact semantic distinctions among "acute comorbidities," "complications," "iatrogenic illnesses," "adverse events," and other similar terms are often unclear. Steel and colleagues (1981) examined charts of 815 patients seen on the medical service of a Boston teaching hospital: 36 percent of patients experienced at least one "iatrogenic illness" and 9 percent sustained "major" events. The most common iatrogenic illnesses were cardiopulmonary, followed by infections, gastrointestinal conditions, and neurologic events. A study of 30,195 patients hospitalized in New York in 1984 found 1,133 "adverse events" (Leape et al. 1991). Among surgical cases, wound infections were most common; among medical cases, drug reactions (e.g., marrow suppression, bleeding, and central nervous system effects) were most frequent.

Whether one must distinguish acute comorbidities related to a natural progression of underlying disease versus those caused by iatrogenic events varies depending on the context, and the ease of making this distinction depends on the data source. For example, Brailer and colleagues (1996) wanted to derive a tool to identify inpatient complications as a quality screen, but they were limited to administrative discharge abstract data. As described in Chapter 3, ICD-9-CM codes for secondary diagnoses typically do not specify whether the condition was present on admission or arose during the hospitalization, perhaps as a complication of care. They impaneled 18 physicians who developed consensus probability estimates that each secondary diagnosis was a complication versus a comorbidity for each potential principal diagnosis. For example, for a patient admitted for simple pneumonia to the general medical service, the panel's probability estimate that specified secondary diagnoses represented complications (not comorbidities) was 0.20 for congestive heart failure, 0.50 for respiratory failure, and 0.90 for urinary tract infection (Brailer et al. 1996, 493).

To be comprehensive, this discussion separated principal diagnoses, comorbidities, and their respective severities into different dimensions of risk. However, to quantify these dimensions, they are often merged into overall assessments of patient severity, "sickness," or "complexity." MedisGroups considered all KCFs including "history of" items (e.g., diabetes mellitus, COPD) in creating logistic regression models predicting in-hospital death. For decades, the Physical Status Classification of the American Society of Anesthesiologists (ASA) has been used in preoperative evaluation of surgical patients. ASA scores rate the risks of perioperative death on a global, subjective, five-point scale, providing this summary assessment of risk that encompasses all aspects of the patient's presentation: I, normal; II, mild disease; III, severe disease limiting activity but not incapacitating; IV, severe, incapacitating, constantly threatening survival; and V, expected to die within 24 hours. Similarly, the CSI not only assigns specific severity scores to each individual diagnosis but also computes an overall severity score, combining the effects of all diagnoses. A study of patients undergoing cholecystectomy, total hip replacement, or transurethral prostatectomy found that increasing ASA scores were generally associated with longer hospital stays, higher complication rates, and more postdischarge physician office visits (Cullen et al. 1994).

Making an inclusive assessment incorporating all diagnoses is especially important in risk adjustment for capitating payment. For instance, ACGs consider the combined effect of all outpatient diagnoses over a year in using branching logic to assign patients to one of 51 mutually exclusive, terminal ACGs (Starfield et al. 1991). The DCG–HCC model considers all inpatient hospital, outpatient hospital, and physician diagnoses from Medicare claims, and sums the incremental predicted payments associated with each diagnosis to produce the total predicted payment over a year. However, the DCG–HCC model designates hierarchies, so that if a patient has multiple diagnoses probably related to the same underlying disease process, only the effect of the single most influential of these interrelated diagnoses is considered (Ellis et al. 1996). For example, COPD is higher in the lung disease hierarchy than pleurisy; if both diagnoses are coded, only the COPD is counted.

Functional Status

As with acute clinical stability, functional status represents a final common pathway. For instance, difficulty walking results from diverse causes, such as congenital deformities, various neurological illnesses, musculoskeletal diseases, arthritis, amputation following long-standing diabetes mellitus, and injury. Functional limitations thus reflect numerous factors—congenital or acquired, permanent or transient, sensory or motor, systemic or localized, physical or psychosocial. Although exact estimates vary, the number of Americans with physical or mental impairments interfering with daily activities is about 35 million—one person in seven. Mobility impairments are the leading cause of functional limitations among adults, with estimated prevalence rising from 40.5 per 1,000 for 18–44-year-olds to 188.4 per 1,000 at ages 85 and older (Pope and Tarlov 1991, 58). Depending on one's purpose, specifying the exact cause of a functional deficit is less important than describing the extent of impairment (Mor in press).

In a comprehensive assessment of patient risk, "functional status" can be distinguished from the concepts of "health status" or "quality of life" described below. However, some find such distinctions spurious, preferring global measures of patient well-being that cut across a variety of areas. Nonetheless, an important distinction is that "functional status" focuses typically on observable behaviors rather than individuals' perceptions of health:

> Functional status . . . encompasses the more limited areas of physical, mental, and social functioning in daily life. Functioning is observable; it consists of everyday behaviors as they occur in a person's home and community life. Measures of functioning include items about daily activities such as eating, dressing, bathing, walking, handling finances, or visiting friends and relatives. Functional status is the end result of a person's health (absence of disease), well-being (capacity to participate fully in life), and coping (capacity to overcome health problems). (Rubenstein et al. 1988, 563)

> Functional status . . . is the concrete, observable, tangible, and objective category of health measures. Measures . . . use a standard external to the individual, such as usual role activity, walking at a certain rate, or customary self-care behaviors . . . It is the concept that has been preferred and best understood until now. (Ware 1991, 777)

Considerable efforts have focused on developing conceptual models relating clinical abnormalities or disease to functional impairment and disability. In a study of the Social Security Disability Insurance program in the early 1960s, Nagi (1991) distinguished four attributes:

1. *Pathology* represents interruption of, or interference with, normal bodily processes or structures. Pathology involves abnormalities at the level of tissues or cells, such as denervation of a leg muscle by trauma.

2. *Impairment* reflects abnormalities or losses of function along specific anatomic, physiological, mental, or emotional dimensions. By definition, all active pathology produces impairment, even if transitory. Impairments can also result from non-active processes, such as congenital malformations, and residual impairments can remain after active pathologic processes have resolved. Impairment concentrates at the level of organs or organ systems, such as atrophy of a leg muscle.

3. *Functional limitations* represent restrictions or inability to perform "normal" activities because of impairments. Limitations focus at the level of the person—for example, inability to use the leg for walking.

4. *Disability* involves limitations or inability to perform activities and roles defined by society and the external physical environment. Disability therefore focuses on the social and cultural contexts.

For example, the person suffering leg trauma may be unable to work and thus be considered disabled.

A competing model suggested by Wood also considers four concepts: disease, impairment, disability, and handicap (Pope and Tarlov 1991). A core component of Wood's conceptualization involves individuals' perceptions and awareness. Under Wood's formulation, for example, a "disease" becomes an "impairment" when the person recognizes its existence; "handicap" represents society's negative response to "impairment" or "disability," limiting the person's ability to fulfill "normal" roles and expectations. In 1980, the World Health Organization (WHO) published the *International Classification of Impairments, Disabilities, and Handicaps,* "a manual of classification relating to the consequences of disease." The WHO categorized nine types of "impairments" or abnormal functions: intellectual; other psychological; language; aural; ocular; visceral; skeletal; disfiguring; and generalized, sensory and other. "Disability," defined as inability to function within the range considered normal for a human being, also had nine categories: behavior, communication, personal care, locomotor, body disposition, dexterity, situational, particular skills, and other activities. Finally, "handicap" was defined as a "disadvantage for a given individual, resulting from an impairment or a disability, that limits or prevents the fulfillment of a role that is normal" (Warren 1987, 336). The seven dimensions of handicap were orientation, physical independence, mobility, occupation, social integration, economic self-sufficiency, and other.

Honing a conceptual model of functional impairment and disability—and choosing the words to describe it—have generated considerable controversy. The word "cripple" is banished; "handicap" is replaced by "disadvantage." Words imply causality and responsibility, individual and societal. The various models of disability shift sequentially from focusing on selected body parts or organ systems to the whole person to society's response. The 1990 passage of the Americans with Disabilities Act codified legal rights and expectations for persons with disabilities, explicitly broadening the concept of disablement to incorporate societal responses to impairment. Nevertheless, as elsewhere in society, laws shift public opinion only slowly, and persons with disabilities continue to confront innumerable societal and other barriers that undoubtedly affect their risks.

Measures of functional status address either specific areas or a range of dimensions. Core components of functional status measures typically include basic activities of daily living (ADLs) (e.g., feeding, bathing, dressing, toileting, walking) and instrumental ADLs (e.g., shopping, cooking, performing other household activities, using transportation). Most comprehensive measures of patient functioning also encompass cognitive abilities (e.g., level of alertness, orientation, long- and short-term memory, capacity for learning and computation), affective health (e.g., happiness, anxiety, depression), and social activities (e.g., visiting friends, sexual relationships). The context of the measurement can make a difference in perceptions of functional ability: For example, "capability" indicates what persons "can do" in controlled settings, whereas "performance" assesses what a person "does do" in everyday life. Capability typically exceeds performance (Young et al. 1996). Numerous functional status measures are available, and extensive literature guides users to relevant instruments (Rubenstein et al. 1988; McDowell and Newell 1987; Spector 1990; Applegate, Blass, and Williams 1990; U.S. Department of Health and Human Services, Public Health Service 1985).

Depending on specific research goals, one analytic consideration is that functional status itself can be the outcome of interest—functional status can appear on both sides of a predictive equation. Over 40 years ago, Karnofsky and colleagues measured patient functioning before and after administration of nitrogen mustard in 35 patients with bronchogenic carcinoma who had either failed radiation therapy or were deemed inoperable (Karnofsky et al. 1948). Their Performance Status measure (p. 635) arrayed patients along a scale from 0 to 100, reflecting ability to pursue normal activities independently and level of reliance on help and nursing care, as follows:

- 0 to 40 percent: Unable to care for self. Requires equivalent of institutional or hospital care. Disease may be progressing rapidly.

- 40 to 70 percent: Unable to work. Able to live at home, care for most personal needs. A varying amount of assistance is needed.

- 70 to 100 percent: Able to carry on normal activity and to work. No special care is needed.

Investigators since then have found a strong relationship: Prior functional status is generally the leading predictor of subsequent functional status.

Functional status is also closely linked with other patient outcomes such as imminent death, complications, and future health services use. Developers of the MMPS found that ambulation (scored as "able to walk," "requires assistance to walk," and "unable to walk") was a significant predictor of mortality 30 days following admission for Medicare beneficiaries with pneumonia and congestive heart failure. In the RAND study of Medicare quality, Keeler and collaborators (1990) found that inability to walk prior to admission was highly predictive of 30-day mortality for pneumonia patients. Patients who have functional impairments have greater risk of postoperative complications. The MICR for noncardiac surgery assigns three points for any condition causing the patient to be chronically bedridden (Goldman 1983, 506).

Results from RAND's 36-item self-administered functional status and health survey strongly predicted total healthcare expenses in the next year, although the subscales measuring physical function and perceived health did best while the subscales for mental health, pain, and energy/fatigue performed poorly (Hornbrook and Goodman 1995, 64). Using data from the Medicare Current Beneficiary Survey, Gruenberg, Kaganova, and Hornbrook (1996) found that 1991 performance on the following functional items were predictive of 1992 Medicare expenses: bathing, toileting, eating, meal preparation assistance, difficulty lifting, and difficulty walking two or three blocks.

Functional status may be more important than traditional clinical measures in assessing risk for acute outcomes. In a study of 366 lung cancer patients, functional status in the month prior to admission was more predictive of in-hospital death (among the 24 percent dying) than the APS of APACHE II, the complete APACHE II score, stage of cancer, and extent of comorbid illness (Iezzoni et al. 1989). Using forward stepwise logistic regression to produce models of in-hospital death for pneumonia and stroke patients, Davis and colleagues (1995) found that nursing assessments of patients' function were more predictive than most laboratory test values and comorbid diseases. Needing total assistance with bathing produced an adjusted odds ratio (95% C.I.) for dying of 6.69 (2.89, 15.49) for stroke patients and 4.98 (2.74, 9.08) for pneumonia patients (Davis et al. 1995, 913, 915). A global assessment by nurses of patients' needs for ADL assistance was a better predictor of in-hospital death among AIDS patients than three validated AIDS mortality measures (Justice et al. 1996).

Clinical and functional status dimensions may convey different information. For example, we studied 296 patients, 185 admitted for AMI and 111 for pneumonia (Iezzoni 1995). In addition to conducting detailed medical record reviews, we interviewed patients, including the 36-item Health Status Questionnaire (HSQ) developed during the Medical Outcomes Study (similar to the Short Form or SF-36, Stewart and Ware 1992). As expected, the eight dimensions within the HSQ were highly positively correlated with each other (Iezzoni 1995; Stewart, Hays, and Ware 1988). In contrast, some, but not all, of the medical record measures were significantly correlated with the HSQ dimensions (Table 2.8). Significant correlations were observed for half of the HSQ dimensions for age and length of stay. An ADL measure abstracted from nursing notes displayed significant positive correlations with each HSQ dimension. In contrast, the APS component of APACHE II showed an important correlation with only one dimension—physical functioning. APACHE II scores were also negatively correlated with several dimensions, possibly because age is used in calculating complete APACHE values. The presence of chronic conditions was strongly negatively linked to four dimensions (physical,

Table 2.8 Correlation Among the HSQ Functional Status Dimensions and Other Attributes

Other Patient Attributes or Findings	HSQ Functional Status Dimensions							
	Physical	Social	Role-physical	Role-emotional	Mental	Energy	Pain	Health
Age	-0.51*	-0.02	-0.20+	-0.02	-0.01	-0.23*	-0.05	0.12‡
Length of stay	-0.12‡	-0.12‡	-0.10	0.06	0.00	-0.11	-0.14‡	-0.14‡
Activities of daily living[a]	0.50*	0.24*	0.23*	0.18§	0.14‡	0.26*	0.13‡	0.28*
Acute physiology score (APACHE II)	-0.17§	-0.08	-0.14‡	0.00	0.04	-0.11	-0.06	-0.12‡
APACHE II score	-0.40*	-0.14‡	-0.26*	-0.04	0.01	-0.26*	-0.12‡	-0.23*
Presence of chronic conditions[b]	-0.38*	-0.15§	-0.22*	-0.07	-0.08	-0.28*	-0.09	-0.21+

Source: Iezzoni 1995.
* $p \leq 0.0001$
+ $p \leq 0.001$
§ $p \leq 0.01$
‡ $p \leq 0.05$

[a] The purpose of this activities of daily living scales was to assess the patients' ability to care for themselves. Scale included feeding, bathing, dressing, bed mobility, ambulation, and bladder and bowel function.

[b] Chronic conditions included AMI within three months prior to admission; congestive heart failure prior to admission; cancer with a poor prognosis; diabetes mellitus; stroke; cirrhosis, portal hypertension, or ascites; chronic renal failure; chronic obstructive pulmonary disease; peripheral vascular disease requiring bypass of leg, arteries or amputation of leg, foot, or toes; psychosis or depression; prior hospitalization within six months; and dementia.

role-physical, energy, and overall health), suggesting that, as the number of chronic conditions increases, patients report worse functioning.

Measuring functional status raises several additional issues. First, the level of functional impairment may be largely independent of patient demographic characteristics and diagnoses: One cannot impute level of disability by simply knowing age, sex, principal diagnosis, and extent of comorbid disease. The Medical Outcomes Study found striking variability in patient functioning within the study groups (Stewart et al. 1989). Controlling for sociodemographic characteristics (age, sex, income, education) and comorbid medical illnesses explained only a fraction of the variation in functional status. As measured by R^2, the amount of variation explained was 24 percent for physical functioning, 20 percent for role functioning, 14 percent for social functioning, 12 percent for mental health, 29 percent for health perceptions, and 14 percent for pain (Stewart et al. 1989, 910).

Second, specific functional status measures may not perform equally well across the entire spectrum of impairment or within selected patient populations. For example, Bindman, Keane, and Lurie (1990) used the Medical Outcomes Study general health survey (MOS-20), an instrument largely designed and tested among ambulatory patients, on 414 patients in poor health admitted to public hospitals. Six months later, patients were asked if their health had changed. At baseline, patients had much lower functional status than did the Medical Outcomes Study subjects, and these poor functioning levels changed little over six months. Nonetheless, over half of the public hospital patients reported that their health status had actually declined. In-depth study suggested that the MOS-20 was insensitive to declining health among very sick patients:

> The floor in the response range leads to an instrument bias against documenting a decline in the health of severely ill patients, the group in which it may be most important to detect it. This problem is obviously less significant when this instrument is used to follow relatively healthy populations. If a sample's initial scores are high, indicating good health, then there is sufficient room for their scores to fall over time if they become ill. The concern in this circumstance might rather be a ceiling effect, as it would be hard to demonstrate improvements in health in a group already reporting high scores. (Bindman, Keane, and Lurie 1990, 1148)

Further examination of Medical Outcomes Study results found problems with the SF-36 measure among the elderly, the poorly educated or impoverished, and patients with both medical and psychiatric comorbidity (McHorney et al. 1994). In addition, ceiling effects were present for younger, relatively healthy patients. A study of HIV-seropositive men found substantial ceiling effects for four of the six SF-20 dimensions among asymptomatic individuals (Holmes, Bix, and Shea 1996). Ceiling effects within the SF-36 may even exist for healthy, community-dwelling elders (Andresen et al. 1995).

Third, the mode of administration of the functional status measure (e.g., face-to-face interview, mail with self-administration, telephone interview) requires consideration. In face-to-face interviews, respondents may be reluctant to reveal their extent of dysfunction. A study of 172 veterans administered the SF-36 found significant differences in patients' reports over the course of a week, depending on the mode of administration. For four of the eight SF-36 dimensions, face-to-face administration elicited a more optimistic view of health than did self-administration (Weinberger et al. 1996).

Fourth, although many functioning measures are independent of diagnoses or the cause of disability, or "generic," disease-specific approaches could be best for some studies. For instance, the Arthritis Impact Measurement Scale (Meenan 1986) and McMaster Health Index Questionnaire (Chambers et al. 1982) were developed to assess functioning for patients with arthritis; the Visual Analogue Pain Scale (McDowell and Newell 1987) pertains to patients with pain; the Tinetti Balance and Gait Evaluation (Tinetti, Williams, and Mayewski 1986) applies to patients with gait abnormalities; and the Activities of Daily Vision Scale focuses on tasks related to vision (Mangione et al. 1992). These condition-specific scales may be more sensitive to change in specified functions (e.g., vision) than generic measures.

Fifth, the current tendency is to seek a single summary number indicating performance—whether it be hospital or health plan quality (see Chapter 11) or patient functioning. However, single numbers may not adequately capture the full range of patient functioning or health (see below). " . . . How can an overall health score be assigned to a person with a serious chronic disease, such as diabetes, who feels well and functions as a productive person with no role or social limitations?" (Stewart and Ware 1992, 22). Stewart, Ware, and Brook (1981) found that three categories (self-care, mobility, and physical activity) could be satisfactorily combined into one functional status index. However, personal and role functioning measures could not be similarly collapsed.

Finally, perceptions about functioning may vary depending on who is asked—patients or physicians. One study examined patients' and physicians' assessment of patient functioning in a hospital-based internal medicine practice in Boston and in selected office-based internal medicine practices in Los Angeles. Dimensions of functioning included basic ADLs, instrumental ADLs, and social activities. Kappa statistics reflecting extent of agreement between patients and physicians (see Chapter 7) ranged from 0.14 to 0.37 in the hospital-based practice and 0.18 to 0.36 in the office-based practice (Calkins et al. 1991, 453). As indicated by these low kappa values, patients and physicians disagreed substantially about patients' functioning. Agreement was generally highest for measures of physical functioning and lowest for indicators of social functioning. Most disagreements involved physicians underestimating patients' functioning.

Psychological, Cognitive, and Psychosocial Functioning

Psychological, cognitive, and psychosocial functioning encompasses a broad range of patient characteristics, including the ability to appreciate and interact with one's surroundings and other persons, the capacity to understand information about one's health and healthcare needs, and having the social support and care of others. These attributes are particularly important when examining outpatient outcomes, outside of controlled institutional environments where staff purportedly oversee all patient needs (e.g., give medications in proper dosages and on schedule). In the community, psychological and cognitive factors can compromise patients' activity levels, self-care, motivation, and perceptions in ways that negatively affect treatment outcomes. For example, Patient C (Table 2.2), who has refused medication to treat profound depression, is at greater risk of a poor postdischarge outcome than Patient A, even though their prostate cancer presentations are identical.

Efforts to measure this aspect of functioning are often combined within scales of overall functioning. However, Applegate, Blass, and Williams (1990, 1210) warned, "Because many elderly persons with mild-to-moderate cognitive impairment often maintain their social skills in terms of superficial interactions, clinically important impairment may remain undetected." Nonetheless, scales of cognitive functioning suffer many of the drawbacks mentioned above, such as floor and ceiling effects (inability to detect small changes in cognitive functioning at either end of the scale). In addition, most cognitive functioning scales are affected by patients' level of education (Applegate, Blass, and Williams 1990). Old people, in particular, may feel threatened when asked to complete cognitive evaluations, such as the Mini-Mental State Examination; they may try to memorize basic recall words to maximize their scores (Kutner et al. 1992).

The Medical Outcomes Study developed a scale explicitly to measure social support, including 19 "support items" such as having someone to show love and affection, confide in, hug, understand problems, have a good time with, prepare meals, and turn to for suggestions (Sherbourne and Stewart 1991). Persons with low social support reported much worse physical functioning and emotional well-being at the start of the study than persons with high social support—a difference that persisted over two years (Sherbourne et al. 1992).

Even without detailed interviews or data collection, basic facts about how patients live offer important insight. One study examined outcomes following AMI for 1,234 patients, focusing on whether patients lived alone (Case et al. 1992). Even after adjusting for such factors as New York Heart Association class, left ventricular ejection fraction, ventricular premature beats, prior infarction, use of β blockers, and education, patients living alone had a higher relative risk of poor outcomes than those living with others—relative risks of 1.54 for recurrent cardiac events and 1.58 for cardiac death. Another study followed 1,368 patients treated medically for coronary artery disease, tracking the occurrence of cardiac death over five years (Williams et al. 1992). Despite controlling for "all known medical prognostic factors," social variables remained important predictors of risk of death. Having a spouse or confidant was the strongest predictor: Unmarried persons without confidants had a relative risk of 3.34 for cardiac death compared to that for other patients. Another study telephoned 2,320 survivors of myocardial infarction, examining mortality 36 months after the acute event (Ruberman et al. 1984). High levels of stress and social isolation independently predicted mortality.

Cultural and Socioeconomic Attributes

Cultural and socioeconomic attributes are often separated from traditional clinical measures, as are related factors such as smoking, seat belt use, sexual practices, societal and domestic violence, illicit drug use, and alcohol consumption. Nonetheless, such attributes clearly affect both short- and long-term patient outcomes.

Low socioeconomic status has been linked to excess mortality rates (Otten et al. 1990), perhaps due to delayed access to medical services or other chronic fundamental deprivations that subtly impair physiological health. This is most obvious in studies of infant mortality and low-birthweight babies—"a mechanism for intergenerational transfer of disadvantage in health because socially deprived women are much more likely to bear low-birthweight infants than are other women" (Starfield 1992, 18). In discussing the chain of events linking poverty to poor health, Starfield (1992, 18) observed:

> The chain of events is complex. Predisposing factors involve environmental conditions, social conditions, and genetic risk factors. Some of these operate directly (such as housing with lead-based paint), and some operate indirectly through mediating factors involving induced behaviors, stress, social isolation, and decreased access to medical care. All risks interact in unknown ways in their effect on health.

Abundant evidence supports income-related risks. For example, cancer survival rates for lower-income people are 10 to 15 percent below rates for others (American Cancer Society 1989). Weissman, Gatsonis, and Epstein (1992) found that uninsured or Medicaid patients in Massachusetts were significantly more likely than privately insured patients to be hospitalized for potentially avoidable causes, such as asthma, cellulitis, diabetic ketoacidosis or coma, gangrene, hypokalemia, malignant hypertension, and bleeding ulcer. Uninsured women and those with Medicaid coverage presented with more advanced stage breast cancer than privately insured women (Ayanian et al. 1993b). One study of 14,557 patients found that Medicaid patients had significantly higher MedisGroups admission scores than other patients; even after controlling for age, sex, MedisGroups admission score, case mix, and hospital, Medicaid patients had significantly longer lengths of stay (Arndt and Bradbury 1995). Possible explanations include greater difficulties arranging discharges for Medicaid patients.

As Bindman and Grumbach (1992, 2427) speculated, "The real story about inequities in access to care in America has more to do with what happens to patients before they are sick enough to require hospitalization. . . ." Bindman and colleagues (1995) examined the association between preventable hospitalizations and access to care in 41 geographic areas within California. They found a four-fold difference in rates of preventable hospitalizations across the 41 areas, with higher rates in areas with more uninsured residents and Medicaid recipients. Self-rated access to care was a significant predictor of preventable hospitalization rates.

A particularly troubling possibility was suggested by Burstin, Lipsitz, and Brennan (1992), who reported that uninsured patients admitted to one of 51 hospitals in New York state were significantly more likely than their insured counterparts to experience injuries due to substandard medical management. Despite this, poor and uninsured patients were much less likely to sue for malpractice, even if they had sustained a medical injury. The adjusted odds ratio (95% C.I.) for submitting a malpractice claim was 0.1 (0.005–0.9) for uninsured compared to privately insured patients and 0.02 (0.03–0.8) for poor compared to higher income persons (Burstin et al. 1993, 1700).

Alcohol and substance abuse also affect patient outcomes. For example, one large teaching facility in Philadelphia was found to have a higher-than-expected morbidity rate for its obstetrical cases, calculated using MedisGroups. When the hospital performed in-depth analyses to determine the source of this discrepancy, they found that most of the unexpected morbidity was concentrated among mothers who were intravenous drug or cocaine abusers. MedisGroups had not adjusted for this maternal risk factor.

People's jobs affect their risks. Occupational exposures cause or heighten susceptibility to certain illnesses, such as respiratory conditions resulting from exposure to dusts, gases, or fumes. For instance, pulmonary fibrosis can be caused by exposure to coal dust, asbestos, silica, talc, and animal proteins; bronchitis may stem from exposure to coal dust, welding fumes, and other compounds; and chronic airways disease can result from exposure to toluene diisocyanate, chromium, grains, animal products, and cotton. Many such conditions are exacerbated further by smoking. Jobs also affect mental well-being; for instance, stresses associated with such occupations as air traffic control and front-line law enforcement are well-documented.

Culture and religion may influence outcomes by affecting compliance with therapy, diet and other daily life activities, and attitudes toward health and medical care. A prominent example is Jehovah's Witnesses' prohibition against blood transfusions regardless of clinical circumstances. Another example involves the dietary cravings of pica particularly during pregnancy—women who desire earth or clay (geophagia), starch (amylophagia), or ice (pagophagia). Pica is particularly common in the South and is associated with maternal anemia and poor birth outcomes.

Overall Assessment of Health Status and Health-Related Quality of Life

As Reiser (1993, 1014) wrote, the interest in outcomes of care is increasingly seeking the patient's voice:

> The modern outcomes movement, which developed in the 1980s and made the consequences of a medical intervention to its recipient a major criterion of determining its value, further enhanced the authenticity and authority of the patient's perspective . . . The objective biological standards of evidence, which had formed the foundation of 20th-century medicine, were found to depict the effects of a medical procedure inadequately. Thus, the medical ethics and outcomes movements both drew their strength from the significance they gave to the patient's view of illness and therapy.

Efforts to articulate patients' perspectives have coalesced into the burgeoning field of health status and quality-of-life assessment. Health status measures generally rely on extensive data obtained directly from patients, encompassing numerous attributes such as severity of illness, physical capabilities, psychosocial and emotional functioning, sense of well-being, and health-related quality of life. A large and growing literature describes numerous measures for a variety of populations and purposes (Lohr 1989, 1992; Stewart and Ware 1992; Guyatt, Feeny, and Patrick 1993; Ware 1995; Streiner and Norman 1995). Table 2.9, taken from Ware (1995, 330), summarizes ten widely used general health surveys—"considered *generic* to the extent that they assess health concepts that represent basic human values relevant to functional status and well-being" (Ware 1995,

Table 2.9 Summary of Information about Widely Used General Health Surveys

	QWB	SIP	HIE	NHP	QLI	COOP	EUROQOL	DUKE	MOS FWBP	MOS SF-36
Concepts[a]										
Physical functioning	✓	✓	✓	✓	✓	✓	✓	✓	✓	✓
Social functioning	✓	✓	✓	✓	✓	✓	✓	✓	✓	✓
Role functioning	✓	✓	✓	✓	✓	✓	✓	✓	✓	✓
Psychological distress		✓	✓	✓	✓	✓	✓	✓	✓	✓
Health perceptions (general)			✓	✓	✓	✓	✓	✓	✓	✓
Pain (bodily)	✓		✓	✓	✓	✓	✓	✓	✓	✓
Energy/fatigue			✓	✓				✓	✓	✓
Psychological well-being		✓	✓	✓				✓	✓	✓
Sleep			✓	✓				✓	✓	
Cognitive functioning		✓						✓	✓	
Quality of life		✓	✓			✓				
Reported health transition						✓		✓	✓	✓
Characteristics										
Administration method (S = self, 1 = interviewer, P = proxy)	I, P	S, I, P	S, P	S, I	S, P	S, I	S	S, I	S, I	S, I, P
Scaling method (L = Likert, R = Rasch, T = Thurstone, U = utility)	U	T	L	T	L	L	U	L	L	L, R
Number of questions	107	136	86	38	5	9	9	17	149	36
Scoring options (P = profile, SS = summary scores, SI = single index)	SI	P, SS, SI	P	P	SI	P	SI	P, SI	P	P, SS

Table 2.9 Continued

QWB = Quality of Well-Being Scale (1973) (Kaplan and Anderson 1988; Patrick, Bush, and Chen 1973)

SIP = Sickness Impact Profile (1976) (Bergner et al. 1981; Bergner et al. 1976)

HIE = Health Insurance Experiment surveys (1979) (Brook et al. 1979; Ware, Avery-Davies, and Brook 1980)

NHP = Nottingham Health Profile (1980) (Hunt and McEwen 1980; Kaplan and Anderson 1988)

QLI = Quality of Life Index (1981) (Spitzer et al. 1981; Wood-Dauphinee and Williams 1987)

COOP = Dartmouth Function Charts (1987) (Landgraf et al. 1990; Nelson et al. 1987)

EUROQOL = European Quality of Life Index (1990) (EuroQOL Group 1990)

DUKE = Duke Health Profile (1990) (Parkerson, Broadhead, and Tse 1990)

MOS FWBP = MOS Functioning and Well-Being Profile (1992) (Stewart and Ware, eds. 1992)

MOS SF-36 = MOS 36-Item Short-Form Health Survey (1992) (Ware and Sherbourne 1992; Ware et al. 1993)

Source: Ware 1995. With permission from the *Annual Review of Public Health*, volume 16, © 1994 by Annual Reviews, Inc.
[a] Note: Rows are ordered in terms of how frequently concepts are represented; only concepts represented in two or more surveys are listed. Columns are roughly ordered in terms of date of first publication. Analyses of content were based on published definitions (Ware 1987).

329). While global assessments of health status frequently are the outcome of interest, they are also important indicators of risk (Steinwachs 1989; Brook et al. 1979). As with functional status, the best predictor of future health status is prior health status.

Over 100 measures of health and functional status and quality of life existed by the end of the 1980s (Reiser 1993). A review of 75 articles involving quality-of-life measurement found that 159 different instruments were cited, with a mean of 3 instruments (range 1 to 19) per article (Gill and Feinstein 1994, 622); Table 2.10 taken from this study shows the variety of instruments available. However, inspection of these 75 articles revealed troubling findings. Authors provided a conceptual definition of quality of life in only 15 percent of articles, and patients were invited to rate their global quality of life separately in only 17 percent of studies. As Gill and Feinstein (1994, 624) observed, "while professing to measure quality of life, many researchers are really measuring various aspects of health status . . . quality of life is something that is perceived by each patient individually. The need to incorporate patients' values and preferences is what distinguishes quality of life from all other measures of health."

Eliciting patients' own values about their health states is central to quality of life measurement—the value that you place on a given health state may differ widely from the value I assign to the same health state. For example, "There is evidence that old people tend to be health optimists, having more favorable health perceptions than their levels of physical functioning objectively allow" (Kutner et al. 1992, 534). The SUPPORT investigators found that the health values of gravely ill patients varied widely and could not be clearly predicted based on the patients' current state of health (Tsevat et al. 1995). Hearing the patient is especially important for persons with disabilities. As one study found:

> . . . Those in what others may perceive to be "poor" health place a relatively high value on their own health since they have adjusted their life styles and expectations to take account of their condition. This may be particularly true of young disabled men and women, since one-quarter of this group of respondents describe their health as "poor" yet value it as "good." Conversely, young people who describe themselves as "healthy" . . . may be reluctant to value their health near the top . . . because they have high expectations about what being in the "best imaginable health state" involves . . . more than one-fifth of respondents [without disabilities] describe their health as "good" yet value it as "poor" (Dolan 1996, 559).

When quality-of-life information is used to guide health policy decisions (e.g., resource allocation), deciding *whose* values to employ is a crucial question.

Despite the obvious appeal of quantifying patients' experiences and perspectives, several caveats remain. First, the explicit effort to be inclusive

Table 2.10 Names of "Quality-of-Life" Instruments from 75 Articles

Ability to Work	EORTC GU Group's Quality	Index of Well-Being
Activities of Daily Living	of Life Form	Inflammatory Bowel Disease
Activity Index	Feelings About Present Life	Symptoms Questionnaire
Additive Daily Activities	(Hard/Easy)	(ISQ)
Profile Test (ADAPT)	Feelings About Present Life	Intellectual Function (ad hoc)
Anamnestic Comparative	(Tied Down/Free)	Jenkins Sleep Dysfunction
Self-Assessment	Functional Disability	Scale
Instrument (ACSA)	Functional Living	Kamofsky Performance
Angina Pectoris Quality of	Index—Cancer (FLIC)	Index
Life Questionnaire	Functional Status (adapted	Katz Adjustment
(APQLQ)	from Sickness Impact	Scale—Relatives' Form
Arthritis Categorical Scale	Profile)	(KAS-R)
Arthritis Ladder Scale	General Health Index	Keitel Assessment
Attitude Towards Warfarin	General Health Perceptions	Kidney Disease
Body Satisfaction Scale	(GHP MOS-13)	Questionnaire
Bradburn Affect-Balance	General Health Perceptions	Ladder Scale (Cantrell) for
Scale	(5-point scale)	Quality of Life
Cancer Instrument (ad hoc)	General Symptoms	Lee Functional Index
Cancer Rehabilitation	General Well-Being	Life Events
Evaluation System	Adjustment Scale	Life Satisfaction (4 domains)
(CARES)	General Well-Being Index	Life Satisfaction (Global with
Center for Epidemiologic	Geriatric Depression Scale	Cantrell Ladder)
Studies Depression	(GDS)	Life Satisfaction
Inventory (CES-D)	Geriatric Mental State	(Likert—7-point scale)
City of Hope Medical Center	Schedule	Life Satisfaction (10-item
Quality of Life Survey	Global Perceived Health	scale)
Chronic Disease Assessment	(adapted from GHP	Life Satisfaction Index
Tool (CDAT) Quality of	MOS-13)	Life Style Questionnaire
Life Scale	Good Days Last Week	Linear Analogue
Chronic Disease Count	Hand Grip Strength	Self-Assessment (LASA)
Cognitive Impairment	Happiness	Locus of Control of Behavior
Colorectal Cancer Quality of	Health Assessment	(LCB)
Life Interview	Questionnaire (HAQ)	McGill Pain Questionnaire
Daily Activities	Health Index	McMaster Health Index
Digit Symbol Substitution	Health Satisfaction	Questionnaire (MHIQ)
Test	Hearing Handicap Inventory	McMaster-Toronto Arthritis
Disease Symptoms	for the Elderly (HHIE)	(MACTAR) Patient
Eating Behavior (adapted	Home Parenteral Nutrition	Function Preference
from Sickness Impact	Questionnaire	Questionnaire
Profile)	HR—Quality of Life	Mental Health Index
Eastern Cooperative	Instrument (using	Mental Status
Oncology Group (ECOG)	Multitrait-Multimethod	Metastatic Breast Cancer
Performance Score	Analysis)	Questionnaire
Emotional Experience	Index of General Affect	MOS-36
(developed from RAND)	Index of Overall Life	Minnesota Multiphasic
Emotional State (ad hoc)	Satisfaction	Personality Inventory
Employment Status	Index of Psychological Affect	(MMPI)

Continued

Table 2.10   Continued

National Institute of Mental Health Depression Questionnaire
Need for Control
Nominal Group Process Technique
Nottingham Health Profile
Other Symptoms
Overall Current Health (adapted from RAND)
Overall Health (Global with Cantrell Ladder)
Overall Health Scale (10 cm)
Overall Life Satisfaction
Pain Index
Pain Ladder Scale
Pain Line (10 cm)
Patient Diary
Patient Utility Measurement Scale (PUMS)
Perceived Health Questionnaire (PHQ)
Perceived Health Status
Perceived Quality of Life Scale (PQOL)
Performance Status Classification
Physical Sense of Well-Being
Physical Status
Physical Symptoms (Standard Questionnaire)
Physical Symptoms Distress Index
Present Pain and Discomfort
Profile of Mood States (POMS)
Psychological Adjustment to Illness Scale (PAIS)
Psychological General Well-Being Schedule (PGWB)

Purpose Designed Questionnaire
QL-Index
Quality of Life Checklist
Quality of Life Index
Quality of Life Index
Quality of Life Index (QALI)
Quality of Life Questionnaire
Quality of Life Questionnaire in Severe CHF (QLQ-SHF)
Quality of Life Scale
Quality of Well-Being (QWB)
Quantified Denver Scale of Communication Function (QDS)
RAND Current Health Assessment
RAND General Health Perceptions Questionnaire
Rey Auditory Verbal Learning Test
Rey-Osterreith Complex Figure Test
Rotterdam Symptom Checklist (RSCL)
Satisfaction with Life Domain Scale (SLDS)
Self Assessment Scale
Self-Evaluation of Life Function (SELF)
Self-Perceived Overall Quality of Life
Sentence Writing (timed)
Serial 7's
Sexual Function
Sexual Symptoms Distress Index
Short Portable Mental Status Questionnaire (SPMSQ)
Sickness Impact Profile

Side Effects and Symptoms (Hypertension)
Side Effects of Chemotherapy (ad hoc)
Sleep, Energy, and Appetite Scale (SEAS)
Social Activity
Social Difficulty Questionnaire
Social Participation Index
Social Participation (Global with Cantrell Ladder)
Standard Gamble Questionnaire
Subjectively Appraised Work Load
Subjective Rating Scale
Symptom Checklist (SCL)-90
Symptom Experience Report (SER)
Taylor Complex Figure Tests
Time Trade Off
Toronto Activities of Daily Living Questionnaire
Unfavorable External Working Conditions
Unfavorable Interpersonal Difficulties
Uniscale
Uremia Quality of Life Questionnaire (ad hoc)
Visual Analogue Scale for Global State of Well-Being
Walking Test
Well-Being Ill-Being Clinical Observation Scale
Willingness to Pay Questionnaire
Word Recall
Work/Daily Role Well-Being Scale

Source: Gill and Feinstein 1994. © 1994, American Medical Association.

frequently yields "megavariable" indices (Feinstein 1992). The importance of specific variables (e.g., particular symptoms that are especially troubling or of prognostic importance) may be overwhelmed by numerous other factors incorporated in the index. In addition, as for some other risk dimensions, certain health status and quality-of-life measures have been developed specifically for patients with particular diseases or conditions, while others are generic (see Table 2.10). No single method suits all research needs (Patrick and Deyo 1989). Choosing an approach depends on the specific research question. Mosteller, Ware, and Levine (1989, S286) recommend routinely using both condition-specific and generic methods; Patrick and Deyo (1989) suggest using standardized, generic instruments with disease-specific supplements.

Second, specific notions of health status and quality of life may also differ for children and adolescents compared to adults:

> Because young people are still developing, ill health may be manifested by decelerations in the rate of attainment of normal features rather than by evidence of abnormal form or function . . . In adults, good health is often defined as the ability to be self-sufficient and economically productive. In contrast, complete self-sufficiency is not expected in children and youths whereas age-appropriate cognitive, psychological, social, and physical development are important considerations (Starfield et al. 1993, 430).

Third, relationships between health status or quality of life and various outcomes may be complex or counterintuitive on first review. For example, using health status to predict resource needs requires caution:

> The relationship of health status to needs for care is not necessarily simple since not all deficits in health status will require health services. The need for care may depend on the severity of the deficit and the potential for timely and appropriate health services to maximize return to the highest level of attainable function. Similarly, individuals with high levels of health status may also have needs for care, including periodic preventive care and counseling on health behaviors that may contribute to future decrements in health status (Steinwachs 1989, S14).

Another important issue involves what to do when patients themselves are incapable of responding for whatever reason (e.g., poor health, cognitive impairment, logistical considerations). One common solution is to ask a proxy—a family member or close friend. The accuracy of a proxy's response in representing patients' perceptions is, however, unclear. For example, one study interviewed 60 pairs of elderly patients and proxies (Epstein et al. 1989). Responses of patients and proxies were generally comparable for overall health and functional status, but proxies reported significantly lower emotional health and satisfaction than did patients. Proxies who spent more than the median time each week with the patient rated the patient's functional status and social activity as more impaired than did the patient.

Finally, as with other dimensions of risk, the conceptual framework, definitions, and clinical meaningfulness require more attention:

> The terms quality of life, health status, and functional status are often used interchangeably and without specific definition . . . Quality of life, just as health or illness, must be assessed specifically . . . Somewhere in the process of deciding on the domains and choosing measures, clinical investigators often start the futile search for the measure, the gold standard that everyone will find appropriate and credible. The bitter truth is that there is no gold standard, there is unlikely ever to be one, and it is unlikely to be desirable to have one (Bergner 1989, S153–S154).

Patient Attitudes and Preferences for Outcomes

Finally, patients' attitudes and preferences often affect their clinical outcomes and thus constitute a dimension of risk. For example, some patients seek more aggressive care than others (Patient H, Table 2.2). Although aggressive interventions may delay death or impairment, such patients are more likely to suffer treatment-related complications than those choosing more palliative options. Most studies suggest that about one-third of patients do not follow their physicians' recommendations, especially for preventive and outpatient care. These failures largely relate to patients' health beliefs (especially personal views of vulnerability and seriousness of their condition), health-related motivations, and perceptions of the psychological and other costs of complying with the recommendations (Becker and Maiman 1975). More than one-third of adult Americans annually seek alternatives to traditional allopathic medicine, especially for chronic conditions, but many do not tell their doctors (Eisenberg et al. 1993).

Patients' attitudes and preferences represent a distillation of a lifetime's experience, beliefs, goals, health status, quality of life, and understanding about prognosis and therapeutic options. As in assessing quality of life (see above), by definition, this process is uniquely personal. Categorizing patients' attitudes and preferences for care is complex. In addition, even the most accurate determinations may vary over time as patients reconsider their desires in light of their changing clinical course and personal circumstances. For instance, one study tracked preferences of 2,073 patients over two years and found that preferences for such interventions as CPR, artificial respiration, and tube feeding frequently altered over time (Danis et al. 1994). Because of these complexities, one might question whether this dimension is necessary—might attitudes and preferences be distributed, for all intents and purposes, randomly across populations, therefore obviating the need to consider them?

Unfortunately, evidence suggests that patients' preferences and attitudes and how providers address patients' desires are distinctly nonrandom. For example, compliance rates are especially poor among patients of low socioeconomic status. In one survey, the highest use of unconventional therapy was reported by non–African Americans, 25 to 49 years of age, who had relatively more education and higher incomes (Eisenberg 1993). Patients who participate more actively in decision making about their care may do better (Kaplan and Ware 1989). One study audiotaped interactions between patients and physicians in different outpatient settings and used this information to rate patients' conversational styles (Kaplan et al. 1989). Patients who assumed control of conversations (e.g., asking more questions, attempting to direct the flow of the discussions and their doctors' behavior) during a baseline office visit reported fewer days lost from work, fewer health problems, lower functional limitations due to health, and higher health status at a follow-up visit. Patients' efforts at conversational control were also linked to physiologic outcome measures: Patients seeking more control had, at follow-up, lower blood glucose and blood pressure readings.

A special case reflecting patients' goals and wishes is the use of "do not resuscitate" (DNR) orders. Not surprisingly, the developers of the MMPS found that admission orders of DNR strongly predicted death for stroke, pneumonia, and AMI, in addition to the severity indicators. However, DNR provisions are not adopted uniformly across patients. Using 1979 to 1982 data, Zimmerman and colleagues (1986) found statistically significant variations in rates of DNR use across 13 hospitals, unexplained by patient age, prior health status, diagnosis, or severity of illness. A companion study using 1988 to 1990 data found that the rate of DNR use had almost doubled overall (9 versus 5.4 percent), but rates still varied across 42 ICUs, ranging from 1.5 to 22 percent (Jayes et al. 1993, 2215). The RAND study of quality of care for Medicare beneficiaries found that, after adjusting for patient and hospital characteristics, DNR orders were assigned more frequently to women and less often to black patients, Medicaid recipients, and rural hospital patients (Wenger et al. 1995).

The SUPPORT investigators found troubling evidence of discordance between patients and physicians around DNR preferences. When patients desired cardiopulmonary resuscitation, physicians' perceptions agreed 56.9 percent of the time; when patients preferred DNR status, physicians' perceptions agreed 47.0 percent of the time (Teno et al. 1995, 182). The Patient Self-Determination Act, implemented in 1991, requires healthcare institutions to notify patients about advance directive provisions.

Nevertheless, the SUPPORT investigators found that use of advance directives and living wills had no significant effect on clinical decision making for seriously ill patients. Of 618 patients who reported having an advance directive, the directive was mentioned in only 5.8 percent of the medical records, and only two patients' directives were actually attached to their charts (Teno et al. 1994, 25). Presence of an advance directive had no significant effect on the likelihood of resuscitation efforts, the hospital bill, average intensity of therapy, or length of stay. DNR orders were written for 52.7 percent of patients stating they wished to forgo resuscitation; having an advance directive did not affect issuance of the DNR order (Teno et al. 1994, 27).

Patients' goals and preferences influence not only clinical outcomes but also costs of their care. For example, we examined the role of purpose of admission in hospitalizations for lung, colon, and breast cancers, using the 1985 Medicare hospital discharge abstract data (Iezzoni et al. 1991b). Six purpose-of-admission categories were created primarily using diagnosis and procedure codes (e.g., surgical intervention plus diagnostic evaluation, diagnostic evaluation only, active medical treatment only, palliation). Average hospitalization charges, per diem charges, lengths of stay, and rates of death varied significantly by purpose. Hospitalizations for major surgery with diagnostic evaluations were much more costly than admissions for palliation. Rural and small hospitals were more likely to admit patients for palliation, while urban and large hospitals admitted relatively more patients for active interventions. Therefore, aggregate hospital costs varied by facility characteristics partially due to differences in patients' goals or the purpose of admissions.

Finally, patient preferences can affect report cards on provider performance using risk-adjusted outcomes (see Chapter 11). One hospital in Pennsylvania found that its MedisGroups severity-adjusted mortality rate for cancer patients was much higher than expected; even more worrisome, death rates were high among patients with admission scores of 0 (indicating mild, if any, clinical instability). Upon investigating, the oncologists found that patients who died with scores of 0 had entered the hospital for pain control and had acknowledged terminal care. Physicians had actively discussed with these patients whether they wanted even routine testing (e.g., phlebotomy to monitor basic serum chemistries), but the patients had requested "comfort measures only." Thus, the standard blood tests used by many severity measures (e.g., serum sodium, potassium, hematocrit, white blood cell count) were not performed (as with Patient I, Table 2.2). Without measurement, no KCFs were identified—hence severity scores of 0. In this circumstance, however, the 0 scores represented not the absence of severe disease but rather the desire of terminally ill patients to maximize their comfort at the end of life.

Additional Considerations

After delineating different dimensions of risk, a number of further issues may require consideration within specific research settings. Three areas are particularly important:

- the unit of analysis (e.g., a particular disease, an individual patient, a group of patients, an individual provider, a group of providers, or a geographic area);
- the time frame or "window of observation" (e.g., a hospitalization; a fixed period, such as 30 days, initiated by admission; an episode of care or illness); and
- the outcome of interest (risk of what?).

The implications of these factors for the risk-adjustment strategy are examined further in Chapter 5.

Special Contexts and Different Professional Perspectives

This discussion of dimensions of risk assumed a general medical context (e.g., a general medical or surgical hospitalization). However, the exact nature of these dimensions could vary within other clinical contexts, such as psychiatry, rehabilitation medicine, long-term care, or hospice care. For example, psychiatry has its own specific rubric for classifying "disease"— the *Diagnostic and Statistical Manual of Mental Disorders*, Fourth Edition (DSM-IV) (American Psychiatric Association 1994). The DSM-IV allows individual cases to be assessed on five axes, each axis representing different aspects of disorders, environmental attributes, and functional considerations that might be overlooked by focusing on a single dimension. The five DSM-IV axes are:

- Axis I—clinical disorders, other conditions that may be a focus of clinical attention;
- Axis II—personality disorders, mental retardation;
- Axis III—general medical conditions;
- Axis IV—psychosocial and environmental problems; and
- Axis V—global assessment of functioning. (American Psychiatric Association 1994, 25)

DSM-IV's guidelines explicitly urge caution when applying this rubric to patients not of Western cultures. Its Appendix I, "Outline for Cultural Formulation and Glossary of Culture-bound Syndromes," provides a nomenclature specifically covering culture-related aspects of behavior (e.g., "spells" or trances in which persons "communicate" with deceased relatives are accepted rituals in other cultures).

In contrast to DSM-IV is the ICD-9-CM, the standard general diagnostic lexicon (see Chapter 3), and its successor ICD-10. Although DSM-IV codes are fully compatible with ICD-9-CM and ICD-10 codes (American Psychiatric Association 1994, xxi), the fundamental organizing principles of the two volumes are very different. The ICD is structured primarily around organ systems or etiologies of disease (e.g., infections, neoplastic disorders), and its coding guidelines do not adopt a multiaxial approach.

The definition of "risk" therefore depends on the professional training or perspectives of who is asked. Not only do physicians vary in their perspectives, but also different healthcare professionals hold divergent views. Smits, Fetter, and McMahon (1984) noted that physicians generally focus on the effect of a particular disease on the physiologic integrity of the patient, asking such questions as, Is a patient more likely to die, become disabled, or experience long-run sequelae than other patients? Psychiatrists concentrate primarily on cognitive dysfunctions, which may or may not include physiologic perturbations. Nurses consider the physiologic perspective of physicians, while adding psychological and dependency attributes of the patient. Physical and occupational therapists target the functional capabilities of patients and their ability to perform ADLs independently. Health economists generally emphasize resource needs, implicitly correlating higher risk with higher intensity or costs. Thus, the challenge facing a multidisciplinary research team is that of bridging differing paradigms of risk.

Resource Needs and Appropriateness

These various dimensions of risk can be synthesized into an overall assessment of patients' needs for services. As suggested above, the relationship may not be linear or monotonic—increasing severity or impairment may not translate neatly into increasing service needs. Nonetheless, the concepts of "appropriateness" and "severity" are flip sides of the same coin.

> Assessing the appropriateness of use of any procedure for a particular clinical indication (scenario) depends on evaluating at a point in time what is known about the probabilities and values (utilities) of the possible outcomes that will occur if the procedure is or is not used. If the value of the benefits (prolonged life, relief of pain, and cure of disease) outweigh the value of the risks (operative mortality, complications, pain, and anxiety), then performing the procedure is appropriate. (Leape et al. 1993)

For example, as described in Chapter 11, for the last few years New York state has annually calculated observed-to-predicted mortality rates for CABG surgery and PTCA using risk-adjustment models derived from a special statewide clinical database, the Cardiac Surgery Reporting System (Hannan et al. 1990, 1992). The state also sponsored studies of the appropriateness of service use for CABG (Leape et al. 1993) and PTCA (Hilborne et al. 1993). These parallel activities of assessing patient risk and the appropriateness of procedures relied on comparable clinical information, although the interpretation varied somewhat. For example, clinical attributes overlapping both the risk and appropriateness assessments for CABG include presence of unstable angina, recent occurrence of an AMI, cardiac ejection fraction, percent stenosis of the left main coronary artery, and presence of congestive heart failure.

Although the clinical factors are similar, the way they are aggregated or judged may differ depending on whether the focus is risk adjustment or appropriateness determinations. For example, in developing the New York state model of CABG mortality, Hannan and collaborators (1990) found that first-order interactions among significant variables were not important, so they were excluded from the final logistic regression model. In contrast, the scenarios created to judge appropriateness often combined multiple variables, sometimes within a branching logic (Leape et al. 1993). For example, the two CABG scenarios that were most frequently judged appropriate were chronic stable angina, class I/II, treated with maximal medical therapy, three-vessel disease, ejection fraction > 35 percent, and low risk; and post-myocardial infarction angina, 6 hours to 21 days, three-vessel disease, ejection fraction > 35 percent, and low risk.

Nature of the Intervention

Beyond risks arising from patients' attributes, the nature of the intervention being studied is also important—the treatment itself may present its own risks. For example, major surgery requiring general anesthesia typically raises more immediate risks than most medical treatments. In some instances, complications (e.g., idiosyncratic but deadly reactions to anesthetic agents) are caused by the procedure itself rather than the underlying disease or patient risk factors. In many circumstances, surgery is not an option for patients with extensive disease in major organ systems, such as the lungs and heart. Thus, the decision to forgo surgical intervention due to serious coexisting diseases could confound comparisons of surgical and medical therapies.

Similarly, certain medical therapies pose more risks than others. Chemotherapy for cancer often generates predictable, even life-threatening side effects, that may be particularly problematic for patients with certain comorbid illnesses (e.g., cardiomyopathy, renal failure). The express goal of most chemotherapeutic regimens is to destroy malignant cells; this process may result in well-anticipated and -defined physiologic derangements. Therefore, among chemotherapy patients, certain acute physiologic derangements (low white blood cell counts, high uric acid or potassium levels due to tumor lysis) may indicate the presumed effectiveness of treatment. Persistence of such abnormalities, however, generates concern. The nature and timing of such intentional abnormalities resulting from treatments must be considered in assessing risks in this setting.

In contrast, treatments such as speech or occupational therapy present few intrinsic clinical risks. Therefore, in this setting, the risk assessment strategy can focus primarily on the severity of the indication for the service.

Random Chance and Unmeasured Sources of Risk

Finally, despite comprehensive efforts to capture patients' risk factors, some important attributes will inevitably elude detection or quantification. In addition, while in some individual clinical settings it is possible to predict, with some assurance, who will die in-hospital (Patient K, Table 2.2), other patients may die unexpectedly (Patient J). This raises the possibility of random chance or "noise":

> Whenever the focus is on outlier events, the group of outliers will be composed of "normals" who experienced bad outcomes by chance and true "abnormals" who actually had a high risk of bad outcomes. This problem arises particularly when patient populations are small and poor outcomes are rare. (Luft and Romano 1993, 336)

For example, one study found that randomness caused the majority of the differences in mortality rates across hospitals (Park et al. 1990). Concerns about interpreting findings based on small sample sizes are particularly pressing when looking at provider-specific, risk-adjusted outcomes, as is happening in states and regions around the country (see Chapters 10 and 11).

References

American Cancer Society. 1989. *Cancer and the Poor: A Report to the Nation.* Atlanta: The Society.

American Psychiatric Association. 1994. *Diagnostic and Statistical Manual of Mental Disorders,* 4th ed. Washington, D.C.: The Association.

Anderson, G. M., K. Grumbach, H. S. Luft, L. L. Roos, C. Mustard, and R. Brook. 1993. "Use of Coronary Artery Bypass Surgery in the United States and Canada. Influence of Age and Income." *Journal of the American Medical Association* 269 (13): 1661–66.

Andresen, E. M., D. L. Patrick, W. B. Carter, and J. A. Malmgren. 1995. "Comparing the Performance of Health Status Measures for Healthy Older Adults." *Journal of the American Geriatrics Society* 43 (9): 1030–34.

Applegate, W. B., J. P. Blass, and T. F. Williams. 1990. "Instruments for the Functional Assessment of Older Patients." *New England Journal of Medicine* 322 (17): 1207–14.

Arndt, M., and R. C. Bradbury. 1995. "Admission Severity of Illness and Resource Utilization: Comparing Medicaid and Privately Insured Patients." *Hospital & Health Services Administration* 40 (2): 210–26.

Averill, R. F., T. E. McGuire, B. E. Manning, D. A. Fowler, S. D. Horn, P. S. Dickson, M. J. Coye, D. L. Knowlton, and J. A. Bender. 1992. "A Study of the Relationship Between Severity of Illness and Hospital Cost in New Jersey Hospitals." *HSR: Health Services Research* 27 (5): 587–606.

Ayanian, J. Z. 1994. "Race, Class, and the Quality of Medical Care." *Journal of the American Medical Association* 271 (15): 1207–8.

Ayanian, J. Z., and A. M. Epstein. 1991. "Differences in the Use of Procedures Between Women and Men Hospitalized for Coronary Heart Disease." *New England Journal of Medicine* 325 (4): 221–25.

Ayanian, J. Z., I. S. Udvarhelyi, C. A. Gatsonis, C. L. Pashos, and A. M. Epstein. 1993a. "Racial Differences in the Use of Revascularization Procedures After Coronary Angiography." *Journal of the American Medical Association* 269 (20): 2642–46.

Ayanian, J. Z., B. A. Kohler, T. Abe, and A. M. Epstein. 1993b. "The Relation Between Health Insurance Coverage and Clinical Outcomes Among Women with Breast Cancer." *New England Journal of Medicine* 329 (5): 326–31.

Ayanian, J. Z., E. Guadagnoli, and P. D. Cleary. 1995. "Physical and Psychosocial Functioning of Women and Men After Coronary Artery Bypass Surgery." *Journal of the American Medical Association* 274 (22): 1767–70.

Becker, M. H., and L. A. Maiman. 1975. "Sociobehavioral Determinants of Compliance with Health and Medical Care Recommendations." *Medical Care* 13 (1): 10–24.

Bennett, C. L., S. Greenfield, H. Aronow, P. Ganz, N. J. Vogelzang, and R. M. Elashoff. 1991. "Patterns of Care Related to Age of Men with Prostate Cancer." *Cancer* 67 (10): 2633–41.

Bergner, M. 1989. "Quality of Life, Health Status, and Clinical Research." *Medical Care* 27 (3) Supplement: S148–56.

Bergner, M., R. A. Bobbitt, S. Kressel, W. E. Pollard, B. S. Gilson, and J. R. Morris. 1976. "The Sickness Impact Profile: Conceptual Formulation and Methodology for the Development of a Health Status Measure." *International Journal of Health Services* 6 (3): 393–415.

Bergner, M., R. A. Bobbitt, W. B. Carter, and B. S. Gilson. 1981. "The Sickness Impact Profile: Development and Final Revision of a Health Status Measure." *Medical Care* 19 (8): 787–805.

Bindman, A. B., D. Keane, and N. Lurie. 1990. "Measuring Health Changes Among Severely Ill Patients. The Floor Phenomenon." *Medical Care* 28 (12): 1142–52.

Bindman, A. B., and K. Grumbach. 1992. "America's Safety Net. The Wrong Place at the Wrong Time?" *Journal of the American Medical Association* 268 (17): 2426–27.

Bindman, A. B., K. Grumbach, D. Osmond, M. Komaromy, K. Vranizan, N. Lurie, J. Billings, and A. Stewart. 1995. "Preventable Hospitalizations and Access to Health Care." *Journal of the American Medical Association* 274 (4): 305–11.

Blumberg, M. S. 1991. "Biased Estimates of Expected Acute Myocardial Infarction Mortality Using MedisGroups Admission Severity Groups." *Journal of the American Medical Association* 265 (22): 2965–70.

Brailer, D. J., E. Kroch, M. V. Pauly, and J. Huang. 1996. "Comorbidity-Adjusted Complication Risk. A New Outcome Quality Measure." *Medical Care* 34 (5): 490–505.

Brook, R. H., J. E. Ware, Jr., A. Davies-Avery, A. L. Stewart, C. A. Donald, W. H. Rogers, K. Williams, and S. A. Johnston. 1979. "Overview of Adult Health Status Measures Fielded in Rand Health Insurance Study." *Medical Care* 17 (7) Supplement: 1–131.

Buckle, J. M., S. D. Horn, V. M. Oates, and H. Abbey. 1992. "Severity of Illness and Resource Use Differences Among White and Black Hospitalized Elderly." *Archives of Internal Medicine* 152 (8): 1596–1603.

Burstin, H. R., W. G. Johnson, S. R. Lipsitz, and T. A. Brennan. 1993. "Do the Poor Sue More? A Case-Control Study of Malpractice Claims and Socioeconomic Status." *Journal of the American Medical Association* 270 (14): 1697–1701.

Burstin, H. R., S. R. Lipsitz, and T. A. Brennan. 1992. "Socioeconomic Status and Risk for Substandard Medical Care." *Journal of the American Medical Association* 268 (17): 2383–87.

Calkins, D. R., L. V. Rubenstein, P. D. Cleary, A. R. Davies, A. M. Jette, A. Fink, J. Kosecoff, R. T. Young, R. H. Brook, and T. L. Delbanco. 1991. "Failure of Physicians to Recognize Functional Disability in Ambulatory Patients." *Annals of Internal Medicine* 114 (6): 451–54.

Case, R. B., A. J. Moss, N. Case, M. McDermott, and S. Eberly. 1992. "Living Alone after Myocardial Infarction: Impact on Prognosis." *Journal of the American Medical Association* 267 (4): 515–19.

Chambers, L. W., L. A. MacDonald, P. Tugwell, W. W. Buchanan, and G. Kraag. 1982. "The McMaster Health Index Questionnaire as a Measure of Quality of Life for Patients with Rheumatoid Disease." *Journal of Rheumatology* 9 (5): 780–84.

Charlson, M. E., P. Pompei, K. L. Ales, and C. R. MacKenzie. 1987. "A New Method of Classifying Prognostic Comorbidity in Longitudinal Studies: Development and Validation." *Journal of Chronic Disease* 40 (5): 373–83.

Concato J., R. I. Horwitz, A. R. Feinstein, J. G. Elmore, and S. F. Schiff. 1992. "Problems of Comorbidity in Mortality After Prostatectomy." *Journal of the American Medical Association* 267 (8): 1077–82.

Cullen, D. J., G. Apolone, S. Greenfield, E. Guadagnoli, and P. Cleary. 1994. "ASA Physical Status and Age Predict Morbidity After Three Surgical Procedures." *Annals of Surgery* 220 (1): 3–9.

Daley, J., S. Jencks, D. Draper, G. Lenhart, N. Thomas, and J. Walker. 1988. "Predicting Hospital-Associated Mortality for Medicare Patients: A Method for Patients with Stroke, Pneumonia, Acute Myocardial Infarction, and Congestive Heart Failure." *Journal of the American Medical Association* 260 (24): 3617–24.

Danis, M., J. Garrett, R. Harris, and D. L. Patrick. 1994. "Stability of Choices about Life-Sustaining Treatments." *Annals of Internal Medicine* 120 (7): 567–73.

Davis, R. B., L. I. Iezzoni, R. S. Phillips, P. Reiley, G. A. Coffman, and C. Safran. 1995. "Predicting In-Hospital Mortality. The Importance of Functional Status Information." *Medical Care* 33 (9): 906–20.

Dolan, P. 1996. "The Effect of Experience of Illness on Health State Valuations." *Journal of Clinical Epidemiology* 49 (5): 551–64.

Eddy, D. M. 1984. "Variations in Physician Practice: The Role of Uncertainty." *Health Affairs* 3 (2): 74–89.

Eisenberg, D. M., R. C. Kessler, C. Foster, F. E. Norlock, D. R. Calkins, and T. L. Delbanco. 1993. "Unconventional Medicine in the United States: Prevalence, Costs, and Patterns of Use." *New England Journal of Medicine* 328 (4): 246–52.

Ellis, R. P., G. C. Pope, L. I. Iezzoni, J. Z. Ayanian, D. W. Bates, H. Burstin, and A. S. Ash. 1996. "Diagnosis-Based Risk Adjustment for Medicare Capitation Payments." *Health Care Financing Review* 17 (3): 101–28.

Epstein, A. M., J. A. Hall, J. Tognetti, L. H. Son, and L. Conant, Jr. 1989. "Using Proxies to Evaluate Quality of Life: Can They Provide Valid Information about Patients' Health Status and Satisfaction with Medical Care?" *Medical Care* 27 (3) Supplement: S91–98.

EuroQol Group. 1990. "EuroQol—A New Facility for the Measurement of Health-Related Quality of Life." *Health Policy* 16 (3): 199–208.

Feinstein, A. R. 1992. "Benefits and Obstacles for Development of Health Status Assessment Measures in Clinical Settings." *Medical Care* 30 (5) Supplement: MS50–56.

———. 1967. *Clinical Judgment.* Baltimore, MD: Williams & Wilkins Company.

Fetter, R. B., Y. Shin, J. L. Freeman, R. F. Averill, and J. D. Thompson. 1980. "Case Mix Definition by Diagnosis-Related Groups." *Medical Care* 18 (2) Supplement: 1–53.

Forman, D. E., A. D. Berman, C. H. McCabe, D. S. Baim, and J. Y. Wei. 1992. "PTCA in the Elderly: The 'Young-Old' Versus the 'Old-Old'." *Journal of the American Geriatric Society* 40 (1): 19–22.

Gertman, P. M., and S. Lowenstein. 1984. "A Research Paradigm for Severity of Illness: Issues for the Diagnosis-Related Group System." *Health Care Financing Review* Annual Supplement: 79–90.

Gill, T. M., and A. R. Feinstein. 1994. "A Critical Appraisal of the Quality of Quality-of-Life Measurements." *Journal of the American Medical Association* 272 (8): 619–26.

Glower, D. D., T. D. Christopher, C. A. Milano, W. D. White, L. R. Smith, R. H. Jones, and D. C. Sabiston, Jr. 1992. "Performance Status and Outcome After Coronary Artery Bypass Grafting in Persons Aged 80 to 93 Years." *American Journal of Cardiology* 70 (6): 567–71.

Goldman, L. 1983. "Cardiac Risks and Complications of Noncardiac Surgery." *Annals of Internal Medicine* 98 (4): 504–13.

Goldman, L., D. L. Caldera, S. R. Nussbaum, F. S. Southwick, D. Krogstad, B. Murray, D. S. Burke, T. A. O'Malley, A. H. Goroll, C. H. Caplan, J. Nolan, B. Carabello, and E. E. Slater. 1977. "Multifactorial Index of Cardiac Risk in Noncardiac Surgical Procedures." *New England Journal of Medicine* 297 (16): 845–50.

Gonnella, J. S., M. C. Hornbrook, and D. Z. Louis. 1984. "Staging of Disease: A Case-Mix Measurement." *Journal of the American Medical Association* 251 (5): 637–44.

Gordon, H. S., D. L. Harper, and G. E. Rosenthal. 1996. "Racial Variation in Predicted and Observed In-Hospital Death. A Regional Analysis." *Journal of the American Medical Association* 276 (20): 1639–44.

Greenfield, S., D. M. Blanco, R. M. Elashoff, and P. A. Ganz. 1987. "Patterns of Care Related to Age of Breast Cancer Patients." *Journal of the American Medical Association* 257 (20): 2766–70.

Greenfield, S., H. U. Aronow, R. M. Elashoff, and D. Watanabe. 1988. "Flaws in Mortality Data: The Hazards of Ignoring Comorbid Disease." *Journal of the American Medical Association* 260 (15): 2253–55.

Greenfield, S., G. Apolone, B. J. McNeil, and P. D. Cleary. 1993. "The Importance of Co-existent Disease in the Occurrence of Postoperative Complications and One-Year Recovery in Patients Undergoing Total Hip Replacement. Comorbidity and Outcomes after Hip Replacement." *Medical Care* 31 (2): 141–54.

Greenfield, S., L. Sullivan, R. A. Silliman, K. Dukes, and S. H. Kaplan. 1994. "Principles and Practice of Case Mix Adjustment: Applications to End-Stage Renal Disease." *American Journal of Kidney Diseases* 24 (2): 298–307.

Gruenberg, L., E. Kaganova, and M. C. Hornbrook. 1996. "Improving the AAPCC With Health-Status Measures From the MCBS." *Health Care Financing Review* 17 (3): 59–75.

Guyatt, G. H., D. H. Feeny, and D. L. Patrick. 1993. "Measuring Health-related Quality of Life." *Annals of Internal Medicine* 118 (8): 622–29.

Hahn, R. A. 1992. "The State of Federal Health Statistics on Racial and Ethnic Groups." *Journal of the American Medical Association* 267 (2): 268–71.

Hahn, R. A., J. Mulinare, and S. M. Teutsch. 1992. "Inconsistencies in Coding of Race and Ethnicity Between Birth and Death in US Infants." *Journal of the American Medical Association* 267 (2): 259–63.

Hahn, R. A., and D. F. Stroup. 1994. "Race and Ethnicity in Public Health Surveillance: Criteria for the Scientific Use of Social Categories." *Public Health Reports* 109 (1): 7–15.

Hannan, E. L., H. Kilburn, Jr., J. F. O'Donnell, G. Lukacik, and E. P. Shields. 1990. "Adult Open Heart Surgery in New York State: An Analysis of Risk Factors and Hospital Mortality Rates." *Journal of the American Medical Association* 264 (21): 2768–74.

Hannan, E. L., D. T. Arani, L. W. Johnson, H. G. Kemp, Jr., and G. Lukacik. 1992. "Percutaneous Transluminal Coronary Angioplasty in New York State: Risk Factors and Outcomes." *Journal of the American Medical Association* 268 (21): 3092–97.

Hannan, E. L., and J. Burke. 1994. "Effect of Age on Mortality in Coronary Artery Bypass Surgery in New York, 1991–1992." *American Heart Journal* 128 (6): 1184–91.

Heuser, M. D., L. D. Case, and W. H. Ettinger. 1992. "Mortality in Intensive Care Patients With Respiratory Disease: Is Age Important?" *Archives of Internal Medicine* 152 (8): 1683–88.

Hilborne, L. H., L. L. Leape, S. J. Bernstein, R. E. Park, M. E. Fiske, C. J. Kamberg, C. P. Roth, and R. H. Brook. 1993. "The Appropriateness of Use of Percutaneous Transluminal Coronary Angioplasty in New York State." *Journal of the American Medical Association* 269 (6): 761–65.

Holmes, W., B. Bix, and J. Shea. 1996. "SF-20 Score and Item Distributions in a Human Immunodeficiency Virus-Seropositive Sample." *Medical Care* 34 (6): 562–69.

Horn, S. D., P. D. Sharkey, J. M. Buckle, J. E. Backofen, R. F. Averill, and R. A. Horn. 1991. "The Relationship Between Severity of Illness and Hospital Length of Stay and Mortality." *Medical Care* 29 (4): 305–17.

Hornbrook, M. C. 1982. "Hospital Case Mix. Its Definition, Measurement and Use: Part II, Review of Alternative Measures." *Medical Care Review* 39 (2): 73–123.

―――. 1985. Techniques for Assessing Hospital Case Mix." *Annual Review of Public Health* 6: 295–324.

Hornbrook, M. C., and M. J. Goodman. 1995. "Assessing Relative Health Plan Risk with the RAND-36 Health Survey." *Inquiry* 32 (1): 56–74.

Hunt, S. M., and J. McEwen. 1980. "The Development of a Subjective Health Indicator." *Sociology of Health and Illness* 2 (3): 231–46.

Hunt, S. M., S. P. McKenna, J. McEwen, J. Williams, and E. Papp. 1981. "The Nottingham Health Profile: Subjective Health Status and Medical Consultations." *Social Science Medicine* 15a (3 pt. 1): 221–9.

Iezzoni, L. I. 1995. "Risk Adjustment for Medical Effectiveness Research: An Overview of Conceptual and Methodological Considerations." *Journal of Investigative Medicine* 43 (2): 136–50.

Iezzoni, L. I, A. S. Ash, G. Coffman, and M. A. Moskowitz. 1991a. "Admission and Mid-Stay MedisGroups Scores as Predictors of Death Within 30 Days of Admission." *American Journal of Public Health* 81 (1): 74–78.

Iezzoni, L. I., and J. Daley. 1992. "A Description and Clinical Assessment of the Computerized Severity Index™." *Quality Review Bulletin* 18 (2): 44–52.

Iezzoni, L. I., M. G. Henderson, A. Bergman, and R. E. Drews. 1991b. "Purpose of Admission and Resource Use During Cancer Hospitalizations." *Health Care Financing Review* 13 (2): 29–40.

Iezzoni, L. I., M. Shwartz, S. Burnside, A. S. Ash, E. Sawitz, and M. A. Moskowitz. 1989. "Diagnostic Mix, Illness Severity, and Costs at Teaching and Nonteaching Hospitals." Springfield, VA: U.S. Department of Commerce, National Technical Information Service (PB 89 184675/AS).

Iezzoni, L. I., M. Shwartz, M. A. Moskowitz, A. S. Ash, E. Sawitz, and S. Burnside. 1990. "Illness Severity and Costs of Admissions at Teaching and Nonteaching Hospitals." *Journal of the American Medical Association* 264 (11): 1426–31.

Iezzoni, L. I., M. Shwartz, A. S. Ash, Y. Mackiernan, and E. K. Hotchkin. 1994. "Risk Adjustment Methods Can Affect Perceptions of Outcomes." *American Journal of Medical Quality* 9 (2): 43–48.

Iezzoni, L. I., M. Shwartz, A. S. Ash, J. S. Hughes, J. Daley, and Y. D. Mackiernan. 1995. "Using Severity-Adjusted Stroke Mortality Rates to Judge Hospitals." *International Journal for Quality in Health Care* 7 (2): 81–94.

Iezzoni, L. I., A. S. Ash, M. Shwartz, J. Daley, J. S. Hughes, and Y. D. Mackiernan. 1996a. "Judging Hospitals by Severity-Adjusted Mortality Rates: The Influence of the Severity-Adjustment Method." *American Journal of Public Health* 86 (10): 1379–87.

Iezzoni, L. I., M. Shwartz, A. S. Ash, J. S. Hughes, J. Daley, and Y. D. Mackiernan.

1996b. "Severity Measurement Methods and Judging Hospital Death Rates for Pneumonia." *Medical Care* 34 (1): 11–28.

Jayes, R. L., J. E. Zimmerman, D. P. Wagner, E. A. Draper, and W. A. Knaus. 1993. "Do-Not-Resuscitate Orders in Intensive Care Units. Current Practices and Recent Changes." *Journal of the American Medical Association* 270 (18): 2213–17.

Justice, A. C., L. H. Aiken, H. L. Smith, and B. J. Turner. 1996. "The Role of Functional Status in Predicting Inpatient Mortality with AIDS: A Comparison with Current Predictors." *Journal of Clinical Epidemiology* 49 (2): 193–201.

Kahn, K. L., M. L. Pearson, E. R. Harrison, K. A. Desmond, W. H. Rogers, L. V. Rubenstein, R. H. Brook, and E. B. Keeler. 1994. "Health Care for Black and Poor Hospitalized Medicare Patients." *Journal of the American Medical Association* 271 (15): 1169–74.

Kaplan, R. M., and J. P. Anderson. 1988. "The Quality of Well-Being Scale: Rationale for a Single Quality of Life Index." In *Quality of Life: Assessment and Application.* Walker, S. R., and R. M. Rosser, eds. pp. 51–78. Lancaster: MTP Press.

Kaplan, S. H., S. Greenfield, and J. E. Ware, Jr. 1989. "Assessing the Effects of Physician-Patient Interactions on the Outcomes of Chronic Disease." *Medical Care* 27 (3) Supplement: S110–27.

Kaplan, S. H., and J. R. Ware, Jr. 1989. "The Patient's Role in Health Care and Quality Assessment." In *Providing Quality Care: The Challenge to Clinicians,* edited by N. Goldfield and D. B. Nash. Philadelphia, PA: American College of Physicians.

Karnofsky, D. A., W. H. Abelmann, L. F. Craver, and J. H. Burchenal. 1948. "The Use of the Nitrogen Mustards in the Palliative Treatment of Carcinoma." *Cancer* 1 (4): 634–56.

Keeler, E. B., K. L. Kahn, D. Draper, M. J. Sherwood, L. V. Rubenstein, E. J. Reinisch, J. Kosecoff, and R. H. Brook. 1990. "Changes in Sickness at Admission Following the Introduction of the Prospective Payment System." *Journal of the American Medical Association* 264 (15): 1962–68.

Knaus, W. A., J. E. Zimmerman, D. P. Wagner, E. A. Draper, and D. E. Lawrence. 1981. "APACHE—Acute Physiology and Chronic Health Evaluation: A Physiologically Based Classification System." *Critical Care Medicine* 9 (8): 591–97.

Knaus, W. A., E. A. Draper, D. P. Wagner, and J. E. Zimmerman. 1985. "APACHE II: A Severity of Disease Classification System." *Critical Care Medicine* 13 (10): 818–29.

Knaus, W. A., D. P. Wagner, E. A. Draper, J. E. Zimmerman, M. Bergner, P. G. Bastos, C. A. Sirio, D. J. Murphy, T. Lotring, A. Damiano, and F. E. Harrell, Jr. 1991. "The APACHE III Prognostic System: Risk Prediction of Hospital Mortality for Critically Ill Hospitalized Adults." *Chest* 100 (6): 1619–36.

Knaus, W. A., F. E. Harrell, Jr., J. Lynn, L. Goldman, R. S. Phillips, A. F. Connors, Jr., N. V. Dawson, W. J. Fulkerson, Jr., R. M. Califf, N. Desbiens, P. Layde, R. K. Oye, P. E. Bellamy, R. B. Hakim, and D. P. Wagner. 1995. "The SUPPORT Prognostic Model: Objective Estimates of Survival for Seriously Ill Hospitalized Adults." *Annals of Internal Medicine* 122 (3): 191–203.

Kroenke, K. 1987. "Preoperative Evaluation: The Assessment and Management of Surgical Risk." *Journal of General Internal Medicine* 2 (4): 257–69.

Krousel-Wood, M. A., A. Abdoh, and R. Re. 1996. "Comparing Comorbid-Illness

Indices Assessing Outcome Variation: The Case of Prostatectomy." *Journal of General Internal Medicine* 11 (1): 32–38.

Kutner, N. G., M. G. Ory, D. I. Baker, K. B. Schechtman, M. C. Hornbrook, and C. D. Mulrow. 1992. "Measuring the Quality of Life of the Elderly in Health Promotion Intervention Clinical Trials." *Public Health Reports* 107 (5): 530–39.

"Lack of Race Data Skews National Discharge Survey." 1995. *Medical Outcomes & Guidelines Alert* 3 (15).

Landgraf, J. M., E. C. Nelson, R. D. Hays, J. H. Wasson, and J. W. Kirk. 1990. "Assessing Function: Does It Really Make a Difference? A Preliminary Evaluation of the Acceptability and Utility of the COOP Function Charts." In *Functional Status Measurement in Primary Care* M. Lipkin, ed. pp. 150–65. New York: Springer-Verlag.

Landon, B., L. I. Iezzoni, A. S. Ash, M. Shwartz, J. Daley, J. S. Hughes, and Y. D. Mackiernan. 1996. "Judging Hospitals by Severity-Adjusted Mortality Rates: The Case of CABG Surgery." *Inquiry* 33 (2): 155–66.

LaVeist, T. A. 1994. "Beyond Dummy Variables and Sample Selection: What Health Services Researchers Ought to Know About Race as a Variable." *HSR: Health Services Research* 29 (1): 1–16.

Leape, L. L., T. A. Brennan, N. Laird, A. G. Lawthers, A. R. Localio, B. A. Barnes, L. Hebert, J. P. Newhouse, P. C. Weiler, and H. Hiatt. 1991. "The Nature of Adverse Events in Hospitalized Patients. Results of the Harvard Medical Practice Study II." *New England Journal of Medicine* 324 (6): 377–84.

Leape, L. L., L. H. Hilborne, R. E. Park, S. J. Bernstein, C. J. Kamberg, M. Sherwood, and R. H. Brook. 1993. "The Appropriateness of Use of Coronary Artery Bypass Graft Surgery in New York State." *Journal of the American Medical Association* 269 (6): 753–60.

Le Gall, J. R., S. Lemeshow, and F. Saulnier. 1993. "A New Simplified Acute Physiology Score (SAPS II) Based on a European/North American Multicenter Study." *Journal of the American Medical Association* 270 (24): 2957–63.

Lemeshow, S., J. Klar, D. Teres, J. S. Avrunin, S. H. Gehlbach, J. Rapoport, and M. Rue. 1994. "Mortality Probability Models for Patients in the Intensive Care Unit for 48 or 72 Hours: A Prospective, Multicenter Study." *Critical Care Medicine* 22 (9): 1351–58.

Lemeshow, S., and J. R. Le Gall. 1994. "Modeling the Severity of Illness of ICU Patients. A Systems Update." *Journal of the American Medical Association* 272 (13): 1049–55.

Lemeshow, S., D. Teres, J. Klar, J. S. Avrunin, S. H. Gehlbach, and J. Rapoport. 1993. "Mortality Probability Models (MPM II) Based on an International Cohort of Intensive Care Unit Patients." *Journal of the American Medical Association* 270 (20): 2478–86.

Lohr, K., ed. 1989. "Advances in Health Status Assessment, Conference Proceedings." *Medical Care* 27 (3) Supplement: S1–294.

———., ed. 1992. "Advances in Health Status Assessment: Fostering the Application of Health Status Measures in Clinical Settings: Proceedings of a Conference." *Medical Care* 30 (5) Supplement: MS1–293.

Luft, H. S., and P. S. Romano. 1993. "Chance, Continuity, and Change in Hospital

Mortality Rates: Coronary Artery Bypass Graft Patients in California Hospitals, 1983 to 1989." *Journal of the American Medical Association* 270 (3): 331–37.

Mangione, C. M., R. S. Phillips, J. M. Seddon, M. G. Lawrence, E. F. Cook, R. Dailey, and L. Goldman. 1992. "Development of the 'Activities of Daily Vision Scale': A Measure of Visual Functional Status." *Medical Care* 30 (12): 1111–26.

Mangione, C. M., E. R. Marcantonio, L. Goldman, E. F. Cook, M. C. Donaldson, D. J. Sugarbaker, R. Poss, and T. H. Lee. 1993. "Influence of Age on Measurement of Health Status in Patients Undergoing Elective Surgery." *Journal of the American Geriatrics Society* 41 (4): 377–83.

Manton, K. G., C. H. Patrick, and K. W. Johnson. 1987. "Health Differentials Between Blacks and Whites: Recent Trends in Mortality and Morbidity." *Milbank Quarterly* 65 Supplement 1: 129–99.

McBean, A. M. and M. Gornick. 1994. "Differences by Race in the Rates of Procedures Performed in Hospitals for Medicare Beneficiaries." *Health Care Financing Review* 15 (4): 77–90.

McDowell, I., and C. Newell. 1987. *Measuring Health: A Guide to Rating Scales and Questionnaires*. New York: Oxford University Press.

McHorney, C. A., J. E. Ware, Jr., J. F. Rachel Lu, and C. D. Sherbourne. 1994. "The MOS 36-Item Short-Form Health Survey (SF-36): III. Tests of Data Quality, Scaling Assumptions, and Reliability Across Diverse Patient Groups." *Medical Care* 32 (1): 40–66.

McKenney, N. R., and C. E. Bennett. 1994. "Issues Regarding Data on Race and Ethnicity: The Census Bureau Experience." *Public Health Reports* 109 (1): 16–25.

MediQual Systems, Inc. 1993. *MedisGroups Scoring Algorithm, January 1993 Version: A Technical Description*. Westborough, MA: MediQual Systems, Inc.

Meenan, R. 1986. "New Approaches to Outcome Assessment: The AIMS Questionnaire for Arthritis." In *Advances in Internal Medicine, Volume 31*, edited by G. Stollerman. Chicago: Year Book Medical Publishers.

Montague, T. J., R. M. Ikuta, R. Y. Wong, K. S. Bay, K. K. Teo, and N. J. Davies. 1991. "Comparison of Risk and Patterns of Practice in Patients Older and Younger Than 70 Years with Acute Myocardial Infarction in a Two-Year Period (1987–1989)." *American Journal of Cardiology* 68 (9): 843–47.

Mort, E. A., E. Guadagnoli, S. A. Schroeder, S. Greenfield, A. G. Mulley, B. J. McNeil, and P. D. Cleary. 1994. "The Influence of Age on Clinical and Patient-Reported Outcomes after Cholecystectomy." *Journal of General Internal Medicine* 9 (2): 61–65.

Mor, V. "A Modern Lexicon of Disability." In *Living in the Community with Disability: Service Needs, Uses and Systems*, edited by S. Allen and V. Mor. New York: Springer, in press.

Mosteller, F., J. E. Ware, Jr., and S. Levine. 1989. "Finale Panel: Comments on the Conference on Advances in Health Status Assessment." *Medical Care* 27 (3) Supplement: S282–94.

Nagi, S. 1991. "Disability Concepts Revisited: Implications for Prevention." In *Disability in America: Toward a National Agenda for Prevention*, edited by A. M. Pope and A. R. Tarlov. Washington, D.C.: Institute of Medicine, National Academy Press.

National Center for Health Statistics. 1996. *Health, United States, 1995.* Hyattsville, MD: Public Health Service.

Navarro, V. 1991. "Race *or* Class or Race *and* Class: Growing Mortality Differentials in the United States." *International Journal of Health Sciences* 21 (2): 229–35.

Nelson, E., J. Wasson, J. Kirk, A. Keller, D. Clark, A. Dietrich, A. Stewart, and M. Zubkoff. 1987. "Assessment of Function in Routine Clinical Practice: Description of the COOP Chart Method and Preliminary Findings." *Journal of Chronic Disease* 40 (Suppl. 1): 55S–62S.

Otten, M. W., Jr., S. M. Teutsch, D. F. Williamson, and J. S. Marks. 1990. "The Effect of Known Risk Factors on the Excess Mortality of Black Adults in the United States." *Journal of the American Medical Association* 263 (6): 845–50.

Park, R. E., R. H. Brook, J. Kosecoff, J. Keesey, L. Rubenstein, E. Keeler, K. L. Kahn, W. H. Rogers, and M. R. Chassin. 1990. "Explaining Variations in Hospital Death Rates. Randomness, Severity of Illness, Quality of Care." *Journal of the American Medical Association* 264 (4): 484–90.

Parkerson, G. R., Jr., W. E. Broadhead, and C. J. Tse. 1990. "The Duke Health Profile. A 17-Item Measure of Health and Dysfunction." *Medical Care* 28 (11): 1056–69.

Patrick, D. L., J. W. Bush, and M. M. Chen. 1973. "Methods for Measuring Levels of Well-being for a Health Status Index." *HSR: Health Services Research* 8 (3): 228–45.

Patrick, D. L., and R. A. Deyo. 1989. "Generic and Disease-Specific Measures in Assessing Health Status and Quality of Life." *Medical Care* 27 (3) Supplement: S217–32.

Pearson, M. L., K. L. Kahn, E. R. Harrison, L. V. Rubenstein, W. H. Rogers, R. H. Brook, and E. B. Keeler. 1992. "Differences in Quality of Care for Hospitalized Elderly Men and Women." *Journal of the American Medical Association* 268 (14): 1883–89.

Perls, T. T., and E. R. Wood. 1996. "Acute Care Costs of the Oldest Old. They Cost Less, Their Care Intensity Is Less, and They Go to Nonteaching Hospitals." *Archives of Internal Medicine* 156 (7): 754–60.

Peterson, E. D., S. M. Wright, J. Daley, and G. E. Thibault. 1994. "Racial Variation in Cardiac Procedure Use and Survival Following Acute Myocardial Infarction in the Department of Veterans Affairs." *Journal of the American Medical Association* 271 (15): 1175–80.

Phillips, R. S., M. B. Hamel, J. M. Teno, P. Bellamy, S. K. Broste, R. M. Califf, H. Vidaillet, R. B. Davis, L. H. Muhlbaier, A. F. Connors, Jr., J. Lynn, and L. Goldman. 1996a. "Race, Resource Use, and Survival in Seriously Ill Hospitalized Adults." *Journal of General Internal Medicine* 11 (7): 387–96.

Phillips, R. S., N. S. Wenger, J. Teno, R. K. Oye, S. Younger, R. Califf, P. Layde, N. Desbiens, A. F. Connors, Jr., and J. Lynn. 1996b. "Choices of Seriously Ill Patients About Cardiopulmonary Resuscitation: Correlates and Outcomes." *American Journal of Medicine* 100 (2): 128–37.

Pollack, M. M., U. E. Ruttimann, and P. R. Getson. 1988. "Pediatric Risk of Mortality (PRISM) Score." *Critical Care Medicine* 16 (11): 1110–16.

Pope, A. M., and A. R. Tarlov, eds. 1991. *Disability in America. Toward a National*

Agenda for Prevention. Washington, D.C.: Institute of Medicine, National Academy Press.

Poses, R. M., D. K. McClish, W. R. Smith, C. Bekes, and W. E. Scott. 1996. "Prediction of Survival of Critically Ill Patients by Admission Comorbidity." *Journal of Clinical Epidemiology* 49 (7): 743–47.

Reiser, S. J. 1993. "The Era of the Patient: Using the Experience of Illness in Shaping the Missions of Health Care." *Journal of the American Medical Association* 269 (8): 1012–17.

Rochon, P. A., J. N. Katz, L. A. Morrow, R. McGlinchey-Berroth, M. M. Ahlquist, M. Sarkarati, and K. L. Minaker. 1996. "Comorbid Illness Is Associated with Survival and Length of Hospital Stay in Patients with Chronic Disability. A Prospective Comparison of Three Comorbidity Indices." *Medical Care* 34 (11): 1093–1101.

Rubenstein, L. V., D. R. Calkins, S. Greenfield, A. M. Jette, R. F. Meenan, M. A. Nevins, L. Z. Rubenstein, J. H. Wasson, and M. E. Williams. 1989. "Health Status Assessment for Elderly Patients: Report of the Society of General Internal Medicine Task Force on Health Assessment." *Journal of the American Geriatric Society* 37 (6): 562–69.

Rubenstein, L. V., N. C. Ward, and S. Greenfield. 1986. "In Pursuit of the Abnormal Serum Alkaline Phosphatase: a Clinical Dilemma." *Journal of General Internal Medicine* 1 (1): 38–43.

Ruberman, W., E. Weinblatt, J. D. Goldberg, and B. S. Chaudhary. 1984. "Psychosocial Influences on Mortality After Myocardial Infarction." *New England Journal of Medicine* 311 (9): 552–59.

Schulman, K. A., L. E. Rubenstein, F. D. Chesley, and J. M. Eisenberg. 1995. "The Roles of Race and Socioeconomic Factors in Health Services Research." *HSR: Health Services Research* 30 (1): 179–95.

Schweiker, R. S. 1982. *Report to Congress: Hospital Prospective Payment for Medicare.* Washington, D.C.: U.S. Department of Health and Human Services.

Sherbourne, C. D., L. S. Meredith, W. Rogers, and J. E. Ware, Jr. 1992. "Social Support and Stressful Life Events: Age Differences in Their Effects on Health-Related Quality of Life Among the Chronically Ill." *Quality of Life Research* 1 (4): 235–46.

Sherbourne, C. D., and A. L. Stewart. 1991. "The MOS Social Support Survey." *Social Science and Medicine* 32 (6): 705–14.

Smits, H. L., R. B. Fetter, and L. F. McMahon, Jr. 1984. "Variation in Resource Use Within Diagnosis-Related Groups: The Severity Issue." *Health Care Financing Review* Annual Supplement: 71–78.

Spector, W. D. 1990. "Functional Disability Scales." In *Quality of Life Assessments in Clinical Trials,* edited by B. Spilker. New York: Raven Press.

Spitzer, W. O., A. J. Dobson, J. Hall, E. Chesterman, J. Levi, R. Shepherd, R. N. Battista, and B. R. Catchlove. 1981. "Measuring the Quality of Life of Cancer Patients. A Concise QL-Index for Use by Physicians." *Journal of Chronic Disease* 34 (12): 585–97.

Starfield, B., J. Weiner, L. Mumford, and D. Steinwachs. 1991. "Ambulatory Care Groups: A Categorization of Diagnoses for Research and Management." *HSR: Health Services Research* 26 (1): 53–74.

Starfield, B. 1992. "Effects of Poverty on Health Status." *Bulletin of the New York Academy of Medicine* 68 (1): 17–24.

Starfield, B., M. Bergner, M. Ensminger, A. Riley, S. Ryan, B. Green, P. McGauhey, A. Skinner, and S. Kim. 1993. "Adolescent Health Status Measurement: Development of the Child Health and Illness Profile." *Pediatrics* 91 (2): 430–35.

Steel, K., P. M. Gertman, C. Crescenzi, and J. Anderson. 1981. "Iatrogenic Illness on a General Medical Service at a University Hospital." *New England Journal of Medicine* 304 (11): 638–42.

Steen, P. M., A. C. Brewster, R. C. Bradbury, E. Estabrook, and J. A. Young. 1993. "Predicted Probabilities of Hospital Death as a Measure of Admission Severity of Illness." *Inquiry* 30 (2): 128–41.

Steen, P. M. 1994. "Approaches to Predictive Modeling." *Annals of Thoracic Surgery* 58 (6): 1836–40.

Steinwachs, D. M. 1989. "Application of Health Status Assessment Measures in Policy Research." *Medical Care* 27 (3) Supplement: S12–26.

Stewart, A. L., S. Greenfield, R. D. Hays, K. Wells, W. H. Rogers, S. D. Berry, E. A. McGlynn, and J. E. Ware, Jr. 1989. "Functional Status and Well-Being of Patients with Chronic Conditions. Results from the Medical Outcomes Study." *Journal of the American Medical Association* 262 (7): 907–13.

Stewart, A. L., R. D. Hays, and J. E. Ware, Jr. 1988. "The MOS Short-Form General Health Survey. Reliability and Validity in a Patient Population." *Medical Care* 26 (7): 724–35.

Stewart, A. L., J. E. Ware, Jr., and R. H. Brook. 1981. "Advances in the Measurement of Functional Status: Construction of Aggregate Indexes." *Medical Care* 19 (5): 473–88.

Stewart, A. L., J. E. Ware, Jr., eds. 1992. *Measuring Functioning and Well-Being: The Medical Outcomes Study Approach.* Durham, NC: Duke University Press.

Streiner, D. L. and G. R. Norman. 1995. *Health Status Measurement Scales. A Practical Guide to Their Development and Use.* 2nd. ed. Oxford: Oxford University Press.

Svensson, C. K. 1989. "Representation of American Blacks in Clinical Trials of New Drugs." *Journal of the American Medical Association* 261 (2): 263–65.

Teno, J. M., R. B. Hakim, W. A. Knaus, N. S. Wenger, R. S. Phillips, A. W. Wu, P. Layde, A. F. Connors, Jr., N. V. Dawson, and J. Lynn. 1995. "Preferences for Cardiopulmonary Resuscitation: Physician-Patient Agreement and Hospital Resource Use." *Journal of General Internal Medicine* 10 (4): 179–86.

Teno, J. M., J. Lynn, R. S. Phillips, D. Murphy, S. J. Youngner, P. Bellamy, A. F. Connors, Jr., N. A. Desbiens, W. Fulkerson, and W. A. Knaus. 1994. "Do Formal Advance Directives Affect Resuscitation Decisions and the Use of Resources for Seriously Ill Patients?" *Journal of Clinical Ethics* 5 (1): 23–30.

Tinetti, M. E., T. F. Williams, and R. Mayewski. 1986. "Fall Risk Index for Elderly Patients Based on Number of Chronic Disabilities." *American Journal of Medicine* 80 (3): 429–34.

Tsevat, J., E. F. Cook, M. L. Green, D. B. Matchar, N. V. Dawson, S. K. Broste, A. W. Wu, R. S. Phillips, R. K. Oye, and L. Goldman. 1995. "Health Values of the Seriously Ill." *Annals of Internal Medicine* 122 (7): 514–20.

Udvarhelyi, I. S., C. Gatsonis, A. M. Epstein, C. L. Pashos, J. P. Newhouse, and B. J.

McNeil. 1992. "Acute Myocardial Infarction in the Medicare Population: Process of Care and Clinical Outcomes." *Journal of the American Medical Association* 268 (18): 2530–36.

U.S. Bureau of the Census. 1992. *Statistical Abstract of the United States: 1992.* Washington, D.C.: The Bureau.

U.S. Department of Health and Human Services, Public Health Service. 1985. "Clearinghouse on Health Indexes." Rockville, MD: National Center for Health Statistics.

U.S. General Accounting Office. 1992. *FDA Needs to Ensure More Study of Gender Differences in Prescription Drug Testing.* Washington, D.C.: U.S. General Accounting Office.

Verbrugge, L. M., and D. L. Patrick. 1995. "Seven Chronic Conditions: Their Impact on US Adults' Activity Levels and Use of Medical Services." *American Journal of Public Health* 85 (2): 173–82.

Vladeck, B. C. 1984. "Medicare Hospital Payment by Diagnosis-Related Groups." *Annals of Internal Medicine* 100 (4): 576–91.

Wagner, D. P., W. A. Knaus, and E. A. Draper. 1986. "Physiologic Abnormalities and Outcome from Acute Disease. Evidence for a Predictable Relationship." *Archives of Internal Medicine* 146 (7): 1389–96.

Ware, J. E., Jr. 1987. "Standards for Validating Health Measures: Definition and Content." *Journal of Chronic Disease* 40 (6): 473–80.

————. 1991. Conceptualizing and Measuring Generic Health Outcomes." *Cancer* 67 (3) Supplement: 774–79.

Ware, J. E., Jr. 1995. "The Status of Health Assessment 1994." *Annual Review of Public Health* 16 327–54.

Ware, J. E., Jr., A. Avery-Davies, and R. H. Brook. 1980. *Conceptualization and Measurement of Health for Adults in the Health Insurance Study: Vol. 1. Model of Health and Methodology.* Santa Monica, CA: Rand Corporation.

Ware, J. E., Jr., and C. D. Sherbourne. 1992. "The MOS 36-Item Short-Form Health Survey (SF-36). I. Conceptual Framework and Item Selection." *Medical Care* 30 (6): 473–81.

Ware, J. E., K. K. Snow, M. Kosinski, and B. Gandek. 1993. *SF-36 Health Survey Manual and Interpretation Guide.* Boston, MA: New England Medical Center Health Institute.

Warren, M.D. 1987. "The Prevalence of Disability: Measuring and Estimating the Number and the Needs of Disabled People in the Community." *Public Health* 101 (5): 333–41.

Weinberger, M., E. Z. Oddone, G. P. Samsa, and P. B. Landsman. 1996. "Are Health-Related Quality-of-Life Measures Affected by the Mode of Administration?" *Journal of Clinical Epidemiology* 49 (2): 135–40.

Weintraub, W. S., J. M. Craver, C. L. Cohen, E. L. Jones, and R. A. Guyton. 1991. "Influence of Age on Results of Coronary Artery Surgery." *Circulation* 84 (5) Supplement III: III-226–III-235.

Weissman, J., C. Gatsonis, and A. M. Epstein. 1992. "Rates of Avoidable Hospitalization by Insurance Status in Massachusetts and Maryland." *Journal of the American Medical Association* 268 (17): 2388–94.

Wenger, N. S., M. L. Pearson, K. A. Desmond, E. R. Harrison, L. V. Rubenstein, W. H. Rogers, and K. L. Kahn. 1995. "Epidemiology of Do-Not-Resuscitate Orders. Disparity by Age, Diagnosis, Gender, Race, and Functional Impairment." *Archives of Internal Medicine* 155 (19): 2056–62.

Wenneker, M. B., and A. M. Epstein. 1989. "Racial Inequalities in the Use of Procedures for Patients with Ischemic Heart Disease in Massachusetts." *Journal of the American Medical Association* 261 (2): 253–57.

Williams, D. R. 1994. "The Concept of Race in *Health Services Research*: 1966 to 1990." *HSR: Health Services Research* 29 (3): 261–74.

———. 1996. "Race/Ethnicity and Socioeconomic Status: Measurement and Methodological Issues." *International Journal of Health Services* 26 (3): 483–505.

Williams, J. F., J. E. Zimmerman, D. P. Wagner, M. Hawkins, and W. A. Knaus. 1995. "African-American and White Patients Admitted to the Intensive Care Unit: Is There a Difference in Therapy and Outcome?" *Critical Care Medicine* 23 (4): 626–36.

Williams, R. B., J. C. Barefoot, R. M. Califf, T. L. Haney, W. B. Saunders, D. B. Pryor, M. A. Hlatky, I. C. Siegler, and D. B. Mark. 1992. "Prognostic Importance of Social and Economic Resources Among Medically Treated Patients with Angiographically Documented Coronary Artery Disease." *Journal of the American Medical Association* 267 (4): 520–24.

Wood, W. R., R. P. Ament, and E. J. Kobrinski. 1981. "A Foundation for Hospital Case Mix Measurement." *Inquiry* 18 (3): 247–54.

Wood-Dauphinee, S., and J. I. Williams. 1987. "Reintegration to Normal Living as a Proxy to Quality of Life." *Journal of Chronic Disease* 40 (6): 491–9.

Working Group on Risk and High Blood Pressure. 1985. "An Epidemiologic Approach to Describing Risk Associated with Blood Pressure Levels." *Hypertension* 7 (4): 641–51.

Young, N. L., J. I. Williams, K. K. Yoshida, C. Bombardier, and J. G. Wright. 1996. "The Context of Measuring Disability: Does It Matter Whether Capability or Performance Is Measured?" *Journal of Clinical Epidemiology* 49 (10): 1097–1101.

Young, W. W. 1993. *Patient Management Categories . . . A Comprehensive Overview*. Pittsburgh, PA: The Pittsburgh Research Institute.

Zimmerman, J. E., W. A. Knaus, S. M. Sharpe, A. S. Anderson, E. A. Draper, and D. P. Wagner. 1986. "The Use and Implications of Do Not Resuscitate Orders in Intensive Care Units." *Journal of the American Medical Association* 255 (3): 351–56.

Exhibit 2.1 Computerized Severity Index

A. Pneumonia

ICD-9-CM Diagnosis codes: 055.1, 112.4, 136.3, 480–486, 506.3, 507–507.1, 516.8, 517–517.1, 518.3, 668–668.04, 997.3, 998.

Category	Complexity Indicator	Level			
		1	2	3	4
Cardiovascular	EKG Rhythm	No EKG ectopy	≥ 6 PVCs per minute; SVT Bigeminy Trigeminy Quadrigeminy Atrial fibrillation PACs or PVCs NOS EKG ectopy NOS Nonsustained ventricular tachycardia Junctional ectopic tachycardia		Runs of ventricular tachycardia
Lab—ABG's	Highest pH	≤ 7.45	≥ 7.46		
	Lowest pO$_2$	≥ 61 mm Hg		51–60 mm Hg	≤ 50 mm Hg
	Lowest pH	≥ 7.35	7.25–7.34	7.10–7.24	≤ 7.09
	Saturation	O$_2$ Sat < 90 with no supplemental oxygen	Able to obtain O$_2$ Sat >90 with 22–50% oxygen	Unable to obtain O$_2$ Sat >90 with 22–50% oxygen Able to obtain O$_2$ Sat >90 with oxygen >50%	Unable to obtain O$_2$ Sat >90 with oxygen >50%

	pO₂/FiO₂ Ratio	≥ 300 Ratio	200–299 Ratio	100–199 Ratio	≤ 99 Ratio
	Lowest O₂ Saturation, Highest FiO₂	≤ 30 Ratio	31–50 Ratio	51–75 Ratio	≥ 76 Ratio
Lab—Hematology	Highest White Blood Cell Count (WBC)	≤ 11.0 K/cu mm	11.1–20.0 K/cu mm	20.1–30.0 K/cu mm	≥ 30.1 K/cu mm
	Highest Bands	≤ 9%	10–20%	21–40%	≥ 41%
	Lowest White Blood Cell Count (WBC)	≥ 4.5 K/cu mm	2.4–4.4 K/cu mm	1.0–2.3 K/cu mm	≤ 0.9 K/cu mm
Neurology	Neurological Status	No unresponsiveness or confusion	Chronic confusion	Acute confusion	Unresponsive
	Lowest Glasgow Coma Scale Score	≥ 12	9–11	6–8	≤ 5
Radiology	Chest X-Ray/Ct Scan	Collapse in >3 lobes	Infiltrate and/or consolidation in ≤ 1 lobe	Infiltrate and/or consolidation in > 1 lobe but ≤ 3 lobes	Infiltrate and/or consolidation > 3 lobes
		Collapse in >1 lobe but ≤ 3 lobes	Localized infiltrate	Extensive infiltrates	Cavitation or necrosis of lung
		Collapse in ≤ 1 lobe	Pleural effusion		
		No lung collapse/ infiltrates/ consolidation/ cavitation/ necrosis/effusion			

Continued

Exhibit 2.1 Continued

Category	Complexity Indicator	Level 1	Level 2	Level 3	Level 4
Respiratory	Cyanosis	No cyanosis		Cyanosis present	
	Sputum/Secretions	White, thin, yellow, and/or mucoid Sputum NOS	Blood-tinged sputum	Frank hemoptysis	
		No sputum production	Purulent and/or frothy Hemoptysis NOS		
	Dyspnea	No dyspnea	Dyspnea on exertion Breathing difficulties NOS	Dyspnea at rest	Apnea
	Stridor	No spasm or stridor	Laryngospasm stridor		
	Rales	No rales	Rales $\leq$ 50% / < 3 lobes	Rales > 50% / $\geq$ 3 lobes	
	Breath Sounds	No decreased or absent breath sounds	Decreased breath sounds $\leq$ 50% / < 3 lobes	Decreased breath sounds > 50% / $\geq$ 3 lobes	Absent breath sounds > 50% / $\geq$ 3 lobes
	Fremitus	Not positive for fremitus (sound conduction)	Positive for fremitus (sound conduction)		

Vitals				
Lowest Pulse Rate	≥ 51 beats/min	41–50 beats/min	31–40 beats/min	≤ 30 beats/min
Lowest Systolic Blood Pressure	≥ 90 mm Hg	80–89 mm Hg	61–79 mm Hg	≤ 60 mm Hg
Highest Temperature	≤ 100.4 Oral °F	100.5–102.0 Oral °F	102.1–103.9 Oral °F	≥ 104.0 Oral °F
Rigors/Chills	Chills / No rigors or chills		Rigors / Rigors and chills	
Lowest Temperature	≥ 96.8 Oral °F	94.0–96.7 Oral °F	90.1–93.9 Oral °F	≤ 90.0 Oral °F
Highest Pulse Rate	≤ 99 beats/min	100–129 beats/min	≥ 130 beats/min	

B. Acute Myocardial Infarction

ICD-9-CM Diagnosis codes: 410–410.92, 429.71–429.79

Cardiovascular				
Heart Blocks	Second degree heart block / First degree heart block / No heart block		Third degree heart block	
Muffled Heart Sounds	No muffled heart sounds	Muffled heart sounds		
Lowest Ejection Fraction	≥ 50%	35–49%	20–34%	≤ 19%
Ischemia by EKG	No ischemic changes by EKG	Acute T wave changes / Newest Onset Q waves / ST Segment changes		

Continued

Exhibit 2.1 Continued

Category	Complexity Indicator	Level			
		1	2	3	4
	EKG Rhythm	No EKG ectopy	≥ 6 PVCs per minutes; SVT Bigeminy Trigeminy Quadrigeminy Atrial fibrillation PACs or PVCs NOS EKG ectopy NOS Nonsustained ventricular tachycardia Junctional ectopic tachycardia		Runs of ventricular tachycardia
Lab— Chemistry	Highest BUN	≤ 23 mg/dl	24–70 mg/dl	71–100 mg/dl	≥ 101 mg/dl
	Highest Creatinine	≤ 1.2 mg/dl	1.3–3.0 mg/dl	3.1–7.0 mg/dl	≥ 7.1 mg/dl
	Highest Male CPK Isoenzyme MB	≤2.5 (xNorm)	2.6–4.0 (xNorm)	4.1–7.9 (xNorm)	≥ 8.0 (xNorm)
	Highest Female CPK Isoenzyme MB	≤2.5 (xNorm)	2.6–4.0 (xNorm)	4.1–7.9 (xNorm)	≥ 8.0 (xNorm)
	Highest Male Total CPK	≤ 4.9 (xNorm)	≥ 5.0 (xNorm)		
	Highest Female Total CPK	≤ 4.9 (xNorm)	≥ 5.0 (xNorm)		

		≤ 11.0 K/cu mm	11.1–20.0 K/cu mm	20.1–30.0 K/cu mm	≥ 30.1 K/cu mm
Lab— Hematology	Highest White Blood Cell Count (WBC)	≤ 11.0 K/cu mm	11.1–20.0 K/cu mm	20.1–30.0 K/cu mm	≥ 30.1 K/cu mm
	Highest Bands	≤ 9%	10–20%	21–40%	≥ 41%
	Highest Erythrocyte Sedimentation Rate (ESR)	≤ 49 mm/hr	≥ 50 mm/hr		
Neurology	Neurological Status	No unresponsiveness or confusion	Chronic confusion	Acute confusion	Unresponsive
	Lowest Glasgow Coma Scale Score	≥ 12	9–11	6–8	≤ 5
Pain	Anginal Pain (Chest Pain)	No angina	Chest pain on the first hospital day	Single episode of chest pain on or after the second hospital day	Multiple episodes of chest pain on or after the second hospital day
Radiology	Chest X-Ray	Cardiac enlargement/Cardiomegaly	Moderate pulmonary vascular congestion	Cardiothoracic ratio ≥ 60%	
		Cardiothoracic ratio < 50%	Venous distention with alveolar edema	Pulmonary edema	
		Normal cardiothoracic ratio	Enlarged pulmonary arteries	Cardiothoracic ratio 55–59%	
		Cardiothoracic ratio 50–54%	Interstitial edema		

Continued

Exhibit 2.1   Continued

Category	Complexity Indicator	Level			
		1	2	3	4
Respiratory	Cyanosis	No cyanosis		Cyanosis present	
	Dyspnea	No dyspnea	Dyspnea on exertion Breathing difficulties NOS	Dyspnea at rest	Apnea
	Rales	No rales	Rales ≤ 50% / < 3 lobes	Rales > 50% / ≥ 3 lobes	
Senses	Conjunctival Involvement	Mucopurulent conjunctival drainage	Conjunctival slough		
		Conjunctival erythema	Bleeding lesions of conjunctiva/conjunctival hemorrhage		
		Conjunctivitis			
		Conjunctival drainage NOS	Conjunctival edema		
		Conjunctival abnormality NOS			
		Normal conjunctiva			

Skin	Diaphoresis	Profuse sweating spells with or without flushing Diaphoretic Night sweats No diaphoresis or night sweats			
Vitals	Lowest Cardiac Output	≥ 4.6 L/min	3.0–4.5 L/min	1.8–2.9 L/min	≤ 1.7 L/min
	Lowest Cardiac Index	≥ 2.1 L/min/m²	1.4–2.0 L/min/m²	0.9–1.3 L/min/m²	≤ 0.8 L/min/m²
	Highest AVO$_2$ Difference	≤ 6.0 ml/dl	6.1–9.0 ml/dl	9.1–10.0 ml/dl	≥ 10.1 ml/dl
	Lowest Pulse Rate	≥ 51 beats/min	41–50 beats/min	31–40 beats/min	≤ 30 beats/min
	Lowest Systolic Blood Pressure	≥ 90 mm Hg	80–89 mm Hg	61–79 mm Hg	≤ 60 mm Hg
	Highest Temperature	≤ 100.4 Oral °F	≥ 100.5 Oral °F		
	Rigors/Chills	Chills No rigors or chills	Rigors Rigors and chills		
	Lowest Urinary Output/24 Hours	≥ 500 cc/24 h		100–499 cc/24 h	≤ 99 cc/24 h
	Highest Pulse Rate	≤ 99 beats/min	100–129 beats/min	≥ 130 beats/min	

Continued

Exhibit 2.1   Continued

C. Malignant Neoplasm of Large Intestine (Proximal)

ICD-9-CM Diagnosis codes: 153–153.1, 153.4–153.7, 211.3

Category	Complexity Indicator	Level			
		1	2	3	4
Cardiovascular	EKG Rhythm	No EKG ectopy	≥ 6 PVCs per minute; SVT Bigeminy Trigeminy Quadrigeminy Atrial fibrillation PACs or PVCs NOS EKG ectopy NOS Nonsustained ventricular tachycardia Junctional ectopic tachycardia		Runs of ventricular tachycardia
Digestive	Nausea/Vomiting	Nausea No nausea or vomiting	Vomiting	Persistent vomiting	
	Stools Per Day During Hospitalization	Diarrhea NOS (≤ 4 stools per day) No diarrhea	Frequent diarrhea (5–10 stools per day)	Continuous diarrhea (> 10 stools per day)	
	Ascites	No ascites	Ascites NOS	Ascites causing dyspnea	

Category					
	Lower Gastrointestinal Bleeding	No rectal hemorrhage, black tarry stools or guaiac positive stools	Guaiac positive stools		Rectal hemorrhage
	Bowel Habits	History of constipation with onset ≤ 4 weeks; Tenesmus; No obstipation/constipation/tenesmus	Constipation	Obstipation	
	Abdominal Mass	Palpable right lower quadrant mass; Palpable right upper quadrant mass; Nodular abdominal mass; No abdominal and/or flank mass; Abdominal mass NOS			
Lab—Chemistry	Lowest Albumin	≥ 3.2 g/dl	2.9–3.1 g/dl	2.5–2.8 g/dl	≤ 2.4 g/dl
Lab—Hematology	Lowest Male Hematocrit (HCT)	≥ 30.0%	20.1–29.9%	15.1–20.0%	≤ 15.0%

Continued

Exhibit 2.1 Continued

Category	Complexity Indicator	Level			
		1	2	3	4
	Lowest Male Hemoglobin (HGB)	≥ 10.0 g/dl	6.6–9.9 g/dl	5.1–6.5 g/dl	≤ 5.0 g/dl
	Lowest Female Hematocrit (HCT)	≥ 30.0%	20.1–29.9%	15.1–20.0%	≤ 15.0%
	Lowest Female Hemoglobin (HGB)	≥ 10.0 g/dl	6.6–9.9 g/dl	5.1–6.5 g/dl	≤ 5.0 g/dl
Vitals	Lowest Pulse Rate	≥ 51 beats/min	41–50 beats/min	31–40 beats/min	≤ 30 beats/min
	Lowest Systolic Blood Pressure	≥ 90 mm Hg	80–89 mm Hg	61–79 mm Hg	≤ 60 mm Hg
	Highest % Weight Loss	≤ 5.9%	6.0–15.9%	16.0–20.9%	≥ 21.0%
	Cachexia	No cachexia	Cachexia		
	Highest Pulse Rate	≤ 99 beats/min	100–129 beats/min	≥ 130 beats/min	

D. Injury of Lower Extremities

ICD-9-CM Diagnosis codes: 808–808.9, 820–828.1, 835–838.19, 890–897.7, 904–904.8, 928–928.9, 956–956.9.

	1	2	3
ADLs	Activities of Daily Living	Independent	Requires assistance	Complete dependence

Cardiovascular	Pulse Characteristics	Bounding peripheral pulses No absent or thready pulses	All peripheral pulses thready Pulses thready in single/several limbs	All peripheral pulses absent Pulses absent in single/several limbs	
	EKG Rhythm	No EKG ectopy	$\geq$ 6 PVCs per minute; SVT Bigeminy Trigeminy Quadrigeminy Atrial fibrillation PCAs or PVCs NOS EKG ectopy NOS Nonsustained ventricular tachycardia Junctional ectopic tachycardia		Runs of ventricular tachycardia
Lab— Hematology	Lowest Male Hematocrit (HCT)	$\geq$ 41.5%	30.0–41.4%	20.1–29.9%	$\leq$ 20.0%
	Lowest Male Hemoglobin (HGB)	$\geq$ 13.8 g/dl	10.0–13.7 g/dl	6.6–9.9 g/dl	$\leq$ 6.5 g/dl

Continued

Exhibit 2.1 Continued

Category	Complexity Indicator	Level 1	2	3	4
	Largest Number of Units Transfused Per 24 Hours	< 6 units transfused per 24 hours / No units transfused		≥ 6 units transfused per 24 hours	
	Lowest Female Hematocrit (HCT)	≥ 36.5%	30.0–36.4%	20.1–29.9%	≤ 20.0%
	Lowest Female Hemoglobin (HGB)	≥ 12.0 g/dl	10.0–11.9 g/dl	6.6–9.9 g/dl	≤ 6.5 g/dl
	Largest Number of Units Transfused Per 24 Hours	< 6 units transfused per 24 hours / No units transfused		≥ 6 units transfused per 24 hours	
Musculo-Skeletal	Number of Fractures	Single fracture of one bone / No fractures	> 1 fracture of single bone	Bilateral bone fracture (excludes hands) and/or multiple fractures (> 1 bone)	
	Displaced Fracture of Pelvis	No displaced fracture of pelvis		Displaced fracture of pelvis	
	Foot Fractures	Single fracture of bone in one or both feet	Multiple fractures of bone in one foot	Multiple fractures of bone in both feet	

Neurology	Motor Strength[a]	No foot fractures
		Complete or marked paralysis
		Incomplete or mild to moderate paresis
		No alteration in motor strength
	Lesion Level[a]	High quadriplegia
		Low quadriplegia
		High paraplegia
		Low paraplegia
		Hemiplegia
		Monoplegia upper extremity
		Monoplegia lower extremity
		No spinal cord lesion
	Time (Weeks) Postinjury[a]	$\leq$ 2 weeks
		$>$ 2 weeks
	Time (Days) Postinjury[a]	$\leq$ 3 days
		$>$ 3 days
	Sensation Alterations	Sensation alteration NOS
		No alteration in sensation
		Complete loss of sensation
		Numbness and/or tingling (paresthesia, dysesthesia)

Continued

Exhibit 2.1 Continued

Category	Complexity Indicator	Level			
		1	2	3	4
Skin	Appearance of Extremity	Cyanosis of extremity Rubor of extremity Pallor of extremity Blanching of extremity Extremity appearance abnormality NOS No extremity appearance abnormality		Grayish white and/or black (necrotic) tissue of extremity Cool and/or patchy blue (mottled) extremity	
	Traumatic Wound Characteristics	No traumatic open wound	Traumatic open wound without obvious contamination	Obvious traumatic wound contamination	
	Protrusion of Bone at Fracture Site	No protrusion of bone at fracture site	Protrusion of bone at fracture site	Bone loss evident on x-ray or exam	
Vitals	Lowest Pulse Rate	$\geq$ 51 beats/min	41–50 beats/min	31–40 beats/min	$\leq$ 30 beats/min
	Lowest Systolic Blood Pressure	$\geq$ 90 mm Hg	80–89 mm Hg	61–79 mm Hg	$\leq$ 60 mm Hg

Lowest Urinary Output/24 Hours	≥ 500 cc/24 h		100–499 cc/24 h	≤ 99 cc/24 h
Highest Pulse Rate	≤ 99 beats/min	100–129 beats/min	≥ 130 beats/min	

a Motor strength, lesion level, and time postinjury are used in a complex algorithm to produce four severity levels. Description is available from Susan D. Horn.

Exhibit 2.2 Disease Staging

A. DISEASE: Bacterial Pneumonia
ETIOLOGY: Infection
DXCAT: RS02

STAGE	DESCRIPTION	DIAGNOSTIC FINDINGS	CODED CRITERIA
1.1	Pneumonia in one lobe ◆	Pneumonia: New infiltrate per chest x-ray report AND infected sputum per Gram stain (presence of many WBCs AND a single predominant organism) OR sputum culture reports growth of pathologic organism OR Legionella titer increase 4 fold ≥ 1:128 per microbiology/serology report OR Legionella direct fluorescent antibody stain of exudate per microbiology/serology report OR history of exposure to birds AND Chlamydia psittaci titer increase 4 fold per microbiology/serology report	482.00–482.90, 481.00, 485.00, 486.00, 483.80;
1.2	Pneumonia with small areas in multiple lobes or bronchopneumonia	Stage 1.1 AND small multilobular infiltrate per chest x-ray report OR bronchopneumonia per chest x-ray report	

1.3	Pneumonia with atelectasis	Stage 1.1–1.2 AND atelectasis per chest x-ray report	S1.1 + 518.00;
2.1	Pneumonia with bacteremia	Stage 1.1–1.3 AND Bacteremia: blood culture reports growth of pathologic bacterial organism(s)	S1.1 + 790.70;
2.2	Pneumonia with empyema	Stage 1.1–2.1 AND empyema per thoracentesis report or effusion culture reports growth of pathologic organism(s)	S1.1 + 510.90;
2.3	Pneumonia with lung abscess or bronchopleural fistula or bronchopleural cutaneous fistula	Stage 1.1–2.2 AND lung abscess per operative/pathology report OR air/fluid level per chest x-ray report OR air/fluid levels in pleural space per chest x-ray report OR cutaneous fistula per chest x-ray report and physical exam	S1.1 + 510.00, 513.00;
2.4	Pneumonia with diffuse involvement of multiple lobes	Stage 1.1–2.3 AND lobular pneumonia in at least 2 lobes per chest x-ray report	

Continued

Exhibit 2.2   Continued

STAGE	DESCRIPTION	DIAGNOSTIC FINDINGS	CODED CRITERIA

3.1	Pneumonia and septicemia	Stage 1.1–2.4
		AND Sepsis
		OR Septicemia
		OR Bacteremia per blood culture reports of pathologic organism growth
		AND temperature $\geq$ 102°F orally or 102.5°F rectally
		AND myalgia
		AND heart rate $\geq$ 110 beats/min
		AND respiratory rate $\geq$ 26/min
		AND band neutrophils $\geq$ 900/mm^3
		AND Hypoxemia:
		    Alveolar-arterial gradient > 15
		    $(693 \times F_1O_2) - (1.2 \times pCO_2) - pO_2 > 15$ calculated from arterial blood gas report values
		    OR $pO_2 < 60$ mm Hg on room air
		    OR Anion gap acidosis: Serum Na$^+$ $-$ (Serum Cl$^-$ + Serum CO$_2$) > 14
		    OR initial pulmonary wedge pressure < 15 mm Hg per pulmonary artery catheter report
		    OR cardiac output reduced $\geq$ 10% from baseline as reported in echocardiogram or nuclear ejection fraction report
		
		Presumptive Diagnostic Findings:
		Stage 1.1–2.4
		AND Bacteremia per blood culture reports of pathologic organism growth
			S1.1 + 038.00–038.90;

AND temperature ≥ 102°F orally or 102.5°F rectally
AND myalgia
AND heart rate ≥ 110 beats/min
AND respiratory rate ≥ 26/min

3.2	Pneumonia with septic arthritis	Stage 1.1–3.1 AND septic arthritis per joint effusion culture reports growth of pathologic organism(s) same as in sputum culture or blood culture	S1.1 + 711.00–711.09;
3.3	Pneumonia and acute osteomyelitis	Stage 1.1–3.2 AND osteomyelitis: growth of pathologic organism(s) per bone culture report OR bone scan, MRI, or x-ray report of involved area consistent with osteomyelitis	S1.1 + 730.00–730.09, 730.20–730.29;
3.4	Pneumonia with peritonitis or subphrenic abscess	Stage 1.1–3.3 AND peritonitis per operative/pathology report or peritoneal fluid culture reports growth of same organism as pneumonia OR subphrenic abscess per operative/pathology report	S1.1 + 567.00–567.90;
3.5	Pneumonia with pericarditis or pericardial effusion	Stage 1.1–3.4 AND Pericarditis per diffuse ST-T findings on EKG report OR diffuse ST-T elevations with ST/T > .25 on EKG AND pericardial friction rub	S1.1 + 420.90, 420.99;

Continued

Exhibit 2.2 Continued

STAGE	DESCRIPTION	DIAGNOSTIC FINDINGS	CODED CRITERIA
		OR purulent pericardial effusion per operative/pathology report or pericardial effusion culture reports growth of same organism as pneumonia or echocardiogram report	
3.6	Pneumonia with endocarditis or meningitis	Stage 1.1–3.5 AND Endocarditis: Fever: temperature ≥ 101°F orally or 101.5°F rectally AND new heart vegetation per echocardiogram OR change in heart murmur OR new heart murmur AND bacteremia: blood culture reports growth of pathologic bacterial organism(s) OR infective endocarditis per culture with growth of pathologic organism(s) from tissue of heart valves, or per operative or pathology report OR Meningitis per growth of pathologic organism(s) on CSF culture report AND CSF glucose < 50% of serum glucose AND CSF proteins > 50 mg/dl AND CSF neutrophils > 1/mm³ per CSF cell count report OR CSF lymphocytes > 8/mm³ per CSF cell count report	S1.1 + 421.00, 421.90, 320.00–320.30, 320.80–320.90;

3.7	Pneumonia with acute respiratory failure	Stage 1.1–3.6 AND Respiratory failure: Hypoxemia: Alveolar-arterial gradient > 15 $(693 \times F_IO_2) - (1.2 \times pCO_2) - pO_2 > 15$ calculated from arterial blood gas report values OR $pO_2 < 60$ mm Hg on room air AND Acidosis: pH < 7.35 per arterial blood gas report AND Hypercarbia: $pCO_2 > 46.5$ mm Hg per arterial blood gas report	S1.1 + 518.81;
3.8	Pneumonia and septic shock	Stage 1.1–3.7 AND Shock: Systolic blood pressure < 90 mm Hg AND urine output < 1000 cc/24 hrs OR urine output < 30 cc/hr	S1.1 + 785.50–785.59;
4.0	Pneumonia and death	Stage 2.1–3.8 AND death	

REFERENCES:

Bone RC. "Sepsis, the Sepsis Syndrome, Multi-Organ Failure: A Plea for Comparable Definitions." *Ann Intern Med*, Feb 1991; 114(4)332–333.

Bone RC. "A Critical Evaluation of New Agents for the Treatment of Sepsis." *JAMA*, Sep 1991; 226(12)1686–1691.

Berkow R, Fletcher AJ, eds. In: *Merck Manual*, 16th Ed. Rahway: Merck & Co., Inc., 1992:681–698.

Duma RJ. "Pneumococcal Pneumonia." In: Wyngaarden JB, Smith Jr LH, Bennett JC, eds. *Cecil Textbook of Medicine*, 19th Ed. Vol 2. Philadelphia: WB Saunders, 1992:1608–1615.

Harris RL, Musher DM, Bloom K, et al. "Manifestations of Sepsis." *Arch Intern Med* Nov 1987; 147(11)1895–1906.

Johanson Jr WG, Harris GD. "Common Gram-Negative Bacillary Pneumonias." In: Braude AI, ed. *Infectious Diseases and Medical Microbiology*, 2nd Ed. Philadelphia: WB Saunders, 1986:799–802.

Reynolds HY. "Pneumonia and Lung Abscess." In: Wilson JD, Braunwald E, Isselbacher KJ, Petersdorf RG, Martin JB, Fauci AS, Root RK, eds. *Harrison's Principles of Internal Medicine*, 12th Ed. New York: McGraw-Hill, 1991:1064–1069.

Stern RC. "Pneumonia." In: Behrman RE, Kliegman RM, Vaughan III VC, Nelson WE, eds. *Nelson Textbook of Pediatrics*, 14th Ed. Philadelphia: WB Saunders, 1992:1077.

Stern RC, Vaughan III VC, Nelson WE. "Bacterial Pneumonia." In: Behrman RE, Kliegman RM, Vaughan III VC, Nelson WE, eds. *Nelson Textbook of Pediatrics*, 14th Ed. Philadelphia: WB Saunders, 1992:1077–1088.

Continued

Exhibit 2.2   Continued

B. DISEASE: **Coronary Artery Disease**
ETIOLOGY: Degenerative, Genetic
DXCAT: CV07

STAGE	DESCRIPTION	DIAGNOSTIC FINDINGS	CODED CRITERIA

1.1	Stable angina pectoris, or old myocardial infarction, coronary atherosclerosis, or chronic ischemic heart disease	ST-T changes at time of pain with exertion per EKG report
		OR positive ischemia per stress test report
		OR old myocardial infarction per EKG report or by history
		OR stable angina pectoris
		OR Angina:
		    ST-T changes at time of pain with exertion per EKG report
		    OR positive ischemia per stress test report
		    OR history of the following with exertion or stress:
		        pressure chest pain
		        OR sharp chest pain
		        OR cutting chest pain
		        OR squeezing chest pain
		        OR chest pain radiating down left arm
		OR positive exercise stress test to $\geq$ 6 metabolic equivalents (METS)
			413.90, 412.00, 414.00, 414.00,
			414.80, 414.90;

2.1	Progressing angina pectoris	Stage 1.1 AND increasing frequency and severity of known angina OR positive exercise stress test to $\geq$ 4 metabolic equivalents (METS) AND positive exercise stress test to < 6 metabolic equivalents (METS)	

Continued

| 2.2 | Angina pectoris with other abnormal cardiac findings | Stage 1.1–2.1
AND hypertrophy per nuclear ejection fraction report or echocardiogram report
OR akinesia per nuclear ejection fraction report or echocardiogram report
OR hypokinesia per nuclear ejection fraction report or echocardiogram report
OR dyskinesia per nuclear ejection fraction report or echocardiogram report
OR murmurs
OR S4 gallop
OR S3 gallop
OR positive exercise stress text to ≥ 2 metabolic equivalents (METS)
AND positive exercise stress test to < 4 metabolic equivalents (METS) | S1.1 + 427.89, 427.90, 429.30, 785.20, 785.00, 429.82; |
| 2.3 | Angina pectoris with congestive heart failure | Stage 1.1–2.2
AND CHF:
initial central venous pressure > 15 cm H_2O per central venous pressure line report or pulmonary artery catheter report
OR initial peak systolic right ventricular pressures > 25 mm Hg
OR initial pulmonary wedge pressure > 18 mm Hg
OR low cardiac output measured by ejection fraction < 50% per echocardiogram or nuclear ejection fraction report, or cardiac output < 4 l/min per cardiac catheterization | S1.1 + 428.00, 428.10; |

Exhibit 2.2 Continued

STAGE	DESCRIPTION	DIAGNOSTIC FINDINGS	CODED CRITERIA

		Presumptive Diagnostic Findings:
		Stage 1.1–2.2
		AND jugular venous distention
		  OR pedal edema ≥ 3+
		  OR S3 gallop
		  OR hepatojugular reflex
		  OR bibasilar rales
		  OR congestive heart failure per chest x-ray report	

2.4	Unstable angina pectoris or Prinzmetal's variant angina ◆	Stage 1.1–2.3
		AND change in nature of onset of symptoms and severity of known anginal pain
		AND past history of angina
		  OR angina occurring at rest
		         AND ST-T elevations at time of pain per EKG report
		  OR Prinzmetal's variant angina (by history)
			411.10, 411.80, 411.81,
			411.89, 413.00, 413.10;

3.1	Acute myocardial infarction	Acute myocardial infarction per EKG report
		  OR CPK-MB > normal per CPK isoenzyme report (in absence of laboratory-specific normal values use CPK-MB > 4.5%)
		         AND LDH1/LDH2 ratio > 1.0 as calculated from LDH isoenzyme report
			410.00–410.92;

3.2	Acute myocardial infarction and heart block or pericarditis	Stage 3.1 AND new heart block per EKG report OR arrhythmias per EKG report	S3.1 + 426.00–426.60, 426.90, 427.00–427.90, 420.90–420.99, 411.00;

3.3	OR Pericarditis per diffuse ST-T findings on EKG report OR diffuse ST-T elevations with ST/T > .25 on EKG AND pericardial friction rub	
Acute myocardial infarction and congestive heart failure	Stage 3.1–3.2 AND CHF: initial central venous pressure > 15 cm H_2O per central venous pressure line report or pulmonary artery catheter report OR initial peak systolic right ventricular pressures > 25 mm Hg OR initial pulmonary wedge pressure > 18 mm Hg OR low cardiac output measured by ejection fraction < 50% per echocardiogram or nuclear ejection fraction report, or cardiac output < 4 l/min per cardiac catheterization *Presumptive Diagnostic Findings:* Stage 3.1–3.2 AND jugular venous distention OR pedal edema ≥ 3+ OR S3 gallop OR hepatojugular reflex OR bibasilar rales OR congestive heart failure per chest x-ray report	S3.1 + 428.00, 428.10;

Continued

Exhibit 2.2   Continued

STAGE	DESCRIPTION	DIAGNOSTIC FINDINGS	CODED CRITERIA
3.4	Acute myocardial infarction and ventricular thrombus formation	Stage 3.1–3.3 AND ventricular thrombus per echocardiogram report or operative/pathology report	S3.1 + 429.79;
3.5	Acute myocardial infarction and ventricular aneurysm	Stage 3.1–3.4 AND ventricular aneurysm per nuclear ejection fraction report or cardiac catheterization report or echocardiogram report	S3.1 + 414.10;
3.6	Acute myocardial infarction and pulmonary embolism or cerebrovascular accident	Stage 3.1–3.5 AND Pulmonary embolism per nuclear ventilation/perfusion scan or pulmonary angiogram report OR new ischemic cerebral infarction per CT scan report	S3.1 + 415.10, 434.00–434.90, 436.00;
3.7	Acute myocardial infarction and papillary muscle rupture or ventricular septal rupture	Stage 3.1–3.6 AND papillary muscle rupture or ventricular septal rupture per operative/pathology report	S3.1 + 429.60;
3.8	Acute myocardial infarction and ventricular fibrillation or shock	Stage 3.1–3.7 AND ventricular fibrillation per EKG report OR ventricular flutter per EKG report OR ventricular tachycardia per EKG report	S3.1 + 427.10, 427.41–427.42, 785.51;

			S3.1 + 427.50;
		OR Shock: Systolic blood pressure < 90 mm Hg AND urine output < 1000 cc/24 hrs OR urine output < 30 cc/hr	
3.9	Acute myocardial infarction and cardiac arrest	Stage 3.1–3.8 AND asystole per EKG report	
4.0	Acute myocardial infarct and death	Stage 3.1–3.9 AND death	

REFERENCES:

Cheitlin MD. "Finding the High-Risk Patient with Coronary Artery Disease." *JAMA* 1988, 259(15)2271–2277.

Cohen LH. "Surgical Treatment of Coronary Artery Disease." In: Wyngaarden JB, Smith Jr LH, Bennett JC, eds. *Cecil Textbook of Medicine*, 19th Ed. Vol 1. Philadelphia: WB Saunders, 1992:318–321.

Cohn PF. "Detection and Prognosis of the Asymptomatic Patient with Silent Myocardial Ischemia." *American Journal of Cardiology* Jan 29, 1988, 61(3)4B–6B.

Froelicher VF, Duarte GM, Oakes DF, Klein J, Dubach PA, Janosi A. "The Prognostic Value of the Exercise Test." *Disease-A-Month* 1988, 34(11)677–735.

Goto Jr AM, Farmer JA. "Risk Factors for Coronary Artery Disease." In: Sabiston Jr DC, ed. *Textbook of Surgery*, 13th Ed. Philadelphia: WB Saunders 1986:1153–1190.

Louis DZ. "Cardiovascular Diseases: Proposed Classification of Impairment." *Veterans Administration Schedule for Rating Disabilities Version.* Center for Research in Medical Education and Health Care, Jefferson Medical College, Philadelphia, October 1988.

Pierard LA, Dubois C, Smeets JP, Boland J, Carlier J, Kulbertus HE. "Prognostic Significance of Angina Pectoris Before First Acute Myocardial." *American Journal of Cardiology* May 1, 1988; 61(13)984–987.

Rogers WJ. "Angina Pectoris." In: Wyngaarden JB, Smith Jr LH, Bennett JC, eds. *Cecil Textbook of Medicine*, 19th Ed. Vol 1. Philadelphia: WB Saunders, 1992:298–304.

Sabiston Jr DC, Rankin JS. "The Coronary Circulation." In Sabiston Jr DC, ed. *Textbook of Surgery*, 14th Ed. Philadelphia: WB Saunders, 1991:1957–1972.

Selwyn AP, Braunwald E, "Ischemic Heart Disease." In: Wilson JD, Braunwald E, Isselbacher KJ, Petersdorf RG, Martin JB, Fauci AS, Root RK, eds. *Harrison's Principles of Internal Medicine*, 12th Ed. New York: McGraw-Hill 1991: 964–971.

Tierney LM. "Blood Vessels & Lymphatics." In: Schroeder SA, Tierney Jr LM, McPhee SJ, Papadakis MA, Krupp MA, eds. *Current Medical Diagnosis & Treatment.* Connecticut: Appleton & Lange, 1992:357–386.

Continued

Exhibit 2.2   Continued

C. DISEASE: Cancer of the Colon and Rectum
ETIOLOGY: Neoplasm
DXCAT: GI24

STAGE	DESCRIPTION	DIAGNOSTIC FINDINGS	CODED CRITERIA
0.0	History of colorectal carcinoma		V10.05, V10.06;
1.1	Colorectal carcinoma limited to the mucosa and submucosa ◆	Colorectal carcinoma limited to mucosa and submucosa OR Duke's classification for colorectal cancer Stage A per operative/pathology report	158.00–154.80, 230.30–230.60;
2.1	Colorectal carcinoma extending to the muscularis or serosa	Colorectal carcinoma limited to muscularis or serosa OR Duke's classification for colorectal cancer Stage B per operative/pathology report	
3.1	Colorectal carcinoma with localized peritonitis or intra-abdominal abscess	Stage 1.1–2.1 AND localized peritonitis per operative/pathology report OR intra-abdominal abscess per operative/pathology report or sonogram report or CT scan report	S1.1 + 569.50, 566.00, 567.20–567.90;
3.2	Colorectal carcinoma with acute bleeding	Stage 1.1–3.1 AND Bleeding: hemoglobin decreases (from patient's baseline) > 1 g/dl in 24 hours, as calculated from CBC reports taken 24 hours apart	S1.1 + 569.30, 578.10, 578.90;
3.3	Colorectal carcinoma with intestinal obstruction	Stage 1.1–3.2 AND intestinal obstruction per KUB x-ray reports small or large bowel obstruction	S1.1 + 560.89, 560.90;

Continued

3.4	Colorectal carcinoma with intussusception or volvulus	Stage 1.1–3.3 AND intussusception or volvulus per operative/pathology report	S1.1 + 560.00, 560.20;
3.5	Colorectal carcinoma extending to the regional lymph nodes	Colorectal carcinoma limited to lymph nodes draining the colon and rectum OR Duke's classification for colorectal cancer Stage C per operative/pathology report	S0.0–S1.1 + 196.20;
3.6	Colorectal carcinoma with fistula formation	Stage 1.1–3.5 AND enteroenteric fistula per barium enema report or UGI series report OR enterovesical fistula per barium enema report or urinalysis reports fecaluria OR enterovaginal fistula per barium enema report or feces and flatus per vagina OR enterocutaneous fistula per barium enema report or feces and flatus per sinus tract	S1.1 + 569.81, 596.10, 619.10, 593.82, 599.10, 565.10;
3.7	Colorectal carcinoma with gross perforation and peritonitis	Stage 1.1–3.6 AND free air within peritoneal cavity per KUB x-ray report or chest x-ray report OR perforation of bowel per barium enema or chest x-ray report OR peritonitis per operative/pathology report or peritoneal fluid culture reports growth of pathologic organism(s)	S3.1 + 569.83;

Exhibit 2.2   Continued

STAGE	DESCRIPTION	DIAGNOSTIC FINDINGS	CODED CRITERIA
3.8	Colorectal carcinoma with metastasis to extracolonic sites	Stage 1.1–3.7 AND mass lesion(s) in liver per CT scan report or MRI report or liver/spleen scan report OR same carcinoma type present in liver per operative/pathology report OR mass lesion(s) in bones per CT scan or bone scan report OR same carcinoma type present in bones per operative/pathology report OR mass lesion(s) in lungs per CT scan or MRI report or chest x-ray report OR same carcinoma type present in lungs per operative/pathology report OR mass lesion(s) in sites other than the colon or rectum per operative/pathology report or CT scan report	S0.0–S1.1 + 196.00– 196.10, 196.30–199.10;
3.9	Colorectal carcinoma and shock	Stage 1.1–3.8 AND Shock: Systolic blood pressure < 90 mm Hg AND urine output < 1000 cc/24 hrs OR urine output < 30 cc/hr	S1.1–S3.8 + 785.50, 785.59;
4.0	Colorectal carcinoma and death	Stage 1.1–3.9 AND death	

REFERENCES: Sarma DP. "Duke's Classification of Rectal Cancer." *Southern Medical Journal* March 1988, 81(3)407–408.

D. DISEASE: **Fracture of the Head or Neck of the Femur**
ETIOLOGY: Trauma
DXCAT: MS09

STAGE	DESCRIPTION	DIAGNOSTIC FINDINGS	CODED CRITERIA
1.1	Stable fracture of the head or neck of the femur ◆	Stress fracture of the head or neck of the femur per x-ray report OR impact fracture of the head or neck of the femur per x-ray report OR linear fracture of the head or neck of the femur per x-ray report OR intertrochanteric fracture of the femur per x-ray report OR transcervical fracture of the femur per x-ray report	820.00–820.09, 820.20–820.21, 820.80;
2.1	Unstable fractures of the head or neck of the femur	Displaced fracture of the head or neck of the femur per x-ray report OR comminuted fracture of the head or neck of the femur per x-ray report	
2.2	Open fracture of the head or neck of the femur	Stage 1.1–2.1 AND exposure of the fracture bone through a skin laceration	820.10–820.19, 820.30–820.31, 820.90;
2.3	Fracture of the head or neck of the femur with avascular necrosis	Stage 1.1–2.2 AND avascular necrosis of the head or neck of the femur per operative/pathology report or x-ray report	S1.1–S2.2 + 733.42;

Continued

Exhibit 2.2   Continued

STAGE	DESCRIPTION	DIAGNOSTIC FINDINGS	CODED CRITERIA
2.4	Fracture of femoral head/neck with deep vein thrombosis	Stage 1.1–2.3 AND DVT: deep vein thrombosis per Doppler ultrasound, nuclear venogram, contrast venography or other venogram report	S1.1–S2.2 + 453.80;
3.1	Fracture of femoral head/neck with pulmonary embolism	Stage 2.1–2.4 AND Pulmonary embolism per nuclear ventilation/perfusion scan or pulmonary angiogram report	S1.1–S2.2 + 415.10, 958.10;
3.2	Fracture of femoral head/neck with respiratory failure	Stage 3.1 AND Respiratory failure: Hypoxemia: Alveolar-arterial gradient > 15 $(693 \times F_iO_2) - (1.2 \times pCO_2) - pO_2 > 15$ calculated from arterial blood gas report values OR $pO_2 < 60$ mm Hg on room air AND Acidosis: pH < 7.35 per arterial blood gas report AND Hypercarbia: $pCO_2 > 46.5$ mm Hg per arterial blood gas report	S1.1–S2.2 + 518.50;
3.3	Fracture of femoral head/neck and shock	Stage 3.1–3.2 AND Shock: Systolic blood pressure < 90 mm Hg AND urine output < 1000 cc/24 hrs OR urine output < 30 cc/hr	S1.1–S2.2 + 958.40, 785.50–785.59;

4.0	Fracture of femoral head/neck and death	Stage 3.1–3.3 AND death

REFERENCES:

Arnoldi CC, Linderholm H. "Fracture of the Femoral Neck—Vascular Disturbances in Different Types of Fractures by Measurements of Intra-Osseous Pressures." *Clinical Orthopedics* May 1972;(84)116–127.

Bernstein SM, Meyers MH. "Fractures of the Femoral Shaft and Associated Ipsilateral Fractures of the Hip and/or Patella." *Journal of Bone and Joint Surgery* 1975;(57A)1029.

Connolly JF. *DePalma's, The Management of Fractures and Dislocations.* 3rd Ed. Philadelphia: WB Saunders, 1981:1407–1455.

Day LV. "The Incidence of Thromboembolic Complications in Hip Fractures: Is Prophylaxis Warranted?" *Journal of Bone and Joint Surgery* 1976;(58A)737.

Day LJ, Bovill Jr EG, Trafton PG, Cohen HA, Johnston JO. "Orthopedics." In: Way LW, ed. *Current Surgical Diagnosis and Treatment,* 9th Ed. Connecticut: Appleton & Lange, 1991:1018–1028.

Rockwood CA, Green DP. "Fractures." Philadelphia: JB Lippincott, 1975:1012–1028.

Rogers PH, Marder VJ. "Thromboembolic Complications of Hip Fractures. *The Orthopaedic Clinics of North America.* 1974;509–521.

Schultz RJ. *The Language of Fractures.* Huntington: Robert E. Krieger Publishing, 1976:30–32.

CLINICAL CRITERIA FOR DISEASE STAGING

Exhibit 2.3   MediQual Systems' Atlas (MedisGroups)

A. Bacterial Lung Infection
A.1. Admission Period Mortality Equations

Independent Variable	Definition or Comments About Key Clinical Finding (KCF)	Coefficient
Age in Years	For patients < 12 months, use 0; for patients 12–23 months, use 1.	0.0276
BUN mg/dL	Use actual value if BUN > 30 mg/dL for either preadmission or admission KCF or imputed normal value of 12.	0.0102
Cancer Group	Group variable—presence of any of: calcium > 11.0 mg/dL, history of cancer, malignant tumor.	0.4968
Coma or Stupor	Coma or stupor as either preadmission or admission KCF.	0.9743
Constant/ Intercept	—	34.983
Diabetes Group	Group variable—presence of any of: current medication insulin, diabetes, glucose < 60 or > 249 mg/dL.	0.3876
Disoriented	Disorientation as either preadmission or admission KCF.	0.4171
Effusion	Effusion of any site as either preadmission or admission KCF.	0.3923
Haemophilus	Any culture positive for Haemophilus as either preadmission or admission KCF.	−1.007
Inflammation Group	Group variable—presence of any of: active herpes, bands > 20%, CSF WBC > 0 c/mm^3, degeneration, history of autoimmune disease, infection, inflammation, oral temperature < 95.5 or > 100.9 °F, WBC < 5 or > 17.0.	0.2983
Malnutrition Group	Group variable—presence of any of: albumin < 3.0 g/dL, severe malnutrition.	0.444
Mechanical Ventilator Days	Requires treatment code for mechanical ventilation. Actual number of days on the ventilator used for scoring. For patients on a ventilator < 1 day, use .5. Patients not on ventilator, impute normal of 0.	0.0514
Na Low	Use actual value if sodium (Na) < 130 for either preadmission or admission KCF or imputed value of 141.	−0.0255
Arterial O$_2$ Saturation %	Use actual value if arterial O$_2$ saturation < 86% for either preadmission or admission KCF or imputed normal of 90.	−0.0232
Oral Temperature °F High	Use actual value if oral temperature > 100.9° F for either preadmission or admission KCF or imputed normal of 98.6°. Records with another unit of measure are converted to °F.	−0.0927

Platelets 10⁹/L	Use actual value if platelets < 100 10^9/L for either preadmission or admission KCF or imputed normal of 250.	−0.0044
Renal Group	Group variable—presence of any of: BUN > 30 mg/dL, chronic renal disease, creatinine > 1.7 mg/dL, urine protein mg/24 hr.	0.3499
Respirations High	Use actual value if respirations > 24 for either preadmission or admission KCF for ages ≥ one month or imputed normal of 18. Value if > 70 for ages 0–30 days or imputed normal of 35.	0.0316
Severe Malnutrition	Severe malnutrition as either preadmission or admission KCF.	0.5027
Streptococcus except β	Any culture positive for Streptococcus except β as either preadmission or admission KCF.	−0.3938
Systolic BP Low	Use actual value if systolic blood pressure < 90 for either preadmission or admission KCF for ages > 17 or < 60 for ages < 18 or imputed normal of 110.	−0.015
pH Arterial Low	Use actual value if arterial pH < 7.35 for either preadmission or admission KCF or imputed normal of 7.38.	−3.2298

A.2. Admission Period Length of Stay Equations

Admission Period Surgery	Surgical procedure in admission period.	1.839301
Age in Years	For patients < 12 months, use 0; for patients 12–23 months, use 1.	0.039654
BUN mg/dL	Use actual value if BUN > 30 mg/dL for either preadmission or admission KCF or imputed normal value of 12.	0.021947
Bands %	Use actual value if bands % > 20 for either preadmission or admission KCF or imputed normal of 0.	0.012884
Blood or Lymph Culture	Positive blood or lymph culture as either preadmission or admission KCF.	0.869017
COPD Group	Group variable—presence of any of: chronic lung disease, FEV1 < 66% predicted.	3.166579
Cancer Group	Group variable—presence of any of: calcium > 11.0 mg/dL, history of cancer, malignant tumor.	0.565674
Central Region Group	Hospital location.	−0.569472
Chronic Lung Disease	Chronic lung disease history KCF.	−2.962102
Chronic Neurological Combination	Group variable—presence of any of: chronic findings of aphasia, apraxia, ataxia, cranial nerve deficit, flaccidity, muscle weakness, paresis, sensory deficit, speech deficit, or tremors; previous head trauma; or previous stroke.	0.306632

Continued

Exhibit 2.3 Continued

Independent Variable	Definition or Comments About Key Clinical Finding (KCF)	Coefficient
Coma Group	Group variable—presence of any of: coma or stupor, coma score < 8	1.077223
Congenital Combination	Group variable—presence of any of: aortic arch abnormality, cerebral palsy, congenital anomaly, congenital heart disease, cystic fibrosis, hypoplastic heart, major cardiac anomaly, mental retardation, open defect, transposition, trisomy.	3.220543
Constant/Intercept	—	13.859507
Current Medication Anticoagulation	Currently on anticoagulation medication.	0.690298
Damage Group	Group variable—presence of any of: AST > 80 U/L, CPK > 150 U/L, damage, tear.	0.690864
Effusion	Effusion of any site as either preadmission or admission KCF.	0.511428
Gender	F=0; M=1	−0.301691
Haemophilus	Any culture positive for Haemophilus as either preadmission or admission KCF.	−0.866488
Hematocrit % Low	Use actual value if hematocrit < 30% for either preadmission or admission KCF for ages ≥ 1 month or imputed normal of 45.5. For ages 0–30 days, use actual value if hematocrit < 40% or imputed normal of 53.	−0.051169
Immunocompromised Group	Group variable—presence of any of: current immunosuppressive medication, HIV positive, immunocompromised, transplant rejection.	0.697046
K mEq/L High	Use actual value if potassium (K) > 5.3 for either preadmission or admission KCF or imputed normal of 4.2.	−0.423959
Malnutrition Group	Group variable—presence of any of: albumin < 3.0 g/dL, severe malnutrition.	1.239122
Mechanical Ventilator Any Days	Treatment code for mechanical ventilation.	3.298172
Na Low	Use actual value if sodium (Na) < 130 for either preadmission or admission KCF or imputed value of 141.	−0.030172
Pseudomonas	Any culture positive for pseudomonas on either preadmission or admission KCF.	0.961088
Pulse High	Use actual value if pulse > 129 for either preadmission or admission KCF or imputed normal of 80 (age > 12 years) or 100 (age < 13 years).	0.010147
Respirations High	Use actual value if respirations > 24 for either preadmission or admission KCF for ages ≥ one month or imputed normal of 18. Value if > 70 for ages 0–30 days or imputed normal of 35.	0.018567

		β
Streptococcus except β	Any culture positive for Streptococcus except β as either preadmission or admission KCF.	-1.023008
Urinary Culture	Positive urinary culture for either preadmission or admission KCF.	0.841017
West Region Group	Hospital location.	-0.83781
pO_2 Arterial	Use actual value if arterial $pO_2 < 75$ for either preadmission or admission KCF or imputed normal of 75.	-0.032519

B. Acute Myocardial Infarction
B.1. Admission Period Mortality Equations

Acute Neurological Combination	Group variable—presence of any of: acute findings of aphasia, apraxia, ataxia, cranial nerve deficit, flaccidity, muscle weakness, paresis, sensory deficit, speech deficit, tremors, gait abnormality, proprioception deficit.	0.5756
Age in Years	For patients < 12 months, use 0; for patients 12–23 months, use 1.	0.0659
Albumin g/dL	Use actual value if albumin < 3.0 g/dL for either preadmission or admission KCF or imputed normal of 4.4.	-0.2491
BUN mg/dL	Use actual value if BUN > 30 mg/dL for either preadmission or admission KCF or imputed normal value of 12.	0.0074
CAD Group	Group variable—presence of any of: circumflex > 49%, ischemia, left anterior descending > 49%, left main > 49%, right coronary artery > 49%, stress test positive.	-0.1706
CHF Group	Group variable—presence of any of: congestive heart failure, edema, effusion respiratory, ejection fraction < 41%, history of CHF, S3 gallop, wedge pressure > 14.	0.4558
CPK U/L	Use actual value if CPK > 150 U/L for either preadmission or admission KCF or imputed normal of 102 (age > 12 years) or > 110 (age < 13 years).	0.0001543
Coagulation Defect Group	Group variable—presence of any of: platelets < 100 10^9/L, PT > 15.5 seconds, PTT > 35.9.	-0.3797
Coma Group	Group variable—presence of any of: coma or stupor, coma score < 8	1.1265
Constant/Intercept	—	22.7669
Damage Group	Group variable—presence of any of: AST > 80 U/L, CPK > 150 U/L, damage, tear.	-0.5749
Diastolic BP	Use actual value if diastolic blood pressure > 119 for either preadmission or admission KCF or imputed normal of 80 (age > 12 years) or 59 (age < 13 years).	-0.0136

Continued

Exhibit 2.3   Continued

Independent Variable	Definition or Comments About Key Clinical Finding (KCF)	Coefficient
Fluid Imbalance Combination	Group variable—presence of any of: K < 2.5 or > 5.3, or Na < 130 or > 150.	0.3645
Glucose mg/dL High	Use actual value if glucose > 249 mg/dL for either preadmission or admission KCF or imputed normal of 80 (ages ≥1 month) or 45 (age 0–30 days).	0.0008749
Left Main	Left main occlusion > 49% for either preadmission or admission KCF.	0.0102
MI	Myocardial infarction as either preadmission or admission KCF.	0.3038
Previous CABG	Previous CABG history KCF.	0.3811
Renal Group	Group variable—presence of any of: BUN > 30 mg/dL, chronic renal disease, creatinine > 1.7 mg/dL, urine protein mg/24 hr.	0.4312
Respiratory High	Use actual value if respirations > 24 for either preadmission or admission KCF for ages ≥ 1 month or imputed normal of 18. For ages 0–30 days, use actual value if > 70 or imputed normal of 35.	0.0282
Resuscitation	Treatment code for resuscitation.	2.3232
Seizure Group	Group variable—presence of any of: previous seizures, seizures.	0.4304
Systolic BP Low	Use actual value if systolic blood pressure < 90 for either preadmission or admission KCF for ages > 17 or < 60 for ages < 18 or imputed normal of 110.	−0.024
WBC High	Use actual value if WBC > 17.0 for either preadmission or admission KCF or imputed normal of 7.5 (age ≥ 1 month) or 21 (ages 0–30 days).	0.0138
pCO$_2$ Arterial	Use actual value if arterial pCO$_2$ > 45 for either preadmission or admission KCF or imputed normal of 40.	−0.0271
pH Arterial Low	Use actual value if arterial pH < 7.35 for either preadmission or admission KCF or imputed normal of 7.38.	−3.2577
pO$_2$ Arterial	Use actual value if arterial pO$_2$ < 75 for either preadmission or admission KCF or imputed normal of 75.	−0.0222

B.2. Admission Period Length of Stay Equations

AST U/L	Use actual value if AST > 80 U/L for either preadmission or admission KCF or imputed normal of 12.	0.001216

Variable	Description	Coefficient
Acute Neurological Combination	Group variable—presence of any of: acute findings of aphasia, apraxia, ataxia, cranial nerve deficit, flaccidity, muscle weakness, paresis, sensory deficit, speech deficit, tremors, gait abnormality, proprioception deficit.	0.660051
Admission Period Surgery	Surgical procedure in admission period.	−0.579638
Age in Years	For patients < 12 months, use 0; for patients 12–23 months, use 1.	0.038516
BUN mg/dL	Use actual value if BUN > 30 mg/dL for either preadmission or admission KCF or imputed normal value of 12.	0.007725
CAD Group	Group variable—presence of any of: circumflex > 49%, ischemia, left anterior descending > 49%, left main > 49%, right coronary artery > 49%, stress test positive.	−1.008663
CHF	CHF as either preadmission or admission KCF.	−0.3935
CHF Group	Group variable—presence of any of: congestive heart failure, edema, effusion respiratory, ejection fraction < 41%, history of CHF, S3 gallop, wedge pressure > 14.	0.539324
COPD Group	Group variable—presence of any of: chronic lung disease, FEV1 < 66% predicted.	0.27014
CPK MB %	Use actual value if CPK MB > 3% for either preadmission or admission KCF or imputed normal of 0.	0.017568
CPK U/L	Use actual value if CPK > 150 U/L for either preadmission or admission KCF or imputed normal of 102 (age > 12 years) or > 110 (age < 13 years).	0.00037897
Central Region Group	Hospital location.	−0.478404
Coma Score 3–15	Use actual value if coma score > 2 for either preadmission or admission KCF or imputed normal of 15.	−0.121311
Constant/Intercept	—	−34.286467
Culture Combination	Group variable—presence of any of: positive blood or lymph culture, gastrointestinal culture, reproductive culture, respiratory culture, skin culture, spinal cord culture, urinary culture.	0.349669
Diabetes	Diabetes history KCF.	0.352596
Effusion	Effusion of any site as either preadmission or admission KCF.	0.642479
Enlarged Heart	Enlarged heart as either preadmission or admission KCF.	0.194145
Fluid Imbalance Combination	Group variable—presence of any of: K < 2.5 or > 5.3, or Na < 130 or > 150.	0.522067
Gender	F=0; M=1	−0.250202

Continued

Exhibit 2.3 Continued

Independent Variable	Definition or Comments About Key Clinical Finding (KCF)	Coefficient
Hemoglobin g/dL Low	Use actual value if hemoglobin < 10 g/dL for either preadmission or admission KCF for ages ≥ 1 month or imputed normal of 12. For ages 0–30 days, use actual value if hemoglobin < 13.4 or imputed normal of 17.5.	−0.258967
History CAD Group	Group variable—presence of any of: current anticoagulant medication, failed PTCA, history of angina, previous CABG, previous PTCA.	0.397191
Inflammation Group	Group variable—presence of any of: active herpes, bands > 20%, CSF WBC > 0 c/mm³, degeneration, history of autoimmune disease, infection, inflammation, oral temperature < 95.5 or > 100.9 °F, WBC < 5 or > 17.0.	0.507799
Ischemia	Ischemia as either preadmission or admission KCF.	0.76654
LAD	Left anterior descending coronary artery occlusion > 49% for either preadmission or admission KCF.	0.010349
Left Main	Left main coronary artery occlusion > 49% for either preadmission or admission KCF.	0.013364
Lesion	Lesion at any site as either preadmission or admission KCF.	0.363275
MI Group	Group variable—presence of any of: CPK MB > 25 ng/ml, CPK MB > 3%, or myocardial infarction	0.305569
Mechanical Ventilator Any Days	Treatment code for mechanical ventilation.	1.872766
Oral Temperature °F Low	Use actual value if oral temperature < 95.5° F for either preadmission or admission KCF or imputed normal of 98.6°. Records with another unit of measure are converted to °F.	0.131809
PTT seconds	Use actual value if PTT > 35.9 for either preadmission or admission KCF or imputed normal of 37.5.	0.007619
Previous Seizures	Previous seizures history KCF.	0.649513
Previous Strokes	Previous stroke history KCF.	0.330871
Pulse Low	Use actual value if pulse < 65 for either preadmission or admission KCF or imputed normal of 80 (ages > 12 years) or 100 (age < 13).	−0.025345
RCA	Right coronary artery occlusion > 49% for either preadmission or admission KCF.	0.005127
S3 Gallop	S3 gallop as either preadmission or admission KCF.	0.45945

Syncope	Syncope history KCF.	0.620428
Systolic BP Low	Use actual value if systolic blood pressure < 90 for either preadmission or admission KCF for ages > 17 or < 60 for ages < 18 or imputed normal of 110.	−0.009604
West Region Group	Hospital location.	−1.328007
pH Arterial High	Use actual value of arterial pH > 7.44 for either preadmission or admission KCF or imputed normal of 7.38.	4.381957

C. Intestinal Disorder
C.1. Admission Period Mortality Predictions

Age Squared	Age in years squared.	0.0003764
Albumin g/dL	Use actual value if albumin < 3.0 g/dL for either preadmission or admission KCF or imputed normal of 4.4.	−0.302
BUN mg/dL	Use actual value if BUN > 30 mg/dL for either preadmission or admission KCF or imputed normal value of 12.	0.0091
Constant/Intercept	—	4.4934
Damage Group	Group variable—presence of any of: AST > 80 U/L, CPK > 150 U/L, damage, tear.	0.6394
History CAD Group	Group variable—presence of any of: current anticoagulant medication, failed PTCA, history of angina, previous CABG, previous PTCA.	0.4084
Immunocompromised Group	Group variable—presence of any of: current immunosuppressive medication, HIV positive, immunocompromised, transplant rejection.	0.896
Mechanical Ventilator Days	Requires treatment code for mechanical ventilation. Actual number of days on the ventilator used for scoring. For patients on a ventilator < 1 day, use .5. Patients not on ventilator, impute normal of 0.	0.1412
Na Low	Use actual value if sodium (Na) < 130 for either preadmission or admission KCF or imputed value of 141.	−0.0401
Pulse High	Use actual value if pulse > 129 for either preadmission or admission KCF or imputed normal of 80 (age > 12 years) or 100 (age < 13 years).	0.0097
Renal Group	Group variable—presence of any of: BUN > 30 mg/dL, chronic renal disease, creatinine > 1.7 mg/dL, urine protein mg/24 hr.	0.7354

Continued

Exhibit 2.3   Continued

Independent Variable	Definition or Comments About Key Clinical Finding (KCF)	Coefficient
Respirations High	Use actual value if respirations > 24 for either preadmission or admission KCF for ages ≥ one month or imputed normal of 18. Value if > 70 for ages 0–30 days or imputed normal of 35.	0.0405
Severe Malnutrition	Severe malnutrition as either preadmission or admission KCF.	1.2101
Stenosis	Stenosis at any site as preadmission or admission KCF.	0.473
Systolic BP Low	Use actual value if systolic blood pressure < 90 for either preadmission or admission KCF for ages > 17 or < 60 for ages < 18 or imputed normal of 110.	-0.0328
pO2 Arterial	Use actual value if arterial pO2 < 75 for either preadmission or admission KCF or imputed normal of 75.	-0.0329

C.2. Admission Period Length of Stay Equations

Independent Variable	Definition or Comments About Key Clinical Finding (KCF)	Coefficient
Admission Period Surgery	Surgical procedure in admission period.	1.342703
Age Squared	Age in years squared.	-0.00026165
Age in Months	For patients age 0–30 days, use the actual number of days divided by 30. For age > 23 months, use 24.	-0.065992
Age in Years	For patients < 12 months, use 0; for patients 12–23 months, use 1.	0.07288
Albumin g/dL	Use actual value if albumin < 3.0 g/dL for either preadmission or admission KCF or imputed normal of 4.4.	-0.704764
BUN mg/dL	Use actual value if BUN > 30 mg/dL for either preadmission or admission KCF or imputed normal value of 12.	0.025332
Bands %	Use actual value if bands % > 20 for either preadmission or admission KCF or imputed normal of 0.	0.023121
CHF Group	Group variable—presence of any of: congestive heart failure, edema, effusion respiratory, ejection fraction < 41%, history of CHF, S3 gallop, wedge pressure > 14.	0.241532
Central Region Group	Hospital location.	-0.378189
Chronic Cranial Nerve Deficit	Chronic cranial nerve deficit as either preadmission or admission KCF.	-0.597467

Variable	Description	Coefficient
Chronic Neurological Combination	Group variable—presence of any of: chronic findings of aphasia, apraxia, ataxia, cranial nerve deficit, flaccidity, muscle weakness, paresis, sensory deficit, speech deficit, or tremors; previous head trauma; or previous stroke.	0.58332
Coagulation Defect Group	Group variable—presence of any of: platelets < 100 10^9/L, PT > 15.5 seconds, PTT > 35.9.	0.265899
Constant/Intercept Group	—	−14.274429
Current Medica-tion Immuno-suppressive	Current immunosuppressive medication KCF.	1.129697
Damage Group	Group variable—presence of any of: AST > 80 U/L, CPK > 150 U/L, damage, tear.	0.398216
Effusion	Effusion of any site as either preadmission or admission KCF.	0.602435
Fluid Imbalance Combination	Group variable—presence of any of: K < 2.5 or > 5.3, or Na < 130 or > 150.	0.572731
Gender	F=0; M=1	−0.356878
Hematocrit % Low	Use actual value if hematocrit < 30% for either preadmission or admission KCF for ages ≥ 1 month or imputed normal of 45.5. For ages 0–30 days, use actual value if hematocrit < 40% or imputed normal of 53.	−0.026788
History of Cancer	Cancer history KCF.	0.356642
Hypoxia Group	Group variable—presence of any of: cyanosis, arterial O_2 saturation < 86%, arterial pO_2 < 75.	0.573408
Infection Group	Group variable—presence of any one of: acinetobacter, bacillus, bacteroides, bordetella, brucella, campylobacter, chlamydia, clostridium, corynebacterium, E. coli, enterobacter, fungus (except candida), haemophilus, klebsiella, legionella, listeria, mixed organisms, neisseria, other organisms (except fungi), proteus, providencia, pseudomonas, salmonella, serratia, shigella, staphylococcus aureus, staphylococcus epidermidis, streptobacillus, streptococcus β, streptococcus except β, yersinia.	0.483418
Inflammation	Inflammation at any site as either a preadmission or admission KCF.	−0.429126
K mEq/L High	Use actual value if potassium (K) > 5.3 for either preadmission or admission KCF or imputed normal of 4.2.	−0.329172
Lesion	Lesion at any site as either preadmission or admission KCF.	0.406699
Lethargy	Lethargy as either a preadmission or admission KCF.	0.365985

Continued

Exhibit 2.3   Continued

Independent Variable	Definition or Comments About Key Clinical Finding (KCF)	Coefficient
Mass Effect Group	Group variable—presence of any one of: mass, papilledema.	0.882369
Mechanical Ventilator Any Days	Treatment code for mechanical ventilation.	3.537941
Oral Temperature °F High	Use actual value if oral temperature > 100.9° F for either preadmission or admission KCF or imputed normal of 98.6°. Records with another unit of measure are converted to °F.	0.217216
Previous Seizures	Previous seizures history KCF.	0.462837
Previous Stroke	Previous stroke history KCF.	−0.345972
Pulse High	Use actual value if pulse > 129 for either preadmission or admission KCF or imputed normal of 80 (age > 12 years) or 100 (age < 13 years).	0.008523
Respirations High	Use actual value if respirations > 24 for either preadmission or admission KCF for ages ≥ one month or imputed normal of 18. Value if > 70 for ages 0–30 days or imputed normal of 35.	0.013658
Severe Malnutrition	Severe malnutrition as either preadmission or admission KCF.	1.087941
Stenosis	Stenosis at any site as preadmission or admission KCF.	0.914973
Tear	Tear of any site as preadmission or admission KCF.	1.614219
WBC High	Use actual value if WBC > 17.0 for either preadmission or admission KCF or imputed normal of 7.5 (age ≥ 1 month) or 21 (ages 0–30 days).	0.01875
West Region Group	Hospital location.	−0.69357

D. Fractures
D.1. Admission Period Mortality Equations

Age Squared	Age in years squared.	0.0003683
BUN mg/dL	Use actual value if BUN > 30 mg/dL for either preadmission or admission KCF or imputed normal value of 12.	0.0311
Cancer Group	Group variable—presence of any of: calcium > 11.0 mg/dL, history of cancer, malignant tumor.	0.9155
Constant/Intercept	—	13.4634
Hypoxia Group	Group variable—presence of any of: cyanosis, arterial O_2 saturation < 86%, arterial pO_2 < 75.	0.9792

Mechanical Ventilator Days	Requires treatment code for mechanical ventilation. Actual number of days on the ventilator used for scoring. For patients on a ventilator < 1 day, use .5. Patients not on ventilator, impute normal of 0.	0.1765
Oral Temperature °F Low	Use actual value if oral temperature < 95.5° F for either preadmission or admission KCF or imputed normal of 98.6°. Records with another unit of measure are converted to °F.	−0.1779
Respirations High	Use actual value if respirations > 24 for either preadmission or admission KCF for ages ≥ one month or imputed normal of 18. Value if > 70 for ages 0–30 days or imputed normal of 35.	0.0596
Systolic BP Low	Use actual value if systolic blood pressure < 90 for either preadmission or admission KCF for ages > 17 or < 60 for ages < 18 or imputed normal of 110.	−0.0376

D.2. Admission Period Length of Stay Equations

AST U/L	Use actual value if AST > 80 U/L for either preadmission or admission KCF or imputed normal of 12.	0.003937
Acute Sensory Deficit	Acute sensory deficit as either preadmission or admission KCF.	0.783062
Admission Period Surgery	Surgical procedure in admission period.	−0.911364
Age Squared	Age in years squared.	0.00023367
Age in Years	For patients < 12 months, use 0; for patients 12–23 months, use 1.	0.026416
COPD Group	Group variable—presence of any of: chronic lung disease, FEV1 < 66% predicted.	0.468456
CPK U/L	Use actual value if CPK > 150 U/L for either preadmission or admission KCF or imputed normal of 102 (age > 12 years) or > 110 (age < 13 years).	0.00041746
Cancer Group	Group variable—presence of any of: calcium > 11.0 mg/dL, history of cancer, malignant tumor.	0.498727
Central Region Group	Hospital location.	−0.734662
Chronic Sensory Deficit	Chronic sensory deficit as either preadmission or admission KCF.	1.220701
Chronic Tremors	Chronic tremors as either preadmission or admission KCF.	0.753342
Constant/Intercept	—	1.173139
Creatinine mg/dL	Use actual value if creatinine > 1.7 mg/dL for either preadmission or admission KCF or imputed normal value of .9.	0.291934

Continued

Exhibit 2.3 Continued

Independent Variable	Definition or Comments About Key Clinical Finding (KCF)	Coefficient
Current Medication Anticoagulation	Currently on anticoagulation medication.	0.804667
Damage Group	Group variable—presence of any of: AST > 80 U/L, CPK > 150 U/L, damage, tear.	0.733232
Diabetes Group	Group variable—presence of any of: current medication insulin, diabetes, glucose < 60 or > 249 mg/dL.	0.512284
E. coli	Any culture positive for E. coli as either preadmission or admission KCF.	−0.955111
Enlarged Heart	Enlarged heart as either preadmission or admission KCF.	1.674252
Gender	F=0; M=1	−0.129063
Hematocrit % Low	Use actual value if hematocrit < 30% for either preadmission or admission KCF for ages ≥ 1 month or imputed normal of 45.5. For ages 0–30 days, use actual value if hematocrit < 40% or imputed normal of 53.	−0.054709
History CAD Group	Group variable—presence of any of: current anticoagulant medication, failed PTCA, history of angina, previous CABG, previous PTCA.	0.400105
Immunocompromised Group	Group variable—presence of any of: current immunosuppressive medication, HIV positive, immunocompromised, transplant rejection.	0.555902
Infection Group	Group variable—presence of any one of: acinetobacter, bacillus, bacteroides, bordetella, brucella, campylobacter, chlamydia, clostridium, corynebacterium, E. coli, enterobacter, fungus (except candida), haemophilus, klebsiella, legionella, listeria, mixed organisms, neisseria, other organisms (except fungi), proteus, providencia, pseudomonas, salmonella, serratia, shigella, staphylococcus aureus, staphylococcus epidermidis, streptobacillus, streptococcus except β, streptococcus except β, yersinia.	1.255161
Inflammation Group	Group variable—presence of any of: active herpes, bands > 20%, CSF WBC > 0 c/mm³, degeneration, history of autoimmune disease, infection, inflammation, oral temperature < 95.5 or > 100.9 °F, WBC < 5 or > 17.0.	1.049288
Lesion	Lesion at any site as either preadmission or admission KCF.	0.521535
Lethargy	Lethargy as either a preadmission or admission finding.	1.012563
Malnutrition Group	Group variable—presence of any of: albumin < 3.0 g/dL, severe malnutrition.	0.519578

Mechanical Ventilation Any Days	Treatment code for mechanical ventilation.	3.420933
Na Low	Use actual value if sodium (Na) < 130 for either preadmission or admission KCF or imputed value of 141.	-0.053778
Open Fracture	Use actual value of open fracture for either preadmission or admission KCF or imputed value of 0.	0.596056
Oral Temperature °F Low	Use actual value if oral temperature < 95.5° F for either preadmission or admission KCF or imputed normal of 98.6°. Records with another unit of measure are converted to °F.	0.204735
Previous Head Trauma	Previous head trauma history KCF.	0.644415
Pulse High	Use actual value if pulse > 129 for either preadmission or admission KCF or imputed normal of 80 (age > 12 years) or 100 (age < 13 years).	0.020415
Respirations High	Use actual value if respirations > 24 for either preadmission or admission KCF for ages ≥ one month or imputed normal of 18. Value if > 70 for ages 0–30 days or imputed normal of 35.	0.03607
Simple Fracture	Simple fracture as either preadmission or admission KCF.	1.688772
Stenosis	Stenosis at any site as preadmission or admission KCF.	0.584336
Systolic BP Low	Use actual value if systolic blood pressure < 90 for either preadmission or admission KCF for ages > 17 or < 60 for ages < 18 or imputed normal of 110.	-0.013835
Tear	Tear of any site as preadmission or admission KCF.	-0.712594
The Trauma Score < 17	Use actual value if Trauma Score < 17 for either preadmission or admission KCF or imputed normal of 16.	-0.362839
West Region Group	Hospital location.	-1.111087
pO$_2$ Arterial	Use actual value of arterial pO$_2$ < 75 for either preadmission or admission KCF or imputed normal of 75.	-0.052764

© MediQual Systems, Inc. 1996.

Exhibit 2.4   Patient Management Categories

A. Respiratory Disorder Module
Sample Patient Management Path
PMC 2404 Respiratory Disorder: Pneumonia with Effusion/Empyema
(1 of 13 Respiratory Disorder PMCs)

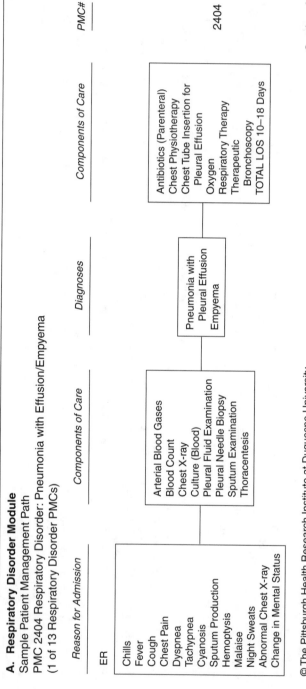

Reason for Admission	Components of Care	Diagnoses	Components of Care	PMC#

ER
 	
Chills
Fever
Cough
Chest Pain
Dyspnea
Tachypnea
Cyanosis
Sputum Production
Hemoptysis
Malaise
Night Sweats
Abnormal Chest X-ray
Change in Mental Status
	Arterial Blood Gases
	Blood Count
	Chest X-ray
	Culture (Blood)
	Pleural Fluid Examination
	Pleural Needle Biopsy
	Sputum Examination
	Thoracentesis
		Pneumonia with
		Pleural Effusion
		Empyema
			Antibiotics (Parenteral)
			Chest Physiotherapy
			Chest Tube Insertion for
			  Pleural Effusion
			Oxygen
			Respiratory Therapy
			Therapeutic
			  Bronchoscopy
			TOTAL LOS 10–18 Days
				2404

© The Pittsburgh Health Research Institute at Duquesne University.

Continued

Exhibit 2.4 Continued

B. Acute Myocardial Infarction Module
Sample Patient Management Paths
PMC 0308 AMI: Cardiogenic Shock
PMC 0390 AMI: Cardiac Catheterization/PCTA
(2 of 8 AMI PMCs)

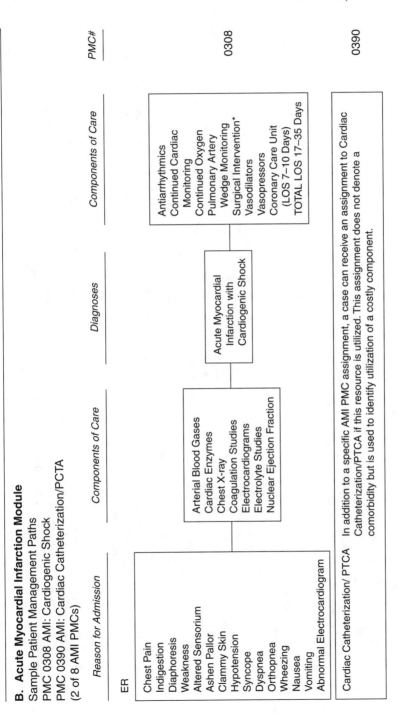

Reason for Admission

ER

Chest Pain
Indigestion
Diaphoresis
Weakness
Altered Sensorium
Ashen Pallor
Clammy Skin
Hypotension
Syncope
Dyspnea
Orthopnea
Wheezing
Nausea
Vomiting
Abnormal Electrocardiogram

Components of Care

Arterial Blood Gases
Cardiac Enzymes
Chest X-ray
Coagulation Studies
Electrocardiograms
Electrolyte Studies
Nuclear Ejection Fraction

Diagnoses

Acute Myocardial
Infarction with
Cardiogenic Shock

Components of Care

Antiarrhythmics
Continued Cardiac
 Monitoring
Continued Oxygen
Pulmonary Artery
 Wedge Monitoring
Surgical Intervention*
Vasodilators
Vasopressors
Coronary Care Unit
 (LOS 7–10 Days)
TOTAL LOS 17–35 Days

PMC#

0308

Cardiac Catheterization/ PTCA   In addition to a specific AMI PMC assignment, a case can receive an assignment to Cardiac Catheterization/PTCA if this resource is utilized. This assignment does not denote a comorbidity but is used to identify utilization of a costly component.

0390

*The surgical intervention indicated is the insertion of an intra-aortic balloon.
© The Pittsburgh Health Research Institute at Duquesne University.

C. Colorectal Neoplasm Module
Sample Patient Management Paths
PMC 0805 Colorectal Neoplasm: GI Metastasis with Obstruction
PMC 0806 Colorectal Neoplasm: GI Metastasis without Obstruction
(2 of 11 Colorectal Neoplasm PMCs)

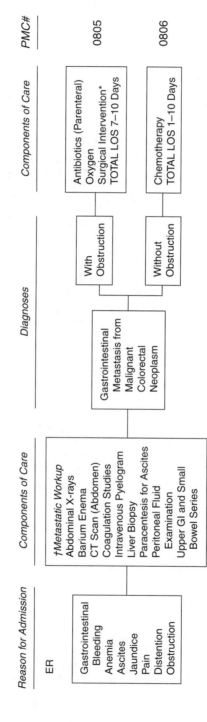

†The standard Metastatic Workup for Colorectal Malignancy includes the following services: Bone Marrow Biopsy, Bone Scan, Carcinoembryonic Antigen, Chest X-ray, Liver Function Studies, Ultrasound.
*The surgical intervention includes one or a combination of the following procedures: colostomy, colon or small bowel resection.
© The Pittsburgh Health Research Institute at Duquesne University.

Continued

Exhibit 2.4 Continued

D. Femur/Pelvic Fracture Module
Sample Patient Management Path
PMC 4807 Femur/Pelvic Fracture: Transcervical/Intertrochanteric Fracture
(1 of 17 Femur/Pelvic Fracture PMCs)

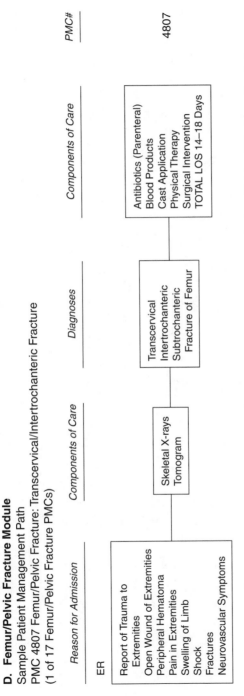

*The surgical intervention includes one or a combination of the following procedures: open reduction with internal fixation, arthroplasty
© The Pittsburgh Health Research Institute at Duquesne University.

Chapter 3

Data Sources and Implications: Administrative Databases

Lisa I. Iezzoni

As described in Chapter 2, the first step in risk adjustment is specifying goals and thus defining "risk"—risk of what outcome? The answer carries tangible practical consequences. To avoid purely theoretical exercises, the outcome itself must be measurable at a reasonable cost. Because the data are readily available, large studies of patient outcomes have typically started with in-hospital deaths, lengths of hospital stay, or dollars spent (see Chapter 11). However, these steps in designing a risk-adjustment strategy are also inextricably tied to data:

- delineating the dimensions of risk to be included in the adjustment; and

- specifying how these dimensions will be captured and quantified.

If necessary data are of poor quality or simply unavailable, the dimension cannot be included in the risk adjustment.

Thus, the content and quality of the data delimit clinical credibility, affect perceptions of validity, and largely determine reliability and accuracy of risk adjustment. The numbers of cases and special attributes of the populations represented (e.g., Medicare beneficiaries, military veterans) influence statistical methods and suggest which patient characteristics must be considered. The data also dictate the scope and strength of inferences that can be drawn from the risk-adjusted outcomes results. Many studies, such as the Patient Outcomes Research Teams (PORTs) funded by the AHCPR, choose their data sources before finalizing the risk-adjustment methodology or specific research questions (Mitchell et al. 1994; Lave et al. 1994).

The first edition of this book drew clear boundaries between these three major data sources frequently used to study patient outcomes:

- *Administrative data*—large, computerized data files generally compiled in billing for healthcare services, such as hospitalizations
- *Medical record information*—data elements abstracted, usually retrospectively, from medical records and obtained from the healthcare provider
- *Patient-derived data*—information collected directly from patients either through interviews or questionnaires

The first edition argued that patient-derived data were rarely used to study outcomes, due to daunting logistical and cost constraints. In the three years since completing the first edition, however, boundaries among these three sources have blurred considerably. Patients are entering data about their health and personal risk factors at computer terminals in doctors' offices; clinical data formerly confined to medical records are increasingly transmitted electronically and stored in central data repositories; the set of data elements contained in routine administrative transmissions for each healthcare encounter is expanding in increasingly clinical directions (Office of Technology Assessment 1995). Although a completely paperless medical record remains elusive, the volume of healthcare data available in electronic form and their clinical scope are growing at a fast and furious pace.

In addition, as suggested by Reiser (see Chapter 2), patients are increasingly valued as the authentic judge of quality of care. Initiatives that target patients' experiences or satisfaction with healthcare routinely collect self-reports of patient functioning and demographic characteristics to use for risk adjustment or stratification. For example, the ongoing Medicare Current Beneficiary Survey not only collects data on respondent expenditures and satisfaction with care but also annually adds queries about performance of ADLs (see Chapter 4). The Boston-based Picker Institute's survey of patients' experiences with hospital care (Cleary et al. 1993; Gerteis et al. 1993), used by programs in St. Louis and New Hampshire to compare hospital performance and by the Department of Veterans Affairs National Customer Feedback Center, collects data on self-reported health status as a risk-stratification variable.

Nonetheless, for convenience, this second edition retains the distinction between administrative databases (discussed in this chapter) and medical record information (Chapter 4), with a brief discussion of patient-generated data in the latter chapter. Note, however, that certain issues, such as developing a uniform nomenclature, coding, and concerns about confidentiality and privacy, cut across all data sources. This chapter starts with current activities involving administrative data sources and ends by looking to the future.

Sources of Administrative Data

The Institute of Medicine (IOM) Committee on Regional Health Data Networks defined a database as "a large collection of data in a computer, organized so that it can be expanded, updated, and retrieved rapidly for various uses" (Donaldson and Lohr 1994, 42). The committee distinguished between "primary records"—information retained by healthcare practitioners in caring for patients—and "secondary records"—information collected for other purposes, such as billing. Administrative databases are the by-product of administering delivery of healthcare services, such as reimbursing hospitals and physicians or determining individual eligibility for an insurance program (e.g., Medicare). The information is aggregated by payors or governmental organizations for reimbursement, monitoring, or other payment-related purposes, such as hospital rate setting.

The three major sources of these databases are the federal government (U.S. Department of Health and Human Services, VA), state governments, and private insurance companies. Initially, administrative data files concentrated primarily on acute care hospitalizations. Information is increasingly compiled from outpatient, long-term care facilities, and home health and hospice programs. While this presentation focuses largely on hospital-derived data as an example of administrative files, concerns raised in the hospital context extend to other healthcare delivery settings.

The Uniform Hospital Discharge Data Set (UHDDS) is the prototype for administrative databases concerning hospital admissions. The UHDDS concept was first formulated in 1972 by the National Committee on Vital and Health Statistics, U.S. Department of Health, Education, and Welfare (DHEW) (1980). The intent underlying the UHDDS was to produce a uniform but "minimum" data set that would facilitate investigation of the cost and quality of short-term hospital services across populations at both local and national levels. In 1974, following initial testing, DHEW mandated submission of UHDDS data for all acute hospital discharges paid through Medicare and Medicaid. In 1979, a committee convened by DHEW further revised the directions for completing the UHDDS, retaining the 14 core data elements recommended 7 years earlier (Table 3.1). Since then, the content of UHDDS has changed little, despite proposals to enhance the data set significantly.

Other efforts to collect information on hospitalizations have generally built around the 14 UHDDS data elements. The most widely used format was the 1982 Uniform Bill (UB-82) required for hospitals submitting reimbursement claims to Medicare, Medicaid, Blue Cross, and

Table 3.1   Contents of the Uniform Hospital Discharge Data Set

Number and Item	*Definition and Comments*
1. Personal identification	"The unique number assigned to each patient within a hospital that distinguishes the patient and his or her hospital record from all others in that institution" (p. 8). Social Security number was not recommended because it is not always unique to an individual. The guidelines recommend using the hospital-assigned medical record number.
2. Date of birth	Date of birth was requested because it was perceived as more accurate than age.
3. Sex	
4. Race and ethnicity	American Indian or Alaskan Native, black, hispanic, white, and other.
5. Residence	Zip code of patient residence. Zip code was viewed as preferable to street address because of lesser concerns about patient confidentiality and because no coding of the information is required.
6. Hospital identification	Medicare provider or some other unique number.
7. Admission date	"An inpatient *admission* begins with the formal acceptance by a hospital of a patient who is to receive physician, dentist, or allied services while receiving room, board, and continuous nursing services" (pp. 10–11).
8. Discharge date	"An inpatient *discharge* occurs with the termination of the room, board, and continuous nursing services, and the formal release of an inpatient by the hospital" (p. 11).
9. Attending physician identification	A unique number within each hospital for "the clinician who is primarily and largely responsible for the care of the patient from the beginning of the hospital episode" (p. 11).
10. Operating physician identification	A unique number within each hospital for "the clinician who performed the principal procedure" (p. 11).
11. Diagnoses	The 1979 recommendation was that a maximum of five diagnoses be recorded including "all diagnoses that affect the current hospital stay." The following definitions were provided (p. 12):
	a. "Principal diagnosis is designated and defined as: the condition established after study to be chiefly responsible for occasioning the admission of the patient to the hospital for care."

Continued

Table 3.1   Continued

Number and Item	Definition and Comments
	b. "Other diagnoses to be designated and defined as associated with the current hospital stay are: all conditions that coexist at the time of admission, that develop subsequently, or that affect the treatment received and/or the length of stay. Diagnoses that relate to an earlier episode which have no bearing on the current hospital stay, are to be excluded."
12. Procedures and dates*	The 1979 recommendation was that all "Class 1, 2, and 3" procedures ("surgery" and "significant procedures") be recorded along with their dates of performance. One procedure was to be designated the principal procedure using the following criteria: "(1) The principal procedure is one that was performed for definitive treatment rather than one performed for diagnostic or exploratory purposes, or was necessary to take care of a complication. (2) The principal procedure is that procedure most related to the principal diagnosis" (p. 12). Until 1992, Medicare allowed only three positions for listing procedures.
13. Disposition of the patient	Discharged to home (routine discharge), left against medical advice, discharged to another short-term hospital, discharged to a long-term institution, died.
14. Expected principal source of payment	Self-pay, worker's compensation, Medicare, Medicaid, maternal and child health, other government payments, Blue Cross, insurance companies, no charge (free, charity, special research, or teaching), other.

Source: National Committee on Vital and Health Statistics, U.S. Department of Health, Education, and Welfare 1980.
*Coded using the *International Classification of Diseases, Ninth Revision, Clinical Modification.*

many commercial health insurance carriers (Gardner 1990). The UB-82 had over 90 data entry fields, including patient identifiers, descriptors of the hospitalization (e.g., admission type—whether emergent, urgent, or elective), insurance coverage information (e.g., deductibles and coinsurance), charge and billing data, and space for five diagnoses (principal plus four others) and three procedures with dates (principal plus two others). As of April 1, 1992, the Health Care Financing Administration (HCFA) increased the number of coding slots to nine diagnosis fields and six procedure fields (*Federal Register* 1991). The electronic version of the 1992 Uniform Bill (UB-92) is now used for 95 percent of hospital claims; with electronic transmittal, providers can repeat the diagnosis records if they wish to convey more than nine diagnoses (National Uniform Billing Committee 1996).

HCFA has been accumulating hospital billing data since 1983 and now has computer files representing over 100 million hospital discharges and billions of other claims.

Medicare Administrative Data Files

Congress established Medicare in 1965 as Title XVIII of the Social Security Act, with benefits for eligible beneficiaries 65 years of age and older beginning July 1, 1966. Amendments in 1972 extended coverage to younger persons with disabilities and persons with end-stage renal disease. Medicare includes two distinct parts: Part A, hospital insurance (coverage for services provided in institutional settings, including hospitals, skilled nursing facilities, hospices, and some home health services), and Part B, supplemental medical insurance (coverage for physician services, outpatient hospital services, certain medical equipment, and other services). Part B enrollment is voluntary. As of 1995, approximately 32.6 million elderly persons and 4.5 million persons with disabilities were enrolled in Medicare Part A, and 31.8 million elderly and 4 million disabled also had Medicare Part B (HCFA 1995, 2–3).

In administering Medicare, HCFA processes massive quantities of beneficiary, institutional, and billing data, much of which is available to qualified researchers through HCFA's Office of Statistics and Data Management, Bureau of Data Management and Strategy (HCFA 1995, 1996). HCFA's data reflect the three primary administrative functions of the Medicare program: (1) enrolling and tracking beneficiaries, (2) designating and monitoring providers and institutions approved to accept Medicare payments, and (3) reimbursing individual services. Processing this enormous volume of information is complex and is described in detail elsewhere (HCFA 1995). Briefly, no claims are submitted directly to HCFA. As of 1991, the country was partitioned into nine distinct processing sectors, each with a designated contractor or "host" producing a Common Working File (CWF). Each beneficiary is assigned to a specific CWF host, who maintains information on that beneficiary's eligibility status and Part A and B utilization records (the Health Insurance Master Records). Institutional provider claims (UB-92) are submitted to the CWF host through a local fiscal intermediary, and physician and supplier claims (HCFA Form 1500) arrive at the CWF through a local carrier. The CWF checks the beneficiary's eligibility status; edits the claim for consistency, remaining beneficiary benefit, and deductibles; and authorizes the fiscal intermediary or carrier to pay or reject the claim or to gather additional documentation. Daily, the nine CWF hosts transmit to the HCFA Bureau of Data Management and Strategy a list of claims processed and updates on each beneficiary's utilization history.

Prior to 1991, claims (then called "bills") were stored at HCFA within a series of separate files (e.g., inpatient, home health, outpatient, physician) that were used to derive other files for various analyses. Since 1991, all institutional provider and physician/supplier claims submitted daily by the nine CWF hosts are entered weekly into the National Claims History (NCH) 100% Nearline File, which is now the only file containing all claims submitted for Medicare beneficiaries, including adjustments, interim claims, and denials. Claims are processed through the NCH Quality Assurance Systems, which apply routine edits for completeness and internal consistency as well as in-depth examination of providers whose billing patterns appear unusually inconsistent or unreliable.

The NCH 100% Nearline File is enormous, containing over 2.5 billion records, with more than 730 million records created in 1994 alone (HCFA 1995, 6). Approximately 160 variables are included. Each record type contains a "fixed portion," consisting of items that occur only once per record (e.g., beneficiary demographics, claim transaction history, diagnosis, payment amounts); and "trailer groups," which vary by record type and can be repeated multiple times. The NCH 100% Nearline File encompasses six record types: four for institutional claims (inpatient/skilled nursing facility, outpatient, home health agency, and hospice); one for physicians or other supplies; and another for durable medical equipment.

Because of this complexity, working with the NCH requires skill and extensive knowledge. Due to beneficiary confidentiality and logistical concerns, the NCH is not a standard public-use file. However, researchers, such as the PORT investigators (Mitchell et al. 1994; Lave et al. 1994), can gain access to NCH information under carefully controlled circumstances. More often, researchers use data extracted from the NCH and configured into analytic files available for public purchase. These files protect beneficiary confidentiality and represent the "final action" for a given event, such as a hospitalization, after all adjustments are finalized (e.g., instead of containing multiple interim claims for a single event).

The file pertaining to inpatient stays is the Medicare Provider Analysis and Review (MEDPAR) file, and MEDPAR data sets are available from 1984 onward. The 1994 MEDPAR file contains roughly 13 million records, including 11.8 million hospitalizations and 1.3 million skilled nursing facility stays (HCFA 1995, 17). MEDPAR contains data elements from the UB-92 hospital claim, including demographic information, principal and other diagnosis codes, procedure codes and dates, charges for a variety of cost centers, and reimbursement information. Since June 1995, MEDPAR has been created from inpatient and skilled nursing facility claims in the NCH 100% Nearline File. Public-use MEDPAR files have encrypted patient identifiers. A national MEDPAR file containing all hospital discharge records for Medicare beneficiaries can be purchased from HCFA's Office of Health Care Information Systems, Bureau of Data Management and Strategy, for $3,415 per year of data (prices in effect from July 1, 1996, to July 1, 1997) (HCFA 1996b).

Information on providers eligible for Medicare reimbursement is also maintained in a variety of files, such as the Hospital Cost Report Information System (HCRIS) and the Provider of Service (POS) File. The HCRIS contains information extracted from the Medicare cost reports submitted annually by participating hospitals, providing not only fiscal information but also data on services rendered and patient volume during the preceding year. The cost report asks about basic structural characteristics of the facility, such as ownership, number of beds, and staff size. It also contains queries about capital expenditures; depreciation expenses; and salaries, malpractice, and activities within a range of cost centers.

The POS File includes information from Medicare certification applications and surveys from hospitals, skilled nursing facilities, home health agencies, independent laboratories, and a range of other facilities. The file, continually updated from recertification applications, contains 2,400 data elements, including information on facility location, bed size, services offered, staff size and professional configuration, and ownership. As of 1993, the POS contained about 61,000 records organized by provider type and number.

Detailed information on Medicare Public Use Files, such as those shown in Table 3.2, can be obtained from HCFA through its home page on the Internet, a case-sensitive address, that can be accessed at http://www. hcfa.gov. Additional information is also available by calling (410) 786–3691 (HCFA 1996a, 2). Price lists for these files are updated at least annually (HCFA 1996b).

Other Federal Sources

Other federal agencies also collect data while administering health services programs. Both the Department of Defense and VA oversee provision of healthcare to large, albeit selected, populations—employees of the uniformed services and their families and military veterans. The Department of Defense, Office of Civilian Health and Medical Program of the Uniformed Services (CHAMPUS) maintains an automated information and reporting system (the CHAMPUS Medical Information System or CMIS) primarily to manage its healthcare delivery system. Founded in 1988, the principal role of CMIS is to provide detailed cost and utilization data to medical treatment facility commanders in the form of both facility-specific and comparative statistics. Diagnosis and procedure data are also available for hospitalizations, including a special DRG database with information aggregated by DRGs. However, most CHAMPUS information is used

Table 3.2   Examples of Public-Use Files from Medicare Databases

Public Use File Name	Description
Standard Analytic Files (SAFs)	These files are available by type of claim. These files contain final action, adjustments-resolved claims and are created every July, for the prior calendar service year. Provider numbers and beneficiary claim numbers are encrypted in the 5% files to protect the privacy of individuals. In the 100% files, the provider number is encrypted and the beneficiary claim number is blocked out. An SAF includes inpatient, outpatient, HHA, hospice, SNF, and physician/supplier Part B information.
Expanded Modified Medicare Provider Analysis and Review—Hospital File (National)	This file contains records for 100% of Medicare beneficiaries using hospital inpatient services. The records are stripped of most data elements that will permit identification of beneficiaries. The hospital is identified by the six-position Medicare billing number. The national file consists of approximately 11 million records.
Physician Sample File	This file contains final action claim line item-level data for services rendered to Medicare beneficiaries by a sample of physicians. The UPIN Validation file is statistically analyzed for the random selection of physicians, which results in an approximate 5% national sample. The file contains service information such as place and type of service, and charge and payment amounts. Provider numbers and claim numbers are encrypted to protect the privacy of individuals.
Annual ZIP Code Enrollment File	This file is derived from the Enrollment Database and contains aged and disabled enrollment data by age, race, and sex in ZIP codes. The file has been edited for conformance with Privacy Act provisions.
Provider of Services Extract File	This file is created from the Online Survey and Certification and Reporting System database. The data include provider number, name, and address, and characterize the participating institutional providers. The data are collected through the HCFA regional offices. The file includes an individual record for each Medicare-approved provider.

Source: Health Care Financing Administration, Bureau of Data Management and Strategy 1995.
HHA = home health agency. SNF = skilled nursing facility. UPIN = Unique Physician Identification Number.

exclusively for managerial purposes or is available on a limited special request basis to support service or command projects. CHAMPUS data are not generally available for health services research studies.

In contrast, VA maintains an active health services research program, drawing extensively from the computerized files created through administering VA hospitals and clinics. Each year, about 2.5 million persons obtain healthcare at a VA facility, with almost 1 million hospitalizations and 25 million outpatient visits at institutions ranging from tertiary medical centers to domiciliaries and nursing homes (Meistrell and Schlehuber 1996, MS92). For decades, VA data systems lagged behind those outside the VA, but in recent years, the VA has become an information system leader. In late 1993, beta testing concluded on the VA's Event Driven Reporting (EDR) system, and it is now being implemented nationwide. Through this system, computerized data maintained at each healthcare facility (e.g., on hospital admissions, clinic visits, procedures) are automatically extracted, transmitted, and entered into the national EDR database every 24 hours. The EDR's goal is to take this facility-generated information and "place it in an accessible repository on which multifacility analyses can be performed" (Meistrell and Schlehuber 1996, MS97).

One data set now derived via EDR is the Patient Treatment File (PTF), a master file that had been 2 to 14 months out of date but with EDR is virtually contemporaneous. The PTF contains information on all persons either receiving inpatient care at a VA facility, nursing home, or domiciliary or obtaining inpatient care elsewhere at VA expense (Lamoreaux 1996). The PTF contains three basic types of information: demographic (social security number, age, gender, race, residence, means test), administrative (hospitalization dates, hospital identifier, number of stays on different clinical "bedsections," number of trips to the operating room), and clinical (DRG, primary and up to nine secondary diagnoses, up to five nonoperating-room procedures). A separate file contains information on up to five surgical procedures (Fleming et al. 1992). Unlike the Medicare program, the VA does not maintain a computerized file that identifies all persons eligible for VA benefits or those using the VA healthcare system.

The VA defines the first-listed hospital diagnosis differently than does UHDDS. Medicare and the UB-92 adopted the UHDDS instructions that the "principal diagnosis is designated and defined as: the condition established after study to be chiefly responsible for occasioning the admission of the patient to the hospital for care" (National Committee on Vital and Health Statistics, DHEW 1980, 11). In contrast, the VA specifies a "primary diagnosis"—the condition that was primarily responsible for the length of the hospitalization.

The following example demonstrates the distinction between principal and primary diagnoses. Suppose a man is admitted for a routine transurethral prostatectomy (TURP) to treat benign prostatic hypertrophy

(BPH). On the day following an uncomplicated TURP, he falls and fractures his hip. He is stabilized and undergoes an open reduction and internal fixation (ORIF) to repair the fracture; postoperatively he begins the slow rehabilitation process. Under UHDDS guidelines, BPH is the principal diagnosis because the patient entered the hospital for BPH treatment. The TURP surgery involved only one or two days, while the ORIF required an additional ten days in-hospital. Thus, hip fracture is the primary diagnosis.

Although in most instances the principal and primary diagnoses are identical, this difference nonetheless confuses comparisons of diagnosis data across the VA and UHDDS-based data systems.

Other Sources of Administrative Data

Most medical effectiveness research using administrative data, such as the PORTs, has concentrated on Medicare databases, due to their ready availability, national scope, and ability to link services performed for individual patients. However, as patient outcomes studies increasingly target younger adults and children, other data sources are necessary. Three types of nonfederal administrative databases offer information on state hospital discharge abstract files, Medicaid databases, and claims files of private insurance companies.

State hospital discharge databases

Thirty-six states systematically collect information from hospitals about costs and admissions (Donaldson and Lohr 1994, 51). The motivation for gathering these data varies across states, including efforts to regulate hospital costs, spur competition across providers, and monitor outcomes of care. Because of this, states also differ in the agencies that oversee data collection and disseminate information. For example, health planning or regulatory agencies are in charge in California, Massachusetts, Maine, and Ohio, while independent data commissions are responsible in Colorado, Florida, Illinois, and Pennsylvania (Epstein 1992). The states vary concerning whether collected data are aggregated at the hospital level and whether information is required only for certain patients (e.g., Medicare and Medicaid beneficiaries, persons insured by private payors) or for all inpatients.

Comparisons across states are hampered by lack of uniformity in data definitions and format (Epstein 1992). States generally use one of three formats for gathering these data: UB-82 or UB-92, UHDDS, or a specific state-designed format (e.g., New York). Despite using common approaches such as UB-92 or UHDDS, data comparability across states is compromised by inconsistency of definitions for data elements and differences in coding.

AHCPR gathered 1993 computerized hospital discharge abstract files and their coding guidelines from 12 states and found tremendous variability in coding even the most basic data elements (Elixhauser et al. 1996). None of the 12 states followed standard coding guidelines, such as UHDDS guidelines.

Some states have expanded the standard recording fields available for certain data elements. For example, California permits recording of the principal plus up to 24 secondary diagnoses and procedures. Some states are also much more aggressive than others in monitoring the quality of coding practices. For instance, the California Office of Statewide Health Planning and Development (OSHPD) periodically publishes the *Discharge Data Review*, containing detailed information about difficult coding topics, definitions of data elements, and new state data regulations. One major difference across states involves the presence of a unique patient identification number (e.g., social security number) that facilitates tracking of individual patients through the healthcare system. Massachusetts, New York, and California include such patient identifiers, but most states do not.

Most importantly, states vary concerning whether patient-level data are available to outside investigators. Most states publish and disseminate aggregated reports based on these data, but some do not allow outside researchers to obtain computerized individual discharge abstract files. For example, the Connecticut Hospital Association owns that state's data and rarely releases files to outsiders. States that do provide files to investigators encrypt medical record numbers and other specific patient identifiers to protect patient confidentiality. In certain instances, however, one can negotiate with a state to obtain individual identifiers to permit study of specific, policy-relevant research questions. For some states, any qualifying outsider can purchase a computerized file containing an entire year of discharge abstracts for as little as $500 to $1,000. For example, in 1994, the *Boston Globe* Spotlight Team purchased a hospital discharge abstract file from the Massachusetts Rate Setting Commission to produce a report card comparing hospital mortality rates (Kong 1994, see Chapter 11).

State discharge abstract files thus offer a relatively inexpensive opportunity to evaluate all or many hospitalizations within a state. Most are limited by the absence of unique patient identifiers. Only a few are able to track postdischarge outcomes, such as mortality (e.g., by linkage with the vital statistics reporting system). Nonetheless, for investigations using the hospitalization as the unit of analysis, state data files can provide useful information.

Medicaid data files

Medicaid is a joint state and federal program, enacted as Title XIX of the Social Security Act amendments of 1965. Medicaid supports inpatient, outpatient, and long-term care services for the poor. To be eligible for Medicaid, persons initially needed to meet welfare program definitions for poverty, blindness, disability, or familial ties to dependent children. In 1986, Congress expanded Medicaid to cover pregnant women and poor children, and in 1990, coverage was extended for Medicare premiums, deductibles, and coinsurance for poor Medicare recipients. Given current political debates, the future fate and form of Medicaid is doubtful, but it is unlikely to become a uniform federal entitlement as is Medicare—Medicaid will retain its state roots.

Details concerning Medicaid eligibility and coverage vary across states, as do the databases (Ku, Ellwood, and Klemm 1990; HCFA 1995). Most mandated Medicaid information involves aggregate reports sent annually to HCFA. However, Medicaid claims databases are also available for some states. These files contain all claims submitted for Medicaid services, taken from the automated Medicaid Management Information Systems files. Included are data on eligibility qualifications, types of services, diagnoses, and payments to providers. Claims sometimes can be linked at the patient level using a unique patient identifier. Because of the volume of claims, state Medicaid files tend to be massive and cumbersome to manipulate, and the "skill of the investigators" is critically important (Bright, Avorn, and Everitt 1989, 944).

In the 1980s, HCFA tried to improve the consistency of data across some states (e.g., through the Tape-to-Tape project involving California, Georgia, Tennessee, Michigan, and New York). Recently, as part of the Medicaid Statistical Information System, HCFA created the Medicaid Valid Tapes File from information voluntarily submitted by states (HCFA 1995). As of December 1994, 26 states were participating, representing a range of geographic regions and population types (e.g., Alaska, California, Iowa, Kentucky, Mississippi, Montana, New Jersey, Vermont). States submit computer files containing information on all persons eligible for Medicaid and adjudicated claims paid (including inpatient, long-term care, and other claims). However, HCFA acknowledged that comparing data across states is impeded by Medicaid programmatic differences (HCFA 1995).

Problems also arise because individuals' eligibility for Medicaid fluctuates—individuals move on and off the Medicaid rolls (e.g., due to changes in financial or work status). In some states, individuals retain the same identification number during all episodes of Medicaid enrollment; in other states, a single recipient may be assigned multiple numbers. This "on again, off again" status of the Medicaid population complicates using these data for population-based studies, such as those performed using Medicare files.

Given these problems, relatively few studies use Medicaid claims files. Inconsistencies across states, the files' sheer size and complexity, and their lower visibility than Medicare files "may have caused some analysts to despair and decide that Medicaid data are hopeless" (Ku, Ellwood, and Klemm 1990, 35). Despite this, one particularly profitable area involves exploration of Medicaid pharmacy data (Ray and Griffin 1989; Gerstman et al. 1990; Bright, Avorn, and Everitt 1989). Medicaid's computerized pharmacy data file contains information on all prescriptions dispensed by pharmacies, including the beneficiary's identification number, prescription date, specific drug (often the National Drug Code number), quantity, prescribing physician, and reimbursement information. The detail of these pharmacy data and the large number of Medicaid enrollees make this file an attractive source of information about prescription drug use.

Data on drug prescriptions in the Medicaid file are reasonably reliable. One study found that 94 percent of pharmacy records matched claims in the Medicaid data set for 1,661 Medicaid beneficiaries (Bright, Avorn, and Everitt 1989). The Medicaid pharmacy data represent prescriptions that were actually filled (instead of prescriptions written but never obtained by the patient). Obviously, however, the Medicaid file does not report compliance with drug regimens (e.g., whether patients took medications as prescribed). In addition, as in most administrative databases, the quality of information not required for reimbursement, such as outpatient diagnoses indicating the indication for a drug, is often questionable (Ray and Griffin 1989).

One final consideration is that Medicaid data represent the experiences of the indigent—persons whose sources of risk may differ from those of more wealthy individuals. Therefore, risk-adjustment methods derived for other populations may not apply equally well to Medicaid recipients. Nonetheless, detailed information on this vulnerable population is an important strength of this database.

Private insurance claims files

As part of processing claims for services, private health insurance companies also create useful administrative databases (Garnick et al. 1996). However, these files are structured for the business purposes of the insurer, not researchers, and can sometimes be dauntingly complicated to handle. Nonetheless, some companies are restructuring these files for analytic use, and some allow researchers access to these generally private and proprietary data. Other insurers, including large self-insured companies, are submitting their data sets to companies that specialize in producing physician practice profiles or other comparative reports. These companies sometimes sell these large, multi-organizational databases to outside researchers after ensuring that the confidentiality of their clients (i.e., the groups that have provided data) is protected.

Private insurance claims offer information on service use by younger, employed adults and their children. Insurance claims files typically include details for each compensated service, including diagnosis and procedure codes, date and place of service, provider and patient identifiers, and charges. Apart from the technical and logistical hurdles of using private insurance claims files for research, however, questions arise concerning the scope and content of these files (Garnick et al. 1996). Claims files do not reflect all utilization of services by patients, generally because patients did not submit claims. This situation relates to the specific insurance provisions—such as whether the service is covered, the patient's deductible, level of coinsurance, and other sources of coverage for the service. Some insurers retain information only on paid claims, deleting information on services below the deductible or above the maximum benefit level. Information on use of prescription drugs is often incomplete: Drugs are commonly covered under separate policies and therefore appear in different claims files.

The content of private insurance claims reflects the mechanism for claims submission and payment (Garnick et al. 1996). For instance, providers may submit "bundled bills" for a series of services, possibly provided on different dates. Dates retained in the claim file may represent the date of payment or payment adjustment, not the date of service. Depending on billing procedures, the provider number listed on the claim can represent various entities—an individual physician, a group of doctors, or an institution. Private insurers frequently require fewer diagnoses on claims than do government payors, such as Medicare. A private insurance claim, even for a hospitalization, may contain only one or two diagnoses.

Because of these problems and difficulties gaining access to private insurance claims files, relatively few outsiders have used them. Nevertheless, creative use of these claims files can yield credible results. For example, Quam and colleagues (1993) found that by linking claims from outpatient medical visits with prescription drug claims, they accurately identified patients with hypertension.

Using Administrative Data to Examine Outcomes of Care

Although they were not originally intended for research, administrative databases have become the mainstay of an entire body of health services research studies (Connell, Diehr, and Hart 1987; Wennberg et al. 1987; Anderson et al. 1990; Center for Evaluative Clinical Studies 1996) and explorations of outcomes of care (Sullivan and Wilensky 1991; Mitchell et al. 1994; Lave et al. 1994). Even the legislation establishing AHCPR (Section

6103 of Omnibus Budget Reconciliation Act of 1989, P.L. 101–239, December 19, 1989) specified use of large administrative files:

> For facilitating research, the Secretary shall . . . (1) conduct and support reviews and evaluations of existing methodologies that utilize large databases in conducting such research . . . (5) conduct and support research and demonstrations on the use of claims data . . . in determining the outcomes, effectiveness, and appropriateness of such treatment, and (6) conduct and support supplementation of existing databases, including collection of new information, to enhance databases for research purposes. [Sec. 1142(c)]

However, after AHCPR spent millions of research dollars using administrative data to evaluate patient outcomes, assessments of their value have been mixed. The U.S. Congress's Office of Technology Assessment (OTA, itself eliminated by recent federal budget cuts) offered a particularly blunt appraisal:

> Contrary to the expectations expressed in the legislation establishing AHCPR and the mandates of the PORTs, *administrative databases generally have not proved useful in answering questions about the comparative effectiveness of alternative medical treatments.* [Italics mine] Administrative databases are very useful for descriptive purposes (e.g., exploring variations in treatment patterns), but the practical and theoretical limitations of this research technique usually prevent it from being able to provide credible answers regarding which technologies, among alternatives, work best. (OTA 1994, 6)

Tracing the roots of this disappointment leads quickly to measures of patient risk. As emphasized in Chapter 1, to assess medical effectiveness using patient outcomes one must first control for patients' risks. For capturing these risks, a database must contain credible clinical information along a range of dimensions (see Chapter 2). Many believe that administrative data are unable to capture patient risk factors adequately.

The IOM Committee on Regional Health Data Networks designated two critical attributes of databases—comprehensiveness (the scope and completeness of data elements pertaining to individual patients) and inclusiveness (the extent to which populations in geographic areas are represented) (Donaldson and Lohr 1994). Their assessment of comprehensiveness encompassed a range of variables, including routine demographic and administrative characteristics as well as health risk factors (e.g., smoking, seat belt use), health status and health-related quality of life, allergies, results of health screening, and past medical history (Donaldson and Lohr 1994, 45). Clearly, administrative data fall short on this attribute.

In current administrative files, most clinical information (beyond age and sex) is in the form of diagnoses coded using the ICD-9-CM (U.S. Public Health Service, Health Care Financing Administration 1980). In addition, many administrative data files derived from hospital reports, including

UB-92, use ICD-9-CM to code procedures. The next sections explore the potential and pitfalls of ICD-9-CM and its application, following a description of its background and structure.

ICD-9-CM and Its Evolution

Background

The ICD-9-CM emerged from international efforts to trace the epidemiology of disease and mortality. Its distant progenitor was conceived at the First Statistical Congress in Brussels in 1853, with a multinational agreement on the need for consistent worldwide coding of causes of death. Two years later in Paris, the congress adopted the general disease classification principles offered by William Farr (see Chapter 1), generally grouping conditions by anatomical site (Israel 1978). Following this basic outline, in 1893 the International Statistical Institute (the successor to the congress) produced the *Classification of Causes of Death*, suggesting that it be revised every ten years. This lexicon evolved into the *International Classification of Diseases* (ICD), and since the 1940s, the World Health Organization (WHO) has been its custodian. WHO convened the International Conference for the Ninth Revision in Geneva in 1977; ICD-9 went into effect January 1979.

Although the ninth revision contained more than three times as many codes as the eighth, some Americans believed that ICD-9 was not sufficiently detailed for use in this country. Chief among the critics was the Council on Clinical Classifications (CCC), composed of the Commission on Professional and Hospital Activities (CPHA) and five major specialty societies, including the American College of Physicians, American Psychiatric Association, and the American Academy of Pediatrics (Slee 1978). These clinicians argued for expanding the coding rubric, especially for pregnancy and childbirth outcomes and mental disorders. The CCC worked with National Center for Health Statistics (NCHS) staff to tailor ICD-9 for broadly defined clinical purposes. The resulting ICD-9-CM contains over 14,000 codes and achieves much of its detail by requiring use of a fifth digit for many diagnosis codes (see below).

In the United States, official coding guidelines are promulgated by the Central Office on ICD-9-CM, after approval by the ICD-9-CM Coordination-Maintenance Committee at NCHS, HCFA, the American Hospital Association (AHA), and the American Health Information Management Association—the "Cooperating Parties" (Sheehy 1991). The NCHS retains primary responsibility for overseeing changes in diagnosis coding; such changes must be coordinated with WHO decisions and must respond primarily to technical or scientific advances in medical knowledge. The procedures volume of ICD-9-CM is used primarily by the United States, and therefore changes in this arena are not channeled through WHO. Instead, HCFA has the principal authority for procedure coding revisions and updates, prompted both by technological advances and reimbursement considerations. The AHA publishes materials both for training ICD-9-CM coders as well as the quarterly newsletter *Coding Clinic* for ICD-9-CM, describing recent changes and providing guidance on proper coding techniques (Brown 1989).

Despite U.S. preferences, ICD-9, the ninth revision without clinical modification, is used by many nations around the world (now superseded by ICD-10 in some countries, see below). While ICD-9-CM codes were designed to collapse neatly into ICD-9 categories, difficulties may arise when using a classification scheme (such as the DRGs) that was derived from the more detailed, clinically modified codes. For example, an Australian study found that some DRGs were not created when applied to ICD-9 data because of missing fifth digits (e.g., DRG 27, traumatic stupor and coma with coma greater than one hour, required the specificity of the five-digit ICD-9-CM code to indicate the duration of coma) (Reid 1991). Thus, comparisons between the United States and other countries can be complicated by use of different ICD-based coding schemes (ICD-9 versus ICD-9-CM).

Organization and Format of ICD-9-CM

ICD-9-CM is organized in three volumes: Volume 1, *Diseases, Tabular List*; Volume 2, *Diseases, Alphabetic Index*; and Volume 3, *Procedures, Tabular List and Alphabetic Index* (U.S. Public Health Service, Health Care Financing Administration 1980).

Volume 1 presents the diagnosis codes in a tabular list, organized within 17 broad categories, some of which harken back to the original grouping by anatomic locations, such as blood and blood-forming organs; nervous system and sense organs; circulatory, digestive, or genitourinary systems; skin and subcutaneous tissue; and musculoskeletal system and connective tissue. Others represent types of conditions from a more pathophysiological perspective, such as infectious and parasitic diseases, neoplasms, congenital anomalies, and injury and poisoning. A final set of categories group a wide variety of conditions, as indicated by their titles: "complications of pregnancy, childbirth, and the puerperium," "certain conditions originating in the perinatal period," and "symptoms, signs, and ill-defined conditions."

ICD-9-CM achieves its diagnostic detail by mandating use of a fifth digit. All codes do not require the full five digits: Three-, four-, and five-digit codes are used as necessary, representing increasing levels of specificity.

For example, the code for pneumococcal pneumonia is three digits long (481), indicating that further detail is not needed. In contrast, the coding of diabetes mellitus spans the full five digits: The three-digit code 250 indicates the presence of diabetes mellitus, while the fourth digit reflects its manifestation (e.g., 250.1, diabetes with ketoacidosis), and the fifth digit specifies the type and whether the diabetes is under control (e.g., 250.13, diabetes with ketoacidosis, type I, uncontrolled).

In addition to the list of numeric codes, two "supplementary classifications" represent a variety of other factors affecting patients' health and other needs. Factors influencing health status and contact with health services are portrayed by codes up to five digits starting with the letter "V." V codes encompass a wide variety of entities, such as a personal history of malignancy of the bronchus and lung (V10.11); family history of trachea, bronchus, or lung cancer (V16.1); personal history of penicillin allergy (V14.0); noncompliance with medical treatment (V15.81); outcomes of delivery (such as single liveborn, V27.0); cardiac pacemaker in situ (V45.0); alcoholism in the family (V61.41); unemployment (V62.0); and refusal of treatment for reasons of religion or conscience (V62.6). Other V codes represent services as the reason for the encounter rather than diagnoses. Examples include routine infant or child health check (V20.2); prescription of oral contraceptives (V25.01); chemotherapy (V58.1); follow-up examination for treatment of a fracture (V67.4); examination for medicolegal reasons, such as blood alcohol tests (V70.4); and examination of eyes and vision (V72.0).

A second supplementary classification lists environmental events, circumstances, and conditions that have caused injury, poisoning, or other adverse events. These factors are represented by codes up to five digits starting with the letter "E." E codes aim to enhance the detail surrounding a patient's condition, but under current UHDDS guidelines, they cannot be listed as the reason for admission or principal diagnosis. Changes to UHDDS proposed in June 1992 (see below) suggest that additional spaces be provided specifically for E codes and to designate whether an injury or poisoning was the cause of the hospitalization (the principal diagnosis). E codes can convey detailed descriptive information, as suggested by the following examples: passenger injured in railway accident involving derailment without antecedent collision (E802.1), crew of commercial aircraft involved in accident at takeoff or landing (E840.2), accidental poisoning by benzodiazepine tranquilizer (E853.2), accidental injury from diving or jumping into a swimming pool (E883.0), excessive cold due to weather conditions (E901.0), criminal abandonment or neglect of infant (E968.4), child abuse by parent (E967.0), bite by centipede or venomous millipede (E905.4), accident involving powered lawn mower (E920.0), and suicide by a hunting rifle (E955.2).

The portion of the tabular list of diseases devoted to "symptoms, signs, and ill-defined conditions" also portrays a broad array of conditions. Coding rules stipulate that signs or symptoms linked definitively to a specific diagnosis generally should not be coded—codes for definitive diagnoses should supersede. Signs and symptoms should be listed, however, when a definitive diagnosis is not established (either because of timing, patients' failures to comply with diagnostic studies, or because a certain diagnosis remains elusive even after testing) or when the symptom represents "important problems in medical care." This series of codes also includes nonspecific indications of abnormal results of a range of diagnostic tests. Examples of these codes include alteration of consciousness (780.0), abnormality of gait (781.2), anorexia (783.0), undiagnosed cardiac murmurs (785.2), precordial chest pain (786.51), incontinence of feces (787.6), oliguria and anuria (788.5), elevated sedimentation rate (790.1), abnormal electrocardiogram (794.31), and sudden infant death syndrome (798.0).

Another interesting group of codes depicts complications resulting from medical care (codes 996–999). Many of these codes are fairly specific about the nature of the problem but not about its causality (e.g., "bad luck" versus negligence). Examples of these codes are mechanical complication due to a heart valve prosthesis (996.02) or an in-dwelling, urethral catheter (996.31); postoperative shock (998.0); accidental puncture or laceration during a procedure (998.2); postoperative infection (998.5); foreign body accidentally left during procedure (998.4); and ABO blood type incompatibility reaction (999.6).

Codes can sometimes enter policy debates. For example, on October 1, 1996, HCFA implemented a new V code (V667) for palliation. The leading advocate for this code was Christine K. Cassel, M.D., chairperson of a task force sponsored by the Milbank Memorial Fund, studying policy options that could improve care for dying patients. As she noted, along with HCFA's administrator, "We hope that the new diagnosis code will legitimize and encourage the use of palliative care" (Cassel and Vladeck 1996, 1233). Dr. Cassel voiced concerns that the role of hospitals in providing palliative care is often forgotten and thus implicitly devalued. In addition, concerns arise about payors' willingness to reimburse for palliative care in-hospital. "Physicians feel that if they really are honest about what's going on in the chart, that the payment will be disallowed and the hospital will be penalized," observed Dr. Cassel (Gianelli 1996, 5). Data using the V667 code will help evaluate the financial implications of palliative care. As another example of codes affecting policy, a small political storm erupted when a lobbying firm apparently representing tobacco interests questioned the E code for secondhand smoke adopted in 1993 (Borzo 1996a). They appealed to the federal Office of Management and Budget (OMB) that ICD-9-CM should be reviewed under the Paperwork Reduction Act. The OMB agreed and has required the Department of Health and Human Services to examine some codes and defend Medicare billing forms that contain space for E codes.

Thus, ICD-9-CM contains codes for many conditions that are technically not "diseases" (Table 3.3)—the name "International Classification of *Diseases*" is a misnomer. According to Vergil N. Slee, the former president of both the CPHA and CCC, this was intentional. ICD-9 specifically included

> ... "problems" that are not diagnoses, many more symptoms, and "other" reasons for seeking health care ... It provides a dual classification, that is, an alternative code for placing certain conditions in classes determined by either cause or manifestation, depending on the interests of the user. (Slee 1978, 425)

ICD-9-CM contains even more such descriptive information and greater detail.

Given this diversity, by putting together the full range of ICD-9-CM codes creatively and with clinical understanding, one can begin to form a fairly broad picture of risk factors and patients' clinical status. For example, Exhibit 3.1 depicts the discharge abstract information taken from a patient admitted to a California hospital in 1987 (Iezzoni et al. 1994a). From this detail, the following story emerges:

> This 64-year-old woman with a history of bowel resection came to the emergency room and was admitted emergently for surgical repair of a malfunctioning enterostomy. On the first hospital day, she underwent repair of a pericolostomy hernia and lysis of peritoneal adhesions. She developed postoperative gastrointestinal complications, and on the sixth hospital day again received surgery for lysis of adhesions. She developed a postoperative infection and became acutely unstable. Starting on the seventh hospital day, she required monitoring of her central venous pressure and pulmonary artery wedge pressures. She also required endotracheal intubation and mechanical respiration. By the 23rd hospital day, however, she had recovered sufficiently to be discharged with home health service support.

Creatively combining ICD-9-CM codes information to create clinical pictures is the approach taken by the staged version of Disease Staging and by PMC (see Chapters 1 and 2).

Some find the detail of ICD-9-CM overwhelming and seek groupings of the codes. For example, the Center for General Health Services Intramural Research at AHCPR (Elixhauser, Andrews, and Fox 1993; Elixhauser and McCarthy 1996) created its "Clinical Classifications for Health Policy Research" by grouping numeric diagnosis codes, V codes, and procedure codes and by eliminating codes that were too general (e.g., V15.81, noncompliance with medical treatment; 780.7, malaise and fatigue). Using the 1987 version of ICD-9-CM, diagnosis codes were first grouped into 18 body

Table 3.3   Type of Information Contained in ICD-9-CM Codes

Type of Information	*Number*	*Code Name*
Clinical diagnosis	250.53	Type I diabetes mellitus with ophthalmic manifestations, uncontrolled
	410.01	AMI of anterolateral wall, initial episode of care
Pathological process	414.01	Coronary atherosclerosis of native coronary artery
	324.0	Intracranial abscess
Symptoms	569.42	Anal or rectal pain
	780.7	Malaise and fatigue
Physical findings	342.0	Flaccid hemiplegia
	786.7	Abnormal chest sounds
Laboratory or other test findings	794.31	Abnormal electrocardiogram
	790.2	Abnormal glucose tolerance test
Severity indicators	427.5	Cardiac arrest
	518.81	Respiratory failure
Potential quality indicators	968.3	Poisoning by intravenous anesthetics
	998.7	Acute reaction to foreign substance accidentally left during a procedure
Psychological factors	308.0	Acute reaction to stress, predominant disturbance of emotions
	V15.4	Psychological trauma
Cognitive factors	290.0	Senile dementia, uncomplicated
	290.13	Presenile dementia with depressive features
Substance abuse	304.21	Continuous cocaine dependency
	303.93	Chronic alcoholism in remission
Personal social factors	V61.1	Marital problems
	V62.0	Unemployment
	V60.0	Lack of housing
Functional status	344.1	Paraplegia
	V53.8	Wheelchair
External environmental factors	E900.0	Excessive heat due to weather conditions
	E965.0	Assault by a handgun

systems and 650 "detailed diagnosis categories"; these were further combined into 185 mutually exclusive "summary diagnosis categories." The 3,500 procedure codes were grouped into 172 mutually exclusive procedure categories. The AHCPR investigators found that these groupings yielded

Exhibit 3.1 Discharge Abstract Information for a Patient Hospitalized in California in 1987

Patient Data	Hospital Data	Admission Data	Disposition Data
ID: XXXXX	Hospital ID: XXXXX	Length of stay: 23 days	Disposition: home health service
Age: 64	Zip code: XXXXX	Admission type: emergency	DRG: 150 (peritoneal adhesiolysis with complication or comorbidity)
Sex: female		Source: emergency room	
Race: white		Total charges: $35,201	
Residence zip code: XXXXX		Payer: Medicare	

DIAGNOSIS AND PROCEDURE CODES AND DAYS FROM ADMISSION TO PROCEDURE

Diagnosis Codes		Procedure Codes		Days
5696	enterostomy malfunction	4642	pericolostomy hernia repair	0
56081	intestinal adhesion with obstruction	545	peritoneal adhesiolysis	0
311	depressive disorder NEC	9112	culture – peritoneum	0
9974	surgical complication-gastrointestinal tract	545	peritoneal adhesiolysis	6
9985	postoperative infection	9608	insert (naso-)intestinal tube	6
		9112	culture – peritoneum	6
		8964	pulmonary artery wedge monitor	7
		8962	central venous pressure monitoring	7
		8763	small bowel series	6
		8744	routine chest x-ray	6
		8819	abdominal x-ray NEC	6
		9604	insert endotracheal tube	6
		9392	mechanical respiratory assistance NEC	0
		9052	culture – blood	0
		9043	culture and sensitivity – lower respiratory tract	0
		8952	electrocardiogram	0

adequate sample sizes using hospital discharge data and a manageable number of categories for analysis.

Clinical Content of ICD-9-CM Codes

Despite the detail implied in the ICD-9-CM codes, questions remain about the clinical definitions of specific ICD-9-CM codes. Neither the *Tabular List* (Volume 1) nor the *Alphabetic Index* (Volume 2) offers clinical descriptions of the conditions represented by ICD-9-CM codes. For example, ICD-9-CM includes 39 four- and five-digit codes for different types of anemia, such as iron deficiency anemia secondary to inadequate dietary iron intake (280.1), thalassemia (282.4), autoimmune hemolytic anemia (283.0), and constitu-tional aplastic anemia (284.0). But nowhere does it specify what level of hematocrit justifies an anemia diagnosis. Similarly, the respiratory failure code (518.81) does not indicate what level of arterial oxygenation, respiratory rate or pattern, or other clinical abnormality merits that "diagnosis."

Because of the absence of operational clinical definitions, assignment of ICD-9-CM codes is highly variable. Coders are instructed to use the terminology noted by the physicians in the medical record. Physicians, however, do not employ a universal or consistent lexicon in charting medical records or other medicolegal documents (e.g., death certificates), further hampering efforts to obtain coherent clinical pictures of patients from diagnosis codes. For example, the same clinical condition was labeled "pulmonary emphysema" in the United States and "chronic bronchitis" in the United Kingdom (Feinstein 1988); Medicare hospital claims data from 1982 showed that "coronary atherosclerosis" was coded more frequently in North Carolina and "angina pectoris" was coded more frequently in New Jersey—the first code representing underlying pathology and the second denoting a clinical syndrome (Iezzoni and Moskowitz 1984). This problem raises serious reservations about the utility of ICD-9-CM diagnostic data for epidemiologic studies, as well as concerns about the precise clinical picture of patients with various ICD-9-CM codes.

In addition, despite the large number of codes, ICD-9-CM does not include certain patient characteristics known to have significant prognostic implications. As stated by Feinstein (1988, 2272):

> The mono-axial orientation of the taxonomy offers a single name for each disease, but prognosis and therapy in modern medicine depend on multiaxial consideration of such cogent features as decompensation of organ systems, severity of illness, rapidity of disease progression, and existence of major comorbid ailments.

For example, the anemia codes merely indicate that anemia was present; they do not specify the hematocrit level or how rapidly anemia developed.

At the other end of the acuity and severity spectrum, ICD-9-CM also fails to reflect the clinical problems typically encountered in an outpatient, primary care practice. One study at Group Health Cooperative of Puget Sound found that physicians were unhappy with the ICD-9-CM representation of an ambulatory care patient's "problem" 45 percent of the time (Payne, Murphy, and Salazar 1993, 654).

In fairness, ICD-9-CM *does* contain many codes for indicating comorbid disease. A number of investigators have developed comorbidity indices for administrative data using these ICD-9-CM codes (Deyo, Cherkin, and Ciol 1992; Romano, Roos, and Jollis 1993a, 1993b; Ghali et al. 1996). In addition, ICD-9-CM offers some severity indicators, such as toxic diffuse goiter with thyroid storm (242.01), intrinsic asthma with status asthmaticus (493.11), and hepatic coma (572.2). However, ICD-9-CM does not specify the clinical context in which these codes should be recorded—for example, which respiratory pattern and arterial blood gas results denote that status asthmaticus is present. In addition, nowhere does ICD-9-CM consider rapidity of disease progression or the interaction of comorbidities. ICD-9-CM also offers little insight into such dimensions of risk as physical or psychological functioning and socioeconomic factors, although V codes provide some information (see above).

Therefore, while ICD-9-CM contains numerous codes representing a variety of clinical conditions, the meaning of specific codes in individual cases is often elusive. The lack of precise clinical definitions encourages variability in the application of codes. Inconsistencies and imprecision in the terms physicians use to document the medical record certainly collude to increase coding variability. Physicians are not trained in ICD-9-CM, and "Many medical record practitioners would say physicians' documentation is the true source of coding problems" (Sheehy 1991, 46). Other sources of concern are the current context of diagnosis coding and questions about motivations for assigning ICD-9-CM codes.

Context of ICD-9-CM Diagnostic Coding and Sources of Error

> Until very recently, the coding function was largely ignored by all but the technical experts and a few scholarly researchers. It was a function of the medical record department; and lacking any evidence to the contrary, it was considered to be a clerical task equivalent to typing and filing. (Weigel and Lewis 1991, 70)

ICD codes have long been used to specify causes of death and, since the introduction of UHDDS in 1974, for hospital indexing and planning health services. The entire context of diagnostic coding in the United States changed, however, with the 1983 enactment of Medicare's prospective payment system, based on DRGs. In 1981 an ominous warning appeared in the *New England Journal of Medicine*:

> This article is intended to provide a case report of "DRG creep," a new phenomenon that is expected to occur in epidemic proportions in the 1980s. DRG creep may be defined as a deliberate and systematic shift in a hospital's reported case mix in order to improve reimbursement . . . Minor diagnostic nuances and slight imprecisions of wording have little practical clinical importance, yet under DRG reimbursement they would have major financial consequences . . . It is hoped that hospitals will refrain from disseminating the more virulent forms of DRG creep; however, the potential for a broad spectrum of manifestations certainly exists. (Simborg 1981, 1602, 1604)

Through DRGs, ICD-9-CM was suddenly vested with powers for which it was never designed—becoming the basis for hospital reimbursement (Vladeck 1984; Fetter et al. 1980). Under DRG-based payment, ICD-9-CM codes translate directly into payment dollars, and thus the demands placed both on the codes and coders have broadened and intensified. New words, such as "optimization" and "maximization," entered the coding vocabulary. Hospital administrators now eagerly focus on coding practices, hoping to maximize their facility's reimbursement. Some hospitals have reorganized, moving medical record departments from general administration to financial divisions (Waterstraat, Barlow, and Newman 1990). The declaration of one coding expert may be closer to present truth than hyperbole: "Coded data is [*sic*] the linchpin that secures a changing mosaic of American healthcare delivery" (Sheehy 1991, 49).

For medical outcomes studies and the development of models of patient risk, concerns about ICD-9-CM codes stem not only from the clinical content of the classification but also from how it is applied. Are diagnosis codes complete, reliable, and accurate?

Steps in coding

In the current payment environment, the diagnosis list is not the only end point of coding—sequencing or ordering the diagnosis codes (differentiating the principal from secondary diagnoses) significantly affects DRG assignment and thus hospital reimbursement. The two major steps in coding a hospital admission are, first, specifying the pertinent diagnoses, and second, determining their order.

Deciding which diagnoses to code requires a review of the medical record, searching for diagnoses established or entertained by the physicians caring for the patient. Coders occasionally need to contact physicians to determine whether particular diagnoses are indicated. Coding guidelines published by the AHA note that physicians do not always list all other pertinent diagnoses in their discharge summary, and they urge coders to review the entire medical record to identify additional relevant conditions (Brown 1989). Consultation with physicians about additional diagnoses is portrayed as the best way to obtain "a more complete listing." ICD-9-CM coding guidelines for the UHDDS require the coding of "all diagnoses that affect the current hospital stay," including the principal diagnosis and "other diagnoses" as follows:

> *Other diagnoses* are designated and defined as all conditions that coexist at the time of admission, that develop subsequently, or that affect the treatment received and/or length of stay. Diagnoses that relate to an earlier episode that have no bearing on the current hospital stay are excluded. (Brown 1989, 22)

In different settings, different rules apply concerning which codes are allowable. For example, some insurance carriers refuse to pay based on codes from Chapter 16 of the ICD-9-CM, "Symptoms, Signs, and Ill-Defined Conditions" (O'Gara 1990). After all codes are established, sequencing occurs. The rules of sequencing are different for different data sets. In the context of UHDDS and Medicare's DRG system, this involves deciding which diagnosis is principal, or responsible for the patient's admission to the hospital. The principal diagnosis is used to assign most cases to a Major Diagnostic Category and then to assign medical DRGs. As noted above, the VA PTF targets the primary diagnosis, or the condition most related to the length of hospitalization. If a patient dies during a hospitalization, the cause of death could be the principal or primary diagnosis, but this is not necessarily so. Cause of death is determined based on mortality classification guidelines from ICD's original use (O'Gara 1990). For Medicare and UHDDS, no specific rule is stipulated for ordering the other diagnoses (Jencks 1992), although the guidelines indicate that "The more significant ones should be sequenced early in the list if there is any likelihood that data entries will be limited" (Brown 1989, 23), as in truncating secondary diagnoses at four codes.

Sequencing can have a profound effect on reimbursement. For example, in his case report warning about the impending epidemic of "DRG creep," Simborg (1981) looked at the financial effect of resequencing decisions at his own institution, the University of California at San Francisco. For 159 patients undergoing major surgery with chronic nephritis, chronic pyelonephritis, or another renal condition listed as a secondary diagnosis, switching the first- and second-listed diagnoses would have shifted total costs by $800,000.

From a clinical perspective, the correct ordering of diagnosis codes is not always obvious. This problem is exacerbated because the DRGs do not consider the clinical overlap among codes relating to different aspects of patients' presentations. For example, coronary atherosclerosis is a pathologic process leading to the clinical syndrome of angina pectoris, manifest by the symptom chest pain (Iezzoni and Moskowitz 1986). The DRGs assign codes representing these three interrelated clinical levels to different DRGs: 132 and 133 (coronary atherosclerosis with and without complications or comorbidities), 140 (angina pectoris), and 143 (chest pain). As suggested by the clinical vignettes in Table 3.4, different DRGs can apply depending on what type of clinical information is listed first. Importantly, one source of confusion between physicians and medical record coders often results from choosing among such clinically interrelated ICD-9-CM codes. From the physician's perspective, all codes accurately represent some aspect of the patient's presentation; the ICD-9-CM coding guidelines that direct sequencing choices may appear arcane and inappropriately dogmatic.

Not surprisingly, therefore, anecdotal information suggests that the productive dialogue between hospital coders and physicians envisioned by the coding guidelines is infrequent. Some hospitals have tried to convey a sense of urgency to their physicians about diagnosis coding. For example, a hospital in New Jersey periodically posts examples in the physicians' lounge documenting the financial effect of coding decisions, such as these:

- If the infectious etiology is not specified for a pneumonia, code 486 will be assigned (pneumonia, organism unspecified), and the case must be grouped in either DRG 89, simple pneumonia and pleurisy with complications or comorbidities (C.C.'s) ($3,497) or DRG 90 without C.C.'s ($2,185). In contrast, if the infectious cause is known and involves selected bacterial agents (e.g., Pseudomonas), specifying that code (482.1) will prompt assignment of DRG 79 or 80, respiratory infections and inflammations with and without C.C.'s ($5,344 and $3,020, respectively).

- Complications or comorbidities often increase payment and should be coded. For example, noting a coexisting chronic lung condition can reassign a patient admitted for acute bacterial bronchitis from DRG 97, bronchitis and asthma without C.C.'s ($1,935) to DRG 96, bronchitis and asthma with C.C.'s ($2,837).

- Sequencing of diagnoses is also important. If a patient is admitted for a urinary tract infection that has seeded the bloodstream, coding urinary tract infection (599.0) as the principal diagnosis with sepsis (038.42, Escherichia coli septicemia) as a secondary diagnosis will result in assignment of DRG 320, urinary tract infection with C.C. ($3,006). Listing the sepsis first prompts assignment of DRG 416, septicemia ($4,592).

As these examples demonstrate, hospitals can benefit financially by assigning more specific codes, making sure that coexisting conditions are

Table 3.4   Examples of Clinical Overlap Among ICD-9-CM Codes

Clinical Presentation	Symptom, Health Problem, or Severity of Illness	Clinical Diagnosis or Pathologic Process
Patient brought into emergency room with weakness of right arm and leg and aphasia; history suggestive of cerebrovascular thrombosis	ICD-9-CM code 342.9 (hemiplegia not otherwise specified) leading to DRG 12 (degenerative nervous system disorders); RW, 0.9550	ICD-9-CM code 434.00 (cerebral thrombosis) leading to DRG 14* (specific cerebrovascular disorders except transient ischemic attack); RW, 1.2160
Patient presents to outpatient clinic, complaining of fatigue and weight loss; examination shows occult blood in stool and low hematocrit; patient is admitted and found to have colon cancer	ICD-9-CM code 280.0 (iron deficiency anemia secondary to chronic blood loss) leading to DRG 395 (red blood cell disorders age > 17); RW, 0.7881	ICD-9-CM code 153.6 (malignant neoplasm of ascending colon) leading to DRG 172* (digestive malignancy with complication or comorbidity); RW, 1.2990
Patient brought into emergency room unresponsive and with depressed respirations; gastric aspirate shows traces of barbiturates	ICD-9-CM code 780.01 (coma) leading to DRG 23* (nontraumatic stupor and coma); RW, 0.8202	ICD-9-CM code 967.0 (barbiturate poisoning) leading to DRG 449 (toxic effects of drugs age > 17 with complication or comorbidity); RW, 0.7889
Patient brought into emergency room in respiratory failure; sputum culture yields *Staphylococcus aureus*, and chest radiograph shows pneumonia	ICD-9-CM code 518.81 (respiratory failure) leading to DRG 87 (pulmonary edema and respiratory failure); RW, 1.3597	ICD-9-CM code 482.4 (staphylococcal pneumonia) leading to DRG 79* (respiratory infections and inflammations age > 17 with complication or comorbidity); RW, 1.7510
Patient is brought into emergency room in shock; evaluation shows bleeding esophageal varices; history confirms alcohol abuse	ICD-9-CM code 785.50 (shock not otherwise specified) leading to DRG 127* (heart failure and shock); RW, 1.0150	ICD-9-CM code 456.0 (esophageal varices with bleeding) leading to DRG 174 (gastrointestinal hemorrhage with complication or comorbidity); RW, 0.9794

Source: Adapted from Iezzoni and Moskowitz 1986. DRG represents Version 10.0 (October 1, 1992–September 30, 1993). DRG relative weights (RW) from *Federal Register,* September 1, 1992, 57 (170): 39879–39893.

*DRG with higher relative weight.

recorded, and paying attention to the order in which codes are listed—but they need their physicians' help to do so.

From the mid-1980s until September 1995, the government made physicians participate actively in ensuring the accuracy of discharge diagnoses. Federal regulations required that physicians "attest" to the accuracy of the discharge diagnoses of Medicare patients prior to hospital submission of bills for payment. The signed statement had to appear in the medical record and declare the following:

> I certify that the narrative descriptions of the principal and secondary diagnoses and the major procedures performed are accurate and complete to the best of my knowledge. [42 CFR §412.46(a)]

However, in July 1995, Vice President Al Gore described the attestation requirements as demeaning and duplicative of discharge summaries already required of doctors. Mr. Gore eliminated the attestation form in September 1995 as part of his broader effort to simplify federal health program paperwork, estimating a savings in physician time of 200,000 hours annually ("Feds Hear Medicine's Plea" 1995, 26). Nonetheless, one year later, worries resurfaced about potential upcoding. Federal regulators were especially concerned about consultants hired by hospitals explicitly to maximize reimbursement through "enhancing" coding. In addition, Medicare's peer review organizations (PROs), which had been required to validate coding, were no longer required to do so because of programmatic changes instituted in the early 1990s. In Philadelphia, the assistant U.S. attorney planned to investigate hospitals coding respiratory and cardiac illnesses at unusually high rates to increase their Medicare reimbursements (Johnsson 1996).

Coding guidelines

The guidelines governing application of diagnosis codes are sometimes arcane and confusing and may have unexpected consequences. One example is the "rule out" rule as stated in the *Coding Clinic for ICD-9-CM* in March–April 1985. For inpatients, abstractors are instructed to code a diagnosis accompanied by such phrases as "rule out," "suspect," or "question" as if the disease had actually occurred in that patient.

AMI was especially susceptible to the "rule out" rule and other coding guidelines. The guidelines for coding AMI had stated that this diagnosis could be coded up to eight weeks following the acute event; AMI could also be coded if it was designated "rule out." This guideline produced unintended consequences, as shown by a study of patients admitted in 1984 and 1985 to 15 hospitals in metropolitan Boston (Iezzoni et al. 1988). Of the 1,003 cases examined, 260 did not meet the clinical criteria for AMI. At tertiary teaching hospitals, 41.7 percent of cases failed to qualify, compared with 9.1 percent at nonteaching institutions. In a large fraction of cases, although an AMI was explicitly "ruled out," the code was nonetheless assigned. An additional 66 teaching hospital cases did not qualify because the patient had been admitted only for coronary angiography after an uneventful, postmyocardial infarction course, with almost one-third of these infarctions occurring five to eight weeks previously (Iezzoni et al. 1988).

On October 1, 1989, coding guidelines for AMI changed, adding a fifth digit specifically to indicate whether the hospitalization was for initial or subsequent treatment of the AMI. In the field, however, change was not immediate—coding modifications typically require time to diffuse throughout the system. For example, Hannan et al. (1992) observed in New York state that in the 15 months following adoption of the AMI coding change 45 percent of codes did not include the fifth digit. A study of 974 patients coded as having AMIs admitted to California hospitals in 1990 and 1991 found that 7.6 percent failed clinical criteria for AMI and 23.7 percent had a "possible" AMI (most of the "possible" cases had either chest pain with borderline cardiac enzymes or positive enzymes without chest pain) (Wilson, Smoley, and Werdegar 1996, 14–23).

A further complication is that "rule out" diagnoses are not permitted for outpatients. Official coding guidelines stipulate that, for outpatients, only confirmed diagnoses should be coded—suspected, probable, and rule-out diagnoses may not be listed. For outpatients, codes must be assigned to their highest level of specificity; for example, if the underlying diagnosis or pathophysiology is unknown, the outpatient diagnosis code must indicate only what is confirmed, such as symptoms or signs (e.g., chest pain). While Medicare and some other payors follow these guidelines, others do not. Some insurers require healthcare practitioners to report presumptive diagnoses justifying tests or services contradicting the guidelines. This inconsistent application of coding guidelines further confuses the meaning of diagnoses listed on outpatient claims.

In June 1992, the committee examining revisions of the UHDDS proposed dropping the "rule out" rule, suggesting its elimination would yield more accurate information (National Committee on Vital and Health Statistics 1992). Furthermore, eliminating that rule would make diagnosis coding for hospitalizations consistent with that for ambulatory visits. Nevertheless, because it is still promulgated by the international body overseeing ICD, the "rule out" rule remains in effect in the United States.

Types of errors in ICD-9-CM coding

ICD-9-CM coding guidelines clearly require complete coding of all conditions addressed during the hospital stay. However, they acknowledge that complete coding may require thorough medical record reviews, a time-consuming and expensive process dependent on the motivation and medical knowledge of individual coders—factors that heighten concern about variability in the extent and quality of coding across institutions and across individual coders. The major sources of diagnosis-coding errors are misspecification, miscoding, incorrect sequencing decisions, and simple clerical mistakes such as transposing digits (Waterstraat, Barlow, and Newman 1990; Hsia et al. 1988).

Misspecification encompasses errors typically resulting from physician failures to document final diagnoses, such as reporting a diagnosis not supported by the medical record, not documenting diagnoses in the medical record, or selecting an incorrect principal diagnosis. Despite physician culpability in misspecification, medical record coders bear some responsibility. In some hospitals, coders are instructed to review the entire medical record before assigning diagnosis codes, and discussions with attending physicians can reduce misspecification. Miscoding refers to the listing of diagnoses not attested to by the attending physician, incorrect application of coding rules, or selection of inappropriately vague codes such as signs or symptoms. Incorrect sequencing—a common cause of erroneous DRG assignment—results when codes are listed as the principal diagnosis when they are probably secondary diagnoses. Finally, clerical mistakes produce a small fraction of coding errors.

Results of Applying ICD-9-CM

Evidence Concerning Errors in Diagnosis Coding

Several studies conducted by the National Academy of Science, Institute of Medicine (IOM) in the late 1970s found alarmingly high rates of inaccurate diagnostic coding (Institute of Medicine 1977a, 1977b). In reviewing the reliability of 1,974 hospital discharge abstracts, they found that the abstracts were almost 100 percent accurate for basic information, such as admission and discharge dates, patient age and sex, and payor. However, agreement on the principal diagnosis between hospitals' reports and the IOM reabstraction was only 65.2 percent (Institute of Medicine 1977a). A major source of this disagreement was vagaries in diagnosis codes, coding guidelines, and sequencing rules pertaining to the coding nomenclature of the time (the eighth revision of ICD, or ICD-8). For 10.7 percent of all cases reviewed, discrepancies were found between hospitals' reports of principal diagnosis and the IOM coding, but the correct code could not be determined. These discrepancies resulted from legitimate professional disagreements in interpreting the medical record and pertinent coding guidelines, particularly problems in sequencing diagnoses (76.5 percent of indeterminate cases).

The IOM study also found that coding accuracy varied by condition, with these diagnoses coded with the indicated accuracy: hypertrophy of tonsils and adenoids, 97.0 percent; cataract, 94.3 percent; hernia without obstruction, 89.1 percent; hernia with obstruction, 81.0 percent; low back pain, 56.3 percent; and chronic ischemic heart disease, 30.2 percent (Institute of Medicine 1977a). For most diagnoses with low accuracy rates, the chief cause of discrepancy involved erroneous sequencing—listing as principal diagnoses a condition that was actually secondary. The IOM investigators concluded: "One must assume that abstracted hospital data contain errors and use them with caution. The seriousness of the error depends on the purpose to which the data are applied" (Institute of Medicine 1977a, 49). Thus, the IOM study provided prescient warnings about the expanded role of discharge abstract data initiated in the early 1980s.

Changes in the case-mix index

One barometer reflecting the effect of coding practices is the Medicare case-mix index (CMI), which reflects the average relative weight of DRGs assigned to hospitalized patients. The CMI is tracked annually by watchdog groups such as the Prospective Payment Assessment Commission (ProPAC), and it has risen continually since Medicare's prospective payment system (PPS) went into effect in October 1983. Higher CMIs represent higher aggregate hospital charges related to the DRG mix of patients. The CMI thus translates directly into governmental payments to hospitals: Each 1 percent increment in the CMI equals $400 million more in hospital revenues and thus higher government expenditures (Carter, Newhouse, and Relles 1990). The CMI has risen 32.4 percent cumulatively from the first year of PPS through 1996 (ProPAC 1996, 61). The largest increases occurred in the two years after PPS was introduced (fiscal years 1984 and 1985) and were a major cause of cost increases for federal hospital payments. In the first two years of PPS, expenditures per hospital discharge rose 18.5 percent and 10.5 percent, respectively, with payments rising by 5 to 6 percent annually up to the ninth year of PPS.

The increases in the CMI suggest that Simborg's 1981 prophesy of DRG creep did come true, but the exact sources of observed changes in DRG mix are not easily proven. The central question is whether coding changes represent "creep" or "optimization." "Creep" implies wilful disregard of coding rules, whereas "optimization" suggests taking lawful advantage of the vagaries of coding and DRG assignment described above. Although some portion of the CMI increases are attributable to code creep, other influential factors include changes in practice patterns (e.g., shifting inpatient to outpatient care, substituting surgical for medical services, developing and diffusing new technologies), heightened oversight of admissions to acute care facilities, aging of the population, hospital structural changes, and changes in the Medicare hospital payment program (Goldfarb and Coffey 1992).

Several studies of CMI increases have assessed the effect of coding changes relative to "real" causes. Investigators at the RAND Corporation tried to "decompose" CMI increases into "true" changes versus coding changes, using data from the organization that assesses PRO performance, the "SuperPRO" (Carter, Newhouse, and Relles 1990, 1991). Until recently, each of approximately 50 PROs across the country had been required to validate ICD-9-CM diagnosis coding for Medicare inpatients (Lohr and Walker 1990). SuperPRO medical record technicians, assisted by physicians, reabstracted a random sample of cases reviewed by each PRO. The RAND studies compared the ICD-9-CM codes assigned by the SuperPRO and the hospitals to determine the extent of DRG creep. The first study found that two-thirds of the 2.4 percent increase in the CMI between 1986 and 1987 was real, with one-third resulting from coding practice changes and modifications in the DRG classification system (Carter, Newhouse, and Relles 1990). A subsequent study, examining the causes of a 3.3 percent increase in the CMI between 1987 and 1988, found that half of the increment was real (Carter, Newhouse, and Relles 1991).

Goldfarb and Coffey (1992) endeavored to disentangle real changes from coding changes in the CMI by distinguishing the effects of Medicare's PPS and its policies from causes due to secular trends, such as shifts in practice patterns and aging of the population (Figure 3.1). They obtained data from 235 short-term, general, nonfederal hospitals from 1980 to 1986 and found that the percent of CMI increases attributable to coding changes varied by fiscal year (FY): FY82, 18.8 percent; FY83, 67.9 percent; FY84, 63.4 percent; FY85, 73.3 percent; and FY86, 42.5 percent. The dramatic decrease between FY85 and FY86 suggested that hospitals had largely completed efforts to improve their coding practices by 1986. In fact, in the tenth and eleventh years of PPS the CMI grew slowly, contributing to the smallest two-year growth in payments since PPS was enacted (3.6 and 3.5 percent respectively) (ProPAC 1996, 64–65).

Although coding changes have contributed significantly to increases in Medicare's CMI, this does not necessarily mean that these changes represent wilful errors, blatant inaccuracies, or fraud. Some changes represent more complete—and therefore accurate—coding of secondary diagnoses and procedures. The impetus for these changes relates directly to modifications in the DRG algorithm. For example, the 1988 DRG Grouper eliminated splits of DRGs based on age above and below 69 years. From that version forward, DRG pairs were split based on the presence of C.C.'s only, not age (with the exception of DRGs pertaining expressly to pediatric populations and a handful split for other reasons, such as patient

Figure 3.1   Sources of Changes in the Medicare Case-Mix Index

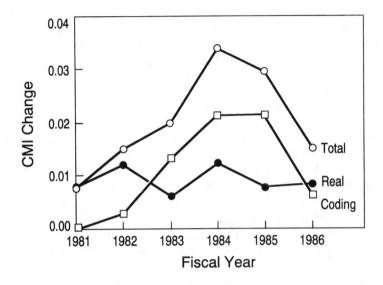

Source: Division of Provider Studies, Center for General Health Services Intramural Research, Agency for Health Care Policy and Research.

death). The 1988 DRG Grouper also introduced special DRGs for patients receiving ventilator support. Not surprisingly, a considerable portion of the CMI changes between 1987 and 1988 was traceable to increased listing of secondary diagnoses representing C.C.'s and ventilator support codes (Carter, Newhouse, and Relles 1991). Despite the legitimacy of many of these coding changes, however, the linkage of ICD-9-CM codes to hospital payment leaves a lingering uneasiness about their clinical credibility.

Studies of coding accuracy

Since the IOM studies, the major nationwide studies of coding accuracy have been performed by the legal overseer of the Medicare program, the Office of the Inspector General (OIG) at the Department of Health and Human Services, and have focused on the coding performance explicitly pertaining to DRG assignment.

The first OIG study sampled Medicare admissions between October 1, 1984, and March 31, 1985, from 239 hospitals across the country (Hsia et al. 1988). Photocopied medical records were reviewed by an OIG contractor, and DRGs originally assigned by the hospitals were compared to those derived from the reabstracted data. Of the 7,050 cases in the final sample, 1,374 changed DRG assignment based on the OIG reabstraction—an average of 20.8 percent changes after reweighting of results by hospital size. Changes were much more common in small (fewer than 100 beds) hospitals (23.6 percent) compared to large (300 beds or more) hospitals (16.6 percent). Most importantly, 61.7 percent of discrepancies financially favored the hospitals (i.e., hospitals had assigned DRGs with higher relative weights), a rate observed across hospitals of all sizes. Of the 1,374 "errors" in hospitals' DRG assignment, 661 were caused by physician misspecification of diagnoses, and 373 were due to problems with sequencing the diagnosis codes. The OIG investigators calculated that, given the identified errors in DRG assignment, HCFA overpaid hospitals by $300 million in fiscal year 1985.

The OIG study (Hsia et al. 1988) focused on the effect of coding problems on DRG assignment. Fisher et al. (1992) reanalyzed these data, looking at the concordance between principal diagnoses and procedures as coded by the hospitals and the OIG contractor. Agreement was assessed for groups of clinically homogeneous codes; within each group, agreement was then measured at the individual ICD-9-CM code level. For principal diagnoses, agreement between hospitals' codes and those assigned by the OIG was 78.2 percent for codes truncated at three digits and 71.5 percent for codes at the fourth digit. When order of the diagnosis code was ignored, however, levels of agreement varied considerably across conditions. For example, the proportion of codes identified by the OIG team that were originally listed by the hospital ranged from 0.58 for peripheral vascular disease to 0.97 for breast cancer. Rates were in the 0.82 to 0.85 range for prostate cancer, diabetes, hypertension, chronic obstructive lung disease, chronic renal failure, and rheumatoid arthritis. As had the IOM, Fisher and colleagues concluded that diagnosis coding is more accurate for some conditions than for others.

The OIG repeated its DRG validation study using 2,451 patient records from 1988 admissions of Medicare beneficiaries (Hsia et al. 1992). In this sample, 14.7 percent of records contained errors that changed DRG assignment. In contrast to the 1985 study, however, coding errors did not disproportionately favor the hospitals: 50.7 percent of errors financially benefited the hospital. Misspecification remained the most common cause of errors (62.9 percent of errors), but the proportion of misspecifications that financially favored the hospitals decreased significantly from the 1985 level. In contrast, missequencing continued to overreimburse hospitals. Hsia et al. (1992, 899) concluded:

> . . . The Prospective Payment Assessment Commission's annual recommendation to Congress for changes in the standardized amount usually included a discount for DRG creep. The present study suggests that regardless of the reasons for decreasing creep, future changes in the standardized amount may not require adjustment for DRG creep.

Despite these encouraging results, it is important to note that this 1988 OIG analysis pertained only to accuracy as it related to DRG assignment. The study by Fisher et al. (1992) suggests that this focus may mask inaccuracies at an individual ICD-9-CM code level. In addition, since eliminating the physician attestation requirement, concerns about coding accuracy have returned (see above).

A few other studies have also looked at coding accuracy. Lloyd and Rissing (1985) examined 1,829 records from patients admitted to five VA hospitals in FY1982. Comparisons of the original PTF information and the reabstraction found discrepancies in 82 percent of records. Some records had multiple errors, and Lloyd and Rissing projected an average of 3.0 errors per record. Physician errors were the most common (70.7 percent of errors) and represented five types: missed procedures, missed diagnoses, inappropriate primary diagnoses, inadequate terminology, and inactive diagnoses called active. These problems may be less relevant today because medical records personnel, not physicians, are responsible for listing diagnoses and procedures at most hospitals (albeit based on complete medical record review and with physician agreement).

As noted earlier, California's OSHPD is particularly active in monitoring that state's hospital coding for all patients (Meux, Stith, and Zach 1990). OSHPD conducted a study involving reabstraction of 2,579 records from discharges from 30 randomly selected hospitals in 1988 across a variety of conditions (including obstetrics, newborn, psychiatric conditions). Like the findings of Fisher et al. (1992), the study found that the accuracy of diagnosis coding varied by condition. For example, the fraction of cases with diagnoses identified by the OSHPD reabstraction that were also present on the original hospital data ranged from 0.545 for old myocardial infarction to 0.979 for any pneumonia and acute cerebrovascular disease (Romano and Luft 1992).

The OSHPD investigators found a particular problem with the underreporting of secondary diagnoses (Meux, Stith, and Zach 1990). In 576 records, the reabstractor coded more secondary diagnoses than in the original hospital list. Secondary diagnoses that were underreported by the hospitals included chronic respiratory conditions (e.g., emphysema, chronic obstructive pulmonary disease, 7.6 percent of underreported conditions), stroke residuals (e.g., hemiplegia, dysphagia, 5.9 percent), arteriosclerotic heart disease (6.1 percent), hypertension (5.9 percent), cardiac dysrhythmias (3.8 percent), and diabetes mellitus (3.6 percent).

Coding of cause of death on death certificates is also suspect, although this was the major original role of ICD (Messite and Stellman 1996). While the federal National Center for Health Statistics furnishes printed instructions and educational videocassettes about coding cause of death, few physicians have seen them. One study comparing coding of six cases supplied in these educational materials found only 56.9 percent agreement among 12 internists on listing cause of death (Messite and Stellman 1996, 795).

Despite these studies, little information is available about the quality of coded diagnostic data in other inpatient settings (e.g., psychiatric or rehabilitation facilities) or outpatient settings. A comparison of Medicare Part B claims from the NCH file with physician office records for 1,596 Maryland patients from 1990 to 1991 produced worrisome results. The Part B claims and physician office record matched on only 40.3 percent of zip codes and 58.5 percent of birthdates (Fowles et al. 1995, 192). The kappa statistics (see Chapter 7) indicating level of agreement between the claim and office record ranged from 0.0 (ketoacidosis) to 0.72 (diabetes mellitus) for the 26 diagnoses examined, and was above 0.40 for only six diagnoses. Claims frequently did not indicate diagnoses noted in the record.

Even less is available about the accuracy of the coded data from a clinical perspective: Do coded conditions accurately and completely reflect the patient's clinical status? As with the concerns about financial motivation for diagnostic coding, this limitation taints the clinical meaningfulness of coded data. However, the true root of this concern is the accuracy of physicians' diagnostic observations. As stated earlier, ICD-9-CM intends only to capture, shorthand, what physicians say.

Implications in Limitations of Coding Slots

Administrative data are submitted in formats that limit the amount of diagnostic information that can be recorded. For example, HCFA's uniform hospital bill (UB-82) permitted coding of only five ICD-9-CM diagnoses and three procedures prior to 1992. While five diagnoses may suffice to describe an uncomplicated admission, they are often inadequate to portray complicated admissions or patients with multiple comorbidities. This situation is compounded by the large number of ICD-9-CM codes describing diseases and their various manifestations. By 1987, almost half of Medicare discharges had all five diagnosis slots filled (Steinwald and Dummit 1989).

A study by Jencks, Williams, and Kay (1988) found that coding of secondary diagnoses was possibly biased due to limitations in the number of coding spaces. Using Medicare data, they examined patient mortality 30 days following admission for stroke, pneumonia, AMI, or congestive heart failure, and discovered the following:

> Patients with recorded [secondary] diagnoses of diabetes mellitus, unspecified anemia, essential hypertension, hypertensive heart disease, old myocardial infarction, angina, ischemic heart disease, mitral valvular disease, ventricular premature beats, and unclassified arrhythmias are significantly

less likely to die within 30 days than patients without these recorded diagnoses . . . These findings are so counterintuitive as to require explanation. The explanation most consistent with the data is a recording bias that reduces the likelihood of a chronic diagnosis being reported if the patient dies . . . Medicare's limit of reporting five diagnoses would then be more likely to truncate chronic diagnoses from the diagnosis list. (Jencks, Williams, and Kay 1988, 2244)

Clinical explanations for the counterintuitive findings have been sought. For example, one hypothesis concerning the apparent "protective" effect of essential hypertension is that these patients take medications, such as β blockers, that are known to improve survival among patients following AMI. Another hypothesis suggests that hypertensive patients have higher blood pressures than others even when experiencing an AMI, and that these higher pressures produce better survival outcomes (Blumberg and Binns 1989). A further hypothesis holds that the "protective" effect of coronary atherosclerosis in AMI results from increased formation of collateral vessels in patients with this chronic condition (Epstein, Quyyumi, and Bonow 1989). A final hypothesis suggests that patients with chronic conditions (e.g., diabetes mellitus, hypertension) have more regular contacts with doctors and thus have their acute illnesses identified at earlier stages or at lower severity.

However, even those advancing these clinical hypotheses admitted reservations—these conditions generally ought to increase patient risk and do so according to studies of comorbid disease (Charlson et al. 1987; Greenfield et al. 1988; Keeler et al. 1990). One study comparing two clinically derived databases with two administrative databases found much lower prevalence of chronic conditions (e.g., mitral insufficiency, cardiomegaly, previous myocardial infarction, hyperlipidemia) using codes from the administrative files (Romano et al. 1994).

The possibility of coding bias due to the limited secondary diagnosis slots prompted pressure for increasing the number of coding spaces. In response, HCFA expanded coding slots to nine diagnoses and six procedures as of April 1, 1992 (*Federal Register* 1991). Figure 3.2 shows the number of diagnoses listed for persons 65 years of age and older admitted to California hospitals in FY1994 using MEDPAR data; Figure 3.3 shows the number of procedures coded in MEDPAR. For comparison, both figures show the number of coding slots filled for persons 65 years of age and older taken from the 1994 hospital discharge abstract database compiled by California's OSHPD. California's data set contains space for 25 diagnosis and 25 procedure codes.

Does expanding the number of diagnosis slots, such as in California, improve the coding completeness for comorbid and chronic conditions? We examined this question using 1988 computerized hospital discharge

Figure 3.2   Number of Diagnoses Listed Per Case in 1994 MEDPAR and California Data

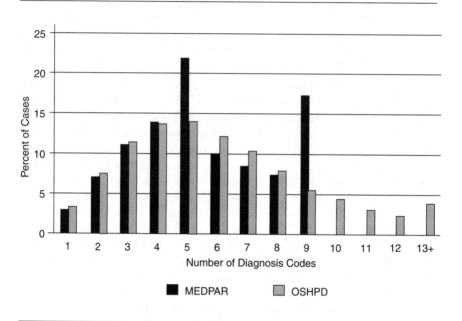

Source: Fiscal Year 1994 MEDPAR data for California; 1994 hospital discharge abstract database from California Office of Statewide Health Planning and Development.

abstract data from California with their 25 diagnosis and 25 procedure coding slots, replicating as closely as possible the study of Jencks, Williams, and Kay (1988). In the California data, the mean number of diagnoses per case was 5.5, and 0.1 percent of cases (106 cases) had all 25 diagnosis coding spaces filled (Iezzoni et al. 1992a). Patients who died had significantly more diagnoses coded than patients who survived hospitalization. The relative risk of in-hospital death was significantly increased by the presence of certain secondary diagnoses, mainly those reflecting acute conditions and possible complications of the principal diagnosis (e.g., cardiac arrest, paroxysmal ventricular tachycardia, congestive heart failure, pneumonia, cardiogenic shock, respiratory failure). For many conditions, however, the relative risk of in-hospital death was significantly less than 1.0 (e.g., Type II diabetes mellitus, essential hypertension, old myocardial infarction, angina, ventricular premature beats). Thus, although in California the average discharge had more than five diagnoses listed and only a few had all 25 coding spaces filled, our findings were generally similar to those of Jencks, Williams, and Kay (1988).

Figure 3.3   Number of Procedures Listed Per Case in 1994
MEDPAR and California Data

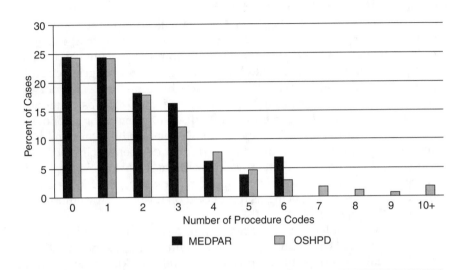

Source: Fiscal Year 1994 MEDPAR data for California; 1994 hospital discharge abstract
database from California Office of Statewide Health Planning and Development.

Our findings differed somewhat from the earlier work, suggesting
that improvement may occur as diagnosis fields are added. Romano and
Mark (1994) analyzed data from the California reabstraction study described above (Meux, Stith, and Zach 1990). When only the first five codes
were examined, "missing comorbidities were significantly more frequent
among deaths than among survivors," 27 percent versus 12 percent ($p <$
0.001) (p. 85). However, when all 25 diagnoses were considered, deaths
and survivors had equal rates of missing comorbidities.

We updated our study of 1988 California data (Iezzoni et al. 1992a),
using California data from 1994. Methods and case identification were
identical (persons 65 years of age and older in four diseases; we used the
fifth digit of the ICD-9-CM codes to select patients undergoing initial AMI
treatment). This time, however, we used multivariable logistic regression
to adjust for age and sex in calculating the odds of in-hospital death given
the presence of specified secondary diagnoses. The 1994 findings were
remarkably similar to those from 1988. As shown in the examples in Table
3.5, some secondary diagnoses significantly decreased the adjusted odds
of death. Examples of diagnoses that generally did not significantly affect
the adjusted odds of death included Type I diabetes mellitus, unspecified

anemia, coronary atherosclerosis, and unspecified ischemic heart disease. Urinary tract infection significantly increased the adjusted odds of dying for pneumonia (1.34) and congestive heart failure (1.46) but decreased the adjusted odds for stroke (0.88) and AMI (0.88).

The reabstraction study of 974 AMI patients admitted to California hospitals in 1990 and 1991 found variation in the validity and reliability of coding of some risk factors, but even important acute conditions were poorly coded. Coding quality was "very good" for congestive heart failure, chronic renal disease, prior coronary bypass surgery, history of pacemaker, complete atrioventricular block, and shock; it was "intermediate" for epilepsy, other cerebrovascular disease, primary or secondary malignancy, and hypertension; and it was "poor" for hypotension, pulmonary edema, other valve disease, nutritional deficiency, chronic liver disease, and late effects of cerebrovascular disease (Wilson, Smoley, and Werdegar 1996, 15–2). California is no longer adjusting for these poorly coded conditions in producing its report card on hospitals' AMI mortality rates (see Chapter 11).

Therefore, undercoding of acute conditions is also a problem. With discharge abstract–based severity measures, clinically appropriate ratings of individual cases depends on coding of *all* relevant diagnoses. In our AHCPR-funded severity study, we abstracted detailed clinical information on 27 patients, including verbatim the information listed on the hospital's face sheet. We asked vendors to rate each case using this information, and we performed scoring for APACHE II (Hughes et al. 1996, Iezzoni et al. 1995c). For the case shown on Table 3.6, the hospital assigned only two codes—*pseudomonas* pneumonia and multiple myeloma. Given the extent of the patient's acute derangements, additional codes could reasonably have been listed, including sepsis, septic shock, and respiratory failure. Several vendors informed us that their severity ratings would have increased by listing such codes. For example, by adding sepsis, the AIM severity class would have risen from 1 to 3, and the predicted length-of-stay from 7.3 to 12.6 days. By adding septicemia and shock, the PMC Severity Score would have risen from 4 to 7, the PMC RIS from 1.66 to 3.011, and the length-of-stay prediction from 8.4 days to 13.0 days. In contrast, because they do not rely on diagnosis coding, the clinically based severity measures assigned fairly severe scores, representing the range of physiologic derangements present on admission.

While complete coding appears an arcane concern, it is nonetheless critical to improving the quality of reports and research that derive from administrative data. Physicians need to become more aware of the uses of discharge diagnosis codes, especially in report cards on their performance (see Chapter 11). In turn, researchers and policymakers must remain aware of the inherent limitations in generating clinical assessments based on listed

Table 3.5   Sample Characteristics and Odds Ratio Adjusted for Age and Sex of In-Hospital Death for Patients with Specified Secondary Diagnoses: 1994 California Hospital Discharge Abstract Data

Sample Characteristics and Secondary Diagnosis	ICD-9-CM Code	Condition			
		Stroke	*Pneumonia*	*AMI*	*Congestive Heart Failure*
Number of cases		35,837	60,066	32,714	54,362
Number of deaths		4,290	7,575	4,329	3,192
Percent died		12.0%	12.6%	13.2%	5.9%
Mean (S.D.) number of diagnosis codes					
Discharged alive		6.3 (2.9)	6.8 (3.2)	6.5 (3.2)	6.7 (2.9)
Discharged dead		6.7 (3.4)	8.6 (3.6)	8.0 (3.6)	8.3 (3.6)

Adjusted Odds Ratio of In-Hospital Death Generally Significantly < 1.0

Essential hypertension	401.9	0.70*	0.69*	0.59*	0.52*
Hypertension with heart disease	402.90	0.70+	0.71+	0.61+	0.49
Old myocardial infarction	412	0.99	0.91	0.78+	0.85#
Angina pectoris	413.9	0.50*	0.56*	0.37*	0.53*

Adjusted Odds Ratio of In-Hospital Death Generally Significantly > 1.0

Dehydration	276.50	1.27*	1.61*	1.77*	3.29*
Paroxysmal ventricular tachycardia	427.1	2.38*	2.26*	2.11*	2.03*
Atrial fibrillation	427.31	1.36*	1.48*	1.25*	1.12+
Cardiac arrest	427.5	47.98*	52.39*	21.64*	58.75*
Pneumonia, organism unspecified	486	2.60*	2.10+	2.04*	2.58*
Chronic obstructive pulmonary disease	496.00	1.16+	0.93+	1.13#	1.17+
Chronic renal failure	585	2.32*	1.98*	2.34*	2.32*
Cardiogenic shock	785.51	24.44*	22.61*	14.20*	23.60*
Respiratory failure	799.1	12.78*	7.95*	8.87*	10.82*

* $p \leq 0.0001$
+ $0.0001 < p \leq 0.01$
# $0.01 < p < 0.05$

ICD-9-CM codes alone. As Romano suggested (1993, 469), "When the reliability or validity of certain variables is suspect, then sensitivity analyses

Table 3.6   Case Presentation, Discharge Abstract Data, and Severity Scores: Effect of Undercoding

Case Presentation

A 54-year-old woman with a 5-year history of multiple myeloma was admitted with dyspnea and diffuse bilateral infiltrates on chest x-ray. She had experienced recurrent paraspinal masses and cord compressions from the multiple myeloma, as well as pathologic fractures, and had received both chemotherapy and radiation therapy. At the time of admission, she was bedbound, cared for at home by her husband, and not receiving active myeloma treatment. On exam, her temperature was 98.6° F, pulse 120, respirations 36, and blood pressure palpable at 92. Arterial blood gas on room air: pH 7.45, pCO_2 39, pO_2 63. Leukocytes were 8.0k with 87 percent segmented forms and no bands. Sputum grew *pseudomonas* and pleural fluid contained malignant cells. The patient initially requested maximal treatment, including intubation and mechanical ventilation. She was treated with intravenous antibiotics but deteriorated rapidly. On Day 3 she became hypoxic, was intubated, and was transferred to the ICU with respiratory failure, necrotizing pneumonia, sepsis, and septic shock. Her respiratory failure worsened, and on Day 5 she became unresponsive. At the family's request, orders for DNR status and comfort measures only were written on Day 5, and she died the next day.

Discharge Abstract Information	
Age: 54 years	Diagnoses listed by hospital:
DRG 475, respiratory system diagnosis with ventilator support	482.1, pneumonia due to *pseudomonas*
	203.0, multiple myeloma
Length of stay: 6 days	
Total charges: $13,800	
Discharge status: expired	
Procedures: 96.04, endotracheal intubation	

Severity Ratings		
Severity Measure	*Patient's Score*	*Range of Scores*
Clinically Based Measures		
APACHE II (worst values from Day 1)		
Acute physiology score	8	0–60
Total APACHE II score	10	0–71
CSI		
Admission score (Days 1 and 2)	3	1–4
Maximum score (worst values from entire stay)	4	1–4

Continued

Table 3.6   Continued

Severity Measure	*Patient's Score*	*Range of Scores*
MedisGroups empirical version		
Admission score (Days 1 and 2)	0.129	0–1.0
Midstay score (Days 3–7)	0.415	0–1.0
Discharge Abstract–Based Measures		
AIM	1	1–5
APR-DRGs	2	1–4
Disease Staging mortality probability	0.054	0–1.0
PMCs Severity Score	4	1–7
PMC RIS	1.66	Base = 1.0
PMC length of stay prediction (days)	8.4	> 0
R-DRGs	B	D,C,B

Adapted from: Hughes et al. 1996.

should be performed to ascertain how the results would be affected by different assumptions."

Retrospective Nature of Discharge Diagnoses

As described earlier, hospital discharge abstract information is retrospective—diagnoses and their sequencing are assigned following patient discharge. Discharge diagnosis codes thus reflect conditions diagnosed or treated during the entire admission, regardless of when they occurred during the hospital stay (Iezzoni 1990). Knowing the timing of diagnoses is, however, crucial for distinguishing risks due to intrinsic patient factors from those due to substandard inpatient care. For instance, suppose a patient had the following discharge diagnoses:

820.21 Closed intertrochanteric fracture of neck of femur

482.4   Staphylococcal pneumonia

599.0   Urinary tract infection, site not specified

250.70 Type II diabetes mellitus with peripheral circulatory disorders, not stated as uncontrolled

The Type II diabetes is obvious preexisting, but either the pneumonia or urinary tract infection could have occurred in-hospital, perhaps as nosocomial infections. The inability to differentiate the timing of diagnoses seriously restricts the utility of discharge abstracts for identifying patients' risk factors prior to medical intervention.

In our AHCPR-funded severity study, discharge abstract–based severity measures (Table 1.9) were sometimes equal or better predictors of in-hospital mortality than measures derived from admission clinical findings (Iezzoni et al. 1995a, 1995b, 1996a; Landon et al. 1996). For example, for AMI patients, discharge abstract–based APR-DRGs and Disease Staging produced slightly higher c statistics than either empirical MedisGroups or the physiology score (Table 3.7). One hypothesis about why discharge abstract–based severity measures sometimes performed well in predicting in-hospital deaths is their reliance on ICD-9-CM codes for conditions, such as cardiac arrest, arising late in the hospital stay. In contrast, the clinically based measures used findings from only the first two hospital days. Thus, we hypothesized that discharge abstract–based measures benefitted from a virtual tautology—using near-death experiences to predict death.

Anecdotal evidence supports this hypothesis. As described above, we abstracted detailed clinical and discharge abstract information on 27 patients and asked vendors to rate each case; we performed scoring for APACHE II (Hughes et al. 1996, Iezzoni et al. 1995c). Several cases suggested that discharge abstract–based measures rely heavily on codes representing serious conditions that might arise late during the hospital stay. The example in Table 3.8 involves an 81-year-old widow admitted for hip fracture repair. She was fairly stable on admission; the clinically based admission severity measures rated her as mildly to moderately severe. Post-operatively, however, she experienced serious complications—Gram-negative septicemia and respiratory failure. PMCs, APR-DRGs, and R-DRGs assigned her high severity scores. The two measures producing

Table 3.7 c-Statistics for Predicting In-Hospital Death

	Condition			
Severity Measure	*AMI*	*CABG*	*Pneumonia*	*Stroke*
Clinically Based Measures				
MedisGroups empirical version	0.83	0.74	0.85	0.87
Physiology Score 2	0.83	0.73	0.82	0.84
Discharge Abstract–Based Measures				
APR-DRGs	0.84	0.83	0.78	0.77
Disease Staging mortality probability	0.86	0.78	0.80	0.74
PMCs Severity Score	0.82	0.81	0.79	0.73

Sources: Iezzoni et al. 1995b, 1996a, 1996c; Landon et al. 1996.

predicted probabilities of in-hospital death are particularly illustrative: The admission MedisGroups probability was 0.009, while Disease Staging's probability was 0.284.

To examine our hypothesis empirically, we used ICD-9-CM diagnosis codes to define findings similar to those represented by MedisGroups KCFs. Given the limitations of ICD-9-CM, this was possible for only selected KCFs (Iezzoni et al. 1996b). For pneumonia patients (see Table 1.9), only six of the clinical findings derived from the ICD-9-CM occurred in at least 1 percent of patients: respiratory failure, 3.6 percent; low sodium, 6.4 percent; acute and chronic renal failure, 1.5 and 2.1 percent respectively; septicemia/bacteremia, 3.3 percent; and cancer, 14.8 percent. All were associated with a much-increased risk of in-hospital death. Viewed alongside admission KCFs, it appeared that these ICD-9-CM codes frequently reflected conditions arising after the first two hospital days. For example, of the 1,145 patients with an ICD-9-CM code for hyponatremia, only 42.9 percent had a KCF indicating low sodium on admission; of the 594 patients with an ICD-9-CM code for septicemia or bacteremia, only 52.2 percent had a KCF indicating a positive blood culture on admission. However, the findings relating to cancer—a condition certainly predating hospitalization—raised concern about how both KCFs and ICD-9-CM codes are determined. Of the 2,666 patients with a cancer code, only 79.7 percent also had a KCF indicating cancer.

Further analysis generally supported the hypothesis that discharge abstract–based severity measures rely heavily on ICD-9-CM codes representing grave conditions potentially arising later in the hospital stay (Iezzoni et al. 1996b). For example, of patients viewed as sicker by Disease Staging's mortality probability model than by Physiology Score 2, 9.5 percent had an ICD-9-CM code representing respiratory failure; in contrast, of patients viewed as sicker by Physiology Score 2 than by Disease Staging, only 0.1 percent had a respiratory failure code. Discharge abstract–based measures also assigned relatively higher scores to patients with a cancer ICD-9-CM code. For example, of patients seen as sicker by Disease Staging than Physiology Score 2, 44.0 percent had a cancer code; of patients seen as sicker by Physiology Score 2 than Disease Staging, only 4.8 percent had a cancer code.

Despite these problems, a number of strategies exist for dealing with timing of diagnoses (Iezzoni 1990). For instance, one could concentrate solely on ICD-9-CM codes representing chronic conditions—diagnoses that are unlikely to arise *de novo* during a hospitalization, such as Type II diabetes mellitus, malignancy, chronic obstructive pulmonary disease, and chronic renal failure (Iezzoni et al. 1994b). Shapiro and colleagues (1994) used a similar approach in comparing mortality rates at municipal and voluntary hospitals in the five boroughs of New York City. They

Table 3.8   Case Presentation, Discharge Abstract Data, and Severity Scores: Comparison of Discharge Abstract– and Clinically Based Measures

Case Presentation

An 81-year-old widow, previously ambulatory and residing at a home for the aged, was admitted after she broke her hip. She had a history of hypertension, a previous syncopal episode with negative diagnostic workup, mitral regurgitation, and aortic regurgitation. Repair of her hip was delayed until Day 4 by a syncopal episode that occurred in the emergency room on admission and by a urinary tract infection. Her postoperative course was complicated by persistent fever, a pleural effusion, and a probable urinary tract infection. Antibiotic coverage was broadened on Day 10, and she was transferred to the intensive care unit on Day 11 due to hypotension (systolic pressure = 80 mm Hg), hypoxia (pO_2 = 66), and possible sepsis. She was intubated and mechanically ventilated but became more hypotensive despite intravenous dopamine and neosynephrine drugs. She died on Day 12.

Discharge Abstract Information

Age: 81 years

DRG 210, hip and femur procedures with complication or comorbidity

Length of stay: 12 days

Total charges: $20,900

Discharge status: expired

Procedures:

79.35, open reduction of femur fracture with internal fixation

Diagnoses:

820.21, pertrochanteric femur fracture, closed, intertrochanteric section

780.2, syncope and collapse

401.9, essential hypertension

599.0, urinary tract infection

038.40, Gram-negative septicemia

518.5, pulmonary insufficiency following trauma and surgery

Severity Ratings		
Severity Measure	*Patient's Score*	*Range of Scores*
Clinically Based Measures		
APACHE II (worst values from Day 1)		
Acute physiology score	1	0–60
Total APACHE II score	7	0–71
CSI		
Admission score (Days 1 and 2)	1	1–4
Maximum score (worst values from entire stay)	4	1–4

Continued

Table 3.8   Continued

Severity Measure	Patient's Score	Range of Scores
MedisGroups empirical version		
Admission score (Days 1 and 2)	0.009	0–1.0
Midstay score (Days 3–7)	0.013	0–1.0

Discharge Abstract–Based Measures		
APR-DRGs	3	1–4
Disease Staging mortality probability	0.284	0–1.0
PMCs Severity Score	7	1–7
R-DRGs	A	D,C,B,A

Adapted from: Hughes et al. 1996.

specified two risk-adjustment models: "full other diagnoses," including 17 categories of other diagnoses; and "limited other diagnoses," eliminating all acute conditions that could potentially represent substandard care (e.g., septicemia, pulmonary embolism, pneumonia, acute tubular necrosis, cardiogenic shock, and respiratory arrest). For most conditions studied, perceptions about whether municipal and voluntary hospitals had different death rates varied across the two risk-adjustment methods.

Another approach involves combining information available within the discharge abstract to attempt inferences about the timing of a diagnosis. One such strategy requires information about when a major procedure was performed during the hospitalization (e.g., date of procedure, length of stay prior to the procedure). For instance, except in unusual situations, surgeons are unlikely to operate on a patient with an active pneumonia. Suppose patients have surgery on Day 1 or 2 of their hospital stays and also have secondary diagnoses of staphylococcal pneumonia. The pneumonia is more likely to represent a postoperative nosocomial infection than a condition present on admission. In designing the Complications Screening Program, we used this approach with administrative data to flag probable in-hospital complications (Iezzoni et al. 1994a, 1994c), such as the patient admitted to a California hospital with alcoholic liver cirrhosis (Exhibit 3.2).

Although playing these probabilities should differentiate preoperative from postoperative conditions across groups of patients, in individual instances, it may not work. In addition, this strategy probably does not hold for conditions that do not pose serious operative risks (e.g., urinary tract infection).

Exhibit 3.2   Case Found Using Discharge Abstract Information to Identify Complications

Patient Data	Hospital Data	Admission Data	Disposition Data
ID: XXXXX	Hospital ID: XXXXX	Length of stay: 86 days	Disposition: routine discharge
Age: 51	Zip code: XXXXX	Admission type: urgent	DRG: 191 (Pancreas, liver and shunt procedures with surgical care)
Sex: female		Source: routine	
Race: white		Total charges: $225,480.00	
Residence zip code: XXXXX		Payer: Medi-cal	

DIAGNOSIS AND PROCEDURE CODES AND DAYS FROM ADMISSION TO PROCEDURE

Diagnosis Codes		Procedure Codes		Days
5712	alcoholic cirrhosis liver	391	intra-abdominal venous shunt	77
45620	bleeding esophageal varices	415	total splenectomy	77
486	pneumonia, organism NOS	4282	suture esophageal laceration	17
9982	accidental operative laceration	3451	decortication of lung	17
5100	empyema with fistula	4291	injection/ligation esophageal varices	3
5990	urinary tract infection NOS	4513	small bowel endoscopy NEC	3
5723	portal hypertension	4291	injection/ligation esophageal varices	5
7895	ascites	4513	small bowel endoscopy NEC	5
2768	hypopotassemia	4513	small bowel endoscopy NEC	1
5119	pleural effusion NOS	3893	venous catheter NEC	5
2874	second thrombocytopenia	3891	arterial catheterization	5
5128	spontaneous pneumothorax NEC	3491	thoracentesis	9
4279	cardiac dysrhythmia NOS	3404	insert intercostal catheter	15
2800	chronic blood loss anemia	8847	contrast abdominal arteriogram NEC	44
4400	aortic atherosclerosis	8801	C.A.T. scan of abdomen	2

Coding Differences across Hospitals

When using administrative data to compare outcomes across hospitals or other providers, a vexing problem is variability in coding across different facilities. Hospitals code with different levels of thoroughness and accuracy. Without additional information, one cannot tell whether these coding differences reflect true differences in the patient mix.

Good circumstantial evidence supports the likelihood of systematic biases in coding practices across facilities. For example, using state discharge abstract data from 1988, we examined patients 65 years of age and older admitted for one of four conditions to California hospitals (Iezzoni et al. 1992a). We arrayed the 441 California hospitals by increasing average number of diagnoses per case, designating the top 10 percent (or 45 hospitals) as "heavy coders." The mean number of diagnoses per case ranged from 2.5 for the lowest coding hospital to 11.7 for the heaviest coder. The 45 hospitals considered "heavy coders" assigned over 8.2 codes to the average case.

Heavy coding hospitals differed from other facilities in several ways. Only 6.7 percent of the heavy coders were public hospitals (compared to 21.5 percent of other institutions) and 35.6 percent were private, for-profit (compared to 28.0 percent, $p = 0.06$ for ownership comparison). Presence of approved residency training programs did not differ across heavy coders and other facilities, but more heavy coders were members of the Council of Teaching Hospitals (11.1 compared to 4.6 percent, $p = 0.06$). Heavy coders were much more likely to be large ($p = 0.01$), with 31.1 percent having 300 or more beds compared to 14.9 percent of other facilities. For three of the four study conditions, death rates were comparable at the heavy coding hospitals, but pneumonia cases died at a 1.1 percent higher rate at heavy coding hospitals.

The reabstraction study of 974 AMI patients admitted to California hospitals in 1990 and 1991 described above was performed in the context of the state's initiative to produce hospital report cards on AMI mortality using administrative data (Wilson, Smoley, and Werdegar 1996, see Chapter 11). Not surprisingly, many criticized these reports because of their data source; in response, California reviewed medical records to validate coding accuracy. Cases were sampled within hospitals stratified into three groups—hospital risk-adjusted AMI mortality better than expected, neither better nor worse, and worse than expected. Some variations in coding accuracy were identified across hospitals.

Overall, at least one clinical risk factor was missing from 65.0 percent of discharge abstracts, and two were missing from 30.9 percent of abstracts (Wilson, Smoley, and Werdegar 1996, 14–6). Hospitals varied from 45 to 87 percent in the fraction of uncoded risk factors. The percent of missing risk factors did not vary across the three hospital mortality categories, but it was more common at high volume than medium volume facilities (68.8 versus 61.2 percent, $p = 0.015$). In contrast, 31.5 percent of the discharge abstracts contained at least one "unsupported risk factor" as determined by the reabstraction study. This overcoding of risk factors was much more common at low-mortality hospitals than at intermediate- or high-mortality hospitals (36.7 percent versus 29.2 percent and 29.0 percent, $p = 0.039$). Overcoding rates ranged from 10 percent at one high-mortality hospital to 74 percent at a low-mortality hospital. Variation in coding accuracy explained part of the differences between high- and low-mortality hospitals (Wilson, Smoley, and Werdegar 1996).

Information about Procedures

The nature of procedures (e.g., technical complexity, anatomic location, time required, anesthesia required) can contribute to the immediate risks of patients (see Chapter 2). For example, an open cholecystectomy typically presents more acute risks to patients than does a laparoscopic procedure. Most risk-adjustment strategies, however, do not incorporate procedures as risk factors—adjusting for procedure use becomes confounded with concerns about technical quality, appropriateness of the surgery, and differences in physicians' practice patterns. Instead, most risk adjustment concentrates on patients' characteristics prior to therapeutic intervention. Nonetheless, procedural information is obviously an essential component of patient outcomes studies.

Procedural Nomenclatures

Unlike for diagnoses, no single procedure classification scheme is used in the United States. Procedure classification and coding differs within different contexts. Hospitals report procedures using the ICD-9-CM for Medicare payment, while physicians employ the HCFA Common Procedure Coding System (HCPCS), which is largely based on the American Medical Association's *Current Procedural Terminology* (CPT). The codes in ICD-9-CM and CPT do not readily link. To complicate matters, insurance carriers occasionally create their procedure codes to amend a basic lexicon such as CPT, compromising further efforts to obtain consistent information about procedures.

The ICD-9-CM procedural nomenclature generates serious reservations. According to McMahon and Smits (1986, 563), one of the key problems with the surgical codes "is that the outcome of surgery is coded and the approach is often ignored." As an example, they cite instances where

ICD-9-CM fails to distinguish the approach for gastrointestinal procedures that are today often performed using endoscopy—for instance, code 42.32 (local excision of other lesion or tissue of esophagus) describes what was done but not how. A particular problem for the PORTs is that ICD-9-CM procedure codes do not identify the side of the body for procedures that could be bilateral. Therefore, it is impossible to track whether sequential hip arthroplasties, for example, are performed on the same or different hips (Mitchell et al. 1994). Despite these problems, ICD-9-CM procedure codes sometimes permit more insight into patients' experiences than CPT and HCPCS, even about possible quality problems (Hannan et al. 1989). For example, ICD-9-CM contains a code for "suture of laceration of uterus," thus indicating that a laceration occurred; HCPCS and CPT contain no such code. However, surgeons sometimes do not charge patients for surgical treatments of operative complications. Therefore, regardless of the procedure coding system, no bill is available marking the event (Mitchell et al. 1994).

CPT provides thousands of codes detailing the approach taken for surgical and diagnostic procedures. One area that generates significant controversy involves coding of outpatient visits and inpatient consultations (Zuber and Henley 1992; Johnsson 1996). Physician billing and coding practices remain continually in flux as HCFA changes Medicare physician reimbursement policies (e.g., the resource-based relative value scale).

Quality of Procedure Coding

In most regions, hospitals have been reimbursed by diagnoses (i.e., DRGs) only since 1983, but payment for specific procedures—represented by relevant procedure codes—is a long-standing practice for physicians. Consequently, one might expect that coding of procedures would be both more complete and accurate than diagnosis coding.

The IOM report on the accuracy of discharge abstract data found better accuracy for ICD-9-CM coding of procedures than for diagnoses. While accuracy of hospitals' reports was only 65.2 percent for the principal diagnosis, it was 73.2 percent for the principal procedure (Institute of Medicine 1977a). Surprisingly, however, determining who coded correctly—the hospital or the IOM reabstractors—was more difficult for principal procedure than for principal diagnosis. For 10.7 percent of all cases reviewed, the correct principal diagnosis was indeterminate compared to 16.3 percent of cases for principal procedure.

In a reanalysis of data collected by the HCFA OIG (Hsia et al. 1988), Fisher et al. (1992) found that agreement between hospitals' principal procedures and those found on reabstraction was 76.2 percent at the two-digit ICD-9-CM procedure code level and 73.8 percent at the three-digit level. When order of the procedure codes was ignored, however, agreement rose considerably and was much higher for procedures than for diagnoses (see above). For example, the proportion of codes identified by the OIG team that were originally listed by the hospital ranged from 0.88 for cardiac catheterization to over 0.95 for 10 of 15 procedures examined. Fisher et al. (1992, 247) suggested that ICD-9-CM procedural data may be more clinically meaningful than diagnostic data.

> The proper clinical interpretation of many coded diagnoses will remain uncertain until clear-cut clinical criteria for their use are established and promulgated. Surgical procedures, because of the precision with which they are defined and the accuracy with which they are coded, pose less difficulty in interpretation.

Lloyd and Rissing (1985) found that physicians commonly failed to document procedures, accounting for 46 percent of physician documentation errors. Underreported procedures were generally not performed in operating rooms, nor did they affect DRG assignment. Coding of nonoperating-room procedures varied greatly across the five facilities included in the study.

Romano and Luft (1992) reanalyzed the findings from the California OSHPD study described above (Meux, Stith, and Zach 1990) to examine the accuracy of procedure coding. For the procedures examined, the procedures as coded originally by the hospital were virtually 100 percent specific (i.e., if the procedure was not listed, the patient in fact had not had the procedure). However, sensitivity (i.e., the percentage of patients with the procedure who had the procedure coded) varied widely by procedure, as follows: chemotherapy, 93.9 percent; mechanical ventilation, 92.1 percent; flexible colonoscopy or sigmoidoscopy, 91.4 percent; computed tomography, head, 89.8 percent; barium enema, 66.7 percent; echocardiography, 66.3 percent; cardiovascular treadmill test, 55.6 percent; electrocardiographic monitor, 39.6 percent; and respiratory nebulizer therapy, 26.4 percent. The procedures coded with lower sensitivity appear to be those associated with lower costs or risks to patients.

One potential problem with procedure coding is the practice of "unbundling"—physicians submitting claims for multiple specific procedures that are all really part of a single procedure. Unbundling is facilitated by the massive detail of CPT: For example, numerous codes for various angiographic procedures and the associated injection of radiographic contrast materials are listed separately. In May 1995, the General Accounting Office suggested that Medicare could save millions of dollars by implementing software to identify unbundled billing. Under Medicare's Correct Coding Initiative, claims are processed through software that flags 83,000 code pairs that are deemed unacceptable. HCFA estimates that this process could result in denials of up to 4 percent of claims, but this initiative is just now under way (Larkin 1996, 7). It is likely to change procedure coding patterns, at least on physician bills.

Nonetheless, although questions remain about the accuracy of procedure coding, they appear less pressing in the inpatient setting than those pertaining to coding of diagnoses. In fact, Romano and Luft (1992, 61) offer this suggestion:

> Procedures also may be used as surrogates for diagnoses when the diagnoses are apt to be coded imprecisely. For example, preoperative use of an intra-aortic balloon pump can be used as a surrogate for severe ventricular dysfunction . . . Obviously, this strategy works only if the date of a secondary procedure relative to the primary procedure is known. Any procedure used as a surrogate for a diagnosis should have relatively clear indications. . . .

The quality of procedure coding for laboratory tests and outpatient interventions is unclear, but one study offered troubling results. This comparison of Medicare Part B claims from the NCH file with physician office records for 1,596 Maryland patients from 1990 to 1991 found that test coding was less accurate than diagnosis coding. Many laboratory tests and procedures were missing from physicians' records. The kappa statistic (see Chapter 7) indicating the agreement between the Part B claims and physician office record ranged from -0.02 for nuclear medicine scans to 0.73 for a hemoglobin A1C (Fowles et al. 1995, 195). Nonetheless, claims-based methods have been developed for profiling physician services (Garnick et al. 1994; Parente et al. 1995).

Structural Attributes of Administrative Data

The principal question about administrative database structure is whether information about service use can be linked at the individual patient level, especially across settings of care (e.g., hospitals, private doctors' offices, nursing homes, homes). Doing so requires a unique patient identification number regardless of payor or provider, raising serious concerns about confidentiality and privacy.

> . . . Databases were at one time discrete—often held in physically secure rooms on tape drives—with identifiers that were unique to a given institution or insurer. Now, however, data from diverse sources can be combined and linked. Once data are stored electronically, networks of databases can be explored almost imperceptibly from remote locations. Unless security systems are designed to record access, the curious, entrepreneurial, or venal can enter databases without leaving evidence of having done so. (Donaldson and Lohr 1994, 141)

Unique patient identifiers are generally available for Medicare, VA, and Medicaid databases but few others. Although a Medicare beneficiary's identification number can change, HCFA has cross-referenced such numbers for some researchers (e.g., the PORTs) (Lave et al. 1994). To protect patient confidentiality, administrative databases obtained for research typically do not contain sufficient information to determine the identity of individual patients. Access to such sensitive information, however, can occasionally be negotiated depending on the nature of the specific research study.

The most commonly used uniform patient identification number is the social security number (SSN), but this use causes consternation among some privacy experts. When social security was mandated in 1935, the SSN was actually the SSAN—the number of a person's social security "account" (Donaldson and Lohr 1994). The number was not intended as a personal identifier. In 1943, President Roosevelt signed an executive order stipulating that all federal agencies implementing new record systems (such as the Internal Revenue Service) use the SSN to identify individuals. States were prohibited from using the SSN by the Privacy Act of 1974, but that prohibition was undermined by the Tax Reform Act of 1976. States with unique patient identifiers attached to hospital discharge abstracts typically use the SSN or some modification of it (such as California and Massachusetts). Actual SSNs are not released to outsiders; California, for example, has developed a careful approach for encrypting SSNs for public-use data files (Meux 1994).

In most instances, the SSN is unique and specific—a single individual has one and only one number—permitting its use for linking records. However, this is not true in certain scenarios. For example, some states may assign a temporary number to persons without a SSN who require immediate Medicaid benefits; a permanent and different number is given later (Bright, Avorn, and Everitt 1989). Family members may be assigned a relative's SSN. For instance, a wife may use her husband's SSN; an unborn child may be given its mother's SSN. These instances of single persons with multiple SSNs and multiple persons with a single SSN complicate record linkage. Nonetheless, these occurrences are relatively uncommon, and ways exist to disentangle instances involving multiple persons with a single SSN (e.g., by tracking other identification information on individual records, such as sex, birthdate, mother's name).

The Health Insurance Portability and Accountability Act of 1996 (P.L. 104–191, Subtitle F, Sec. 1173(b)(1), see below) stipulates that "the Secretary [of the Department of Health and Human Services] shall adopt standards providing for a standard unique health identifier for each individual, employer, health plan, and health care provider for use in the health care system." The act also requires the Secretary to protect individual privacy concerns. At this time, it is unclear how these two potentially competing goals will be reconciled and achieved.

Even without a unique, patient-level number it is often possible to link records, with some degree of certainty, if adequate demographic and administrative information is available. A variety of computerized algorithms are now available that match records agreeing exactly on specified characteristics (deterministic linkage). Algorithms automatically calculate a probability that a given pair of records refer to the same individual (probabilistic linkage) when they agree only on certain characteristics (Roos et al. 1996).

Having patient-level, linked data can solve some of the problems with individual hospital discharge abstract information described above. With linked data, one can identify conditions treated previously that could thus be considered chronic or preexisting. One can also look at patterns of diagnoses over previous hospitalizations or healthcare encounters to draw inferences about the course of illness. For example, in the patient described above with a principal discharge diagnosis of closed intertrochanteric fracture of neck of femur (820.21), prior outpatient visits for staphylococcal pneumonia (482.4) or urinary tract infection (599.0) provide important clues about the timing of events. Linking Medicare Part A and B records provide an opportunity for "internal validation" of the quality of Medicare data—seeing whether hospital and physician claims agree on listed diagnoses and procedures (Baron et al. 1994).

Linkage over time is another important structural attribute. For example, using multiple years of Medicare data, one can track patients not only across services but over time. The ability of some administrative files to provide a longitudinal record of patients offers a tool that, in certain situations, can be more powerful than a primary data collection effort:

> Primary data collection must deal with both inability to locate individuals and refusal to participate; even well-run surveys employing multiple call-backs usually have 10–15% nonresponse. A database designed to capture utilization by an entire population "solves" the problem by registering ("locating") individuals and ensuring that utilization ("participation") results in a claim. (Roos, Nicol, and Cageorge 1987, 43)

Tracking patients through longitudinal administrative databases can minimize concerns about bias due to differences among nonrespondents that plague primary data–based studies.

Databases such as the Medicare and VA files link readily with eligibility records that indicate patients' vital status. Other data sets generally do not have a mechanism to track dates of death. In certain situations, one option for tracking whether patients are still alive is the National Death Index (NDI), a computerized record based on state vital statistics information that has been maintained by the National Center for Health Statistics since 1979 (Edlavitch, Feinleib, and Anello 1985). The matching criteria for the NDI include SSN, patient's first and last names, patient's father's surname, and patient's birthdate. The NDI is updated approximately annually, on receipt of reports from states. Although the NDI offers an attractive adjunct to databases without vital status information, to use it one must have data that are often withheld from investigators for confidentiality reasons (e.g., valid SSNs, not encrypted; names; and birthdates).

Another crucial structural question is whether the data are population based and denominators can be determined. As suggested above, detailed Medicare enrollment files are kept and often updated; in addition, once individuals participate in Medicare, participation is generally "permanent" (i.e., patients do not often relinquish their Medicare participation). Thus, population denominators are fairly easily delineated for Medicare patients. In contrast, eligibility for Medicaid tends to wax and wane for many individuals, depending on their changing financial and employment status. Therefore, when using Medicaid data, it is important to determine the eligibility status of the population under study over time.

A major problem with state databases involves border crossing by patients for services and residential migration across states—more likely in some states than in others. For instance, patients living in small states next to states with large, renowned, tertiary medical centers often cross state borders to obtain sophisticated services. These out-of-state services are not included in the database of the state where the patient resides. Thus, the numerator of procedure rate calculations, for example, in the small state would be biased downward by border crossing. Determining population denominators is a particular problem for states with large numbers of illegal immigrants or migrant workers.

Determining the population covered by private insurance claims files is challenging (Garnick et al. 1996). Many insurers update their enrollment files only once a year, when groups renew coverage. In addition, most carriers only retain files on groups that are actively covered by their plans. Therefore, no information is retrievable on persons whose companies had dropped the insurance policy.

Finally, the size of administrative databases has both logistical and conceptual implications. From a practical perspective, one must have computer facilities that can handle large volumes and other technical requirements (e.g., tape drives to download the data). Conceptually, huge sample sizes mean that even small differences appear statistically significant. Thus, *a priori* hypotheses about expected findings and associations are essential, as well as a practical sense about what magnitude of differences is clinically meaningful.

Administrative Data in the Future

As stated at the outset of this chapter, the boundaries between traditional administrative data (e.g., the contents of a claim or bill) and more clinical information are increasingly blurred. Information generated during patient care or testing can often now be transmitted automatically into central electronic data repositories, at least within institutions (OTA 1995). For example, the Regenstrief Medical Record System at Indiana University Medical Center gathers data from three hospitals, 30 clinics, and other settings of care into one network, capturing data from a clinician order-entry system, nursing notes, certain bedside monitors, laboratory, pharmacy, and various administrative sources. The VA now continuously updates central repositories containing data transmitted from institutions nationwide (Meistrell and Schlehuber 1996). However, in most places, only "islands of automation" exist—digital health information remains cloistered within departments, institutions, or communities (OTA 1995, 30).

Nonetheless, in the future, an enormous volume of electronic clinical information will likely accumulate as a routine byproduct of patient care. Several provisions within the Health Insurance Portability and Accountability Act of 1996 (the Kassebaum/Kennedy Bill), signed by President Clinton on August 21, 1996, give the federal government a leading role in determining data transmission standards, mechanisms for protecting privacy, and ways of coding the specified data elements. Title II—Subtitle F, "Administrative Simplification" (H.R. 3103) of the act requires nationally uniform standards for electronic exchange of administrative data by all health plans and providers. Transaction and security standards are to be specified within 18 months of the act's signing.

This chapter concludes by touching briefly on several considerations that will shape the future of "administrative" data.

Standardization of Data Capture and Transmission

"Standards are agreements on how to implement technologies" (OTA 1995, 68). To share data electronically, data must be technically produced and transmitted in a standard fashion. Promulgation of such standards in the banking industry now allows travelers to obtain cash from automatic teller machines worldwide. In healthcare, messaging standards will permit data exchanges across entire health systems, drawing from such sources as bedside computers, physiologic monitors, billing systems, and outside knowledge bases.

Development of consensus standards for healthcare is actively proceeding in the United States and internationally by committees representing an array of stakeholders (e.g., technology vendors, government, medical representatives, unions). Standards committees are accredited by organizations such as the American Society for Testing and Materials (ASTM) and the American National Standards Institute (ANSI). Committees trying to build consensus typically meet over several years, seeking external review and comment on draft standards before submitting them to a vote. The resulting standards, on the surface a baffling assortment of acronyms, are often interrelated (OTA 1995, 69): For example, the ANSI X12 standard directs communication of financial data to insurers and others outside healthcare organizations, HL7 standards (written by the Health Level Seven committee) govern sharing of clinical data, and E1467 standards (developed by the ASTM E31.16 subcommittee) guide exchange of neurophysiological data from physiological monitors (these messages use identical syntax and most of the same segments as HL7 messages, but they incorporate data structures for continuous waveforms, such as electroencephalogram tracings). To coordinate standards development, in 1993 ANSI created the Health Informatics Standards Planning Panel.

Standards are moot without something to standardize. Therefore, a central activity of some standards committees involves specifying the data elements to be captured. Although little is yet finalized, certain standards committees (e.g., those addressing claims) appear interested in introducing more clinical information alongside the standard financial data elements. Once data elements are identified, those that are language based (e.g., not an electronic waveform) must be coded. Various organizations are therefore considering the content of data sets and new coding approaches.

Subtitle F, Sec. 261, of the Kassebaum/Kennedy Bill (P.L. 104–191) views standards as the means for administrative simplification:

> It is the purpose of this subtitle to improve the Medicare program under title XVIII of the Social Security Act, the Medicaid program under title XIX of such Act, and the efficiency and effectiveness of the health care system, by encouraging the development of a health information system through the establishment of standards and requirements for the electronic transmission of certain health information.

Content of Data Sets

Even with established data transmission standards, the content of data sets can still be diverse. For example, the National Uniform Billing Committee created the UB-92 form. To encourage electronic claims transmission, in 1992 HCFA offered direct electronic payment for providers submitting at least 90 percent of their claims this way. However, each state adds its own data elements to the electronic form. Some payors and software vendors therefore must support almost 50 versions of UB-92 (OTA 1995, 93). The electronic data interchange standard for claims (X12.837) can structure UB-92 data differently—so while the transmission standard remains intact, the precise content varies.

HCFA stipulated that all Medicare claims be transmitted using the standard form by 1996, and HCFA is aiming for 100 percent electronic transmission of claims by the year 2000. Electronic physician claims will be required to use the ANSI 837 or National Standards Format (Tokarski 1996). HCFA's action is expected to move the entire industry into conformance (OTA 1995). The new automated Medicare Transaction System will integrate Part A and B claims data, and it will replace fiscal intermediaries and local claims processors with two national processing centers (Tokarski 1996).

However, the future content of claims and other standard information sets on health and healthcare remains actively debated. No single group has yet assumed leadership on deliberations on the content of data sets. The AMA chairs the National Uniform Claim Committee (NUCC), established in 1995 to develop a uniform set of data elements for electronic transmission on claims (Borzo 1996b). Some NUCC members apparently want to add to claims selected data elements not available elsewhere, such as patients' self-reported functional status. AMA representatives are opposed. As the AMA director of medical practice and financing said, "Just because we're no longer restricted to an 8½-by-11-inch sheet of paper doesn't mean the sky's the limit" (Borzo 1996b, 8). Another AMA official concurred: "We don't want to burden physicians with extra work or clutter up the claims form with superfluous information" (Borzo 1996b, 8). Two activities of the National Committee on Vital and Health Statistics (NCVHS) have addressed the future of data set content.

The Future of UHDDS

The UHDDS's initial intent was to collect the "minimum" information necessary for "planning, monitoring, evaluation, and adjustment of the health services system" (NCVHS 1980, 1). In the early 1990s, increasing interest in monitoring patient outcomes prompted a reassessment of the content of UHDDS by the NCVHS, in conjunction with the National Uniform Billing Committee. A proposal for revising the UHDDS was submitted in June 1992 (NCVHS 1992). Although none of the proposed changes have yet been adopted, they offer a roadmap on how UHDDS might be improved.

The NCVHS advocated adoption of a unique patient identification number that could track individuals across settings of care, regardless of payor. SSN, with a modifier as necessary, was considered the best candidate number, with encryption when files are offered for outside use. The NCVHS further proposed unique identifiers for hospitals and physicians using the Medicare Unique Physician Identification Number (UPIN), with UPINs listed for both attending and operating physicians. These changes would permit tracking providers across databases, regardless of payor source.

The NCVHS proposed adding several new data elements to UHDDS: birth weight of newborns, preferably in grams; total charges billed by the facility; and a socioeconomic indicator, such as years of education completed. The listing of diagnoses generated several proposals, most importantly adding a new data element—an "alpha" qualifier indicating whether the onset of the diagnosis preceded or followed admission to the hospital. This proposal was based on prior experience at the Mayo Clinic and New York state, where it added a "modest additional cost" to data collection. The NCVHS also recommended specifying the primary in addition to the principal diagnosis and adding a special place to code external cause of injury (E codes, see above).

Core Data Elements Project

In 1994, the U.S. Department of Health and Human Services requested that the NCVHS provide advice about data elements pertaining to individuals and to healthcare encounters that are important to meeting the Department's responsibilities (Centers for Disease Control and Prevention 1996). Specifically, NCVHS was asked to review the state of the art in collecting person- and encounter-level data and to obtain input from key users of healthcare information around the country about core data elements. Between 1994 and 1996, NCVHS reviewed standard governmental data sets (e.g., UB-92, the HCFA 1500 form), data sets prepared by standards organizations (e.g., ANSI 834 format, for health plan enrollment transactions; ANSI 837 format, for health claims and encounters), and data routinely collected by major insurers and health plans. NCVHS also held several hearings, soliciting input from governmental and private producers and users of health data, standards-setting organization representatives, and reports on international health data efforts.

A major finding of NCVHS's study involved the process of decision making—many different organizations (e.g., governments, standards committees, private health plans) are making decisions *now* about data elements to collect routinely, without a recognized leader to promote consensus. Therefore, this situation raises the immediate risk of a cacophony of diverse, competing approaches. The NCVHS recommended a public-private working group to further consensus among interested parties. Forty-two core data elements were identified. While general agreement on their importance was apparent on many basic data elements (such as those already included in UHDDS), considerable diversity persisted in preferred definitions. Data elements, such as patients' health status and functional status, were included among core data elements by many organizations, but there was no standard definition for these attributes.

The ironic warning embedded in this NCVHS study is the threat of fragmentation—that despite new information technologies (or perhaps because of them), we could spiral away from achieving truly comparable information across the entire healthcare delivery system. This possibility parallels the trend arising following the demise of federal healthcare reform (see Chapter 1). Without a single, nationwide strategy for healthcare financing and delivery—or data policy—many individual stakeholders are making disparate decisions meeting their own specific needs.

ICD-10 and Other Coding Approaches

Standards are also essential for describing diagnoses, procedures, and other nonnumeric clinical information. ICD-9-CM, HCPCS, and CPT are examples of such coding schemes, but there are others. For example, the *International Classification of Primary Care* aims explicitly to classify the three elements of a healthcare encounter: the reason for the encounter, the diagnoses or problems presented, and the process of care (Lamberts and Wood 1989). In addition, several efforts are under way to define medical terms consistently. For instance, the Systematized Nomenclature of Medicine (SNOMED) plans to standardize vocabulary and definitions of medical terms. The National Library of Medicine is meshing SNOMED and over 20 other standardized medical vocabularies into the Unified Medical Language System (UMLS) (McCray and Divita 1995). The UMLS Metathesaurus hopes to link terms with common meanings.

Despite its massive size, even the UMLS Metathesaurus will not address all needs. For example, investigators at Group Health Cooperative of Puget Sound found that many terms desired by clinicians for a problem-list vocabulary were missing from the UMLS Metathesaurus, and the method's internal linkages were ill suited to their needs (Payne and Martin 1994). They concluded that many terms would need to be added for their specific clinical setting. Nonetheless, the hope is that methods like the UMLS Metathesaurus, which is repeatedly updated and enhanced, will facilitate searches of healthcare databases created by different groups for different purposes.

In the meantime, the WHO has pursued its mandated responsibility to revise the ICD nomenclature periodically (Weigel and Lewis 1991). Proposals for revisions from around the world were reviewed by WHO and its various advisory bodies from 1984 through 1987 before it produced a draft revision—the ICD-10. Delegates from 43 countries gathered in Geneva in 1989 to review these ICD-10 drafts, and the final version of ICD-10 was approved by the World Health Assembly in May 1990. ICD-10 looks, on the surface, quite different from ICD-9, with its alphanumeric numbering scheme and new chapter titles (V codes and E codes, formerly supplementary listings, are now integrated into the main classification rubric). To underscore the statistical purpose of the nomenclature and its expanded scope, ICD-10's official title is the *International Statistical Classification of Diseases and Related Health Problems*. The target date for worldwide implementation of ICD-10 was January 1993.

By international treaty, the United States is required to report mortality statistics using ICD-10. Therefore, the federal National Center for Health Statistics, which oversees vital statistics reporting in the United States, has geared up for the transition to ICD-10, with retroactive recoding of cases to 1993. But, as described above, diagnosis coding in the United States serves multiple purposes. The sheer mechanics of a full-scale transition from ICD-9-CM to ICD-10 will be very expensive and logistically complicated—requiring reprogramming of computers and retraining of thousands of coders from private doctors' offices to health clinics to hospitals. In addition, as with ICD-9, Americans may wish to "clinically modify" ICD-10, creating a volume that contains more detail; a federal contractor hired by the National Center for Health Statistics is currently examining this possibility. ICD-10 does not have a procedure classification. HCFA has hired 3M Health Information Systems, the vendor of APR-DRGs, to create a new procedure nomenclature—an ICD-10 procedure classification.

Widespread implementation of ICD-10 (or an ICD-10-CM) in the United States will have far-reaching ramifications. For example, HCFA will need to ensure that this shift will not significantly increase DRG-based hospital payment simply as a coding artifact. At this time, future plans for moving to ICD-10 for morbidity reporting in the United States are unclear.

Organizations Involved in Data Production and Dissemination

Rapidly developing telecommunications and networking technologies increasingly facilitate linkages of diverse data systems. The vision of community health information networks (CHINs) and community health management information systems (CHMIS) is to link within regions various clinical institutions, public health officials, private medical practices, payors and insurers, and academic institutions (OTA 1995). The two forms—CHINs and CHMISs—share many features but have slightly different emphases. CHINs aim initially to facilitate connections and data transport across organizations within regions, while CHMISs typically concentrate on creating central data repositories for evaluating provider and health plan performance. Nonetheless, both types of networks are envisioned as systems allowing the "seamless exchange of clinical or administrative information among health care providers, payers, and other authorized users" (OTA 1995, 95).

Roughly 100 CHINs and CHMISs are under development around the country. Technology is not usually the limiting factor: Many new methods are available that permit easy transportation of large quantities of health data, even at the patient level (e.g., "smart cards" containing integrated circuit chips or laser optical cards that can contain up to 2.5 megabytes of digital information). Instead, advancement of these organizations is typically slowed by concerns about confidentiality and privacy, organization and ownership control, and network design and data management. For example, in 1994, the Iowa legislature created the Community Health Management Information System requiring all providers and payors to use uniform electronic claims and eligibility verification by July 1996. This deadline was extended for a year due to delays caused by "overzealousness and poor planning . . . [and] trying to lead in a field fraught with conflicting agendas, increasing competition and rapidly developing technologies at a time when health care faces pressing demands to contain costs" (Borzo 1996c, 4). According to a representative of the local medical society, "This project has caused a lot of confusion and concern for physicians. Physicians didn't know what they had to do, how to go about it or how much it would cost" (Borzo 1996c, 4).

Some are concerned that, as more managed care organizations become integrated delivery systems, the attractions of CHINs and CHMISs will diminish (OTA 1995, 103). Not only will such integrated systems "wire" their extensive network of providers, but competing organizations will be unwilling to share information. Others counter that large purchasers of healthcare services will force public release of comparable information across plans.

Changes in the Organization and Payment of Healthcare Delivery

Finally, capitated payment plans, such as HMOs, are expanding rapidly in some healthcare marketplaces. Annual capitation payments are determined by some actuarial formula, perhaps involving risk adjustment (e.g., using the ACGs or DCGs–HCCs). Providers therefore do not submit bills for individual services. For example, Part B claims are not produced for Medicare beneficiaries enrolled in HMOs; Part A hospital claims are submitted only for beneficiaries enrolled in cost-based HMOs (Mitchell et al. 1994). As more Medicare beneficiaries are encouraged to join HMOs, HCFA is currently undecided about what reporting standards to require. For example, should HMOs document services provided to Medicare beneficiaries during their year of enrollment? While such data appear central to HCFA fiduciary responsibility to ensure quality of care for Medicare beneficiaries, handling claims—even electronically—is costly.

Some HMOs argue vehemently against requiring reports about individual services, saying it would increase their administrative expenses and thus defeat a major purpose of capitation. Others recognize that some information tracking the services provided to enrollees must be produced, at least for internal business purposes (e.g., planning, monitoring utilization, profiling physicians). Nonetheless, if HMOs face no external reporting requirements, the databases developed for their internal use are likely to diverge in content and scope, thus impeding comparisons across plans. In addition, HMOs may view these internal data as proprietary, prohibiting outside use or cross-plan comparisons. Either way, current trends in the financing and organization of healthcare delivery lessen the potential for useful, comparative administrative data from a burgeoning sector of the marketplace.

Summary

Administrative databases clearly offer important advantages. They are relatively inexpensive and readily available; they generally cover either populations or large groups of persons whose numbers are known; and from creative and clinically informed use of ICD-9-CM codes, one can get a sense—albeit preliminary—of the clinical status of patients. If longitudinal, patient-level data are available, administrative databases also minimize problems in tracking study subjects over time and remove the reliance on patients' recall of service use (Roos, Nicol, and Cageorge 1987).

However, administrative data also have important drawbacks. From a clinical perspective, limitations of the ICD-9-CM coding nomenclature itself are of particular concern: From ICD-9-CM, one cannot obtain a complete clinical picture of the extent and nature of all "dimensions of risk" outlined in Chapter 2. Troubling questions are also raised by limitations in the way ICD-9-CM is applied and the retrospective nature of discharge diagnoses. Because of these difficulties, one may not be able to use administrative data adequately to address important research or policy questions. The next step often involves collecting data directly from medical records or patients, as described in Chapter 4.

References

Anderson, G., E. P. Steinberg, J. Whittle, N. R. Powe, S. Antebi, and R. Herbert. 1990. "Development of Clinical and Economic Prognoses From Medicare Claims Data." *Journal of the American Medical Association* 263 (7): 967–72.

Baron, J. A., G. Lu-Yao, J. Barrett, D. McLerran, and E. S. Fisher. 1994. "Internal Validation of Medicare Claims Data." *Epidemiology* 5 (5): 541–44.

Blumberg, M. S., and G. S. Binns. 1989. *Risk-Adjusted 30-Day Mortality of Fresh Acute Myocardial Infarctions: The Technical Report.* Chicago: The Hospital Research and Educational Trust of the American Hospital Association.

Borzo, G. 1996a. "Breaking the E-code." *American Medical News* 39 (14): 1, 27.

———. 1996b. "AMA Wants Role in Evolving System for Billing Payers." *American Medical News* 39 (27): 7–8.

———. 1996c. "Iowa Delays, Scales Back Electronic Billing Plan." *American Medical News* 39 (28): 4–5.

Bright, R. A., J. Avorn, and D. E. Everitt. 1989. "Medicaid Data as a Resource for Epidemiologic Studies: Strengths and Limitations." *Journal of Clinical Epidemiology* 42 (10): 937–45.

Brown, F. 1989. *ICD-9-CM Coding Handbook, Without Answers. Revised Edition.* Chicago: American Hospital Publishing, Inc., Division of Quality Control Management of the American Hospital Association.

Carter, G. M., J. P. Newhouse, and D. A. Relles. 1990. *How Much Change in the Case Mix Index Is DRG Creep?* R-3826-HCFA Santa Monica, CA: RAND Corporation.

———. 1991. *Has DRG Creep Crept Up? Decomposing the Case Mix Index Change between 1987 and 1988.* R-4098-HCFA/ProPAC. Santa Monica, CA: RAND Corporation.

Cassel, C. K., and B. C. Vladeck. 1996."ICD-9 Code for Palliative or Terminal Care." *New England Journal of Medicine* 335 (16): 1232–34.

Centers for Disease Control and Prevention, National Center for Health Statistics. 1996. *Report of the National Committee on Vital and Health Statistics. Core Health Data Elements.* Washington, D.C.: U.S. Government Printing Office.

Center for Evaluative Clinical Studies, Dartmouth Medical School. 1996. *The Dartmouth Atlas of Health Care.* Chicago: American Hospital Association.

Charlson, M. E., P. Pompei, K. L. Ales, and C. R. MacKenzie. 1987. "A New Method of Classifying Prognostic Comorbidity in Longitudinal Studies: Development and Validation." *Journal of Chronic Disease* 40 (5): 373–83.

Cleary, P. D., S. Edgman-Levitan, J. O. Walker, M. Gerteis, and T. L. Delbanco. 1993. "Using Patient Reports to Improve Medical Care: A Preliminary Report From 10 Hospitals." *Quality Management in Health Care* 2 (1): 31–38.

Connell, F. A., P. Diehr, and L. G. Hart. 1987. "The Use of Large Data Bases in Health Care Studies." *Annual Review of Public Health* 8: 51–74.

Deyo, R. A., D. C. Cherkin, and M. A. Ciol. 1992. "Adapting a Clinical Comorbidity Index for Use With ICD-9-CM Administrative Databases." *Journal of Clinical Epidemiology* 45 (6): 613–19.

Donaldson, M. S., and K. N. Lohr, eds. 1994. *Health Data in the Information Age. Use, Disclosure, and Privacy.* Washington, D.C.: National Academy Press.

Edlavitch, S. A., M. Feinleib, and C. Anello. 1985. "A Potential Use of the National Death Index for Postmarketing Drug Surveillance." *Journal of the American Medical Association* 253 (9): 1292–95.

Elixhauser, A., R. M. Andrews, and S. Fox. 1993. *Clinical Classifications for Health Policy Research: Discharge Statistics by Principal Diagnosis and Procedure.* (AHCPR

Publication No. 93–0043). Division of Provider Studies Research Note 17. Rockville, MD: Agency for Health Care Policy and Research, Public Health Service.

Elixhauser, A., R. Andrews, J. Ball, R. Coffey, M. Johantgen, and P. Purcell. 1996. "Lessons for National Standards on Health Data: State Practices in Building Databases on Hospital Inpatient Stays." In *Data Needs in an Era of Health Reform*, 359. Proceedings of the 25th Public Health Conference on Records and Statistics and the National Committee on Vital and Health Statistics 45th Anniversary Symposium. Washington, D.C.: U. S. Department of Health and Human Services.

Elixhauser, A., and E. McCarthy. 1996. *Clinical Classifications for Health Policy Research, Version 2: Hospital Inpatient Statistics.* (AHCPR Publication No. 96–0017). Healthcare Cost and Utilization Project (HCUP-3) Research Note 1. Rockville, MD: Agency for Healthcare Policy and Research.

Epstein, M. H. 1992. "Guest Alliance: Uses of State-Level Hospital Discharge Databases." *Journal of the American Health Information Management Association* 63 (4): 32–37.

Epstein, S. E., A. A. Quyyumi, and R. O. Bonow. 1989. "Sudden Cardiac Death without Warning: Possible Mechanisms and Implications for Screening Asymptomatic Populations." *New England Journal of Medicine* 321 (5): 320–24.

Federal Register. 1991. "Rules and Regulations." 58 (169): 43213–15.

"Feds Hear Medicine's Plea, Drop One Medicare Form." 1995. *American Medical News* 38 (27): 26.

Feinstein, A. R. 1988. "ICD, POR, and DRG. Unsolved Scientific Problems in the Nosology of Clinical Medicine." *Archives of Internal Medicine* 148 (10): 2269–74.

Fetter, R. B., Y. Shin, J. L. Freeman, R. F. Averill, and J. D. Thompson. 1980. "Case Mix Definition by Diagnosis Related Groups." *Medical Care* 18 (2) Supplement: 1–53.

Fisher, E. S., F. S. Whaley, W. M. Krushat, D. J. Malenka, C. Fleming, J. A. Baron, and D. C. Hsia. 1992. "The Accuracy of Medicare's Hospital Claims Data: Progress Has Been Made, but Problems Remain." *American Journal of Public Health* 82 (2): 243–48.

Fleming, C., E. S. Fisher, C. H. Chang, T. A. Bubolz, and D. J. Malenka. 1992. "Studying Outcomes and Hospital Utilization in the Elderly: The Advantages of a Merged Data Base for Medicare and Veterans Affairs Hospitals." *Medical Care* 30 (5): 377–88.

Fowles, J. B., A. G. Lawthers, J. P. Weiner, D. W. Garnick, D. S. Petrie, and R. H. Palmer. 1995. "Agreement Between Physicians' Office Records and Medicare Part B Claims Data." *Health Care Financing Review* 16 (4): 189–99.

Gardner, E. 1990. "UB-82 Forms Offer Wealth of Information, Misinformation." *Modern Healthcare* 20 (38): 18–19, 24–29.

Garnick, D. W., J. Fowles, A. G. Lawthers, J. P. Weiner, S. T. Parente, and R. H. Palmer. 1994. "Focus on Quality: Profiling Physicians' Practice Patterns." *Journal of Ambulatory Care Management* 17 (3): 44–75.

Garnick, D. W., A. M. Hendricks, C. B. Comstock, and D. B. Pryor. 1996. "A Guide to Using Administrative Data for Medical Effectiveness Research." *Journal of Outcomes Management* 3 (1): 18–23.

Gerstman, B. B., F. E. Lundin, B. V. Stadel, and G. A. Faich. 1990. "A Method of

Pharmacoepidemiologic Analysis That Uses Computerized Medicaid." *Journal of Clinical Epidemiology* 43 (12): 1387–93.

Gerteis, M., S. Edgman-Levitan, J. D. Walker, D. M. Stokes, P. D. Cleary, and T. L. Delbanco. 1993. "What Patients Really Want." *Health Management Quarterly* 15 (2): 2–6.

Ghali, W. A., R. E. Hall, A. K. Rosen, A. S. Ash, and M. A. Moskowitz. 1996. "Searching for an Improved Clinical Comorbidity Index for Use With ICD-9-CM Administrative Data." *Journal of Clinical Epidemiology* 49 (3): 273–78.

Gianelli, D. M. 1996. "New Diagnosis Code Will Track Palliative Care in Hospitals." *American Medical News* 39 (35): 5.

Goldfarb, M. G., and R. M. Coffey. 1992. "Change in the Medicare Case-Mix Index in the 1980s and the Effect of the Prospective Payment System." *HSR: Health Services Research* 27 (3): 385–415.

Greenfield, S., H. U. Aronow, R. M. Elashoff, and D. Watanabe. 1988. "Flaws in Mortality Data: The Hazards of Ignoring Comorbid Disease." *Journal of the American Medical Association* 260 (15): 2253–55.

Hannan, E. L., H. R. Bernard, J. F. O'Donnell, and H. Kilburn, Jr. 1989. "A Methodology for Targeting Hospital Cases for Quality of Care Record Reviews." *American Journal of Public Health* 79 (4): 430–36.

Hannan, E. L., H. Kilburn, Jr., M. L. Lindsey, and R. Lewis. 1992. "Clinical Versus Administrative Data Bases for CABG Surgery: Does It Matter?" *Medical Care* 30 (10): 892–907.

Health Care Financing Administration, Bureau of Data Management and Strategy. 1995. *Data Users Reference Guide.* Baltimore, MD: U.S. Department of Health and Human Services.

———. 1996a. *Overview of Health Care Financing Administration Data. Resource Guide.* Baltimore, MD: U.S. Department of Health and Human Services.

Health Care Financing Administration, Bureau of Data Management and Strategy, Office of Health Care Information Systems. 1996b. *Public Use Files Catalog. Medicare/Medicaid Data Files.* Baltimore, MD: U.S. Department of Health and Human Services.

Hsia, D. C., C. A. Ahern, B. P. Ritchie, L. M. Moscoe, and W. M. Krushat. 1992. "Medicare Reimbursement Accuracy under the Prospective Payment System, 1985 to 1988." *Journal of the American Medical Association* 268 (7): 896–99.

Hsia, D. C., W. M. Krushat, A. B. Fagan, J. A. Tebbutt, and R. P. Kusserow. 1988. "Accuracy of Diagnostic Coding for Medicare Patients under the Prospective-Payment System." *New England Journal of Medicine* 318 (6): 352–55.

Hughes, J. S., L. I. Iezzoni, J. Daley, and L. Greenberg. 1996. "How Severity Measures Rate Hospitalized Patients." *Journal of General Internal Medicine* 11 (5): 303–11.

Iezzoni, L. I. 1990. "Using Administrative Diagnostic Data to Assess the Quality of Hospital Care: The Pitfalls and Potential of ICD-9-CM." *International Journal of Technology Assessment in Health Care* 6 (2): 272–81.

Iezzoni, L. I., A. S. Ash, M. Shwartz, J. Daley, J. S. Hughes, and Y. D. Mackiernan. 1995a. "Predicting Who Dies Depends on How Severity is Measured: Implications for Evaluating Patient Outcomes." *Annals of Internal Medicine* 123 (10): 763–70.

Iezzoni, L. I., S. Burnside, L. Sickles, M. A. Moskowitz, E. Sawitz, and P. A.

Levine. 1988. "Coding of Acute Myocardial Infarction: Clinical and Policy Implications." *Annals of Internal Medicine* 109 (9): 745–51.

Iezzoni, L. I., J. Daley, T. Heeren, S. M. Foley, E. S. Fisher, C. Duncan, J. S. Hughes, and G. A. Coffman. 1994a. "Identifying Complications of Care Using Administrative Data." *Medical Care* 32 (7): 700–15.

Iezzoni, L. I., S. M. Foley, J. Daley, J. Hughes, E. S. Fisher, and T. Heeren. 1992a. "Comorbidities, Complications, and Coding Bias: Does the Number of Diagnosis Codes Matter in Predicting In-Hospital Mortality?" *Journal of the American Medical Association* 267 (16): 2197–2203.

Iezzoni, L. I., T. Heeren, S. M. Foley, J. Daley, J. Hughes, and G. A. Coffman. 1994b. "Chronic Conditions and Risk of In-hospital Death." *HSR: Health Services Research* 29 (4): 435–60.

Iezzoni, L. I., and M. A. Moskowitz. 1984. *The Clinical Impact of DRG-Based Physician Reimbursement.* Prepared for the Health Care Financing Administration under Cooperative Agreement (18-C-98526/1–01), Health Policy Research Consortium.

———. 1986. "Clinical Overlap among Medical Diagnosis-Related Groups." *Journal of the American Medical Association* 255 (7): 927–29.

Iezzoni, L. I., M. Shwartz, A. S. Ash, J. S. Hughes, J. Daley, and Y. D. Mackiernan. 1995b. "Using Severity-adjusted Stroke Mortality Rates to Judge Hospitals." *International Journal for Quality in Health Care* 7 (2): 81–94.

———. 1996a. "Severity Measurement Methods and Judging Hospital Death Rates for Pneumonia." *Medical Care* 34 (1): 11–28.

Iezzoni, L. I., M. Shwartz, A. S. Ash, J. S. Hughes, J. Daley, Y. D. Mackiernan, and D. Stone. 1995c. *Evaluating Severity Adjustors for Patient Outcome Studies: Final Report.* Prepared for the Agency for Health Care Policy and Research under grant no. HS06742. Boston, MA: Beth Israel Hospital.

Iezzoni, L. I., M. Shwartz, A. S. Ash, and Y. D. Mackiernan. 1996b. "Using Severity Measures to Predict the Likelihood of Death for Pneumonia Inpatients." *Journal of General Internal Medicine* 11 (1): 23–31.

Iezzoni, L. I., A. S. Ash, M. Shwartz, J. Daley, J. S. Hughes, and Y. D. Mackiernan. 1996c. "Judging Hospitals by Severity-Adjusted Mortality Rates: The Influence of the Severity-Adjustment Method." *American Journal of Public Health* 86 (10): 1379–87.

Institute of Medicine. 1977a. *Reliability of Hospital Discharge Abstracts.* Washington, D.C.: National Academy of Sciences.

———. 1977b. *Reliability of Medicare Hospital Discharge Records.* Washington, D.C.: National Academy of Sciences.

Israel, R. A. 1978. "The International Classification of Diseases: Two Hundred Years of Development." *Public Health Reports* 93 (2): 150–52.

Jencks, S. F. 1992. "Accuracy in Recorded Diagnoses." *Journal of the American Medical Association* 267 (16): 2238–39.

Jencks, S. F., D. K. Williams, and T. L. Kay. 1988. "Assessing Hospital-Associated Deaths from Discharge Data: The Role of Length of Stay and Comorbidities." *Journal of the American Medical Association* 260 (15): 2240–46.

Johnsson, J. 1996. "Crackdown on Coding Ahead." *American Medical News* 39 (24): 28.

Keeler, E. B., K. L. Kahn, D. Draper, M. J. Sherwood, L. V. Rubenstein, E. J. Reinisch, J. Kosecoff, and R. H. Brook. 1990. "Changes in Sickness at Admission Following the Introduction of the Prospective Payment System." *Journal of the American Medical Association* 264 (15): 1962–68.

Kong, D. "High Hospital Death Rates," *Boston Globe,* October 3, 1994, 1, 6, 7.

Ku, L., M. R. Ellwood, and J. Klemm. 1990. "Deciphering Medicaid Data: Issues and Needs." *Health Care Financing Review* Annual Supplement: 35–45.

Lamberts, H., and M. Wood. 1989. *International Classification of Primary Care.* Oxford: Oxford University Press.

Lamoreaux, J. 1996. "The Organizational Structure for Medical Information Management in the Department of Veterans Affairs. An Overview of Major Health Care Databases." *Medical Care* 34 (3): MS31-MS44.

Landon, B., L. I. Iezzoni, A. S. Ash, M. Shwartz, J. Daley, J. S. Hughes, and Y. D. Mackiernan. 1996. "Judging Hospitals by Severity-Adjusted Mortality Rates: The Case of CABG Surgery." *Inquiry* 33 (2): 155–66.

Larkin, H. 1996. "AMA, HCFA Vow to Correct Medicare Coding." *American Medical News* 39 (27): 7–8.

Lave, J. R., C. L. Pashos, G. F. Anderson, D. Brailer, T. Bubolz, D. Conrad, D. A. Freund, S. H. Fox, E. Keeler, J. Lipscomb, H. S. Luft, and G. Provenzano. 1994. "Costing Medical Care: Using Medicare Administrative Data." *Medical Care* 32 (7): JS77-JS89.

Lloyd, S. S., and J. P. Rissing. 1985. "Physician and Coding Errors in Patient Records." *Journal of the American Medical Association* 254 (10): 1330–36.

Lohr, K. N., and A. J. Walker. 1990. "The Utilization and Quality Control Peer Review Organization Program." In *Medicare: A Strategy for Quality Assurance: Volume II, Sources and Methods,* edited by K. N. Lohr. Washington, D.C.: Institute of Medicine, National Academy Press.

McCray, A. T., and G. Divita. 1995. "ASN.1: Defining a Grammar for the UMLS Knowledge Sources." *Proceedings of the Annual Symposium on Computer Applications in Medical Care:* 868–72.

McMahon, L. F., Jr., and H. L. Smits. 1986. "Can Medicare Prospective Payment Survive the ICD-9-CM Disease Classification System?" *Annals of Internal Medicine* 104 (4): 562–66.

Meistrell, M., and C. Schlehuber. 1996. "Adopting a Corporate Perspective on Databases: Improving Support for Research and Decision Making." *Medical Care* 34 (3): MS91-MS102.

Messite, J., and S. D. Stellman. 1996. "Accuracy of Death Certificate Completion. The Need for Formalized Physician Training." *Journal of the American Medical Association* 275 (10): 794–96.

Meux, E. 1994. "Encrypting Personal Identifiers." *HSR: Health Services Research* 29 (2): 247–56.

Meux, E. F., S. A. Stith, and A. Zach. 1990. *Report of Results from the OSHPD Reabstracting Project: An Evaluation of the Reliability of Selected Patient Discharge Data, July through December 1988.* Sacramento, CA: Office of Statewide Health Planning and Development.

Mitchell, J.B., T. Bubolz, J. E. Paul, C. L. Pashos, J. J. Escarce, L. H. Muhlbaier, J. M.

Wiesman, W. W. Young, R. S. Epstein, and J. C. Javitt. 1994. "Using Medicare Claims for Outcomes Research." *Medical Care* 32 (7): JS38-JS51.

National Committee on Vital and Health Statistics (NCVHS), Subcommittee on Ambulatory and Hospital Care Statistics. 1992. *Proposed Revision to the Uniform Hospital Discharge Data Set.* Washington, D.C.: National Committee on Vital and Health Statistics.

National Committee on Vital and Health Statistics, U.S. Department of Health, Education, and Welfare. 1980. *Uniform Hospital Discharge Data Minimum Data Set.* DHWQ Pub. (PHS) 80–1157. Hyattsville, MD: U.S. Department of Health, Education, and Welfare.

National Uniform Billing Committee. 1996. *UB-92. Data Element Specifications as Developed by the National Uniform Billing Committee.*

Office of Technology Assessment, U.S. Congress (OTA). 1994. *Identifying Health Technologies That Work: Searching for Evidence.* OTA-H-608. Washington, D.C.: U.S. Government Printing Office.

———. 1995. *Bringing Health Care Online. The Role of Information Technologies.* OTA-ITC-624. Washington, D.C.: U.S. Government Printing Office.

O'Gara, S. 1990. "Data Sets and Coding Guidelines: Sequencing vs. Classification Rules." *Journal of the American Medical Record Review Association* 61 (2): 20–21.

Parente, S. T., J. P. Weiner, D. W. Garnick, T. M. Richards, J. Fowles, A. G. Lawthers, P. Chandler, and R. H. Palmer. 1995. "Developing a Quality Improvement Database Using Health Insurance Data: A Guided Tour With Application to Medicare's National Claims History File." *American Journal of Medical Quality* 10 (4): 162–76.

Payne, T. H., and D. R. Martin. 1994. "How Useful is the UMLS Metathesaurus in Developing a Controlled Vocabulary for an Automated Problem List?" *Proceedings of the Annual Symposium on Computer Applications in Medical Care:* 705–9.

Payne, T. H., G. R. Murphy, and A. A. Salazar. 1993. "How Well Does ICD9 Represent Phrases Used in the Medical Record Problem List?" *Proceedings of the Annual Symposium on Computer Applications in Medical Care:* 654–57.

Prospective Payment Assessment Commission (ProPAC).1996. *Medicare and the American Health Care System. Report to the Congress.* Washington, D.C.: Prospective Payment Assessment Commission.

Quam, L., L. B. M. Ellis, P. Venus, J. Clouse, C. G. Taylor, and S. Leatherman. 1993. "Using Claims Data for Epidemiologic Research: The Concordance of Claims-Based Criteria with the Medical Record and Patient Survey for Identifying a Hypertensive Population." *Medical Care* 31 (6): 498–507.

Ray, W. A., and M. R. Griffin. 1989. "Use of Medicaid Data for Pharmacoepidemiology." *American Journal of Epidemiology* 129 (4): 837–49.

Reid, B. 1991. "The Impact of Different Coding Systems on DRG Assignment and Data." *Health Policy* 17 (2): 133–49.

Romano, P. S. 1993. "Can Administrative Data Be Used to Compare the Quality of Health Care?" *Medical Care Review* 50 (4): 451–77.

Romano, P. S., and H. S. Luft. 1992. *Getting the Most Out of Messy Data: Problems and Approaches for Dealing with Large Administrative Data Sets. Proceedings of*

Medical Effectiveness Research Data Methods Conference. Rockville, MD: Agency for Health Care Policy and Research, Public Health Service.

Romano, P. S., and D. H. Mark. 1994. "Bias in the Coding of Hospital Discharge Data and Its Implications for Quality Assessment." *Medical Care* 32 (1): 81–90.

Romano, P. S., L. L. Roos, H. S. Luft, J. G. Jollis, K. Doliszny, and the Ischemic Heart Disease Patient Outcomes Research Team. 1994. "A Comparison of Administrative Versus Clinical Data: Coronary Artery Bypass Surgery as an Example." *Journal of Clinical Epidemiology* 47 (3): 249–60.

Romano, P. S., L. L. Roos, and J. G. Jollis. 1993a. "Adapting a Clinical Comorbidity Index for Use With ICD-9-CM Administrative Data: Differing Perspectives." *Journal of Clinical Epidemiology* 46 (10): 1075–79.

———. 1993b. "Further Evidence Concerning the Use of a Clinical Comorbidity Index With ICD-9-CM Administrative Data." *Journal of Clinical Epidemiology* 46 (10): 1085–90.

Roos, L. L., J. P. Nicol, and S. M. Cageorge. 1987. "Using Administrative Data for Longitudinal Research: Comparisons with Primary Data Collection." *Journal of Chronic Disease* 40 (1): 41–49.

Roos, L. L., R. Walld, A. Wajda, R. Bond, and K. Hartford. 1996. "Record Linkage Strategies, Outpatient Procedures, and Administrative Data." *Medical Care* 34 (6): 570–82.

Shapiro, M. F., R. E. Park, J. Keesey, and R. H. Brook. 1994. "The Effect of Alternative Case-Mix Adjustments on Mortality Differences between Municipal and Voluntary Hospitals in New York City." *HSR: Health Services Research* 29 (1): 95–112.

Sheehy, K. H. 1991. "White Paper: Coding and Classification Systems—Implications for the Profession." *Journal of the American Medical Record Association* 62 (2): 44–49.

Simborg, D. W. 1981. "DRG Creep: A New Hospital-Acquired Disease." *New England Journal of Medicine* 304 (26): 1602–4.

Slee, V. N. 1978. "The International Classification of Diseases: 9th Revision (ICD-9)." *Annals of Internal Medicine* 88 (3): 424–26.

Steinwald, B., and L. A. Dummit. 1989. "Hospital Case-Mix Change. Sicker Patients or DRG Creep?" *Health Affairs* 8 (2): 35–47.

Sullivan, L. W., and G. R. Wilensky. 1991. *Medicare Hospital Mortality Information. 1987, 1988, 1989.* Washington, D.C.: U.S. Department of Health and Human Services, Health Care Financing Administration.

Tokarski, C. 1996. "HCFA Aims for Faster Claims." *American Medical News* 39 (27): 7.

U.S. Public Health Service, Health Care Financing Administration. 1980. *The International Classification of Diseases, 9th Revision, Clinical Modification.* PHS 80–1260. Washington, D.C.: U.S. Department of Health and Human Services.

Vladeck, B. C. 1984. "Medicare Hospital Payment by Diagnosis-Related Groups." *Annals of Internal Medicine* 100 (4): 576–91.

Waterstraat, F. L., J. Barlow, and F. Newman. 1990. "Diagnostic Coding Quality and Its Impact on Healthcare Reimbursement: Research Perspectives." *Journal of the American Record Association* 61 (9): 52–59.

Weigel, K. M., and C. A. Lewis. 1991. "Forum: In Sickness and in Health—The Role of the ICD in the United States Health Care Data and ICD-10." *Topics in Health Record Management* 12 (1): 70–82.

Wennberg, J. E., N. Roos, L. Sola, A. Schori, and R. Jaffe. 1987. "Use of Claims Data Systems to Evaluate Health Care Outcomes: Mortality and Reoperation Following Prostatectomy." *Journal of the American Medical Association* 257 (7): 933–36.

Wilson, P., S. R. Smoley, and D. Werdegar. 1996. *Second Report of the California Hospital Outcomes Project. Acute Myocardial Infarction. Volume Two: Technical Appendix.* Sacramento, CA: Office of Statewide Health Planning and Development.

Zuber, T. J., and D. E. Henley. 1992. "New CPT Codes: Hospital, Consultation, Emergency and Nursing Facility Services." *American Family Physician* 45 (3): 1277–83.

Chapter 4

Data Sources and Implications: Information from Medical Records and Patients

Lisa I. Iezzoni

Studies of patient outcomes often start with administrative data because they are readily available, computer readable, and inexpensive to acquire. As mentioned in Chapter 1, a prominent early example was HCFA's publication of hospital mortality rates for Medicare beneficiaries (Sullivan and Wilensky 1991). These HCFA reports relied on the computerized claims accumulated while administering Medicare and paying hospitals (Chapter 3), but this data source also prompted increasing reservations about the validity of the mortality comparisons. In June 1993, newly appointed HCFA administrator Bruce Vladeck halted production of the Medicare hospital mortality reports, concerned that they unfairly penalized inner-city public institutions (Podolsky and Beddingfield 1993). The administrative data did not allow adjustment for critical risk factors associated with poverty and medical indigence.

Elsewhere in the country, some initiatives comparing hospital performance believed they needed to move beyond administrative data (Chapter 11). Regional and statewide programs (e.g., in Pennsylvania, New York state, Cleveland, and St. Louis) mandated widespread collection of clinical severity information from medical records (Iezzoni, Shwartz, and Restuccia 1991; Iezzoni and Greenberg 1994). These programs were motivated by reservations about the clinical content of administrative databases, especially their ability to capture patients' risk factors. According to Walter McClure, a leading proponent of these data mandates, "There is no other way than to go in and abstract the clinical findings from the chart. Let's stop fooling ourselves that we can compare patient severity by claims" (Iglehart 1988, 82).

Medical records offer a rich source of information about patients and their care. Especially in teaching hospitals, records from a single admission can consume hundreds of pages and multiple volumes, with notations from dozens of clinicians and reports from numerous tests and procedures. At a minimum, hospital records generally document patients' histories, chief complaints, presenting symptoms, physical examinations, clinical assessments and diagnoses, diagnostic laboratory results, procedures, medications, in-hospital responses to therapy, day-by-day or hour-by-hour clinical courses, and discharge plans. In most institutions, paper medical records remain the vehicle for clinicians to document and share their immediate clinical impressions and plans and to transmit important information across the variety of persons caring for patients.

Medical records, therefore, are an invaluable source of information about both risk factors and outcomes of care. However, medical records are "second hand" in the sense that all observations have been filtered through the clinician—questions are asked and answers are recorded by clinicians rather than by patients. Medical records thus reflect the realities of human discourse—forces pertaining both to patients and physicians—such as faulty memories, communication failures, subjective judgments, and conscious and unconscious distortions. Thus, medical records do not always yield a straightforward, complete, and objective accounting of patients' risks, especially their preferences for care (Chapter 2). For these reasons, some efforts to evaluate risks and outcomes are turning directly to patients, collecting data from the most primary source.

This chapter examines medical record information and touches briefly on patient-generated data. As with administrative data, new information technologies have the potential to revolutionize the collection and transmission of both clinician- and patient-generated information. The chapter therefore concludes with the future, but starts with the past.

Background

Medical records, as we know them today, are a fairly new creation. Until recently, information about individual patients was dispersed throughout records, not aggregated in a single place. In the early nineteenth century, American hospitals kept records in bound volumes, organized chronologically by admissions, not by patients. In conducting rounds, physicians would walk from bed to bed, writing brief assessments of patients consecutively by bed order. Notations rarely offered diagnostic speculation, emphasizing instead symptoms as described by the patient, with scanty information on physical findings and treatment. Some notes were very brief, such as the following from Massachusetts General Hospital on August 18, 1824:

> Skin nearly natural, tongue rather dry, with moist red edges. Countenance good. Took hasty pudding at 10 a.m. (Massachusetts General Hospital 1824)

In contrast, other notes were longer, containing colorful descriptions of patients' symptoms and physical findings, but generally offering no diagnosis, as in the following notation about a woman of unspecified age, also from the Massachusetts General Hospital on August 18, 1824:

> Sense of fullness and oppression in the Chest. Dyspnea increased by exercise and by recumbent position. Sense of tightness across thorax. Pains in left side, not constant, but often darting to the epigastric region and to left shoulder. Inability of lying on left side, which brought on great distress and sense of suffocation. Tongue has thin pale coat . . . Skin now cool and moist, says she has sweat much at times. Thinks she has not lost much flesh, being much swelled.

Despite the absence of diagnostic conjecture in 1824, the description of symptoms is compelling, permitting speculation today about the patient's ailment—probable congestive heart failure with episodes of angina pectoris.

Even in the late nineteenth century, medical record notes remained primarily descriptive. For example, the Mayo brothers in Rochester, Minnesota, generally did not record physical examinations, diagnoses, or treatments. In most cases, their medical record notations contained only the date, the patient's age, residence, and descriptions of symptoms, such as "gas on the stomach and poor sleep" and "night terrors—wetting bed" (Clapesattle 1941, 385). Patient-centered medical records did not debut until the early twentieth century. The so-called unit medical record, which accumulates all information on an individual patient in a single record, was not fully implemented until 1916, at the Presbyterian Hospital in New York (Kurtz 1943, 2–10).

Concerns about the quality of medical records are not new. Even in the early 1900s, the American College of Surgeons (ACS), in particular, focused considerable attention on what they deemed shoddy medical record-keeping practices. In 1917, the ACS Conference on Hospital Standardization expounded, "If good records are kept, it is almost certain that good work will be done" (Hornsby 1917, 7). The conference judged medical records as "valueless" at 75 percent of hospitals, due to missing information on physical examinations, patients' histories, and diagnoses. The conference was unabashedly direct in assigning blame for these problems, describing the absence of diagnostic information as "premeditated" and "intended to cover up and hide carelessness or incapacity on the part of the surgeon to diagnose the disease. . . ." (Hornsby 1917, 7).

Ernest Amory Codman of Boston, a founder of the ACS (see Chapter 1), envisioned a heretical new use for the medical record, suggesting, "Our record system should enable us to fix responsibility . . . for the success or failure of each case treated" (Codman 1917). He noted the need for "clear, honest records, no matter how brief, if they fearlessly face the facts" (Codman 1917). One suggestion stipulated that progress notes be written at least once every three days (Ramsey and Kingswood 1923). Raymond Pearl, the statistician to The Johns Hopkins Hospital, argued strongly for standardized, printed forms, bemoaning the wide variety of medical record formats used by individual physicians. He observed, "The general scheme or outline which a history is to follow resides, far too often, in the head of the history writer, and there only. And heads, especially of human beings, do vary so!" (Pearl 1921, 187). However, the ACS offered the broadest vision for the role of medical records, arguing in 1918 that they be used to evaluate medical and surgical outcomes:

> Consistent and fearless review of case records by the hospital staff, as here suggested, is a just and effective means to deal with incompetent medical and surgical work in a hospital. Facts are not debatable . . . If the facts establish evidence that a physician or surgeon is unsafe in judgment, unworthy in character, untrained, lax, lazy, or careless, in all honor and decency that individual should either overcome his deficiencies or withdraw from practice . . . A wise use of honest case records points the way to great advance in the medical profession. (American College of Surgeons 1918, 2)

Despite these exhortations, the medical record did not change significantly until the 1960s. One reason for the inertia was the self-proclaimed independence of physicians, who railed against any hint of standardization or uniformity. When change did come, it was largely motivated by the compelling arguments of Lawrence Weed, who observed:

> It will be necessary to develop a more organized approach to the medical record, a more rational acceptance and use of paramedical personnel and a more positive attitude about the computer in medicine. Eventually, for every physician all three areas will be an obligatory part of his professional environment if he is to play a significant part in the total health-care job that will have to be done . . . Among physicians there has been uncritical adherence to tradition in the first phase of medical action, which is the collection of data, upon which complete formulation and management of all the patient's problems depends. (Weed 1968b, 593, 595)

Weed believed that collection of clinical data should be as comprehensive as possible, limited only by the "discomfort, danger and expense to the patient" (Weed 1968b, 595). He noted that, to formulate care plans, physicians had to read through records that were poorly organized and often illegible—a process that was generally performed in an inconsistent and unreliable fashion across clinicians. He suggested focusing documentation around a "problem list," a dynamic inventory of the major clinical issues that required attention. The list could be separated into "active" and "inactive" problems, with all pertinent observations, orders, and plans aggregated around specific problems. Weed echoed Codman's call for using the medical record to audit the quality of care, believing that a problem-oriented medical record clarified the clinical evidence and logic employed in making diagnostic and therapeutic decisions (Weed 1968a).

Weed's further formulation contributed to development of the so-called SOAP notation within the problem list (Weed 1971), organizing information under these four major headings:

- *Subjective:* descriptions of symptoms and subjective feeling, capturing the patients' viewpoint not only about their health status but also about the care they are receiving

- *Objective:* documentation of "objective" clinical findings (e.g., from the physical examination, laboratory testing, diagnostic procedures)

- *Assessment:* physicians' conclusions about the status of the problem based on the subjective and objective evidence

- *Plan:* diagnostic, therapeutic, monitoring, and other activities to address the problems described in the clinicians' assessment

Weed believed that this logical ordering of information would assist in handling the increasing threat of information overload—requiring physicians to process massive quantities of clinical data without logical, organizing principles.

The problem-oriented medical record and the SOAP approach advocated by Weed were widely adopted, but the structure and content of written medical records has changed little in the ensuing two decades despite the explosion of technology. For many years, Weed's pleas for computerization were largely ignored. The potential for information overload persists and expands as technology grows. Some medical records now encompass multiple volumes and hundreds of pages. Information is recorded in various formats, including handwritten free text, such as physician and nursing notes; handwritten graphic displays, such as vital signs charting; handwritten reports on standardized forms (e.g., intraoperative anesthesia records, medication and physician order sheets); typed narrative summaries, including discharge summaries, operative reports, and reports from testing (e.g., radiology or pathology); and typed numerical values arranged often by date and time (e.g., laboratory results). Despite being the source of jokes, illegibility of handwritten notations is a serious problem, especially for retrospective reviews of medical records. Most hospitals are moving toward increasing computerization and electronic transmission of printed documents containing numerical information and test reports—clinical laboratory values and radiology reports, in particular (see below). Nevertheless, some smaller facilities still do much of their internal reporting by hand (e.g., laboratory results are handwritten on individual slips of paper and pasted in the medical record). Even at the largest facilities, the narrative reports of providers caring for patients (e.g., daily progress reports) are rarely computerized or typed. Records in individual physicians' private offices are even more variable than those of hospitals.

The Quality of Clinical Information

As the millennium closes, debate persists about whether medicine is an art or a science. The implicit assumption is that a "science" of medicine leads to discovery of "truth" or "hard facts." However, the so-called objective findings underlying medical practice, such as diagnostic test results and physical examination findings, are often fraught with vagaries and wide variations among observers (Anderson, Hill, and Key 1989). Poor interobserver reliability is common even for many tests that appear technologically sophisticated and machine driven. As Eddy (1984) wrote, "Uncertainty creeps into medical practice through every pore . . . And the ambiguities grow worse as medical technology expands" (75, 76).

This concern about interobserver variation is not only academic. "Unreliable observations are unlikely to be accurate" (Koran 1976, 69), a variation that can significantly affect research findings—and patients:

> For the many phenomena in clinical medicine that are not easily measured and that lack a convenient or definitive "gold standard," the consequences of observer variability may be dramatic. A radiologist's interpretation of a mass lesion may lead to an expensive and invasive diagnostic work-up; a pathologist's reading of a tissue slide may determine whether a woman keeps her breast or loses it; a research technician's decision about primary clinical data may affect the final results of a research project. (Elmore and Feinstein 1992, 567)

The medical literature documents numerous instances of physicians disagreeing among themselves about the presence of a physical finding, the interpretation of common tests (e.g., chest radiographs, electrocardiograms), and sophisticated tests (e.g., endoscopy, angiography, radionuclide imaging). Studies have noted tremendous intraphysician variability—physicians disagreeing with themselves on re-review of a physical examination or a test. In their "Bibliography of Publications on Observer

Variability (Final Installment)," Elmore and Feinstein (1992) listed 431 citations from the clinical literature in English where observer variation was the primary topic. This 1992 list did not overlap with a similarly extensive 1985 bibliography (Feinstein 1985) on the same topic!

A few examples convey the scope of this problem. One study evaluating the results of microscopic cytological examinations for women with cervical abnormalities found that pathologists agreed with each other only 51 percent of the time and with themselves only 68 percent of the time (Eddy 1984, 78). Another study involved examinations of patients with established pulmonary diagnoses by six sets of four physicians each; the four physicians agreed about patients' physical signs only 55 percent of the time (Spiteri, Cook, and Clarke 1988, 873). In a study of classification of trochanteric fractures, six physicians reviewed hip films from 50 patients. All observers classified the fractures identically for only 11 cases; the percentage of fractures considered "stable" ranged from 29 to 55 percent across physicians (Andersen, Jørgensen, and Hededam 1990).

Questions also arise about findings that require physicians to interpret patients' experiences subjectively. For example, as described in Chapter 2, patients' and physicians' assessment of patient functioning may disagree. One study of agreement between ambulatory patients and their physicians found kappa values ranging from 0.14 to 0.37, reflecting substantial disagreement between patients and physicians in perceptions of patient functioning (Calkins et al. 1991, 453). Agreement between patients and doctors was generally highest for measures of physical functioning and lowest for indicators of social functioning. The majority of disagreements involved physicians' underestimation of patients' disabilities.

For research studies relying on clinical factors taken from medical records, investigators may need to re-review or reinterpret critical tests or findings. For example, investigators could independently interpret pertinent radiographs or electrocardiograms. Without explicit review criteria, however, investigators are not automatically immune from bias or interobserver variation. To the extent possible, investigators performing such reviews should be blinded about patients' outcomes or other critical criteria that could bias their interpretations. This strategy pertains only to those clinical findings where hard copies of data exist that can be retrieved and reviewed retrospectively. This will not be possible for evaluating dimensions of risk where findings are ephemeral or transitory, or require patients to be available for examination (e.g., physical findings, functional status).

A risk-adjustment methodology that relies heavily on clinical findings from the medical record is the CSI (see Exhibit 2.1). Roughly half of the CSI's clinical factors represent numeric values, such as vital signs or laboratory findings, while most of the others are more descriptive and qualitative (Iezzoni and Daley 1992). Many factors indicate findings that are often measured unreliably, such as jugular venous distention, Kussmaul respiration, rales, and pulsus paradoxus. Other items require patient reports and thus depend on the vagaries of recall and other patient attributes, such as thresholds for pain and complaint, acuity in self-observation, and willingness to reveal certain personal facts. Examples include nausea, anorexia, numbness, tingling, and severe headache. While most of the differences in the patients' reports of such factors probably vary randomly across providers, systematic differences could occur across patient populations in the detail and nature of such self-reports relating to language, culture, education, and socioeconomic status (Zola 1966).

The CSI example illustrates the dilemma surrounding use of potentially unreliable clinical findings in risk assessment. First, regardless of whether such findings are unreliable, they are what doctors and other clinicians use to make therapeutic and prognostic judgments about patients. Therefore, disregarding entirely these types of findings in judging risk would be inappropriate. Second, when using such findings, one must remember that they are inherently subjective, representing clinicians' interpretations—albeit highly educated interpretations. Finally, given these two considerations, the major question is whether a potential for bias exists: Could assessments of risk, based on these clinical findings, be biased by any systematic factors affecting this subjective interpretation of clinicians? For example, interns and residents are generally more likely to commit "errors" than senior physicians (Wiener and Nathanson 1976; Johnson and Carpenter 1986). All potential sources of bias must be explored.

Accuracy and Validity of Medical Records

> The clarity and logic of medical recording is a direct reflection of the clarity and logic (or lack thereof) of the medical practitioner's thoughts. An ambiguous, illegible chart with a confusion of orders and counter-orders, incomplete physical examinations, and absence of clear impressions or plans most likely reflects the same confusion in that patient's physician. (Bradbury 1990, 25)

The completeness, accuracy, and validity of medical records—as a chronicle of patients' healthcare experiences—are critically important. Errors or incomplete information could influence judgments of patients' risk. However, measuring the magnitude of this problem is complicated. A thorough and flawless investigation requires an omniscient observer continually monitoring providers who are unaware of being observed and also performing independent and objective evaluations of patients. Clearly, this is impossible. Therefore, it is not surprising that relatively little has been published on this topic. This limited literature suggests that the medical record is sufficient for certain purposes but that it often does not completely or accurately represent the care rendered to patients or certain aspects of their diseases that could significantly affect risk (Romm and Putnam 1981; Starfield et al. 1979; Feigl et al. 1988; Kosecoff et al. 1987).

Studies of Medical Record Accuracy, Completeness, and Validity

Feigl et al. (1988) compared inpatient and radiation therapy records for patients diagnosed with certain cancers. While laboratory and other diagnostic test results, consultations, and specific inpatient treatments were well documented in the inpatient record, important information obtained in outpatient settings about the extent of the cancer (e.g., mammography results) was poorly documented. Another study examined the accuracy of the medication histories documented in the medical records of 122 elderly persons admitted to two teaching hospitals in Los Angeles (Beers, Munekata, and Storrie 1990). Within 48 hours of admission, the investigators independently interviewed all subjects and abstracted the medication history recorded by the admitting intern or attending physician. "Errors" represented failures to record a medication the patient reported taking, not differences in dosages or administration schedules. When all medications were included in the analyses, at least one error occurred for 83 percent of subjects; 46 percent had more than two errors. Considering only "important" medications, 60 percent of subjects had at least one error, while 18 percent had more than two.

Several studies have compared medical record information with audiotapes or independent observations of encounters. Romm and Putnam (1981) compared transcripts of audiotapes to medical records of 55 patient encounters in a general medicine outpatient clinic. Agreement between the transcripts and records was best (92 percent) for patients' chief complaints, with approximately 70 percent agreement for history of the present illness, impression, tests, and therapy (Romm and Putnam 1981, 310). For concerns stated by the patient but not considered part of their chief complaint, agreement was only 29 percent.

Another study also involved audiotaping outpatient encounters, this time in clinics caring for children under 13 years of age (Zuckerman et al. 1975). Of the 51 visits evaluated, about one-third were for follow-up of preexisting acute or chronic ailments. Chief complaints were coded with 96 percent concordance between the audiotape and the written record; agreement was 67 percent for diagnosis. However, agreement was only 4 percent for compliance, 10 percent for cause of illness, and 10 percent for indications for follow-up.

An additional study involved anesthesiologists observing intraoperative recording of standard data by other anesthesiologists for 197 surgeries in New Zealand (Rowe, Galletly, and Henderson 1992). Important information was commonly omitted, including American Society of Anesthesiology score (22 percent of the time), allergies (55 percent), intravenous fluid type (27 percent), and preoperative condition (72 percent). This study illustrates a hazard of this type of investigation—in one case, the observing anesthesiologist briefly took over care while the subject anesthesiologist responded to an emergency!

One study observed hundreds of patient visits to a primary care pediatric clinic but focused on whether the doctors (interns and residents) recorded information using a free text medical record versus a structured encounter form (Duggan, Starfield, and DeAngelis 1990). The structured form had been a routine part of clinical practice and was used in approximately two-thirds of visits for well child care, although its use varied widely among physicians. During the observation period, the choice of the form was left to the provider. For visits during which the structured form was used, recording was significantly ($p < 0.001$) better across all dimensions examined (overall care, history, physical examination, developmental assessment, guidance, and follow-up). However, when the structured form was used, the recorded performance for the physical examination was significantly more comprehensive than the observed performance, leading the investigators to conclude that, at least for certain areas of care, "use of the structured form exerted a greater impact on recording than on performance" (Duggan, Starfield, and DeAngelis 1990, 111).

Differences in Medical Records by Hospital Characteristics

Completeness of documentation may vary by hospital type. A study of approximately 4,500 medical record reviews at 15 metropolitan Boston hospitals revealed anecdotal evidence of differences in completeness of documentation across teaching and nonteaching hospitals (Iezzoni et al. 1989, 1990). Physician notes at nonteaching hospitals generally focused exclusively on the acute presenting illness. To gather information on chronic comorbidities, such as non-insulin-dependent diabetes mellitus or hypertension, we needed to review nursing notes and medication logs. We hypothesized that physicians at nonteaching hospitals did not document chronic coexisting diseases because they were generally patients' primary providers, with an intimate knowledge of the patients from prior encounters. In addition, these physicians were likely to supervise all care during the hospitalization, therefore making it unnecessary for them to inform other doctors about the patient's history through extensive notations.

In contrast, at teaching hospitals, physicians' notes contained copious information on both acute and chronic conditions. We hypothesized that these documentation differences reflected differences in roles between teaching and nonteaching physicians. At teaching hospitals, the admission note is generally written by an intern or resident unfamiliar with the patient. Therefore, this note contains information extracted during a comprehensive review of patients' clinical histories. In addition, interns and residents provide extensive cross-coverage for each other on weekends and evenings. The medical record serves as the means for transmitting important information to covering doctors who are unfamiliar with patients but may need to make critical care decisions.

Functional status and social history information was minimal at both teaching and nonteaching hospitals. For example, we had aimed to derive a measure of patients' living situations (e.g., whether they lived alone or with others) but were unable to do so from medical record documentation. If functional and social information was recorded, it was more likely in nurses' than physicians' notations. Other investigators also have found fault with recording of relevant social history information. For example, despite the importance of occupational exposures, one study found that recorded occupation for lung cancer patients agreed with only one-third of patients' reports from independent interviews (McDiarmid, Bonanni, and Finocchiaro 1991). A review of 155 medical records found that only 30 percent noted patients' marital status and 15 percent listed occupation (Mansfield 1986).

Missing Records

Finally, a separate but important issue involves records that are missing altogether. In any study using medical records, some records inevitably will not be found or are unavailable for some reason. Are patients and experiences represented by missing records significantly different than for records that are found? A study of obstetrical outcomes at one hospital could not locate 25 percent of medical records (Westgren et al. 1986). Available demographic data suggested that missing records probably chronicled a larger fraction of newborns with low birth weight and low gestational age than did records that were found. The investigators believed that missing records significantly biased their findings.

Experiences in other investigations have been less worrisome. The Harvard Medical Practice Study sampled 31,429 medical records in 51 hospitals in New York state, and 96 percent of records were initially located (30,195 records). At a later date, an additional 578 records were located. Of the remaining 656 records (2.1 percent of the original sample) that were never found, 90 were mismatches with the New York discharge data set used for sampling, 470 were declared by record rooms to be lost, and 96 were found but not available in time for review (Lawthers 1993). In a study by the Department of Health and Human Services Office of the Inspector General, Hsia et al. (1992) found 91.5 percent of the records requested.

Showstack, Schroeder, and Matsumoto (1982) also found 91 percent of the requested hospital records.

Given this experience, it seems reasonable to expect to locate over 90 percent of hospital records. Nonetheless, the question remains concerning whether these patients are different in any way. Evidence from the missing records study conducted by the Harvard Medical Practice Study suggests that the missing charts are unlikely to be substantially different from the located charts. The three groups of records (classified as "initially found," "found on follow-up," and "never found") did not differ with respect to age, gender, or DRG. A slightly higher percentage of black and Medicaid patients were found at follow-up, but the difference was not significant (Harvard Medical Practice Study 1990).

Medical Records and the Current Healthcare Environment

The medical record still serves primarily to support the clinical care of individual patients. Other traditional roles for these records include research and medical education. However, the medical record is increasingly assuming a variety of newer roles, involving utilization review, quality assurance, cost containment, medicolegal activities, and other administrative purposes. Thus, many people not directly involved in caring for patients have access to their records.

Privacy Concerns

This access to medical records seems antithetical to the commonly held notion that medical records are private. Nonetheless, no explicit right to privacy is guaranteed by the U.S. Constitution. A presumed right to privacy as the basis for a civil action stems from a legal opinion written in 1890 by Justice Louis D. Brandeis, as well as various amendments to the Bill of Rights (Donaldson and Lohr 1994). However, patients are frequently unaware that they have authorized individuals, such as health insurance company representatives, to obtain access to their medical records.

> A patient may be asked to accede to disclosure by signing a blanket consent form when applying for insurance or employment. In such cases, however, consent cannot be truly voluntary or informed. Such authorizations are often not *voluntary* because the patient feels compelled to sign the authorization or forgo the benefit sought, and they are not *informed* because the patient cannot know in advance what information will be in the record, who will subsequently have access to it, or how it will be used. (Donaldson and Lohr 1994, 150)

Confidentiality of the record is theoretically guaranteed by the Uniform Health Care Information Act, which stipulates that providers cannot give any information about patients or their healthcare to a third party without the patient's consent (McCabe 1988). The Uniform Health Care Information Act delineates exceptions to the patient consent requirement, through which providers can release medical records or health information without specific consent. However, the guiding principle is that such exceptions be in the patient's best interest (e.g., the ability of doctors to share records in a healthcare emergency) (McCabe 1988). Nonetheless:

> As a practical matter, policing redisclosure of one's personal health information is difficult and may be impossible. At a minimum, such policing requires substantial resources and commitment. With the use of computer and telecommunications networks, an individual may never discover that a particular disclosure has occurred, even though he or she suffers significant harm—such as inability to obtain employment, credit, housing, or insurance—as a result of such disclosure. Pursuing legal remedies may result in additional disclosure of the individual's private health information. (Donaldson and Lohr 1994, 17)

Despite this legislation, many more persons not directly involved in patients' care now have access to their records. As noted by Fleming and Fleming (1989–1990, 36):

> An increasing number of third party payers for health care have been exercising some form of utilization management. As a result, there has been an erosion of the physician-patient privilege and patient confidentiality. The kinds of medical information obtained by third party payers under the guise of prior authorizations, concurrent review, post-utilization review, and claims processing and administration (including audits), violate the spirit if not the actual laws pertaining to physician-patient communication.

Consequences for Medical Record Documentation

Some observers believe that these shifts have led to subtle and not-so-subtle changes in the content and character of medical record documentation. These changes could affect the utility of medical records for assessing patients' risk. Burnum (1989, 483) lamented the current state of the medical record:

> The loss of confidentiality of medical records has caused physicians and patients alike to withhold clinically important, but sensitive, personal information from medical records that might harm the patient if brought to public view. Furthermore, physicians are being forced to censor essential chart information patients might find objectionable now that patients have the right to read their own records.

Specific areas affected by these concerns include documentation of psychological disorders or symptoms, cognitive dysfunctions (such as dementia), substance abuse, sexual practices, and information about the human immunodeficiency virus—important risk factors for many outcomes. Word choices and terminology have become biased, with language modified to meet expectations of those now anticipated to have access to medical records (e.g., utilization reviewers, "peer" reviewers, billing offices, lawyers, patients). For example, Burnum (1989, 483) observed that, to justify a patient's continued hospital stay, "chart notes have become increasingly gloomy."

Patients' access to their own records generates strong ambivalence among healthcare providers. On one hand, society is increasingly supporting consumers' rights, including the rights of healthcare consumers. But on the other hand, as suggested above, knowing that patients can read their records may constrain what physicians record. According to one expert in the Uniform Health Care Information Act, "There's still a great deal of unhappiness in the medical community over the issue of patient's privacy rights and patient access to records. Almost every state has some sort of patient access statute or upholds this right by virtue of common law" (McCabe 1988, 24). Consequently, physicians may modulate the tone or censor altogether their assessments of patients' clinical status or prognoses that they record in the medical chart.

Effect of "Report Cards"

As described in Chapters 10 and 11, an increasing number of organizations are publicly releasing information about hospital and physician performance. Especially when doctors are identified individually by name, incentives to color documentation of patient risk factors may prove irresistible—doctors are human, too. If surgeons, for example, experience numerous postoperative deaths, they will try to prove that their patients are severely ill, and therefore at high risk, regardless of treatment.

Whether such documentation shifts occur—and whether they reflect fact or fiction—is difficult to know. Since 1990, New York state has published statistics on in-hospital deaths among coronary artery bypass graft (CABG) patients, adjusting for risk using clinical data furnished by surgeons and hospitals (see Chapter 11). CABG risk factors were specified by clinicians consulting with the state Department of Health and reflect clinical factors known to affect CABG risk, such as low cardiac ejection fraction, stenosis of the left main coronary artery, unstable angina, New York Heart Association functional class, and a variety of chronic illnesses (Hannan et al. 1990). In 1991, *Newsday* published information on CABG volumes and mortality by surgeon name, after suing the state under its

Freedom of Information Act. The resultant publicity highlighted further the importance of the CABG risk factor reports to public perceptions of surgeon performance.

Green and Wintfeld (1995) analyzed the prevalence of reported risk factors by quarterly periods around these public releases of the New York CABG mortality data. They found that "the reported prevalence of chronic obstructive pulmonary disease, unstable angina, and low ejection fraction increased sharply in the first quarter of 1990, just after the first mortality report had been distributed to hospitals" (Green and Wintfeld 1995, 1230–31). For example, in the years 1989, 1990, and 1991, reported prevalence of chronic obstructive pulmonary disease was 6.9, 12.4, and 17.4 percent respectively; prevalence of unstable angina was 14.9, 21.1, and 21.8 percent respectively (Green and Wintfeld 1995, 1231). Some of this increase was due to changes in variable definitions, but:

> Patterns in the data suggested that some institutions outpaced the overall trend toward an increased reporting of risk factors. For example, at one hospital, the reported prevalence of chronic obstructive pulmonary disease increased from 1.8 to 52.9 percent; at another hospital, the reported prevalence of unstable angina increased from 1.9 to 20.8 percent. Variation in the reporting of some risk factors was far greater each year than could reasonably be attributed to differences in case mix. For example, in 1991 the prevalence of chronic obstructive pulmonary disease reported by surgeons ranged from 1.4 to 60.6 percent, and for unstable angina, the range was 0.7 to 61.4 percent. (Green and Wintfeld 1995, 1231)

New York state officials were also concerned about shifts in reporting of risk factors, and they instituted mechanisms to monitor this practice.

> The department ensures the accuracy of data with an independent audit of a sample of data from a sample of hospitals that compares the data in the registry with the information in the medical records. The first such audit was conducted in 1989. Annual audits began in 1992. . . .
>
> We scrutinize the results of each individual hospital's audit. If discrepancies are considered to be substantial, the hospital is asked to explain the audited results. If the explanation is inadequate, the hospital is asked to recode its data. This has happened twice, in 1992 and 1993 . . . Since 1991, the prevalence of each risk factor except congestive heart failure has remained stable; for that risk factor the definition has continued to be refined.
>
> Changing definitions, together with some underreporting of risk factors in 1989 (documented in the first audit and largely resolved by 1990), account for these changes in prevalence. There will always be some room for judgment, however, in determining whether a patient has certain risk factors. (Chassin, Hannan, and DeBuono 1996, 396)

Therefore, a lingering concern about monitoring some risk factors is the subjectivity involved in their assessment (e.g., New York Heart Association functional class). To evaluate accuracy of such factors, it is almost necessary to perform independent examinations of the patients. Re-review of medical records may not suffice.

Implications of Practice Patterns and Dependence on Technology

Differences in practice patterns across providers are well documented (see Chapter 1), including variations in use of diagnostic tests, such as those used to evaluate patients' risk factors. If nonrandom variations occur in practice patterns involving pertinent tests, these variations could affect the ability to produce unbiased assessments of patients' risks across providers. Even at the most mundane level, if a physiologic value is not measured, it cannot contribute to a patient's severity rating.

An anecdotal example of this concern is the story told in Chapter 2 concerning outcomes of cancer patients at a hospital in Pennsylvania, where all hospitals are required to report MedisGroups severity information. MedisGroups rates severity using extensive KCFs abstracted from medical records (Brewster et al. 1985; Iezzoni and Moskowitz 1988; Steen et al. 1993). This hospital was told by state officials that its MedisGroups severity-adjusted mortality rate for cancer patients was much higher than expected; most worrisome was that numerous deaths occurred among patients who had the lowest severity scores (0 or 1). When oncologists at this hospital investigated, they found that these deaths occurred among patients, often with widely metastatic disease, who desired comfort measures only—even routine blood drawing for serum chemistry (e.g., sodium, potassium) and hematology testing (e.g., hematocrit, white blood cell counts) was not desired. Therefore, no test values were available to indicate the patients' "true" severity.

A related issue involves whether indicators of risk are derived from performing specific tests or using sophisticated technology. While using the myriad test results available in medical records is tempting, this could potentially bias risk estimates across patients and providers. For example, MedisGroups tried to minimize reliance on inherently unreliable findings by seeking information from the putatively most "objective" source, such as technologically sophisticated diagnostic tests (Iezzoni and Moskowitz 1988). Most KCFs used in the new, empirically derived version of Medis-Groups involve fairly routine tests (Steen et al. 1993). Nevertheless, results of some sophisticated tests, such as number of vessels occluded determined through coronary angiography, are used as predictors in deriving the severity score (see Exhibit 2.3).

An unintentional consequence of this strategy could involve potentially biasing comparisons across providers, especially if different hospitals have different technological capabilities—such as academic medical centers versus small community hospitals. Identical patients could receive different severity ratings depending on the availability and use of a specific diagnostic test. Practice patterns could thus confound comparisons of severity scores.

As an example, suppose two hospitals perform carotid endarterectomies on patients mildly symptomatic from transient ischemic attacks (Iezzoni and Moskowitz 1988). The patients on admission have no clinical findings used in producing the severity scores. At the first hospital, patients are admitted for angiography with a finding of arterial stenosis, and the patients then receive surgery during the same admission. Under the older version of MedisGroups, the angiography findings contributed to an admission severity score of 1. At the second hospital, patients have angiography during an initial diagnostic admission, which thus receives a score of 1. During the subsequent surgical admission, no KCFs are identified that contribute to admission severity, and admission scores are 0 for the surgical hospitalization at the second hospital.

Practice patterns about the timing of testing could also influence identification of risk factors, especially when risk factors must come from a narrow window of time, such as during the hospitalization or within a week of admission. In these circumstances, risk assessments could be biased if some hospitals split diagnostic and therapeutic admissions or perform diagnostic testing in outpatients earlier than the permissible window of observation (e.g., when preadmission test results are considered only if they occur within specified time periods prior to admission). This sort of procedural artifact could hamper comparisons across facilities.

One final concern about practice patterns has been raised in some locales that have mandated use of severity measures based on chart review (see Chapter 11)—the possibility of increased testing to identify abnormalities that could contribute to severity findings. As mentioned earlier, if a physiologic parameter is not tested, its value cannot contribute to the severity rating. Where providers feel particularly pressured to demonstrate that their patients are very ill, they may be motivated to perform more diagnostic tests than warranted. Although this phenomenon is as yet unproven, the possibility has raised concerns, particularly in competitive healthcare marketplaces.

Preliminary evidence does suggest, however, that access to predicted probabilities of patient outcomes might alter physicians' therapeutic choices. One study from four centers in Great Britain examined treatments and outcomes for patients with severe head injuries who were either comatose or required surgical evacuation of an intracranial hematoma (Murray et al. 1993). During a one-year intervention period, the medical staff was given predictions of patient outcomes based on empirically derived prediction models. Patients' outcomes did not differ between intervention and control periods. Nevertheless, when patients were stratified into prognostic groups, use of therapeutic interventions varied between the intervention and control periods. During the intervention, patients with good to moderate prognoses were treated more aggressively (e.g., with intubation or ventilation, intracranial pressure monitoring). In contrast, patients with poor prognoses received less intense treatment than during the control periods. Thus, the act of providing systematic risk assessments in the clinical setting could itself affect practices.

Chart Documentation Patterns and the Data Collection Approach

Differences across institutions in chart documentation practices could bias comparisons of patient risk across hospitals. As suggested above, an obvious example is the comparison of teaching and nonteaching facilities—multiple physicians document records at teaching hospitals, while single physicians generally document records at nonteaching facilities. Trainees tend to leave copious individual notes. In addition, there are often multiple levels of trainees (ranging from interns to specialty fellows) who all document patients' records, as well as multiple attending physicians (e.g., patients' primary doctors, specialist consultants), resulting frequently in inconsistencies among different physicians' assessments of patients. Nonetheless, the information needed for risk adjustment may thus be more available at tertiary teaching institutions, leading to the possibility of bias in the risk judgment by hospital teaching status.

Data collection guidelines also affect the information available to judge risk. For example, MedisGroups stipulated that most information be taken from physician notes (exceptions involve vital sign KCFs). This practice may expedite the chart reviews, but it could affect comparisons across hospitals with different levels of physician coverage. Patients at tertiary teaching hospitals, with round-the-clock teams of physicians, could have multiple physician notes, whereas identical patients at a small community hospital could receive only one daily physician note. This documentation difference may be particularly important for clinical findings that tend to wax and wane, such as wheezing, pericardial friction rubs, or S3 gallop heart sounds.

What should be done when physician notes disagree? Again, this problem primarily pertains to academic medical centers. We encountered this situation during a study in which research nurses employed by us used MedisGroups to review medical records (Iezzoni et al. 1992a). These reviews involved records at tertiary teaching institutions of often-complicated patients. MedisGroups staff instructed reviewers to take clinical information from the notes of the most senior physician (e.g., the attending physician's note took precedence over that of the intern). However, not unexpectedly, the reviewers encountered instances where senior physicians, such as specialists from different disciplines, disagreed about their clinical observations. This occurrence compromised our ability to meet the designated MedisGroups data collection reliability target (see Chapter 7).

When physicians' notes do not contain complete information about patients' medical histories (e.g., chronic coexisting conditions), one strategy to overcome this absence is using notes of clinicians other than physicians to gather information about risk factors. For example, the CSI uses all provider documentation in the medical record, including countersigned notes of trainees (Iezzoni and Daley 1992). Disadvantages of this approach involve time-consuming reviews and questions about interdisciplinary variability in assessing patient findings. Nonetheless, it facilitates inclusion of a potentially broader range of information. For example, nurses may be more likely to note patient functional status than physicians.

Clinical Versus Administrative Data for Risk Adjustment

A few studies have compared the performance of clinical versus administrative data for measuring healthcare outcomes. All have supported the relative advantages of clinical information, but several suggest that relatively small numbers of clinical variables convey the majority of the benefit. In other words, a handful of clinical variables can be equally useful as dozens of variables abstracted from medical records.

We explored the ability of six different models to predict in-hospital death of patients 65 years of age admitted to 24 MedisGroups-member hospitals (Iezzoni et al. 1992b). One model used only administrative information, including age, sex, and comorbid illnesses defined by ICD-9-CM diagnosis codes (Table 4.1). The other five models used the values of KCFs abstracted during the first few hospital days using the MedisGroups chart review protocol. From over 500 potential KCFs, we identified, for each condition, KCFs present in at least 1 percent of the cases or those clinically judged to be important (e.g., ventricular fibrillation). Between 40 and 65 KCFs were identified in each condition. As described in Table 4.1, three models were derived empirically using multivariable regression (Iezzoni et al. 1992b).

Table 4.1 Performance for Predicting In-Hospital Mortality for Six Models within Five Conditions

Model	Stroke	Lung Cancer	Pneu-monia	AMI	CHF
		Cross-validated $R^2 \times 100$			
Administrative: age; age squared; sex; principal diagnosis; and comorbidities defined by ICD-9-CM codes (diabetes, chronic pulmonary disease, cancer, chronic liver disease, chronic renal disease, cerebrovascular degeneration or chronic psychosis, hypertensive disease, and chronic cardiovascular disease)	2.3	2.4	6.1	6.5	2.3
Original MEDISGROUPS Score: 0, 1, 2, 3, and 4 (see Table 1.7)	9.6	5.8	15.4	19.5	7.5
P-APS: pseudo version of APACHE II acute physiology score (APS) constructed from MedisGroups KCF values for twelve physiologic variables	22.4	14.9	16.4	15.0	13.7
APSKCFs: values of the 12 APS physiologic variables plus age and sex in a regression analysis predicting in-hospital death within each condition	23.5	20.7	22.1	17.4	18.3
10KCFs: first ten KCFs to enter forward step-wise regression following age and sex within each condition	23.3	24.2	24.3	18.0	19.6
ALLKCFs: all 40 to 65 KCFs plus age and sex in a regression analysis predicting in-hospital death within each condition	20.8	5.4	24.0	15.7	19.6

Adapted from: Iezzoni et al. 1992b.

The "administrative" model performed least well, yielding cross-validated R^2 values ($\times$ 100) from 2.3 to 6.5 (Table 4.1). Despite being based on numerous KCFs, MedisGroups did better than the pseudo–APACHE II Acute Physiology Score models for only one condition, AMI. The "ALLKCFs" model never had a better cross-validated performance than the "10KCFs" model. In lung cancer, the R^2 for the "ALLKCFs" model produced on the fitting data set (34.4) was much higher than that following cross validation (5.4) (see Chapter 6). Although some "ALLKCFs" models, with 40 or more explanatory variables each, achieved high R^2 values, these models were initially overspecified: In the cross-validation analyses, they performed no better, and in lung cancer did far worse, than models based on the ten most important clinical variables (10KCFs).

As described in Chapter 3, our AHCPR-funded severity study found that code-based severity measures occasionally outperformed clinically based severity measures, although clinical approaches were clearly better for pneumonia and stroke (see Table 3.7). But an equally striking finding was how little the predictive performance differed between the MedisGroups versions (derived from dozens of clinical variables) and the physiology scores (based on 12 and 17 physiologic variables) (Iezzoni et al. 1995, 1996a, 1996b; Landon et al. 1996) (Table 4.2). On average, collecting the data required for the physiology scores would undoubtedly cost less than gathering MedisGroups information.

Hannan and colleagues (1992) compared the ability to predict in-hospital death for coronary artery bypass graft (CABG) surgery using two data sources: a clinical database gathered through the Cardiac Surgery Reporting System (CSRS) and an administrative file produced by the New

Table 4.2 c-Statistics for Predicting In-Hospital Death

Severity Measure	Condition			
	AMI	*CABG*	*Pneumonia*	*Stroke*
Many Clinical Variables				
Original MedisGroups	0.80	0.73	0.81	0.80
Empirical MedisGroups	0.83	0.74	0.85	0.87
Relatively Few Clinical Variables				
Physiology score 1	0.82	0.73	0.78	0.80
Physiology score 2	0.83	0.73	0.82	0.84

Sources: Iezzoni et al. 1995, 1996a, 1996b; Landon et al. 1996.

York Statewide Planning and Research Cooperative Systems (SPARCS). The CSRS contained detailed CABG risk factors, including left ventricular ejection fraction, percent narrowing of the left main coronary artery, unstable angina, and previous myocardial infarction (see Chapter 11). In contrast, SPARCS included standard administrative information, including up to five ICD-9-CM diagnosis and procedure codes. The CSRS was significantly better able to discriminate deaths than the SPARCS model ($c = 0.788$ versus 0.721, respectively, $p < 0.001$) (Hannan et al. 1992, 898). Adding only three of the CSRS risk factors (reoperation, ejection fraction, and > 90 percent narrowing of the left main trunk) significantly improved the predictive ability of the SPARCS model.

When ranking hospitals based on their adjusted CABG mortality profiles, the CSRS and SPARCS models produced somewhat different assessments about which facilities were high and low outliers (Hannan et al. 1992).

> Thus, it can be argued that the importance of using a clinical data base rather than an administrative data base for CABG surgery is dependent on the purposes of the data base. If the information is used for internal quality assurance purposes or to target hospitals for state or federal site visits, the administrative data base may suffice. However, if the information is used to inform consumers of relative quality of hospital care, the differences in hospital ratings between the two systems as well as the potential damage to a hospital's reputation are probably too great to risk using an administrative data base. (Hannan et al. 1992, 903)

Finally, for several years HCFA experimented with a massive computerized tool to abstract clinical information from hospital records of Medicare beneficiaries, the Uniform Clinical Data Set System (UCDSS). A pilot test, conducted by Medicare peer review organizations (PROs) in six states, found that individual chart abstractions sometimes required hours. The UCDSS data entry software could capture 1,800 different data items, although the PRO pilot found that pneumonia patients averaged 365 items and stroke patients 371 items (Hartz et al. 1994, 883). Interestingly, UCDSS did not collect functional status items, such as the need for assistance with bathing, feeding, ambulation, or toileting.

One study empirically derived predictive models for hospital length of stay and occurrence of adverse events for pneumonia and stroke patients (Hartz et al. 1994). The models used either UCDSS data alone or UHDSS data supplemented with information on functional status and other non-UHDSS data items specially abstracted from medical records at a study hospital. Interestingly, despite the hundreds of candidate predictor variables, only a handful were statistically significant and retained in the final models. For example, only four factors were included in the model predicting adverse events for stroke: lethargy, stupor, or coma; labored or abnormal breathing; increase in pulse rate of 20 beats per minute; and ischemic heart disease (Hartz et al. 1994, 890). When available, functional status items (need for bathing assistance, restrictions on out-of-bed movement) were among the items retained for two of the four models. The UHDSS-based models had better predictive ability than models based on UB-82 administrative information.

This UHDSS experiment provides a cautionary tale, on several levels. First, even though a data abstraction tool contains almost 2,000 data elements, it might not include important factors (e.g., functional status information). Second, predictive models may distill hundreds of data elements down to a handful. Finally, data-gathering initiatives can die of their own weight. The expense of the UHDSS was an important factor when HCFA finally abandoned this global approach for a more focused, "minimum data set"-type strategy to help the PROs target their quality improvement projects.

Patient-Generated Information

As described in Chapters 2 and 11, views of patients are increasingly valued in identifying and evaluating outcomes of care. For example, the Foundation for Accountability, a coalition of consumer and purchaser groups, explicitly plans to capture information on patient functional status and satisfaction with care (Prager 1996). Not only are patient-reported observations used as outcome measures (e.g., self-reported health status), but patient-generated information also provides the necessary risk factors. Sometimes the complexities of conducting a clinically credible outcomes study prove so daunting that obtaining information directly from patients seems much simpler. For example, in 1995, the Massachusetts Health Quality Partnership (MHQP) debated which quality measures to adopt for its new initiative comparing hospital performance, immediately dismissing administrative data-based approaches as insufficient. Initial thoughts involved looking at mortality rates following selected hospital admissions (e.g., for heart attack), but deliberations ground to a halt around the conceptual and logistical complexities of risk adjustment. MHQP decided that starting with comparisons of patients' experiences and satisfaction with care was easier, and it selected the Picker Institute survey of patients' experiences (Cleary et al. 1991, 1993), which uses patient-reported health status as its major risk adjuster.

Obtaining data directly from patients is not cheap, however, and the logistics are not simple. Some efforts will be expensive due to their expansive vision. For example, the Henry Ford Health System in Detroit is developing information systems for tracking the long-term functional outcomes of patients, as well as their satisfaction with care, throughout its extensive care network (Donaldson and Lohr 1994). While this will undoubtedly produce an invaluably rich data source, it is certainly costly. Equally pressing, however, are questions about the quality of the data: How good are patient reports?

In one sense, patient-generated data are the *only* authentic data about patients' perceptions, functioning, health status, and quality of life. While recognizing this absolute validity, appreciating nuances within these reports may be important. For example, as described in Chapter 2, persons who others may view as in "poor" health often place relatively high values on their health, having adjusted their lifestyles and expectations to their capabilities. Conversely, young, apparently healthy people may devalue their health, given high and possibly unrealistic expectations about what optimal health should be (Dolan 1996).

A few studies have compared patients' reports to outside "gold standard" measures. For example, one study compared patients' reports of cardiovascular disease risk factors obtained through a telephone interview with findings during a subsequent clinic visit with trained physicians and nurses (Bowlin et al. 1996). "Objective" tests were run for each risk factor (e.g., exhaled carbon monoxide levels were assayed to identify smokers, blood pressure was measured three times using an American Heart Association protocol, serum total cholesterol was quantified on fasting venous blood). Compared with these clinical gold standards, approximately half the subjects with hypertension and hypercholesterolemia misclassified themselves as without the risk factor. Patients' reports of smoking were generally accurate. In the Medical Outcomes Study, doctors' reports of "tracer" diagnoses (e.g., diabetes mellitus) agreed better with confirmatory laboratory data (e.g., glycosylated hemoglobin) than did patients' reports on self-administered questionnaires or face-to-face interviews (Kravitz, Greenfield, and Rogers 1993).

Comparisons of self-reported resource use to medical records show that patients' memories are often inaccurate. Even though hospitalizations would seem a memorable event, comparisons of patients' reports with administrative records show that patients systematically underreport hospital admissions (Clark, Ricketts, and McHugo 1996). Not surprisingly, patients' memories are especially faulty if considerable time has elapsed. The accuracy of patient-reported service use was examined for 500 men participating in the Olmsted County Study of Urinary Symptoms and Health Status (Roberts et al. 1996). The accuracy of self-reports was best for the number of inpatient nights in the prior year (roughly 90 percent of respondents accurately reported 0 nights), but it fell considerably when asked about the number of physician visits in the prior year. Patients underreported the number of doctor visits, especially when six or more visits had actually occurred.

Nonetheless, investigators have used patient-reported risk factors in risk adjusting a variety of outcomes. For example, in an analysis of mortality over seven years for Medical Outcomes Study patients with hypertension or Type II diabetes mellitus, investigators adjusted for comorbidities based on patients' reports about 29 comorbid conditions (Greenfield et al. 1995a). In the Type II Diabetes PORT, funded by AHCPR, researchers were concerned by the irregularity of laboratory testing and missing chart data. They therefore developed a method to judge the severity of diabetes mellitus and comorbid illness using patients' reports (Greenfield et al. 1995b). A composite, global measure was produced by aggregating 15 individual severity scales, using data from a patient questionnaire containing 130 items and taking about 15 minutes to complete (Greenfield et al. 1995b).

Katz and colleagues (1996) were concerned about the logistics and expense of paying trained nurse abstractors to gather medical record information for the Charlson comorbidity index (see Chapter 2). They developed a questionnaire containing the Charlson comorbidity factors that was either self-administered or answered during an interview. Charlson scores from patient-generated data produced a Spearman correlation coefficient of 0.63 when compared with medical record-derived scores (Katz et al. 1996, 77). Kappa statistics indicating agreement between patients' reports of individual comorbidities and medical record evidence of comorbidities ranged from 0.35 to 0.85 (see Chapter 7). Relative costs of the various versions were estimated as follows: $0.93 for mailed, self-report questionnaires; $1.67 for patient interviews; and $3.50 for chart abstraction (Katz et al. 1996, 79).

Numerous logistical concerns are raised by obtaining information directly from patients. As described in Chapter 2, some patients may be physically or cognitively unable to respond. Many studies, such as that of Katz et al. (1996), limit themselves to respondents who speak English, given the costs and linguistic challenges of translating questionnaires (i.e., ensuring that the translation has the same meaning as the English version). Cross-cultural differences in attitudes toward health, symptoms, and disease are crucial considerations in translating surveys for use across nations or across linguistic groups within populations (Ware et al. 1995; Mathias, Fifer, and Patrick 1994). Telephone interviews must recognize that while 93 percent of Americans have telephones, those who do not may differ in important ways (e.g., socioeconomic status, psychosocial factors) from those who do (Gfroerer and Hughes 1991).

While mailed questionnaires are cheaper than interviews for obtaining information from patients, concerns about respondent literacy complicate matters. Troubling reports periodically appear, documenting the functional illiteracy of large numbers of adult Americans. The Type II Diabetes PORT developed an 11-question "questionnaire literacy screen" (QLS) to judge the ability of their study subjects to complete self-administered questionnaires about their diabetes and other characteristics (Sullivan et al. 1995). Based on the QLS results, subjects were assigned to an appropriate modality of survey administration. Thus, interviews were conducted only when necessary. In their urban, Midwestern, teaching hospital clinical population, 35 percent of respondents failed the QLS (Sullivan et al. 1995, AS187).

Information Technologies and the Future

A concerted impetus in the 1990s is the trend toward entirely computerized, or "paperless," medical records (Dick and Steen 1991; Office of Technology Assessment 1995). Computerized medical records could offer significant advantages, such as improved organization of massive quantities of data, easy access to individual data elements within the record, the potential to motivate and organize collection of data from providers (e.g., complete physical examination findings), the ability to insert pictorial representations (e.g., radiographs), legibility, and decreased space requirements for storage and processing. Nonetheless, many technical, conceptual, and cultural challenges must be addressed before computerized records will be widely used. As described at the end of Chapter 3, technical challenges range from establishing electronic transmission standards to developing standardized vocabularies. Practical challenges involve expense and changing physician behavior.

Hospitals are increasingly moving toward electronic transmission of laboratory reports and radiological and other diagnostic tests—data that can be directly downloaded into the computerized record.

> Most of the benefits of computerizing the patient record are realized when information is *delivered* to the caregiver or patient, but most of the expense and problems of computerizing the patient record are realized when the information is *collected*. In general, converting raw data into electronic information that can be shared requires that caregivers spend extra time and lose some flexibility in their recordkeeping—at least initially—and it requires institutional investments for training, maintenance of standards, and redesigning work processes. (Office of Technology Assessment 1995, 41)

Much of clinicians' contribution to computerized records is in unstructured free text that remains problematic to analyze and interpret (e.g., due to ill-defined terms and inconsistencies). Doubts and financial concerns of doctors about computerized records are especially pressing for private or small group practices.

> The assumption that computerized recordkeeping and data management will allow physicians to deliver high quality care at a lower cost is shared by many in Medical Informatics. Although this assumption is widely accepted,

there are virtually no systems in wide-spread use, regardless of cost, that deliver the desired results. The most convincing demonstrations . . . are beyond the reach of the average practitioner. (Essin and Lincoln 1995, 431)

Nevertheless, computerized records offer numerous potential advantages. For example, computerized rule-based alerts, reminders, and suggestions for care of specific patients in real time can be programmed into medical logic modules (Fitzmaurice 1995). Rind and colleagues (1994) sent computerized alerts to physicians about rising creatinine levels in their hospitalized patients receiving nephrotoxic or renally excreted medications. Alerts were generated automatically from electronic laboratory reports and pharmacy records. The mean interval between an event and change or discontinuation of a medication was 21.6 hours shorter after institution of the alerts than before. The relative risk of serious renal impairment was 0.45 (95% confidence interval, 0.22 to 0.94) compared to the period prior to instituting the alerts (Rind et al. 1994, 1513, 1511). Of physicians who responded to a questionnaire, 44 percent said that the alerts helped them care for their patients, while 28 percent found them annoying.

One of the most advanced computerized hospital information systems is the HELP (Health Evaluation through Logical Processing) system at LDS Hospital in Salt Lake City (Kuperman, Gardner, and Pryor 1991). The HELP system obtains electronic data from numerous sources throughout the hospital, including the laboratory, pharmacy, computerized nursing charting, and computerized respiratory care charting (for persons on ventilators). For persons receiving open-heart surgery, intraoperative physiologic data are automatically captured; for ICU patients being hemodynamically monitored, HELP regularly captures information directly from the physiologic probes on cardiac output, blood pressure, and pulmonary pressures, and from pumps administering intravenous medications. ICU rounds often start with reviews of computer printouts to see trends in physiologic parameters as well as drug administration. Algorithms take data elements from within the HELP system and automatically calculate APACHE scores for ICU patients. Other decision rules alert physicians about such problems as the occurrence of a nosocomial infection or adverse drug events. HELP data are also aggregated to assist in quality assurance and managerial functions.

Patients can also directly enter information into their medical records. At my hospital in Boston, Wald and colleagues (1995) designed a "Health History Interview" that asked patients questions about the medical review of systems, psychiatric symptoms, preventive health, habits and risk factors, and other areas. New patients were asked to come early for their scheduled appointment, and prior to their doctor visit, they sat at terminals in the clinic waiting room. The information they entered was directly downloaded into their computerized medical record, and paper copies were printed for the patient and doctor. The interview took an average of 27 minutes, and although 42 percent of the older patients had no prior keyboard experience, patients saw the computerized interview as positive; 65 percent actually preferred a computer-administered survey, compared to the 15 percent that preferred a face-to-face interview (Wald et al. 1995, 149). Patients conveyed fairly sensitive information: For example, 13 percent reported risk of potentially serious domestic violence in the prior 12 months, and 16 percent reported suicidal thoughts.

However, even if medical records were completely computerized, it is unlikely that their general content or problem orientation would change dramatically (Bradbury 1990). They will continue to report providers' impressions, assessments, and plans concerning patients and their treatments. One study in Great Britain videotaped visits to general practitioners and examined the types of information recorded in manual medical records versus computerized medical records (Pringle, Ward, and Chilvers 1995). These practices had been identified by the computer software vendor as those having a high commitment to recording data on the computer. Diagnoses and prescriptions were extensively documented in the computer records; in fact, more diagnoses were listed on the computer than had even been noted through reviewing the videotapes of the patient encounters. However, duration of symptoms, site of symptoms, and preventive services were rarely recorded on the computer; compared to the videotape impression, these items were recorded about half the time in the manual records.

Therefore, regardless of their format, questions will remain about the reliability, objectivity, and completeness of the clinical information.

Computerized Medical Records and Confidentiality Concerns

The ready access to detailed clinical information has generated escalating concern among privacy advocates. At one extreme is the obvious question when big producers of patient-level clinical information sell computerized files to health information vendors, pharmaceutical companies, credit record organizations, and other large data banks (Kolata 1995). Often those selling the records (e.g., health clinics, pharmacies) fail to remove patient names and other uniquely identifying information. At the other end are concerns that even doctors caring for individual patients have access to portions of the record the patient wishes to keep confidential, primarily mental health records (Page 1996). For example, Harvard Pilgrim Health Care, a large managed care plan in Boston, has kept detailed clinical information in computer-based records for 20 years, sometimes including verbatim transcripts of psychotherapy sessions. Controversy erupted when a patient seeking treatment for a broken leg found that clinicians also had complete access to his mental health records.

The Health Insurance Portability and Accountability Act of 1996 (P.L. 104-191, the Kassebaum/Kennedy Bill), signed by President Clinton on August 21, 1996, mandates that the federal government develop confidentiality standards and explore computerized medical record systems. A variety of standards from this mandate are scheduled to emerge within the next several years.

Conclusions

Despite the reservations described above, clinical variables obtained from medical records are conceptually appealing indicators of risk. They represent the types of information that physicians and other providers use daily to make diagnostic, therapeutic, and prognostic judgments. Therefore, eliminating all such variables from consideration is counterproductive. Instead, in designing a risk-adjustment strategy based on these data, several fundamental questions must be answered:

- Does the nature of the data elements (e.g., technology dependence) lead to bias?
- Is the data collection approach biased against certain types of providers or patients?
- Can the clinical data be manipulated to bias the severity findings (e.g., by increasing testing)?

Studies must be structured to avoid measurement bias in the variables contributing to risk assessment.

This last question is of particular concern in states and regions that have mandated collection of additional severity information from medical records, such as New York and Pennsylvania (see Chapter 11). The developers of these methods based on chart review attempted to build safeguards into their severity algorithms to minimize the opportunity for manipulation. Nevertheless, it is certainly possible to manipulate these systems, for example, by shifting testing or documentation patterns. Given current medical technologies, even physiologic parameters can be "normalized" or modulated in gravely ill patients: " 'Aggressive' treatment may mask extreme changes in physiology that would be identified in another ICU that waits and reacts to changes in patients' physiology" (Teres and Lemeshow 1994, 95). Some "manipulation" will be subliminal or a reflection of the honest uncertainty characteristic of much of clinical practice. For instance, if during a manual blood pressure reading the Korotkoff sounds disappear around 104 to 106 mm Hg, the decision about which value to record could be subconsciously affected by knowing that a diastolic pressure of 105 mm Hg or greater results in a higher severity score. Therefore, the incentives imposed by any data collection structure may have an important effect on the "quality" of the data.

Finally, application of chart-based risk-adjustment methodologies is more expensive than use of existing administrative databases. Data collection is often the major limiting expense of research studies. As described in Chapter 11, concerns about cost also reach into the policy debate about what information is essential for monitoring patient outcomes. For instance, the Institute of Medicine committee examining Medicare quality assessment strategies expressed explicit concern about the potential high cost of HCFA's UCDSS (Lohr, Donaldson, and Harris-Wehling 1992). As described above, the UCDSS considered over 1,800 variables, and the goal was to gather UCDSS information on a 10 percent sample of Medicare discharges. However, in test sites, abstraction times averaged from 67 to 115 minutes per discharge (Jencks and Wilensky 1992, 901). Expense was a major factor in HCFA's decision to abandon widespread UCDSS implementation. In many instances, hospitals must absorb costs of state-mandated data collections. According to one administrator at a hospital in Dubuque, Iowa, that had spent $200,000 on gathering severity data, "No third-party payer is reimbursing us for the [costs of MedisGroups], which means we are taking dollars away from patient care" ("Iowa's Experiment with Severity Software" 1992, 106). These costs were a major reason that Iowa switched from MedisGroups to administrative data–based APR-DRGs in 1994. Thus, costs of data are likely to be a central topic in policy debates about risk-adjusted outcomes information (see Chapter 11).

References

American College of Surgeons. 1918. "Standard of Efficiency for the First Hospital Survey of the College." *Bulletin of American College of Surgeons* 3: 1–4.

Andersen, E., L. G. Jørgensen, and L. T. Hededam. 1990. "Evans' Classification of Trochanteric Fractures: An Assessment of the Interobserver and Intraobserver Reliability." *Inquiry* 21 (6): 337–38.

Anderson, R. E., R. B. Hill, and C. R. Key. 1989. "The Sensitivity and Specificity of Clinical Diagnostics During Five Decades: Toward an Understanding of Necessary Fallibility." *Journal of the American Medical Association* 261 (11): 1610–17.

Beers, M. H., M. Munekata, and M. Storrie. 1990. "The Accuracy of Medication Histories in the Hospital Medical Records of Elderly Persons." *Journal of the American Geriatric Society* 38 (11): 1183–87.

Bowlin, S. J., B. D. Morrill, A. N. Nafziger, C. Lewis, and T. A. Pearson. 1996. "Reliability and Changes in Validity of Self-Reported Cardiovascular Disease

Risk Factors Using Dual Response: The Behavioral Risk Factor Survey." *Journal of Clinical Epidemiology* 49 (5): 511–17.

Bradbury, A. 1990. "Computerized Medical Records: The Need for a Standard." *Journal of the American Medical Record Association* 61 (3): 25–35.

Brewster, A. C., B. G. Karlin, L. A. Hyde, C. M. Jacobs, R. C. Bradbury, and Y. M. Chae. 1985. "MEDISGRPS®: A Clinically Based Approach to Classifying Hospital Patients at Admission." *Inquiry* 22 (4): 377–87.

Burnum, J. F. 1989. "The Misinformation Era: The Fall of the Medical Record." *Annals of Internal Medicine* 110 (6): 482–84.

Calkins, D. R., L. V. Rubenstein, P. D. Cleary, A. R. Davies, A. M. Jette, A. Fink, J. Kosecoff, R. T. Young, R. H. Brook, and T. L. Delbanco. 1991. "Failure of Physicians to Recognize Functional Disability in Ambulatory Patients." *Annals of Internal Medicine* 114 (6): 451–54.

Chassin, M. R., E. L. Hannan, and B. A. DeBuono. 1996. "Benefits and Hazards of Reporting Medical Outcomes Publicly." *New England Journal of Medicine* 334 (6): 394–98.

Clapesattle, H. 1941. *The Doctors Mayo.* Minneapolis, MN: The University of Minnesota.

Clark, R. E., S. K. Ricketts, and G. J. McHugo. 1996. "Measuring Hospital Use Without Claims: A Comparison of Patient and Provider Reports." *HSR: Health Services Research* 31 (2): 153–69.

Cleary P. D., S. Edgman-Levitan, M. Roberts, T. W. Moloney, W. McMullen, J. D. Walker, and T. L. Delbanco. 1991. "Patients Evaluate Their Hospital Care: A National Survey." *Health Affairs* 10 (4): 254–67.

Cleary P. D., S. Edgman-Levitan, J. F. Walker, M. Gerteis, T. L. Delbanco. 1993. "Using Patient Reports to Improve Medical Care: A Preliminary Report from Ten Hospitals." *Quality in Managed Health Care* 2 (1): 31–38.

Codman, E. A. 1917. "Case-Records and Their Value." *Bulletin of American College of Surgeons* 3 (1): 24–27.

Dick, R. S. and E. B. Steen, eds. 1991. *The Computer-Based Patient Record: An Essential Technology for Health Care.* Washington, D.C.: National Academy Press.

Dolan, P. 1996. "The Effect of Experience of Illness on Health State Valuations." *Journal of Clinical Epidemiology* 49 (5): 551–64.

Donaldson, M. S., and K. N. Lohr. 1994. *Health Data in the Information Age. Use, Disclosure, and Privacy.* Washington, D.C.: National Academy Press.

Duggan, A. K., B. Starfield, and C. DeAngelis. 1990. "Structured Encounter Form: The Impact on Provider Performance and Recording of Well-Child Care." *Pediatrics* 85 (1): 104–13.

Eddy, D. M. 1984. "Variations in Physician Practice: The Role of Uncertainty." *Health Affairs* 3 (2): 74–89.

Elmore, J. G., and A. R. Feinstein. 1992. "A Bibliography of Publications on Observer Variability (Final Installment)." *Journal of Clinical Epidemiology* 45 (6): 567–80.

Essin, D. J., and T. L. Lincoln. 1995. "Implementing a Low-Cost Computer-Based Patient Record: A Controlled Vocabulary Reduces Database Design Complexity." *Proceedings of the Annual Symposium for Computer Applications to Medical Care* 431–35.

Feigl, P., G. Glaefke, L. Ford, P. Diehr, and J. Chu. 1988. "Studying Patterns of Cancer Care: How Useful Is the Medical Record?" *American Journal of Public Health* 78 (5): 526–33.

Feinstein, A. R. 1985. "A Bibliography of Publications on Observer Variability." *Journal of Chronic Disease* 38 (8): 619–32.

Fleming, D. G., and N. S. Fleming. 1989–1990. "The Erosion of Physician-Patient Privilege and Patient Confidentiality." *Health Matrix* 7 (4): 36–40.

Fitzmaurice, J. M. 1995. "Computer-Based Patient Records." In *The Biomedical Engineering Handbook*, edited by J. D. Bronzino. Boca Raton, FL: CRC Press, Inc.

Gfroerer, J. C., and A. L. Hughes. 1991. "The Feasibility of Collecting Drug Abuse Data by Telephone." *Public Health Reports* 106 (4): 384–93.

Green, J., and N. Wintfeld. 1995. "Report Cards on Cardiac Surgeons: Assessing New York State's Approach." *New England Journal of Medicine* 332 (18): 1229–32.

Greenfield, S., W. Rogers, M. Mangotich, M. F. Carney, and A. R. Tarlov. 1995a. "Outcomes of Patients with Hypertension and Non-Insulin-Dependent Diabetes Mellitus Treated by Different Systems and Specialties. Results from the Medical Outcomes Study." *Journal of the American Medical Association* 274 (18): 1436–44.

Greenfield, S., L. Sullivan, K. A. Dukes, R. Silliman, R. D'Agostino, and S. H. Kaplan. 1995b. "Development and Testing of a New Measure of Case Mix for Use in Office Practice." *Medical Care* 33 (4): AS47–AS55.

Hannan, E. L., H. Kilburn, Jr., J. F. O'Donnell, G. Lukacik, and E. P. Shields. 1990. "Adult Open Heart Surgery in New York State: An Analysis of Risk Factors and Hospital Mortality Rates." *Journal of the American Medical Association* 264 (21): 2768–74.

Hannan, E. L., H. Kilburn, Jr., M. L. Lindsey, and R. Lewis. 1992. "Clinical Versus Administrative Data Bases for CABG Surgery: Does It Matter?" *Medical Care* 30 (10): 892–907.

Hartz, A. J., C. Guse, P. Sigmann, H. Krakauer, R. S. Goldman, and T. C. Hagen. 1994. "Severity of Illness Measures Derived From the Uniform Clinical Data Set (UCDSS)." *Medical Care* 32 (9): 881–901.

Harvard Medical Practice Study. 1990. *Patients, Doctors, and Lawyers: Studies of Medical Injury, Malpractice Litigation, and Patient Compensation in New York.* Cambridge, MA: President and Fellows of Harvard College.

Hornsby, J. A. 1917. "The Hospital Problem of Today—What Is It?" *Bulletin of American College of Surgeons* 3 (1): 4–11.

Hsia, D. C., C. A. Ahern, B. P. Ritchie, L. M. Moscoe, and W. M. Krushat. 1992. "Medicare Reimbursement Accuracy Under the Prospective Payment System, 1985 to 1988." *Journal of the American Medical Association* 268 (7): 896–99.

Iezzoni, L. I., and J. Daley. 1992. "A Description and Clinical Assessment of the Computerized Severity Index." *Quality Review Bulletin* 18 (2): 44–52.

Iezzoni, L. I., and M. A. Moskowitz. 1988. "A Clinical Assessment of MedisGroups." *Journal of the American Medical Association* 260 (21): 3159–63.

Iezzoni, L. I., M. Shwartz, S. Burnside, A. S. Ash, E. Sawitz, and M. A. Moskowitz. 1989. *Diagnostic Mix, Illness Severity, and Costs at Teaching and Nonteaching Hospitals.* Springfield, VA: U.S. Department of Commerce, National Technical Information Service (PB 89 184675/AS).

Iezzoni, L. I., M. Shwartz, M. A. Moskowitz, A. S. Ash, E. Sawitz, and S. Burnside. 1990. "Illness Severity and Costs of Admissions at Teaching and Nonteaching Hospitals." *Journal of the American Medical Association* 264 (11): 1426–31.

Iezzoni, L. I., M. Shwartz, and J. Restuccia. 1991. "The Role of Severity Information in Health Policy Debates: A Survey of State and Regional Concerns." *Inquiry* 28 (2): 117–28.

Iezzoni, L. I., J. D. Restuccia, M. Shwartz, D. Schaumburg, G. A. Coffman, B. E. Kreger, J. R. Butterly, and H. P. Selker. 1992a. "The Utility of Severity of Illness Information in Assessing the Quality of Hospital Care: The Role of the Clinical Trajectory." *Medical Care* 30 (5): 428–44.

Iezzoni, L. I., A. S. Ash, G. A. Coffman, and M. A. Moskowitz. 1992b. "Predicting In-Hospital Mortality: A Comparison of Severity Measurement Approaches." *Medical Care* 30 (4): 347–59.

Iezzoni, L. I., and L. G. Greenberg. 1994. "Widespread Assessment of Risk-Adjusted Outcomes: Lessons from Local Initiatives." *Journal on Quality Improvement* 20 (6): 305–16.

Iezzoni, L. I., M. Shwartz, A. S. Ash, J. S. Hughes, J. Daley, and Y. D. Mackiernan. 1995. "Using Severity-adjusted Stroke Mortality Rates to Judge Hospitals." *International Journal for Quality in Health Care* 7 (2): 81–94.

———. 1996a. "Severity Measurement Methods and Judging Hospital Death Rates for Pneumonia." *Medical Care* 34 (1): 11–28.

Iezzoni, L. I., A. S. Ash, M. Shwartz, J. Daley, J. S. Hughes, and Y. D. Mackiernan. 1996b. "Judging Hospitals by Severity-Adjusted Mortality Rates: The Influence of the Severity-Adjustment Method." *American Journal of Public Health* 86 (10): 1379–87.

Iglehart, J. K. 1988. "Competition and the Pursuit of Quality: A Conversation with Walter McClure." *Health Affairs* 7 (1): 79–90.

"Iowa's Experiment with Severity Software Provides Good Report Card But May Cost Too Much." 1992. *Medicare Policy & Payment Report* (July): 106–13.

Jencks, S. F., and G. R. Wilensky. 1992. "The Health Care Quality Improvement Initiative: A New Approach to Quality Assurance in Medicare." *Journal of the American Medical Association* 268 (7): 900–3.

Johnson, J. E., and J. L. Carpenter. 1986. "Medical House Staff Performance in Physical Examination." *Archives of Internal Medicine* 146 (5): 937–41.

Katz, J. N., L. C. Chang, O. Sangha, A. H. Fossel, and D. W. Bates. 1996. "Can Comorbidity be Measured by Questionnaire Rather than Medical Record Review?" *Medical Care* 34 (1): 73–84.

Kolata, G. "When Patients' Records Are Commodities for Sale," *New York Times,* November 15, 1995, A1, C14.

Koran, L. M. 1976. "Increasing the Reliability of Clinical Data and Judgments." *Annals of Clinical Research* 8 (2): 69–73.

Kosecoff, J., A. Fink, R. H. Brook, and M. R. Chassin. 1987. "The Appropriateness of Using a Medical Procedure: Is Information in the Medical Record Valid?" *Medical Care* 25 (3): 196–201.

Kravitz, R. L., S. Greenfield, and W. H. Rogers. 1993. "Patient Mix and Utilization of Resources: In Reply to the Editor." *Journal of the American Medical Association* 269 (1): 44.

Kuperman, G. J., R. M. Gardner, and T. A. Pryor. 1991. *HELP: A Dynamic Hospital Information System.* New York: Springer-Verlag.

Kurtz, D. L. 1943. *Unit Medical Records in Hospital and Clinic.* New York: Columbia University Press.

Landon, B., L. I. Iezzoni, A. S. Ash, M. Shwartz, J. Daley, J. S. Hughes, and Y. D. Mackiernan. 1996. "Judging Hospitals by Severity-Adjusted Mortality Rates: The Case of CABG Surgery." *Inquiry* 33 (2): 155–66.

Lawthers, Ann. 1993. Personal communication, January 20.

Lohr, K. N., M. S. Donaldson, and J. Harris-Wehling. 1992. "Medicare: A Strategy for Quality Assurance, V: Quality of Care in a Changing Health Care Environment." *Quality Review Bulletin* 18 (4): 120–26.

Mansfield, B. G. 1986. "How Bad Are Medical Records? A Review of the Notes Received by a Practice." *Journal of the Royal College of General Practitioners* 36 (290): 405–6.

Massachusetts General Hospital. August 18, 1824. *Medical Case Records.* Boston, MA. Unpublished.

Mathias, S. D., S. K. Fifer, and D. L. Patrick. 1994. "Rapid Transition of Quality of Life Measures for International Clinical Trials: Avoiding Errors in the Minimalist Approach." *Quality of Life Research* 3 (6): 403–12.

McCabe, J. 1988. "The Uniform Health-Care Information Act: Current Status, Part II. [Interview by Joan Banach]." *Journal of the American Medical Record Association* 59 (10): 23–25.

McDiarmid, M. A., R. Bonanni, and M. Finocchiaro. 1991. "Poor Agreement of Occupational Data between a Hospital-Based Cancer Registry and Interview." *Journal of Occupational Medicine* 33 (6): 726–29.

Murray, L. S., G. M. Teasdale, G. D. Murray, B. Jennett, J. D. Miller, J. D. Pickard, M. D. Shaw, J. Achilles, S. Bailey, P. Jones, D. Kelly, and J. Lacey. 1993. "Does Prediction of Outcome Alter Patient Management?" *Lancet* 341 (8859): 1487–91.

Office of Technology Assessment, U.S. Congress. 1995. *Bringing Health Care Online. The Role of Information Technologies.* OTA-ITC-624. Washington, D.C.: U.S. Government Printing Office.

Page, L. 1996. "Managed Care Files Pose Privacy Risks." *American Medical News* 39 (22): 3, 12.

Pearl, R. 1921. "Modern Methods in Handling Hospital Statistics." *Bulletin of the Johns Hopkins Hospital* 32 (364): 184–94.

Podolsky, D., and K. T. Beddingfield. 1993. "America's Best Hospitals." *U.S. News and World Report* 115 (22): 66–70, 74.

Prager, L. O. 1996. "As Pressure Grows, Plan Performance Measures Move Toward Outcomes." *American Medical News* 39 (25): 3, 30.

Pringle, M., P. Ward, and C. Chilvers. 1995. "Assessment of the Completeness and Accuracy of Computer Medical Records in Four Practices Committed to Recording Data on Computer." *British Journal of General Practice* 45 (399): 537–41.

Ramsey, G. A., and R. C. Kingswood. 1923. "Case Records." *Bulletin of the American College of Surgeons* 7 (2): 22–24.

Rind, D. M., C. Safran, R. S. Phillips, Q. Wang, D. R. Calkins, T. L. Delbanco, H. L. Bleich, and W. V. Slack. 1994. "Effect of Computer-Based Alerts on the Treatment and Outcomes of Hospitalized Patients." *Archives of Internal Medicine* 154 (13): 1511–17.

Roberts, R. O., E. J. Bergstralh, L. Schmidt, and S. J. Jacobsen. 1996. "Comparison of Self-Reported and Medical Record Health Care Utilization Measures." *Journal of Clinical Epidemiology* 49 (9): 989–95.

Romm, F. J., and S. M. Putnam. 1981. "The Validity of the Medical Record." *Medical Care* 19 (3): 310–15.

Rowe, L., D. C. Galletly, and R. S. Henderson. 1992. "Accuracy of Text Entries Within a Manually Compiled Anaesthetic Record." *British Journal of Anaesthesia* 68 (4): 381–87.

Showstack, J. A., S. A. Schroeder, and M. F. Matsumoto. 1982. "Changes in the Use of Medical Technologies, 1972–1977: A Study of 10 Inpatient Diagnoses." *New England Journal of Medicine* 306 (12): 706–12.

Spiteri, M. A., D. G. Cook, and S. W. Clarke. 1988. "Reliability of Eliciting Physical Signs in Examination of the Chest." *Lancet* 1 (8590): 873–75.

Starfield, B., D. Steinwachs, I. Morris, G. Bause, S. Siebert, and C. Westin. 1979. "Concordance Between Medical Records and Observations Regarding Information on Coordination of Care." *Medical Care* 17 (7): 758–66.

Steen, P. M., A. C. Brewster, R. C. Bradbury, E. Estabrook, J. A. Young. 1993. "Predicted Probabilities of Hospital Death as a Measure of Admission Severity of Illness." *Inquiry* 30 (2): 128–41.

Sullivan, L. W., and G. R. Wilensky. 1991. *Medicare Hospital Mortality Information: 1987, 1988, 1989.* Washington, D.C.: U.S. Department of Health and Human Services, Health Care Financing Administration.

Sullivan, L. M., K. A. Dukes, L. Harris, R. S. Dittus, S. Greenfield, and S. H. Kaplan. 1995. "A Comparison of Various Methods of Collecting Self-Reported Health Outcomes Data Among Low-Income and Minority Patients." *Medical Care* 33 (4): AS183-AS193.

Teres, D., and S. Lemeshow. 1994. "Why Severity Models Should Be Used With Caution." *Critical Care Clinics* 10 (1): 93–110.

Wald, J. S., D. Rind, C. Safran, H. Kowaloff, R. Barker, and W. V. Slack. 1995. "Patient Entries in the Electronic Medical Record: An Interactive Interview Used in Primary Care." *Proceedings of the Annual Symposium for Computer Applications to Medical Care:* 147–51.

Ware, Jr., J. E., S. D. Keller, B. Gandek, J. E. Brazier, and M. Sullivan. 1995. "Evaluating Translations of Health Status Questionnaires: Methods from the IQOLA Project." *International Journal of Technology Assessment in Health Care* 11 (3): 525–51.

Weed, L. L. 1968a. "Medical Records That Guide and Teach." *New England Journal of Medicine* 278 (11): 593–600.

———. 1968b. "Medical Records That Guide and Teach (Concluded): Implementation of More Comprehensive Care through the Medical Record and the Computer." *New England Journal of Medicine* 278 (12): 652–57.

———. 1971. "Quality Control and the Medical Record." *Archives of Internal Medicine* 127 (1): 101–5.

Westgren, M., M. Divon, J. Greenspoon, and R. Paul. 1986. "Missing Hospital

Records: A Confounding Variable in Retrospective Studies." *American Journal of Obstetric Gynecology* 155 (2): 269–71.

Wiener, S., and M. Nathanson. 1976. "Physical Examination: Frequently Observed Errors." *Journal of the American Medical Association* 236 (7): 852–55.

Zola, I. K. 1966. "Culture and Symptoms—An Analysis of Patients' Presenting Complaints." *American Sociological Review* 31 (5): 615–30.

Zuckerman, A. E., B. Starfield, C. Hochreiter, and B. Kovasznay. 1975. "Validating the Content of Pediatric Outpatient Medical Records by Means of Tape-Recording Doctor-Patient Encounters." *Pediatrics* 56 (3): 407–11.

Chapter 5

Developing Risk-Adjustment Methods

Jennifer Daley and Michael Shwartz

Developing risk-adjustment methods is challenging but essential for understanding the significance of variations in healthcare outcomes. As suggested in Chapter 1, risk adjustment is especially important for studies of medical effectiveness—outcomes resulting from care provided by typical clinicians employing usual practices under customary conditions. One tenet of medical effectiveness research is to avoid the narrow selection criteria often imposed in randomized clinical trials (Roper et al. 1988). Given the clinical heterogeneity of humans, controlling for differences in patient characteristics is crucial when assessing the outcomes of care.

This chapter describes important considerations in developing a risk-adjustment strategy for studying healthcare outcomes. It is intended for persons developing a risk-adjustment method, as well as for those seeking to understand the development process and the consequent strengths and limitations of a risk-adjustment method. We address a range of issues, including the implications of the purpose of risk adjustment, how predictor variables should be defined, the role of clinical judgment, and empirical modeling techniques. As stated throughout this book, however, detailed technical discussions available elsewhere (e.g., on multivariable modeling techniques) are not replicated. Instead, we focus on issues especially pertinent to creating risk measures. We draw examples from the literature on the severity measures introduced in Chapter 1, as well as from one author's experience developing risk-adjustment systems using Medicare mortality data—the MMPS (Daley et al. 1988)—and for adverse surgical outcomes in a large, multicenter, observational study in the Department of Veterans Affairs (VA)—the National Veterans Affairs Surgical Risk Study (Khuri et al. 1995).

Purpose of Risk Adjustment

The first step in developing a risk-adjustment approach is defining one's purpose (see Chapter 1) as Hornbrook (1982, 3) wrote, "A measure is not independent of the purpose for which it was devised. . . ." To assess risk, one must initially answer the question, risk of what? Narrowly defined, risk adjustment in outcomes research seeks to account for *patient* factors existing prior to medical interventions that could affect outcomes, variously defined (see below). Broadly construed, however, risk adjustment attempts to account for *all* factors, other than the healthcare intervention itself or the process of care (i.e., what was done for the patient), that may explain variation in patient outcomes.

Four factors generally account for observed differences in patient outcomes:

- differences in significant risk factors among patients (see Chapter 2);

- differences in how well available data sources represent reality and these risk factors (see Chapters 3 and 4);

- random variation (see Chapter 10); and

- differences in the effectiveness of the health services provided or the quality of care.

Medical effectiveness research, as well as report cards on healthcare providers (see Chapters 10 and 11), are most interested in isolating this last quantity—the effect of specific healthcare interventions or provider performance. To isolate effectiveness or quality of care, risk-adjustment models therefore attempt to incorporate all patient-specific risk factors that could significantly influence the outcome of interest. The risk measure should rely on data that are pertinent, accurate, and unbiased. Making inferences about effectiveness or quality after adjusting for risk also requires appropriate consideration of random variation (Blumberg 1986), as discussed in detail in Chapter 10.

Which Outcomes?

As described in Chapters 3 and 4, studies are generally confined to outcomes available from existing data sources, which typically include in-hospital mortality, postdischarge mortality, provider costs (or charges), length of stay, use of specific procedures or services, and complications or adverse events recorded in the database—a modest subset of the range of potentially important outcomes (see Table 1.1). For investigations using administrative data files, measurable outcomes are especially limited (see

Chapter 3). Although information derived from medical records offers significantly more clinical detail than administrative sources, information about outcomes is only marginally more comprehensive. Information about complications and potentially avoidable adverse events can generally be extracted from medical charts, but little is systematically recorded about patients' baseline functional status, quality of life, symptoms, or goals of treatment (see Chapter 4). Even less is recorded about changes in these factors during the hospital stay, and obviously, postdischarge information is unavailable—a critical gap, given the dramatic shortening of hospital stays.

Recently, some healthcare organizations and researchers are beginning systematically to collect information prospectively from patients prior to their medical treatment. Patients are then followed for a predetermined period after the medical intervention to determine the prevalence of adverse outcomes and, in a proactive effort to improve health status, to assess changes in physical function and health-related quality of life. In the National VA Surgical Risk Study, patients undergoing major surgery are identified preoperatively, and selected preoperative risk factors are assessed prior to the surgery. Nurse reviewers then follow the patients for 30 days postoperatively to determine mortality status and the incidence of 21 predefined postoperative adverse events. Many hospitals also assess the generic or disease-specific functional status of patients on admission to the hospital and follow patients for weeks to months after their discharge to determine changes in health status. For example, at some hospitals, patients admitted for total hip replacement complete a generic health status instrument, such as the SF-36 (Stewart, Hays, and Ware 1988; Stewart et al. 1989; Ware and Sherbourne 1992), and are then resurveyed at three or six months postoperatively. Other researchers and institutions use a disease- or symptom-specific measure, such as the Specific Activities Scale (Goldman et al. 1981), the Duke Activity Status Index (Hlatky et al. 1989), or the Seattle Angina Questionnaire (Spertus et al. 1995).

Prospective collection of risk and outcomes information overcomes many of the limitations of using administrative or retrospective chart review data described in Chapters 3 and 4, but still does not typically incorporate relevant information about patients' preferences for treatment options or clinical outcomes. For example, in the National VA Surgical Risk Study, the presence of a do-not-resuscitate (DNR) order prior to major surgery is a significant predictor of 30-day mortality. Determining patients' preferences about tradeoffs between potential improvements in functional status and the risks of major surgery will require tools to elicit patients' preferences in a reliable, valid, and feasible fashion. These issues and their methodological implications are an active focus of the current clinical decision-making literature.

From both an individual patient's and societal perspectives, the most relevant outcomes are those achieved after patients leave hospitals for homes and communities. These outcomes include a patient's ability to function independently, to interact with families and friends, and to return to work and daily routines. As mentioned above, in-hospital outcomes diminish in importance as lengths of stay decrease under pressures to control healthcare costs, and as patients are increasingly treated as outpatients for many conditions (e.g., cataract extraction, inguinal herniorrhaphy, uncomplicated pneumonia, angina pectoris). Out-of-hospital outcomes must be obtained through painstaking review of office records dispersed at multiple sites or through prospective data collection directly from patients or providers. Some outcomes, such as posthospitalization mortality and readmissions, may be determined from longitudinal administrative data. As described in Chapter 3, Medicare and VA beneficiaries are identified by social security number (or a variation thereof) within their respective databases. This permits both the construction of longitudinal episodes of care, linkage between utilization and mortality information (e.g., death benefits), and linkage between the Medicare and VA databases to achieve a full picture of all care received regardless of payor (Medicare or VA). Such linked databases have been used to study services and mortality for acute myocardial infarction (AMI) patients across the Medicare and VA systems (Wright et al. 1997a, 1997b).

Another longitudinal outcome of interest is total resource consumption over a period of time. As capitated payment becomes more common and as HMOs grow, assessing annual costs of care (e.g., a year of utilization for a "covered life") has become a priority—both to ensure fair payment and reduce incentives for "cream skimming." For example, Ambulatory Care Groups (ACGs, see Chapter 1) use the diagnoses found in billing data to classify people according to the nature and number of medical problems under treatment (Starfield et al. 1991; Weiner et al. 1991). ACGs are used to estimate the expected resource utilization for groups of people (e.g., those being seen at a certain clinic) as a function of the disease burden in the population. The original ACG models were developed using ambulatory data to identify expected total costs within the same year that the diagnoses were observed in outpatient settings. However, ACGs' developers have extended their work to include inpatient diagnoses and to predict total costs in a subsequent year for a general population.

Diagnostic Cost Groups (DCGs, see Chapter 1) also use diagnoses from billing data to identify expected healthcare costs (Ash et al. 1989; Ellis et al. 1996). In the original DCG model, developed to tailor payments to Medicare HMOs to the sickness of enrolled persons, the principal inpatient diagnosis associated with the most expensive single medical problem one year was used to predict a person's expected cost the next year. In subsequent versions, DCG models have been fit to other populations, used to estimate concurrent costs, and extended to accommodate multiple diagnoses noted from either inpatient or ambulatory bills.

Investigating a spectrum of relevant outcomes (both positive and negative) is optimal for fully assessing the effectiveness of care, despite difficulties obtaining data. Positive outcomes include amelioration of symptoms, improvement in functional status, prevention of death, and lowered costs. Adverse outcomes include complications of treatment, morbidity, mortality, and higher costs. Trade-offs among these outcomes may be necessary, especially when melding interests in both clinical results and resource use. In some scenarios, better clinical outcomes (e.g., survival, functional ability) may be achieved but at a high price (e.g., prolonged intensive care), such as lengthy stays in neonatal intensive care for low-birthweight neonates.

What Is the Unit of Analysis?

Examination of outcomes is inherently a comparative exercise, but, again, the most appropriate comparisons depend on one's purpose. The unit of observation can vary by context. Options include individual patients, individual providers, groups of providers (e.g., those practicing in capitated versus fee-for-service arrangements), hospitals, groups of hospitals (e.g., teaching versus nonteaching facilities), or geographic areas (Whiting-O'Keefe, Henke, and Simborg 1984). These units are not mutually exclusive; smaller units are often nested within larger units as suggested by the order of the list of options.

Units of analysis defined by the window of observation depend on what is available in the data set. As described above, when using hospital discharge abstract data that cannot be linked at the patient level (as in many state databases), the only available unit of analysis is the individual hospitalization. In databases with linked longitudinal information, the unit can be an individual patient observed during an episode of illness or over a set time period (e.g., a year).

Choice of the unit of analysis has important analytic implications. In particular, questions about the need for hierarchical modeling and "nested" designs may arise (Bryk and Raudenbush 1992; Gatsonis et al. 1993). For example, when comparing patient outcomes across groups of hospitals (e.g., teaching versus nonteaching institutions), one must consider that individual patients are clustered or "nested" within specific hospitals and that individual hospitals are nested within groups of institutions reflecting teaching intensity (e.g., tertiary teaching versus nonteaching).

For example, suppose that we observe 1,000 hospital admissions, half occurring in five teaching hospitals and half in five nonteaching hospitals. Our goal is to compare complication rates at teaching versus nonteaching hospitals. This study is basically a two-sample comparison, with five observations in each sample; this would remain a two-sample comparison even if we observed 100,000 admissions at each of the ten hospitals. More observations per hospital permit more accurate estimations of individual hospitals' complication rates, but our ability to discriminate between the two *types* of hospitals relies on comparing the five teaching hospital averages to the five nonteaching hospital averages.

We cannot determine whether teaching and nonteaching hospitals differ without recognizing the structure of the data (i.e., individual observations are nested within specific hospitals, which are in turn nested within hospital type). This hierarchical structure is typically addressed through so-called "mixed models," which examine the evidence for a *fixed* effect of lasting interest (here, hospital teaching status) in the presence of the *random* effect (or "statistical noise") caused by selecting particular hospitals as representatives of their type. The evidence that hospitals differ by teaching status is strongest when differences among hospitals with the same teaching status are small compared to the differences across hospital groups (see Figure 5.1). For example, Iezzoni and colleagues (1989, 1990) examined whether severity and severity-adjusted costs differed across five tertiary teaching, five other teaching, and five nonteaching hospitals in metropolitan Boston. Equal numbers of patients were studied at each of the 15 hospitals. When analyses disregarded variability among the five institutions within each of the three hospital types, numerous statistically significant differences were found by hospital teaching status. However, in many instances, wide variability existed among the five hospitals within each teaching category. When this variability was considered through nested analyses, many of the statistically significant differences by hospital teaching status disappeared.

Researchers are refining tools for valid modeling of hierarchical data, as described in Chapter 10. No consensus yet exists about the best way to model such data, nor is there a clear appreciation of how sensitive analytic findings are to different modeling approaches.

What Is the Focus of Analysis?

The characteristics of the study population has implications for the risk-adjustment strategy. For example, research targeting one particular disease will not need to adjust for the presence of the disease, although one may wish to adjust for disease-specific severity. The larger the population under study (e.g., comparisons across states or regions), the less necessary it is to adjust for dimensions of risk that can plausibly be assumed to be evenly distributed across large patient populations (Gatsonis et al. 1995).

Figure 5.1   Two Scenarios in Which Mean Performance of Teaching
and Nonteaching Hospitals Differs by the Same Amount

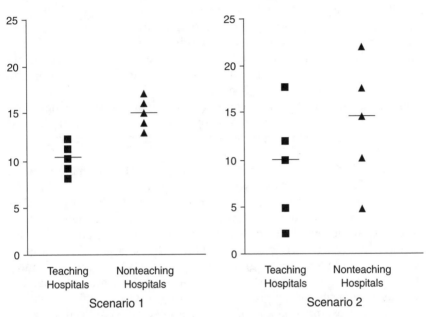

Scenario 1

Individual hospital averages vary little by teaching status compared to average differences between patients at the two types of hospitals; this suggests that teaching status is an important predictor.

Scenario 2

Individual hospital averages vary widely within teaching strata; the importance of teaching status is less clear than in Scenario 1.

However, one should not assume that patients with a particular diagnosis admitted to specific hospitals in different regions of the country are similar, even if *across all hospitals in the different areas* the populations are similar.

Different risk-adjustment strategies have been designed for different units of observation. For example, the clinical criteria version of Disease Staging assigns a severity stage to each disease experienced by a patient. Thus, patients with several coexisting conditions could have multiple severity ratings (Gonnella, Hornbrook, and Louis 1984). Scores are not necessarily equivalent across diseases. For instance, a Stage 3.2 prostate cancer may not carry the same risk of short-term mortality as a Stage 3.2 pneumonia. This version of Disease Staging does not compute an overall severity score for the patient—diseases are scored, not patients. Other versions of Disease Staging, however, combine this disease-specific information to generate overall scores for patients (see Exhibit 2.2 and accompanying discussion in Chapter 2).

Some studies investigate outcomes for patients with specific clinical conditions. These analyses focus primarily on examining the effect of differences in the process of care for patients with the particular condition. Examples of this approach include the AHCPR-funded Patient Outcome Research Teams (PORTs) studying AMI, benign prostatic hyperplasia, cataract surgery, low back pain, hip and knee replacement, pneumonia, chronic ischemic heart disease, and other prevalent conditions. As mentioned above, concentrating on patients within a single condition obviates the need to control for disease itself; the focus instead shifts to disease severity, comorbid illness, and other pertinent dimensions of risk.

In the policy context (see Chapter 11), often the ultimate goals of risk-adjusted outcome analyses are to evaluate quality of care and to motivate quality improvement (Chassin, Hannan, and DeBuono 1996). This motivation has important implications for the risk-adjustment strategy. Especially when quality of care is the ultimate interest, controlling for patients' characteristics *prior to medical intervention* is crucial. Comparisons across a range of patient types grouped by provider introduce considerable clinical heterogeneity. In addition, such aggregations may obscure important differences among providers or across services within individual hospitals. For example, in an analysis of in-hospital complications based on administrative data, we found that the relative observed-to-expected complication rates within and across hospitals varied significantly depending on whether surgical or medical cases were analyzed (Iezzoni et al. 1994). As another example, after adjusting for severity and a variety of other factors, a hospital's relative ranking by cost per case depended on the specific condition examined (e.g., cardiovascular disease versus hip fracture) (Iezzoni et al. 1990).

Most existing severity measures were intended to be used across groups of patients and are not well suited to making inferences about individual cases. A potential but controversial exception is APACHE III, a measure that aims to predict imminent death among ICU patients. APACHE III is increasingly touted as one additional piece of prognostic information (e.g., as are laboratory tests) to assist individual clinical decision making. For example, APACHE III's predictions of in-hospital death may be used to guide decisions about which patients would benefit most from ICU care, transferring recovering patients out of ICUs, or possibly withdrawing ICU care when the prognosis is grim (Knaus et al. 1991, 1993). APACHE III's developers see their system as a way to improve consistency and comparability in assessing risks across ICU patients. "Physicians are already deciding what is hopeless. We are already deciding who gets what when,"

Knaus argues (Brown 1992, A8). The ethical implications of using risk-adjustment measures such as APACHE III in allocating scarce resources at the individual patient level are considerable: "Is your hopeless the same as my hopeless? Are you quitting at the same threshold that I am?" (Brown 1992, A8).

Furthermore, a logical problem arises in using severity scores for individual patient care: Predicted probabilities of mortality calculated by a tool such as APACHE reflect what outcomes were historically, *given the care that was rendered at the facilities participating in developing the severity algorithm*. The scores tell us little about what would happen if practice changes or if care is very different from practices at the institutions used to develop the measure. In general, when processes of care are modified in response to empirically derived expectations about outcomes, the real probabilities of outcomes change in ways that are difficult to measure. Also, the performance characteristics (see Chapter 9) of existing risk-adjustment methods are insufficient to support making such individual decisions solely on the basis of these measures (Chang 1989; Hadorn et al. 1992). Use of severity scores for making individual patient decisions therefore requires caution (Teres and Lemeshow 1994).

Condition-Specific versus Generic Risk Adjustment

Whether risk adjustment should be condition-specific or generic (diagnosis-independent) remains controversial and again depends on one's purpose. Some severity measures are structured within a diagnostic framework while others are not (see Table 1.5). Disease Staging, for instance, specified separate clinical criteria within each of 420 conditions (Gonnella, Hornbrook, and Louis 1984). As described above, the risk represented by numerically identical substages is not necessarily comparable across diagnoses. As a result, using this Disease Staging methodology, patients with different diagnoses cannot be aggregated into identical risk groups, although other versions of Disease Staging do rate all patients on the same scale (e.g., by expected resource intensity).

In the original version of MedisGroups, admission severity scores from 0 through 4 were assigned regardless of patients' diseases (Brewster et al. 1985; Iezzoni and Moskowitz 1988). MedisGroups' developers intended that the likelihood of imminent risk of organ failure, as indicated by the five ordinal categories, would be comparable for all patients. Nonetheless, despite using the same scoring method, diagnosis-specific differences were observed: Among patients with a MedisGroups score of 2, for example, AMI patients had a substantially higher probability of death (15.4 percent) than patients undergoing prostate surgery (2.5 percent) (Iezzoni et al. 1991, 75). Using a disease-specific approach, the CSI has "severity matrices" associated with over 820 disease groups (Iezzoni and Daley 1992); four such matrices appear in Exhibit 2.1.

With increasing sophistication in risk-adjustment methods and improvement in data quality, the recent trend has been toward developing disease-specific risk models. The evolution of APACHE is illustrative. Developed to predict the probability of in-hospital death for ICU patients, the original APACHE computed a generic score combining information about age, chronic diseases, and acute physiologic parameters (Knaus et al. 1981). The most recent revision, APACHE III, calculates the same APACHE score for any patient admitted to an ICU; however, the algorithm for predicting probability of in-hospital death with this score considers 78 disease groups (Knaus et al. 1991). Similarly, MedisGroups has developed a new scoring system that generates a probability of in-hospital death from KCFs within over 60 different disease groups (Steen et al. 1993; MediQual Systems, Inc. 1993). Nonetheless, although both APACHE III and MedisGroups now use predictive equations that consider disease group, each method generates a predicted probability of death that ranges from 0 to 1. This prediction carries the same implications about patients' risks of dying regardless of diagnosis. However, the relationship between predictions and what actually happened (i.e., the "quality" of the prediction) usually differs by disease group (see Chapter 9).

Relationships of Risks to Outcomes

After specifying the outcome or outcomes of interest, a conceptual model of how risks relate to the particular outcomes is needed. As suggested in Chapter 2, this relationship often is complex. Several aspects of the relationship are particularly important. Does the relative importance of the specific risk variables vary across different outcomes? What is the time frame or window of observation for the outcome of interest? Does the nature of the intervention under study affect the relationship between risk factors and the outcome? What are the implications of these relationships for measuring risk factors? These areas are discussed below.

Patient Risk Factors and Individual Outcomes

Some argue that a "minimum" or "core" set of risk factors can be used within a single condition to adjust for patient risks of various different outcomes—mortality, morbidity, length of stay, and resource use. Considerable research has assessed this hypothesis. Although pertinent individual risk variables are often similar across different outcomes, relationships between these factors and the outcomes (e.g., the "weights," the empirical parameter estimates) vary by outcome. One study used forward stepwise regression techniques to select the ten most statistically important Medis-Groups KCFs to predict hospitalization costs and in-hospital death (Iezzoni, Moskowitz, and Ash 1988, 119–120, 128–29). The database included patients 65 years of age and older admitted between 1984 and 1986 to one of 24 hospitals that routinely used MedisGroups. Results from three conditions suggest that the ten most important predictors vary widely depending on whether cost or death is the outcome of interest (Table 5.1). Both MedisGroups and APACHE have developed risk-adjustment models that predict both in-hospital mortality, resource utilization, and length of stay; the weights assigned to the predictor variables differ by outcome (Knaus et al. 1993; Becker et al. 1995).

In the National VA Surgical Risk Study, risk-adjustment models were developed to predict postoperative 30-day mortality, morbidity (21 adverse events), and length of stay. Although considerable overlap exists among the patient risk variables for all three outcomes, two issues become clear from examining the ten most predictive risk variables. First, four patient risk variables are among the ten most predictive risk variables across the three outcomes: serum albumin, American Society of Anesthesiology class, emergency surgery, and patient age. The other six variables from the top ten predictive risk factors vary across outcomes. Second, the relative weights (coefficients) of the common variables in each model differ.

Such differences become increasingly evident as other outcomes, such as functional status, are examined (Greenfield et al. 1993, 1995; Wu et al. 1995). Thus, those who seek a global risk-adjustment system that predicts equally well across all outcomes of interest will be disappointed. It is critically important to develop specific hypotheses about patient risk for each different outcome of interest. Failure to do so may result in risk models with poor predictive validity (see Chapter 6).

Time Frame: Window of Observation

The time frame, or window of observation, significantly affects which dimensions of risk are of greatest importance. Options for this time window include:

- a hospitalization or stay at some other healthcare facility (e.g., nursing home);
- a fixed period (e.g., 30 or 180 days) initiated by admission, by a procedure, or by diagnosis of a condition;
- an episode of care or illness, often defined by a constellation of health events or series of services, and possibly of varying duration from patient to patient;

Table 5.1 Top Ten Key Clinical Findings Entering Stepwise Regression Models to Predict Costs and In-Hospital Death for Three Conditions

	Stroke		Pneumonia		AMI	
Step	Cost	Death	Cost	Death	Cost	Death
1	oxygenation	coma	oxygenation	BUN	congestive heart failure	cardiac arrest
2	lethargy	respiratory rate	hematocrit	cardiac arrest	BUN	BUN
3	creatinine	cardiac arrest	calcium	systolic blood pressure	cardiac arrest	oxygenation
4	myocardial ischemia	stupor	carbon dioxide	arterial pH	creatinine phosphokinase	systolic blood pressure
5	edema	glucose	calcium squared	stupor	positive sputum culture	coma
6	potassium	pulse	cardiac arrest	respiratory rate	cardiomegaly	bundle branch block on ECG
7	wheezing	BUN	lethargy	coma	calcium	AMI on ECG
8	partial thromboplastin time	high density brain mass	premature ventricular contractions	alkaline phosphatase	potassium	stupor
9	calcium	systolic blood pressure	sodium	pleural effusion	pulse	atrial flutter
10	AMI on ECG	history of diabetes	blood in stool	arterial pH squared	AMI on ECG	positive sputum culture

Notes: For physiologic parameters that can have both high and low abnormal values, the value of the parameter squared as well as the raw value were entered into the model.

BUN = blood urea nitrogen.   ECG = electrocardiogram.

- a variable period initiated by admission, by a procedure, or by diagnosis of a condition, with the length of observation determined by methods of patient follow-up or specific time constraints of the particular study; and

- a fixed period, often defined by a calendar or fiscal year, covered by an insurance or capitated health plan.

In general, acute clinical stability and acute attributes of the principal diagnosis and coexisting conditions are the most important components of risk for studies involving short time frames (see Chapter 2). In contrast, chronic disability, physical functioning, and various nonclinical factors increase in importance as the time window expands.

Many severity measures (Table 1.3) focus on the short term—the hospital stay or 30 days following admission. One exception is the chronic disease measure developed by Charlson and colleagues (1987), widely used in the PORT studies (Patrick and Deyo 1989; Deyo, Cherkin, and Ciol 1992). This measure attempts to predict death within one year of an index hospitalization for patients admitted to a medical service. Risk-adjustment measures that adjust utilization and costs for use in capitated payment systems also typically use a one-year window of observation (e.g., ACGs, DCGs). Even longer time periods may be required for certain purposes. One example is the clinical staging systems used in oncology. Cancer-staging criteria are often delineated based on risk of three- to five-year survival. Often clinical responses following cancer therapy are couched in terms of disease-free survival periods, and conjectures about "cures" are not even ventured until after five or more years without evidence of disease. Cox proportional hazards regression models (Cox 1972), discussed briefly below, model survival and are increasingly used for risk adjustment when longer-term, follow-up data are available (e.g., Knaus et al. 1995). However, relatively little systematic information is available about sources of long-term patient risks for conditions other than cancer.

For some conditions, such as AMI, early interventions (e.g., thrombolytic therapy, primary angioplasty) greatly affect survival and the development of complications. In these instances, risk factors relating to mortality and the development of acute complications within the first hours to days of the onset of illness are very important. When studying the longer-term outcomes of this condition (e.g., functional status, quality of life, persistent chest pain, disability from congestive heart failure), one must consider the most appropriate time to measure these outcomes and which risk factors on initial presentation affect these longer-term results.

As another example, the outcomes of greatest interest for hip fracture patients immediately after hospitalization are mortality and complications related to the patient's general medical status (e.g., deep venous thrombosis, pulmonary embolism, bleeding, cardiac or respiratory failure). Risk factors for these outcomes differ from those related to longer-term outcomes, such as return to baseline functional status. Similar considerations apply to other diseases, such as stroke, in which the risk of mortality is high during the first days after the acute event. Other outcomes, such as functional status, become more important in the ensuing weeks and months.

Risk factors may have different relationships to the same outcome when that outcome is measured at different times after the acute event. For example, different risk factors (or different weights for the same risk factors) may arise when examining mortality after AMI, depending on when deaths occur (e.g., in-hospital, 30 days after the acute event, 180 days, one year, two years). This is particularly important to consider when mortality is very common immediately after the acute event, such as stroke, pneumonia, congestive heart failure, and AMI. Risk models that adjust for variations in mortality during the acute period may differ considerably from those for patients who survive that acute time window.

Timing of Collection of Risk Factors

For evaluating the effectiveness of a specific intervention, one must specify *a priori* hypotheses about timing and the relationships among the risk factors, specific outcome, and clinical practice under study. The nature of the particular intervention or process of care being examined significantly affects the information required for judging risk and when during the clinical course risk factors are collected. It also suggests the most relevant form for the risk models.

For example, for APACHE II (Knaus et al. 1985) and III (Knaus et al. 1991), the outcome of interest is in-hospital death, the intervention is medical and surgical ICU care, and patient risk is defined by the structure of the APACHE scoring system. Because most physiologic parameters are measured repeatedly in ICUs, numerous values are typically available. Which value of these physiologic parameters should be used for risk adjustment? The first? The worst over some time period? What time period?

The answer to these questions must be viewed within the research and clinical contexts, but the implications for data collection may also need to be considered. Although APACHE's developers recommend using the most abnormal value in the first day of ICU treatment, studies of cases at their own institution showed that in 88 percent of the physiologic measurements, the worst value was that observed on ICU admission (Knaus et al. 1985, 825). Depending on the time interval considered, worst values may reflect the results of therapeutic or diagnostic mishaps. For example, blood pressure may become further deranged from its admission value because of incorrect therapeutic decisions. In addition, from a practical perspective, identifying the first value is easier than finding the worst value; reviewers require less training, and data abstraction reliability is thus probably higher (see Chapter 7). Extensive analyses by APACHE's developers have shown no significant difference in APACHE risk models based on physiologic parameters collected initially versus those gathered within the first 24 hours. However, calculating APACHE prognostic estimates daily during an ICU stay usefully tracks patients' clinical trajectories, differentiating patients who are improving from those who are worsening (Wagner et al. 1994).

The MMPS was developed to predict risk of mortality within 30 days of hospital admission in four conditions with high death rates among Medicare beneficiaries: stroke, pneumonia, congestive heart failure, and AMI (Daley et al. 1988). In MMPS, the intervention of interest was hospitalization, and the outcome was mortality 30 days after admission. Risk was measured using patient-specific variables obtained within 24 hours of admission and retrospectively abstracted from medical records. We chose the first 24 hours of admission to allow a reasonable period for data collection regarding the patient's status before hospitalization, but to eliminate information from later in the hospitalization that might reflect the process of hospital care—the intervention of interest. In addition, we were concerned that using worst values was virtually equivalent to identifying patients who died. Worst values could include apnea, asystole, and absent blood pressure—certain clues about imminent death.

In the National VA Surgical Risk Study, the intervention of interest was major surgery, the outcomes of interest were 30-day postoperative morbidity and mortality, and risk was measured using 65 patient risk factors measured prior to surgery. Preoperative risk variables were measured as close as possible to when the patient entered the operating room, but some information was sought from up to 14 days prior to surgery. For example, the most recent hematocrit and white blood cell count values were sought, but to accommodate elective surgery where patients underwent ambulatory preoperative clearance the most recent value in the previous 14 days was collected.

The longer the period from which data are collected, the greater the possibility of confounding the quality of care with patient risk before treatment. If the time period is too short, however, levels of missing information may be unacceptably high. One study to predict in-hospital mortality at a tertiary teaching hospital used information from a computerized repository of all laboratory test results obtained on hospitalized patients (Davis et al. 1995). To avoid confounding quality with patients' risk factors, the investigators initially desired to include only laboratory values from the first 12 hours of the hospital stay: They were convinced that the house staff thoroughly worked up patients immediately on admission at their facility. However, to their chagrin, they needed to expand the time window to the first 48 hours of hospitalization. Otherwise, too many values were missing—even from routine laboratory tests. Continuing declines in hospital lengths of stays, however, may change timing of testing and the availability of certain test results during the hospitalization.

As described in Chapter 3, a significant limitation of risk adjustment based on administrative data is the inability to distinguish among secondary discharge diagnoses representing conditions existing before versus those developing during the hospitalization. For example, pneumonia, congestive heart failure, or pyelonephritis may be present when a patient is admitted for hip fracture. These conditions are risk factors for poor outcomes, but they also represent significant complications in patients who develop them after being admitted for hip fracture. From most administrative data files, one cannot definitively distinguish discharge diagnoses codes that represent preexisting risk factors from adverse outcomes or complications. In the AMI PORT's studies using administrative data of the effect of coronary revascularization on one- and two-year mortality, risk models were developed conditional on 30-day survival to eliminate risk factors for early death from AMI. Because the primary interest involved the decision to perform cardiac catheterization followed by revascularization (either with percutaneous transluminal coronary angioplasty or coronary artery bypass graft), all patient factors present before cardiac catheterization were candidates for the analysis. Data collection need not be restricted to the first 24 or 48 hours after admission (Normand et al. 1995). Chapter 3 described further approaches that have been adopted for addressing timing of risk factors using administrative data.

Selecting Risk Factors

Having defined the outcomes of interest, the intervention(s) of interest, the temporal relationships between the outcomes and the intervention, and when the risk factors should be measured, which patient risk factors should be identified? Because hospital-associated mortality and resource consumption have been studied intensively over the last decade, patient factors associated with these outcomes are somewhat understood—both generically and for specific conditions. Less is currently known about risk factors for longer-term mortality, functional status, or health-related quality of life.

The clinical literature from randomized trials and other studies may be helpful in identifying important patient risk factors, especially for short-term mortality for certain illnesses and interventions (e.g., see Tables 6.3 and 6.4). For example, the clinical literature in the medical management of ischemic heart disease, AMI, and surgical treatment of coronary artery disease is particularly extensive. However, the clinical literature from randomized trials is relatively limited—one of the explicit motivations for the interest in effectiveness research. Randomized controlled trials generally provide little information about patient risk factors for predicting resource consumption, functional status, and quality of life.

Another common way to elicit lists of potential risk factors is by asking clinical experts or panels of practicing clinicians. Clinical knowledge, based on clinicians' experience in patient care as well as their synthesis of the literature, is important in informing model development. As described in Chapter 2, good models of risk must be medically meaningful. Involving clinicians in their development helps achieve this clinical credibility. In developing the MMPS, we convened subspecialty panels and provided them with a full literature review of patient risk factors for short-term (30-day) mortality. Panelists were recommended by subspecialty societies and principal investigators of prior large studies of stroke, myocardial infarction, congestive heart failure, and pneumonia. In the National VA Surgical Risk Study, we convened expert panels to identify patient risk factors for mortality and morbidity after surgery and to group similar surgical procedures according to likelihood of adverse outcomes.

In working with clinicians to identify risk factors, one must keep them focused on the specific outcomes and time frames considered by the intended analysis. Frequent reminders to discriminate among specific risk factors relevant to each outcome are important. Information from reviews of the clinical literature and interviews with clinical experts can generate hypotheses about important risk factors. For example, we developed the MMPS to provide hospitals with an easily implemented chart review instrument for risk adjusting their Medicare hospital mortality data. To determine a parsimonious set of risk variables, we asked panelists to suggest a limited number of risk factors predictive of mortality in all four conditions and, in addition, to suggest several condition-specific variables.

Clinicians can also assist in defining the specific structure of the relationship between the risk factor and the outcome. For example, in developing the MMPS, clinicians noted the importance of fever and extremes of body temperature in predicting the likelihood of imminent death in pneumonia. They also specified that the presence of a very low temperature in certain circumstances might reflect increased likelihood of in-hospital mortality for some pneumonia patients. In the National VA Surgical Risk Study, panels of clinicians reviewed all the candidate risk factors and suggested the relationship of each risk factor to postoperative mortality, morbidity, and length of stay. They were also asked to draw on a rough graph their predictions regarding the relationship between the continuous variables (e.g., laboratory variables, age) and the outcomes of interest. By a rough sketch, clinicians can succinctly summarize their thinking about the relationships of outcomes and a continuous variable at all values of that variable. For example, a U-shaped curve suggests that the continuous variable increases risk at both high and low abnormal values.

Some potentially important risk factors cannot easily be captured from existing data sources (see Chapters 3 and 4). Translating clinically important concepts into variables that can be measured reliably and validly using available data is one of the greatest challenges in developing risk-adjustment models. For example, clinicians and the literature report that the presence of cardiogenic shock on admission for AMI is a leading predictor of in-hospital death. "Cardiogenic shock," however, is a complex clinical entity, with its full clinical definition requiring evidence of diminished cardiac output or assessment of hypotension relative to the patient's premorbid mean blood pressure *and* clinical evidence of hypoperfusion of at least one vital organ (i.e., brain, heart, kidneys, or peripheral tissues), sometimes accompanied by evidence of lactic acidosis. Using a secondary data source containing ICD-9-CM diagnosis codes (Chapter 3), several codes can indicate cardiogenic shock: hypotension, unspecified (458.9); shock without mention of trauma (785.5); cardiogenic shock (785.51); or shock, unspecified (785.50). By the strictest and most accurate application of ICD-9-CM coding rules, only 785.51 should be used for cardiogenic shock. Nevertheless, given the limitations of administrative data, ICD-9-CM codes, and the coding process, some investigators may include some or all of these other codes to denote cardiogenic shock. While these additional ICD-9-CM codes will identify more patients, expanding the definition may include patients with other forms of shock (e.g., hypovolemic, septic) with a different relationship to the outcome, disease, or intervention under study.

Data from retrospective medical record reviews also present challenges. Continuing the example of cardiogenic shock, a recording of diminished cardiac output calculated from an intracardiac pulmonary artery pressure monitor is probably the best objective indicator of cardiogenic shock. Not every patient has, or should have, this invasive monitoring. Therefore, collecting diminished cardiac output measured this way will result in many missing values. Alternatively, one could use the peripheral arterial blood pressure measured by arm cuff because it is assessed in nearly every patient. Peripheral arterial blood pressure does not, however, always reflect whether the patient is in cardiogenic shock. In this example, finding a variable—in this case, blood pressure—measured in most patients does not capture the full complexity of the original clinical concept of the patient-specific risk factor, cardiogenic shock. Other proxies for the presence of cardiogenic shock, such as the left ventricular ejection fraction or the Killip classification, are not always measured or consistently noted in medical records.

The National VA Surgical Risk Study was initiated in 1991 after analysis of discharge abstract data and retrospective medical record reviews failed to provide findings with clinical credibility acceptable to surgeons practicing in VA facilities. Analysis of the VA discharge abstract database, the Patient Treatment File, was hindered by inconsistent coding patterns across the 123 hospitals performing major surgery and the inability of discharge abstracts to distinguish among patient risk factors present prior to major surgery and those occurring postoperatively. Retrospective chart review of six major surgical operations in a sample of VA medical centers was limited by poor reliability among raters and the lack of important risk factors being recorded in the charts.

The Department of Veterans Affairs and VA surgeons decided that having trained nurse reviewers prospectively collect data using consistent risk factor and outcome definitions across all medical centers performing major surgery was the only way to ensure reliability, validity, and acceptance by clinicians of the results. The costs of prospective data collection, analysis, and reporting—about $50 per case—were deemed worthwhile for reliable, valid, comparative information that could be provided to each chief of surgery. The ongoing implementation of a systemwide computerized information system, the Decentralized Hospital Computer Plan (DHCP), to all VA hospitals made data collection, data transmittal for analysis, and communication among the sites possible. The Surgical Risk Study module in the Surgical Package of DHCP permits data entry, range checks, verification, and reporting of surgical volume, risk assessment, and operative information at each site. Some patient risk variables (e.g., preoperative laboratory results) are captured directly from the clinical laboratory reporting systems in DHCP and transmitted for analysis.

Thus, operationalizing a risk concept in a clinically credible and reliable fashion can require new and potentially costly data collection. The appropriate trade-off between clinical credibility and data-gathering expense must be decided within each context. For example, the leaders of the National VA Surgical Risk Study decided that prospective data collection was worth the cost to produce information acceptable to the target audience—chiefs of surgery. In all contexts, however, when developing a risk-adjustment method, one must first define carefully the patient-specific risk factors (e.g., cardiogenic shock, sepsis, liver failure, altered mental status), then identify clinical measures of their presence (e.g., low blood pressure, low cardiac output, positive blood cultures, prolonged prothrombin time, elevated bilirubin, decreased serum albumin, hepatic coma, abnormal mental status exam). A systematic evaluation is then required to decide whether these variables (or acceptable surrogates) can be taken from existing sources or will require additional data collection.

Depending on data availability and willingness to pay for data gathering, some risk factors may just not be feasible to include.

In developing the MMPS AMI models, the anatomic location of the AMI (anterior versus inferior or posterior) and the presence of a transmural (Q-wave) as opposed to a subendocardial (non-Q-wave) infarction were proposed as important predictors of mortality. However, retrieving both items from the official interpretations of the electrocardiograms (ECGs) was very difficult. In some hospitals, interpretations were not recorded on the ECGs; other hospitals used computer readings of the tracings that did not provide a definitive anatomic location or type of infarct. We also noted considerable regional differences in the nomenclature of reading ECGs by cardiologists, which made standardization of the definitions difficult. Similarly, although the neurology panelists viewed the extent of the initial neurological deficits from a stroke as prognostic of likelihood of death (e.g., dense hemiparesis versus mild weakness of one hand), it was very difficult to determine the full extent of the initial deficit from the medical record. Therefore, we could not derive a standard measure of neurological deficit across all the patients and hospitals in the study.

Review of the contents of a secondary database or pilot data collection efforts can be very helpful. For studies using administrative databases, a thorough understanding of pertinent ICD-9-CM codes and coding conventions is necessary (see Chapter 3). For studies using retrospective medical record reviews, a sample of charts should be examined to determine the level of detail contained in a typical record. Prospective data collection, although generally more reliable and valid, also requires a pretesting of data collection procedures and protocols. For example, in the National VA Surgical Risk Study, pilot data collection of wound, blood, sputum, and urine culture bacteriology results revealed a wide variation in practices of reporting culture results that prevented collecting these data prospectively across the multiple sites. Thus, differing practices for obtaining specific tests or measurements may preclude using some variables. For example, policies or practice patterns about standard preoperative testing (e.g., blood tests, ECGs, chest radiographs) may influence decisions about which variables are feasible to collect.

As suggested in Chapter 4, considerable interobserver variation occurs in assessment of many clinical variables. Reliable and valid measures of acute physiological disturbances, however, are increasingly available for medical and surgical patients. Measures of comorbid illnesses have been developed by several investigators, although their predictive performance for various outcomes has not been demonstrated, with a few exceptions (Charlson et al. 1987; Greenfield et al. 1993). Less available are well-validated measures of patient functional status before medical intervention; measures of acute and chronic neurological, psychiatric, and mental status; and measures of patient preferences for outcome. Even established measures (Stewart, Hays, and Ware 1988; Stewart et al. 1989; Ware and Sherbourne 1992) are rarely routinely collected and recorded in patients' charts—they never appear in administrative data files.

Lack of standardization among common diagnostic procedures is also a limitation. In developing the MMPS pneumonia models, the number of lobes involved with infiltrate was suggested as a predictor of likelihood of death. We were unable to collect this information routinely from the chest x-ray reports for two reasons. First, among this sick elderly population, many chest radiographs were portable anterior-posterior films in which the number of lobes could not be assessed. Second, even among those patients with posterior-anterior and lateral films, the radiologists' readings rarely noted the number of lobes involved with pneumonia. Although the patients' physicians may have known the number of lobes involved by physical examination or through their reviews of the radiographs, we could not obtain this information on retrospective chart review. In the National VA Surgical Risk Study, we restricted patient risk factors to those readily recorded as part of the preoperative assessment and laboratory evaluation. As in the development of MMPS, a six-hospital pilot study confirmed that ECG results were too time-consuming to collect. Laboratory values were collected through software programs that automatically scan laboratory databases in each hospital and transmit the information for analysis. In such a large-scale observational study, we avoided using the results of cardiac, pulmonary, or vascular testing in developing candidate risk factors (e.g., results of noninvasive cardiac testing, pulmonary function tests) because we knew that only a small proportion of patients undergoing major surgery have these tests performed, that results and interpretations across multiple facilities would be inconsistent, and that securing the results would require considerable effort by the nurse reviewers.

Finally, one must carefully consider each risk indicator specifically to ensure that it reflects only patient risk and not some component of process of care. Treatment choices can affect one's ability to measure risk. Variables representing both patient risk and treatment choices can confound risk with processes of care. For example, collecting information obtained from invasive testing implicitly conveys the decision to obtain the test. As suggested in Chapter 4, if important clinical variables can be captured only by means of specific tests (e.g., left ventricular ejection fraction measured by pulmonary artery catheter, nuclear medicine studies, or echocardiography), using such variables may bias analysis and even lead to undesirable changes in clinical practice—especially when the data are used to produce provider "report cards" (see Chapters 10 and 11). For example, equally ill patients at a hospital that avoid using these technologies may erroneously appear less ill. Risk-adjustment models that incorporate therapies, such as whether a patient has been treated with a particular medication or procedure, may similarly confound risk factors with process of care. For example, APACHE III incorporates several process-related variables in its models to predict the probability of in-hospital death: the patient's location before ICU admission (e.g., emergency room, floor, other ICU, or other hospital), time spent in the emergency room, and whether the patient had emergency surgery (Knaus et al. 1991). These variables certainly relate to patient risk but may have different implications in different delivery systems. They reflect what happened to the patient—the process of care.

Feasibility Considerations

The first steps in developing a risk-adjustment strategy are to define the appropriate conceptual construct of "risk" and to identify variables that capture that construct. Next, as suggested above, data considerations dominate: Available data sources often dictate what can go into the risk models. For example, use of administrative hospital discharge abstract data requires making the best possible match between the ICD-9-CM diagnosis and procedures codes and the indicators of risk in the conceptual model. As described in Chapter 3, this translation is often imperfect for a variety of reasons (e.g., intrinsic limitations of the ICD-9-CM nomenclature and coding conventions, poor coding reliability exacerbated by reimbursement incentives in code assignment, sloppiness of physician terminology, limitations in coding spaces).

In considering retrospective data collection from medical records, several feasibility questions arise:

- Do most charts contain the variable of interest? How will missing values affect the analysis? If data are missing, is there a basis for imputing a value?
- How reliably can the variable be abstracted from the records?
- If the variable is recorded in several different places in the chart, what value should be used? How will instructions for locating the variable be given?
- How sensitive is a particular variable to the characteristics of the person collecting it (e.g., staff physician, training physician, nurse) or where it is recorded (e.g., at a teaching hospital versus a community hospital)?
- How difficult is it to obtain the variable from the medical record?

Some variables are such important determinants of risk that it is reasonable to devote considerable time and effort to identify them. In contrast, if a risk factor is only marginally useful, the energy expended may outweigh the benefit of having it.

In developing MMPS, we conducted feasibility studies to determine the most reliable sources of risk information in the chart, which led to a hierarchy specifying where data abstractors should obtain particular pieces of information. Because we were interested in the first values of vital signs obtained in the hospital, for example, we focused on the emergency room information first and then reviewed the initial admission history and physical examination. All progress notes in the first 24 hours were then examined. In teaching hospitals, we abstracted information from the attending physician, the resident, the intern, and the medical student—in that order.

We also collected variables that we considered important, but difficult to abstract, from records: functional status and DNR status. Functional status information was available in only two-thirds of the charts and was rarely noted by the physicians. The initial nursing admission note, however, often contained basic information about patients' capacity to ambulate and feed themselves. We therefore used nurses' notes as the source of functional status information. We collected DNR status only if it were present on admission. DNR status was usually indicated both on the emergency room admitting sheet and in the admitting orders, but it was designated in very different ways across different hospitals (e.g., "DNR," "do not resuscitate," "care and comfort only," "no code 99," "no code blue"). Therefore, we specified synonyms that qualified as DNR orders.

As suggested above, prospective data collection can solve some problems relating to variable definition, standardization, reliability, and validity. Data collection instruments and guidelines are written in advance, and data collectors are taught and tested during the training period. Nevertheless, concerns about the marginal cost of collecting individual risk variables remain—too much effort may be expended collecting information of marginal utility. Thus, a pilot study of the prospective data collection procedures can determine the feasibility of collecting specific data elements.

For example, the National VA Surgical Risk Study involves prospective data collection. As noted above, most laboratory data are gathered through automated software that downloads required information directly from the hospitals' laboratory systems. ECG results, however, are not available in the automated system. In a feasibility study, data collectors spent unacceptably long periods of time retrieving ECG results from patient charts and the ECG laboratories, to the detriment of collecting other important data elements. In addition, despite clear definitions of what constituted a nosocomial infection (e.g., postoperative wound infection), ascertainment bias was evident across the sites because of different practices for obtaining wound cultures. Adoption of the Centers for Disease Control definitions for superficial and deep wound infections and pneumonia and urinary tract infections, which are also used as the infection control definitions systematically throughout the VA, permitted standard case finding.

Certain important risk factors involve sensitive information that is difficult to obtain reliably, regardless of how data are gathered. For example, although sexual behaviors and use of illicit drugs are associated with selected outcomes, they are sensitive items. This type of information is often underreported in medical records (see Chapter 4). In prospective data gathering, respondents often refuse to answer, lie, or are so offended by being asked such personal information that they refuse to answer subsequent questions.

Building the Risk Model

How should models of risk be developed? Experience has convinced most researchers that combining clinical judgment and empirical modeling is better than either approach alone. Different severity measures have emphasized different development approaches, often depending on whether large data sets are available for empirical modeling (Table 1.6). Based on their experiences, clinicians can help identify factors likely to be important, but they are generally unable to quantify the effects of these factors. Methodologists without clinical training generally need help in designating which variables to collect and how best to code these variables for clinical meaningfulness. Evaluating the resultant models for face validity also requires clinical input (see Chapter 6).

Therefore, to maximize both the statistical performance of the model (Chapters 8 and 9) as well as its acceptance by the clinical community, one should meld the knowledge and expertise of clinicians and the powerful techniques of empirical model building in deriving risk adjustors. Relying solely on empirical modeling of relationships deprives the risk-outcome model of valuable input from the medical literature and clinical practice. Without *a priori* clinical hypotheses about risk-outcome relationships, empirical model building can become a data-dredging exercise, yielding relationships that are unique functions of that particular database. Resultant models can lack clinical credibility or face validity (see Chapter 6). On the other hand, models built solely using clinical judgment lack the ability to explore the complex interactions of multiple clinical variables in patients with specific illnesses and specific outcomes.

In conducting empirical modeling, clinicians should be involved in identifying and specifying the risk variables. Clinicians are also helpful in reviewing the empirical models for clinical face validity and plausibility (see Chapter 6). Clinicians, however, tend to think in terms of risk relating to morbidity, mortality, and functional status, rather than outcomes such as length of stay, resource use, or costs over a year.

Another way to involve clinicians is to ask them to offer specific hypotheses about the effect of each variable on the outcomes before empirical analysis begins (Keeler et al. 1990). For example, what effect will age have on mortality 30 days after admission in AMI? What is the relationship of body temperature on admission to the likelihood of death in pneumonia? What is the relationship of blood pressure on admission to mortality in AMI compared to stroke? To clarify their thoughts, clinicians should whenever possible graphically represent the relationship of the predictor variable with the outcome. Is it a linear, U-shaped, or J-shaped relationship? If it is linear, is it increasing or decreasing? During empirical modeling, these hypotheses about the predicted relationships should be compared to those observed in the database. Empirical relationships different from these prior expectations should be inspected carefully. These clinical hypotheses, however, should be generated *before* seeing the empirical modeling results; *a posteriori* clinical hypothesis generation suggests questions for future research, but it is of limited value in reaching conclusions in a given study.

APACHE was originally based solely on clinical judgment, using clinical variables and weights assigned by clinicians (Knaus et al. 1981). APACHE II was also derived primarily using the clinical judgment of its developers and their consultants (Knaus et al. 1985). In contrast, APACHE III was developed empirically using a large database (Knaus et al. 1991). This third version incorporates a few new acute physiology risk indicators—such as blood glucose, blood urea nitrogen (BUN), total bilirubin, serum albumin, urine output—and the weights assigned all variables were calculated using a database of 17,440 patients admitted to 40 ICUs across the country. In creating the comorbidity component of APACHE III, the developers considered "the magnitude and direction of the influence of each comorbid chronic disease variable on mortality (a coefficient of .05) and the overall statistical significance of the influence (t ratio > 2)" (Knaus et al. 1991, 1633). These considerations guided selection of the seven chronic conditions included in APACHE III from among 34 candidate conditions (see Table 2.7). Thus, as data became available, APACHE evolved from a solely clinically based system to one that relies heavily on empirical modeling techniques.

MedisGroups represents another example of this evolution. Medis-Groups' scores originally used weights for KCFs assigned by clinicians (Iezzoni and Moskowitz 1988). Recent revisions to the MedisGroups scoring system have relied primarily on the large MedisGroups Comparative Database, an enormous computer file containing all KCF information on hundreds of thousands of patients admitted to over 100 hospitals using MedisGroups. The new MedisGroups algorithms incorporate KCFs designated as clinically relevant by physician developers, but empirical modeling techniques are used to identify the most predictive KCFs and assign them weights for predicting the probability of in-hospital death (Steen et al. 1993) or other outcomes (e.g., length of stay).

In the National VA Surgical Risk Study, patient risk factors were suggested by review of the surgical literature and the suggestions of expert panels of surgical subspecialists. Feasibility studies in six pilot hospitals eliminated some clinical variables as either too unreliable, difficult, or time-consuming to include in the data collection protocol. In the final Phase I protocol, 65 preoperative patient risk variables were collected. Univariate relationships to the outcomes of interest (30-day mortality, morbidity, and length of stay) were examined, and variables in which the relationship to the outcome was as expected and statistically significant ($P < 0.05$) were included in the modeling.

In the VA study, one clinical variable, smoking in the two weeks prior to major surgery, demonstrated an unexpected relationship to mortality. Patients who reported *not* smoking in the two weeks prior to surgery had much higher mortality rates than those who did report smoking. This relationship was the opposite of what we had predicted. Therefore, we examined the other risk factors of nonsmokers compared to smokers and discovered that the nonsmokers had a much higher risk profile (i.e., more diabetes mellitus, ischemic heart disease, chronic pulmonary disease) than those reporting smoking in the two weeks prior to surgery. Contrary to our initial hypothesis, nonsmokers appeared to be much sicker—they appeared physically unable to smoke in the two preoperative weeks. We did not include smoking in our final multivariate models and have subsequently changed the determination of smoking status. We now ask about whether patients smoked in the year prior to surgery and how many packs per year they have smoked.

In developing the MMPS, we first chose variables as follows:

> In selecting clinical variables for field testing, we required clinical credibility, empirical research evidence that the variable does predict short-term mortality, independence of the treatment rendered, availability of the data for most patients with the condition, and reliability of abstraction by medical record personnel . . . We used both literature review and expert panels of clinicians and health services researchers . . . to select candidate predictor variables. (Daley et al. 1988, 3619)

Therefore, although we ultimately relied on empirical techniques to make final decisions about the structure of the models, clinical and data considerations guided much of our work. In the final specification of the models, we included a few clinical variables in each of the models that added little at the margin to the predictive validity of the model but had important clinical meaningfulness to the expert panelists and in the clinical literature (e.g., presence of positive blood cultures in pneumonia). We also removed some variables that had predictive value in the empirical modeling, but the relationship was the opposite of what clinical panelists had suggested. For example, in AMI, an elevated serum SGOT was associated with a decreased likelihood of death. Because this finding did not correspond to the expected relationship, we eliminated it from the AMI model.

Another example of combining clinical and statistical criteria is the RAND measure of "sickness at admission." Keeler and collaborators (1990, 1963–64) first

> . . . screened variables for use in the final regressions to predict mortality according to a rule that combined clinical judgment with statistical evidence. Variables were rated 1, 2, 3, and 4 by clinicians for their expected association with a poor outcome. Using this rating, variables were kept for possible inclusion in the scale (1) if they were a strong predictor of 30- or 180-day postadmission mortality (t statistic > 2.5) in regressions that also included systolic blood pressure, age and the APACHE II APS scale; (2) if they were a medium predictor (t statistic > 2) with a clinical score of 1 or 2; or (3) if the t statistic was greater than 1.5 and the clinicians expected a strong relationship with death (clinical score of 3 or 4).

Assembling an Analytic Data Set

Unless it is based solely on clinical judgment, developing a model of risk requires a data set. Obtaining the data may be only the first step—data often require "cleaning." Standard data cleaning involves range checks (e.g., looking for values that are not plausible, such as centigrade temperatures of 102°), identifying impossible occurrences (e.g., female patients admitted for prostate surgery), finding invalid data elements (e.g., ICD-9-CM codes that have no meaning in the current version of the coding system), and describing the frequencies of missing or poorly specified data elements (e.g., the frequency of missing values for liver function tests in patients undergoing cholecystectomy). Multivariate checks should also be analyzed: Is the systolic blood pressure always higher than the diastolic blood pressure? Is the most extreme or worst value during the first 24 hours of admission always higher or lower than the first recorded value of risk variable X? Analysts acquire a valuable in-depth knowledge of their data sets through this process.

How much a raw data file needs cleaning and editing depends on the source of the data. In general, more cleaning is needed when the data have not been used before for a similar purpose. Some analysts obtain administrative data files that have already gone through extensive data checks (e.g., by the state agency that compiled the data). For example, one study (Iezzoni et al. 1994) used the 1988 statewide computerized hospital discharge abstract data set obtained from the California Office of Statewide Health Planning and Development and found that these key data elements were missing or invalid less than 0.001 percent of the time: age, sex, discharge disposition (e.g., death), and principal diagnosis (no cases were missing principal diagnosis). The state had performed routine editing before releasing the data.

If the data were entered using computer software that includes internal range checks, implausible values may have been rejected as the data were gathered. In developing MMPS, we created data entry computer software that has internal data consistency checks and ranges of permissible values, thus preventing the entry of illogical or invalid values for many parameters. Some data files from chart review or prospective data collection may require considerable data cleaning. When data are acquired from external sources, clarifying variable definitions and coding conventions assessing missing data, and organizing the data set is often necessary. Clinical consultants may especially assist this process. For example, clinicians can specify ranges for clinical variables that are physiologically impossible and therefore represent data errors.

Treatment of Missing Values

In most data sets, values of some variables are missing. This problem is encountered most frequently in data collected from retrospective medical record review, but it also occurs in administrative databases and even with information that is gathered prospectively (Marshall et al. 1995). This problem invariably raises questions about how to handle missing information. The literature on severity measures addresses missing data concerns most commonly in the context of acute physiologic parameters (see Chapter 2). These variables are typically clinical guideposts for physicians caring for acutely ill patients, and most (e.g., vital signs, complete blood counts, serum chemistries) are measured routinely and with minimal technologic intervention (e.g., venipuncture). One reason that certain variables were eliminated in creating APACHE II was that they were measured infrequently (e.g., serum osmolarity, lactic acid level, skin testing for anergy), whereas others reflected a treatment decision (e.g., right atrial pressure measured through a central venous pressure line). Fortunately, the remaining variables—albeit generally available and easily measured—yielded good ability to predict in-hospital death (Knaus et al. 1985).

While most acute physiologic parameters are routinely assessed in ICU patients, some—especially arterial blood gas findings (e.g., arterial oxygenation, arterial pH)—may not be measured in non-ICU patients. Nonetheless, most of these parameters will be measured in non-ICU patients, and some (e.g., blood pressure) are captured even in many ambulatory care encounters. For example, one study reviewed medical records to gather APACHE II data for 4,463 adult patients admitted primarily to general medical or surgical (not ICU) services at one of fifteen metropolitan Boston hospitals (Iezzoni et al. 1989, 1990). As shown in Table 5.2, arterial blood gases were missing in 70 percent of cases. But over 99 percent of cases had complete vital sign information, and over 90 percent of cases had both serum electrolyte and hematology findings (Iezzoni et al. 1993).

Given that most of these physiologic parameters are measured routinely, how should one interpret missing data? *A priori*, this question has no correct response; it must be answered in both the research and clinical contexts. For example, APACHE assumes that unmeasured parameters are likely to be normal. This assumption is reasonable, because APACHE pertains explicitly to ICU patients who are generally aggressively treated and monitored. The MMPS also substitutes normal values for missing values; our analyses suggested that this choice maximizes predictive accuracy and replicability (Daley et al. 1988).

The approach toward missing values, however, may differ in other clinical contexts. For instance, gravely ill patients, such as those with widely metastatic cancer, may explicitly refuse even routine monitoring by blood tests—accepting so-called "comfort measures only" (e.g., intravenous morphine for pain control). In this setting, absence of information about serum

Table 5.2 Percent of Cases in Which APACHE II Variables Had Been Measured ($n = 4,463$)

APACHE II Physiologic Variable	*Percent with Recorded Value*
Temperature	99.4%
Heart rate	99.9
Respiratory rate	99.3
Blood pressure	99.9
Arterial oxygenation	30.0
Arterial pH	30.0
Serum sodium	91.8
Serum potassium	92.1
Creatinine	84.3
Hematocrit	97.4
White blood cell count	97.1
Notations concerning level of consciousness (for Glasgow Coma Score)	98.9

Source: Iezzoni et al. 1993.

electrolytes or hematologic indices reflects patient preferences, not physiologic status. In still other clinical contexts, missing data result when patients die before tests can be performed, which may explain Blumberg's findings that AMI patients with missing laboratory values are more likely to die within 30 days of admission than patients with complete information on routine tests (Blumberg 1991).

Depending on the database used to assess acute physiologic parameters, two further explanations for missing values require consideration. As discussed in Chapter 4, practice patterns vary, even for collecting routine physiologic information (Selker 1993). For example, in a study of 15 metropolitan Boston hospitals, reported in Table 5.2 (Iezzoni et al. 1989), important differences were apparent in even routine testing across teaching and nonteaching hospitals. For instance, among cerebrovascular disease cases, at least one of APACHE II's serum chemistry tests was missing in 2 percent of tertiary teaching, 10 percent of other teaching, and 28 percent of nonteaching hospital cases; for patients admitted for low back problems, serum chemistry values were missing in 20 percent of teaching hospital cases and 66 percent of cases from nonteaching facilities. The severity of the cerebrovascular disease and low back conditions, however, was comparable across hospital types. In analyzing outcomes of general surgical patients, the availability of preoperative ECGs varies considerably with patient age, hospital-specific policies about routine preoperative ECGs, and the preoperative risk status of the patient.

Some information is recorded less consistently and reliably in medical records but has important predictive value as a risk factor. As described in Chapter 4, functional status information may be recorded in only a fraction of charts, but it may have significant predictive capacity in outcomes such as mortality. For instance, in the MMPS data set, only two-thirds of the patients had a simple measure of functional status (ability to ambulate independently) recorded in their charts, usually in the nursing notes (Daley et al. 1988). This variable was included in the analysis and was a significant predictor in some models. Assuming that the absence of functional status information implied full ability to ambulate independently, we substituted "fully independent" for the missing values.

Another source of missing data can be the specific data collection protocol, such as that used in constructing the MedisGroups Comparative Database. The data include demographic, diagnostic, procedural, and KCF information collected on hospitalized patients during medical record reviews (Iezzoni et al. 1993). Despite the many KCFs gathered by Medis-Groups, one aspect of the data collection process limited its usefulness: Reviewers were instructed not to record values of clinical findings if they were in a "normal" range, as determined by the MedisGroups glossary. This strategy was designed to make feasible the abstraction of literally hundreds of data elements; however, it had two potentially problematic results. First, if a KCF was absent in the MedisGroups data, it was impossible to determine whether a test was not performed or whether its result was in a normal range. Second, because MedisGroups' normal ranges tended to be very broad (e.g., systolic blood pressures were recorded only if they were less than 90 mm Hg), many cases had nonrecorded or missing values even for routine physiologic parameters.

These concerns lead to questions about how well the clinical information contained in the MedisGroups Comparative Database would perform in predicting some outcomes (Iezzoni et al. 1993). As shown in Table 5.3, many common variables often were missing when data recording was censored around a MedisGroups-defined normal range. More recent versions of MedisGroups permit the data collectors to collect all values, not just those outside the defined normal ranges. New MedisGroups software that uses data downloaded directly from computerized laboratory information systems increases the feasibility—and decreases the costs—of gathering all values, at least of laboratory variables.

Finally, indicators of acute clinical stability are often easily manipulated by medical interventions—indeed, the immediate goal of therapy is generally to resolve acute physiologic abnormalities even if underlying disease remains. For example, a patient with diabetic ketoacidosis may

Table 5.3 MedisGroups "Abnormal" Ranges and Percent of Cases with Missing Values (*n* = 4,463)

Clinical Variable	MedisGroups Guidelines	Percent of Cases with Missing Values: Censored Data Base
Temperature C° (oral)	< 35.3 or > 38.2	96.3%
Heart rate (beats per minute)	< 40 or > 129	97.0
Respiratory rate (breaths per minute)	< 10 or > 24	83.5
pO$_2$ (arterial)	< 75.0	83.7
Systolic blood pressure (mm Hg)	< 90	97.1
Diastolic blood pressure (mm Hg)	> 119	97.1
Arterial pH	< 7.35 or > 7.45	87.6
Sodium (mMol/l)	< 130 or > 150	97.5
Potassium (mMol/l)	< 2.5 or > 5.3	98.3
Creatinine (mg/dl)	> 1.7	94.0
Hematocrit (%)	< 30 or > 59.9	97.3
White blood cell count (cc/mm)	< 5.0 or > 17.0	91.3
Glasgow Coma Score	record all values	1.1

Source: Iezzoni et al. 1993.

have wildly aberrant physiologic findings that resolve relatively quickly to insulin and supportive therapy. Even patients who cannot breathe on their own can have arterial blood gas findings normalized through ventilator support. The concern is whether some short-term or palliative treatment is masking serious underlying disease. For example, for a time, aspirin can lower a patient's temperature, and administration of oxygen generally immediately improves arterial oxygenation.

In addition to the clinical and data collection implications of missing values, the way those values are handled may dictate how many cases will be available for analysis using some modeling techniques. For example, many computerized statistical routines drop cases with any missing value among any of the variables in the model. Even if each variable is missing for only a few cases, many cases will have at least one missing value if numerous variables are considered. Thus, many cases could be eliminated during statistical modeling in data sets with numerous missing values. This situation may bias the models toward characteristics of that subset of patients with complete data—patients who are unlikely to be a random sample. In addition, when examining two models—one with few explanatory variables and a second with many—the second model may actually be fit to a much smaller data set (i.e., the subset of patients without any missing values). This argues for using the same standard data set when comparing models built with different variables.

Given the potential confounding of patient risk with data quality, availability, and practice patterns, how one treats missing data assumes some significance. Several sources provide helpful technical guidance on how to handle missing information (Buck 1960; Dempster, Laird, and Rubin 1977; Rubin 1987; Rubin 1993). Computer algorithms are also available in statistical software packages for dealing with missing values (e.g., Roberts and Capalbo 1987). In developing risk measures, several analytic approaches have been proposed for resolving this issue. Most commonly, normal values are substituted for missing values of clinical measurements, under the assumption that abnormalities would be recorded in the medical record. We used this approach in devising the MMPS, justifying this decision by observing that "studies . . . on other data sets indicate that this rule maximizes predictive accuracy and replicability" (Daley et al. 1988, 3620).

Some studies have specifically evaluated the practice of assigning normal values for missing values. For instance, in developing APACHE III, Knaus et al. (1991, 1633)

> . . . examined our practice of assigning a weight of zero [or normal] to missing physiologic variables. We did this by examining the pattern of missing values and by using dummy variables to estimate the most appropriate weight to impute to a missing physiologic value . . . Analysis indicated that the proportion of missing values was directly related to physiologic stability

as determined by vital sign data. Patients with normal or near normal vital signs had the largest proportion of missing laboratory tests . . . Based on estimation fill-in values, with dummy variables, missing physiologic variables were assumed normal and assigned zero weights.

In the National VA Surgical Risk Study, all patient preoperative risk factors were over 99 percent complete, except the preoperative laboratory values. Most of the preoperative laboratory variables (e.g., complete blood count, serum sodium, blood urea nitrogen) were over 95 percent complete, but a handful of preoperative laboratory values (serum albumin, serum bilirubin, SGOT) were missing in a substantial minority of cases (e.g., serum albumin was missing for 39 percent of cases). Analyses demonstrated that patients with missing albumin and liver function tests were less sick (e.g., lower incidence of other risk factors) and had lower mortality, morbidity, and shorter length of stay than those patients with values for those laboratory tests. Extensive analyses compared incorporating imputed missing values using a regression procedure with substituting a normal value for each missing laboratory variable. These comparisons found similar results for the modeling and variations analyses.

In certain contexts, especially regions with aggressive "report card" initiatives (see Chapter 11), how missing values are handled could have practical consequences. If missing values are assumed to be normal, clinicians will learn that, in order to have their patients classified as "sick," they must record the problems they find. This could affect testing practices, for example, increasing laboratory testing even when clinical suspicions of an abnormal result are low.

Structure of Continuous Independent Variables

Exploring the effect of the form of each risk factor—whether it is entered into the model as a categorical or continuous independent variable—requires thought. Age, the most common continuous risk factor (see Chapter 2), is a case in point. The relationship of age to outcomes (e.g., in-hospital mortality, length of stay, or charges) is unlikely to follow a simple straight line, especially over a wide age range. Age can be treated as a continuously valued variable or categorized into two or more groups. For example, as described in Chapter 2, the Pediatric Risk of Mortality Score (PRISM) weights physiologic values differently for two age levels, infants and children, thus incorporating an interaction between age and physiologic status (Pollack, Ruttimann, and Getson 1988). APACHE III assigns points for patients in different age categories (Knaus et al. 1991). Different risk-adjustment measures use different ways of weighting age with regard to outcomes.

Other clinical variables, such as blood pressure and temperature, have complex relationships to various outcomes, including death. For instance, the very high and low extremes of blood pressure are associated with increased likelihood of imminent death as compared to the middle or normal ranges. However, although high blood pressure is a risk factor for long-term mortality, it may not be highly predictive of 30-day mortality; low blood pressure is associated with short-term mortality (see, for example, Lemeshow et al. 1985). U-shaped relationships with mortality may not be symmetrical for high and low values of some variables. For instance, the likelihood of death may be much higher for incremental decreases in temperature and blood pressure than similar incremental increases above normal values. In pneumonia, for example, we modified the APACHE II scoring system for the MMPS to account for the much increased likelihood of death in the Medicare elderly presenting with very low body temperatures (Daley et al. 1988).

Most clinical variables have a nonlinear relationship with the outcome. In general, clinical judgment combined with statistical analyses are used to determine ranges for continuous variables and relationships with the outcome within these ranges. Computer-based "smoothing techniques" can help delineate these relationships. For example, Le Gall (1993) used the LOWESS (locally weighted least squares) smoothing function (Cleveland 1979) to produce a smoothed plot of the relationship between outcomes and candidate independent variables. "Cut points" in the smoothed function (points where a large change in outcome occurs for small changes in independent variables) can be used to define categories of independent variables, which are then represented in the final model by dummy variables. Cubic splines (Harrell, Lee, and Pollock 1988) are also used to produce smoothed functions. For example, in developing APACHE III, Knaus et al. (1991, 1632) did this:

> The physiologic variables were divided into clinically appropriate ranges based partly on cell size and partly on clinical judgment. They were then incorporated into the analysis as a series of separate predictor variables for each range. The initial results from these analyses were compared with basic clinical and physiologic relationships. Where discrepancies existed . . . we adjusted the ranges. Most of these variations were due to small sample sizes in the original designated ranges. In a few cases where the results of the analyses remained incompatible with established physiologic patterns, we adjusted the estimated weights using clinical judgment. Patterns of weights were also checked using restricted cubic splines functions. Cubic splines is a statistical smoothing technique that allows assignment of a continuous varying weight to a physiologic variable . . . In this data base, however, the use of cubic splines did not substantially increase total explanatory power.

In the National VA Surgical Risk Study, panels of clinicians were asked to sketch the relationship between the outcomes of interest and the continuous variables of age and preoperative laboratory tests. Age and serum albumin, empirically and by clinical judgment, demonstrated a linear relationship to the outcomes. Selected laboratory variables (e.g., serum sodium, serum potassium, white blood cell count) demonstrated a U-shaped relationship to the outcomes and were trichotomized for the final analyses (i.e., serum sodium less than 136 mEq/ml, serum sodium greater than 148 mEq/ml, and a reference group of serum sodium > 136 mEq/ml and < 148 mEq/ml).

A continuous variable that often appears in many disease-specific mortality prediction models is the serum BUN. In healthy patients, BUN ranges from 2 to 20 mg/dl, but in patients with multiple cardiac, renal, and metabolic abnormalities, BUN may rise to 500 mg/dl. In the MMPS, BUN was transformed and standardized to values greater than 40 mg/dl, and a continuous function of BUN above 40 mg/dl was constructed. In the National VA Surgical Risk Study, a similar relationship was found, and BUN greater than 40 mg/dl was used in all of the risk models.

Need for Data Reduction

Despite the many data limitations described in Chapters 3 and 4, much useful information is nonetheless available for deriving risk-adjustment models. The quantity of information can be overwhelming, and researchers may actually need to reduce the data set to a reasonable number of potential risk factors for modeling.

An example of the potential perils of incorporating too many predictors was demonstrated by a study that modeled in-hospital mortality for 16,855 patients 65 years of age or older discharged from 24 MedisGroups-member hospitals (Iezzoni et al. 1992). Several risk models were examined (Table 5.4). The first model was the five-level old MedisGroups admission score (a categorical variable with values from 0 through 4). The second and third models used KCFs specified within each condition to derive empirically a model for predicting in-hospital death. From the over 500 potential KCFs contained in that early version of MedisGroups, the investigators identified, for each condition, those KCFs that were present in at least 1 percent of the cases or that were viewed clinically as important predictors of death (e.g., ventricular fibrillation). Between 40 and 65 KCFs were identified in each of the five conditions. The second model relied only on the first ten KCFs to enter a stepwise regression following age and sex within each condition. The third model used all 40 to 65 KCFs plus age and sex within each condition.

Table 5.4   Fitting and Cross-Validating Model Performance in Predicting In-Hospital Mortality (R^2)

		Model Performance (R^2)		
Condition	Sample Used for Model Performance	Admission MedisGroups Score	Top 10 KCFs	All KCFs
Stroke	Fitting	.122	.299	.330
	Cross-validating	.096	.233	.208
Lung cancer	Fitting	.049	.280	.344
	Cross-validating	.058	.242	.054
Pneumonia	Fitting	.137	.247	.278
	Cross-validating	.154	.243	.240
Acute myocardial infarction	Fitting	.204	.243	.276
	Cross-validating	.195	.180	.157
Congestive heart failure	Fitting	.069	.208	.234
	Cross-validating	.075	.196	.196
All cases	Fitting	.134	.260	.293
	Cross-validating	.133	.225	.195

Source: Iezzoni et al. 1992.

The R^2 statistic from an ordinary least squares regression was used to compare the utility of different models in predicting death (see Chapter 9). R^2 values were first computed on half of the data used to derive the model, then validated on the remaining half. The two empirically derived models had the best fits (i.e., highest R^2 values). Although the model with all KCFs fit the development data somewhat better than the model using only ten KCFs, its cross-validated performance was never superior to that of the ten-KCFs model. In lung cancer (total $n = 1,244$, 23.9 percent in-hospital deaths), the drop for the all KCF model from the fitting R^2 value (0.344) to the cross-validated value (0.054) was particularly striking. Thus, although the models with 40 or more explanatory variables each achieved the highest R^2 values, these models appear to have been overspecified: In the cross-validation analyses, they performed no better, and in one instance did far worse, than the models based on the ten most important clinical variables (Iezzoni et al. 1992).

A variety of approaches are available to trim the number of predictor variables prior to modeling (Marshall et al. 1995). For example, as in the study described above, inspection of the frequency distributions of the variables may reveal items that appear too infrequently to be retained in the analysis. Removing variables that are of suspicious quality or of poor reliability is prudent, apart from statistical concerns. Examining univariate associations between individual predictors and the outcomes is a common approach. Model development then employs only those factors that are statistically significant at a prespecified level (e.g., $P = 0.10$).

Another example using MedisGroups, with its dozens of KCFs as potential explanatory variables, illustrates the approach of starting with univariate analyses. Van Ruiswyk and colleagues (1993) employed these MedisGroups KCF data to develop a model to predict 30-day mortality for AMI patients. Chi-square tests were used to identify individual predictors of 30-day mortality. However, "when several univariate predictors represented the same physiologic abnormality, a composite variable was formed that indicated an abnormality in any of the findings" (Van Ruiswyk et al. 1993, 154). After eliminating variables that revealed abnormalities in under 0.5 percent of the sample, the remaining univariate predictors were entered into a backward stepwise logistic regression to create an empirical model of risk (see below).

Two distinct concerns arise when using rare risk factors as predictors. One is that too few cases may be present in the model development data set to assess accurately the association between the rare risk factor and the outcome. For example, with 3,000 cases for modeling, a risk factor present in less than 0.5 percent of the cases occurs fewer than 15 times. This problem is minimized by a sufficiently large data set for model fitting.

The other problem, however, is practical. If data are gathered through chart review, do we want to expend costly effort finding rare risk factors? The answer may be yes in three instances: First, the rare risk factor is strongly associated with the outcome; second, it independently predicts outcome even after other variables are included in the model; and third, clinicians feel that failure to include it either substantially reduces clinical credibility of the model or penalizes certain providers who see a disproportionate number of rare cases.

As suggested earlier, statistically significant univariate associations between risk factors and outcomes that appear opposite to the clinically hypothesized relationships must be carefully reviewed. They may reveal problems with the original data sources, the database itself, or the coding of the independent variables. In addition, problems with multiple comparisons may arise: If one examines 100 univariate associations with variables that have no real association, and a $P = 0.05$ is used to identify statistically significant variables, about five variables will be flagged simply by random chance.

A variety of computer-intensive approaches are increasingly used to identify important variables to include in models. Normand and colleagues (1996) used such an approach to identify candidate variables for a logistic regression model predicting 30-day postadmission mortality of AMI patients. From an initial sample of 14,581 patients, three 25 percent subsamples of patients were selected. For each of the three subsamples, 20 "random starting models" were identified. In each of the 60 models (three subsamples times 20 starting models), four clinical variables closely related to left ventricular ejection fraction were forced into the model. Using a step-wise procedure, other statistically significant independent variables were stepped into the model. For each of the three subsamples, the model with the best fit among the 20 random starting models (measured by the likelihood estimate) was selected. The set of variables from these three "best fit" models then became candidate variables for further regression models.

Similarly, Hornbrook and Goodman (1996) used a computer-intensive approach to analyze the importance of self-reported illness, functional status, perceived health status, and demographic characteristics in predicting annual HMO expenses. They made 25 random splits of the overall database. For each split, one-half of the data was used for model development and the other half for model validation (see Chapter 6). Thus, 25 multiple regression models were produced. The sign and statistical significance of the coefficients, as well as variance across the 25 replications, were examined. Conclusions about the predictive role of specific variables were viewed as more reliable when their coefficients consistently had the same sign, consistent statistical significance, and low variance across the 25 replications.

Other techniques for data reduction include principal components analysis and factor analysis. Excellent discussions of technical considerations in the general area of data reduction approaches are available elsewhere (Jolliffe 1986; Harrell et al. 1984).

Multivariable Modeling Techniques

Detailed descriptions of multivariable modeling techniques, their underlying assumptions, strengths and weaknesses, and appropriate diagnostic measures are beyond the scope of this volume. Readers are referred to standard texts of statistical methods for detailed consideration of different approaches (see citations in Chapters 8 and 9). Here we provide examples of applying these techniques to risk adjustment to demonstrate how they are used in this setting.

Several analytic techniques have been used for modeling long-term outcomes in which there may be time-dependent variation in risk, changing hazards, or repeated observations: Markov models (Beck and Pauker 1983), Bailey-Makeham models (Bailey, Homer, and Summe 1977; Bailey 1988), Kalman filtering (Meinhold and Singpurwalla 1983), and proportional hazards modeling (Hopkins 1983; Brown, Hollander, and Korwar

1974). Different analytic techniques are available for modeling the relationship of risk factors and dichotomous outcomes. The most frequently modeled dichotomous outcome is death. Multiple techniques have been employed, stepwise logistic regression being the most popular (Cox 1972; Harrell et al. 1984; Harrell and Lee 1985; Harrell et al. 1988; Hosmer and Lemeshow 1989). Other approaches include two methods of data reduction prior to stepwise logistic regression—cluster analysis and principal components analysis (Jolliffe 1986), a subjective sickness score, an additive model of odds ratios or relative risks, Bayesian models, and recursive partitioning (Breiman et al. 1984; Cook and Goldman 1984). In studies of operative mortality after cardiac surgery, stepwise logistic regression performed as well as the other methods, provided the number of events (e.g., deaths) was at least ten times greater than the number of predictive variables (Marshall et al. 1994). Likewise, other studies have shown that logistic regression models perform well compared to alternative approaches (Selker et al. 1995; Hadorn et al., 1992).

Briefly, forward stepwise regression procedures build the model by adding one variable at a time. At each stage, the variable added is the one that contributes the most to model fit at that step. The backward elimination approach begins with all variables in the model, and then, one by one, eliminates those variables that contribute the least to model fit. Using each technique, options allow variables previously added to be dropped (forward elimination) or variables previously dropped to be added (backward selection). In addition, some "stopping rule" is necessary. Usually modeling is considered complete when the variables added to the model are statistically significant at a $P = 0.05$ or 0.10 level (or those dropped are insignificant at one of these levels).

Harrell and colleagues (1984) performed simulations demonstrating that, if logistic regression models are built on data sets with less than 1,000 observations, significant deterioration of the c-statistic (see Chapter 9) can occur on model validation for models developed using stepwise procedures. With a dichotomous outcome such as mortality, the number of cases in the smaller of the two groups (i.e., those with or without the outcome) is usually the limiting factor. The work of Harrell and colleagues (1984) suggests that first clustering the variables and then developing indices from each cluster (using all the variables, a subset of variables, or both) performs better than traditional stepwise procedures. Most severity models have been developed on large data sets, with well over 2,000 cases, where stepwise procedures seem to validate as well as other approaches.

Examples of clustering are available in the literature. Krakauer and collaborators (1992) used cluster analysis to identify diagnostic, administrative, and clinical variables that tended to occur together. They formed twelve clusters. Then, within each, they used backward stepwise logistic regression to identify variables that were statistically significantly associated with the probability of death within 30 days of admission. In the final backward stepwise regression analysis, the selected variables were added to demographic data and variables pertaining to prior admissions.

A major challenge in developing a model is to identify important interactions, or nonadditive effects, among predictor variables. Even when a moderate number of predictors are under consideration, there are generally far too many possible interactions to use unguided statistical exploration to detect the important interactions. For example, ten predictors generate 45 possible paired interactions and 120 three-way interactions. Knaus and colleagues (1991) used logistic regression results plus clinical judgment to study interactions among physiologic variables in APACHE III, evaluating both individual and combined weighting of variables. An important example involved the variables reflecting clinical acid-base disturbances (i.e., serum pH, pCO_2, and bicarbonate). Using their database including over 17,000 ICU admissions, Knaus and colleagues (1991, 1621) found empirical relationships incompatible with established physiologic principles:

> The computer-derived weights for serum pCO_2 above 50 mm Hg were consistently estimated as having little or no significant relationship to risk of death. We hypothesized that this was because the appropriate weighting for pCO_2 is also dependent on the associated serum pH (i.e., whether there is a primary or secondary respiratory disorder). Therefore, we developed a combined variable, which included serum pH and pCO_2 to establish weights for common acid-base disorders.

They then derived the weight for this combined variable as they had for individual variables. Knaus and colleagues (1991, 1621) also found important statistical interactions between urine output and serum creatinine, and among respiratory rate, PaO_2, and ventilator use. Combined variables were created from each of these sets. The weights assigned to the combined and individual variables were compared for their clinical validity.

As suggested earlier, a major concern in model development is model "overfitting"—including variables that may be useful predictors in the development database, but do not have the same relationship to the outcome in other databases. The lung cancer example in Table 5.4 illustrates this problem (Iezzoni et al. 1992): Using all MedisGroups KCFs in stepwise regression models resulted in models that did not validate as well as simpler models. These issues are discussed further in Chapters 8 and 9. Briefly, however, two main tactics are used to guard against model overfitting: First, employing both clinical and statistical criteria in making decisions about which variables to include; and second, limiting the number of candidate variables. For example, when predicting a continuous variable, the number of independent variables should never be more than one-tenth of the number of cases. A ratio of at least 30 cases to each predictor variable is preferable. When predicting a dichotomous variable, the number of candidate independent variables should be less than 10 percent of the number of cases that experienced the event of interest. Using no more than one predictor for every 20 positive cases is safer.

One must decide not only about the number of independent variables to include but also whether to transform them before adding them to the model. Again, a combination of clinical judgment and statistical criteria underlie this decision. For example, in developing MMPS, we used the first 600 cases to select variables and choose the form in which each variable was expressed (i.e., APACHE II points, logarithm of the variable, or some other transformation), using goodness of fit measured by chi-square analysis (Daley et al. 1988). Using an additional 300 cases, we next tested a few models, examining the overall goodness of fit but not the coefficients of individual variables. Only after the final functional form for the model was produced did we determine coefficients from the entire sample.

After a model is fit, one often must turn its output into a scale or score. In some cases, the results of the logistic regression model (e.g., parameter estimates, intercept terms) are used directly as the risk score. An example is the empirical version of MedisGroups that produces a probability of in-hospital death directly from the output of validated logistic regression equations (see Exhibit 2.3). In other cases, however, modifications are made. For example, to produce a score for predicting morbidity and mortality for coronary artery bypass patients, Higgins et al. (1992) first ran logistic regression models. Each significant variable was then assigned a score of 1 to 6 points based on the univariate odds ratio, the level of significance in the logistic model, and clinical input. "Different weights were evaluated for each factor to optimize performance of the clinical model" (Higgins et al. 1992, 2345). Keeler and collaborators (1990) used logistic regression to assign initial weights to variables considered for inclusion in their model. Final weights for each variable were determined by dividing the logistic regression coefficient for the variable by the coefficient for the APACHE II Acute Physiology Score in the model and then rounding to the nearest integer. Variables that were not statistically significant were eliminated. Finally, as did the APACHE III developers, Keeler and colleagues (1990) evaluated whether the statistical findings were clinically plausible. They dropped six factors that had been empirically identified but were viewed as clinically unlikely predictors of lower mortality.

Most risk-adjustment measures introduced in Chapter 1 used stepwise procedures to identify candidate variables for inclusion in their model. An exception involves the Risk-Adjusted Mortality Index (RAMI).

RAMI's development illustrates the challenges in using alternative modeling techniques (DesHarnais et al. 1988, 1991). Development started by distinguishing two categories of DRG clusters (aggregations of DRGs that previously had been divided based on age, comorbidities and complications, or death) based on whether their death rates were greater than 5 percent. For clusters with death rates under 5 percent, contingency tables became the basis for predicting mortality. Specifically, for each condition, a 2 × 3 table was created by crossing three age categories (0–64, 65–74, and over 75) with two comorbidity (but not complication) categories (i.e., comorbidities present or absent). Within each cell, the predicted death rate was the actual death rate present in the development database, a file from the Commission on Professional and Hospital Activities including 6 million admissions to 776 hospitals in 1983.

For the 64 clusters with higher death rates, logistic regression was used to develop predictive models, one for each cluster. Independent variables were age, sex, race, presence of any secondary diagnosis, presence of any cancer except skin cancer as a secondary diagnosis, risk of death associated with the principal diagnosis, risk of death associated with Class I operative procedures, risk associated with the comorbidity having the highest risk, and the number of secondary diagnoses with a risk of death greater for the secondary diagnosis than for the DRG cluster itself. To derive the risks for the last three variables, separate risk estimates were made for each secondary diagnosis in each Major Diagnostic Category (MDC). Once variables were defined, 64 logistic regressions were run, one for each condition.

One problem with this approach is that few cases may be available for making estimates (e.g., to estimate the probability of death for each individual secondary diagnosis in each MDC). In a study for the Prospective Payment Assessment Commission to analyze changes in within-DRG case complexity, SysteMetrics developed a within-DRG complexity weight for patients with specified characteristics that was proportional to the mean of standardized charges for these patients. The patient characteristics, defined within each DRG, included the Disease Stage of the principal disease and whether there were 0, 1–2, or 3+ comorbidities for persons within each principal diagnosis stage (Houchens and Briscoe 1992). In developing RAMI, DesHarnais and colleagues (1988) needed to estimate the mortality risk associated with comorbidities.

In these instances, a logical estimate would be the average value (the mean) of the variable of interest in each of the cells (e.g., mean charges among patients in DRG 5 with principal diagnosis at Stage 2, and 1–2 comorbidities; or average risk of death of patients in MDC 4 with some particular comorbidity). However, many cells in these analyses contain few observations. With small numbers in a cell, estimates using the average value are not very accurate.

In these circumstances, an increasingly popular approach involves taking a weighted average of the observed cell mean and some overall grand mean—to "shrink" the observed cell mean toward the overall mean (see Chapter 10). The weight given to the observed overall mean depends on the reliability of estimates in the cell. For cells with few observations, more weight is given to the overall mean and less to the cell mean, resulting in more shrinkage. In contrast, for cells with many observations, more weight is given to the cell mean, resulting in less shrinkage. Efron and Morris (1973, 1975, 1977) describe this approach and provide a theoretical justification.

Applying this approach requires judgment in deciding on the overall mean toward which the cell mean should be shrunk. For example, in determining within-DRG complexity weights, the stage/number of comorbidities cell mean could be shrunk toward a mean calculated by averaging over the comorbidity categories 0, 1–2, and 3+ within each stage of the principal disease. The alternative was to calculate a separate mean for each comorbidity class by averaging over all stages of the principal diagnosis (Houchens and Briscoe 1992). Thus, for example, within each DRG, there is one mean for 0 comorbidities, one for 1–2 comorbidities, and one for 3+ comorbidities. The shrunk estimate of complexity for a person in Disease Stage 1 in DRG 1 with 0 comorbidities is a weighted average of the mean charge for persons in that cell and the average of all persons with 0 comorbidities in DRG 1. In developing RAMI, "we adjusted the observed risk of death associated with each secondary diagnosis in any specific MDC toward the observed risk of that same secondary diagnosis in all MDCs" (DesHarnais et al. 1988, 1138).

Cox proportional hazards models are also increasingly used for risk adjustment (Cox 1972). To clarify the nature of the dependent variable in this model, one should recognize that the probability that an event (e.g., death) occurs in a small interval of time (t to $t + \Delta$) is the product of two probabilities: First, the probability that death does not occur prior to time t; and second, the conditional probability that a person who has survived until time t, dies prior to $t + \Delta$. This latter probability is called a hazard rate. For example, consider 100 patients alive at time 0. In the first six months, 40 patients die. In the next week after the six months, six more patients die. The probability of surviving six months is 0.6 and the hazard rate (for Δ equal one week) is 0.10 (6/60), the probability of death among those 60 patients who lived to the start of the interval. The product of the two probabilities ($0.6 \times 0.10 = 0.06$) is the observed probability of death in the interval six months to six months plus one week. Thus, 0.06 reflects the deaths of six of the 100 patients in the interval of interest.

The dependent variable in the Cox proportional hazard model is the "instantaneous" hazard rate at time t (i.e., the hazard rate as Δ becomes very, very small). This is expressed as a function of some baseline hazard (which is a nuisance parameter) and other independent variables of interest. The main assumption in the simple version of the model is that each independent variable increases the baseline hazard by a constant multiple. The statistical question is whether the observed increase is large enough to conclude that it is "real."

Similarly to multiple regression models, stepwise procedures can be used to build proportional hazards models. Proportional hazards models allow outputs to be converted into a survival function—the probability that a person survives different amount of time as a function of their values for the independent variables included in the model. Thus, in contrast to a logistic regression model, which gives a predicted probability of death within some time period, the proportional hazards model gives a predicted probability of death over all time intervals for which follow-up data are available.

In their Medicare mortality models, HCFA (see Chapters 1 and 11) has used a sophisticated version of the proportional hazards model, the Bailey-Makeham model. This model expresses the hazard rate as a function of three parameters, each of which is then expressed as a function of independent variables of interest (Sullivan and Wilensky 1991, A-3). More recently, Knaus and colleagues (1995) used a proportional hazards model to build the SUPPORT prognostic model, which predicts 180-day survival for seriously ill, hospitalized patients.

Conclusions

The basic message of the work to date in developing severity measures is that empirical techniques should be used whenever appropriate data are available. No matter how sophisticated, however, empirical methods are generally not enough—clinical judgment is also required. For example, both Knaus and colleagues (1991) and Keeler and collaborators (1990) used state-of-the-art statistical approaches and very large databases, yet both experienced instances where the empirical findings were clinically implausible. A model that is not clinically sensible (i.e., that contradicts established physiologic principles) is not valid, regardless of the statistical rigor used in its derivation. Studies that use clinically credible risk-adjustment strategies are far more likely to yield findings that will be trusted, believed—and acted upon. Because assessment of healthcare outcomes attempts ultimately to affect clinical practice, believability of the risk-adjustment method is essential.

Validity is thus a crucial attribute that encompasses both clinical and statistical considerations. Chapter 6 focuses on validity measurement primarily from a clinical perspective, while Chapters 8 and 9 address statistical measures of predictive validity.

References

Ash, A., F. Porell, L. Gruenberg, E. Sawitz, and A. Beiser. 1989. "Adjusting Medicare Capitation Payments Using Prior Hospitalization Data." *Health Care Financing Review* 10 (4): 17–29.

Bailey, R. C. 1988. "Some Uses of a Modified Makeham Model to Evaluate Medical Practice." *Journal of the Washington Academy of Sciences* 78 (4): 338–52.

Bailey, R. C., L. D. Homer, and J. P. Summe. 1977. "A Proposal for the Analysis of Kidney Graft Survival." *Transplantation* 24 (5): 309–15.

Beck, J. R., and S. G. Pauker. 1983. "The Markov Process in Medical Prognosis." *Medical Decision Making* 3 (4): 419–58.

Becker, R. B., J. E. Zimmerman, W. A. Knaus, D. P. Wagner, M. G. Seneff, E. A. Draper, T. L. Higgins, F. G. Estafanous, and F. D. Loop. 1995. "The Use of Apache III to Evaluate ICU Length of Stay, Resource Use, and Mortality After Coronary Artery By-pass Surgery." *Journal of Cardiovascular Surgery* 36 (1): 1–11.

Blumberg, M. S. 1986. "Risk Adjusting Health Care Outcomes: A Methodologic Review." *Medical Care Review* 43 (2): 351–93.

———. 1991. "Biased Estimates of Expected Acute Myocardial Infarction Mortality Using MedisGroups Admission Severity Groups." *Journal of the American Medical Association* 265 (22): 2965–70.

Breiman, L., J. H. Friedman, R. A. Olshen, and C. J. Stone. 1984. *Classification and Regression Trees.* Belmont, CA: Wadsworth International Group.

Brewster, A. C., B. G. Karlin, L. A. Hyde, C. M. Jacobs, R. C. Bradbury, and Y. M. Chae. 1985. "MEDISGRPS®: A Clinically Based Approach to Classifying Hospital Patients at Admission." *Inquiry* 22 (4): 377–87.

Brown, D. "Computers' 'Second Opinions' Help Guide Medical Treatment," *Washington Post* January 1, 1992: A1.

Brown, B. W., M. Hollander, and R. M. Korwar. 1974. "Nonparametric Tests of Independence for Censored Data, with Application to Heart Transplant Studies." In *Reliability and Biometry,* edited by F. Proschan and R. J. Serfling Philadelphia, PA: SIAM.

Bryk, A. S., and S. W. Raudenbush. 1992. *Hierarchical Linear Models: Applications and Data Analysis Methods.* Newbury Park, CA: Sage Publications.

Buck, S. F. 1960. "A Method of Estimation of Missing Values in Multivariate Data suitable for use with an Electronic Computer." *Journal of the Royal Statistical Society, Series B* 22 (2): 302–6.

Chang, R. W. 1989. "Individual Outcome Prediction Models for Intensive Care Units." *Lancet* 2 (8655): 143–6.

Charlson, M. E., P. Pompei, K. L. Ales, and C. R. MacKenzie. 1987. "A New Method of Classifying Prognostic Comorbidity in Longitudinal Studies: Development and Validation." *Journal of Chronic Diseases* 40 (5): 373–83.

Chassin, M. R., E. L. Hannan, and B. A. DeBuono. 1996. "Benefits and Hazards of Reporting Medical Outcomes Publicly." *New England Journal of Medicine* 334 (6): 394–98.

Cleveland, W. S. 1979. "Robust Locally Weighted Regression and Smoothing Scatterplots." *Journal of the American Statistical Association* 74 (368): 829–36.

Cook, E. F., and L. Goldman. 1984. "Empiric Comparison of Multivariate Analytic Techniques: Advantages and Disadvantages of Recursive Partitioning Analysis." *Journal of Chronic Diseases* 37 (9–10): 721–31. Published erratum appears in 1986, 39 (20): 157.

Cox, D. R. 1972. "Regression Models and Life-Tables." *Journal of the Royal Statistical Society, Series B* 34 (2): 187–220.

Daley, J., S. Jencks, D. Draper, G. Lenhart, N. Thomas, and J. Walker. 1988. "Predicting Hospital-Associated Mortality for Medicare Patients. A Method for Patients With Stroke, Pneumonia, Acute Myocardial Infarction, and Congestive Heart Failure." *Journal of the American Medical Association* 260 (24): 3617–24.

Davis, R. B., L. I. Iezzoni, R. S. Phillips, P. Reiley, C. Safran, G. A. Coffman. 1995. "Predicting in-hospital mortality: The importance of functional status information." *Medical Care* 33 (9): 906–21.

Dempster, A. P., N. M. Laird, and D. R. Rubin. 1977. "Maximum Likelihood Estimation from Incomplete Data via the EM Algorithm." *Journal of the Royal Statistical Society, Series B* 39 (1): 1–22, discussion 22–38.

DesHarnais, S. I., J. D. Chesney, R. T. Wroblewski, S. T. Fleming, and L. F. McMahon, Jr. 1988. "The Risk-Adjusted Mortality Index: A New Measure of Hospital Performance." *Medical Care* 26 (12): 1129–48.

DesHarnais, S. I., L. F. McMahon, Jr., and R. T. Wroblewski. 1991. "Measuring Outcomes of Hospital Care Using Multiple Risk-Adjusted Indexes." *HSR: Health Services Research* 26 (4): 425–45.

Deyo, R. A., D. C. Cherkin, and M. A. Ciol. 1992. "Adapting a Clinical Comorbidity Index for Use With ICD-9-CM Administrative Databases." *Journal of Clinical Epidemiology* 45 (6): 613–19.

Efron, B., and C. Morris. 1973. "Stein's Estimation Rule and Its Competitors—An Empirical Bayes Approach." *Journal of the American Statistical Association* 68 (341): 117–30.

———. 1975. "Data Analysis Using Stein's Estimator and Its Generalizations." *Journal of the American Statistical Association* 70 (350): 311–19.

———. 1977. "Stein's Paradox in Statistics." *Scientific American* 236 (5): 119–27.

Ellis, R. P., G. C. Pope, L. I. Iezzoni, J. Z. Ayanian, D. W. Bates, H. Burstin, and A. S. Ash. 1996. "Diagnosis-Based Risk Adjustment for Medicare Capitation Payments." *Health Care Financing Review* 17 (3): 101–28.

Gatsonis, C., S. L. Normand, C. Liu, and C. Morris. 1993. "Geographic Variation of Procedure Utilization. A Hierarchical Model Approach." *Medical Care* 31 (5) Supplement: YS54–YS59.

Gatsonis, C. A., A. M. Epstein, J. P. Newhouse, S. L. Normand, and B. J. McNeil. 1995. "Variations in the Utilization of Coronary Angiography for Elderly Patients With an Acute Myocardial Infarction. An Analysis Using Hierarchical Logistic Regression." *Medical Care* 33 (6): 625–42.

Goldman, L., B. Hashimoto, F. Cook, and A. Loscalzo. 1981. "Comparative Reproducibility and Validity of Systems for Assessing Cardiovascular Functional Class: Advantages of a New Specific Activity Scale." *Circulation* 64 (6): 1227–34.

Gonnella, J. S., M. C. Hornbrook, and D. Z. Louis. 1984. "Staging of Disease. A Case-Mix Measurement." *Journal of the American Medical Association* 251 (5): 637–44.

Greenfield, S., G. Apolone, B. J. McNeil, and P. D. Cleary. 1993. "The Importance of Co-existent Disease in the Occurrence of Postoperative Complications and One-Year Recovery in Patients Undergoing Total Hip Replacement. Comorbidity and Outcomes After Hip Replacement." *Medical Care* 31 (2): 141–54.

Greenfield, S., L. Sullivan, K. A. Dukes, R. Silliman, R. D'Agostino, and S. H. Kaplan. 1995. "Development and Testing of a New Measure of Case Mix for Use in Office Practice." *Medical Care* 33 (4) Supplement: AS47–AS55.

Hadorn, D. C., D. Draper, W. H. Rogers, E. B. Keeler, and R. H. Brook. 1992. "Cross-Validation Performance of Mortality Prediction Models." *Statistics in Medicine* 11 (4): 475–89.

Harrell, F. E., Jr., and K. L. Lee. 1985. "The Practical Value of Logistic Regression." *SAS Users Group International* 9: 1031–36.

Harrell, F. E., Jr., K. L. Lee, R. M. Califf, D. B. Pryor, and R. A. Rosati. 1984. "Regression Modelling Strategies for Improved Prognostic Prediction." *Statistics in Medicine* 3 (2): 143–52.

Harrell, F. E., Jr., K. L. Lee, and B. G. Pollock. 1988. "Regression Models in Clinical Studies: Determining Relationships Between Predictors and Response." *Journal of the National Cancer Institute* 80 (15): 1198–1202.

Higgins, T. L., F. G. Estafanous, F. D. Loop, G. J. Beck, J. M. Blum, and L. Paranandi. 1992. "Stratification of Morbidity and Mortality Outcome by Preoperative Risk Factors in Coronary Artery Bypass Patients. A Clinical Severity Score." *Journal of the American Medical Association* 267 (17): 2344–48.

Hlatky, M., R. E. Boineau, M. B. Higginbotham, K. L. Lee, D. B. Mark, R. M. Califf, F. R. Cobb, and D. B. Pryor. 1989. "A Brief Self-administered Questionnaire to Determine Functional Capacity (the Duke Activity Scale Index)." *American Journal of Cardiology* 64 (10): 651–54.

Hopkins, A. 1983. "BMDP2L: Survival Analysis with Covariates—Cox Models." In *BMDP Statistical Software*, edited by W. J. Dixon, 576–94. Berkeley, CA: Health Sciences Computing Facility.

Hornbrook, M. C. 1982. "Hospital Case Mix: Its Definition, Measurement and Use: Part I. The Conceptual Framework." *Medical Care Review* 39 (1): 1–43.

Hornbrook, M. C., and M. J. Goodman. 1996. "Chronic Disease, Functional Health Status, and Demographics: A Multi-Dimensional Approach to Risk Adjustment." *HSR: Health Services Research* 31 (3): 283–307.

Hosmer, D. W., and S. Lemeshow. 1989. *Applied Logistic Regression.* New York: John Wiley and Sons.

Houchens, R. L., and W. W. Briscoe. 1992. *Within DRG Case Complexity Change in Fiscal Year 1990.* Extramural Report E-92–04, April 1992, submitted to the Prospective Payment Assessment Commission. Santa Barbara, CA: SysteMetrics.

Iezzoni, L. I., A. S. Ash, G. A. Coffman, and M. A. Moskowitz. 1991. "Admission and Mid-Stay MedisGroups® Scores as Predictors of Death Within 30 Days of Hospital Admission." *American Journal of Public Health* 81 (1): 74–78.

———. 1992. "Predicting In-Hospital Mortality. A Comparison of Severity Measurement Approaches." *Medical Care* 30 (4): 347–59.

Iezzoni, L. I., and J. Daley. 1992. "A Description and Clinical Assessment of the Computerized Severity Index." *Quality Review Bulletin* 18 (2): 44–52.

Iezzoni, L. I., J. Daley, T. Heeren, S. M. Foley, J. S. Hughes, E. S. Fisher, C. C. Duncan, and G. A. Coffman. 1994. "Using Administrative Data to Screen Hospitals for High Complication Rates." *Inquiry* 31 (1): 40–55.

Iezzoni, L. I., E. K. Hotchkin, A. S. Ash, M. Shwartz, and Y. Mackiernan. 1993. "MedisGroups Data Bases. The Impact of Data Collection Guidelines on Predicting In-Hospital Mortality." *Medical Care* 31 (3): 277–83.

Iezzoni, L. I., and M. A. Moskowitz. 1988. "A Clinical Assessment of MedisGroups." *Journal of the American Medical Association* 260 (21): 3159–63.

Iezzoni, L. I., M. A. Moskowitz, and A. S. Ash. 1988. *The Ability of MedisGroups and Its Clinical Variables to Predict Cost and In-Hospital Death.* Report prepared for the Health Care Financing Administration under Cooperative Agreement No. 18-C-98526/1–04. Boston, MA: Health Care Research Unit, Boston University Medical Center.

Iezzoni, L. I., M. Shwartz, S. Burnside, A. S. Ash, E. Sawitz, and M. A. Moskowitz. 1989. "Diagnostic Mix, Illness Severity, and Costs at Teaching and Nonteaching Hospitals." Springfield, VA: U.S. Department of Commerce, National Technical Information Service (PB 89 184675/AS).

Iezzoni, L. I., M. Shwartz, M. A. Moskowitz, A. S. Ash, E. Sawitz, and S. Burnside. 1990. "Illness Severity and Costs of Admissions at Teaching and Nonteaching Hospitals." *Journal of the American Medical Association* 264 (11): 1426–31.

Jolliffe, I. T. 1986. *Principal Components Analysis.* New York: Springer-Verlag.

Keeler, E. B., K. L. Kahn, D. Draper, M. J. Sherwood, L. V. Rubenstein, E. J. Reinisch, J. Kosecoff, and R. H. Brook. 1990. "Changes in Sickness at Admission Following the Introduction of the Prospective Payment System." *Journal of the American Medical Association* 264 (15): 1962–68.

Khuri, S. F., J. Daley, W. G. Henderson, G. Barbour, P. Lowry, G. Irvin, J. Gibbs, F. Grover, K. E. Hammermeister, J. F. Stremple, J. B. Aust, J. Demakis, D. Deykin, and G. McDonald, and the participants in the National Veterans Administration Surgical Risk Study. 1995. "The National Veterans Administration Surgical Risk Study: Risk Adjustment for the Comparative Assessment of the Quality of Surgical Care." *Journal of the American College of Surgeons* 180 (5): 519–31.

Knaus, W. A., E. A. Draper, D. P. Wagner, and J. E. Zimmerman. 1985. "APACHE II: A Severity of Disease Classification System." *Critical Care Medicine* 13 (10): 818–29.

Knaus, W. A., F. E. Harrell Jr., J. Lynn, L. Goldman, R. S. Phillips, A. F. Connors Jr., N. V. Dawson, W. J. Fulkerson, Jr., R. M. Califf, N. Desbiens, P. Layde, R. K. Oye, P. E. Bellamy, R. B. Hakim, and D. P. Wagner. 1995. "The SUPPORT Prognostic Model: Objective Estimates of Survival for Seriously Ill Hospitalized Adults." *Annals of Internal Medicine* 122 (3): 191–203.

Knaus, W. A., D. P. Wagner, E. A. Draper, J. E. Zimmerman, M. Bergner, P. G. Bastos,

C. A. Sirio, D. J. Murphy, T. Lotring, A. Damiano, and F. E. Harrell, Jr. 1991. "The APACHE III Prognostic System. Risk Prediction of Hospital Mortality for Critically Ill Hospitalized Adults." *Chest* 100 (6): 1619–36.

Knaus, W. A., D. P. Wagner, J. E. Zimmerman, and E. A. Draper. 1993. "Variations in Mortality and Length of Stay in Intensive Care Units." *Annals of Internal Medicine* 118 (10): 753–61.

Knaus, W. A., J. E. Zimmerman, D. P. Wagner, E. A. Draper, and D. E. Lawrence. 1981. "APACHE—Acute Physiology and Chronic Health Evaluation: A Physiologically Based Classification System." *Critical Care Medicine* 9 (8): 591–97.

Krakauer, H., R. C. Bailey, K. J. Skellan, J. D. Stewart, A. J. Hartz, E. M. Kuhn, and A. A. Rimm. 1992. "Evaluation of the HCFA Model for the Analysis of Mortality Following Hospitalization." *HSR: Health Services Research* 27 (3): 317–35.

Le Gall, J. R., S. Lemeshow, and F. Saulnier. 1993. "A New Simplified Acute Physiology Score (SAPS II) Based on a European/North American Multicenter Study." *Journal of the American Medical Association* 270 (24): 2957–63.

Lemeshow, S., D. Teres, H. Pastides, J. S. Avrunin, and J. S. Steingrub. 1985. "A Method for Predicting Survival and Mortality of ICU Patients Using Objectively Derived Weights." *Critical Care Medicine* 13 (7): 519–25.

Marshall, G., F. L. Grover, W. G. Henderson, and K. E. Hammermeister. 1994. "Assessment of Predictive Models for Binary Outcomes: An Empirical Approach Using Operative Death from Cardiac Surgery." *Statistics in Medicine* 13 (15): 1501–11.

Marshall, G., W. G. Henderson, T. E. Moritz, A. L. Shroyer, F. L. Grover, and K. E. Hammermeister. 1995. "Statistical Methods and Strategies for Working with Large Data Bases." *Medical Care* 33 (10) Supplement: OS35–OS42.

MediQual Systems, Inc. 1993. *MedisGroups Scoring Algorithm, January 1993 Version: A Technical Description.* Westborough, MA: MediQual Systems.

Meinhold, R. J., and N. D. Singpurwalla. 1983. "Understanding the Kalman Filter." *American Statistician* 37 (2): 123–27.

Normand, S. L. T., M. E. Glickman, G. V. R. K. Sharma, and B. J. McNeil. 1996. "Using Admission Characteristics to Predict Short-term Mortality from Myocardial Infarction in Elderly Patients: Results from the Cooperative Cardiovascular Project." *Journal of the American Medical Association* 275 (17): 1322–28.

Normand, S. L. T., C. N. Morris, K. S. Fung, B. J. McNeil, and A. M. Epstein. 1995. "Development and Validation of a Claims Based Index for Adjusting for Risk of Mortality: The Case of Acute Myocardial Infarction." *Journal of Clinical Epidemiology* 48 (2): 229–43.

Patrick, D. L., and R. A. Deyo. 1989. "Generic and Disease-Specific Measures in Assessing Health Status and Quality of Life." *Medical Care* 27 (3) Supplement: S217–S32.

Pollack, M. M., U. E. Ruttimann, and P. R. Getson. 1988. "Pediatric Risk of Mortality (PRISM) Score." *Critical Care Medicine* 16 (11): 1110–16.

Roberts, J. S., and G. M. Capalbo. 1987. *A SAS Macro for Estimating Missing Values in Multivariate Data.* Dallas, TX: SAS Users Group International Twelfth Conference Proceedings.

Roper, W. L., W. Winkenwerder, G. M. Hackbarth, and H. Krakauer. 1988. "Effectiveness in Health Care. An Initiative to Evaluate and Improve Medical Practice." *New England Journal of Medicine* 319 (18): 1197–202.

Rubin, D. B. 1987. *Multiple Imputation for Nonresponse in Surveys.* New York: John Wiley & Sons.

———. 1993. "Tasks in Statistical Inference for Studying Variation in Medicine." *Medical Care* 31 (5) Supplement: YS103–YS10.

Selker, H. P. 1993. "Systems for Comparing Actual and Predicted Mortality Rates: Characteristics to Promote Cooperation in Improving Hospital Care." *Annals of Internal Medicine* 118 (10): 820–22.

Selker, H. P., J. L. Griffith, S. Patil, W. J. Long, and R. B. D'Agostino. 1995. "A Comparison of Performance of Mathematical Predictive Methods for Medical Diagnosis: Identifying Acute Cardiac Ischemia Among Emergency Department Patients." *Journal of Investigative Medicine* 43 (5): 468–76.

Spertus, J. A., J. A. Winder, T. A. Dewhurst, R. A. Deyo, J. Prodzinski, M. McDonell, and S. D. Fihn. 1995. "Development and Evaluation of the Seattle Angina Questionnaire: A New Functional Status Measure for Coronary Artery Disease. *Journal of the American College of Cardiology* 25 (2): 333–41.

Starfield, B., J. Weiner, L. Mumford, and D. Steinwachs. 1991. "Ambulatory Care Groups: A Categorization of Diagnoses for Research and Management." *HSR: Health Services Research* 26 (1): 53–74

Steen, P. M., A. C. Brewster, R. C. Bradbury, E. Estabrook, and J. A. Young. 1993. "Predicted Probabilities of Hospital Death as a Measure of Admission Severity of Illness." *Inquiry* 30 (2): 128–41.

Stewart, A. L., S. Greenfield, R. D. Hays, K. Wells, W. H. Rogers, S. D. Berry, E. A. McGlynn, and J. E. Ware, Jr. 1989. "Functional Status and Well-Being of Patients with Chronic Conditions: Results from the Medical Outcomes Study." *Journal of the American Medical Association* 262 (7): 907–13. Published erratum November 10, 1989, 262 (18): 2542.

Stewart, A. L., R. D. Hays, and J. E. Ware, Jr. 1988. "The MOS Short-Form General Health Survey: Reliability and Validity in a Patient Population." *Medical Care* 26 (7): 724–35.

Sullivan, L. W. and G. R. Wilensky. *Medicare Hospital Mortality Information. 1987, 1988, 1989.* Washington, D.C.: U.S. Department of Health and Human Services, Health Care Financing Administration.

Teres, D., and S. Lemeshow. 1994. "Why Severity Models Should be Used With Caution." *Critical Care Clinics* 10 (1): 93–110.

Van Ruiswyk, J., A. Hartz, E. Kuhn, H. Krakauer, M. Young, and A. Rimm. 1993. "A Measure of Mortality Risk for Elderly Patients with Acute Myocardial Infarction." *Medical Decision Making* 13 (2): 152–60.

Wagner, D. P., W. A. Knaus, F. E. Harrell, Jr., J. E. Zimmerman, and C. Watts. 1994. "Daily Prognostic Estimates for Critically Ill Adults in Intensive Care Units: Results from a Prospective, Multicenter, Inception Cohort Analysis." *Critical Care Medicine* 22 (9): 1359–72.

Ware, J. E., Jr., and C. D. Sherbourne. 1992. "The MOS 36-Item Short-Form Health Survey (SF-36): I. Conceptual Framework and Item Selection." *Medical Care* 30 (6): 473–83.

Weiner, J. P., B. H. Starfield, D. M. Steinwachs, and L. M. Mumford. 1991. "Development and Application of a Population-Oriented Measure of Ambulatory Care Case-Mix." *Medical Care* 29 (5): 452–72.

Whiting-O'Keefe, Q. E., C. Henke, and D. W. Simborg. 1984. "Choosing the Correct Unit of Analysis in Medical Care Experiments." *Medical Care* 22 (12): 1101–14.

Wright, S. M., J. Daley, E. Peterson, and G. E. Thibault. 1997a. "Outcomes of Acute Myocardial Infarction in the Department of Veterans Affairs: Does Regionalization in Health Care Work?" *Medical Care* 35 (2): 128–41.

Wright, S. M., J. Daley, E. S. Fisher, and G. E. Thibault. 1997b. "Where Do Elderly Veterans Obtain Care for Acute Myocardial Infarction: Department of Veterans Affairs or Medicare?" *HSR: Health Services Research* 31 (6): 739–54.

Wu, A. W., A. M. Damiano, J. Lynn, C. Alzola, J. Teno, C. S. Landefeld, N. Desbiens, J. Tsevat, A. Mayer-Oakes, F. E. Harrell, Jr., and W. A. Knaus. 1995. "Predicting Future Functional Status for Seriously Ill Hospitalized Adults. The SUPPORT Prognostic Model." *Annals of Internal Medicine* 122 (5): 342–50.

Chapter 6

Validity of Risk-Adjustment Methods

Jennifer Daley

As described in Chapter 2, everyone believes he or she understands the word "severity," although no single meaning exists. The same is true with the word "validity." Obviously risk-adjustment methodologies should be valid, although there is little consensus about exactly how to demonstrate validity. In mathematics, a proof is either valid or it is not—a dichotomous judgment. Thus, in mathematics, it is inappropriate to ask, "How valid is a proof?" In observational studies, however, "validity" has a graded meaning. The validity of a finding is improved by decreasing experimental error, reducing systematic error, or by eliminating plausible alternative explanations for the finding. When considering the validity of a risk-adjustment method, the important question is not, "Is this risk-adjustment method valid?" but, "How believable is this finding when we use risk-adjustment method X in the following way to answer question Y?"

As with severity, one difficulty is that validity is truly a multidimensional concept. According to Donabedian (1980, 101),

> The concept of validity is itself made up of many parts; and there is no precise way of saying what belongs to it, or what belongs more appropriately under another heading . . . I would say that the question of validity covers two large domains. The first has to do with the accuracy of the data and the precision of the measures that are constructed with these data. The second has to do with the justifiability of the inferences that are drawn from the data and the measurements.

This chapter discusses ways for assessing validity of risk-adjustment methods. Before doing so, however, one of Donabedian's points deserves emphasis: It is sometimes difficult to distinguish which attributes fall under the rubric of "validity" and which are more appropriately categorized elsewhere. A good example stems from Donabedian's concern about data accuracy. For instance, as described in Chapter 4, many physical examination findings (e.g., S3 gallop heart sounds, pericardial friction rubs, jugular venous distension, rales) are used in daily clinical practice as indicators of patients' cardiac or pulmonary status but are measured unreliably across physicians. Does this make them invalid as measures of risk? Is this a problem with "validity" or with "reliability"? If the differences involve random errors, then only accuracy is affected. If systematic differences occur among groups of policy relevance, then validity is threatened. "Reliability" is therefore another word that can have more than one meaning (Chapter 7), most meaningful to define not as a stand-alone concept, but as part of the phrase "reliability for the purpose of X." For example, temperature readings taken to the nearest one-tenth of one degree Fahrenheit are unlikely to be identical twice in a row, yet the majority of repeat readings will probably yield the same conclusion about whether 101.5° F is exceeded.

Many of the severity measures introduced in Chapter 1 are frequently revised or updated (Table 6.1). The explicit purpose of these changes is *to improve the validity of the measures*—along a variety of dimensions. As these severity measures change, perceptions of their validity may change. Assessments of validity may also alter over time even if severity measures are not revised, because of new discoveries in clinical medicine, new understanding concerning disease and its treatments, or changes in the comprehensiveness and accuracy of data sources. Therefore, validity is a dynamic characteristic.

In the ensuing discussion of validity, we raise a range of concerns that some may prefer to group elsewhere—for example, with reliability. In this book, however, our overarching goal is to be comprehensive across chapters in identifying issues raised in designing a risk-adjustment strategy. While this chapter focuses on validity, broadly defined, Chapter 7 examines concerns pertaining to reliability and its measurement.

Overview

As repeated throughout this book, one cannot divorce the concept of risk—or the validity of a measure—from its purpose. In examining outcomes, the goal of risk adjustment is to account for pertinent patient characteristics before making inferences about the effectiveness of care (Chapter 1). As previously described, outcomes research examines the effect of medical interventions on patients' health status. Particular outcomes result from various patient attributes prior to care, what is done to and for the patient, and chance (Figure 2.1). Examining outcomes for many patients reduces the contribution of chance (see Chapter 10). Accurately quantifying the level of risk patients bring to each healthcare encounter is central to assessing the effect of care on outcomes.

Table 6.1   Revision Schedules and Purposes for Severity Measures

System	Revision Schedule	Purpose
ACGs	Continuous updating	Respond to changes in ICD-9-CM coding and user input; refine clinical homogeneity of groupings
AIM	Annual	Respond to changes in ICD-9-CM coding and concerns about appropriate case classification
APACHE		
I	Not applicable	
II	Not applicable	
III	Periodic*	Remain current and improve predictive validity
APR-DRGs	Every 18–24 months	Respond to changes in ICD-9-CM coding and findings from empirical analyses using new data bases
CSI	Continuous review of clinical criteria and weighting	Improve clinical credibility and ability of system to predict length of stay, cost, mortality, and usefulness for clinical practice improvement
DCGs–HCCs	Periodic	Limit inappropriate incentives and sensitivity to coding practices when used for capitated reimbursement
DRGs	Annual	Respond to changes in ICD-9-CM coding and concerns about appropriate case classification; produce new relative weights for payment
DS		
Clinical	Periodic	Improve clinical credibility
Coded	Annual	Respond to changes in ICD-9-CM coding and improve clinical credibility
Staging Scale	Annual	Improve predictive validity
MMPS	Not applicable	
MPM	Periodic	Improve predictive validity

Continued

Table 6.1   Continued

System	Revision Schedule	Purpose
MedisGroups		
Original	Annual; original now replaced by empirical version	Improve predictive validity and review KCFs to improve clinical credibility
Empirical	Periodic	Improve predictive validity and review KCFs to improve clinical credibility
NY CABG	As needed	
PMCs		
Categories	Annual	Respond to changes in ICD-9-CM coding and refine categories to improve clinical credibility
Path	Annual	Update to reflect changes in medical practice
RIS	Annual	Improve predictive validity
Severity Score	Annual	Improve predictive validity
PRISM	As needed	
RAND	Not applicable	
RAMI	Periodic	Respond to changes in ICD-9-CM coding and improve predictive validity
RACI	Periodic	Respond to changes in ICD-9-CM coding and improve predictive validity
RARI	Periodic	Respond to changes in ICD-9-CM coding and improve predictive validity
R-DRGs	Annual	Respond to changes in ICD-9-CM coding and concerns about appropriate case classification; produce new relative weights for payment

* Periodic indicates intervals that are less frequent than every year.

Evaluating the validity of a risk-adjustment methodology therefore involves the following question: How well does the adjustment method account for patients' *true* risk? Here the specific purpose is again important: risk of what? As shown in Table 1.4, existing measures use different definitions of what constitutes "severity of illness" and consequently how patient risk is defined. Concepts of patient risk vary depending on the outcome of interest. Given different notions of risk and outcome, assessing the validity of a risk-adjustment methodology requires careful attention to the fundamental conceptualization of risk, illness, outcome, and the goals of the analysis.

Determining the validity of scales or classification systems is the study of psychometrics or clinimetrics (Stewart, Hays, and Ware 1992; Feinstein 1987). Methodologists have distinguished numerous different dimensions of validity; Table 6.2 summarizes eight of these. Distinctions across these different dimensions, however, often become blurred. For example, in assessing "criterion validity," it is unclear what should serve as the gold standard and how this dimension differs from "construct validity."

Although considering each type of validity separately is useful, definitions overlap in many ways. In assessing the validity of risk-adjustment methods, the most important are face validity, content validity, criterion and construct validity, predictive validity, and attributional validity. As with methodological discussions elsewhere in this book, we do not recreate detailed technical reviews. Instead, we discuss each of these five validity dimensions, highlighting those issues most crucial in risk adjustment.

Face Validity

Face validity indicates whether a method—on the face of it—appears to measure what it claims to measure. In other words, will whoever uses the method accept it as "valid" in the everyday sense of the word? Although face validity is not a rigorous concept, it is critically important. Poor face validity is a serious barrier to overall acceptance, especially by practicing clinicians who have little knowledge of technical considerations in developing risk-adjustment approaches. Clinicians generally evaluate the acceptability of a severity measure against their own internal standards: How does this fit with my personal judgments about how sick a patient is?

Clinicians will be skeptical of a risk-adjustment method that fails to incorporate clinical concepts of risk, such as a measure that assigns a low likelihood of death to patients generally understood to be at high risk of dying. For example, when hospitalized for acute medical or surgical intervention, patients with chronic renal failure requiring dialysis are known to be at higher risk of death and complications than otherwise healthy patients. Risk-adjustment methods that rely solely on the serum BUN as a measure of renal failure may underestimate the likelihood of death for patients on hemodialysis (the dialysis machine lowers the BUN, which, without dialysis, would be grossly elevated). Risk-adjustment methods that calculate both admission and subsequent scores, such as the Computerized Severity

Table 6.2 Different Dimensions of Validity

Validity Dimension	Definition	Example
Face validity	A measure contains the types of variables that will allow it to do what it aims to do	A method for adjusting for in-hospital mortality for acute myocardial infarction (AMI) includes clinical variables that on "face value" are the types of variables clinicians consider important risk factors
Content validity	A measure contains all relevant concepts	A method for adjusting for in-hospital mortality from AMI includes all clinical variables that are important risk factors
Construct validity	A measure correlates with actual indicators of risk in the expected way	A method for adjusting for in-hospital mortality from AMI correlates with actual measures of cardiac function
Convergent validity	A measure has a positive correlation with other indicators of actual risk	When a method for adjusting for in-hospital mortality from AMI shows increasing risk, actual measures of cardiac functioning also show increasing risk
Discriminant validity	A measure has a stronger correlation with indicators specific to its purpose rather than with other indicators	A method for adjusting for in-hospital mortality from AMI correlates more strongly with actual measures of cardiac function than with measures of ambulation
Criterion validity	A measure correlates with the "gold standard" measure	A method for adjusting for in-hospital mortality from AMI correlates with a clinical scale derived from intensive, continuous cardiac monitoring
Predictive validity	A measure explains variations in outcomes	A method for adjusting for in-hospital mortality from AMI predicts accurately which patients have died
Attributional validity	Findings using the measure permit one to make statements about the causes of what is observed	In-hospital mortality rates, adjusted using the measure, permit one to attribute differences to effectiveness or quality of care

Sources: Donabedian 1980; Thomas, Ashcraft, and Zimmerman 1986; Stewart, Hays, and Ware 1992.

Index and MedisGroups, may also miscalculate risk for patients whose BUNs fluctuate dramatically with each dialysis treatment. Such measures may not accurately capture risk over time for dialysis-dependent patients. These considerations raise concerns about using such measures to evaluate patient outcomes at hospitals that serve large numbers of chronic renal failure patients.

Examining face validity of risk-adjustment methods requires several components. First, open access to the individual variables and their weights for evaluation by both clinicians and methodologists permits critical appraisal of the strengths and weaknesses of the risk-adjustment method (Iezzoni 1991; Selker 1993). Second, clinicians must compare their knowledge with the variables included in the risk-adjustment method. The inclusion of important variables is critical to acceptance by clinicians. Third, clinicians must assess the direction and weight of each variable with respect to the outcome. They should look for relationships of the risk factor to the outcome that contradict their knowledge and experience. Clinicians can accept or reject the whole enterprise of risk adjustment and outcome measurement on that basis (see discussion on the development of APACHE III in Chapter 5).

A fourth aspect of assessing face validity may be the most difficult—translating the risk structure implicit in a particular model into something accessible to clinicians, so that they can test it against their clinical experience. This process is especially difficult for risk models that include highly correlated factors and numerous interaction terms. In these situations it is very difficult to determine how much and in what manner weight is being attributed to the effect of different independent variables. Graphic representations of the independent effects of a variable on the outcome can be a useful and intuitive way to explain the model to clinicians (see Chapter 5).

Content Validity

Content validity refers to the extent to which the risk factors incorporated in the risk methodology include the universe of risk factors that should have been included. A model of risk can always include more factors (see Chapter 2). Examining content validity asks whether important risk factors are missing. Information to judge this dimension is typically drawn from the clinical literature and experts. For example, in acute myocardial infarction (AMI), the literature suggests that important predictors of in-hospital death include cardiogenic shock on admission, diminished left ventricular function, malignant ventricular arrhythmias, and the anatomical location of the AMI (Table 6.3). In acute stroke, significant predictors of

Table 6.3 Clinical Predictors of Outcomes for Acute Myocardial Infarction

Variables	Literature Indicating Predictive Utility of Variable
APACHE II Acute Physiology Score (APS) Variables	
Temperature	1, 2, 3, 4
Heart rate	1, 2, 3, 4, 5, 9
Respiratory rate	1, 2, 3
Systolic blood pressure	1, 2, 3, 4, 6, 9
Diastolic blood pressure	1, 2, 3, 4, 6
Serum sodium	1, 2, 3
Serum potassium	1, 2
Serum creatinine	1, 2, 3
Hematocrit	1, 2, 3
White blood cell count	1, 2, 3
Arterial oxygenation	1, 2, 3, 6
Arterial carbon dioxide	1, 2, 3
Arterial pH	1, 2, 3, 6
Level of consciousness (Glasgow Coma Scale)	1, 2, 3, 6
Additional APACHE III APS Variables	
Albumin	3
Blood urea nitrogen	3, 4, 6, 7, 7
Glucose	3
Total bilirubin	3
Urine output	3
Other Variables	
Demographics:	
Age	4, 5, 6
Sex	4
Clinical variables:	
2° or 3° atrioventricular block	8
Acute myocardial infarction on electrocardiogram (Q-waves)	6, 7, 9, 10
Arrest	7, 7
Arrhythmia	10
Atrial fibrillation	7
Bundle branch block	6
Calcium	7, 7

Continued

Table 6.3   Continued

Variables	Literature Indicating Predictive Utility of Variable
Cardiogenic shock	8
Cardiomegaly	**7**
Cardiomyopathy	7
Creatinine kinase score (CPK)	5, **7**
Intubation	5
Location of myocardial infarction	5, 8
Pulmonary function test	**7**
Serum aspartate aminotransferase	5
Sputum culture, positive	7, **7**
Subendocardial infarction	4
Ventricular fibrillation	8
Witnessed seizure	6
History variables:	
Coronary artery disease (on cardiac catheterization)	**7**
Congestive heart failure	4, 5, **7**, 8, 10
Diffuse metastatic cancer	4
DNR order on admission	4
Left ventricular hypertrophy on EKG	7
Old MI on EKG	7, **7**
Unable to walk	4
Unstable angina	10

Note: Citations in regular type face pertain to the ability of the variable to predict mortality; citations in **bold and underlined** indicate the ability of the variable to predict resource consumption (length of stay, hospitalization costs or charges).

1. Knaus et al. 1985.
2. Wagner, Knaus, and Draper 1986.
3. Knaus et al. 1991.
4. Daley et al. 1988.
5. Keeler et al. 1990.
6. Iezzoni et al. 1992.
7. Iezzoni, Moskowitz, and Ash 1988.
8. Moreau et al. 1989.
9. Selker, Griffith, and D'Agostino 1991.
10. Teskey, Calvin, and McPhail 1991.

in-hospital death include coma, the extent of acute neurologic impairment, and intracerebral edema causing a midline intracerebral shift (Table 6.4).

Examining the content validity of a severity measure for risk of in-hospital death for AMI or stroke requires an assessment of how well the

Table 6.4   Clinical Predictors of Outcomes for Stroke

Variables	Literature Indicating Predictive Utility of Variable
APACHE II Acute Physiology Score (APS) Variables	
Temperature	1, 2, 3, 5
Heart rate	1, 2, 3, 7, 8
Respiratory rate	1, 2, 3, 7, 8
Systolic blood pressure	1, 2, 3, 5, 7, 8, 9
Diastolic blood pressure	1, 2, 3, 5, 7, 8, 9
Serum sodium	1, 2, 3
Serum potassium	1, 2
Serum creatinine	1, 2, 3
Hematocrit	1, 2, 3
White blood cell count	1, 2, 3
Arterial oxygenation	1, 2, 3
Arterial carbon dioxide	1, 2, 3, 8
Arterial pH	1, 2, 3
Level of consciousness (Glasgow Coma Scale)	1, 2, 3, 4, 5, 7, 8, 9
Additional APACHE III APS Variables	
Albumin	3
Blood urea nitrogen	3, 5, 6, 7
Glucose	3, 6, 7, 8
Total bilirubin	3
Urine output	3
Additional Variables	
Demographics:	
Age	4, 5
Sex	5
Clinical variables:	
Alkaline phosphatase	8
Aspiration pneumonitis	4
Calcium	<u>6</u>
Cardiac arrest (AMI)	6, <u>6</u>
Cardiomegaly	<u>6</u>
Edema	<u>6</u>
Hemiplegia	4
Infiltrate (on chest radiograph)	6, 7, 8
Intraventricular hemorrhage extension	4, 9

Continued

Table 6.4 Continued

Variables	Literature Indicating Predictive Utility of Variable
Ischemia on ECG	**6**
Mass effect on CT or MRI scan	4, 5, 7
Massive/multiple lesions on CT scan (brain lesion)	4, 6
Partial thromboplastin time	**6**
Pleural effusion	6
Seizures in-hospital	4, 6
Sputum culture positive	**6**
Wheezing	6, **6**
History variables:	
Cardiovascular disease	8
Diffuse/metastatic cancer	5
DNR order on admission	5
History of diabetes mellitus	6, 7
History of seizures	6
History of syncope	**6**
Previous stroke	4
Activities of daily living:	
Acute motor deficit	**6**
Unable to walk	5

Note: Citations in regular type face pertain to the ability of the variable to predict mortality; citations in **bold and underlined** indicate the ability of the variable to predict resource consumption (length of stay, hospitalization costs or charges).

1. Knaus et al. 1985.
2. Wagner, Knaus, and Draper 1986.
3. Knaus et al. 1991.
4. Rodrigues and Joshi 1991.
5. Daley et al. 1988.
6. Iezzoni, Moskowitz, and Ash 1988.
7. Keeler et al. 1990.
8. Smith et al. 1991.
9. Tuhrim et al. 1991.

variables included in the model capture these clinical characteristics. As shown in Tables 6.3 and 6.4, for example, the Acute Physiology Scores (APS) of APACHE II and III contain clinical variables noted in much of the literature. Disease-specific factors, however, are not included in APACHE because of its developers' intention to create a generic indicator of risk among all patients in ICUs, regardless of diagnosis.

Tables 6.3 and 6.4 also suggest that identifying relevant risk factors depends on the outcome of interest. Risk factors for in-hospital mortality differ from those for resource consumption. These tables also highlight that the literature for certain outcomes may be modest, at best. For instance, the literature cited in these tables was distilled from items found on extensive, computerized bibliographic searches of the clinical literature in 1993. While the literature for predicting in-hospital death was relatively rich, few articles had been published concerning resource consumption, especially for stroke.

Assessment of content validity is complicated by highly correlated independent variables. Certain variables that clinicians view as important may be excluded from the model because of their correlation with included variables. For example, in the National VA Surgical Risk Study, general surgeons examining the variables included in the final risk models for 30-day mortality and morbidity often commented on the presence or absence of laboratory values, such as bilirubin and liver function tests in assessing the presence of acute and chronic hepatobiliary disease. Initially, the surgeons were skeptical because the models did not include serum bilirubin and hepatic transaminases, and they questioned the validity of the models. After further examining the models, however, they appreciated that the serum albumin level (an included variable) was an excellent predictor of surgical outcome and was a single patient-specific variable representing risk from both hepatobiliary disease and poor nutritional status. Therefore, although certain variables may not appear in a final prediction model, the effect of these clinical risk factors may be captured by other closely related variables.

Beyond the statistical finding of strong correlations, individual clinical parameters often capture a range of clinical concerns, as in the albumin example above. One clinical variable that appears in many risk-adjustment models, serum BUN, similarly reflects a variety of clinical causes—intravascular volume depletion, diminished cardiac output, renal insufficiency, significant gastrointestinal bleeding, or an increased catabolic state. In some situations, however, multiple risk factors are required to represent fully the clinical risk concept. For example, the constellation of very low or very high body temperature, low blood pressure, very high or very low peripheral white blood cell count, and the presence of positive blood cultures is a highly valid representation of sepsis or septic shock. Each of these variables, however, alone or in combination with only one or two of the others, does not have the same significance in defining the risk of death from sepsis.

Other risk variables may only weakly represent the risk concept. For example, in congestive heart failure and AMI, acute neurological damage or diminished levels of consciousness are important risk factors for early hospital-associated mortality. The Glasgow Coma Score, developed as a measure of severity of acute coma in patients admitted to neurological and neurosurgical ICUs, is used as a surrogate for acute neurological damage, as well as a measure of coma, in some risk-adjustment approaches (Knaus et al. 1985; Daley et al. 1988). Although the Glasgow Coma Score does identify patients with acutely diminished levels of consciousness, it poorly represents other aspects of neurological damage, such as paralysis, paresis, or chronic mental status changes. The APACHE III investigators have also noted that, although the Glasgow Coma Score predicts mortality risk, it lacks sensitivity in its intermediate ranges; furthermore, variations in the use of sedatives in different ICUs introduces treatment bias in outcome predictions (Bastos et al. 1993).

The content of risk-adjustment methods is inevitably limited by the data sources used, generally either administrative files (Chapter 3) or medical records (Chapter 4). Many important risk factors are not available in these sources. For example, administrative data contain no functional status information, and the quality of such information in medical charts is very uneven. The absence of measures for more complex and subjective risk concepts, such as patient-perceived functional status and psychological, cognitive, and psychosocial functioning, continues to limit the content of risk-adjustment methods.

Criterion and Construct Validity

Obviously, having a "gold standard," or criterion against which to measure validity, is desirable. As discussed previously, for abstract, multidimensional concepts, such as "risk" and "severity of illness," no such standard exists nor is there even common agreement about how these terms should be defined. Criterion validation is thus not possible. Several alternative validation procedures, however, may be used. Construct or correlation validation assesses how well the measurement correlates with other measures of the same concept. To determine validity, hypotheses are generated about how the levels of risk measured by the method under study will correlate with other measures or variables. Confirmation of these hypotheses provides evidence of the measure's validity. One strategy for establishing construct validity is to examine the correlations between a risk rating and the determinations of risk by a panel of expert physicians.

Only a few published studies compare physicians' ratings and risk scores. Because APACHE II scores may be calculated prospectively when patients are admitted to an ICU, several studies have compared the APACHE II prediction of likelihood of death with the clinical judgment of physicians and nurses. Kruse, Thill-Baharozian, and Carlson (1988) compared the predictions of 57 physicians and 33 critical care nurses with the APACHE II score on 366 patients admitted to an ICU; they found no significant differences between the accuracy of the clinical judgments and the APACHE II score. Both had high predictive validity (i.e., were accurate predictors of which patients died). A similar study found different results: Brannen, Godfrey, and Goetter (1989) compared the predictions of critical care physicians in one medical ICU with the predictions from the APACHE II score. They found that physicians did significantly better than the APACHE II score in predicting mortality. They concluded that APACHE II predictions were still useful, however, especially in patients whose predicted likelihood of death was less than 30 percent.

In one surgical ICU, 578 patients were evaluated within 24 hours of admission by the ICU attending physician, who predicted whether the patient would live or die in-hospital (Meyer et al. 1992). An APACHE II score was calculated at the same time. Of the 40 patients who died, death was correctly predicted by the ICU attending for 22 (sensitivity 55.0 percent); of the 538 patients who lived, survival was correctly predicted by the attending for 528 (98.2 percent specificity for the prediction of death). Overall accuracy for the clinical assessment was 95.2 percent. Because the APACHE II score is continuous, an APACHE II score of 20 or greater was chosen as an optimal score to divide predicted survivors from nonsurvivors based on a receiver-operator curve of APACHE II predictions (see Chapter 9). Based on this break point, the APACHE II prediction was correct in 527 of the 578 patients (overall accuracy 90.2 percent). Of the 40 patients who died, death was correctly predicted for 23 (sensitivity 57.5 percent); of the 538 patients who lived, survival was correctly predicted by the APACHE II for 504 (93.7 percent specificity). The authors concluded that the clinical prediction was slightly better than the APACHE II prediction. Significantly, both physician and APACHE II predictions misclassified 40 percent of patients as likely to die who subsequently lived.

In the SUPPORT project, 4,028 patients had physician estimates of their 180-day survival, as well as estimates from the empirically derived model (Knaus et al. 1995, 195). The area under a receiver-operating characteristic curve (see Chapter 9) was identical for the physician and model predictions, 0.78. However, the physicians were more pessimistic than the empirical model. Physicians judged more patients to be at high risk of dying (< 0.15 likelihood of survival) than did the SUPPORT model ($n = 753$ for physicians; $n = 471$ for the model).

Comparison of scores among risk-adjustment measures is another way to investigate construct validity. Different risk-adjustment scores have rarely been compared, however, partially because of the proprietary ownership of many methods in widespread use. As a result, with few exceptions (see discussion about our AHCPR-funded severity study below), direct comparison among risk adjustors have usually not been conducted on the same cases or patients. Comparing performance on different cases can be misleading (see Chapters 8 and 9). To be meaningful, such comparisons require careful examination of the definition of patient populations, similar outcome measures and statistical approaches for assessing predictive validity, careful attention to data sources, and roughly comparable distributions of the dependent and independent variables. Sample sizes also must be adequate to account for random variation at the chosen level of analysis (e.g., patient, institution, groups of institutions). Finally, the goal of the analysis must be considered. Methods for validating risk-adjustment measures may differ when considering the accuracy of predictions for individual patients as opposed to accuracy for groups of patients (Chang 1989; Hornbrook and Goodman 1995).

As in comparing nurse and physician clinical predictions with APACHE scores, most direct comparisons of risk-adjustment methods have been made in ICU patients. Gross and colleagues (1991) compared APACHE II, the CSI, McCabe-Jackson, and the American Society of Anesthesiologists (ASA) scores with the number of comorbidities in 107 patients admitted to a combined medical ICU/coronary care unit. They concluded that all scores correlated well with the number of comorbidities and that APACHE II, CSI, and McCabe-Jackson scores appeared to be comparable predictors of comorbidity in medical ICU patients. Correlation was less with the ASA class.

Rocca and colleagues (1989) compared four severity scores in 70 patients with head trauma in one neurosurgical intensive care unit: The APS, the Simplified Acute Physiology Score, the Glasgow Coma Score, and the Therapeutic Intervention Scoring System (TISS). They concluded that the Glasgow Coma Score was superior for predicting mortality for head trauma patients, while the TISS system was best for predicting the level of care needed by the patients. After considering the time and effort needed to collect the data, they concluded that the Glasgow Coma Score was the best measure overall.

Given the public availability of the APACHE II algorithms, much effort has focused on the validity of APACHE II, developed on ICU patients in the United States, for other populations of patients, including ICU patients in different countries. Given that ICU practices vary internationally, APACHE II's generalizability and validity must be studied anew in different environments, and research using APACHE II has come from several countries, including Canada (Wong et al. 1995), Singapore (Chen, Koh, and Goh 1993), Israel (Porath et al. 1994), Britain and Ireland (Rowan et al. 1993, 1994), and Switzerland (Berger et al. 1992). In general, APACHE II demonstrated validity in these international comparisons. Variable results have arisen from attempts to validate APACHE II in specific diagnosis-

or procedure-based populations, such as breast cancer patients (Headley, Theriault, and Smith 1992), neurosurgical patients (Hartley et al. 1995), AMI patients (Ludwigs and Hulting 1995), and trauma patients (Vassar and Holcroft 1992, 1994; Rutledge et al. 1993).

Aside from studies of different risk-adjustment methods for predicting ICU mortality, few comparative studies of risk-adjustment methods have been conducted. Thomas and Ashcraft (1991) compared the ability of six severity measures—APACHE II, MedisGroups, CSI, Disease Staging, PMCs, and Acuity Index Method—to explain variations in estimated costs of hospitalized patients in 11 selected adjacent DRGs in 5 hospitals. Although all measures improved on DRGs in explaining variation in costs in some diagnostic categories (e.g., coronary artery bypass surgery), little or no improvement was noted by any measures in other diagnostic categories (e.g., major large and small bowel procedures and esophagitis, gastroenteritis, and miscellaneous digestive disorders). Risk estimates based on maximum scores, such as the maximum CSI score, had better predictive ability than admission scores or ratings based on administrative data. Without detailed information about the individual risk variables that are most highly predictive of high or low hospital costs, a careful examination of content validity of each risk measure was not feasible.

Iezzoni and colleagues (1992) compared six models in predicting in-hospital mortality in five medical conditions. Models included one based on administrative data, the original MedisGroups admission score, an approximation of the APS from APACHE II, and three models empirically derived from MedisGroups data. For the empirically derived models (produced using forward stepwise regression), most important predictor variables were physiologic measures (e.g., levels of consciousness, vital signs, BUN) common across all five conditions. There were only a few condition-specific predictor variables. Significantly, physiologic variables common to all five conditions had different weights in the models with the best predictive validity, suggesting that disease-specific modeling produces the strongest predictive models.

Assessing Construct Validity in the AHCPR-Funded Severity Study

As described above, construct and correlation validation assesses how well one measure correlates with other measures of the same concept. Given that our database contained numerous different severity measures for the same patients (see Chapter 1), we had a unique opportunity to assess construct validity. Selected results from these investigations are summarized below.

We report here on four conditions with sufficient numbers of in-hospital deaths for meaningful statistical analysis, as follows (see Table 1.9): medically treated AMI, 11,880 patients from 100 hospitals with 1,574 (13.2 percent) in-hospital deaths (Iezzoni et al. 1995a, 1996a); coronary artery bypass graft (CABG) surgery, 7,765 patients from 38 hospitals with 252 (3.2 percent) in-hospital deaths (Landon et al. 1996); pneumonia, 18,016 patients from 105 hospitals with 1,732 (9.6 percent) in-hospital deaths (Iezzoni et al. 1996b, 1996c); and medically treated stroke, 9,407 patients from 94 hospitals with 916 (9.7 percent) in-hospital deaths (Iezzoni et al. 1995b, 1996d).

Logistic regressions were run within each condition to predict death using patient age, sex, and severity scores (Iezzoni et al. 1995c). Separate models were produced for each severity measure (the results presented here involve the empirical version of MedisGroups and the physiology score patterned after APACHE III, see Table 1.8). Three measures were based on administrative data: Disease Staging, PMCs, and APR-DRGs. Each model produced a predicted probability of in-hospital death for each patient, which we added to determine expected death rates for each hospital. We calculated a z-score for each hospital as follows:

$$z = \frac{(\text{observed number of deaths}) - (\text{expected number of deaths})}{(\text{square root of the variance in the number of deaths})}.$$

We ranked hospitals from lowest (fewer deaths than expected) to highest (more deaths than expected) based on these z-scores.

We first examined the following question: Do different severity measures predict different likelihoods of in-hospital death for the same patients? There are a variety of ways to flag patients viewed as having different predicted probabilities of death, but regardless of the approach, the answer to this question was yes—many patients were scored very differently by different severity measures (Iezzoni et al. 1995a, 1996b, 1996d).

For the analysis presented here, we compared the odds ratios of death calculated by each severity measure (e.g., the odds of dying predicted by MedisGroups divided by the odds predicted by Disease Staging). When this ratio was less than 0.5 or greater than 2.0, we viewed a patient as having a very different probability of death predicted by the two measures (Table 6.5). The most startling finding was how often patients had dissimilar predictions of dying (Iezzoni et al. 1995a, 1996b, 1996d). Thus, for individual patients, their predicted likelihood of death calculated by one severity measure often was very different from that by another measure.

Patterns varied across conditions. For example, agreement between MedisGroups and physiology scores was high for AMI, but predictions

Table 6.5 Percent of Patients with Different Odds of Death Calculated by Pairs of Severity Measures[a]

Severity Measures		Conditions			
		AMI	CABG	Pneumonia	Stroke
		Percent of Patients with Different Predicted Odds			
MedisGroups	Physiology Score	19.5%	4.1%	30.2%	17.8%
MedisGroups	Disease Staging	51.4	32.8	47.6	57.8
MedisGroups	PMC Severity Score	45.6	42.0	46.9	61.6
MedisGroups	APR-DRGs	46.1	65.8	47.9	48.4
Physiology Score	Disease Staging	51.6	32.3	38.9	52.0
Physiology Score	PMC Severity Score	44.2	40.9	30.4	44.0
Physiology Score	APR-DRGs	44.9	68.5	32.0	31.0
Disease Staging	PMC Severity Score	51.8	40.2	31.0	32.9
Disease Staging	APR-DRGs	49.5	56.4	30.4	41.3
PMC Severity Score	APR-DRGs	27.5	60.7	21.2	20.1

Sources: Iezzoni et al. 1995a, 1995c, 1996b, 1996d.
Note: MedisGroups = empirical version; Physiology Score = version 2.
[a] Comparisons were based on the ratio = (odds of death predicted by first severity measure)/(odds of death predicted by second severity measure). If this ratio were < 0.5 or > 2.0, then the odds predicted by the two severity measures was viewed as very different.

diverged for almost one-third of pneumonia patients. Not surprisingly, code-based measures disagreed frequently with clinically based measures, but code-based measures also differed from one another. For instance, PMCs and APR-DRGs disagreed for 60.7 percent of CABG patients.

Given these differences, an obvious question is which severity measures makes more clinical sense. Because we could not return to medical records to explore this question, we conducted a preliminary investigation using MedisGroups admission KCFs. We reviewed the medical literature to identify clinical characteristics viewed as prognostic of in-hospital death, and found the MedisGroups KCF that best captured each. We then looked at patterns of these KCFs for patients with discordant predictions of dying by pairs of severity measures (Iezzoni et al. 1995a, 1996b). Not surprisingly, we found that clinically based measures generally had more clinical credibility than code-based measures, except for CABG, where clinical and code-based measures were comparable.

Finding differences across severity measures at the level of individual patients led to the second question: Would judgments about whether hospitals look particularly good or bad differ using different severity measures to risk adjust mortality rates?

Again, the answer to this question is yes, but the findings are more subtle than at the patient level (Iezzoni et al. 1995b, 1996a, 1996c; Landon et al. 1996). As before, there are several ways to address this question. Here we used severity-adjusted death rates the way hospitals or health insurers may employ the information (see Chapters 10 and 11). The z-scores described above identified hospitals falling into these two extremes.

- The best 10 percent: hospitals with the lowest severity-adjusted death rates. These hospitals could be designated as exemplar facilities and thus serve as benchmarking targets in quality improvement initiatives.

- The worst 10 percent: hospitals with the highest severity-adjusted death rates. Insurers may choose not to contract with these institutions.

Table 6.6 shows how often pairs of severity measures agreed about which hospitals fell into the best and worst 10 percent. Table 6.6 also includes hospital rankings based on z-scores associated with raw mortality rates (unadjusted for age, sex, or severity). The immediate impression is that severity measures often flagged different hospitals than unadjusted mortality rates, but different severity measures also frequently flagged different hospitals (Iezzoni et al. 1995b, 1996a, 1996c; Landon et al. 1996). No clear pattern emerged suggesting that code-based measures agreed more with each other than they agreed with the clinically based measures; nor was agreement better for flagging the best 10 percent than the worst 10 percent. Again, there were differences by condition: For example, MedisGroups and PMCs agreed relatively well for pneumonia but poorly for stroke.

When disagreements occurred, hospitals ranked in the top or bottom 10 percent by one severity measure often appeared in the next 10 percent (11 to 20 percent or 81 to 90 percent) ranked by the other measure. Sometimes differences in rankings were larger. For example, MedisGroups and Disease Staging agreed about 5 of 11 hospitals ranked among the top 10 percent for pneumonia. The remaining six, ranked in descending order by MedisGroups (1 = best), had the following rankings by Disease Staging (MedisGroups rankings are in parentheses): 57 (4), 66 (7), 25 (8), 27 (9), 43 (10), and 30 (11). Hospitals with widely discrepant rankings were not low volume, where small numbers could yield volatile results. For instance, the hospital ranked 7th by MedisGroups but 66th by Disease Staging had 266 pneumonia patients with 20 deaths.

Interestingly, agreement in flagging hospitals between severity-adjusted and unadjusted mortality rates was often better than agreement between pairs of severity measures. For example, MedisGroups and Disease Staging agreed on only three of the ten worst hospitals for AMI, while MedisGroups and unadjusted rankings agreed on six hospitals. Therefore, one set of severity-adjusted findings was not obviously better than another or than unadjusted rankings.

For each pair of severity measures, we calculated a kappa statistic based on whether individual hospitals were flagged as among the best or worst 10 percent by one, both, or neither measure. Kappa assesses whether the observed agreement is greater than expected by chance (see Chapter 7). The kappa values showed fair to excellent agreement among severity measures in flagging hospitals (Iezzoni et al. 1995b, 1996a, 1996c). For example, MedisGroups and Disease Staging agreed on only 5 of the 11 worst hospitals for pneumonia patients (Table 6.6), for a kappa of 0.39, indicating fair agreement (Iezzoni et al. 1996c). In contrast, Physiology Score 2 and PMC's Severity Score agreed on 9 of the 11 worst hospitals, for a kappa of 0.80, suggesting substantial agreement.

Overall, these analyses suggest that individual hospitals could care greatly about which mortality rates are examined—unadjusted versus severity-adjusted rates—and about which severity measure is used. While severity measures agreed about flagging hospitals more often than chance, rankings for some hospitals differed dramatically across severity measures. Thus, these construct analyses suggest that—at both individual patient and hospital levels—agreement across severity measures was often modest. As mentioned below, the central question is still unresolved: Which severity measure best isolates that residual quantity—quality of care differences—across hospitals?

Table 6.6 Number of Times Pairs of Severity Measures Agreed on the Ten Percent of Hospitals with the Best and Worst Mortality Performance

Severity Measures, Including Unadjusted Mortality rates		AMI (n = 10)		CABG (n = 4)		Pneumonia (n = 11)		Stroke (n = 9)	
		Best	Worst	Best	Worst	Best	Worst	Best	Worst
		Number of Hospitals on Which Severity Measures Agreed							
MedisGroups	Physiology Score	9	10	4	4	6	8	7	6
MedisGroups	Disease Staging	6	3	2	3	5	5	5	3
MedisGroups	PMC Severity Score	7	5	2	2	6	8	4	3
MedisGroups	APR-DRGs	6	4	1	2	6	7	6	4
MedisGroups	Unadjusted rates	5	6	3	4	3	6	3	5
Physiology Score	Disease Staging	5	3	2	3	4	7	5	3
Physiology Score	PMC Severity Score	6	5	2	2	7	9	6	3
Physiology Score	APR-DRGs	6	4	1	2	5	8	6	3
Physiology Score	Unadjusted rates	6	6	3	4	3	9	5	5
Disease Staging	PMC Severity Score	7	5	3	2	4	7	6	3
Disease Staging	APR-DRGs	7	5	2	2	4	6	7	3
Disease Staging	Unadjusted rates	5	4	1	3	1	7	5	5
PMC Severity Score	APR-DRGs	8	9	2	2	7	10	7	7
PMC Severity Score	Unadjusted rates	4	6	1	2	5	7	7	6
APR-DRGs	Unadjusted rates	6	6	1	2	5	7	6	5

Conditions and Number of Hospitals in Best and Worst 10%

Sources: Iezzoni et al. 1995b, 1996a, 1996c; Landon 1996.
Note: MedisGroups = empirical version; Physiology Score = version 2.
n = Number of hospitals in best and worst 10%.

Predictive Validity

Predictive validity refers to how well a measure predicts an outcome of interest. Chapters 8 and 9 discuss statistical measures of performance of predictive models, such as risk-adjustment methods. Here, we discuss the more general conceptual issues in measuring predictive validity.

When considering predictive validity, one must distinguish between the data set used to develop the model and the data set used for model validation. As discussed in more detail in Chapters 8 and 9, risk-adjustment models typically perform better when predicting outcomes in the data set used to develop the approach than they do on other data sets. The most important test of a model is how well it works on data that were not used in its development.

The more data that are used in developing a risk-adjustment model, the better one can identify the most important risk factors and accurately quantify risks. If all the data are used in model development, however, none remain for independent validation. The same data can be used to develop and to validate a model, but it is harder to know how well the model will perform in an independent validation when new data are not used in the validation. Using the development data set to provide estimates of independent validation is called "cross-validation."

The cross-validation approach depends primarily on the size of the data set. If the database is sufficiently large, one cross-validation method is as follows. First, divide the data randomly in half; in doing so, however, it may be reasonable to ensure that the events of interest (e.g., deaths) are equally distributed in each half (e.g., by repeating the random splits until the two halves have roughly the same number of deaths). Second, develop a model on one half and compare its predictions to actual outcomes in the other half. Any summary measure of model fit, such as R^2, computed from paired "observed and predicted" outcomes, can be calculated to produce a cross-validated measure of the model's performance. Optionally, the roles of the two halves may then be reversed, and the model development and validation process repeated (e.g., Iezzoni et al. 1992).

Although this cross-validation approach is appealing, it has drawbacks. For instance, only half of the data are used in model development. If the final model was actually developed using the entire database (as often occurs), the validation results will not directly pertain to this final model. Fortunately, the validation results are conservative, because theory suggests that a model developed on twice as many cases will validate even better. Another problem is that results may be affected by imbalances that sometimes occur when data are randomly split, producing disturbing discrepancies between the models developed on the two halves or in two validation results.

When the data set is too small to develop good models on half of the cases, the data may be divided into smaller subsets, such as ten groups each containing 10 percent of the cases. One then successively "holds out" each 10 percent subset while fitting the model to the remaining 90 percent of cases. Each time, the fitted model from the main body of data is used to predict values for each observation in the smaller hold-out subset. Finally, discrepancies between actual and predicted values are pooled across all ten subsets to evaluate predictive fit. This approach has been used by several developers of risk-adjustment approaches (Daley et al. 1988; Keeler et al. 1990; Knaus et al. 1991; Naessens et al. 1992).

An extreme example of this approach is useful with very small data sets. It involves holding out individual cases and then fitting successive models to all other cases, an approach called Predicted Sum of Squares (Neter, Wasserman, and Kutner 1990). With this strategy, if there are n total patients, n successive models are developed on each subset of the data of size $n - 1$ created by holding out just one case; each such model is used to predict the outcome for the case that was held out when that model was developed. Thomas and Ashcraft (1991) employed this approach to determine cross-validated R^2 values.

Regardless of the size of the hold-out samples, the principle is similar. First, predicted values are determined for each case using a model that does not include that case in model development, then measures of performance, such as R^2 values and c-statistics, are calculated through comparing predicted and actual values (see Chapters 8 and 9).

Another technique for cross-validation is "bootstrapping," named after the "pulling yourself up by your bootstraps" aphorism (Efron 1979). Before describing this approach, suppose that we had access to the (enormously large) "parent" population for which a particular sample of n patients (the development database) is a representative random sample. In this situation, we could create multiple databases similar to our actual database by taking repeated random samples of size n from the parent population. We could develop a model from each of these samples and compute performance measures for each model. By comparing the variables found to be important in each model, their coefficients, and resultant measures of model performance, we could quantify the uncertainty present in the single analysis of our particular data.

Because we typically do not have access to the parent population, we "pull ourselves up by the bootstraps"—we use what we do have (the n cases in our development data set) as a best guess about what the parent population looks like. To replicate creating multiple samples of size n drawn from this population, we carry out repeated sampling *with replacement* from the development database. We can examine various aspects of model development and validation by refitting the model to each database replication and calculating measures of predictive validity. In this way, for example, we can determine confidence intervals for statistics of interest, such as R^2 or c, based on the distributions of these statistics across the different replications. For instance, we can construct a 95 percent confidence interval for R^2 using the fifth from the lowest and the fifth from the highest values of R^2 that occur in 200 repeated samplings.

Separate from deciding how to cross-validate measures of predictive validity is the question of the extent to which the entire model development procedure must be validated (see Chapter 5). For example, when cross-validating a model developed using stepwise procedures, one approach is first to use the entire database to identify variables for use in modeling and to validate only the coefficients that occur when the model is fit. An alternative is to repeat the entire procedure, starting with the complete set of potential variables as candidates in stepwise procedures run on subsets of the data. In interpreting results from cross-validations, it is important to consider whether the entire model-building procedure is validated versus only certain components of the process.

As mentioned above, external validation with an entirely independent data set provides the strongest test of predictive validity. Given the great expense and practical challenges of data collection and the desire to use the available data as completely as possible in model development, however, totally independent data sets are rarely available. Despite the value of external validation, using an entirely different data set introduces important questions. Independent development and validation databases are likely to differ much more than randomly subdivided subsets of a single database. For instance, the average value of the dependent variable will probably differ more between two independent data sets than between randomly chosen halves of the same data set. To what extent is it appropriate to make adjustments to the predictions to account for differences in average outcomes in different databases? Unless a model is developed on an extremely large and representative data set (e.g., such as the Medicare database), expecting correct calibration across data sets may be unrealistic. Nevertheless, this correction of calibration is necessary to say that a provider's patients experience "too many deaths" given the expected number. As described in Chapter 9, these issues have been explored in some depth for models used to predict dichotomous outcomes.

Attributional Validity

Finally, Donabedian (1980) described a critical concept that he called "attributional validity." In the context of risk adjustment for studying healthcare outcomes, attributional validity applies to the extent to which it is appropriate to make inferences about the causes of variations in outcomes across patients (e.g., about the reason for differences in mortality rates). Attributional validity examines whether the risk adjustment is sufficient for one to say that variations were *not* related to intrinsic patient characteristics. Instead, observed variations were attributable to another cause, such as differences in treatment effectiveness or quality of care.

> When outcomes are used to make inferences about the quality of care, it is necessary first to establish that the outcomes can, in fact, be attributed to that care. We may call this the problem of "attribution," and its satisfactory solution may be said to confirm "attributional validity." (Donabedian 1980, 103)

Clearly, when using risk-adjusted outcome information to motivate practice changes or to monitor providers, attributional validity is key. It may, however, also be difficult to measure. In the health policy arena, many now assume that if a severity adjustment system meets other standards (e.g., a certain level of predictive power or R^2), it is safe to draw inferences about other causes from studies which used that measure for risk adjustment (see Chapter 10). That is not necessarily so, even if the risk adjustor performs well in all other dimensions of validity. One study showed that there is little relationship between the proportion of outcome variance explained by the risk-adjustment models and the strength of the relationship between quality of care—as measured by peer review organizations (PROs)—and risk-adjusted mortality (Thomas, Holloway, and Guire 1993). Interpreting the cause of variations in risk-adjusted outcomes—even with the "best" measure for risk—must be pursued cautiously.

Several studies have assessed the relationship of risk-adjusted mortality to effectiveness and quality of care with conflicting results. Dubois and colleagues investigated the relationship among hospitals that were high and low outliers in an analysis of in-hospital mortality (Dubois, Brook, and Rogers 1987). After adjusting for the patients' risk of dying on admission using APACHE II, hospitals with higher death rates were noted to take care of a sicker population of patients than hospitals with lower mortality rates in three high-mortality conditions: pneumonia, stroke, and AMI (Dubois et al. 1987). Explicit and implicit chart reviews were conducted on a sample of cases in each disease category from high- and low-mortality outlier hospitals (Dubois and Brook 1988). Explicit reviews detected no apparent differences in effectiveness of care. After adjusting for differences in patient risk, implicit reviews demonstrated that patients with stroke and pneumonia had a 5 percent incidence of preventable deaths in high-mortality outlier hospitals compared with 1 percent preventable deaths in low-mortality outlier hospitals. The authors concluded that high-mortality outlier hospitals may have both sicker patients and less effective care.

Subsequent detailed studies of variations in risk-adjusted mortality and their association with quality of care and effectiveness have been d in cardiovascular surgery. Open-heart surgery lends itself to dies because of its frequency and relatively high mortality risk—ing about 4 percent in-hospital mortality in most series.

Hannan and colleagues (1990) analyzed data from a prospective registry of all open-heart surgery performed in New York state (see Chapters 10 and 11). After developing an empirical risk-adjustment model for patients undergoing CABG surgery, expected mortality rates were calculated for the 28 hospitals that perform CABGs in New York state. These rates were compared with the observed mortality rates. Three hospitals were identified as having lower-than-expected mortality rates; four hospitals were identified as having higher-than-expected mortality rates. The hospitals identified as having the highest and lowest risk-adjusted mortality rates were not necessarily those with the highest and lowest observed crude rates. Severity differences were significant enough among the hospitals that the rank order correlation coefficient between risk-adjusted rates and the crude rates was only 0.67. Using a combination of site visits and chart reviews by board-certified specialists blinded to the high or low outlier status of a hospital, quality of care was assessed at the outlier hospitals. Eighteen (45 percent) of the 40 deaths in the high outlier hospitals were noted to have quality of care problems in contrast to 1 (4.4 percent) of the 23 cases reviewed in the low outlier hospitals (Hannan et al. 1990, 2773).

A similar study was conducted among the five hospitals that perform CABG surgery in northern New England (O'Connor et al. 1991). After developing a risk-adjustment model and clinical prediction rule (O'Connor et al. 1992), observed and predicted in-hospital mortality rates were compared among the five medical centers and among individual surgeons. After adjusting for clinical risk, significant variability persisted among both medical centers (2.5-fold between the highest and lowest medical center rates) and among surgeons (4.2-fold between the highest and lowest surgeon's rates). To understand these differences further, the group compared processes of care among the five hospitals, reviewing all subprocesses of CABG surgery (Kasper, Plume, and O'Connor 1992). Site visits were conducted with the five medical center teams to observe several aspects of the process of care, including the technical process of care, process ownership and leadership, communication among and between participants, decision making, use and recording of data, and underlying factors (e.g., training levels, staff fatigue, and environmental characteristics). Considerable variation was observed in many dimensions of process of care across the five sites. Additional process analyses of the technical aspects of care using detailed chart review was also conducted, and a series of process improvement steps were instituted. Subsequent measures of adverse outcome, including risk-adjusted mortality rates, decreased after process improvement (O'Connor et al. 1996).

Investigators studying the effect of the implementation of the DRG-based prospective payment system implemented by Medicare in 1983 on the quality of care to Medicare beneficiaries used 30-day mortality after admission for five prevalent illnesses—congestive heart failure, AMI, pneumonia, stroke, and hip fracture (Keeler et al. 1992). After adjusting for sickness on admission, they studied the process of care using both implicit and explicit criteria. Both at an individual patient level and for groups of hospitals, the investigators demonstrated a relationship between risk-adjusted mortality rates and measures of process of care by both implicit and explicit review criteria—hospitals with lower risk-adjusted mortality rates had better process of care based on chart review. Using Medicare administrative data, Hartz and colleagues correlated the risk-adjusted mortality rates among hospitals caring for Medicare beneficiaries in 1987 with the rates of quality problems reported by 38 PROs for the same hospitals. They found a weak but statistically significant relationship between the PROs' rating of the hospitals and the risk-adjusted mortality rates. These findings were even more striking for groups of hospitals with similar characteristics (e.g., teaching status, size, urban location) (Hartz et al. 1993).

Thomas and colleagues (1993) studied the relationship between risk-adjusted hospital mortality rates for selected cardiac disease (ischemic heart disease, coronary artery disease, angina, and left ventricular aneurysm), AMI, and sepsis and PRO quality ratings. They found a strong relationship between risk-adjusted mortality and quality in cardiac disease, a weak relationship in AMI, and no relationship in sepsis (Thomas et al. 1993). In addition, Thomas (1996) looked at the relationship of quality, as determined by PRO record reviews and risk-adjusted hospital rates of readmission within four time windows. He studied 12 conditions, using the PMCs and Medicare discharge abstract data for Michigan hospitals for risk adjustment. Thomas found little relationship between readmission rates and quality of care.

In the National VA Surgical Risk Study, attributional validity was assessed in two ways. A sample of charts from surgical services with higher- and lower-than-expected mortality and complication rates were reviewed by panels of surgical subspecialists using a structured implicit review instrument modeled after that used by the RAND investigators (Kahn et al. 1992). In addition, because many structural and process of care attributes of surgical practice within institutions cannot be evaluated through chart reviews, we visited 20 outlier institutions: Ten surgical services with the highest risk-adjusted mortality or complication rates, and ten surgical services with the lowest mortality or complication rates. Site visit teams consisted of a chief of surgery, a surgical ICU nurse specialist, and a study investigator, and they spent two days observing and interviewing staff at each surgical service. The site visit teams focused on the technology, equipment, and physical structure of the service; the technical competence of the surgery, anesthesiology, nursing, and house staff; the relationship with the affiliated university teaching programs; the relationships with all other patient care services in the hospital (e.g., internal medicine, radiology, laboratory); quality monitoring and improvement activities on the surgical service; communication and coordination among surgery, nursing, and anesthesia; and leadership in surgery and the institution. The site visitors identified significant differences between the high and low outliers in several dimensions. The surgical services with better-than-expected outcomes were more likely to have better technology and equipment (e.g., more up-to-date anesthesia equipment and monitoring equipment in the surgical ICU). Communication and coordination practices in the low outlier institutions were more likely to include standardized approaches to routine patient care, such as practice guidelines or clinical pathways for routine operations. The site visitors, who were unaware of the outlier status of the surgical services at the time of the site visits, rated the overall quality of care higher among the ten low outlier surgical services than among the ten high outlier services.

Other similar and related studies to explore the relationship of processes and effectiveness of care and risk-adjusted outcomes will undoubtedly appear as the field of outcomes research matures. Assessing attributional validity will require both careful methodology and cautious interpretation of the results to avoid drawing invalid or inappropriately generalized results. For example, one should be cautious about drawing conclusions about the attributional validity of the models described above in cardiac surgery to other surgical practices or to medical patients. Similarly, the attributional validity of a risk-adjustment method for one outcome, such as mortality, may not apply to other studies using the same risk-adjustment approach for assessing different outcomes, such as functional status or satisfaction with care.

References

Bastos, P. G., X. Sun, D. P. Wagner, A. W. Wu, and W. A. Knaus. 1993. "Glasgow Coma Scale Score in the Evaluation of Outcome in the Intensive Care Unit: Findings from the Acute Physiology and Chronic Health Evaluation III Study." *Critical Care Medicine* 21 (10): 1459–65.

Berger, M. M., A. Marazzi, J. Freeman, and R. Chiolero. 1992. "Evaluation of the Consistency of Acute Physiology and Chronic Health Evaluation (APACHE II) Scoring in a Surgical Intensive Care Unit." *Critical Care Medicine* 20 (12): 1681–87.

Brannen, A. L., II, L. J. Godfrey, and W. E. Goetter. 1989. "Prediction of Outcome from Critical Illness. A Comparison of Clinical Judgment With a Prediction Rule." *Archives of Internal Medicine* 149 (5): 1083–86.

Chang, R. W. 1989. "Individual Outcome Prediction Models for Intensive Care Units." *Lancet* 2 (8655): 143–46.

Chen, F. G., K. F. Koh, and M. H. Goh. 1993. "Validation of APACHE II Score in a Surgical Intensive Care Unit." *Singapore Medical Journal* 34 (4): 322–24.

Daley, J., S. Jencks, D. Draper, G. Lenhart, N. Thomas, and J. Walker. 1988. "Predicting Hospital-Associated Mortality for Medicare Patients. A Method for Patients with Stroke, Pneumonia, Acute Myocardial Infarction, and Congestive Heart Failure." *Journal of the American Medical Association* 260 (24): 3617–24.

Donabedian, A. 1980. *Explorations in Quality Assessment and Monitoring. Volume 1. The Definition of Quality and Approaches to Its Assessment.* Ann Arbor, MI: Health Administration Press.

Dubois, R. W., and R. H. Brook. 1988. "Preventable Deaths: Who, How Often, and Why?" *Annals of Internal Medicine* 109 (7): 582–89.

Dubois, R. W., R. H. Brook, and W. H. Rogers. 1987. "Adjusted Hospital Death Rates. A Potential Screen For Quality of Medical Care." *American Journal of Public Health* 77 (9): 1162–66.

Dubois, R. W., W. H. Rogers, J. H. Moxley, III, D. Draper, and R. H. Brook. 1987. "Hospital Inpatient Mortality: Is It a Predictor of Quality?" *New England Journal of Medicine* 317 (26): 1674–80.

Efron, B. 1979. "Bootstrap Methods: Another Look at the Jacknife." *Annals of Statistics* 7: 1–26.

Feinstein, A. R. 1987. *Clinimetrics.* New Haven, CT: Yale University Press.

Gross, P. A., M. R. Stein, C. van Antwerpen, P. J. DeMauro, J. R. Boscamp, W. Hess, and S. Wallenstein. 1991. "Comparison of Severity of Illness Indicators in an Intensive Care Unit." *Archives of Internal Medicine* 151 (11): 2201–5.

Hannan, E. L., H. Kilburn, Jr., J. F. O'Donnell, G. Lukacik, and E. P. Shields. 1990. "Adult Open Heart Surgery in New York State. An Analysis of Risk Factors and Hospital Mortality Rates." *Journal of the American Medical Association* 264 (21): 2768–74.

Hartley, C., A. Cozens, A. D. Mendelow, and J. C. Stevenson. 1995. "The APACHE II Scoring System in Neurosurgical Patients: A Comparison with Simple Glasgow Coma Scoring." *British Journal of Neurosurgery* 9 (2): 179–87.

Hartz, A. J., M. S. Gottlieb, E. M. Kuhn, and A. A. Rimm. 1993. "The Relationship Between Adjusted Hospital Mortality and the Results of Peer Review." *HSR: Health Services Research* 27 (6): 765–77.

Headley, J., R. Theriault, and T. L. Smith. 1992. "Independent Validation of APACHE II Severity of Illness Score for Predicting Mortality in Patients with Breast Cancer Admitted to the Intensive Care Unit." *Cancer* 70 (2): 497–503.

Hornbrook, M. C., and M. J. Goodman. 1995. "Assessing Relative Health Plan Risk with the RAND-36 Health Survey." *Inquiry* 32 (1): 56–74.

Iezzoni, L. I. 1991. " 'Black Box' Medical Information Systems. A Technology Needing Assessment." *Journal of the American Medical Association* 265 (22): 3006–7.

Iezzoni, L. I., M. A. Moskowitz, and A. S. Ash. 1988. *The Ability of MedisGroups and*

Its Clinical Variables to Predict Cost and In-Hospital Death. Boston, MA: Health Care Research Unit, Section of Internal Medicine, Boston University Medical Center.

Iezzoni, L. I., A. S. Ash, G. A. Coffman, and M. A. Moskowitz. 1992. "Predicting In-Hospital Mortality. A Comparison of Severity Measurement Approaches." *Medical Care* 30 (4): 347–59.

Iezzoni, L. I., A. S. Ash, M. Shwartz, J. Daley, J. S. Hughes, and Y. D. Mackiernan. 1995a. "Predicting Who Dies Depends on How Severity Is Measured: Implications for Evaluating Patient Outcomes." *Annals of Internal Medicine* 123 (10): 763–70.

Iezzoni, L. I., M. Shwartz, A. S. Ash, J. S. Hughes, J. Daley, and Y. D. Mackiernan. 1995b. "Using Severity-adjusted Stroke Mortality Rates to Judge Hospitals." *International Journal for Quality in Health Care* 7 (2): 81–94.

Iezzoni, L. I., M. Shwartz, A. S. Ash, J. S. Hughes, J. Daley, Y. D. Mackiernan, and D. Stone. 1995c. *Evaluating Severity Adjustors for Patient Outcome Studies. Final Report.* Prepared for the Agency for Health Care Policy and Research under grant no. RO1-HS06742. Boston, MA: Beth Israel Hospital.

Iezzoni, L. I., A. S. Ash, M. Shwartz, J. Daley, J. S. Hughes, and Y. D. Mackiernan. 1996a. "Judging Hospitals by Severity-Adjusted Mortality Rates: The Influence of the Severity-Adjustment Method." *American Journal of Public Health* 86 (10): 1379–87.

Iezzoni, L. I., M. Shwartz, A. S. Ash, and Y. D. Mackiernan. 1996b. "Using Severity Measures to Predict the Likelihood of Death for Pneumonia Inpatients." *Journal of General Internal Medicine* 11 (1): 23–31.

Iezzoni, L. I., M. Shwartz, A. S. Ash, J. S. Hughes, J. Daley, and Y. D. Mackiernan. 1996c. "Severity Measurement Methods and Judging Hospital Death Rates for Pneumonia." *Medical Care* 34 (1): 11–28.

Iezzoni, L. I., M. Shwartz, A. S. Ash, and Y. D. Mackiernan. 1996d. "Predicting In-Hospital Mortality for Stroke Patients: Results Differ Across Severity–measurement Systems." *Medical Decision Making* 16 (4): 348–56.

Kahn, K. L., D. Draper, E. B. Keeler, W. H. Rogers, L. V. Rubenstein, J. Kosecoff, M. J. Sherwood, E. J. Reinisch, M. F. Carney, C. J. Kamberg, S. S. Bentow, K. B. Wells, H. Allen, D. Reboussin, C. P. Roth, C. Chew, and R. H. Brook. 1992. *The Effects of the DRG-Based Prospective Payment System on Quality of Care for Hospitalized Medicare Payments.* Publication no. R-3931-HCFA. Santa Monica, CA: RAND.

Kasper, J. F., S. K. Plume, and G. T. O'Connor. 1992. "A Methodology for QI in the Coronary Artery Bypass Grafting Procedure Involving Comparative Process Analysis." *Quality Review Bulletin* 18 (4): 129–33.

Keeler, E. B., K. L. Kahn, D. Draper, M. J. Sherwood, L. V. Rubenstein, E. J. Reinisch, J. Kosecoff, and R. H. Brook. 1990. "Changes in Sickness at Admission Following the Introduction of the Prospective Payment System." *Journal of the American Medical Association* 264 (15): 1962–68.

Keeler, E. B., L. V. Rubenstein, K. L. Kahn, D. Draper, E. R. Harrison, M. J. McGinty, W. H. Rogers, and R. H. Brook. 1992. "Hospital Characteristics and Quality of Care." *Journal of the American Medical Association* 268 (13): 1709–14.

Knaus, W. A., E. A. Draper, D. P. Wagner, and J. E. Zimmerman. 1985. "APACHE II: A Severity of Disease Classification System." *Critical Care Medicine* 13 (10): 818–29.

Knaus, W. A., D. P. Wagner, E. A. Draper, J. E. Zimmerman, M. Bergner, P. G. Bastos, C. A. Sirio, D. J. Murphy, T. Lotring, A. Damiano, and F. E. Harrell, Jr. 1991. "The APACHE III Prognostic System: Risk Prediction of Hospital Mortality for Critically Ill Hospitalized Adults." *Chest* 100 (6): 1619–36.

Knaus, W. A., F. E. Harrell, Jr., J. Lynn, L. Goldman, R. S. Phillips, A. F. Connors, Jr., N. V. Dawson, W. J. Fulkerson, Jr., R. M. Califf, N. Desbiens, P. Layde, R. K. Oye, P. E. Bellamy, R. B. Hakim, and D. P. Wagner. 1995. "The SUPPORT Prognostic Model: Objective Estimates of Survival for Seriously Ill Hospitalized Adults." *Annals of Internal Medicine* 122 (3): 191–203.

Kruse, J. A., M. C. Thill-Baharozian, and R. W. Carlson. 1988. "Comparison of Clinical Assessment with APACHE II for Predicting Mortality Risk in Patients Admitted to a Medical Intensive Care Unit." *Journal of the American Medical Association* 260 (12): 1739–42.

Landon, B., L. I. Iezzoni, A. S. Ash, M. Shwartz, J. Daley, J. S. Hughes, and Y. D. Mackiernan. 1996. "Judging Hospitals by Severity-adjusted Mortality Rates: The Case of CABG Surgery." *Inquiry* 33 (2): 155–66.

Ludwigs, U., and J. Hulting. 1995. "Acute Physiology and Chronic Health Evaluation II Scoring System in Acute Myocardial Infarction: A Prospective Validation Study." *Critical Care Medicine* 23 (5): 854–59.

Meyer, A. A., W. J. Messick, P. Young, C. C. Baker, S. Fakhry, F. Muakkassa, E. J. Rutherford, L. M. Napolitano, and R. Rutledge. 1992. "Prospective Comparison of Clinical Judgment and APACHE II Score in Predicting the Outcome in Critically Ill Surgical Patients." *Journal of Trauma* 32 (6): 747–53.

Moreau, R., T. Soupison, P. Vauquelin, S. Derrida, H. Beaucour, and C. Sicot. 1989. "Comparison of Two Simplified Severity Scores (SAPS and APACHE II) for Patients with Acute Myocardial Infarction." *Critical Care Medicine* 17 (5): 409–13.

Naessens, J. M., C. L. Leibson, I. Krishan, and D. J. Ballard. 1992. "Contribution of a Measure of Disease Complexity (COMPLEX) to Prediction of Outcome and Charges among Hospitalized Patients." *Mayo Clinic Proceedings,* 67 (12): 1140–49.

Neter, J., W. Wasserman, and M. H. Kutner. 1990. *Applied Linear Statistical Models: Regression, Analysis of Variance, and Experimental Design.* 3rd ed. Homewood, IL: Richard D. Irwin.

O'Connor, G. T., S. K. Plume, E. M. Olmstead, L. H. Coffin, J. R. Morton, C. T. Maloney, E. R. Nowicki, J. F. Tryzelaar, F. Hernandez, L. Adrian, K. J. Casey, D. N. Soule, C. A. S. Marrin, W. C. Nugent, D. C. Charlesworth, R. Clough, S. Katz, B. J. Leavitt, and J. E. Wennberg for the Northern New England Cardiovascular Disease Study Group. 1991. "A Regional Prospective Study of In-Hospital Mortality Associated with Coronary Artery Bypass Grafting." *Journal of the American Medical Association* 266 (6): 803–9.

O'Connor, G. T., S. K. Plume, E. M. Olmstead, L. H. Coffin, J. R. Morton, C. T. Maloney, E. R. Nowicki, D. G. Levy, J. F. Tryzelaar, F. Hernandez, L. Adrian, K. J.

Casey, D. Bundy, D. N. Soule, C. A. S. Marrin, W. C. Nugent, D. C. Charlesworth, R. Clough, S. Katz, B. J. Leavitt, and J. E. Wennberg for the Northern New England Cardiovascular Disease Study Group. 1992. "Multivariate Prediction of In-Hospital Mortality Associated with Coronary Artery Bypass Graft Surgery." *Circulation* 85 (6): 2110–18.

O'Connor, G. T., S. K. Plume, E. M. Olmstead, J. R. Morton, C. T. Maloney, W. C. Nugent, F. Hernandez, Jr., R. Clough, B. J. Leavitt, L. H. Coffin, C. A. S. Marrin, D. Wennberg, J. D. Birkmeyer, D. C. Charlesworth, D. J. Malenka, H. B. Quinton, and J. F. Kasper for the Northern New England Cardiovascular Disease Study Group. 1996. "A Regional Intervention to Improve the Hospital Mortality Associated with Coronary Artery Bypass Graft Surgery." *Journal of the American Medical Association* 275 (11): 841–46.

Porath, A., N. Eldar, I. Harman-Bohem, and G. Gurman. 1994. "Evaluation of the APACHE II Scoring System in an Israeli Intensive Care Unit. *Israel Journal of Medical Sciences* 30 (7): 514–20.

Rocca, B., C. Martin, X. Viviand, P. F. Bidet, H. L. Saint-Gilles, and A. Chevalier. 1989. "Comparison of Four Severity Scores in Patients with Head Trauma." *Journal of Trauma* 29 (3): 299–305.

Rodrigues, C. J., and V. R. Joshi. 1991. "Predicting the Immediate Outcome of Patients with Cerebrovascular Accident. A Prognostic Score." *Journal of the Association of Physicians of India* 39 (2): 175–80.

Rowan, K. M., J. H. Kerr, E. Major, K. McPherson, A. Short, and M. P. Vessey. 1993. "Intensive Care Society's APACHE II Study in Britain and Ireland—II: Outcome Comparisons of Intensive Care Units After Adjustment for Case Mix by the American APACHE II Method." *British Medical Journal* 307 (6910): 977–81.

———. 1994. "Intensive Care Society's Acute Physiology and Chronic Health Evaluation (APACHE II) study in Britain and Ireland: A Prospective, Multicenter, Cohort Study Comparing Two Methods for Predicting Outcome for Adult Intensive Care Patients." *Critical Care Medicine* 22 (9): 1392–1401.

Rutledge, R., S. Fakhry, E. Rutherford, F. Muakkassa, and A. Meyer. 1993. "Comparison of APACHE II, Trauma Score, and Injury Severity Score as Predictors of Outcome in Critically Injured Trauma Patients." *American Journal of Surgery* 166 (3): 244–47.

Selker, H. P. 1993. "Systems for Comparing Actual and Predicted Mortality Rates: Characteristics to Promote Cooperation in Improving Hospital Care." *Annals of Internal Medicine* 118 (10): 820–22.

Selker, H. P., J. L. Griffith, and R. B. D'Agostino. 1991. "A Time-Insensitive Predictive Instrument for Acute Myocardial Infarction Mortality: A Multicenter Study." *Medical Care* 29 (12): 1196–1211.

Smith, D. W., M. Pine, R. C. Bailey, B. Jones, A. Brewster, and H. Krakauer. 1991. "Using Clinical Variables to Estimate the Risk of Patient Mortality." *Medical Care* 29 (11): 1108–29.

Stewart, A. L., R. D. Hays, and J. E. Ware, Jr. 1992. "Methods of Validating MOS Health Measures." In *Measuring Functioning and Well-Being. The Medical Outcomes Study Approach*, edited by A. L. Stewart and J. E. Ware, Jr., Durham, NC: Duke University Press.

Teskey, R. J., J. E. Calvin, and I. McPhail. 1991. "Disease Severity in the Coronary Care Unit." *Chest* 100 (6): 1637–42.

Thomas, J. W. 1996. "Does Risk-Adjusted Readmission Rate Provide Valid Information on Hospital Quality?" *Inquiry* 33 (3): 258–70.

Thomas, J. W., and M. L. F. Ashcraft. 1991. "Measuring Severity of Illness: Six Severity Systems and Their Ability to Explain Cost Variations." *Inquiry* 28 (1): 39–55.

Thomas, J. W., J. J. Holloway, and K. E. Guire. 1993. "Validating Risk-Adjusted Mortality as an Indicator for Quality of Care." *Inquiry* 30 (1): 6–22.

Tuhrim, S., J. M. Dambrosia, T. R. Price, J. P. Mohr, P. A. Wolf, D. B. Hier, and C. S. Kase. 1991. "Intracerebral Hemorrhage: External Validation and Extension of a Model for Prediction of 30-Day Survival." *Annals of Neurology* 29 (6): 658–63.

Vassar, M. J., C. L. Wilkerson, P. J. Duram, C. A. Perry, and J. W. Holcroft. 1992. "Comparison of APACHE II, TRISS, and a Proposed 24-hour ICU Point System for Prediction of Outcome in ICU Trauma Patients. *Journal of Trauma* 32 (4): 490–500.

Vassar, M. J., and J. W. Holcroft. 1994. "The Case Against Using the APACHE System to Predict Intensive Care Unit Outcome in Trauma Patients." *Critical Care Clinics* 10 (1): 117–26.

Wagner, D. P., W. A. Knaus, and E. A. Draper. 1986. "Physiologic Abnormalities and Outcome from Acute Disease: Evidence for a Predictable Relationship." *Archives of Internal Medicine* 146 (7): 1389–96.

Wong, D. T., S. L. Crofts, M. Gomez, G. P. McGuire, and R. J. Byrick. 1995. "Evaluation of Predictive Ability of APACHE II System and Hospital Outcome in Canadian Intensive Care Unit Patients." *Critical Care Medicine* 23 (7): 1177–83.

Chapter 7

Reliability of Risk-Adjustment Methods

John S. Hughes and Arlene S. Ash

One important indicator of the quality of a scientific measure is its ability to yield consistent, reproducible results. Statisticians call this characteristic "precision," while psychologists, social scientists, and health services researchers know it as "reliability." Both terms address this basic question: If a process were repeated—possibly by someone else—following identical rules, would the same results occur?

Consistency and reproducibility assume special significance in examining risk-adjustment measures. Ordinarily, the worth of a scientific analysis is primarily determined by its accuracy, or how closely its results represent biological or scientific "truth." For risk adjustment, however, no "gold standard" measure of true risk exists (see Chapter 6).

> The crucial quality of scientific data is not accuracy, but reproducibility. There is no such thing as absolute accuracy, any more than there is an absolute vacuum, an absolute number of chemical elements, an absolute limit to the size of particles into which matter can be finely divided, or absolute truth. (Feinstein 1967, 345)

> No matter how the observations are made and described, the data will have scientific quality if the results of the observational process can be consistently reproduced by the same or another observer. (Feinstein 1987, 170)

Risk-adjustment methods can be reapplied by the same observer or rater (as a test of intrarater reliability) or by different raters (interrater reliability). Agreement among different raters is a more rigorous test and is generally the approach used for reliability analyses.

This chapter explores reliability as it pertains to risk adjustment. We consider why risk-adjustment measures may be unreliable, suggest conceptual considerations in assessing reliability, and introduce specific methods for quantifying reliability. As in other chapters, our goal is not to provide a comprehensive review of technical considerations in assessing reliability.

Implications of the Data Source for Reliability

As shown in Table 1.6, risk-adjustment methods fall into two major types, depending on their data source: those applied to large adminis-trative databases using computerized algorithms (code-based measures); and those requiring collection of information, generally retrospectively and manually, from medical records (chart-based measures). These two data sources pose different implications for the strategies used to assess reliability.

Administrative data are derived from what is documented in the medical record. As described in Chapter 3, chart abstractors rely on clin-ician notations to code diagnoses and procedures. Therefore, code-based measures ultimately depend on the contents of medical records. However, ratings from code-based measures remain the same when the computer-ized scoring algorithm is applied repeatedly to the same administrative data set. Therefore, the real focus of reliability questions for code-based measures involves how accurately and completely the coded information from the medical record was gathered—that is, how well diagnosis and procedure codes were assigned. Unfortunately, logistical constraints usu-ally prevent reliability testing for most studies involving administrative data. Returning to medical records to determine whether reabstractions would yield identical results is generally infeasible. The reliability of code-based risk adjustors is thus not tested directly but only inferred from reports of other investigations addressing coding accuracy, typically in different administrative databases. As detailed in Chapter 3, the accuracy of data contained in administrative files for both inpatient and outpatient care is often questionable (Institute of Medicine 1977; Hsia et al. 1988; Fisher et al. 1992; Fowles et al. 1995; Wilson, Smoley, and Werdegar 1996). This imperfect approach to reliability measurement is a concession to the realities and costs of data collection.

For chart-based risk-adjustment approaches, reliability considera-tions are somewhat different. The number of data elements required is gen-erally larger, data collection and handling processes are more complicated, and both persons and protocols involved in abstraction and rating are more diverse than for code-based measures. However, although more individual data items are often required, the elements can frequently be identified more readily and with less subjective interpretation than diagnosis codes (e.g., laboratory test values). The greater complexity therefore does not necessarily translate into greater unreliability. A practical advantage for assessing reliability of chart-based measures is that the original medical records are frequently accessible for re-review (e.g., as in studies using photocopied records).

Sources of Variation

A range of factors contribute to the reliability of a risk-adjustment measure. Variability may be inherent within the underlying data elements, such as laboratory tests or self-reported functional status (see Chapter 4), it may be intrinsic to performing the risk-adjustment itself, or it may result from those applying the method. Feinstein (1987) observed that no standard nomenclature exists for these three sources of variation; he called them "input variability," "procedure variability," and "user variability." Various aspects of each are explored below, recognizing that the boundaries among them may blur.

Input Variability

In evaluating a biological variable—serum cortisol, for example—repeated samples from an individual vary throughout the day, due to diurnal variation, among other factors. Requiring that samples be taken at a specific time of day could reduce the effect of diurnal variation. Similarly, repeated assessments of a demented person using an index of mental function (e.g., the Folstein mini-mental status test) may yield different scores from day to day. These differences can occur due to the person's mood, use of sedating medications, or adequacy of sleep the night before the test. These two examples illustrate variation in the entity under evaluation, or "substrate."

For a risk-adjustment methodology, the analogous entity under evaluation is the medical record. Therefore, input variability of chart-based measures pertains largely to the reproducibility of information in the medical record. Although medical records, once created, should not change, several sources contribute to variability during its creation, including the setting and type of organization generating the record (e.g., tertiary teaching hospital, individual physician office), organizational documentation practices, the management of information at the organization, the structure and size of the medical record, and the types of illness under consideration. The next sections examine these contributions to input variability.

Setting of care and documentation patterns

As suggested in Chapters 3 and 4, different organizations devote varying levels of resources to diagnosis and procedure coding and medical record documentation. Variability is especially marked across ambulatory care settings: Solo practitioners with minimal administrative support may use very different coding procedures than those at large, multispecialty clinics. These factors affect the reliability of risk adjustment because they influence both the quantity and quality of the data. They can also potentially bias assessments of risk across different institutions or providers.

An important example involves comparing patients at teaching and nonteaching hospitals. As described in Chapter 4, one study found anecdotal evidence of important differences in documentation patterns across these two institutional types (Iezzoni et al. 1989, 1990). Physician notes at nonteaching hospitals generally focused exclusively on the acute presenting illness with sketchy information on chronic comorbidities. In contrast, copious physicians' notes at teaching hospitals documented both acute and chronic conditions. Reliably abstracting comparable information on chronic illnesses across these two hospital types is thus complicated by differences in documentation styles.

Teaching and nonteaching hospitals also differ in the quantity of documentation. As discussed in Chapter 4, several tiers of physicians document records at teaching hospitals, while single physicians generally document records at nonteaching facilities. Trainees tend to leave voluminous notes, and often multiple levels of trainees (ranging from interns to specialty fellows) all contribute to patients' records, in addition to various attending physicians—from the primary care doctor to specialist consultants. When different clinicians document patients' records, inconsistencies commonly arise among their assessments of patients, a factor that compromises data abstraction reliability.

The sheer volume of many medical records, especially at tertiary teaching hospitals, can undermine the reliability of data abstraction. This was particularly apparent during a study in which research nurses employed by the investigators used the MedisGroups data abstraction protocol to review medical records at tertiary teaching hospitals (Iezzoni et al. 1992b). Patients with complicated conditions underwent numerous tests and procedures and thus had lengthy records. Frequently, one reviewer or another would miss a particular notation or laboratory report in these voluminous records. In addition, the handling of inconsistencies in notations among the same tier of clinicians (e.g., variability among specialist consultants) was itself inconsistent. Largely because of these factors, the research nurses never met the designated MedisGroups data collection target of 95 percent accuracy.

Coding

Problems with the reliability of ICD-9-CM coding deserve particular mention (see Chapter 3). The appropriate diagnosis code may not be clear, even to the attending clinician. As an example, consider a patient with decompensation of chronic lung disease. ICD-9-CM codes might legitimately reflect chronic obstructive lung disease (491.2), chronic bronchitis (491.9), emphysema (492.8), acute bronchitis (466.0), or even respiratory failure (799.1). Other conditions have more straightforward diagnostic labels (e.g., acute appendicitis, hip fracture); coding of these types of conditions would therefore be more consistent and thus reliable.

As described in Chapter 3, for hospital payment, the list of discharge diagnoses typically must be sequenced, or ordered, to differentiate the principal from secondary diagnoses. This order considerably affects not only payment based on DRGs, but also results using other code-based risk adjustors. The correct ordering of diagnosis codes is not always obvious to clinicians caring for the patient, and it is even less apparent to the chart abstractor. For example, if a patient is admitted for postobstructive pneumonia relating to lung cancer, which is the principal diagnosis, pneumonia or lung cancer? What about sequencing of diagnoses for a patient admitted with both sepsis and respiratory failure?

In the outpatient setting, coding is even more variable. Documentation and coding procedures vary widely across settings, such as private physicians' offices, managed care groups, large multispecialty clinics, and hospital-based clinics where residents provide care under attending physician supervision. The process for assigning diagnosis codes for outpatient visits is highly variable. Patients often have several chronic conditions, which individually and in combination influence their outcomes. Although several of these problems might be addressed during an office visit, only one diagnosis is usually coded, because only one is required for billing. Little incentive thus exists to submit more diagnoses because generally no additional payment is generated.

How physicians decide what to code for outpatients is unclear. Anecdotal evidence suggests that the choice depends heavily on codes physicians have memorized and use commonly. For example, most primary care physicians see innumerable patients with urinary tract infections and therefore have memorized its ICD-9-CM code—599.0. In addition, many offices and clinics list common diagnoses and their codes on the back of the visit ticket (the form that initiates the billing process). Physicians tick off a diagnosis from this list and rarely add other, less common conditions. Whether this choice is reliable is unclear. As outpatient appointment times increasingly shorten under current economic pressures, physicians have less time for administrative tasks, such as assigning multiple diagnosis codes to individual outpatient visits.

Information management

The modern hospital chart can be voluminous, accumulating information from numerous departments throughout the institution (e.g., radiology, laboratories, pathology). Strategies for managing massive quantities of data vary widely across hospitals, with a substantial effect on reliability. As described in Chapter 4, the structure and content of the medical record can promote or hinder the consistency of information gathered from the record. Handwritten free text (e.g., notes from providers) is common, as well as handwritten graphic displays (e.g., vital signs charting) and reports on standardized forms (e.g., intraoperative anesthesia records, medication and physician order sheets). Typically, only laboratory and other official test reports and discharge and other procedure summaries are typed. While most hospitals are moving toward computerization and electronic transmission of printed documents containing numerical information and test results, some hospitals still rely on individual laboratory test slips containing handwritten reports. In some institutions, timeliness is particularly worrisome, with procedure reports wending slowly and sporadically to the medical record. Although this problem generally lessens in hospitals with computerized laboratory and reporting systems, it raises yet another nonrandom consideration in comparing reliability across institutions.

For physical findings (e.g., the presence of pulmonary rales or an S3 gallop heart sound), reliability is compromised by needing to interpret physicians' handwriting, compounding the problem of dealing with inconsistencies among multiple contributors to the chart. Legibility and other concerns about medical record organization and completeness are magnified when chart abstractions are performed outside the hospital using photocopied medical records. Thomas and Ashcraft (1989, 487), for example, found that 40 percent of the 431 charts they reviewed in a study of reliability could not be abstracted for MedisGroups, which requires detailed information from physicians' notes. Photocopying made key elements in the clinical record unreadable.

Outpatient records, especially for primary care doctors, raise additional concerns. Testing, such as radiological studies, is often performed outside of the doctor's office; therefore, test reports must travel from other sites before reaching the chart. If an outpatient sees a specialist in consultation, reports from that visit must also be generated in and arrive from another office. Keeping track of all the disparate pieces of information about an individual patient (e.g., what document has arrived, what is still missing) is a daunting task.

Type of illness

The type of illness or reason for the healthcare encounter considerably affects the documentation generated, and hence affects the data abstraction reliability. For example, outpatient clinic records for travel immunization are much easier to abstract reliably than records from patients admitted for open-heart surgery.

Physicians are often inconsistent in their diagnostic terminology (see Chapter 4). They also vary widely in their diligence in recording patients' coexisting or comorbid conditions, particularly if the hospital course was especially complicated or if the coexisting conditions were not a major focus of the hospitalization. Furthermore, many risk-adjustment methods, even for extremely complicated hospitalizations, require identification of one principal diagnosis as the first and most important classification step. As suggested above, physicians' notes may not clarify which of several clinical problems addressed during the hospitalization should be given paramount importance. Such uncertainty is compounded by the redundancy, ambiguity, and uncertainty built into ICD-9-CM (see Chapter 3).

In the outpatient setting, a note for an individual visit may pertain only to the presenting problem. Especially if the patient is well known to the physician, the doctor may not document fully at each visit all the patients' problems. Well-child visits or routine adult check-ups will generate very different documentation than visits for outpatient chemotherapy. Specialized outpatient settings, such as chemotherapy or dialysis units, may have a fairly standard battery of items they document. Electronic outpatient medical records often provide space for a "problem list" that documents all relevant health conditions and is updated over time.

Variability of diagnostic and therapeutic actions

Variability also results from differences in *what happened* during an encounter (e.g., a hospitalization or outpatient visit), not just from the differences in *documenting* what happened. For example, just as some hospitals document charts and code more aggressively than others, some hospitals diagnose and treat more aggressively than others. A patient with a moderately severe pneumonia may be admitted at one hospital and sent home at another. A patient with an asthma attack may have several arterial blood gas analyses obtained at one hospital but none at another. The effect of such inconsistencies in the choice of actions, rather than the documentation of actions, cannot be resolved by risk-adjustment methodologies.

Systematic differences in patterns of missing data for patients treated for the same condition in different settings is a serious problem (see Chapter 5). This difficulty argues against including certain data items (especially those derived from procedures or pharmaceutical use) in the risk measure, even if they are helpful in pinpointing risk. For example, depending on the context, it may be inappropriate to include evidence determined from a test (e.g., magnetic resonance imaging of the brain in stroke) that may be performed routinely in some hospitals but not in others. Similarly, one should be cautious about using items with highly variable documentation, such as functional status measures.

Procedure Variability

The analogy to Feinstein's procedure variability arises in applying risk-adjustment methodologies to the medical record. It relates both to extracting information from charts and to applying the formula or algorithm that generates the risk score. Procedure variability arises *after* creation of the medical record; input variability arises *during* the creation of the medical record. The following sections describe several components of procedure variability.

Inherent unreliability of data elements

As suggested in Chapters 3 and 4, some data elements are inherently less reliable than others. Although this source of unreliability can be lessened by sufficient diligence by well-trained and closely monitored data abstracters, it can never be eliminated. In a hierarchy of reproducibility, demographic data (e.g., age, gender, zip code) and administrative information (e.g., patients' discharge status, alive or dead) are the most reliably recorded. Perhaps next in order of reliability are laboratory data, particularly those that are computer generated and reported. Further behind come abstracted diagnosis codes. The identification of procedures is more reliable—questions rarely arise about whether the procedure was done. As suggested above, sequencing is even less reproducible than the codes themselves. The greatest inconsistency occurs among data elements that must be extracted from doctors' and nurses' (often handwritten) clinical notes.

Variability of the rating mechanism: Replicability

"Replicability" refers to whether other users can follow abstraction and rating procedures as readily as the original developers of a risk-adjustment method. Consistency is lessened if procedures are poorly understood and if instructions and criteria are vague, ambiguous, or incomplete. Replicability also suffers when risk-adjustment methods move from a research and development setting into the real world, such as a peer review organization or third party payor. An example of poor replicability occurred when Schumacher and colleagues (1987) evaluated the reliability of the Severity of Illness Index, or SOII (Horn, Horn, and Sharkey 1984; Horn et al. 1985a, 1985b; Horn, Horn, and Moses 1986; Horn et al. 1986), which is no longer widely used. The creators of the SOII reported excellent interrater agreement (Horn et al. 1985a, 1985b; Horn and Horn 1986). Similarly, the chart abstractors in Schumacher's study achieved excellent agreement during SOII training sessions. However, their reliability fell dramatically once active chart abstraction began. Only seven of the 13 rater pairs reached a minimally acceptable kappa score of 0.4 or greater.

Fragility

"Fragility" reflects how susceptible the risk score is to a few influential data elements. A measure is fragile if one or two isolated or idiosyncratic findings, particularly those that are unreliably detected, dramatically alter the risk score.

Evaluating fragility of a code-based measure involves examining how ratings of risk change following modifications in the choice and ordering of diagnosis codes. In part of a larger study evaluating the performance of risk-adjustment measures, Thomas and Ashcraft (1989) compared the reliability of three code-based approaches—DRGs, PMCs, and the Disease Staging Q-Scale—by reabstracting hospital charts. They found substantially higher reliability scores for DRGs than for PMCs or Disease Staging. Thomas and Ashcraft attributed this finding to the frequent dependence of risk category assignments for PMCs and Disease Staging on a single diagnosis code. Thus, a single inconsistency in diagnosis coding could significantly effect the risk assignment. In contrast, DRGs were much less susceptible to coding variation because any one of a number of similar (and sometimes not-so-similar) diagnoses often yielded the same assignment. DRGs were, in effect, more forgiving, less fragile, and therefore more reliable.

Chart-based methods face similar concerns about fragility of their rating mechanisms. Although many opportunities for inconsistency occur in collecting data elements, this is less important than the effect of those inconsistencies on the final risk score. Concerns about fragility contributed to a decision by the developers of the CSI to require two or more clinical criteria to be met at a severity level before the patient would be assigned to that level (Horn et al. 1991; Iezzoni and Daley 1992). For example, as shown in Exhibit 2.1A, for pneumonia patients, an oral temperature $\geq 104.0°$ F is assigned to severity level 4. Two temperature readings of this magnitude must be present for this level 4 criterion to be met. Because of this requirement, a single deranged value that may be a measurement error cannot dictate the severity score.

Other issues in procedure variability

Certain types of abstraction strategies are more inconsistent than others. APACHE is based on the most deranged physiologic values from the first

24 hours of ICU admission (Knaus et al. 1985, 1991). ICU patients are typically tested frequently, especially during their initial care; therefore, a single patient could have multiple tests within the first 24 hours. Determining which values are the most deranged is itself complicated, requiring well-trained reviewers. The challenges of reliably collecting this information increase if reviewers must sift through individual, handwritten laboratory slips.

Certain risk measures depend heavily on raters' subjective interpretations of clinical information. The chart-based manual version of the SOII (Horn, Horn, and Sharkey 1984; Horn et al. 1985a, 1985b; Horn and Horn 1986; Horn, Horn, and Moses 1986; Horn et al. 1986) relied largely on subjective judgments. The SOII scored patients on a four-point scale, independent of diagnosis. It required review of the medical record to rate the patient along seven dimensions:

1. stage of principal diagnosis at admission;
2. complications of the principal diagnosis;
3. interactions with comorbidities;
4. patient dependency on intensive services;
5. nonoperating room procedures (particularly the use of life-support services);
6. rate of response to therapy; and
7. residual symptoms at discharge.

Reviewers implicitly generated ratings on these seven dimensions after scanning the entire record and then subjectively integrated them to produce an overall score. This subjectivity of the SOII chart review process worried critics. Schumacher and colleagues (1987) partially attributed the poor reliability of SOII to the number of subjective judgments required.

User Variability

Chart abstractors bring their own variability to the process. Their individual performance is influenced by various factors, including who employs them, how they perceive their role, what motivates them, how they were trained, how they are monitored, how much time pressure they feel, their work environment (e.g., ventilation, lighting), the nature of their working relationships, and organizational culture.

Hospital influences

As described in Chapter 3, ICD-9-CM coders must identify and record principal and secondary diagnoses based on physicians' notations. However, many hospitals require medical record staff to review the chart in detail to optimize coding, which could add to the diagnoses a physician has listed in a discharge summary. Hospitals clearly have different coding practices (Iezzoni et al. 1992a; Wilson, Smoley, and Werdegar 1996). The aggressiveness with which hospitals pursue comprehensive coding varies, driven increasingly by fiscal considerations (extra coding effort may be rewarded by higher payment from Medicare) and concerns about external publication of report cards (see Chapters 10 and 11). Financially vulnerable facilities can afford less time per chart abstraction than more solvent institutions. Additional variation stems from the skill and diligence of individual abstractors and the quality of their training.

The influence of externally published report cards is a recent concern. Hospitals, as do individuals, want to "look good" on report cards. Somehow, hospitals may be able to transmit this concern to their coding staff and thus influence coding. For example, as described in Chapter 3, California published report cards derived from administrative data on the mortality rate of heart attack patients at individual hospitals (Wilson, Smoley, and Werdegar 1996). A reabstraction study examined the accuracy of coding of secondary diagnoses used as risk factors in the mortality prediction model. The study found that 31.5 percent of the discharge abstracts contained at least one "unsupported risk factor" (i.e., coding factors that were unjustified by the medical record documentation). Overcoding of risk factors was much more common at "low mortality" hospitals than at "intermediate" or "high mortality" hospitals, ranging from 10 percent at one high-mortality hospital to 74 percent at a low-mortality hospital. Variation in coding accuracy explained part of the differences between high- and low-mortality hospitals.

Type of rater

The training and professional background of the person reviewing the record is critically important. For diagnosis and procedure coding using ICD-9-CM, extensive training is required in specific coding guidelines promulgated by the World Health Organization, the United States government, and the American Hospital Association. Some training programs lead to registered record administrator (RRA) or accredited record technician (ART) degrees, recipients of which can staff medical record departments and can generally perform the validation of ICD-9-CM coding for external organizations.

Although routine hospital discharge coding is usually done by RRAs and ARTs, research studies and other data collection initiatives draw reviewers from a variety of other disciplines, including nursing, medicine, and persons without specific professional backgrounds who are specially trained for particular studies. The implications for reliability of data abstraction vary across disciplines, separately from the issue of specific training.

For example, in the study described above where the investigators hired their own research staff to abstract medical records with Medis-Groups (Iezzoni et al. 1992b), the background of the reviewers became an impediment to achieving the reliability target. The reviewers were registered nurses, with additional postgraduate-level training. Because of their educational backgrounds, the reviewers were uncomfortable following strict data collection protocols established by MedisGroups' developers to achieve high levels of reliability. (The guidelines often detail the specific words that must be found in the record to identify various key clinical findings.) Instead, the reviewers wanted to use their extensive knowledge to interpret findings or reflect their own clinical sense of what was important. A cultural clash was therefore inevitable between highly trained health-care providers wishing to impose their own subjective interpretations and a protocol requiring rigid adherence to detailed abstraction guidelines. While independent judgment is highly valued in clinical care, it can be a major source of inconsistency in applying a risk-adjustment measure.

Other organizational influences

Interrater comparisons among reviewers employed by a hospital and abstracting charts at that hospital should exhibit more consistency than comparisons involving reviewers from multiple sites, because of shared work habits, frequent communication and commiseration, common coding conventions and strategies, and similar familiarity with the intricacies of the hospital's medical record. However, as suggested by the California example above, bias is also possible—hospital employees may treat records from their home institution differently from records at another facility (i.e., they may not be unbiased observers of records from their own hospital).

A more rigorous test of a measure's reliability involves comparing abstractors who work for different employers. Differences in the type of organization conducting the chart review can produce systematic differences in ratings between hospital-based reviewers and nonhospital-based reviewers (e.g., insurance company or research project employees) (Lloyd and Rissing 1985). Such differences result from variations in the type and extent of training, the use of specific coding strategies, the amount of time allotted for each chart abstraction, and financial motivations.

Reliability Measurement Methods

As noted above, the reliability of a risk-adjustment method cannot be determined by comparing its results with a "gold standard." In this setting, reliability instead relates to reproducibility across two or more applications of an imperfect instrument. Reliability assessment aims to determine the amount of agreement resulting from repeated application of the instrument. Reliability does not ensure validity—whether higher measured risk actually identifies patients with higher risks (Chapter 6).

A simple approach involves measuring the percentage agreement between reviewers or raters, as in the accuracy ratings reported by the developers of MedisGroups (Brewster, Bradbury, and Jacobs 1985). As part of their training, new MedisGroups chart reviewers must match the KCFs they extract from charts with KCFs identified by their instructor (an expert MedisGroups reviewer). Agreement between the two lists must be at least 95 percent before the trainee qualifies as a MedisGroups reviewer. Reviewers are reportedly tested periodically afterwards.

Measuring percent exact agreement neglects one important possibility: Reviewers may agree simply by chance rather than due to their skill or the instrument's reliability. A more useful measurement of reliability corrects for the amount of agreement that would occur by chance. To illustrate this concern, consider a method that dichotomizes patients as "high risk" or "low risk." If one observer randomly rated 70 percent of patients as high risk, and another observer randomly rated 60 percent as high risk, then the expected agreement on the high-risk rating would be 42 percent ($0.6 \times 0.7 = 0.42$). In addition, by chance alone, the reviewers would be expected to agree on a low-risk rating 12 percent of the time ($0.3 \times 0.4 = 0.12$). Thus, the total chance agreement would equal 54 percent ($0.42 + 0.12 = 0.54$).

Cohen's Kappa

The most common measure of the reliability of instruments with categorical and ordinal scales is kappa (Cohen 1960), which can take several forms. The simplest formulation measures how much the level of agreement between two observers exceeds the amount of agreement expected by chance alone, computed as:

$$K = \frac{P_o - P_c}{1 - P_c}$$

where P_o is the observed agreement and P_c is the agreement that would have occurred by chance. In the previous example of two observers using a two-level scale, if the overall agreement rate had been 70 percent, then kappa would be

$$\frac{.70 - .54}{1 - .54} = .35.$$

How good is a kappa score of 0.35? Landis and Koch (1977) offered a performance assessment of kappa that has become a standard in the literature. According to them, the strength of agreement represented by kappa statistics is as follows: kappa < 0.0, poor agreement; kappa 0.0–0.2, slight agreement; kappa 0.21–0.4, fair agreement; kappa 0.41–0.6, moderate agreement; kappa 0.61–0.8, substantial agreement; and kappa 0.81–1.0, almost perfect agreement. Based on this Landis and Koch (1977) assessment, a kappa of 0.35 is only fair because the level of agreement was not substantially greater than agreement that would have been achieved by chance alone.

Although kappa is an improvement over percentage agreement, it is unstable when the prevalence of a problem is small. For example, suppose two raters each reviewed the same 100 cases and each found two problems. Three scenarios are possible with respect to the reliability of the assessment of problems (illustrated in Table 7.1):

- both found the same two problem cases;
- they agreed on just one of the two cases; or
- each found two different cases.

Percent exact agreement for these three scenarios is 100 percent, 98 percent, and 96 percent, respectively. Kappa is 1.00, 0.49, and −0.01, respectively. As shown in this example, a shift in one or two cases can cause the kappa to vary over the entire range of possible values.

The simple form of kappa applies when assessing agreement between two raters. With more than two raters, kappa scores for each pair of raters are computed, and these kappas are averaged.

Weighted Kappa

One weakness of the basic form of kappa is that all disagreements among raters are rated the same, regardless of the magnitude of the individual disagreements. This is not a problem when the raters are only choosing one

Table 7.1   Example of Two Raters When Prevalence of Problem Is Small

| | Rater 1 | | | | | |
| | Scenario 1 | | Scenario 2 | | Scenario 3 | |
Rater 2	No	Yes	No	Yes	No	Yes
No	98	0	97	1	96	2
Yes	0	2	1	1	2	0

of two ratings, such as the presence or absence of a diagnosis. Problems arise when the raters have three or more choices on an ordinal scale, such as a rating of edema (or swelling) that ranges from "one plus" (1+) to "four plus" (4+). The basic formulation of kappa can still be used in this situation, but it could obscure important differences in reliability. For example, suppose there are two ordinal scales, each yielding possible scores from 1 to 4 and both producing 70 percent agreement between two raters. For one scale, all disagreements are within one point; for the other, disagreements are frequently two or three points apart. Using the basic form of kappa, both scales achieve the same score, although the sizes of the disagreements for one of the scales is much greater.

Landis and Koch (1977) proposed mechanisms for weighting kappa to give partial credit for lesser discrepancies. Weighted kappa overcomes some of the limitations of simple kappa by either giving partial credit for near misses or increasing the penalty as the magnitude of the discrepancy in ratings increases. For example, in a situation in which exact agreement is given a value of 1, ratings for an individual case that were within 1 rank might be given a ½; those within 2 ranks given a ¼; and those more than two ranks apart given a 0. Another approach is to base the score on the square of the amount of disagreement, which causes the penalty for disagreement to increase geometrically as the discrepancy in ratings increases. Because this form of weighted kappa is based on the squared value of the difference in ratings, it can be viewed as an analysis of variance (ANOVA) procedure, providing opportunities for other statistical manipulations.

Other Variations of Kappa

When evaluating reliability among several raters, Horn et al. (1985a, 21; 1985b, 1196) compared individual rater's agreement with a modal rating of all the other raters for an individual case. This approach is a legitimate analytic strategy. However, it produces a systematically higher number than the average kappa among all pairwise comparisons.

Intraclass Correlation Coefficient

The intraclass correlation coefficient (ICC), or interrater reliability coefficient (R_I), is based on one-way ANOVA and can be used in one of several forms to assess the degree of agreement among two or more raters. Because it is a proportion, the ICC ranges from 0 (complete disagreement) to 1 (complete agreement).

Shrout and Fleiss (1979) developed several types of calculations for ICC, each formed as a ratio of variance estimates. In each, the variance of ratings for different cases, or targets—the *between-mean square* (BMS)—is divided by a sum of BMS plus other variance components, depending on the purpose of the particular analysis. The BMS derives from the *between-targets sum of squares*, which is calculated as the sum of squared differences between the mean rating for each case and the overall average of ratings for all cases (the *grand mean*). The other major components of variance for the ICC may be summarized as follows:

- *Judge-mean square* (JMS) is derived from the *between-judges sum of squares* (JSSQ)—the sum of the squared differences, for all judges, between the mean rating for each judge and the grand mean.

- *Within-mean square* (WMS) is derived from the *within-targets sum of squares* (WSSQ)—the sum of the squared differences, for all cases, between the individual ratings for each case and the mean rating for that case.

- *Error-mean square* (EMS) is a residual variance and derives from the *error sum of squares* (ESSQ)—the difference of the within-targets sum of squares and the between-judges sum of squares, that is, WSSQ − JSSQ.

Two situations described below illustrate different forms of the ICC. In both situations, each member of one panel of judges gives one rating to each case. In the first situation, the panel of judges is considered representative of a larger population of potential judges. This situation permits an examination of how these ratings might differ if other judges were doing the rating, for which Shrout and Fleiss (1979) suggest the following formula:

$$ICC = \frac{BMS - EMS}{BMS + (JMS - EMS)}.$$

In this equation, as the magnitude of the variance between judges (JMS) increases, the ICC decreases. A higher ICC reflects greater similarity among the judges' ratings.

In the second situation, we suppose that the ratings by this particular panel of judges are the only ones of interest, with no concern that these judges represent a larger population of judges. We further assume that differences in the *actual* ratings given by the judges would not be of concern as long as their *relative* ratings were similar. For example, if one judge's ratings were always exactly three points higher than a second judge's, this would be considered perfect agreement. In this case, the following formula applies:

$$ICC = \frac{BMS - EMS}{BMS}.$$

In this equation the smaller the error mean square, the larger the ICC. Because EMS and JMS vary inversely, the EMS is smaller when most of the within-targets variance is caused by a high level of between-judges variance (JMS), meaning that although the judges differed in their average ratings their relative ratings were similar. In this situation, the major focus is the usefulness of the mean rating rather than the reliability of future individual ratings for the case.

One choice of variance components yields the weighted kappa score based on squared error described above. Because the ICC is based on one-way ANOVA, it treats the risk scales being evaluated as interval scales. Because many severity measures produce ordinal scales (see Table 1.7), reliability results using the ICC potentially could be misinterpreted. Shrout and Fleiss (1979) provide an excellent discussion of considerations in selecting the appropriate form of the ICC.

Gamma

Gamma is useful in evaluating ordinal scales because it measures the degree to which cases are ranked in similar order by two different observers. Gamma can be calculated by taking all possible pairs of cases and noting how often the pairs have concordant and discordant rankings (ties are not counted). The formula is as follows:

$$\Gamma = \frac{N_s - N_d}{N_s + N_d}.$$

where N_s equals the concordant pairs (pairs of cases ranked in the same order by both observers) and N_d equals the discordant pairs (those ranked in opposite order by the two observers). The gamma score can range from -1.0 (implying total disagreement) to 1.0 (total agreement). When no ties occur, there is a simple relationship between gamma and the c-statistic (see Chapter 9).

Tau-B

Tau-B is based on the same principle as gamma, but considers ties. A tie occurs when a pair of cases is given the same rank by one of the observers. Because the distribution of tau-B is known, under the assumption that the ratings are independent, inferences about statistical significance are possible:

$$T_B = \frac{N_s - N_d}{\left[(N_s + N_d + T_y)(N_s + N_d + T_x)\right]^{\frac{1}{2}}}.$$

where T_x and T_y are the number of ties assigned by observer x and observer y, respectively. Gamma and tau-B both are not affected by systematic bias in the application of a risk-adjustment method, such as when one rater consistently gives higher ratings. The scale will appear to perform well as long as the relative scoring among observers or raters is consistent. Depending on the context, this may or may not be a desirable feature.

Additional Considerations in Reliability Assessments

Different approaches quantify risk along ordinal or interval scales (Table 1.7), a distinction with important implications for reliability measurement. An interval scale provides a continuum of values, and it implies that a given increase in the scale always has the same implication for increased risk. On an interval scale, for example, the difference between scores of 5 and 10 intends to convey the same increased risk as the difference between scores of 25 and 30. PMCs Relative Intensity Score and the Disease Staging scaled versions are examples of interval-scaled measures; both generate a score that is designed to be proportional to the cost (resource intensity) of the patient's care. PMCs produce a normative cost weight; and one version of Disease Staging creates a scale reflecting expected charges (or costs), while another scaled version predicts length of stay. As severity of illness (and consequently cost) rises, the score produced by both methods should increase in directly proportional amounts. For example, if one patient's score for either of these measures is twice as high as another's, his or her resource use should be twice as high.

In contrast, an ordinal scale conveys only a ranking of the score levels without specifying the magnitude of the differences between the levels. A higher score simply indicates greater risk. For example, using an ordinal scale, a patient with a score of 3 is at higher risk than one with a score of 2, but the difference between scores 2 and 3 is not necessarily equivalent to the difference between scores 3 and 4.

The reliability of a measure is, to some extent, an artifact. For example, suppose that two raters each rate 100 persons on a three-point scale, with the results shown in Table 7.2.

The kappa for Table 7.2 is $(60 - 34)/(100 - 34) = 0.39$, which is "fair" by the standards of Landis and Koch. However, one can boost kappa to 0.52 ("moderate") by collapsing the observations to a two-point scale, as shown in Table 7.3.

The perceived improvement is somewhat real, because many of the misclassifications in the first table relate to distinctions between the scores 1 and 2. While one can often improve reliability by collapsing scores, reducing the number of categories can also cause kappa to fall. This would happen in the above example by using a different two-point scale, as shown in Table 7.4. For this table, the kappa drops to 0.38.

Table 7.2   Example of Two Raters and a Three-Point Scale

Scores of Rater 2	Scores of Rater 1			
	1	2	3	*All*
1	25	10	5	40
2	10	15	5	30
3	5	5	20	30
All	40	30	30	100

Table 7.3   Example of Two Raters and a Three-Point Scale Collapsed to a Two-Point Scale: Case 1

Scores of Rater 2	Scores of Rater 1		
	< 3	*3*	*All*
< 3	60	10	70
3	10	20	30
All	70	30	100

The most important lesson is not to rely too much on the precise value of kappa and not to compare kappas for two measures with very different distributions of cases in their scale categories. It would be particularly inappropriate to compare a simple kappa for APACHE II, with 72 scores (from 0 to 71), with a simple kappa for a 4- or 5-category method, such as the original CSI or the initial version of MedisGroups. This comparison is unfair for this reason: It is much easier for APACHE II to be off by one or more points than for the other methods to be off by an entire category.

In their comparison of the reliability of several severity measures, Thomas and Ashcraft (1989) dealt with these issues by stratifying APACHE II, PMC Normative Cost Weights, and the Disease Staging Q-Scale, as well as DRG weights, into the same number of categories as MedisGroups—five. They determined the cutpoints for the APACHE II score in two ways. First, they approximated the distribution of rankings among the five MedisGroups categories; second, they determined the optimal cutpoints using the Automated Interaction Detector computer program to minimize variance (Thomas, Ashcraft, and Zimmerman 1986). With the latter method of recoding, the 90 percent of patients with scores of 15 or less were divided among the lowest four categories, while the remaining patients with scores ranging from 16 to 71 made up the fifth category.

Table 7.4   Example of Two Raters and a Three-Point Scale Collapsed to a
Two-Point Scale: Case 2

Scores of Rater 2	*Scores of Rater 1*		
	1	*>1*	*All*
1	25	15	40
>1	15	45	60
All	40	60	100

Reliability is best compared between two measures using the first approach of categorizing the more finely differentiated scale, such as APACHE II in contrast to MedisGroups. For example, if 35 percent of cases are in MedisGroups' lowest category, then the lowest category of APACHE II would include numbers 0 through x, where x is chosen to encompass approximately 35 percent of the cases. If MedisGroups' second-lowest category has 25 percent of the cases, APACHE II scores $x + 1$ through y would form the second category, where y is chosen to encompass approximately the next 25 percent of cases.

Studies of Reliability

With a few exceptions, neither independent investigators nor the creators of commercially available risk adjustors have focused on assessing reliability. Horn and colleagues reported reliability figures for the SOII as described earlier. More recently, Horn and collaborators (1991) reported remarkably good agreement between two raters for their latest severity measure, the CSI. In this study at five hospitals, a random sample of 237 cases was rated independently by a second reviewer. This rerating occurred toward the end of the data abstraction, so the abstractors were experienced (Horn et al. 1991, 316). The quality of the information appeared excellent: Plain percent agreement was 95 percent for both admission and maximum CSI scores, with kappa values of 0.80.

As noted earlier, the creators of MedisGroups have reported accuracy ratings of greater than 95 percent for identifying KCFs by newly trained raters when compared with an experienced rater (Brewster et al. 1985; Steen et al. 1993). Although this degree of agreement is impressive, it alone is not a complete test of reliability without correcting for chance agreement. For the Acute Physiology Score component of APACHE II, Strauss and colleagues (1986) reported that two raters' scores were within two points of each other for each of 30 charts. In the SUPPORT project, exact agreement was 87 percent for physiologic variables and 82 percent for coexisting comorbidities (Knaus et al. 1995, 193).

In a comprehensive independent assessment, Thomas and Ashcraft (1986, 1989) examined the reliability of several major severity measures. Their study included two chart-based methods, APACHE and Medis-Groups, both of which produced ordinal scales, and two automated measures that produced interval-scaled results, PMC Normative Cost Weights and the Disease Staging Q-Scale. They used medical records from 11 adjacent DRGs from three teaching and two community hospitals, and they submitted a subsample of 431 charts to a second review and rating process. For APACHE and MedisGroups, both the initial abstraction and a repeat by a second rater used a photocopied chart. APACHE abstraction and reabstraction were performed by project research staff, while both abstractions for MedisGroups were performed by the vendor, MediQual Systems, Inc. Due to problems of legibility, 18 charts were eliminated from the APACHE analysis, and 174 charts were excluded from the MedisGroups analysis because of MedisGroups' requirement for detailed information from doctors' progress notes. For the two automated systems (PMCs and the Q-Scale) and for DRGs, discharge diagnosis and procedure codes were reabstracted from the chart and submitted to the computerized algorithm by research project staff. Results were compared with those from the original abstractions performed by hospital staff.

Using various tests of reliability, including kappa, the interrater reliability coefficient, gamma, and tau-B, Thomas and Ashcraft found that the two chart-based methods, MedisGroups and APACHE II, had very high reliability, while PMCs and Disease Staging Q-Scale (two code-based measures) had only fair to good reliability. By contrast, DRGs (a code-based method) had excellent reproducibility on reabstraction. As noted earlier, Thomas and Ashcraft attributed the greater reliability of DRGs to the more frequent dependence of PMCs and the Q-Scale risk assignments on the presence of one particular diagnosis code.

Despite its generally robust research design, Thomas and Ashcraft's work has an important limitation due largely to the practical realities of this type of study—they used different configurations of abstractors for the different measures. This meant that they could not create an entirely level playing field for comparing reliability across the different risk measures. DRGs, Disease Staging, and PMCs were abstracted by two different groups (originally by hospital staffs outside of a research environment, with reabstraction by research project staff). In contrast, initial and repeat abstractions were performed by one set of abstractors each for APACHE and MedisGroups, which might have produced a more consistent performance. In addition, the MedisGroups testing was performed by the method's developer, as opposed to research project staff, due to proprietary and practical constraints.

Nevertheless, the work by Thomas and Ashcraft (1989) stands virtually alone in comparative reliability assessment for severity measures. Since it appeared in 1989, most of the severity measures have been revised, without systematic reexamination of their reliability. As Thomas and Ashcraft emphasized, reliability assessment must be an ongoing process.

Conducting Reliability Studies

When contemplating an assessment of the reliability of risk-adjustment methods, several questions must be answered:

- Who should perform the chart abstraction?
- What type of time and organizational constraints should the abstractors face?
- What data sets and medical records should be included?
- Who should sponsor and organize the reliability test?

The choice of the chart abstractors can profoundly affect the evaluation. The staff of the developer of the risk measure will have a greater familiarity with the method, plus more frequent practice and monitoring. Nonetheless, a perception of bias may linger. An independent researcher's staff may be more typical of abstractors for a hospital records department but may have sufficiently different training, talents, and sense of mission to influence results. To approximate the real-world circumstances of the hospital record department, abstractors for evaluation projects should be selected either from actual work sites or from a pool of workers with similar qualifications and backgrounds.

Similarly, the time, setting, and organizational constraints confronted by the abstractors must be as similar to the real world as possible. For example, does the developer promise ten minutes per chart abstraction, and does the hospital record department expect that level of productivity? If so, the test circumstances must impose the same constraints. The selection of medical records for testing is also critical. Depending on one's purpose, the records must represent a range of hospitals, the level of complexity of records, and the types of illnesses that the measure ultimately will be used to review.

Subsuming all of the choices of who, where, what, and how that confront the evaluation of a risk measure is the question of who should sponsor and organize evaluation studies. In many instances, they have been performed by the developers of the risk measure. Often, the developer's results and those obtained by an independent evaluation disagree.

Developers' reports of efficiency and reliability have provoked skepticism among other users of their systems. For example, Horn and colleagues (1991) reported an average of ten minutes to abstract both admission and maximum CSI severity scores. The short abstraction time was perplexing given the time required for scoring other chart-based severity measures (e.g., APACHE, MedisGroups). The claim raised questions about the level of complexity of the charts under review and whether such results would be obtainable under ordinary circumstances in hospital record rooms.

This skepticism cannot be answered by the original developers, no matter how meticulous their attention to methodological detail. These are questions of credibility that require rigorous and independent answers. One impediment to conducting independent evaluations is the increasingly proprietary ownership of widely used severity measures and the reluctance of some vendors to subject their methods to head-to-head comparisons with others. In addition, conducting such reviews is costly and may require multiple sets of reviewers. For example, in the study cited above where the investigators hired nurses to conduct MedisGroups reviews, another set of nurses was employed to review the same records using the CSI (Iezzoni et al. 1992b). Because the instructions for reviewers and the abstraction protocols are so dramatically different, it was unrealistic to expect the same reviewers to be trained simultaneously for both MedisGroups and the CSI. Each method's abstraction protocol required a totally different mindset.

Conclusions

Reliability testing is crucial for judging the merit of a risk-adjustment approach. Deciding how to measure reliability, however, raises numerous conceptual and logistical questions. A single measure of interrater reliability is generally insufficient. Although Thomas and Ashcraft (1989) demonstrated strong correlations among all the reliability methods tested, they suggested that reliability analyses should employ several techniques simultaneously.

Strategies for measuring reliability invoke comparisons with the contrast between efficacy and effectiveness studies described in Chapter 1. The ultimate test of reliability for any risk-adjustment approach is not how well it performs under laboratory conditions but rather how well it does in the real world. As Soeken and Prescott (1986) suggested, a measure of risk should be tested over the broad range of settings, raters, and subjects for which it is proposed. A complete evaluation of a risk measure must therefore encompass many types of tests of reliability performed with data sets that include multiple reviewers, settings, and patient types. Reliability of risk-adjustment measures is essential to maximize the utility of the information for both research and policy applications (see Chapter 11).

References

Brewster, A. C., R. C. Bradbury, and C. M. Jacobs. 1985. "Measuring the Effect of Illness Severity on Revenue under DRGs." *Healthcare Financial Management* 39 (7): 52–53, 56–60.

Cohen, J. A. 1960. "A Coefficient of Agreement for Nominal Scales." *Educational and Psychological Measurement* 20 (1): 37–46.

Feinstein, A. R. 1967. *Clinical Judgment*. Baltimore, MD: Williams & Wilkins Company.

———. 1987. *Clinimetrics*. New Haven, CT: Yale University Press.

Fisher, E. S., F. S. Whaley, W. M. Krushat, D. J. Malenka, C. Fleming, J. A. Baron, and D. C. Hsia. 1992. "The Accuracy of Medicare's Hospital Claims Data: Progress Has Been Made, but Problems Remain." *American Journal of Public Health* 82 (2): 243–48.

Fowles J. B., A. G. Lawthers, J. P. Weiner, D. W. Garnick, D. S. Petrie, and R. H. Palmer. 1995. "Agreement Between Physicians' Office Records and Medicare Part B Claims Data." *Health Care Financing Review* 16 (4): 189–99.

Horn, S. D., R. A. Horn, and P. D. Sharkey. 1984. "The Severity of Illness Index as a Severity Adjustment to Diagnosis-Related Groups." *Health Care Financing Review* Supplement: 33–45.

Horn, S. D., G. Bulkley, P. D. Sharkey, A. F. Chambers, R. A. Horn, and C. J. Schramm. 1985a. "Interhospital Differences in Severity of Illness: Problems for Prospective Payment Based on Diagnosis-Related Groups (DRGs)." *New England Journal of Medicine* 313 (1): 20–24.

Horn, S. D., P. D. Sharkey, A. F. Chambers, and R. A. Horn. 1985b. "Severity of Illness within DRGs: Impact on Prospective Payment." *American Journal of Public Health* 75 (10): 1195–99.

Horn, S. D., and R. A. Horn. 1986. "Reliability and Validity of the Severity of Illness Index." *Medical Care* 24 (2): 159–78.

Horn, S. D., R. A. Horn, and H. Moses. 1986. "Profiles of Physician Practice and Patient Severity of Illness." *American Journal of Public Health* 76 (5): 532–35.

Horn, S. D., R. A. Horn, P. D. Sharkey, and A. F. Chambers. 1986. "Severity of Illness within DRGs. Homogeneity Study." *Medical Care* 24 (3): 225–35.

Horn, S. D., P. D. Sharkey, J. M. Buckle, J. E. Backofen, R. F. Averill, and R. A. Horn. 1991. "The Relationship between Severity of Illness and Hospital Length of Stay and Mortality." *Medical Care* 29 (4): 305–17.

Hsia, D. C., W. M. Krushat, A. B. Fagan, J. A. Tebbutt, and R. P. Kusserow. 1988. "Accuracy of Diagnostic Coding for Medicare Patients under the Prospective-Payment System." *New England Journal of Medicine* 318 (6): 352–55. Published erratum appears in 1990, 322 (21): 1540.

Iezzoni, L. I., M. Shwartz, S. Burnside, A. S. Ash, E. Sawitz, and M. A. Moskowitz. 1989. *Diagnostic Mix, Illness Severity, and Costs at Teaching and Nonteaching*

Hospitals. Springfield, VA: U.S. Department of Commerce, National Technical Information Service (PB 89 184675/AS).

Iezzoni, L. I., M. Shwartz, M. A. Moskowitz, A. S. Ash, E. Sawitz, and S. Burnside. 1990. "Illness Severity and Costs of Admissions at Teaching and Nonteaching Hospitals." *Journal of the American Medical Association* 264 (11): 1426–31.

Iezzoni, L. I., and J. Daley. 1992. "A Description and Clinical Assessment of the Computerized Severity Index™." *Quality Review Bulletin* 18 (2): 44–52.

Iezzoni, L. I., S. M. Foley, J. Daley, J. Hughes, E. S. Fisher, and T. Heeren. 1992a. "Comorbidities, Complications, and Coding Bias. Does the Number of Diagnosis Codes Matter in Predicting In-Hospital Mortality?" *Journal of the American Medical Association* 267 (16): 2197–203.

Iezzoni, L. I., J. D. Restuccia, M. Shwartz, D. Schaumburg, G. A. Coffman, B. E. Kreger, J. R. Butterly, and H. P. Selker. 1992b. "The Utility of Severity of Illness Information in Assessing the Quality of Hospital Care. The Role of the Clinical Trajectory." *Medical Care* 30 (5): 428–44.

Institute of Medicine. 1977. *Reliability of Hospital Discharge Abstracts*. Washington, D.C.: National Academy of Sciences.

Knaus, W. A., E. A. Draper, D. P. Wagner, and J. E. Zimmerman. 1985. "APACHE II: A Severity of Disease Classification System." *Critical Care Medicine* 13 (10): 818–29.

Knaus, W. A., D. P. Wagner, E. A. Draper, J. E. Zimmerman, M. Bergner, P. G. Bastos, C. A. Sirio, D. J. Murphy, T. Lotring, A. Damiano, and F. E. Harrell, Jr. 1991. "The APACHE III Prognostic System. Risk Prediction of Hospital Mortality for Critically Ill Hospitalized Adults." *Chest* 100 (6): 1619–36.

Knaus, W. A., F. E. Harrell, Jr., J. Lynn, L. Goldman, R. S. Phillips, A. F. Connors, Jr., N. V. Dawson, W. J. Fulkerson, Jr., R. M. Califf, N. Desbiens, P. Layde, R. K. Oye, P. E. Bellamy, R. B. Hakim, and D. P. Wagner. 1995. "The SUPPORT Prognostic Model. Objective Estimates of Survival for Seriously Ill Hospitalized Adults." *Annals of Internal Medicine* 122 (3): 191–203.

Landis, J. R., and G. G. Koch. 1977. "The Measurement of Observer Agreement for Categorical Data." *Biometrics* 33 (1): 159–74.

Lloyd, S. S., and J. P. Rissing. 1985. "Physician and Coding Errors in Patient Records." *Journal of the American Medical Association* 254 (10): 1330–36.

Schumacher, D. N., B. Parker, V. Kofie, and J. M. Munns. 1987. "Severity of Illness Index and the Adverse Patient Occurrence Index. A Reliability Study and Policy Implications." *Medical Care* 25 (8): 695–704.

Shrout, P. E., and J. L. Fleiss. 1979. "Intraclass Correlation: Uses in Assessing Rater Reliability." *Psychological Bulletin* 86 (2): 420–28.

Soeken, K. L., and P. A. Prescott. 1986. "Issues in the Use of Kappa to Estimate Reliability." *Medical Care* 24 (8): 733–41.

Steen, P. M., A. C. Brewster, R. C. Bradbury, E. Estabrook, and J. A. Young. 1993. "Predicted Probabilities of Hospital Death as a Measure of Admission Severity of Illness." *Inquiry* 30 (2): 128–41.

Strauss, M. J., J. P. LoGerfo, J. A. Yeltatzie, N. Tempkin, and L. D. Hudson. 1986. "Rationing of Intensive Care Units: An Everyday Occurrence." *Journal of the American Medical Association* 255 (9): 1143–46.

Thomas, J. W., and M. L. F. Ashcraft. 1986. *An Evaluation of Alternative Severity of Illness Measures for Use by University Hospitals*. Ann Arbor, MI: Department of Health Services Management and Policy, School of Public Health, The University of Michigan.

Thomas, J. W., M. L. F. Ashcraft, and J. Zimmerman. 1986. *An Evaluation of Alternative Severity of Illness Measures for Use by University Hospitals: Volume II, Technical Report*. Ann Arbor, MI: Department of Health Services Management and Policy, School of Public Health, The University of Michigan.

Thomas, J. W., and M. L. F. Ashcraft. 1989. "Measuring Severity of Illness: A Comparison of Interrater Reliability Among Severity Methodologies." *Inquiry* 26 (4): 483–92.

Wilson P., S. R. Smoley, and D. Werdegar. 1996. *Second Report of the California Hospital Outcomes Project. Acute Myocardial Infarction. Volume Two: Technical Appendix*. Sacramento, CA: Office of Statewide Health Planning and Development.

Chapter 8

Evaluating the Performance of Risk-Adjustment Methods: Continuous Outcomes

Michael Shwartz and Arlene S. Ash

As described in previous chapters, many factors must be considered when selecting a risk-adjustment approach—the range of clinical dimensions captured, data demands, content and face validity, and reliability. Important conceptual questions include:

- Risk of what outcome (e.g., death, functional impairment, prolonged length of stay, resource consumption)?
- Risk for whom (e.g., older versus younger patients, patients with particular conditions, patients in particular settings of care)?
- Risk during what time period (e.g., during a hospitalization, within the first 30 days following admission, over a year)?
- Risk attributable to what factors (e.g., a particular intervention, therapeutic approach, provider or institution)?

After addressing these specific concerns, however, a critical global question remains: How well does the approach account for differences in patient risk? This question is usually addressed by comparing risk-adjusted predictions of patients' outcomes to actual outcomes. In the terminology of Chapter 6, what is the predictive validity?

In contrast to qualitative judgments about clinical content and face validity, performance in predicting outcomes can be quantified. Nonetheless, interpreting objective measures of performance still requires judgment. Which questions can be addressed are constrained by the data available. As indicated in Chapter 3, the data delimit the content of risk-adjustment approaches and the outcomes that can be examined. Database characteristics also establish the context for interpreting performance.

Performance measures are usually derived from multivariable modeling. Most aspects of developing and evaluating performance of risk-adjustment methods are common to all multivariable modeling endeavors, including the need to examine the data carefully using basic descriptive approaches (e.g., frequency distributions, histograms, boxplots, and scatterplots). Many excellent textbooks provide clear and comprehensive information on the principles and practice of modeling, such as classic works by Draper and Smith (1981); Neter and Wasserman (1974); Mosteller and Tukey (1977); and Box, Hunter, and Hunter (1978).

Here, we focus on issues of special concern in risk adjustment for assessing healthcare outcomes. Chapters 8 and 9 examine quantitative measures of predictive validity—that is, how well risk-adjustment methods perform. Chapter 8 focuses on predicting continuous outcomes (e.g., number of days spent in-hospital, total charges), while Chapter 9 concentrates on dichotomous outcomes (e.g., death, use of specified procedures). Throughout, we draw examples from existing severity measures (see Table 1.3) and from our own work.

Approach to Evaluating Performance: Multivariable Modeling

Translating a Risk Score into a Predicted Outcome

The term "risk adjustment" implies an ability to estimate expected outcomes for individual patients based on assessing their specific risk characteristics. With certain severity measures, determining a predicted or expected outcome from the risk score is relatively straightforward *for the outcome addressed by the measure* (see Table 1.4). For example, the empirically derived MedisGroups method uses a patient's KCFs to assign a score that estimates the predicted probability of in-hospital death for that patient (Steen et al. 1993). The expected number of deaths among a group of patients can then be computed as the sum of their individual predicted probabilities of dying.

To illustrate this approach, Exhibit 2.3B shows the coefficients associated with variables in the MedisGroups admission severity models to predict the likelihood of in-hospital death for acute myocardial infarction (AMI) patients. These coefficients allow information about each patient's clinical characteristics (i.e., which KCFs the patient has) to be converted to a probability of death. The actual death rate in any group can then be compared to its risk-adjusted expected death rate, computed as the average of the group's predicted probabilities of death. Another version of MedisGroups was developed to predict the length of hospital stays (also see Exhibit 2.3). Expected length of stay for a group of patients is computed as the average of the predicted values for each patient.

However, even when risk scores are derived explicitly for a particular outcome, adjustments might be useful, depending on the purpose of the analysis. For example, the MedisGroups models to predict in-hospital death shown in Exhibit 2.3 were developed using the MedisGroups Comparative Database, compiled from selected hospitals, largely from Pennsylvania (see Chapters 10 and 11), which use the MedisGroups severity method. The relationship between KCFs and the likelihood of death determined from patients in this database may or may not generalize well to other patients.

As an illustration, suppose that 13 percent of 10,000 AMI patients hospitalized in Florida in 1996 died but that their MedisGroups-based expected death rate was 15 percent. If the unadjusted MedisGroups predictions provide an appropriate standard (because patients in the Medis-Groups Comparative Database sample are sufficiently similar to patients in Florida), then the results are reasonably viewed as better than expected. This may be due to better-than-average quality of care, although other plausible causes exist. Identifying a single leading cause of such a difference is difficult and controversial. For example, declines in coronary artery bypass graft (CABG) mortality in New York state following publication of risk-adjusted mortality rates by hospital and surgeon (see Chapter 11) have been attributed both to improved performance (Hannan et al. 1995; Chassin, Hannan, and DeBuono 1996) and to various factors not related to quality (Green and Wintfeld 1995).

Perhaps models based on the MedisGroups Comparative Database are not a good standard for Florida's population. Recalibration can make a model developed elsewhere fit a new data set. Here, "recalibration" means systematically changing predictions to make the average of expected outcomes equal to actual average outcomes in a population. More generally, recalibration involves revaluing a set of predictions so that the new predictions more closely match the outcomes in a data set. Recalibration can be accomplished several ways, including adding the same amount (e.g., 2 percent) to each score, multiplying each score by the same amount (e.g., 13/15), or using regression techniques. When predictions are recalibrated, however, they lose their value as an external standard. Nonetheless, recalibrated predications can still be used to examine risk-adjusted differences in outcomes for policy-relevant groups of patients, for example, between Medicaid and private pay patients in Florida (see Chapter 9).

The Relative Intensity Score (RIS), one of several measures provided by PMCs, illustrates another type of adjustment that may be needed when using a risk score to predict an outcome. The RIS measures expected relative resource intensity for patients with a particular combination of PMCs. A patient with an RIS of 1.2, for example, is expected to be 20 percent more resource intensive than a standard patient. However, determining the cost of a standard patient is still necessary before predictions can be compared to actual costs. If cost is proportional to RIS, we can estimate the constant of proportionality and convert scores to predicted costs by regressing cost on RIS in a model with no intercept. Other relationships between cost and RIS can also be modeled with regression.

As described in Chapter 5, risk-adjustment methods have used various search procedures, often stepwise ordinary least squares (OLS) regression or stepwise logistic regression, to identify important factors and to build models from data. The resulting equations specify the coefficients for each explanatory variable included in the model. Examples are APACHE III (Knaus et al. 1991), the MMPS (Daley et al. 1988), and the RAND score of sickness at admission (Keeler et al. 1990). From a list of variables and their coefficients, one can calculate a risk score for each case. However, translating the score into a predicted outcome may require calibration and further analysis. For example, APACHE III scores per se are neither predicted nor expected values of a specific outcome. Regressing an outcome on such scores (or on score and score squared) is one way to translate APACHE III scores into predictions. Another way is to collapse the many possible individual scores into several categories (e.g., 0, 1 to 5, 6 to 10, and so on) with adequate numbers of cases within each category and then to regress the outcome on categorical dummy variables (discussed in the next section). This approach is equivalent to setting the probability of an event for patients in each category equal to the fraction of patients experiencing the event in that category. Several considerations raised by making such cuts are discussed later in this chapter and in Chapter 5.

Some measures assign patients to ordinal risk categories, such as 0 to 4 in the older version of MedisGroups (with 4 being the highest-risk group) or 1 to 5 in the Acuity Index Method (AIM). When many cases fall into a category, calculating the risk for these patients as the average of their outcomes is reasonable. If other factors, such as age and sex, are also considered in predicting outcomes, regression can quantify risk as a combined function of risk category and such other factors.

However, relating severity to outcomes is more complicated for measures that do not assign single scores to individual patients, such as the Disease Staging version that assigns a separate stage to each condition the patient has (Gonnella, Hornbrook, and Louis 1984). For patients with multiple coexisting conditions, translating the different stages of these conditions into an overall risk score requires sophisticated analysis of very large databases, guided by both clinical judgment and an understanding of the limits of empirical analyses.

This kind of problem has been addressed by researchers seeking to characterize persons by their various medical problems during a one-year period. For example, Ambulatory Care Groups (ACGs) were developed originally to estimate the resources needed annually to treat medical problems in ambulatory care settings as a function of the number and nature of patients' medical problems (Weiner et al. 1991; Starfield et al. 1991). The ACG algorithm requires several steps to assign persons to a specific ACG. First, Ambulatory Diagnosis Groups (ADGs) classify individual *diagnoses* into 34 groups, such as "time-limited: major" and "likely to recur: discrete." Each person is then classified into one of 51 mutually exclusive ACGs, based on age, sex, presence or absence of certain individual ADGs, and number of individual ADGs. Examples of ACGs are "acute minor conditions(s) only, age less than two" and "four or five different ADGs, age 17–44."

ACGs' developers propose two main ways to regress outcomes (such as number of visits, ambulatory charges, and all charges this year) on predictors. Their primary recommendation is to regress the outcome on ADGs, age, and sex; a second method is to regress the outcome on dummy variables that distinguish the 51 ACGs. The ADG/ACG methodology has been extended to other patient populations to predict next year's costs and to incorporate information on the medical problems treated in both inpatient and ambulatory settings (Weiner et al. 1996).

Diagnostic Cost Group (DCG) models originally sought to predict next year's costs for elderly Medicare beneficiaries based on their principal inpatient diagnoses (Ash et al. 1989). Patients with multiple hospitalizations could have multiple principal diagnoses. In this instance, DCGs predicted costs based on the patient's "worst" diagnosis—the single diagnosis associated with the highest average costs next year.

DCG methods have since been extended (Ellis et al. 1996) to consider both ambulatory and inpatient diagnoses and to estimate concurrent as well as future costs. Also, a new family of models, Hierarchical Coexisting Condition (HCC), bases predictions on the full set of medical conditions being treated (Ellis et al. 1996). HCC modeling tries to account for the multiple medical problems that individuals have, while limiting the model's sensitivity to coding idiosyncracies and code proliferation. Multiple, interrelated ICD-9-CM diagnosis codes for common conditions are grouped and arrayed in a hierarchy based on expense, and individual patients are assigned to the highest group within each hierarchy. For example, codes for metastatic malignancy override all site-specific cancers; when coexisting, the more expensive lung cancer ("Higher-Cost Cancers") would be chosen rather than breast or prostate cancer ("Lower-Cost Cancers"). Predictions are produced by regressing cost on age and sex categories as well as on dummy variables representing each of around 50 coexisting categories (e.g., "High-Cost Infectious Diseases," "Renal Failure," "Chronic Obstructive Pulmonary Disease").

Translating a Risk Score into a Predicted Outcome Using Multivariable Modeling

Multivariable modeling provides a framework for translating risk scores, risk categories, or specific variables into predicted outcomes. For each patient, we know the actual value of the variable to be predicted (the "dependent" variable), labeled Y_i for the ith patient. For a dichotomous outcome, this is coded as a 0/1 variable (1 if the event occurs and 0 if it does not). We also know the values of variables that are associated with the outcome and are variously called "predictor," "explanatory," or "independent" variables. For example, X_i could be the value of a risk score for the ith patient. If the risk adjustor defines categories numbered 1, 2, 3, and 4, three independent dummy variables (also called "indicator," "marker," or "0/1" variables) could be defined as X_{ij}, with $j = 1, 2,$ or 3. With this coding, category 4, referred to as the omitted category, is treated as the base situation; if patient i is in category 4, the three X_{ij} variables are all set equal to 0. For a patient in risk category 2, variable X_{i2} equals 1 and the other two categorical variables equal 0. The coefficients of each dummy variable measure the average difference in risk between cases in that category and cases in category 4.

The independent variables (i.e., X_{ij}'s) may capture demographic or clinical information and may be either continuous or categorical. In chapter 5, we discuss the considerations that go into identifying the independent variables in a model; whatever the number and nature of predictors, however, the model form most widely used with a continuous outcome is:

$$E(Y_i) = a + \sum_j b_j X_{ij}$$

where $E(Y_i)$ is the expected value of the dependent variable for the ith patient, a is a constant (called the "intercept"), and the b_j's are coefficients associated with the independent variables (the X_{ij}'s). Statisticians call such a model "linear" (that is, "additive") because its predictions are formed by summing terms. This sometimes causes confusion because the variables in a linear model can be nonlinear functions of the data (e.g., age squared). The model only becomes nonlinear when its structural form changes, for example, in

$$E(Y_i) = a * C_{i1}^{b1} * C_{i2}^{b2}.$$

The estimated model parameters (i.e., the number $\hat{a}$ and the $\hat{b}_j$'s, where "^" indicates an estimate of an underlying parameter) in a linear model are chosen to make the predicted values close to the actual outcomes, most commonly in the sense that they minimize the sum of the squared deviations or "errors" between observed and expected; that is, they minimize

$$SSE = \sum_i (Y_i - \hat{Y}_i)^2$$

where $\hat{Y}_i = \hat{a} + \sum_j \hat{b}_j X_{ij}$. OLS regression is named for its property of identifying those coefficients that minimize the SSE. Although OLS modeling can be applied to any data, its properties are best understood and the statistical inferences underlying standard statistical tests are most trustworthy when:

- the distribution of the dependent variable is approximately "normal"—that is, the histogram for the Y_i's looks like a bell-shaped curve;
- the variance of the dependent variable is reasonably similar for all observations—the assumption of "homoskedasticity"; and
- observations are independent.

If the first two assumptions are seriously violated, data transformations (e.g., taking logarithms of the dependent variable) or non-OLS regression may be used (see below).

Violations of independence often occur when data are clustered (i.e., observations are grouped, such as patients treated at the same hospital or by the same physician). With clustered observations, the predictor variables fail to capture fully how such observations are more like each other than they are like other cases. In Chapter 10, we address this issue further in the context of comparing differences across providers within which patients are clustered.

Linear regression models have been widely used in risk adjustment. For example, we were interested in examining how well differences in severity of illness explained differences in patient costs among tertiary teaching, other teaching, and nonteaching hospitals (Iezzoni et al. 1990). We collected data on over 4,400 patients with one of eight conditions (cerebrovascular disease, respiratory malignancy, acute and chronic bronchitis and asthma, AMI, coronary artery disease without AMI, prostate disease, hip and femur fracture, and low back disorder) admitted to five tertiary teaching, five other teaching, and five nonteaching hospitals in metropolitan Boston. In one analysis, we used stepwise regression to identify comorbidities with a statistically significant relationship to cost (Shwartz et al. 1996a), after including a categorical variable representing the patient's DRG. Table 8.1 shows the regression coefficients for comorbidities that entered the model listed by order of entry. The coefficient of each

Table 8.1   Prevalence and Regression Coefficients for Comorbidities Entering a Stepwise Regression Model to Predict Costs

Comorbidity	Prevalence (%)	Coefficient
Intubation ≥ 24 hours	2.3%	3794
Congestive heart failure (active problem)	3.6	2115
Stroke (active problem)	0.2	5721
Moderate dementia	8.7	1011
Chronic pulmonary disease (active problem)	6.1	860
Ventricular tachycardia (active problem)	0.7	2416
Atrial arrhythmias or premature ventricular contractions (active problem)	10.0	732
Severe dementia	1.7	1486
Ventricular couplets	0.3	2938
Occult blood in stool (active problem)	0.4	2364
Angina (active problem)	2.7	650
Hypertension (active problem)	6.7	497
Malignancy with poor prognosis	1.9	853
Chronic renal failure (active problem)	1.6	821
Transient ischemic attack (history only)	2.6	669
Stroke (history only)	5.6	−496
Deep venous thrombosis (active problem)	1.6	1982
Diabetes not requiring insulin (active problem)	1.6	710
Acute myocardial infarction (active problem)	0.2	1817
Nonmalignant bradyrhythmias or tachyrhythmias (active problem)	6.1	320
Hip fracture (history only)	2.3	471
Cardiac arrest	7.2	−563
Diabetes requiring insulin	6.1	285

Note: Comorbidities could be (1) present only as medical history, (2) an active problem addressed during the hospitalization, or (3) considered regardless of whether present as history only or an active problem.

comorbidity estimates its contribution to a patient's cost, and effects are assumed to be additive. For example, the predicted cost of a patient with moderate dementia and angina is 1,661 (i.e., 1,011 + 650) higher than it would be for a similar patient without these two problems.

In our AHCPR-funded severity project, we used OLS regression to build models predicting length of stay (LOS) for patients hospitalized for pneumonia (Iezzoni et al. 1996). Severity score was entered as one or more independent variables (depending on the nature of the score), along with age, age squared, sex, and dummy variables for DRG (cases in DRGs 79, 80,

89, and 90 were included in the analysis). Separate models were built for each severity measure (Table 8.3). Severity scores were entered as either continuous variables or as categorical variables (see Table 1.8). For the two measures that rate severity as a predicted probability of death ($\hat{p}$), we included both ($\hat{p}$) and ($\hat{p}$) squared in the model. This allowed for the possibility that both the least and most severe patients (i.e., those with the lowest and the highest predicted likelihood of death) have shorter LOSs than those at intermediate risk. For methods that measure severity within DRGs (AIM, APR-DRGs, and R-DRGs), we also considered models with "interaction" terms for severity and DRG: terms of the form: $X_{ij} * DRG_i$ A. Such a term equals 1 only when patient i is both in the jth severity category and DRG A; otherwise it is 0. The coefficient associated with this term reflects differences in the effect of severity on LOS for patients in DRG A as opposed to patients in a reference DRG (the omitted category).

We examined interactions between age categories and sex in developing models to predict LOS of patients hospitalized for hip fracture, using eight age categories (18–44, 45–54, 55–64, 65–69, 70–74, 75–79, 80–84, and 85 and older) interacted with a dummy variable for gender (Shwartz et al. 1996b). If variables AGE1, . . . , AGE8 indicate the eight age categories and F represents female sex, a fully interacted age-sex model requires sixteen interaction terms (i.e., F, AGE2, . . . , AGE8, F*AGE1, F*AGE2, . . . , F*AGE8). Although AGE1 is the omitted category, the variable F*AGE1 allows for the possibility that outcomes differ for men and women in age category 1. If the coefficient of F*AGE1 is 0.2, for example, then the average outcome is 0.2 higher for women in AGE1 than for men in AGE1. Using interaction terms is one way to adapt simple linear models to more complex realities.

In certain situations, the cases available for modeling are selectively sampled to contain a disproportionate fraction of persons from specific subgroups of the population (e.g., outliers—cases with particularly high or low values). Weighted least squares (WLS) modeling may be used here, attempting to replicate regression results that would occur if OLS modeling is used in a random sample of the general population. The weights make cases that come from undersampled parts of the population count more heavily in the analysis. Although WLS is discussed in standard texts (e.g., Draper and Smith 1981), proper implementation requires care. A good discussion of the issues involved can be found in the reference manual for the Stata statistical analysis software (Computer Resource Center 1992). A well-founded concern is that most statistical packages generally provide inadequate support for sampling weights. The developers of MMPS (Daley et al. 1988) demonstrated how data gathered using a complex sampling scheme could be modeled using WLS.

Chapter 6 draws the distinction between:

- how a model performs on the data to which it is fit, often called the "development" data set; and
- how a previously developed model performs when it is applied to new data, called a "validation" data set.

The more variables considered in the model, the more important it is to compute measures of performance on a validation data set. Thus, for example, in using a preformed summary score X (e.g., the RIS score from PMCs), one might use the following model to translate RIS into a predicted cost:

$$\hat{Y}_i = \hat{a} + \hat{b}X_i$$

where $\hat{Y}_i$ is the predicted cost for the ith patient and X_i is the RIS score.

With only two coefficients to fit to a large data set, "overmodeling" is not a major concern (Chapter 5). However, in many situations, the same data set is used both to specify the model (i.e., to determine which of many factors to include and the form in which to include them) and to estimate coefficients for each included variable. In this setting, the possibility of overfitting is real. As described in Table 5.4, overfitting occurs when variables are identified and parameters estimated that fit the particular development data set (and its idiosyncracies) too closely. An overfit model can perform substantially poorer when used to make predictions on new data. For example, in Table 8.1, several of the comorbidities in the model were relatively rare, occurring in under 20 cases. The large size of the data set is irrelevant; the coefficient associated with a rare factor is determined by the outcomes among the cases in which it occurs. This can be heavily influenced by a single high-cost case in the development data and may not reflect a recurring relationship.

For outcomes that are approximately normally distributed, 30 cases are generally considered enough to establish coefficients reliably; for highly skewed outcomes, hundreds of cases may be needed. For example, the total healthcare costs of a general population during a fixed time period typically contains many zeros (for people who use no services); a large majority of cases with low costs (those with minor, ambulatory ailments only); and a small fraction (less than 20 percent in the elderly) with high costs, consisting of people who are hospitalized or otherwise seriously ill. Furthermore, within this last group, a few have extremely high costs. For example, in Medicare in 1994, average program payments per enrollee were about $4,900, but about 11 percent of beneficiaries—those with costs greater than $10,000—accounted for almost 75 percent of program dollars (Health Care Financing Administration 1996a, 1996b). With such data, the average cost of a group of even 100 people is subject to substantial variation.

A practical impediment to validation is the lack of independent data. As described in Chapter 6, a variety of techniques can be used to estimate what performance would be on a validation data set by creatively using the data that were employed for model development. We illustrate such approaches later in this chapter.

Definition of R^2

R^2, which is also called the coefficient of determination, is the standard summary measure of model performance when the dependent variable is continuous. Although several alternative definitions of R^2 exist, the one most widely used is

$$R^2 = 1 - \left[\sum_i (Y_i - \hat{Y}_i)^2 / \sum_i (Y_i - \bar{Y})^2 \right]$$

where $\bar{Y}$ is the average of the Y_i's. In the term subtracted from 1, the numerator sum of squared terms is called the sum of squared errors (SSE); the denominator is called the sum of squares total (SST). SST is determined by the data alone and not by the model and measures the variability of the outcome Y in the data. SSE measures the variability in Y that is not accounted for by differences that the model can predict. When OLS is used to estimate model parameters (a and the b_j's), SSE is minimized, and thus R^2 is maximized. Therefore, when OLS methods are used to fit models, R^2 is a particularly appropriate measure of model performance.

However, R^2 can still be computed and may be a useful summary measure of performance even if predicted values are developed some other way, such as using the binary split algorithm CART© (Salford Systems, San Diego, California; based on methods originally developed by Breiman et al. 1984). In particular, examining the same measure is often desirable when comparing the performance of models constructed with different algorithms. When using R^2 for such comparisons, remember that other algorithms do not choose coefficients with the goal of maximizing R^2.

R^2 is often described as the fraction of total variability in the dependent variable explained by or attributed to differences in risk among cases included in the model. Sometimes R^2 is multiplied by 100 and described as percent of variation explained. Thus, for example, in the comorbidity model, DRGs were able to explain 42 percent of the variability in cost among patients. When the 23 comorbidity variables in Table 8.1 were added to the model, 50 percent of the variability was explained, indicating that comorbidities increased the variability explained by roughly 20 percent ($[(50 - 42) / 42] \times 100$) over that explained by DRGs alone.

Most investigators routinely report R^2 as a measure of the performance of risk-adjustment models used to explain either length of stay, hospital charges, or costs. For example, Thomas and Ashcraft (1991) used R^2 to measure how well different severity measures explained variations in estimated costs among patients hospitalized in each of eleven conditions. Six severity methods were evaluated: AIM, APACHE II, the CSI admission and maximum scores, Disease Staging, the original MedisGroups admission and morbidity ratings, and PMCs. Analyses were performed twice, once on all cases and once with outliers eliminated (see below). Two forms of models were considered: first, assuming simple linear relationships between severity and costs (therefore entering a single, continuous variable into the model); and second, allowing for nonlinear relationships (modeled with categorical risk variables). Modeling was performed separately within each of the eleven conditions.

Table 8.2 shows the R^2 values from the nonlinear models used to predict cost, averaged across the eleven conditions from the Thomas and Ashcraft study (1991). The relative performance of different severity measures depended on whether outliers were included in the analysis and whether R^2 was calculated from the model fit to the development data set or a validation R^2 was estimated. The validation R^2 was estimated using PRESS (see Chapter 6). R^2 values varied greatly from condition to condition (data not shown). Table 8.2 prompts the following question: What are meaningful differences in R^2 values? We address this point later.

Table 8.2 R^2 for Predicting Cost by Risk-Adjustment System*

| | R^2 | | | |
| | Development R^2 | | Validation R^2† | |
Severity System	All Cases (N = 1,714)	Inliers (N = 1,379)	All Cases	Inliers
DRGs	.061	.079	.052	.056
Disease Staging	.188	.131	.146	.103
PMCs	.141	.136	.113	.101
AIM	.104	.078	.076	.060
APACHE II	.132	.108	.096	.084
MedisGroups: admission score	.129	.118	.090	.091
CSI: admission score	.115	.110	.081	.067
MedisGroups: morbidity score	.215	.181	.166	.136
CSI: maximum score	.228	.217	.165	.177

Source: Data from Thomas and Ashcraft (1991), Table 3, p. 47, nonlinear model.
*Data relate to cases in 11 adjacent DRGs, and R^2 values are a weighted average of the R^2 values in the 11 conditions.
†Calculated using PRESS (see Chapter 6) (Neter, Wasserman, and Kutner 1990).

Using a sample of approximately 76,000 cases abstracted from 25 hospitals in New Jersey, Averill and colleagues (1992) examined the relationship between maximum CSI score and hospital costs. Results were reported for 76 DRGs, selected based on preliminary analyses that identified DRGs in which severity affected patient costs. Only inlier patients (i.e., those without extreme outcome values) were analyzed. For 34 DRGs, the R^2 was between 0.10 and 0.19; for 25 DRGs, it was between 0.20 and 0.29; and for 17 DRGs, R^2 was greater than or equal to 0.30. Averill and colleagues referred to the R^2 value as the "reduction in variance." The appropriateness of this characterization is demonstrated by rewriting the formula as

$$R^2 = (SST/n - SSE/n)/(SST/n)$$

where n is the number of cases in the database. Because SST/n is an estimate of the variance of the outcome variable and SSE/n is the residual variance after fitting the model, the numerator can be viewed as a reduction in variance.

Freeman and colleagues (1995) revised DRGs through more refined uses of diagnosis- and procedure-specific sets of comorbidities and complications that represented different levels of resource use. The resulting refined DRGs (R-DRGs) explained 38.1 percent of the variation in charges among all discharges in the Medicare Provider Analysis and Review subsample of about one million cases used in the analysis and 45.6 percent of the variation among the nonextreme charges (i.e., after outliers were eliminated).

Table 8.3 shows R^2 and cross-validated R^2, both using untrimmed data (all cases) and trimmed data (outliers eliminated), for severity measures used in our study (see Table 1.8) as well as for a model using only age, sex, and DRG (Iezzoni et al. 1996). The severity methods varied in their statistical performance, but all performed somewhat better on trimmed than untrimmed data and all did better than the model including only age, sex, and DRG. R^2 values ranged from 0.079 to 0.142 (R-DRGs).

Although R^2 is a valuable summary measure of model performance, it provides little intuitive feel for the ability of a model to discriminate among cases with high and low values for the dependent variable. To provide such insight, we also examined actual and predicted mean LOS within deciles of predicted LOS. For example, Table 8.4 shows that for AIM, which had an R^2 of 0.125 (Table 8.3), the predicted mean LOS of patients in the lowest decile was 5.5 days; the predicted mean LOS of patients in the highest decile was 12.8 days, slightly over twice as long. For R-DRGs, with an R^2 of 0.142 percent, the comparable LOS values were 4.1 days and 13.2 days, over a three-fold difference. Table 8.4 also shows the actual mean LOS values in

Table 8.3 R^2 and Cross-Validated R^2 for Predicting Length of Stay: Untrimmed and Trimmed Data for Pneumonia Patients

Severity Adjustment Method	Untrimmed Data		Trimmed Data	
	R^2	Cross-Validated R^2	R^2	Cross-Validated R^2
AIM[a]	0.125	0.122	0.140	0.139
APR-DRGs[a]	0.126	0.123	0.147	0.145
Disease Staging RRS	0.128	0.125	0.144	0.143
PMC RIS	0.103	0.102	0.122	0.120
R-DRGs	0.142	0.140	0.170	0.169
Disease Staging mortality probability	0.091	0.089	0.107	0.105
PMC severity score	0.104	0.101	0.122	0.119
Body Systems Count	0.118	0.113	0.133	0.129
Comorbidity Index	0.085	0.083	0.103	0.099
MedisGroups	0.091	0.090	0.109	0.108
Physiology score	0.082	0.080	0.099	0.098
Age, sex, and DRG only	0.079	0.078	0.097	0.096

Source: Iezzoni et al. 1996.
[a] From model with severity score interacted with DRG.

each decile. In general, predicted mean LOS values in the extreme deciles were closer together than actual mean LOS values in these deciles.

R^2 is sometimes said to range between 0 and 1, but these boundaries can be misleading, as described below.

The Minimum Value for R^2

In the development data set, the R^2 of a linear model is never less than zero. This value is achieved by letting $\hat{a}$ equal $\bar{Y}$ and all the $\hat{b}_j$'s equal zero. The $\hat{Y}_i$ is always predicted to be $\bar{Y}$, SSE equals SST, and R^2 equals zero. Because OLS finds numbers $\hat{a}$ and $\hat{b}_j$'s that make SSE as small as possible, OLS never has an R^2 value lower than zero.

However, in a validation data set, there is no guarantee that a model developed elsewhere will yield an SSE at least as small as SST. For example, assume that the average outcomes in the development and validation data set, designated as $\bar{Y}_{dev}$ and $\bar{Y}_{val}$, are not identical. Then, the model that predicts $\bar{Y}_{dev}$ for every case in the validation data set will yield a negative R^2 in that data set. More generally, a negative R^2 will result anytime the $\hat{Y}_i$'s, as determined in the development data, are further from the Y_i's (in the sense of "sum of squared differences") than the constant prediction $\bar{Y}_{val}$ is from the Y_i's. This is strong evidence of poor predictive power.

Table 8.4   Actual and Predicted Mean Lengths of Stay within Deciles of Predicted Lengths of Stay: Trimmed Data

Severity Adjustment Method	Decile of Predicted Lengths of Stay			
	1	2	9	10
	Mean Actual LOS (Mean Predicted LOS)			
AIM[a]	5.1 (5.5)	6.6 (6.8)	11.1 (10.9)	13.2 (12.8)
APR-DRGs[a]	5.0 (5.5)	6.6 (6.7)	11.6 (10.9)	13.0 (12.8)
Disease Staging RRS	5.1 (5.3)	6.4 (6.6)	11.2 (11.2)	13.4 (13.6)
PMC RIS	5.2 (5.2)	6.4 (6.8)	11.0 (11.2)	12.6 (12.9)
R-DRGs	4.0 (4.1)	6.2 (6.5)	11.4 (11.5)	13.2 (13.2)
Disease Staging mortality probability	5.2 (5.3)	6.6 (6.9)	10.8 (11.0)	12.5 (12.6)
PMC severity score	5.1 (5.3)	6.5 (6.6)	10.8 (11.0)	12.6 (12.8)
Body Systems Count	5.1 (5.1)	6.5 (6.7)	11.0 (11.3)	13.0 (13.1)
Comorbidity Index	5.2 (5.3)	6.7 (6.9)	10.9 (11.0)	12.2 (12.5)
MedisGroups	5.2 (5.2)	6.5 (6.9)	10.7 (11.1)	12.4 (12.6)
Physiology score	5.1 (5.3)	6.7 (7.0)	10.6 (11.0)	12.1 (12.4)
Age, sex, and DRG only	5.2 (5.3)	6.8 (7.0)	11.0 (11.0)	11.9 (12.4)

Source: Iezzoni et al. 1996.
[a] From model with severity score interacted with DRG.

The Maximum Achievable Value for R^2

R^2 achieves its maximum value of 1.0 if all of its predictions are perfect—if every $\hat{Y}_i$ equals the actual Y_i . In most situations, however, this goal is unrealistic.

For a given set of variables used to measure risk in a particular sample of cases, the maximum achievable R^2 is generally much less than 1.0. To illustrate this, consider a situation in which all independent predictor variables are categorical. If all possible combinations of the predictor variables are included as independent variables in a model, the model is said to be fully saturated (i.e., to include all interactions). In this situation, each case falls uniquely in one of the cells defined by the interactions. For example, assume a model includes sex and severity class, which can take on one of five values. A fully saturated model would include ten (i.e., 2×5) variables (i.e., nine dummy variables and a constant term). One cell, for instance, would contain the data for all women in severity class 2.

In a fully saturated, least squares model, the predicted value of each case equals the average value of the dependent variable for all cases in the same cell. One assumption of a linear regression model is that the variance of the outcome variable is the same for different combinations of independent variables. Under this assumption, cases in each cell have the same variance around their cell average. The maximum R^2 for any model that cannot make finer distinctions than those defined by these ten cells is given by

$$\max R^2 = 1 - \frac{\text{(average variance of the outcome within each cell)}}{\text{(variance of the outcome in the whole population)}}.$$

This can be estimated by

$$1 - \frac{(n - 10)\, s^2}{\text{SST}}$$

where n is the number of cases in the data set and s^2 is the pooled estimate of the common variance of the outcome variable among cases in each cell. No model can eliminate the variability measured by s^2 unless it uses other information to distinguish cases within each cell further.

The more interaction terms a model includes, the closer R^2 will be to its maximum. When risk is defined generically across conditions, comparing R^2 to maximum R^2 helps quantify the loss of predictive power associated with a model that is not condition specific. For instance, some versions of Disease Staging are condition specific. In any model, separate independent variables must be included for each severity stage within each condition, because the stages for different conditions are not comparable (Conklin et al. 1984). If condition and stage are the only variables included in a model, then the only sensible model is fully interacted. In this situation, R^2 and maximum R^2 are the same.

In contrast, in the older version of MedisGroups, five generic (i.e., diagnosis independent) severity levels were determined. When using old MedisGroups with data from ten conditions, for example, one has two choices: (1) to include a separate interaction term for each level of severity within each condition; or (2) to include only nine separate variables to distinguish among the ten conditions, and four variables to distinguish the five severity classes. The first choice results in 49 dummy variables in the model, the second choice results in only 13. Under the second choice, R^2 will differ from the maximum R^2 to the extent that the effect of severity level on outcome differs depending on the condition.

The concept of "maximum R^2" rarely appears in the published risk-adjustment literature. We believe it is useful for two reasons. First, it allows one to distinguish two types of poor fit: (1) poor fit because a simpler model is used rather than one containing all possible interactions (measured by the difference between maximum R^2 and actual R^2); and (2) poor fit due to variation of the dependent variable within the cells defined by the independent variables used in modeling (measured by the difference between the maximum R^2 and 1.0) (Korn and Simon 1991). As discussed in Chapter 9, identifying the source of poor model fit is particularly useful in interpreting R^2 values calculated on models with a dichotomous dependent variable. Second, the maximum R^2 is, in some sense, a measure of how hard a specific data set is to model with a particular set of variables, which suggests that reporting maximum R^2 for a standard, agreed-upon set of variables might be a useful way of characterizing data sets.

Grouped R^2

In the traditional R^2 (= 1 − SSE/SST), each difference between a person's actual and predicted costs contributes to the model's error and reduces the R^2. However, in many settings, the important purpose of risk adjustment is not to produce correct averages for each person but to produce correct averages within policy-relevant subgroups of the population, such as people enrolling in different health plans.

The concept of a "grouped R^2" was developed to measure a model's ability to match average predicted and actual costs within specified subgroups of the population (Ash et al, 1989). With the traditional R^2 for example, predicting \$1,500 for each of two people, one of whom costs nothing and the other, \$3,000 leads to a "penalty" of $(1500)^2$ for each. However, with the grouped R^2 there is no penalty *if both belong to the same subgroup*. Within the same subgroup, positive and negative individual errors of prediction are allowed to cancel each other out.

Unlike the traditional R^2, a grouped R^2 is not an intrinsic property of a population but depends on how the population is partitioned into subgroups (also called a "binning") such that each case belongs in one and only one bin. Specifically, the grouped R^2 for a partition (with B bins in total and n_b cases in the bth bin) is defined as

$$\text{Grouped } R^2 = 1 - \frac{\text{GSS(Model)}}{\text{GSS(Total)}}, \text{ where}$$

$$\text{GSS(Model)} = \sum_{b=1}^{B} n_b \times \left(\text{Ave}_b(\hat{Y}) - \text{Ave}_b(Y)\right)^2, \text{ and}$$

$$\text{GSS(Total)} = \sum_{b=1}^{B} n_b \times \left(\text{Ave}(Y) - \text{Ave}_b(Y)\right)^2.$$

Different values of the grouped R^2 result with different rules for defining the subgroups. One should decide, preferably in advance, on a few ways of binning the population of greatest interest. (This same issue applies to the Hosmer-Lemeshow tests, described in Chapter 9.) Thus, for example, to see how well a model predicts next year's cost as a function of this year's, we could use quintiles of current cost to form the bins. In this instance, the grouped R^2 measures how much of the variation in next year's costs that exists for people on the basis of this year's cost is explained by the model.

Interpreting Measures of Performance

Analytic Context

Only experience suggests what values of R^2 "good" models should have, and the notion of a good R^2 varies depending on the context. For example, when predicting next year's healthcare costs for a Medicare enrollee from information available this year, models with R^2 values of 0.05 are considered useful by actuaries and policymakers; when predicting one year's salary from employee characteristics, models with R^2 values around 0.80 are the norm (Ash et al. 1989; Epstein and Cumella 1988; Scott 1977).

The most recent work with ACG-type models to predict 1992 total annual costs to Medicare has achieved R^2 values in the range of 5.5 percent to 6.3 percent (for the so-called ADG-Hosdom and ADG-MDC models, respectively) (Weiner et al. 1996). The most recently reported DCG-type models applied to the same database have similar explanatory power, in particular, 6.3 percent for the strictly hierarchical DCG model that uses ambulatory as well as inpatient diagnoses, and 8.1 percent for the HCC payment model (Ellis et al 1996).

Many people are unimpressed by models that explain less than 10 percent of the variation in cost. However, context is all-important. Models predicting next year's costs will never have high R^2 values largely because they cannot know which specific individuals will incur catastrophic expenses next year. Nonetheless, such models may still be helpful depending on the policy context.

The following example illustrates a context in which low R^2 values do not necessarily negate the value of a model. When using age and sex alone to predict (and pay for) next year's healthcare, costs for the 20 percent of people with the lowest expenses this year are overpaid by a factor of 2.5, while the most expensive 20 percent are underpaid by half. Obviously, under this age- and sex-adjusted payment system, people who were expensive in the past would not be attractive risks for capitated health plans. However, the HCC risk-adjustment model substantially reduces these payment errors (Ellis et al. 1996). The HCC approach overpays only

30 percent for the lowest quintile of this year's cost and underpays only 15 percent for the highest quintile. Risk-adjusted payments attempt to reduce the disincentive for health plans to enroll chronically ill persons with predictably high future expenses. Although not a complete solution, the HCC model helps address that problem, despite its low R^2.

Context is not always simple to evaluate when interpreting R^2 values for risk-adjustment methods. APACHE II was developed explicitly for use in ICUs, although it also has been employed as one dimension of severity in non-ICU populations (Daley et al. 1988; Iezzoni et al. 1990; Keeler et al. 1990). APACHE III yielded an R^2 (cross-validated, see Chapter 5) of 0.15 to predict ICU LOS (Knaus et al. 1993). The analysis was based on data drawn from a stratified random sample of 26 hospitals, plus 14 other volunteer hospitals that were primarily tertiary teaching facilities. Location of patients (in the ICU) and the predominance of tertiary teaching hospitals affect context, and it is unclear what R^2 to expect when using APACHE III in a different setting.

In the 1992 MedisGroups Comparative Database used in our AHCPR-funded severity project, the hospital sample was not nationally representative. Pennsylvania hospitals were overrepresented (55 percent of the hospitals in the database versus 4 percent nationally), as were hospitals with over 300 beds (51 versus 18 percent) and teaching hospitals (49 versus 19 percent). The generalizability of conclusions drawn from analyzing this database is unclear. Unfortunately, this is often the case (i.e., the effect of context on model performance is usually unknown).

In some investigations, diseases are chosen specifically because severity adjustment is likely to affect cost or length of stay. R^2 values for models developed for such conditions will tend to be larger than R^2 values for a random selection of cases, or for cases from conditions selected for other reasons. For example, in choosing conditions for study with Disease Staging, Conklin and colleagues (1984, 17) used as one selection criterion that the DRGs be "characterized by a high degree of variability in cost per stay." Averill and collaborators (1992) focused on DRGs for which severity significantly affected patient cost. Thomas and Ashcraft (1991, 42–43) selected conditions from four university hospitals and one community hospital "based on frequency of occurrence (relatively high), costs (high and/or highly variable), clinical specificity of DRG definitions (both very specific and not very specific), and major treatment modality (medical and surgical)." In each study, one criterion was the potential of severity to explain outcome. The R^2 values should be interpreted in light of this choice.

Hardness of the Data to Model

As discussed in the section on maximum R^2, measures of performance depend on the cases in the database as well as on the variables available for modeling. Two database characteristics have a major effect on the R^2—the dispersion of the independent variables and the dispersion of the dependent variable. Figure 8.1 shows three schematic diagrams of models to predict Y from a single variable X, where we assume that larger values for X indicate a sicker person. Graph A shows the classic bivariate normal situation. R^2 is approximately equal to

$$1 - \frac{\text{variance } (Y - \hat{Y})}{\text{variance in } Y} \, .$$

The other two graphs in Figure 8.1 show what happens when only some of the data are available for modeling. In Graph B, cases with extreme values of X have been eliminated, leading to less variation in Y but with no change in the variation in $(Y - \hat{Y})$ for the remaining cases. In this situation, we expect R^2 to decrease. In Graph C, cases with extreme values of Y are removed, which reduces both kinds of variation. The net effect on R^2 is unpredictable.

As another illustration of the effect of the data set's characteristics, suppose two risk adjustors are applied to two different data sets and are equally accurate in predicting outcomes for cases across the range of independent variables (i.e., SSE/n is the same for each system). The method applied to the data set with more variability in the outcome variable will generate a higher SST and, thus, the R^2 will be higher (Korn and Simon 1991). The higher R^2 leads to a misleading conclusion about the superior performance of the method.

As suggested above, in certain data sets, cases are sampled nonrandomly: For example, certain types of cases are oversampled to increase the amount of information available about them (e.g., cost outliers, patients who died, the uninsured). The average level of the outcome for these oversampled patients often differs greatly from that in the general population. The result is artificially large variability of the dependent variable, usually leading to a higher value of R^2 than would be encountered in a general population. Such concerns led some to conclude that R^2 is not suitable for comparing models developed on different data sets (Cox and Wermuth 1992). More generally, one must remain aware that comparing model performance on different data sets can be misleading, even with measures of model performance other than R^2.

Figure 8.1 How Differences in the Data Modeled Affect R^2

Graph A

Graph B

Graph C

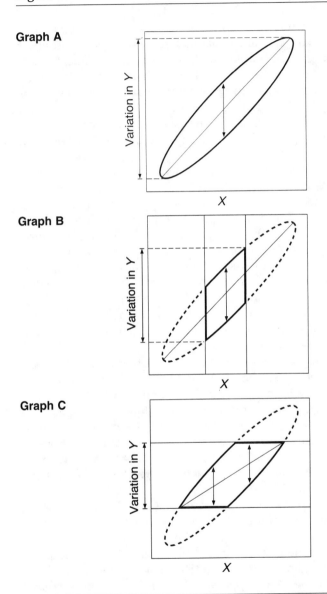

Graph A shows a regression line fit to a schematic scatterplot of bivariate normal data. In graph B, cases with extreme values of X have been removed; in graph C, cases with extreme values of Y have been removed. The shorter, vertical arrows in the body of each graph indicate variation in $(Y - \hat{Y})$. The smaller the ratio of variation in $(Y - \hat{Y})$ to variation in Y, the larger is R^2.

Trimming the Data

Because general linear models are fit specifically to minimize the square of the error term, particularly deviant values in the data set have a large effect on parameter estimates. For example, a payor may not care whether $10,000 in excess costs occurs because the observed cost of a single case exceeds the predicted by $10,000, or because the observed cost for each of ten patients exceeds expected by $1,000. However, the squared term associated with one large error is far greater than the sum of squares associated with a number of smaller errors that add to the same amount: $1 \times (10,000)^2$ is ten times larger than $10 \times (1,000)^2$.

This is one reason for "trimming," in which certain types of cases are eliminated before analysis. Cost "outliers" (i.e., very high cost or very low cost cases) are often trimmed. Trimming's effect on R^2 is not obvious. Both SSE and SST are reduced by dropping outlier cases. Because R^2 is determined from the ratio of these two values, the effect of eliminating outliers depends on the relative magnitude of changes in the two terms.

Data can be trimmed in a variety of ways. In studies where the outcome is hospital resource use, a common strategy involves defining either cost or length of stay outliers similarly to Medicare's policy under DRG-based prospective payment (Conklin et al. 1984; Thomas and Ashcraft 1991; Iezzoni et al. 1991). In such studies, analyses are often performed both including and excluding outlier cases.

Other studies have defined outliers using rules that are less sensitive to extreme values than those promulgated by Medicare. For example, McGuire (1991) employed a nonparametric trimming algorithm derived from the first and third quartile points of the data. McMahon and colleagues (1992) developed a modification of APACHE, called APACHE-L, which uses the laboratory values of the APACHE score to explain variations in LOS and ancillary resource use. They used Cook's D-statistic to identify influential observations on ancillary resource use, which were then eliminated (Cook and Weisberg 1982, 116–17).

In our AHCPR-funded severity study, we considered two strategies to identify high LOS outliers: (1) HCFA's approach, which flagged all cases more than three standard deviations from the mean on a log scale; and (2) a robust approach (one less sensitive to the actual distribution of the data) proposed by Hoaglin and Iglewicz (1987). For hip fracture patients (Shwartz et al. 1996b), the HCFA approach eliminated 57 outliers (from a sample of 5,721), reducing the average LOS from 11.9 days to 11.5 days; the Hoaglin-Iglewicz approach eliminated 414 outliers, shortening average LOS to 10.3 days. Using the Hoaglin-Iglewicz approach, R^2 was higher on trimmed cases for only one of the 14 severity methods considered; for eight methods, R^2 was almost 50 percent higher using the HCFA trim points

(Shwartz et al. 1996b). Likewise, in the study of pneumonia cases (Iezzoni et al. 1996), R^2 was higher using the HCFA trim points for all severity measures but one.

Other studies have not eliminated outliers but have reset outlier values to a prespecified, less extreme value, a practice called "Winsorizing" (D'Agostino and Lee 1977) or truncating. For example, one study that examined the relationship between a measure of disease complexity and hospital charges set all charges that exceeded the 95th percentile to the value of the 95th percentile (in that case, $61,000) (Naessens et al. 1992). In deriving APACHE III models to predict ICU LOS, Knaus and colleagues (1993) capped all ICU LOSs at 40 days.

As with trimming, Winsorizing data raises some concern. Both methods ignore some of the variability in the outcome measure, and they change its mean value. Trimming completely eliminates outliers, while Winsorizing pulls them in closer to the center of the data. For many applications, these methods do not cause problems. However, if the models are being developed to predict outcomes for new individuals, they are likely to perform poorly in the regions trimmed or Winsorized (i.e., the mean will not be valued correctly).

In addition, the effect of eliminating (or truncating) outliers may vary depending on how the risk adjustor is constructed. Methods that generate only a few categories (e.g., that assign scores of 1 to 5) may have focused on identifying a highest-risk category with few cases that are likely to result in the highest values of the dependent variable. In theory, risk-adjustment approaches designed in this way should perform relatively better when outliers are included in the analysis than when they are excluded. Risk-adjustment approaches employing a continuous scale may distinguish better among nonoutlier cases but may not perform as well when cases with extreme values are included.

In the study by Thomas and Ashcraft (1991, Table 8.2), no consistent picture was found concerning the effect of trimming the data on the R^2 associated with different types of risk-adjustment methods. Focusing on the validated R^2, DRGs, CSI maximum scores, and MedisGroups admission scores had higher R^2 levels with outliers excluded; the other methods had higher R^2 values using all cases. Iezzoni and colleagues (1991) likewise found no consistent pattern across conditions in terms of whether admission score or midstay reviews using MedisGroups had higher R^2 values using trimmed or untrimmed data. In our studies of pneumonia cases and of hip fracture cases, R^2 values were noticeably higher on the trimmed data sets (Iezzoni et al. 1996; Shwartz et al. 1996b).

How and whether to trim data is best decided in a policy context. For example, when predicting costs, dropping cases over $100,000 is consistent with a payment system that covers all costs below this threshold but pays for cases that cost more out of a separate pool. If only the costs exceeding $100,000 are handled separately, then Winsorizing costs (rather than dropping cases) is appropriate. Any trimming understates costs (that is, produces predictions that are systematically smaller than actual outcomes) and can be misleading in a payment system with no special mechanism for separately handling outliers.

Form of the Risk Measure

As shown in Tables 1.7 and 1.8, some risk-adjustment approaches produce categorical measures of risk and others a continuous value. To capture complex relationships between risk and outcome, continuous values of a risk-adjustment score are sometimes recoded as discrete categories. How this is done and whether outliers are included in the analysis can affect the R^2.

Categories can be defined expressly to distribute cases relatively evenly among them (e.g., by defining five quintiles of increasing risk). In this instance, models are likely to perform better when outliers are excluded. In contrast, the top category may be defined to contain a small percentage of all cases but nonetheless to capture relatively rare cases with the highest values of the outcome of interest. Such a model is likely to perform better with outliers included.

To some extent, the value of different methods depends on how they will be used. Suppose that two risk-adjustment methods each have risk categories 1, 2, 3, and 4. Suppose further that Method A's four categories have 1, 3, 4, and 10 percent problem rates respectively. Method B's four categories have 0.5, 3, 4, and 25 percent problem rates respectively. At first glance, Method B seems to discriminate better. Suppose, however, that you discovered that 25 percent of cases were in each of Method A's four categories, while only 1 percent of cases were in Method B's lowest and highest risk groups (categories 1 and 4). For many purposes, Method A is more useful because it can meaningfully discriminate relatively large numbers of people. In other situations, if finding the 1 percent of the population at lowest and highest risk is important, Method B would be much better.

In comparing performance measures across approaches for which discrete categories have been created from a continuous scale, one must understand how the categories were defined and how cases were distributed across categories. If the category definitions were chosen to maximize model performance in a development data set, the model's performance could deteriorate when used with new data. A simple way to examine how much discrimination is achieved in a categorical model (i.e., one that assigns cases to a small number of risk categories) is to tabulate the percentage of cases and the average value of the outcome variable in each risk category. Better models have larger fractions of the whole population identified in risk categories with either very low or very high average outcomes.

To convert APACHE II to a five-level ordinal scale, Thomas and Ashcraft (1991) sought cutpoints to yield a distribution of APACHE II scores similar to the overall distribution across MedisGroups admission scores and CSI admission scores. This categorization was first performed across all cases, regardless of diagnosis. However, they discovered that condition-specific cutpoints not tied to the distribution of patients in other methods worked better. To define the condition-specific cutpoints, they used the Automatic Interaction Detector algorithm (Morgan and Sonquist 1963), which groups cases into categories with the goal of reducing within-category variation in the dependent variable. In their study, the criterion used to form the classes was to minimize within-category variation in hospitalization costs. This approach was also used to define cutpoints for other severity measures that are continuous (a version of Disease Staging's scaled indices). In such instances, one must remain aware that the same data were used both to modify the methods and to evaluate their performance.

Chapter 5 discusses the use of computer-based approaches (e.g., LOWESS and cubic splines) for producing a smoothed plot of the relationship between an outcome and a candidate independent variable. Change points in the smoothed function (places where the change in outcome is large for a small change in the independent variable) can be used to define cutpoints for categories of independent variables, which are then represented in the final model by dummy variables.

Data Transformations

Continuous outcome variables, such as LOS and hospital charges, are often skewed, possessing "long right tails." This situation generates two major problems:

- The underlying distributional assumptions of certain statistical tests—that outcomes are normally distributed—are violated.
- A few unusually high values can significantly affect parameter estimates and measures of performance.

As a way to limit the influence of high-value cases, an alternative to trimming involves transforming the dependent variable. Often a logarithmic transformation is used (i.e., the actual value of the dependent variable is replaced by its natural logarithm). A more general approach involves a range of possible transformations, such as the Box-Cox models. A logarithmic transformation is one member of the family of Box-Cox transformations (Box, Hunter, and Hunter 1978; Atkinson 1985; Spitzer 1982). The transformed data more closely conform to the assumptions of OLS modeling, making the approach most appropriate when the goal is to identify significant predictors of the outcome. However, when models are used to predict the value of the dependent variable, predicting the log of the outcome is less useful.

Predictions based on a transformed outcome variable must be retransformed to the original scale before calculating performance measures. In particular, it is inappropriate to compare the R^2 values associated with predicting logged and unlogged outcomes. As discussed above, OLS maximizes R^2 for the data to which the model is fit—whether the original or a transformed scale. Regardless of this choice, the R^2 to judge model performance should be computed in the original scale (e.g., dollars, days).

Duan's smearing estimator is a widely used, theoretically attractive approach for retransforming log-transformed data (Duan 1983). This estimator is a number (the average of the retransformed residuals) by which each prediction is multiplied in an attempt to correct for the known bias associated with the retransformation. However, the retransformed predictions often fail to achieve as high an R^2 as a model fit directly to the untransformed data. Consequently, it is important to evaluate performance measures using the actual scale of interest (e.g., dollars, days) and not to report only R^2 values from modeling with transformed data as if they were comparable to those achieved when predicting the actual outcome.

In our severity project, we evaluated R^2 both on untransformed LOS data and log transformed data, using Duan's smearing estimator to retransform predictions before calculating R^2. For both pneumonia cases and hip fracture cases (Iezzoni et al. 1996; Shwartz et al. 1996b), R^2 values were as high or higher using LOS rather than log(LOS) and retransforming as the dependent variables.

Nonlinear Models

The generalized linear model (GLM) provides a versatile framework for dealing with data that do not meet the assumptions for OLS regression. Although the relationship between the outcome and the predictor variables may be far from linear, some function of the outcome, called a "link" function, may be modeled as a linear function of the predictors. The GLM framework also allows for independent specification of how variances are expected to change as a function of the mean value of the outcome (because we know, for example, that costs for expensive cases tend to vary more than costs for inexpensive ones). An advantage of using GLM to predict the cost, using the log function as a link, as opposed to using OLS to predict log(cost) is that the GLM algorithm seeks parameters to predict actual dollars directly, rather than log(dollars). Generalized linear models are described in a classic but sophisticated text by McCullagh and Nelder (1989), which requires an understanding of mathematical likelihood. Several books describe generalized linear models via their implementation in the S programming language (Chambers and Hastie 1993; Ripley and Venable 1994).

The most commonly used GLM is logistic regression for predicting a dichotomous outcome, in which the link function is the logit of the probability of a problem: log $(p/1-p)$. The variance of an outcome is specified as being proportional to $p*(1-p)$. We discuss the logistic model in Chapter 9.

Dudley and colleagues (1993) studied five different analytic methods for examining a dollar-based outcome: OLS to predict dollars; OLS to predict log(dollars); logistic regression (to predict whether a case would be high cost); and two survival modeling approaches, a parametric (Weibull) approach and a nonparametric (proportional hazards) approach. Survival modeling, usually used to predict the time to an event (such as death), can be used to predict any non-negative outcome, in this case total hospital charges for an admission for CABG surgery. In their analyses, the choice of model substantially affected which variables appeared to predict charges. Their paper provides a good discussion of the issues involved in interpreting the results of the different analyses.

In using survival models (see Chapter 5) to predict dollars (rather than time to an event), observations are viewed as continuing to accumulate charges until they become "complete" at the time of live discharge from the hospital. If, however, the patient dies, the observation becomes "censored" (because we do not see the additional costs that might have occurred before discharge). This framework adapts well to the reality that costs tend to be lowest for both the very sickest persons (because they die before many resources are consumed) and the least sick (whose cases are relatively uncomplicated), and to the highly skewed distributions found in health cost outcomes data. However, survival models are difficult to interpret when (as here) the censored observations (cases that die) systematically differ from complete cases (cases discharged alive), a problem technically referred to as "informative censoring." Furthermore, the importance of the construct "what patients would likely have cost had they not died" is not obvious. Thus, if a substantial fraction of cases are censored (die), survival modeling to predict costs becomes problematic.

Model Validation

Calibration

When OLS is used to estimate model parameters in a development data set, the average of the predicted values from the model [AVE($\hat{Y}_i$)] is equal to the average of the actual values of the dependent variable [AVE(Y_i)]. However, when the model is applied to another data set, AVE($\hat{Y}_i$) is likely to differ from AVE(Y_i). As discussed earlier, the significance of this difference depends on the purpose of the comparison. Assuming the goal is to assess model validity, one might then consider the difference between AVE($\hat{Y}_i$) and AVE(Y_i) as a measure of model calibration. One indicator of model performance is therefore how well it calibrates in a validation data set. As discussed at the start of this chapter, in some situations it is reasonable to adjust the model to ensure calibration—for example, by reestimating the constant term or by multiplying each of the estimates by AVE(Y_i)/AVE($\hat{Y}_i$) to force the observed and expected averages to coincide.

In addition to examining overall calibration, assessing calibration for certain subgroups of interest using both development and validation data sets is valuable. For example, consider this: How much higher are costs in teaching hospitals compared to nonteaching hospitals after adjusting for differences in severity of illness of patients? Such an analysis is typically performed first by running a regression model with variables to reflect severity of illness and a dummy variable to indicate hospital teaching status. The coefficient associated with the teaching status variable is interpreted as a measure of the magnitude of the cost difference after adjusting for severity differences (Iezzoni et al. 1990). In a slightly different context, this is the same issue as discussed earlier in the chapter, using the example of myocardial infarction patients in Florida. For the teaching status question, we assume that the severity measure is equally valid in teaching and nonteaching hospitals. As described in Chapter 4, because of the more extensive documentation in teaching hospital medical records, this assumption may be faulty.

Subgroups of interest can be specified in different ways, such as urban versus rural hospitals, public versus private hospitals, Medicaid versus Blue Cross as a payor, insured versus uninsured. In each example, concerns arise about differences in the performance of a risk-adjustment measure in the subgroups under consideration.

Subgroup fit can be examined, for example, to determine if the relationship between severity and the outcome changes in the same way when an analysis is performed within subgroups. However, as discussed at the end of Chapter 9, the question of the validity of a severity measure in subgroups of interest raises difficult issues about performance that ultimately rest on dimensions other than predictive validity (see Chapter 6).

One should distinguish subgroups formed *a priori* (using similar variables to those available for making predictions) from subgroups of patients formed on the basis of their outcomes. A typical example of the latter is patients distinguished because they have a particularly high (or low) value of the outcome variable. Concerns have arisen about the failure of risk-adjustment methods to calibrate well on these particular subgroups, a problem sometimes called "compression." However, when groups are formed *post hoc*, based on extreme outcomes, the mean expected value of the group should be less extreme than the actual group value. This is especially easy to see when considering models to predict the total cost of next year's health services for a group of persons (see Chapter 10). For example, about 40 percent of Medicare beneficiaries generate no healthcare costs over one year. However, no Medicare recipients have expected costs during a year of enrollment of zero dollars. No matter how healthy a group of people was in a particular year, some costs are likely to be generated in the next year. Similarly, no matter how expensive, on average, a group of persons is expected to be next year because of problems observed this year, their actual costs will not be as high as the highest among all Medicare recipients in the next year. Patients with the very highest or lowest costs in any one period are expected to have costs in the next period that are closer to the overall average in that period, a phenomenon called "regression to the mean" (Bailar and Mosteller 1986, 87).

Little analysis of subgroup calibration in the context of evaluating model performance has occurred when predicting a continuous dependent variable. The usual assumption is that the risk-adjustment approach applies equally well to subgroups of interest. Thus, subgroup differences after adjusting for risk are assumed to be unrelated to different levels of overall fit in the subgroups but instead are due to other characteristics of the subgroups (e.g., differences in the quality of care). As discussed in Chapter 9, this issue has been studied more in models predicting death.

Cross-Validated R^2 Values

In discussing predictive validity, Chapter 6 described approaches for validating predictions when a second data set for external validation is unavailable. When the data set is large enough, the simplest approach is to use a portion (e.g., one-half or two-thirds) of the data to develop the model and the remaining portion (e.g., one-half or one-third) to validate the model. We used such an approach to validate the comorbidity prediction model described earlier (Shwartz et al. 1996a). In this validation, we focused on the increase in R^2 from adding the comorbidity variables to a model that included only DRGs. On the first half of the data, the R^2 associated with the model including only DRGs was 0.44; adding the comorbidity variables increased the R^2 20 percent to 0.53. When this model was validated on the second half of the data, the increase in R^2 from adding the comorbidity variables was 16 percent (from 0.38 to 0.44). When the roles of the development and validation groups were reversed, the increase in R^2 in the validation set was again 16 percent (from 0.41 to 0.48). As noted above, when the entire data set was used, the increase in R^2 was about 20 percent (from 0.42 to 0.50). This analysis suggests that most of the increase in R^2 from adding the comorbidity variables to a model that already includes DRGs is real, not an artifact of model overfitting.

In our AHCPR-funded severity project, we performed cross-validation as follows. First, we randomly split the data in half, into samples 1 and 2, and fit models to each. In sample 1, we computed SSE1 and SST1, as

> SSE_1 = the sum (within sample 1) of squared differences between each Y and the $\hat{Y}$ predicted for it by the model that was fit to sample 2; and

> SST_1 = the sum (within sample 1) of squared differences between the individual Y's and the average Y in sample 1.

From these we computed validated R^2, denoted CVR_1^2, as $1 - SSE_1/SST_1$. We repeated this process, reversing the roles of samples 1 and 2, to get CVR_2^2, a validated R^2 for the sample 2 data. We then computed a summary CVR^2 as the average of these two values. This method gave us insight into the variation associated with the resulting value. However, if a single number is required, another approach is to calculate a single CVR^2 value on the whole database, using

> SSE = SSE1 + SSE2 = the sum (over all cases) of squared differences between each Y and the $\hat{Y}$ predicted for it by the model that was fit to the sample that did not contain it; and

> SST = the sum (over all cases) of squared differences between the individual Y's and the average Y in the whole population. Note that SST does not equal SST1 + SST2.

An advantage of this approach is that it generalizes readily to settings where too little data are available to hold out half for model validation. In this situation, a popular cross-validation approach is to divide the data into a number of approximately equal parts (e.g., ten) and to fit models successively on all of the data except one part. Each model developed (e.g., on 90 percent of the data) is used to make predictions for the held-out part. Thus, the prediction for each case that goes into the SSE is made based on the unique model that did not include that case in parameter estimation. Cross-validated R^2 values are then calculated from the actual and predicted values for all the cases, as in the second method described above (see Chapter 6).

Knaus and colleagues (1993) held out successive tenths of cases in estimating the cross-validated R^2 for predictions of length of stay using APACHE III. Naessens and colleagues (1992) used the same approach in validating the ability of a complexity indicator to explain hospital charges. Thomas and Ashcraft (1991) used a single case hold-out approach to determine validated R^2 in their analyses.

In general, the smaller the hold-out sample, the more concern arises about falsely assessing model validity. As noted, if only small subsets are held out during each iteration, the main body of the data is similar for each successive model fit (Picard and Berk 1990). Thus, the models are unlikely to differ much from a model fit to the entire database. Nevertheless, as shown in Table 8.2, cross-validated R^2 values can differ substantially from R^2 values in the development data set even when only one case is held out (Thomas and Ashcraft 1991), suggesting the large effect even a single case can have when the sample used for modeling is modest. In our severity project, with large sample sizes (see Table 1.9), cross-validated R^2 values were very similar to values developed on the entire data set (e.g., Table 8.3).

As noted earlier, Table 8.2 prompts the question, What is the variability in the estimate of the R^2 associated with the different models? Answers would allow one to determine which models have R^2 values that are statistically significantly higher than those of other models. Chapter 6 discussed "bootstrapping" as an approach to estimate confidence intervals for statistics such as the R^2, whose distributional properties are not well characterized. To construct a bootstrap estimate for a model's R^2, sampling with replacement is used to select from the original data a large number (e.g., 1,000) of simulated populations, each of the same size as the original population. The model is fit to the data in each simulated population, and the R^2 calculated. Confidence intervals for R^2 can be constructed from the distribution of the 1,000 R^2 values. For example, if the 5th and 95th percentiles (that is, the 50th from the lowest and 50th from the highest values of R^2) were 0.15 and 0.23, respectively, then [0.15, 0.23] is a 90 percent confidence interval for R^2.

As part of an analysis of the contributions of severity of illness to explaining cost differences between tertiary teaching and nonteaching hospitals, we estimated that severity plus other patient characteristics (e.g., admission source, discharge destination, transfer status, purpose of admission) explained 18 percent of the higher costs at teaching hospitals. We used bootstrapping to determine a 90 percent confidence interval for this estimate, which was 4 percent to 33 percent (Iezzoni et al. 1990).

Hornbrook and Goodman (1995) validated models developed to predict next year's total health expenses in order to risk adjust when setting capitated payment rates. They randomly split their overall data set 25 times and, for each of the 25 times, they used one half of the data for model estimation and the other half for model validation (i.e., predictions for each case in the validation sample were generated from a model fit to the estimation sample). In each of the 25 validation samples, five criteria were used to evaluate performance: (1) average prediction error, where smaller is better; (2) variance of the predicted values, where larger is better (to shift more dollars around); (3) a comparison of the distribution of predicted values to the distribution of observed values; (4) correlation between errors in prediction and risk factors included in the model and other policy relevant attributes (e.g., race), the less correlation the better; and (5) good "group" predictions, because the purpose of the model is to set payment rates for groups, not individuals. To examine group predictions, in each validation sample, cases were sorted from highest to lowest by predicted expenses and then divided into 50 groups, differing in terms of their predicted risk. The R^2 from a model that regressed average predicted value for each of the 50 groups on the average observed expense for the group served as a validated measure of goodness of fit. The approach is similar to the grouped R^2 discussed above.

Conclusions

R^2 is the standard measure of performance in models with a continuous dependent variable. In this chapter we highlighted factors that must be considered when interpreting a particular value of R^2 reported for analyses involving risk adjustment, including these:

- the maximum value for R^2 that could realistically be achieved using the risk-adjustment variables on a particular data set;
- the specific context or origin of the sample under study (e.g., type of hospitals, whether certain groups were oversampled);
- the variability in the dependent and independent variables in the data set;
- whether outliers are included in the analysis;
- whether the risk adjustor is a continuous variable and, if so, whether and how discrete categories were formed for this analysis;
- whether data transformations were performed and, if so, whether the R^2 is reported on the retransformed data; and
- whether R^2 estimates were validated or confidence intervals reported.

Reported R^2 values must be interpreted in light of such factors—many of which require judgment. Therefore, although R^2 is a numeric value, knowing what to make of it requires subjective evaluation of a range of issues. As noted in Chapter 9, many identical issues arise when evaluating the performance of models for dichotomous outcomes.

References

Ash, A., F. Porell, L. Gruenberg, E. Sawitz, and A. Beiser. 1989. "Adjusting Medicare Capitation Payments Using Prior Hospitalization Data." *Health Care Financing Review* 10 (4): 17–29.

Atkinson, A. C. 1985. *Plots, Transformations, and Regression: An Introduction to Graphical Methods of Diagnostic Regression Analysis.* Oxford: Clarendon Press.

Averill, R. F., T. E. McGuire, B. E. Manning, D. A. Fowler, S. D. Horn, P. S. Dickson, M. J. Coye, D. L. Knowlton, and J. A. Bender. 1992. "A Study of the Relationship Between Severity of Illness and Hospital Cost in New Jersey Hospitals." *HSR: Health Services Research* 27 (5): 587–606.

Bailar, J. C., III, and F. Mosteller. 1986. *Medical Uses of Statistics.* Waltham, MA: NEJM Books.

Box, G. E. P., W. G. Hunter, and J. S. Hunter. 1978. *Statistics for Experimenters. An Introduction to Design, Data Analysis, and Model Building.* New York: John Wiley & Sons.

Breiman, L., J. H. Friedman, R. A. Olshen, and C. J. Stone. 1984. *Classification and Regression Trees.* Belmont, CA: Wadsworth International Group.

Chambers, J. M., and T. J. Hastie, EDS. 1993. *Statistical Models in S. In Chapman and Hall Computer Science Series.* New York: Chapman and Hall.

Chassin, M. R., E. L. Hannan, and B. A. DeBuono. 1996. "Benefits and Hazards of Reporting Medical Outcomes Publicly." *New England Journal of Medicine*, 334 (6): 394–98.

Computer Resource Center. 1992. *Stata Reference Manual: Release 3. 5th Edition. Volume 1.* Santa Monica, CA: The Center.

Conklin, J. E., J. V. Lieberman, C. A. Barnes, and D. Z. Louis. 1984. "Disease Staging: Implications for Hospital Reimbursement and Management." *Health Care Financing Review* Annual Supplement: 13–22.

Cook, R. D., and S. Weisberg. 1982. *Residuals and Influence in Regression.* New York: Chapman and Hall.

Cox, D. R., and N. Wermuth. 1992. "A Comment on the Coefficient of Determination for Binary Responses." *American Statistician* 46 (1): 1–4.

D'Agostino, R. B., and A. F. S. Lee. 1977. "Robustness of Location Estimators Under Changes of Population Kurtosis." *Journal of the American Statistical Association* 72 (358): 393–96.

Daley, J., S. Jencks, D. Draper, G. Lenhart, N. Thomas, and J. Walker. 1988. "Predicting Hospital-Associated Mortality for Medicare Patients. A Method for Patients with Stroke, Pneumonia, Acute Myocardial Infarction, and Congestive Heart Failure." *Journal of the American Medical Association* 260 (24): 3617–24.

Draper, N. R., and H. Smith. 1981. *Applied Regression Analysis*, 2nd ed. New York: Wiley.

Duan, N. 1983. "Smearing Estimate: A Nonparametric Retransformation Method." *Journal of the American Statistical Association* 78 (383): 605–10.

Dudley, R. A., F. E. Harrell, Jr., L. R. Smith, D. B. Mark, R. M. Califf, D. B. Pryor, D. Glower, J. Lipscomb, and M. Hlatky. 1993. "Comparison of Analytic Models for Estimating the Effect of Clinical Factors on the Cost of Coronary Artery Bypass Graft Surgery." *Journal of Clinical Epidemiology* 46 (3): 261–71.

Ellis, R. P., G. C. Pope, L. I. Iezzoni, J. Z. Ayanian, D. W. Bates, H. Burstin, and A. S. Ash. 1996. "Diagnosis-Based Risk Adjustment for Medicare Capitation Payments." *Health Care Financing Review* 17 (3): 101–28.

Epstein, A. M., and E. J. Cumella. 1988. "Capitation Payment: Using Predictors for Medical Utilization to Adjust Rates." *Health Care Financing Review* 10 (1): 51–69.

Freeman, J. L., R. B. Fetter, H. Park, K. C. Schneider, J. L. Lichtenstein, J. S. Hughes, W. A. Bauman, C. C. Duncan, D. H. Freeman, Jr., and G. R. Palmer. 1995. "Diagnosis-Related Group Refinement with Diagnosis- and Procedure-Specific Comorbidities and Complications." *Medical Care* 33 (8): 806–27.

Gonnella, J. S., M. C. Hornbrook, and D. Z. Louis. 1984. "Staging of Disease. A Case-Mix Measurement." *Journal of the American Medical Association* 251 (5): 637–44.

Green, J. and N. Wintfeld. 1995. "Report Cards on Cardiac Surgeons. Assessing New York State's Approach." *New England Journal of Medicine* 332 (18): 1229–32.

Hannan, E. L., A. L. Siu, D. Kuman, H. Kilburn, and M. R. Chassin. 1995. "The Decline in Coronary Artery Bypass Graft Surgery Mortality in New York State." *Journal of the American Medical Association* 273 (3): 209–13.

Hoaglin, D. C. and B. Iglewicz. 1987. "Fine-Tuning Some Resistant Rules for Outlier Labeling." *Journal of the American Statistical Association* 82 (400): 1147–49.

Health Care Financing Administration. 1996a. "High-Cost Users of Medicare Services." *Health Care Financing Review*, Medicare and Medicaid Statistical Supplement: 32.

Health Care Financing Administration. 1996b. "Table 17. Persons Served Under Medicare and Program Payments, by Type of High-Cost User: Calendar Year 1994." *Health Care Financing Review*, Medicare and Medicaid Statistical Supplement: 220.

Hornbrook, M.C., and Goodman, M.J. 1995. "Assessing Relative Health Plan Risk with the RAND-36 Health Survey." *Inquiry* 32 (1): 56–74.

Iezzoni, L. I., M. Shwartz, M. A. Moskowitz, A. S. Ash, E. Sawitz, and S. Burnside. 1990. "Illness Severity and Costs of Admissions at Teaching and Nonteaching Hospitals." *Journal of the American Medical Association* 264 (11): 1426–31.

Iezzoni, L. I., A. S. Ash, G. A. Coffman, and M. A. Moskowitz. 1991. "Admission and Mid-Stay MedisGroups® Scores as Predictors of Hospitalization Charges." *Medical Care* 29 (3): 210–20.

Iezzoni, L. I., M. Shwartz, A. S. Ash, and Y. D. Mackiernan. 1996. "Does Severity Explain Differences in Hospital Length of Stay for Pneumonia Patients?" *Journal of Health Services Research and Policy* 1 (2): 65–76.

Keeler, E. B., K. L. Kahn, D. Draper, M. J. Sherwood, L. V. Rubenstein, E. J. Reinisch,

J. Kosecoff, and R. H. Brook. 1990. "Changes in Sickness at Admission Following the Introduction of the Prospective Payment System." *Journal of the American Medical Association* 264 (15): 1962–68.

Knaus, W. A., D. P. Wagner, E. A. Draper, J. E. Zimmerman, M. Bergner, P. G. Bastos, C. A. Sirio, D. J. Murphy, T. Lotring, A. Damiano, and F. E. Harrell, Jr. 1991. "The APACHE III Prognostic System. Risk Prediction of Hospital Mortality for Critically Ill Hospitalized Adults." *Chest* 100 (6): 1619–36.

Knaus, W. A., D. P. Wagner, J. E. Zimmerman, and E. A. Draper. 1993. "Variations in Mortality and Length of Stay in Intensive Care Units." *Annals of Internal Medicine* 118 (10): 753–61.

Korn, E. L., and R. Simon. 1991. "Explained Residual Variation, Explained Risk, and Goodness of Fit." *American Statistician* 45 (3): 201–6.

McCullagh, P., and J. A. Nelder. 1989. *Generalized Linear Models*, 2nd Ed. London: Chapman and Hall.

McGuire, T. E. 1991. "An Evaluation of Diagnosis-Related Group Severity and Complexity Refinement." *Health Care Financing Review* 12 (4): 49–60.

McMahon, L. F., Jr., R. A. Hayward, A. M. Bernard, J. S. Rosevear, and L. A. Weissfeld. 1992. "APACHE-L: A New Severity of Illness Adjuster for Inpatient Medical Care." *Medical Care* 30 (5): 445–52.

Morgan, J. N., and J. A. Sonquist. 1963. "Problems in the Analysis of Survey Data, and a Proposal." *Journal of the American Statistical Association* 58 (302): 415–34.

Mosteller, F., and J. W. Tukey. 1977. *Data Analysis and Regression: A Second Course in Statistics*. Reading, MA: Addison-Wesley Publishing Co.

Naessens, J. M., C. L. Leibson, I. Krishan, and D. J. Ballard. 1992. "Contribution of a Measure of Disease Complexity (COMPLEX) to Prediction of Outcome and Charges Among Hospitalized Patients." *Mayo Clinic Proceedings* 67 (12): 1140–49.

Neter, J., and W. Wasserman. 1974. *Applied Linear Statistical Models: Regression, Analysis of Variance, and Experimental Design*. Homewood, IL: Richard D. Irwin.

Picard, R. R., and K. N. Berk. 1990. "Data Splitting." *American Statistician* 40 (2): 140–47.

Ripley, B. D. and W. N. Venable. 1994. *Modern Applied Statistics with S-Plus*. New York: Springer-Verlag.

Scott, E. L. 1977. *Higher Education Salary Evaluation Kit*. Washington, D.C.: American Association of University Professors.

Shwartz, M., L. I. Iezzoni, M. A. Moskowitz, A. S. Ash, and E. Sawitz. 1996a. "The Importance of Comorbidities in Explaining Differences in Patient Costs." *Medical Care* 34 (8): 767–79.

Shwartz, M., L. I. Iezzoni, A. S. Ash, and Y. D. Mackiernan. 1996b. "Do Severity Measures Explain Differences in Length of Hospital Stay? The Case of Hip Fracture." *HSR: Health Services Research* 31 (4): 365–85.

Spitzer, J. J. 1982. "A Primer on Box-Cox Estimation." *Review of Economics and Statistics* 64 (2): 307–13.

Steen, P. M., A. C. Brewster, R. C. Bradbury, E. Estabrook, and J. A. Young. 1993. "Predicted Probabilities of Hospital Death as a Measure of Admission Severity of Illness." *Inquiry* 30 (2): 128–41.

Starfield, B., J. Weiner, L. Mumford, and D. Steinwachs. 1991. "Ambulatory Care Groups: A Categorization of Diagnosis for Research and Management." *HSR: Health Services Research* 26 (1): 53–74.

Thomas, J. W., and M. L. F. Ashcraft. 1991. "Measuring Severity of Illness: Six Severity Systems and Their Ability to Explain Cost Variations." *Inquiry* 28 (1): 39–55.

Weiner, J. P., B. H. Starfield, D. M. Steinwachs, and L. M. Mumford. 1991. "Development and Application of a Population-Oriented Measure of Ambulatory Care Case-Mix." *Medical Care*, 29 (5): 452–72.

Weiner, J. P., A. Dobson, S. L. Maxwell, K. Coleman, B. H. Starfield, and G. F. Anderson. 1996. "Risk-Adjusted Medicare Capitation Rates Using Ambulatory and Inpatient Diagnoses." *Health Care Financing Review* 17 (3): 77–99.

Chapter 9

Evaluating the Performance of Risk-Adjustment Methods: Dichotomous Outcomes

Arlene S. Ash and Michael Shwartz

As discussed in Chapter 8, R^2 is used nearly universally to measure the performance of models with continuous variables as outcomes. However, many important healthcare outcomes are dichotomous or binary—that is, either the event did or did not occur (e.g., in-hospital death, readmission within 30 days, development of a complication, use of open heart surgery). There is less agreement about how best to measure performance for models that predict binary outcomes. In this chapter, we introduce common performance measures for models with a dichotomous outcome and discuss issues raised in interpreting the values of these measures. As an example, we use death (coded as 1 when it occurs and 0, otherwise) as our dichotomous outcome, but our comments relate to all binary outcomes.

A Simple Situation to Introduce Concepts

Suppose we compute a score measuring risk of in-hospital death and establish a cutoff such that we predict that patients will die if their scores exceed this cutoff. Patients with lower scores are predicted to live. We can array such data in a two-by-two table as shown in Table 9.1, leading to several useful quantities:

- True positive cases = A
- False positive cases = B
- True negative cases = D

- False negative cases = C
- Prevalence = (A + C) / (A + B + C + D)
- Sensitivity = A / (A + C)
- Specificity = D / (B + D)
- Predictive value positive = PV+ = A / (A + B)
- Predictive value negative = PV− = D / (C + D)

The last four quantities measure the percent of cases correctly classified, taking different perspectives. Sensitivity is the percent of deaths correctly classified by the prediction rule, while specificity is the percent of live patients correctly classified. The predictive value positive is the percent of patients predicted to die who are classified correctly, while predictive value negative measures the percent of those predicted to live who are classified correctly.

The cases used in denominators of PV+ and PV− depend on the classification rule. This complicates comparisons of different classification rules based on PV+ and PV−. In contrast, sensitivity (the "true positive rate") and specificity (the "true negative rate") use denominators defined by the death rate within the population under study. This makes sensitivity and specificity more suitable for comparisons of different classification rules involving the same population. The "false negative rate" is defined as 1 − sensitivity, and the "false positive rate," as 1 − specificity.

Lemeshow and colleagues (1988) developed models to predict the probability of in-hospital death, using data on 2,644 patients admitted to an ICU in a large tertiary teaching hospital. Three models were created, based on clinical findings at ICU admission, 24 hours into the ICU stay, or 48 hours into the ICU stay. The admission model, MPM_0 (Mortality Prediction Model with data from time zero), used data on 11 variables collected at ICU admission. Patients were predicted to die if the probability of death calculated from the MPM_0 model was greater than 0.50. In evaluating the

Table 9.1   Layout for Comparing a Dichotomous Outcome with a Dichotomized Prediction

Risk Score Prediction	Patient Outcome		
	Dead	*Alive*	*All Cases*
Dead	A	B	A + B
Alive	C	D	C + D
All Cases	A + C	B + D	A + B + C + D

performance of the MPM_0 model (using the 0.50 classification rule), they reported this:

- Sensitivity = 0.448
- Specificity = 0.966
- Predictive value for dying = 0.762
- Predictive value for surviving = 0.879

Thus, this classification identified 44.8 percent of all cases who died, while misclassifying only 3.4 percent of those who lived (1 − 0.966). Of those predicted to die, 76.2 percent did die; while of those predicted to live, 87.9 percent did live.

Two-by-two classification tables are used often to evaluate diagnostic rules in clinical practice. In this context, it is important to note that the prevalence of a problem in a population affects the predictive values of a test (Ingelfinger et al. 1987). For example, the PV+ and PV− values for the above MPM_0 classification rule were computed in a population with just below 20 percent deaths. In a population with more deaths, a test with the same sensitivity and specificity would yield higher PV+ and lower PV− values. For instance, with 50 percent deaths, the PV+ and PV− are 0.929 and 0.636, respectively. Conversely, when the outcome is rare, PV+ falls while PV− rises. With a 1 percent death rate, for example, PV+ is 0.117, and PV− is 99.4. Thus, in a population where nearly everyone lives, predicting that a patient will live is very likely to be correct; accurately identifying those few who will die is much harder.

Sensitivity and specificity thus describe the properties of tests in the abstract, whereas PV+ and PV− address the consequences of using a particular test in a specific population.

A major problem with using sensitivity and specificity, determined from two-by-two tables, to measure model performance is that a cutoff must be selected to dichotomize the risk score. For some purposes, defining such a cutoff is useful, such as if the score is intended to identify a manageable number of high-risk patients to receive special follow-up. However, the "right" cutoff is situation specific, depending on such factors as the funds available to monitor the targeted patients. Typically, no single cutoff is unequivocally "best."

The two-by-two table is poorly suited to deciding which risk adjustment method is better. One problem is that when different researchers describe performance of their method, each using a different cutpoint, reported sensitivities could vary widely, making it difficult to compare the specificities. When the cutpoints are chosen so that sensitivities are identical, one can compare specificities. However, which model is judged better may depend on the value of sensitivity used to establish the cutpoint.

For example, one model may accurately identify a few cases in which death is very likely, while not discriminating well in the general population; another model may identify a substantial fraction of cases where the chance of death is much higher than average, but still unlikely. In language defined later in this chapter, inconsistent judgments are possible whenever the receiver operating characteristic (ROC) curves for the different risk-adjustment models cross.

In the next sections, we discuss briefly the analytical methods used to develop models with dichotomous outcomes, and we consider several ways to provide more global assessments of how well such models perform.

Analytic Methods

Logistic regression is the most widely used approach for modeling dichotomous dependent variables. It performs favorably even compared with other, more complex, modeling approaches (Feinstein, Wells, and Walter 1990; Hadorn et al. 1992b; Selker et al. 1995). In logistic regression, the dependent variable is the (natural) logarithm of the odds (ln O) of an event. If p is the probability of an event and $q = 1 - p$ is the probability that the event will not occur, then the odds of the event is p/q. For example, if the chance of an event is 3 in 4, then $p = 3/4$, $q = 1/4$, and the odds of the event are 3 to 1, or 3.00. Letting p_i be the probability of the event in the ith case, the logistic regression model is:

$$\ln O_i = \ln \left[p_i/(1 - p_i) \right] = a + \sum_j b_j X_{ij}.$$

As with the multiple regression model discussed in Chapter 8, the X_{ij}'s may be (1) dummy variables representing risk classes; (2) covariates plus the risk classes; (3) covariates plus a single risk score; or (4) a subset of significant variables identified using a selection procedure, such as stepwise regression. With a continuous outcome variable, such as cost, the outcome of the ith person is viewed as an estimate (with error) of the expected value of cost, $E(Y_i)$. In logistic regression, the result for the ith person also estimates the expected value of the outcome for the ith person, in this case, p_i, the probability of death for the ith person. However, single observations can only be 0 or 1; thus they never equal their expected value, p_i.

From an estimate of $\ln O_i$ (designated as $\widehat{\ln O_i}$), the predicted probability of the event for the ith case is:

$$PRED_i = \frac{e^{\widehat{\ln O_i}}}{(1 + e^{\widehat{\ln O_i}})}.$$

Methods other than logistic regression may be used to estimate the numbers $PRED_i$, such as binary splits algorithms (e.g., CART©, California Statistical Software, Lafayette, California; based on techniques developed by Breiman et al. 1984), probit models, ordinary least squares (OLS) models (Cleary and Angel 1984), determinations by panels of clinical experts, and Cox proportional hazards regression models (Knaus et al. 1995).

Many measures of model performance, including the traditional R^2 and the c-statistic (see below), are determined from the set of pairs of numbers, one for each case, consisting of:

- the estimated probability of the event of interest for that case (its $PRED_i$); and
- the actual outcome Y_i (coded as a 0 or a 1).

Several other measures of model fit are based on the "likelihood" of the observed data (L) as predicted by the model. For a particular model, L is obtained by multiplying together the predicted probabilities of living ($1 - PRED$) for each case who lived and the predicted probabilities of dying ($PRED$) for each case who died. Better models have larger $1 - PRED$ values for cases who lived and larger $PRED$s for those who died—thus, they have larger likelihoods. The Akaike Information Criterion (AIC) uses the likelihood to measure the deviance between the actual data and the model, building in a penalty for model complexity (Akaike 1973). Neither the likelihood nor the AIC is standardized to a common, interpretable scale, such as the 0 to 1.0 interval containing the c-statistic (see below). One likelihood-based measure that is standardized is a generalization of R^2. Similarly to the traditional R^2, it summarizes the improvement in model fit for the full model over an intercept-only model (Nagelkerke 1991). Likelihood-based measures of model performance are not as common as R^2 and c in the health services research literature.

As with OLS modeling for predicting continuous outcome variables (Chapter 8), inferences based on logistic modeling are fully valid only when certain assumptions hold true. However, both logistic and OLS modeling are often used when these assumptions are known to be violated. This is acceptable partly because the techniques are "robust" to many common departures from the ideal situation. More importantly, these algorithms for transforming measures of risk into predictions of outcomes are judged primarily by how closely their predictions match reality, rather than the extent to which underlying assumptions are met. When employed with care, these modeling procedures yield reasonable and useful predictions.

Model Calibration and Model Discrimination

As discussed in Chapter 8, a model is said to be calibrated to a data set when the average of the predicted values matches the average of the actual outcomes. In the notation of Chapter 8, overall calibration error is measured as $[AVE(Y_i) - AVE(\hat{Y}_i)]$, where $\hat{Y}_i$ is the predicted value of Y for person i. For a dichotomous outcome, Y_i records the presence of a death: It is 1 if the patient dies and 0 if the patient lives. With this coding, the average Y_i is the death rate, and the $\hat{Y}_i$ is often called $PRED_i$ because it is the *predicted* probability that the ith case will die.

A statement such as "The model was calibrated to a set of data" likely means that the parameters of the model were derived by fitting the model to the data. If the fitting was done using OLS, the resulting calibration error is zero. However, if some other fitting approach is used (e.g., the maximum likelihood method used in logistic regression computer software packages), the actual and predicted death rates may differ somewhat.

Model discrimination is the extent to which the model predicts higher probabilities of death (higher $PRED$s) for patients who die. Discrimination can be usefully portrayed by drawing two histograms of the predicted probabilities on the same scale: one for patients who die and the other for those who live. The histogram for patients who live should lie to the left of the histogram for patients who die. Figure 9.1 illustrates two such histograms, scaled for a situation where four times as many cases live as die (i.e., a 20 percent death rate). Such a picture is called a covariance graph (Yates 1982). When discrimination is better, the two histograms overlap less.

While good model calibration is desirable, discrimination is more important. To see why, imagine a population with a 10 percent death rate. A model that assigns $PRED = 0.10$ to every person is perfectly calibrated, but it is unable to distinguish patients who live from those who die. On the other hand, suppose that a second model assigns $PRED = 0.80$ to every patient who lives and $PRED = 0.90$ to the patients who die. Although the numerical predictions of this second model are entirely wrong, the model can perfectly predict the outcome. While the problem with the second model can be fixed through recalibration, no simple change is going to make the first model useful for identifying patients who die.

Measure of Model Discrimination: The *c*-Statistic

As stated above, no consensus exists about the most appropriate performance measure for models predicting a dichotomous outcome. Nevertheless, most agree that the *c*-statistic, one measure of performance, should be reported (Harrell et al. 1984).

The *c*-statistic has several equivalent definitions. To illustrate one, consider all possible pairs that can be formed, such that one patient dies and the other lives. The *c*-statistic equals the proportion of pairs in which

Figure 9.1   Schematic Drawing of a Covariance Graph: Comparative Histograms for the Predicted Probability of a Problem (*PRED*) by Actual Outcome

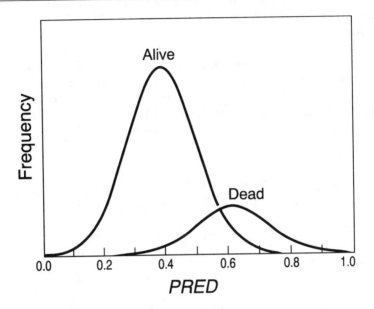

the predicted probability of death is higher for the patient who died than for the patient who lived. Each tied pair counts as one-half.

The c-statistic also equals the area under a ROC curve, which can be generated by converting the information in a covariance graph into a series of two-by-two tables, such as Table 9.1, and then plotting sensitivity versus (1 − specificity) from each table. The following illustrates the ROC curve in terms of the covariance graph. First, the two histograms are converted to distributions by rescaling each curve so that it has an area of 1.00. Given a predicted probability of death for each case ($PRED_i$) and a specified cutoff (t), we make a rule as follows: If $PRED_i$ is greater than t, patients are expected to die; and if $PRED_i$ is less than t, patients are expected to live. For a particular value of t, the consequences of this rule are displayed in Figure 9.2. The true positive rate (i.e., sensitivity) is the area to the right of t and under the curve for the patients who die. The false positive rate (i.e., 1 − specificity) is the area to the right of t and under the curve for the patients who live. In this way, each t is associated with a pair of numbers as follows: $P(t) = (x(t), y(t)) = (1 − specificity(t), (sensitivity(t))$. The ROC curve is the set of points $P(t)$ that are traced on a unit square as t is allowed to vary from its lowest to its highest value (see Figure 9.3). When *t* is zero, all cases are declared positive, and the pair (1,1) is generated. As the cutoff *t* increases, the vertical line in Figure 9.2 shifts to the right, and fewer cases are called positive. Thus, both the true and false positive rates decrease, and the new point lies to the left and down from the previous point. When *t* is one, all cases are declared "negative," and the pair (0,0) is generated.

A model with good discrimination has a high true positive rate while the false positive rate remains low; this generates a curve that passes close to the upper left corner of the plot—the point (0,1) (see Figure 9.3). The area under this curve, which is equivalent to the *c*-statistic associated with the model generating the covariance graph, is close to 1. The particular point, P(*t*), on this curve that comes from using the cutpoint *t* illustrated in Figure 9.2 is marked.

Figure 9.2   Distribution of *PRED* by Actual Outcome with Indications of True and False Positive Rates as Determined by a Cutpoint *t*

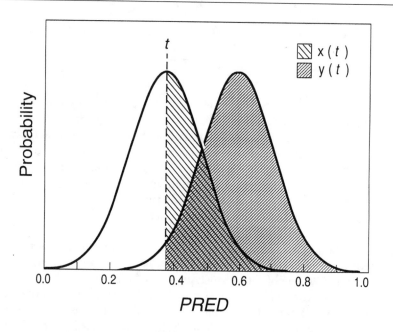

x(*t*) = fraction of cases that live for which *PRED* > *t*
      = 1 − specificity
y(*t*) = fraction of cases that die for which *PRED* > *t*
      = sensitivity

Figure 9.3   ROC Curve Associated with Distributions Shown in Figure 9.2

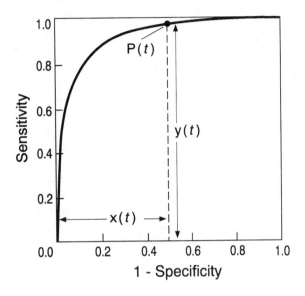

$P(t) = (x(t), y(t))$ is determined using the particular cutpoint t shown on Figure 9.2. As t increases from 0 to 1, the ROC curve is traced out, starting in the northeast corner (1,1) and finishing in the southwest (0,0).

Most risk prediction models provide a fairly continuous distribution of predicted values. In this instance, drawing the ROC curve is relatively straightforward. However, models with a small number of categorical independent variables generate only a few pairs of $(x(t), y(t))$. Alternative approaches are available for estimating a presumed-continuous, underlying ROC curve under these circumstances. The two most common such approaches are compared in Centor and Schwartz (1985).

More insight into what the c-statistic measures results from knowing the relationship between c and the rank sum statistic, S, which is used to test the following hypothesis (H_0):

> The median value of *PRED* is the same for patients who live and for patients who die.

S is formed by combining the n_0 cases who live with the n_1 cases who die and assigning ranks according to the values of *PRED*. The case with the lowest value of *PRED* gets rank 1, the case with the second lowest value gets a 2, and so on up to $n_0 + n_1$, the rank assigned to the case with the highest value of *PRED*. For cases with the same value of *PRED*, the ranks are averaged. For example, if four cases share the same, lowest value of *PRED*, each is assigned 2.5 (which equals $[1 + 2 + 3 + 4]/4$).

The rank sum statistic S is formed by adding the ranks of all n_1 patients who die. The smallest possible value for S is achieved when all patients who die have a predicted probability of death *PRED* that is less than the cases who live. Then, $S_{min} = 1 + 2 + \ldots + n_1$. It can be shown that $S_{min} = n_1(n_1 + 1)/2$. This model has perfect discrimination, but it is wrong—those who die have the lowest predicted probabilities of death and those who live have the highest. The largest possible value of S comes when the n_0 cases who live have ranks 1 to n_0, leading to $S_{max} = (n_0 + 1) + (n_0 + 2) + \ldots + (n_0 + n_1)$. The sum of these n_1 numbers is $S_{min} + n_0 n_1$. Such a model also has perfect discrimination, and it is right— the deaths have the highest predicted probabilities. Whatever the value of S, c may be computed as the following unique linear function of S:

$$c = \frac{(S - S_{min})}{(S_{max} - S_{min})}.$$

When $S = S_{min}$, $c = 0$; when $S = S_{max}$, $c = 1$. When the average rank of *PRED* is the same for both cases who lived and died (i.e., when S equals S_{mid}, a number halfway between its minimum and maximum), $c = 0.50$.

The sum of the ranks S illustrates the relationship between c and another measure of model discrimination—the overlap index (OI), which was defined by Hartz (1984) to have a value of 1 when S equals S_{mid}, a situation of maximum overlap. The OI drops to zero (as a simple linear function of S) as S moves further out to its most extreme values of S_{min} or S_{max} (see Figure 9.4). Any reasonable model has a value of S bigger than S_{mid}. In that case, the relation between c and the OI is given by $c = 1 - 0.5 \, OI$.

The c-statistic depends only on the ranks of predictions, not on their actual values. Therefore, a model that assigns a probability of death of 0.20 to each patient who dies and 0.19 to each patient who lives has a c-statistic of 1.00. The value of c is unaffected by how close the average of the predicted values $[AVE(PRED_i)]$ is to the average of the actual values $[AVE(Y_i)]$. Thus, c provides no information about model calibration.

In summary, the c-statistic measures model discrimination, achieving its maximum value of 1.00 when all *PRED*s for patients who die are higher than any *PRED*s for patients who live. When the model has no ability to discriminate (e.g., because it randomly assigns probabilities to patients who live and those who die), the expected value of the c-statistic is 0.5. A c-statistic much less than 0.5 indicates model discrimination but with improper coding of the risk scores. Presumably, this could be fixed by

Figure 9.4　The *c*-Statistic and the Overlap Index (OI), as Functions of the Rank Sum Statistic *S*

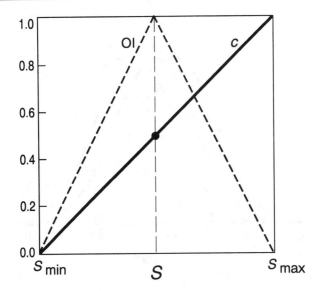

reassigning risk scores (values of *PRED*) that go in the other direction (e.g., each person's *PRED* would become one minus the predicted probability from the model).

To provide some feel for how *c* values relate to varying levels of discrimination, Figure 9.5 shows overlapping normal distribution curves when the distribution for the patients who die is shifted rightward from the distribution for patients who live by 0.5, 1.0, 1.5, and 2.0 standard deviations. Figure 9.6 shows the four ROC curves for the shifted distributions. The values of *c* associated with these shifts are 0.64, 0.76, 0.86, and 0.92, respectively.

The *c*-statistic and ROC curve derive from measures of sensitivity and specificity. As noted at the start of the chapter, these measures do not depend on the prevalence of the condition (e.g., the death rate in the population), a fact that has led to criticism of *c*. Hilden (1991) argues that because the value of a diagnostic test to a diagnostician does depend on the prevalence of the problem in the population being tested, insensitivity to prevalence is a weakness of *c* and the ordinary ROC curve. He proposed using ROC-like pictures that are scaled for prevalence (thus affecting total numbers of misclassified cases) and possibly for different "costs" (to the patient and/or society) of false positive versus false negative errors. Such graphs make it easier to see the tradeoffs associated with using

Figure 9.5   Overlapping Normal Distribution Curves Displaying
Various Amounts of Shift

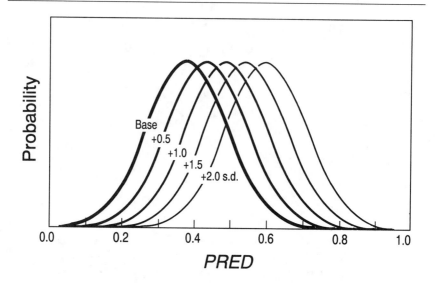

different cutpoints for deciding when to call a case positive. Hilden (1991) also provided a disturbing example of two procedures that are logically equivalent yet lead to different ROC curves and different *c*-statistics.

The *c*-statistic is commonly reported for risk-adjustment models involving a dichotomous outcome variable. For example, Krakauer and colleagues (1992) examined almost 43,000 Medicare cases sampled from 84 hospitals throughout the country. They used logistic regression to develop two models to predict mortality rates, one from claims data submitted to Medicare for hospital payment and another from clinical data abstracted with the older version of MedisGroups. The *c*-statistic for the claims-based model was 0.84; for the clinical model, 0.90. They are one of the few groups to report the value of the overlap index: 0.33 for the model using claims data and 0.21 for the clinical model.

Chapter 8 described reported R^2 values when APACHE III was used to predict lengths of stay in the ICU. However, APACHE III was developed to predict the likelihood of in-hospital death, not length of stay, for patients in the ICU. Knaus and colleagues (1991) reported a *c*-statistic of 0.90 for predicting death from APACHE III, based on the same 17,440 patients from 40 hospitals used to develop the model. They also reported sensitivity, specificity, predictive value positive, and predictive value negative for three different cutpoints used to predict whether a patient would die:

Figure 9.6   ROC Curves for Four Different Amounts of Shift between *PREDs* for Cases Who Live and *PREDs* for Cases Who Die

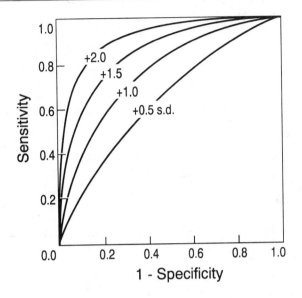

The areas under the four curves are 0.64, 0.76, 0.86, and 0.92, for shifts of 0.5, 1.0, 1.5, and 2.0 s.d.'s, respectively.

model-predicted probabilities greater than 0.10, greater than 0.50, and greater than 0.90. Moving from the lowest to highest cutpoint, sensitivity fell from 0.891 to 0.130 as specificity increased from 0.711 to 0.998.

In our AHCPR-funded severity project, we used the *c*-statistic as one summary measure of model performance when predicting in-hospital deaths for acute myocardial infarction (AMI) cases (Table 9.2, Iezzoni et al. 1996a, 1383), pneumonia cases (Table 9.3, Iezzoni et al. 1996b, 19), and stroke cases (Table 9.4, Iezzoni 1995a, 86). For AMI cases, all severity measures except the comorbidity index yielded much larger *c*-statistics than the model with only age and sex (from 0.79 to 0.86, compared to 0.69). For pneumonia patients, nine severity measures had *c*-statistics less than 0.80, compared to 0.71 for the model with only age, sex, and DRG; five severity measures achieved *c*-statistics of 0.80 or higher. For stroke patients, the age and sex model had a *c*-statistic of 0.60; three severity measures produced similar *c* values—Disease Staging's stage version (0.60), the comorbidity index (0.61), and the Acuity Index Method (0.66). All other

Table 9.2   Measures of Model Performance for Predicting In-Hospital Death and Percent of Patients Who Died in the Top Two and Bottom Two Deciles of Predicted Probability of Death: Acute Myocardial Infarction

System	c-Statistic	R²	Decile Rank Based on Predicted Probability of Death			
			1	2	9	10
			Percent of Patients Who Died			
MedisGroups						
Original version	0.80	0.17	0.5	1.9	24.4	46.0
Empirical version	0.83	0.23	0.5	1.3	25.9	53.7
Physiology Score 1	0.82	0.18	0.3	1.4	28.3	46.9
Physiology Score 2	0.83	0.23	0.3	1.3	23.8	54.7
Comorbidity Index	0.70	0.06	1.4	4.0	24.5	26.3
Disease Staging						
Mortality probability	0.86	0.27	0.3	0.4	26.7	58.4
Stage	0.79	0.17	1.4	2.9	22.1	49.7
PMCs—Severity Score	0.82	0.18	0.2	0.8	27.3	47.3
APR-DRGs	0.84	0.20	0.0	0.9	36.3	45.0
R-DRGs	0.80	0.15	1.0	1.9	29.6	42.2
Age and sex, interacted	0.69	0.05	1.4	4.3	23.2	25.6

Source: Iezzoni et al. 1996a. © 1996 American Public Health Association.

severity measures exhibited substantially greater ability to discriminate (with c values ranging from 0.73 to 0.87).

As described in Chapter 11, New York state developed a risk-adjustment model (with $c = 0.79$) for predicting death following coronary artery bypass graft surgery (CABG) using data from a report form completed (prospectively) by the department performing the surgery (Hannan et al. 1994, 763). Publication of risk-adjusted mortality statistics for individual hospitals and surgeons may have contributed to reductions in CABG-related mortality in New York. In our AHCPR-funded severity project, c-statistics for models predicting death during an admission for CABG surgery ranged from 0.85 for R-DRGs to 0.70 for the comorbidity index (Landon et al. 1996, 161).

As noted in Chapter 3, the relatively high c-statistics produced by severity measures based on discharge abstract data (see Table 1.8 and Tables 9.2 through 9.4) may result from their use of diagnosis codes indicating near-death events, such as cardiac arrest, regardless of when they occurred during the hospitalization (Iezzoni et al. 1995b, 1996c, 1996d). This produces a virtual tautology—near-death events predicting death. In contrast,

Table 9.3　Measures of Model Performance for Predicting In-Hospital Death and Percent of Patients Who Died in the Top Two and Bottom Two Deciles of Predicted Probability of Death: Pneumonia

Method	c-Statistic	R^2	Decile Rank Based on Predicted Probability of Death			
			1	2	9	10
			Percent of Patients Who Died			
MedisGroups						
Original version	0.81	0.13	0.1	0.7	20.8	34.4
Empirical version	0.85	0.19	0.1	0.3	20.1	42.8
Physiology Score 1	0.78	0.10	0.1	1.1	18.7	33.5
Physiology Score 2	0.82	0.15	0.2	0.8	20.0	38.5
Body Systems Count	0.71	0.05	0.3	1.8	16.1	23.0
Comorbidity Index	0.74	0.06	0.2	2.2	17.6	25.3
Disease Staging						
Mortality Probability	0.80	0.13	0.2	1.1	19.5	35.0
Stage	0.75	0.08	0.3	1.6	16.4	30.1
Comorbidities	0.76	0.08	0.3	1.7	18.6	29.0
PMCs—Severity Score	0.79	0.11	0.2	1.2	19.6	34.3
AIM	0.73	0.05	0.4	1.8	16.7	24.5
APR-DRGs	0.78	0.10	0.2	1.1	22.0	31.1
PMC-RIS	0.78	0.10	0.2	1.4	19.4	31.8
R-DRGs	0.83	0.28	0.2	1.7	17.3	42.7
Age and sex, interacted	0.67	0.03	1.3	3.9	16.8	17.4
Age and sex, interacted, plus DRG	0.71	0.04	0.4	2.1	16.5	22.5

Source: Iezzoni et al. 1996b.

the clinical data-based measures (MedisGroups and the physiology scores) relied on information drawn from the first two hospital days. Obviously, if risk-adjusted death rates are being used to make inferences about quality of care, adjusting only for preexisting conditions (i.e., patients' characteristics prior to treatment) is best (see Chapter 11).

As described in Chapters 3 and 11, California developed several models using administrative data to predict 30-day in-hospital mortality for AMI patients (Wilson, Smoley, and Werdegar 1996). Model A included only clinical risk factors judged to be almost "certainly present" when the patient entered the hospital, which therefore reflected health on admission. Model B also included additional risk factors: clinical characteristics that

Table 9.4   Measures of Model Performance for Predicting In-Hospital Death and Percent of Patients Who Died in the Top Two and Bottom Two Deciles of Predicted Probability of Death: Stroke

System	c-Statistic	R^2	\multicolumn{4}{c}{Decile Rank Based on Predicted Probability of Death}
			1	2	9	10
			\multicolumn{4}{c}{Percent of Patients Who Died}
MedisGroups						
Original version	0.80	0.15	0.6	1.7	19.7	33.7
Empirical version	0.87	0.27	0.3	1.1	21.1	49.6
Physiology Score 1	0.80	0.17	0.9	2.6	17.7	42.4
Physiology Score 2	0.84	0.24	0.9	2.3	18.3	48.2
Comorbidity Index	0.61	0.01	4.4	6.0	15.1	15.0
Disease Staging						
Mortality probability	0.74	0.11	3.1	3.5	16.5	32.8
Stage	0.60	0.01	4.8	6.6	14.8	14.3
PMCs—Severity Score	0.73	0.10	2.9	2.7	11.9	36.6
AIM	0.66	0.03	2.8	4.3	16.4	18.2
APR-DRGs	0.77	0.10	1.2	3.1	19.0	33.7
R-DRGs	0.74	0.07	2.7	2.6	22.3	26.5
Age and sex, interacted	0.60	0.01	4.6	6.4	14.7	14.6

Reprinted from *International Journal for Quality in Health Care*, volume 7, Iezzoni, L.I., M. Shwartz, A. S. Ash, J. S. Hughes, J. Daley and Y. D. Mackiernan, 81–94, Copyright 1996, with kind permission from Elsevier Science Ltd., The Boulevard, Langford Lane, Kidlington OX5 1GB, UK.

may have been either comorbidities (present at admission) or complications (conditions arising perhaps due to poor care), and nonclinical characteristics where associations with mortality may have represented "confounded or unreliable measures" (e.g., race, expected principal source of payment, and source and type of admission). Model A ran the risk of not adjusting enough—it may not have given adequate credit to hospitals with a particularly complex mix of patients. In contrast, Model B may have adjusted too much, by having given credit for factors unrelated to patients' health at admission, factors due possibly to poor care—the very quantity of interest to California's policymakers (see Chapter 11).

For both Models A and B, California's investigators developed one version on patients with a prior hospitalization within eight weeks of the index admission (in this situation, the presence of preexisting conditions on admission to the index hospitalization could be confirmed) and a second version on the remaining patients. These c-statistics were reported: for the cases with prior hospitalizations, Model A's $c = 0.76$ and Model B's $c = 0.83$; among cases without prior hospitalizations, Model A's $c = 0.77$ and Model B's $c = 0.86$ (Wilson, Smoley, and Werdegar 1996, 10–15). Thus, in each data set, the models with the full array of risk factors (Model B) produced higher c values.

Other Views of Discrimination

Some authors summarize the ability of a model to discriminate between cases who live and die by contrasting the average of the predicted probabilities in the two groups. For example, Daley and colleagues (1988) developed the MMPS models to predict mortality within 30 days of hospital admission for Medicare patients in each of four conditions (see Table 1.4 and Chapter 5). They reported the average predicted probability of death for survivors and nonsurvivors in the study conditions: stroke (0.14 versus 0.39), pneumonia (0.14 versus 0.32), myocardial infarction (0.19 versus 0.33), and congestive heart failure (0.12 versus 0.27). These averages were weighted to reflect the fact that some cases were more likely to enter the sample than others but were not cross-validated (see Chapter 6 for a discussion of cross-validation).

Working with the same database as Krakauer and colleagues (1992), Smith and collaborators (1991) used logistic regression to predict mortality. To describe the difference between the two distributions of $PRED$, they employed yet another measure—the ratio of average $PRED$ for nonsurvivors (AVE_1) to average $PRED$ for survivors (AVE_0). We let RATIO = AVE_1 / AVE_0. A $RATIO$ of 1.0 represents no discrimination: It says that the two averages are identical, just as $c = 0.5$ says that the average rank of the predictions in the two populations is the same. The higher the value of $RATIO$, the better the discrimination. $RATIO$ is equivalent to percent increase in AVE_0, because AVE_1 is $100 \times (RATIO - 1)$ percent larger than AVE_0. For example, if $RATIO$ is 1.5, then AVE_1 is 50 percent larger than AVE_0. The literature provides little guidance about interpreting values of $RATIO$. In addition, ratios are unstable when the denominator is small, which is expected for conditions with low death rates.

If a single summary measure is produced to represent the difference of two averages, their difference (that is, $DIFF = AVE_1 - AVE_0$) is another potential measure. $DIFF$ reports the amount of increase in AVE_0, and, as discussed below, it is closely associated with R^2. However, both $RATIO$ and $DIFF$ are problematic. $RATIO$ may undervalue an important difference between two models when AVE_0 is large, and $DIFF$ may undervalue an important difference when AVE_0 is small. Because of these problems, researchers should avoid reporting only a single-number summary of the difference between AVE_0 and AVE_1. If prevalence for the population (i.e., $AVE(Y_i)$) is reported, as well as AVE_0 and AVE_1 for each model under consideration, then readers can compute for themselves whatever summary measure(s) seem most meaningful.

Methods for Measuring Model Calibration

The calibration curve graphically compares predicted probabilities with actual outcomes (Yates 1982). To construct the curve, patients are divided into groups based on similar predicted probabilities of death. The average of the predicted probabilities for patients in each group are compared to the frequency of actual outcomes in the group.

Lemeshow and Hosmer (1982) proposed a χ^2 (chi-square) test derived from data organized similarly to the calibration curve. This Hosmer-Lemeshow χ^2 is often used in evaluations of severity measures to examine model calibration across the range of predicted probabilities. It does not check directly for overall calibration (i.e., that the average of predicted deaths in the whole population is close to the actual population death rate). Instead it addresses whether average and predicted rates are similar within population subgroups. Although the Hosmer-Lemeshow method can be performed in several ways, the following four steps represent an increasingly standard application:

1. Data are divided into ten subgroups based on deciles of predicted risk (*PRED*).

2. Within each subgroup, deviations between observed and expected numbers of deaths (O_{die} and E_{die}) and observed and expected numbers of live cases (O_{live} and E_{live}) are measured using a statistic reminiscent of a χ^2 calculation:

$$\frac{(O_{die} - E_{die})^2}{E_{die}} + \frac{(O_{live} - E_{live})^2}{E_{live}} = \frac{(O_{die} - E_{die})^2}{npq}$$

where n = the number of cases in the subgroup, p = the predicted death rate for these n cases, and $q = 1 - p$. The expected numbers are determined from the *PRED*s.

3. To determine whether deviations are larger than expected (under the hypothesis that each prediction is correct), these deviations are summed over the ten subgroups. The result is compared to a χ^2 distribution with eight degrees of freedom.

4. The model is accepted if the P value for this test is reasonably large (i.e., the observed deviations from the model predictions are fully

consistent with the size of chance deviations that would occur if the model were correct).

As for any χ^2 test, a serious concern when using this or any version of the Hosmer-Lemeshow approach is that the decision about the adequacy of model fit depends heavily on the number of observations available. When the sample size is large, even small discrepancies between the model's predictions and observed death rates (which may have little practical significance) can cause the model to be rejected. In contrast, the null hypothesis (that the model is correct) may be accepted despite large differences between the expected and observed values when few cases are available.

Other versions of this test involve rules other than deciles of predicted risk for putting observations into subgroups or strata. For example, with fewer cases available, one might split the data into only five quintiles of predicted risk. Another situation requiring different methods for grouping cases arises when large fractions of the cases have very similar predicted probabilities. For example, if the PREDs for the healthiest half of the population are all similarly low, the lowest subgroup might be the 50 percent of cases with the lowest PRED values.

In general, strata do not need equal numbers of cases, but a reasonably straightforward rationale for the grouping rule is desirable, and the distribution of cases among the subgroups should be shown. With k strata, the χ^2 with k minus two degrees of freedom is the test statistic. The outcome of the test (i.e., the decision about whether the model is calibrated) can depend on the rule for grouping patients into strata.

Another concern with the Hosmer-Lemeshow χ^2 test, as described above, is that npq overestimates the variance of the deviations under the null hypothesis. Let n equal the number of cases in each decile, p equal the average predicted probability of death in the decile, $q = 1 - p$, p_i equal the predicted probability of death of the ith person in the decile, and $q_i = 1 - p_i$. In the Hosmer-Lemeshow statistic, variance in each cell is estimated as npq rather than the sum of the p_iq_i's, which is a better estimate of the variance. (If the p_i were known to be correct, rather than simply estimates, it would be exactly right.) Furthermore, npq is generally larger than the sum of the p_iq_i's.

If the subgroups are formed using deciles of predicted risk, then npq and the sum of the p_iq_i are likely to be very similar, and little harm is done. However, when the subgroups contain cases with widely dispersed probabilities of death, the Hosmer-Lemeshow statistic is noticeably smaller than it should be—leading to the inappropriate acceptance of models with predictions that deviate greatly from actual outcomes. For example, if there are 50 cases with $p_i = 0.90$ and 50 with $p_i = 0.10$, then the sum of the p_iq_i

equals 9 while $npq = 25$. So, $(O_{die} - E_{die})/npq$ will be only 36 percent as large as would be correct (because $9/25 = 0.36$). On the other hand, if the p_i's are split into two groups of 50 with more similar probabilities, say 0.40 and 0.60, then the sum of the p_iq_i's equals 24, which is fully 96 percent as large as npq. To avoid this problem, one should use the sum of the p_iq_i's instead of npq in calculating the test statistic.

In developing the MPM for ICU patients, Lemeshow and colleagues (1988) used this test extensively to measure overall model fit. For the New York state CABG model (Hannan et al. 1994, 763), the P value for the Hosmer-Lemeshow chi-square statistic was 0.16, indicating good fit, particularly in light of the large number of cases used (over 57,000). The California AMI models did not calibrate as well (Wilson, Smoley, and Werdegar 1996, 10–14): The Hosmer-Lemeshow statistic for Model A with the "no prior admissions" cases yielded a P value of 0.015 ($n = 62,570$); for cases with prior admissions, the P value was 0.061 ($n = 5,442$). In light of the many cases used, P values near or less than 0.05 may not indicate worrisome amounts of miscalibration. The California report notes that the models "do not demonstrate a significant, consistent pattern of bias across risk strata" (Wilson, Smoley, and Werdegar 1996). The two Model B versions did not calibrate as well, each yielding P values less than 0.0001. This reflects overestimates of risk in the lowest-risk decile and underestimates in the highest-risk group.

In summary, the Hosmer-Lemeshow test has drawbacks. Whether a deviation between observed and expected rates across strata is viewed as evidence of model misfit depends heavily on the number of cases studied and possibly on the rule for assigning cases to subgroups. We therefore believe that the most valuable and appropriate use of this methodology is exploratory. Examining calibration tables directly allows for a rich comparison of actual and expected results across the range of predictions (see below).

A More Detailed View of Model Performance within Subgroups

The Hosmer-Lemeshow statistic forms a single summary measure of the match between predicted and actual death rates within subgroups of the data. If the summary fit is poor, the pairs of observed and predicted death rates can be examined individually to see which deciles contribute most to the poor fit. Whether or not the Hosmer-Lemeshow *test* is performed, the table showing the number of actual and predicted deaths in each subgroup provides valuable insights into model performance.

Ash and colleagues (1990) used a deciles-of-risk calibration table to illustrate the ability of a model, developed using administrative data available at the time of hospital admission, to predict the likelihood that the admission would be deemed inappropriate by utilization reviewers. The final model was fit to the whole data set after models fit to two halves of a split sample were shown to be similar, to perform well, and to lose little explanatory power when cross-validated. Calibration of the full model was examined in deciles, as illustrated in Table 9.5.

Calibration within deciles is checked by looking across the rows of Table 9.5. Except for deciles 5, 9, and possibly 7, the observed and predicted problem rates are very close. The final column, which records each decile's contribution to the Hosmer-Lemeshow statistic, confirms that the other rows are not widely discordant. For the Hosmer-Lemeshow statistic not to reject the model fit, the sum of the numbers in the last column must add to less than 15.5, which is the 95th percentile for a χ^2 distribution with eight degrees of freedom. For a model to pass this test, only a few of the ten summands can be as large as two. Here the numbers add to 12.0, and the model passes this test of calibration.

Examining the observed percent problems column of Table 9.5 provides further insight into model discrimination. If the model had no explanatory power, approximately 8.3 percent of the cases in each decile

Table 9.5 A Deciles-of-Risk Calibration Table

Decile	Predicted % Problems	Observed % Problems	Contribution to the Hosmer-Lemeshow Statistic
1	0.3	0.1	1.3
2	1.4	1.6	0.2
3	2.7	2.3	0.6
4	4.0	4.1	0.0
5	6.1	7.5	3.6
6	6.9	6.5	0.3
7	7.8	9.0	2.3
8	8.7	8.1	0.5
9	11.4	9.7	3.0
10	34.1	34.5	0.1

Note: The contribution to the Hosmer-Lemeshow statistic for decile i is $(O_i - E_i)^2 / n_i p_i q_i$, where O_i is the observed number of problem cases in decile i, E_i is the expected number of problem cases in decile i, n_i is the number of cases in decile i, p_i is aver (*PRED*) in decile i, and q_i is 1 − aver (*PRED*) in decile i. The number of cases in decile i (n_i) is always within one of 1,030.5, since $N = 10,305$ is the full population size. The Hosmer-Lemeshow statistic is 12.0, the sum of the numbers in the last column. The probability that a χ^2 statistic with eight degrees of freedom is greater than 12.0 exceeds 10%. Thus, the model is not rejected, $P > 0.10$. Observed problem rate = 8.334%. Predicted problem rate = 8.336%.

would be problematic. Obviously, the problem rate was dramatically higher for cases in the top decile than for other cases, and very few problem cases occurred in the lowest four deciles. Cases in deciles 5 through 9 had problem rates relatively close to the problem rate of 8.3 percent for the whole population.

The fraction of all problem cases that occur in a decile or a group of deciles can be computed by adding the observed percent of problems for these deciles and dividing by the sum of all the percentages (83.34 for Table 9.5). This computation addresses useful practical questions such as, What percentage of all the problem cases were found by looking at the 10 percent of the cases thought to be most likely to be problematic? Using the data from Table 9.5, the answer is over 40 percent, because 34.5/83.34 = 0.41. In contrast, fewer than 10 percent of the problems were located in the bottom four risk deciles.

A similar analysis was reported by Keeler and colleagues (1990) when using their "sickness at admission" measures to predict mortality. These investigators compared differences in the death rate between the healthiest and sickest quartiles of patients based on their predicted probabilities of death. For example, they noted, " . . . of those patients whose admission characteristics put them in the healthiest 25% of patients who had a cerebrovascular accident, 3% percent died in the 30 days that followed admission, whereas 55% of patients in the sickest quartile died" (Keeler et al. 1990, 1,965). Hannan et al. (1994, 765), in examining the validity of the New York state CABG risk-adjustment model, used the Hosmer-Lemeshow statistic computed in deciles of predicted risk as the basis for concluding "There was a reasonably good correspondence between actual deaths and expected deaths in each of the individual intervals." They noted that in the highest decile, predicted mortality was 36 percent and actual mortality was 32 percent; thus, the model appears to adjust sufficiently for the most severe cases.

As discussed in Chapter 8, examining outcomes by decile of predicted outcome provides more insight than do simple summary measures into how well models discriminate risk among cases. The right-most columns of Tables 9.2 through 9.4 show such data for AMI, pneumonia, and stroke cases, respectively. To illustrate for AMI cases, with an overall death rate of 13.2 percent (Table 9.2), the original version of MedisGroups yielded a c-statistic of 0.80 and identified, at the low extreme, 10 percent of cases with a death rate of 0.5 percent, and at the high extreme, 10 percent of cases with a death rate of 46.0 percent. Disease Staging's mortality probability score (with a c-statistic of 0.86) distinguished deciles of cases with death rates of 0.3 versus 58.4 percent at either extreme. Thus, the higher c statistic associated with Disease Staging is reflected in the greater differences in death rates between extreme deciles.

The ability to discriminate by decile depends partially on the death rate in the population under study. The death rate for stroke cases was 9.7 percent. Both MedisGroups' original version and Physiology Score 1 had c-statistics of 0.80 for predicting death in stroke. For MedisGroups, extreme decile death rates were 0.6 and 33.7 percent; for Physiology Score 1, they were 0.9 and 42.4 percent. For both severity measures, the difference in death rates between extreme deciles is less than when original MedisGroups was used with AMI cases, even though the c-statistics were similar (0.80). Comparable c-statistics result in less discrimination when the death rate is lower. In addition, although the c-statistics were similar for original MedisGroups and Physiology Score 1 for stroke patients, the extreme decile death rates differed. This is yet another confirmation of the fact that single-number summaries cannot capture all important aspects of how models perform.

Rather than classify groups of patients based on their predicted probability of death, Krakauer and colleagues (1992) classified hospitals by the average predicted mortality of their cases. They then examined the differences in predicted mortality between the top and bottom 5 percent of hospitals. A model using administrative data alone resulted in a twofold difference in predicted probabilities, versus a threefold difference produced by a model using clinical variables, suggesting that the clinical model provided better discrimination than the model using administrative data. The authors did not report the difference in actual mortality between hospitals in the extreme groups.

The same kind of table may be constructed for other divisions of the data into subgroups (such as by age or payor class), with the goal of identifying types of cases whose rate of death is not predicted well by the model. The crucial next step is to understand why the model does not predict well for these cases.

Model Discrimination versus Calibration

Lemeshow and Hosmer (1982) argued that if models do not calibrate well, examining discrimination is worthless. A more popular view is expressed well by Harrell and colleagues (1984, 144):

> The reason we argue for first priority to discrimination in judging a model's relative performance is that if discrimination deteriorates, no adjustment or calibration can correct the model. On the other hand with good discrimination, one can calibrate the predictor to attain reliability without sacrificing discrimination.

If the model is used to distinguish those who died from those who lived, the actual values of *PRED* are not important. However, if the model is used to determine an expected death rate for comparison with an actual death rate (e.g., in an attempt to identify hospitals with higher-than-expected mortality; see Chapter 10), then calibration is more important than discrimination. Both calibration and discrimination should be addressed when evaluating model performance.

R^2 and Dichotomous Outcomes

The Debate

As for continuous outcome variables, R^2 has several definitions. This is the one known best, and the one that we use:

$$R^2 = 1 - \left[\frac{\sum_i (Y_i - PRED_i)^2}{\sum_i (Y_i - \bar{Y})^2} \right].$$

The predicted probabilities ($PRED_i$) can come from any method of modeling, including OLS or logistic regression. If the model is fit using OLS, R^2 exactly equals the amount by which the average predicted probability of death among those who died (AVE_1) exceeds the average predicted probability of death among those who lived (AVE_0), a quantity referred to as $DIFF$ above. We have found that when the predictions are derived using a logistic regression model, R^2 closely approximates this difference.

The same issues associated with using R^2 to measure performance for modeling continuous outcomes (see Chapter 8) are present when modeling dichotomous outcomes. However, when the outcome variable is dichotomous and modeling other than OLS is performed, less precedent supports the use and interpretation of R^2. Models to predict 0/1 outcomes have R^2 values that are much lower than generally result when predicting continuous outcomes; in the 0/1 setting, R^2 values as large as 0.30 are rare. In addition, the size of R^2 that a 0/1 model can achieve is affected by the prevalence of the outcome (e.g., the death rate) in the population to which the model is applied. This observation has led some to conclude that R^2 is not a useful measure of model performance for dichotomous dependent variables (Cox and Wermuth 1992). However, recall Hilden's contention (1991) that the insensitivity of the c-statistic to prevalence is a problem with that measure.

Such criticisms should not be made exclusively in the setting of using R^2 to evaluate a 0/1 model. In Chapter 8, we noted that models to predict next year's medical expenses for Medicare beneficiaries also have small R^2 values (Ash et al. 1989; Epstein and Cumella 1988). These models are nevertheless helpful to policymakers and persons designing reimbursement systems for capitated health plans. In any particular context, it is necessary to develop experience with both models and measures in order to benchmark the findings.

The concept of maximum R^2 introduced in Chapter 8 is a useful device for explaining the lower R^2 values observed with 0/1 outcomes. First, consider the case of a continuous dependent variable such as hospitalization costs. In a model with several explanatory variables, the data can be partitioned into cells, defined by each unique combination of the values of each explanatory variable. When no more data are available for making finer distinctions among cases within these cells, no model can achieve an R^2 larger than that achieved by the so-called "fully saturated" model, which predicts for each case in a cell the average ($\bar{Y}$) for all cases in that cell. Thus, the R^2 for the fully saturated model is the maximum R^2 that is achievable with these explanatory factors in this data set. Typically, the maximum R^2 is less than 1 because cases in the same cell do not all have identical outcomes.

Next, consider predicting the probability of a binary outcome (e.g., death). If within each cell defined by a unique combination of predictor variables, all cases have the same outcome, then the fully saturated model can be made perfect (assigning $PRED = 0$ to all cases who live and $PRED = 1$ to all who die) and the maximum R^2 will be 1. Just as with a continuous outcome, however, we do not expect the same outcome for all cases in the same cell. The best to be expected is that within-cell variation in the outcome is much reduced from the variation in the outcome present among all the cases (that is, each cell will contain either mostly all 0's or mostly all 1's). For example, if the death rate in a population is 50 percent, it would be useful to sort cases into cells where either 70 or 30 percent died. However, the R^2 for a model that could do this would only be

$$1 - \frac{(.3)(.7)}{(.5)(.5)} = .18 .$$

The maximum R^2 for a binary outcome is thus limited by the fact that, within the finest breakdown of cases into cells that the explanatory data allow, the death rates differ from 0 and 1. In a model to predict a dichotomous outcome, then, the model can be perfect in the sense that every case has its probability of death correctly predicted, but unless these predictions can be made quite close to 0 or to 1, its R^2 will not be large.

Many of the warnings about interpreting R^2 introduced in Chapter 8 apply here, as well as to interpreting the c-statistic. In particular, one should be wary of comparisons using either measure with analyses performed on different data sets. Comparisons are most problematic when different protocols for defining the population of interest, trimming outliers, or oversampling difficult cases have led to populations that vary markedly in the amount of total variability that the model attempts to explain.

This problem arises when trying to compare R^2 values for models to predict death in two populations with very different death rates. In general, one expects a model to discriminate among cases better in a population where there is more variation—both in the independent characteristics that are used to specify risk and in the outcome. For a 0/1 outcome, variation is greatest when prevalence is around 50 percent; then the population standard deviation (σ) is 0.5. When prevalence is 10 percent (or 90 percent), σ drops to 0.3. At a prevalence of 1 percent (or 99 percent), σ is 0.1, only one-fifth as large as when cases are split 50–50 between the two possibilities.

Comparisons of the performance of models fit to different populations face the following fundamental limitation: The level of performance achieved by a model on a population largely depends on various attributes of this population, especially the variance of important predictor variables and of the outcome. Many researchers fail to appreciate that this limitation pertains to the c-statistic as well as to R^2 and other measures (Hadorn et al. 1992a). When prevalence differs between populations, measures of model performance developed on them are often not comparable.

The problem of noncomparability may be partially addressed with a weighted analysis, most successfully if there is a well-documented and objectively quantified reason for the discrepancy between the populations (e.g., use of stratified sampling). While dissimilarity in the outcomes of two populations clearly suggests noncomparability, similarity does not guarantee that two populations are equally easy to model, as is shown by Hadorn and colleagues (1992a). With these warnings in mind, we list below R^2 values attained in selected published studies, to provide a sense of typical R^2 values for dichotomous outcomes.

Cross-validated R^2 values (determined for successive 10 percent sets of the data from the remaining 90 percent of the data, as described in Chapter 6) for the MMPS models, which predict death within 30 days of hospital admission, were stroke, 0.25; pneumonia, 0.18; AMI, 0.14; and congestive heart failure, 0.15 (Daley et al. 1988). Keeler and colleagues (1990) reported the following cross-validated R^2 values (determined similarly as for the MMPS models) for the RAND "sickness at admission" models: congestive heart failure, 0.12; AMI, 0.22; pneumonia, 0.26; cerebrovascular accident, 0.30; and hip fracture, 0.06.

Green and collaborators (1990) focused on the improvement in R^2 (determined using OLS regression) when severity variables (using the stage of principal diagnosis at admission component of the Severity of Illness Index, Horn and Horn 1986) were added to regression models using only administrative data. Their models were developed from data on 34,252 Medicare patients from 13 hospitals using the Severity of Illness Index (Green et al. 1990). Models were developed for cancer, severe acute heart disease, stroke, pulmonary disease, and low-risk heart disease. For the models based on administrative data, the weighted R^2 (among the five conditions considered) was 0.025 versus 0.215 when severity was added.

Wagner and colleagues (1994) produced models to predict risk of hospital death for patients in the ICU that included as independent variables current APACHE III score and score change from the previous day, ICU admission diagnosis, age, chronic health status, and treatment before ICU admissions. These models achieved R^2 values of 0.34 (when predictions were made on day 6 of the ICU stay) and 0.40 (when predictions were made on day 1), and c-statistics ranged from 0.84 to 0.90 (Wagner et al. 1994, 1365).

Tables 9.2 through 9.4 from our severity study show the R^2 values for the different severity measures, as well as the c-statistics. For AMI cases, R^2 values for the ten different severity systems included in the analysis ranged from 0.15 to 0.27 (with the exception of the comorbidity index); for pneumonia cases, for the comparable ten severity measures in the AMI analysis, R^2 values ranged from 0.08 to 0.28 (again excluding the comorbidity index); for stroke cases, from 0.01 to 0.27. One cannot map c-statistics to R^2 values; in fact, severity measures with higher c-statistics can even have lower R^2 values, although this is rare. For example, for AMI cases, Physiology Score 2 had $c = 0.83$ and $R^2 = 0.23$; APR-DRGs had $c = 0.84$ and $R^2 = 0.20$. For stroke cases, both the PMC Severity Score and APR-DRGs had R^2 values of 0.10, but the former had a c of 0.73 while the latter had a c of 0.77. Nonetheless, models with higher c-statistics generally have higher R^2 values.

Finally, an interesting public dialogue about R^2 and c-statistics occured regarding New York state's CABG model. In 1995, the *New England Journal of Medicine* published an article with this criticism of the New York model:

> The validity of risk-adjusted mortality as an indicator of the quality of care depends on the ability of a mathematical model to quantify base-line differences in case mix among providers accurately. Our analysis of predicted and observed outcomes revealed that the capacity of [New York's] model to do this was limited. Predicted mortality rates assigned to surgeons by the model explained only a small portion of the variance in mortality ($R^2 = 7.3$ percent); the R^2 value for hospital was negligible (0.4 percent). The power of the model to predict outcomes for individual patients was also low ($R^2 = 8.0$ percent). (Green and Wintfeld 1995, 1230)

In their critique, Green and Wintfeld never mentioned c-statistics. In their last sentence they warned, "To help ensure that report cards provide fair and informative comparisons, the data and methods used to generate them should regularly undergo a thorough, independent statistical evaluation" (Green and Wintfeld 1995, 1232).

In 1996, New York officials responded, again in the *New England Journal of Medicine*:

> Statistically, the fit of a logistic-regression model is typically assessed on the basis of discrimination . . . The R^2 statistic, or the square of the multiple correlation coefficient, is a measure typically used to assess linear regression models in which the dependent variable is continuous. In theory, values for R^2 range from 0 (representing no association between the predicted and observed values) to a 1 (representing a perfect association). In logistic-regression models in which the overall mortality rate ranges from 2 percent to 4 percent, however, R^2 is almost always less than 0.2. This limitation arises from the nature of logistic regression, in which the dependent variable must have one of only two values (in this case, survival or death). When the difference between actual and predicted mortality rates is calculated for each person (as part of the calculation of R^2), no matter how accurate the prediction is, the difference between the predicted value and the observed value for the mortality will be large, since the observed mortality must be either 0 or 1 and the prediction is a proportion between 0 and 1.
>
> Discrimination in logistic regression, therefore, is usually measured by the C statistic . . . In analyses of the New York data, the C statistic has typically been approximately 0.80; for 1992, it was 0.826. This value compares favorably with the C statistics reported for other models of CABG-associated mortality, which range from 0.74 to 0.814.
>
> It has been argued that the New York model does not accurately predict the future performance of hospitals or physicians and that therefore it functions poorly. Predicting performance is not a test of the model's validity, however, because it was not designed to foretell the future. Instead, the model was constructed to help hospitals and physicians improve their performance, precisely to avoid repeating problems encountered in the past. (Chassin, Hannan, and DeBuono 1996, 396–97)

The bottom line is that both c and R^2 are useful measures of the performance of models predicting dichotomous outcomes. With binary outcomes, however, presenting only R^2 can give a misleading impression that a model performs poorly—an impression that can be used in support of policy arguments.

The Merit of R^2

Two models applied to a single data set often have c-statistics that seem similar while their R^2 values seem different. We illustrate this situation here as an example of findings to suggest that the c-statistic is less sensitive to real differences between models than R^2. First, two models to predict in-hospital death were fit to a sample of 17,577 AMI patients from the MedisGroups 1991 Comparative Database (Iezzoni et al. 1994). These data included information from 112 U.S. hospitals that used MedisGroups; the in-hospital death rate was 13.5 percent. Model 1 included dummy variables for the five original MedisGroups severity classes. Model 2 was based on administrative data only; it included 8 dummy variables for age categories and 12 dummy variables to represent the presence of 12 chronic conditions defined using discharge diagnosis codes (see Chapter 2 and Table 2.3).

For Model 1, the R^2 was 0.15 and c was 0.76 (Iezzoni et al. 1994, 45). In contrast, the R^2 for Model 2 was 0.07 and its c-statistic was 0.72. Therefore, by looking either at R^2 or at c, Model 1 (the MedisGroups model) appeared clearly superior to Model 2 (the model based on administrative data). We used bootstrapping (see Chapter 6) to determine empirically the distributions of, and construct 95 percent confidence intervals around, c and R^2 for each of the models. Because of the large sample size, these confidence intervals were narrow, and the evidence for a difference between models was overwhelmingly statistically significant using either measure. But the superiority of Model 1 was more striking using the R^2 as compared to the c-statistic (0.15 versus 0.07 as opposed to 0.76 versus 0.72). Furthermore, when each difference was standardized by dividing by a pooled estimate of its standard deviation, the two R^2 measures differed by ten standard deviations, while the two c-statistics differed by only six. With a smaller sample size—and if c were the only performance measure considered—the superiority of Model 1 might not have been detected. Thus, R^2 may convey information about model fit more strongly than c.

Other Measures of Model Performance

As described in Chapter 5, DesHarnais and colleagues (1988) developed the Risk-Adjusted Mortality Index (RAMI), an empirically derived model based on hospital discharge abstract data. They reported correlations between the actual and predicted number of deaths and actual and predicted death rates at the over 300 hospitals represented in the data used to build the model. In 1983, the year of data used to develop the RAMI, the correlation between actual and predicted number of deaths was 0.98; the correlation of death rates was 0.84. To validate the RAMI, the model fit to the 1983 data was applied to 1984 data. The correlation between actual and predicted number of deaths was again 0.98; correlation of death rates was 0.81. At a finer level, they compared actual and predicted deaths and death rates within condition within each hospital. Using the 1984 data, correlation in number of deaths was 0.95, and correlation of death rates was 0.85. Correlations near 1.00 for expected versus observed *numbers* of deaths are not surprising because both numbers are principally determined by variations in hospital size. Hospitals in the study varied in patient volume, and those with more cases had higher expected, as well as actual, numbers of deaths. An information-free model—for example, one that predicts a 10 percent probability of death for every patient—will perform well on this measure.

The finding that expected death rates correlate well with observed rates is more interesting. It suggests that the predictors in the model were differently distributed among hospitals and that these differences accounted for much of the variation among hospitals in their mortality rates. Because they are averages, rates are more stable (i.e., they are less affected by random error) than individual observations, making it easier to achieve high correlations between predicted and actual death rates for *groups* of patients than for *individuals*. Thus, even though R^2 can be computed by squaring the correlation (e.g., if $r = 0.80$ then $R^2 = 0.64$), the resulting hospital-level R^2 values from predictions about hospitals are not comparable to the individual-level R^2 values mentioned earlier.

Other investigators have used correlations and hospital rankings to examine the effect of different risk-adjustment models. Hannan and colleagues (1992) used both a claims database and a clinical database on over 22,000 patients in New York state to develop models to predict in-hospital mortality from CABG surgery. Correlations between predicted hospital mortality rates using the two models were only moderately high (0.75 to 0.80). We expect the clinical model to find fewer outlier hospitals if it uses factors not captured in the administrative model that both affect risk and differ among hospitals. Thus, by adding clinical information, some hospitals identified as outliers by the administrative data model might be resolved. In fact, the administrative data model did identify a few more outlier hospitals (nine low and four high outliers) than the clinical model (four low and three high).

Krakauer and colleagues (1992) compared HCFA's mortality prediction model (which uses administrative data to predict death within 30 days of admission) to a model developed using MedisGroups KCFs. They entered dummy variables for hospitals in a regression model fit to a data set of almost 43,000 Medicare patients from 84 hospitals. The two models were compared several ways:

1. "The correlations of hospital rank [first] as determined by their regression [coefficient] and [then their] standardized regression coefficients (regression coefficients divided by their standard errors)";

2. "The proportion of hospitals estimated to have statistically significantly high regression coefficients by means of the claims model but not by the more complete clinical model"; and

3. "The changes in decile ranks of hospitals caused by the inclusion of clinical variables." (Krakauer et al. 1992, 322)

The correlation of hospital ranks was 0.91 based on the regression coefficients and 0.87 based on the standardized regression coefficients. Of the

33 hospitals identified as high outliers by the administrative data model, 12 were not considered high outliers by the clinical model; however, five hospitals were newly identified as outliers by the clinical model. In terms of decile rankings, only one hospital in the extreme two deciles at either end changed by as much as two deciles. Krakauer and colleagues (1992) concluded that administrative data models are useful to rank hospitals in terms of adjusted mortality but less useful for defining a cutpoint beyond which hospitals should be considered outliers.

Measuring calibration and discrimination with logistic regression models

Lee and colleagues (1986) compared prognostic predictions of survival in patients with coronary artery disease made by senior cardiologists to predictions from a multivariable statistical model (specifically, a Cox proportional hazard model; see Chapter 6). To evaluate the predictions, they fit the following logistic regression model:

$$\ln\left[\frac{p}{(1-p)}\right] = a + b\ln\left[\frac{PRED}{(1-PRED)}\right].$$

The p's represent each patient's probability of death; the PREDs are the predicted values, whether from the clinician or from the multivariable model. The investigators were interested in assessing which predictions had the strongest relationship to actual outcomes—those of physicians or those from the statistical model. In addition, they determined whether one set of predictions added prognostic information to the other set of predictions, by using the log odds of the PRED produced by each of the models in their regression as well as modeling separately with each PRED. Focusing on c-statistics, Lee and colleagues (1986) generally found a stronger relationship with the outcome for the model's predictions than for those of the clinicians. Also, the model's predictions contributed significantly to the clinicians' predictions, while the converse was not true for four of the five clinicians.

Miller and colleagues (1993) formalized a framework for assessing both model calibration and discrimination. Referring to the above equation, the parameter a measures model calibration. If $a < 0$, the predicted probabilities are too high; if $a > 0$, the predicted probabilities are too low. The parameter b measures discrimination. If $|b| > 1$, the PREDs do not vary enough; if $0 < |b| < 1$, the PREDs vary too much. If b is positive, higher PREDs go with cases more likely to die; negative b means that the PREDs go in the wrong direction.

Miller and colleagues (1993) described three tests for assessing the fit of the predicted probabilities:

1. an overall test of the quality of predictions ($a = 0$ and $b = 1$);
2. a test of incorrect calibration given appropriate discrimination ($a = 0$ given $b = 1$); and
3. a test of discrimination given corrected calibration ($b = 1$ given a).

In addition, they suggested regression diagnostics to identify cases that exert exceptional influence on the estimated calibration and discrimination terms. While this approach has not been used to evaluate risk-adjustment models, it could be a useful tool for evaluating model performance.

The Brier Score

The Brier score was developed initially to evaluate the quality of a model that makes dichotomous weather predictions (Brier 1950). It is the mean square error (MSE) of the model (i.e., SSE/n). Because R^2 can be written as

$$1 - n \times \frac{\text{MSE}}{\text{SST}}$$

and n and SST are solely functions of the data rather than the model, then the Brier score is a linear function of R^2 for a given data set. Given this derivation, the Brier score moves in the opposite direction from R^2: Better models (i.e., those with higher R^2 values) have lower Brier scores.

Brier scores must lie between 0 and 1. However, one should always be able to achieve a better Brier score than that produced by guessing $PRED = 0.5$ for all cases. With $PRED = 0.5$ for everybody, this uninformative model yields a Brier score of 0.25, because each of the squared errors is either $(1 - 0.5)^2$ or $(0 - 0.5)^2$. It should also be possible to improve on constantly guessing $PRED = p$, where p is the true death rate with an associated Brier score of $p(1 - p)$.

One useful feature of the Brier score is that it can be decomposed in several informative ways. Yates (1982) provides a comprehensive discussion of various decompositions of the Brier score, their relations to each other, and their utility in analyzing the comparative strengths and weaknesses of models along the several dimensions (such as calibration and discrimination) that contribute to good performance. A helpful discussion of these ideas is contained in Poses, Cebul, and Centor (1988), which also considers statistical tests to compare the performance of different medical prediction methods. The so-called covariance decomposition of the Brier score described by Yates (1982) is a sum of components as follows:

1. The variance of the observed values or $p(1 - p)$. This variance is not under the control of the forecaster but illustrates that the score depends on characteristics of the data set.

2. The squared difference between the average predicted rate of death, AVE($PRED$), and the actual rate, AVE(Y) or p. This measures overall model calibration.

3. The negative of $2(AVE_1 - AVE_0)\,p(1 - p)$, where AVE_1 is the average predicted value among patients who died and AVE_0 is the average predicted value among patients who lived. This component is driven by the difference in the average predicted probabilities for the two outcome groups, a measure of model discrimination called *DIFF* above.

4. The variance of the predicted values, which can be further split into two components: One that depends on *DIFF*, and one that depends on how spread out the actual predicted probabilities in each group are around their averages.

The Brier score has not been calculated in most evaluations of risk-adjustment methods, although it has been used in evaluating clinicians' predictions of certain events. For example, in assessing clinicians' subjective probability estimates made in response to different clinical scenarios derived from medical records, Dolan, Bordley, and Mushlin (1986) reported a range of Brier scores from 0.05 to 0.57. Objectively determined probabilities achieved a Brier score of 0.11. This score was better than the score achieved by 96 percent of the clinicians. They also examined a decomposition of the Brier score, focusing on the improved calibration and lower variability of the objectively determined probabilities.

Lee and colleagues (1986) used Brier scores, among other measures, to compare expert clinicians' predictions of survival from coronary disease to predictions produced by a multivariate statistical model (Cox proportional hazard model). The average and median Brier scores were lower for the model than for four of the five clinicians. McClish and Powell (1989) compared clinicians' predictions of mortality in an ICU to predictions based on APACHE II; they decomposed the Brier score into a calibration component and a discrimination component. The c-statistic was 0.89 for physicians and 0.83 for APACHE II. The discrimination component of the Brier score was 0.10 for physicians and 0.13 for APACHE, which also suggests that physicians did better. However, APACHE II was better calibrated than the physicians' predictions (0.003 versus 0.021, respectively). Arkes and colleagues (1995) published a well-written expository article exploring the information contained in the various components of the Brier—or the probability score, as they call it—for comparing the prognostic estimates of physicians, patients, and patient surrogates.

Model Validation

Overall Model Validation

Chapter 6 discusses issues in both cross-validation and external validation, while Chapter 8 provides examples of validation when the dependent variable is continuous. Here we provide several examples of validation for a dichotomous outcome.

Daley and colleagues (1988) used successive subsamples of 90 percent of the data to make predictions for the hold-out 10 percent subsamples. R^2 values were calculated from the predictions in the hold-out subsamples. Keeler and colleagues (1990) used the same approach. DesHarnais and collaborators (1988) explicitly evaluated face validity of their RAMI predictions at the hospital level (as opposed to face validity of the individual variables included in the model and their coefficients). Reports were prepared for 16 hospitals, meetings were held with the medical directors and quality assurance personnel, and reactions were solicited. "In no cases did these reviews yield information that questioned the credibility of the results. In several cases the reports flagged problems that the hospital representatives were able to confirm through their reviews" (DesHarnais et al. 1988, 1142).

Higgins and colleagues (1992) developed a model using patient severity (measured by a series of clinical variables) to predict death following CABG at the Cleveland Clinic. The model was developed based on about 5,000 patients and then validated on a cohort of about 4,200 new patients treated subsequently at the Cleveland Clinic. Using an independent sample for validation raises the issue of calibration discussed in Chapter 8. Severity scores differed significantly in the two data sets, with more higher-risk patients in the validation group. However, morbidity was lower in the validation data set (12.1 versus 13.5 percent). Thus, in the validation set, the lower confidence bound on the predicted morbidity rate was higher than the observed rate in four out of nine severity score categories, primarily in the higher-risk groups. The investigators suggested that the model may not have validated prospectively due to improvements in clinical management over time. Another possibility is that more intensive coding of risk factors in the later data may have produced higher predicted probabilities of morbidity with no real increase in patient risk. The data do not allow for a test of either hypothesis.

The important lesson is that discrepancies between reality and model predictions are easy to document, but the reasons for these differences usually require further study. This lesson rarely is considered in policy discussions surrounding public releases of risk-adjusted outcome information (see Chapter 11).

Van Ruiswyk and colleagues (1993) performed an external validation study of their model to predict mortality for elderly patients with AMI. The model was developed on data collected by Medicare's peer review organizations (PROs) in seven states in 1985 and validated using the 1988 MedisGroups Comparative Database. The PRO database included 30-day postadmission mortality information, while the MedisGroups database contained only in-hospital mortality. To account for this difference, the constant term in the logistic regression model developed from the PRO database was rescaled by a factor relating in-hospital to 30-day mortality in the development database. The constant term has no effect on the ranks of observations and thus on the c-statistic. In the validation data set, the c-statistic was 0.76, only slightly less than in the development data set (0.77).

Iezzoni and colleagues (1992) illustrated the use of split-sample cross-validation using MedisGroups data (see Table 5.4). The analyses were conducted on almost 135,000 patients 65 years and older from 24 Medis-Groups-member hospitals who had one of these conditions: stroke, lung cancer, congestive heart failure, pneumonia, and AMI. As described in Chapter 5, the number of KCFs (i.e., the candidate explanatory variables) ranged from 40 to 65. To test for model overfitting, the data were randomly divided into even and odd subsets. Models were fit to the even half of the data and then used to make predictions for each observation in the odd half of the data. Within each condition, the ten KCFs that were first to enter in the stepwise procedure were also subjected to cross-validation. Most of the variables appearing among the first ten KCFs were the same when models were fit to the two halves of the data.

Another finding from this study illustrates the deterioration of performance under cross-validation for more complex models. Although in each condition the model developed using all KCFs fit the data better than the model that used only the top ten KCFs, it never had a higher cross-validated R^2 than did the ten-KCF model (see Table 5.4). Performance measures without cross-validation generally give an inappropriately optimistic view of the ability of complex models to predict outcomes.

Bootstrapping (see Chapter 6) has been used in several validations of mortality prediction models. In developing their "sickness at admission" measure, Keeler and colleagues (1990) repeated their modeling on five bootstrap replicates of the data sets for each condition and reported that the "average pairwise correlation of predicted death probabilities from the different models was .94" (p. 1964).

Closely related to the validity of performance measures is the question of the uncertainty associated with the measure. As discussed in

Chapter 8, confidence intervals for R^2 are usually estimated from bootstrap replications. Hanley and McNeil (1982, 1983) provide methods for analytically calculating confidence intervals for c-statistics and for differences in two c-statistics calculated using either the same or different data. In our severity study, we reported 95 percent confidence intervals for the c-statistic and the R^2 statistic for each of the severity measures for predicting in-hospital AMI deaths (Iezzoni et al. 1996a). Confidence intervals were generated by replicating the analyses (i.e., fitting the models and calculating performance measures) 80 times using bootstrapping techniques. Because of the large sample size (13,800 patients), confidence intervals were narrow.

The California hospital mortality report mentioned above has undertaken extensive validation of their risk-adjustment models for AMI patients (see Chapters 3 and 11). To validate the models, which were developed from discharge abstract data, a two-stage probability sample was used to select slightly over 1,000 hospital records for reabstracting (Wilson, Smoley, and Werdegar 1996). Reabstracted information included core demographic variables, diagnosis codes, procedure codes and dates, additional clinical risk factors, and the use of various therapies. A variety of validation analyses were performed, including: (1) a determination of the proportion of cases for whom AMI was incorrectly reported or incorrectly diagnosed (definitely 2.2 percent and possibly another 7.2 percent); (2) a study of coding quality, which concluded that the original coding ranged from excellent (sensitivity > 80 percent and kappa > 0.8) for some conditions (infarct site and diabetes) to very good (sensitivity > 60 percent and kappa > 0.6) for such conditions as congestive heart failure and chronic renal disease, to poor (sensitivity < 40 percent and kappa < 0.45) for such conditions as chronic liver disease and pulmonary edema; and (3) a study that found no consistent differences in the coding accuracy for specific risk factors across hospital mortality and volume categories (Wilson, Smoley, and Werdegar 1996, 15-2–3). However, when the original data were replaced by the reabstracted data, the difference in risk-adjusted mortality between low- and high-mortality outlier hospitals shrank by 19 percent to 29 percent using Model B and by 0 percent to 12 percent using Model A (in a variety of alternative analyses). Nevertheless, even in Model B, over 70 percent of the spread in risk-adjusted mortality was not explained by coding variation.

Hardness of the Data to Model

As discussed above and in Chapter 8, performance measures vary due to characteristics of the data set as well as of the model. Some data sets are harder to model than others. For example, suppose we seek to validate two different models with the same initial R^2 values on a development data set. The first model is validated on a data set with a lower dispersion of independent variables than the second. Therefore, the first model appears to validate less well. However, this apparent difference in model performance really reflects the increased difficulty in explaining variation in outcomes when independent variables are less dispersed (as illustrated in Figure 8.1).

Hadorn and colleagues (1992a) explored the effect of the "hardness" of the data set on performance measures when modeling a dichotomous outcome. Based on predictions from a logistic regression model developed to predict mortality within 30 days of admission for patients with AMI, the overall data set was divided into subsets that differed in the dispersion of the predicted probabilities. Both a good and a poor model were run on the harder and easier subsets of the data. They found that measures of performance of poor models on easy data often exceeded measures for good models on difficult data, illustrating well why judgments based on comparisons of model performance measured in different data sets are potentially problematic (Hadorn et al. 1992a).

Validations Using Subgroups of the Data

Suppose that a model developed to predict death is then applied to some subgroup of cases, either a subset of the model development data set or to new cases that share a particular characteristic (as opposed to a randomly sampled validation data set). Suppose further that the observed death rate in the group being studied is significantly different from what the model predicts. If we believe that the model fairly captures and accounts for all important factors affecting patient risk, we then begin to look for some other factor causing the difference, such as low- or high-quality care. However, systematic misprediction of mortality for classes of patients may reflect problems with the model.

Blumberg (1991) examined the problem of poor subgroup fit, which he referred to as "biased estimation," using the old version of the Medis-Groups admission severity score to adjust for 30-day mortality of AMI patients. He found that estimates of expected mortality differed significantly from actual outcomes in subgroups formed using several patient attributes (e.g., age, location of infarction in the myocardium, history of congestive heart failure, serum potassium level, serum urea nitrogen level, pulse rate, and blood pressure). To illustrate the problem, consider the variable "age." Blumberg reported 38.4 deaths among 289 patients 85 years of age and older versus an expected number of deaths of 27.2 based on the distribution of MedisGroups admission scores. From this, Blumberg concluded that this version of the MedisGroups severity score was biased, in that it did not properly account for the independent effect of age on mortality risk. The new empirical version of MedisGroups specifically includes age in its prediction models (Steen et al. 1993). Other evidence also supports the supposition that age is an independent risk factor for mortality (see Chapter 2). However, another hypothesis consistent with Blumberg's finding is that, after adjusting for risk, quality of care is lower for the very old, resulting in more deaths than expected.

How discrepancies between observed and expected outcomes are interpreted is a very serious issue, as highlighted in Chapter 11. For example, suppose that death rates in public hospitals are significantly higher than expected after risk adjustment using some particular set of variables to measure risk. Whether this difference indicates that care in such hospitals is poor, or that patients seen in public hospitals are sicker than patients in other hospitals *in ways not measured by the model*, is critical to understanding this finding. The public discourse around such findings is not always objective—providers with worse-than-expected outcomes typically claim that this is due to unmeasured excess risk, while providers with better-than-expected outcomes willingly believe that quality differences are responsible.

One might attempt to validate the model separately on subgroups of the data. However, interpreting performance measures is a special case of the general problem discussed above; due to intrinsic differences in the hardness of the data for modeling, performance measures for models applied to different subgroups should not be directly compared. To illustrate this further, consider a situation where patients representing three different diseases are included in a single data set. If predictions are modeled separately within each disease subgroup, then the R^2 for making predictions in the whole data set is a sum of two quantities: the average of the three R^2 values for the three subsets and the R^2 for a model that assigns the average death rate for each disease to each patient with that disease. Thus, if the three diseases have very different death rates, the overall R^2 could be large simply because which disease a person has is very predictive, even if the ability to distinguish risk among patients with the same disease is negligible.

Given the growing public desire to compare risk-adjusted outcomes across providers (see Chapters 10 and 11), interest in the performance of risk prediction models will increase. Of particular concern is the claim that worse-than-expected outcomes reflect the inadequacy of risk adjustment. The only way to test this claim is to collect data on the unmeasured factors believed responsible for the discrepancies and to see how much of the difference is explained. Although theoretically attractive, this test is often not practical. As suggested in Chapter 2, myriad factors affect patients' risk of various healthcare outcomes. Without further studies, one must rely on judgments about the face and content validity of the risk-adjustment approach (Chapter 6), and judgments about whether the effects of unmeasured risk factors are likely to explain observed discrepancies. Thus, as noted at the start of Chapter 8, interpreting "objective" measures of performance must partially rely on subjective assessments.

Conclusions

Chapters 8 and 9 addressed issues raised in interpreting quantitative measures of the performance of risk-adjustment approaches. When modeling a continuous outcome variable, R^2 is the main measure of performance. When modeling a dichotomous variable, a variety of measures summarize how well a model's predictions fit a particular set of data. Regardless of the perceived advantages of some new way of measuring model fit, the scientific community will be best served if all reports present a set of measures in common. Our short list of important measures includes the c-statistic, the traditional R^2, the mean *PRED* for cases who live and for those who die, and a decile-of-predicted-risk table.

Nevertheless, as mentioned at the outset of Chapter 8, interpreting these quantitative measures of performance is not always straightforward, and subjective judgments are often required. For both continuous and dichotomous outcome measures, many issues must be considered in interpreting the statistics. The important questions for interpreting models of continuous outcomes listed at the conclusion of Chapter 8 are also important for dichotomous outcomes. Given these various considerations, the way risk-adjusted outcomes information is used in the current health policy environment raises concern, as described in Chapters 10 and 11.

References

Akaike, H. 1973. "Information Theory and an Extension of the Maximum Likelihood Principle." In *Second International Symposium on Information Theory*, edited by B.N. Petrov and F. Csaki. Budapest: Akademia Kiado.

Arkes, H. R., N. V. Dawson, T. Speroff, F. E. Harrell, Jr., C. Alzola, R. Phillips, N. Desbiens, R. K. Oye, W. Knaus, A. F. Connors, Jr., and the SUPPORT Investigators. 1995. "The Covariance Decomposition of the Probability Score and Its Use in Evaluating Prognostic Estimates." *Medical Decision Making* 15 (2): 120–31.

Ash, A., F. Porell, L. Gruenberg, E. Sawitz, and A. Beiser. 1989. "Adjusting Medicare Capitation Payments Using Prior Hospitalization Data." *Health Care Financing Review* 10 (4): 17–29.

Ash, A., M. Shwartz, S. M. C. Payne, and J. D. Restuccia. 1990. "The Self-Adapting Focused Review System. Probability Sampling of Medical Records to Monitor Utilization and Quality of Care." *Medical Care* 28 (11): 1025–39.

Blumberg, M. S. 1991. "Biased Estimates of Expected Acute Myocardial Infarction Mortality Using MedisGroups Admission Severity Groups." *Journal of the American Medical Association* 265 (22): 2965–70.

Breiman, L., J. H. Friedman, R. A. Olshen, and C. J. Stone. 1984. *Classification and Regression Trees.* Belmont, CA: Wadsworth International Group.

Brier, G. W. 1950. "Verification of Forecasts Expressed in Terms of Probability." *Monthly Weather Review* 78 (1): 1–3.

Centor, R. M., and J. S. Schwartz. 1985. "An Evaluation of Methods for Estimating the Area Under the Receiver Operating Characteristic (ROC) Curve." *Medical Decision Making* 5 (2): 149–56.

Chassin, M. R., E. L. Hannan, and B. A. DeBuono. 1996. "Benefits and Hazards of Reporting Medical Outcomes Publicly." *New England Journal of Medicine* 334 (6): 394–98.

Cleary, P. D., and R. Angel. 1984. "The Analysis of Relationships Involving Dichotomous Dependent Variables." *Journal of Health and Social Behavior* 25 (3): 334–48.

Cox, D. R., and N. Wermuth. 1992. "A Comment on the Coefficient of Determination for Binary Responses." *American Statistician* 46 (1): 1–4.

Daley, J., S. Jencks, D. Draper, G. Lenhart, N. Thomas, and J. Walker. 1988. "Predicting Hospital-Associated Mortality for Medicare Patients. A Method for Patients with Stroke, Pneumonia, Acute Myocardial Infarction, and Congestive Heart Failure." *Journal of the American Medical Association* 260 (24): 3617–24.

DesHarnais, S. I., J. D. Chesney, R. T. Wroblewski, S. T. Fleming, and L. F. McMahon, Jr. 1988. "The Risk-Adjusted Mortality Index. A New Measure of Hospital Performance." *Medical Care* 26 (12): 1129–48.

Dolan, J. G., D. R. Bordley, and A. I. Mushlin. 1986. "An Evaluation of Clinicians' Subjective Prior Probability Estimates." *Medical Decision Making* 6 (4): 216–23.

Epstein, A. M., and E. J. Cumella. 1988. "Capitation Payment: Using Predictors of Medical Utilization to Adjust Rates." *Health Care Financing Review* 10 (1): 51–69.

Feinstein, A.R., C.K. Wells, and S. D. Walter. 1990. "A Comparison of Multivariable Mathematical Models for Predicting Survival. I. Introduction, Rationale, and General Strategy." *Journal of Clinical Epidemiology* 43 (4): 339–47.

Green, J. and N. Wintfeld. 1995. "Report Cards on Cardiac Surgeons—Assessing New York State's Approach." *New England Journal of Medicine* 332 (18): 1229–32.

Green, J., N. Wintfeld, P. Sharkey, and L. J. Passman. 1990. "The Importance of Severity of Illness in Assessing Hospital Mortality." *Journal of the American Medical Association* 263 (2): 241–46.

Hadorn, D., E. Keeler, W. Rogers, and R. Brook. 1992a. "Proposed Standards for Measuring the Performance of Clinical Prediction Models." Discussion Paper for RAND/HCFA Meeting.

Hadorn, D. C., D. Draper, W. H. Rogers, E. B. Keeler, and R. H. Brook. 1992b. "Cross-Validation Performance of Mortality Prediction Models." *Statistics in Medicine* 11 (4): 475–89.

Hanley, J. A., and B. J. McNeil. 1982. "The Meaning and Use of the Area under a Receiver Operating Characteristic (ROC) Curve." *Radiology* 143 (1): 29–36.

————. 1983. "A Method of Comparing the Area under Receiver Operating Characteristic Curves Derived from the Same Cases." *Radiology* 148 (3): 839–43.

Hannan, E. L., H. Kilburn, Jr., M. Racz, E. Shields, and M. R. Chassin. 1994. "Improving the Outcomes of Coronary Artery Bypass Surgery in New York State." *Journal of the American Medical Association* 271 (10): 761–66.

Hannan, E. L., H. Kilburn, Jr., M. L. Lindsey, and R. Lewis. 1992. "Clinical Versus Administrative Data Bases for CABG Surgery. Does It Matter?" *Medical Care* 30 (10): 892–907.

Harrell, F. E., Jr., K. L. Lee, R. M. Califf, D. B. Pryor, and R. A. Rosati. 1984. "Regression Modelling Strategies for Improved Prognostic Prediction." *Statistics in Medicine* 3 (2): 143–52.

Hartz, A. J. 1984. "Overlap Index. An Alternative to Sensitivity and Specificity in Comparing the Utility of a Laboratory Test." *Archives of Pathology and Laboratory Medicine* 108 (1): 65–67.

Higgins, T. L., F. G. Estafanous, F. D. Loop, G. J. Beck, J. M. Blum, and L. Paranandi. 1992. "Stratification of Morbidity and Mortality Outcome by Preoperative Risk Factors in Coronary Artery Bypass Patients. A Clinical Severity Score." *Journal of the American Medical Association* 267 (17): 2344–48. Published erratum appears in 1992, 268 (14): 1860.

Hilden, J. 1991. "The Area under the ROC Curve and Its Competitors." *Medical Decision Making* 11 (2): 95–101.

Horn, S. D., and R. A. Horn. 1986. "Reliability and Validity of the Severity of Illness Index." *Medical Care* 24 (2): 159–78.

Iezzoni, L. I., A. S. Ash, G. A. Coffman, and M. A. Moskowitz. 1992. "Predicting In-Hospital Mortality. A Comparison of Severity Measurement Approaches." *Medical Care* 30 (4): 347–59.

Iezzoni, L. I., M. Shwartz, A. S. Ash, Y. D. Mackiernan, and E. K. Hotchkin. 1994. "Risk Adjustment Methods Can Affect Perceptions of Outcomes." *American Journal of Medical Quality* 9 (2): 43–48.

Iezzoni, L. I., M. Shwartz, A. S. Ash, J. S. Hughes, J. Daley, and Y. D. Mackiernan. 1995a. "Using Severity-Adjusted Stroke Mortality Rates to Judge Hospitals. *International Journal for Quality in Health Care* 7 (2): 81–94.

Iezzoni, L. I., A. S. Ash, M. Shwartz, J. Daley, J. S. Hughes, and Y. D. Mackiernan. 1995b. "Predicting Who Dies Depends on How Severity is Measured: Implications for Evaluating Patient Outcomes." *Annals of Internal Medicine* 123 (10): 763–70.

————. 1996a. "Judging Hospitals by Severity-Adjusted Mortality Rates: The Influence of the Severity-Adjustment Method." *American Journal of Public Health* 86 (10): 1379–87.

Iezzoni, L. I., M. Shwartz, A. S. Ash, J. S. Hughes, J. Daley, and Y. D. Mackiernan. 1996b. "Severity Measurement Methods and Judging Hospital Death Rates for Pneumonia." *Medical Care* 34 (1): 11–28.

Iezzoni, L. I., M. Shwartz, A. S. Ash, and Y. D. Mackiernan. 1996c. "Using Severity Measures to Predict the Likelihood of Death for Pneumonia Inpatients." *Journal of General Internal Medicine* 11 (1): 23–31.

Iezzoni, L. I., M. Shwartz, A. S. Ash, and Y. D. Mackiernan. 1996d. "Predicting In-hospital Mortality for Stroke Patients: Results Differ Across Severity–measurement Methods." *Medical Decision Making* 16 (4): 348–56.

Ingelfinger, J. A., F. Mosteller, L. A. Thibodeau, and J. H. Ware. 1987. *Biostatistics in Clinical Medicine.* New York: Macmillan Publishing Co.

Keeler, E. B., K. L. Kahn, D. Draper, M. J. Sherwood, L. V. Rubenstein, E. J. Reinisch, J. Kosecoff, and R. H. Brook. 1990. "Changes in Sickness at Admission Following the Introduction of the Prospective Payment System." *Journal of the American Medical Association* 264 (15): 1962–68.

Knaus, W. A., F. E. Harrell, Jr., J. Lynn, L. Goldman, R. S. Phillips, A. F. Connors, Jr., N. V. Dawson, W. J. Faulkerson, Jr., R. M. Califf, N. Debians, P. Layde, R. K. Oye, P. E. Bellamy, R. B. Hakim, and D. P. Wagner. 1995. "The SUPPORT Prognostic Model. Objective Estimates of Survival for Seriously Ill Hospitalized Adults." *Annals of Internal Medicine* 122 (3): 191–203.

Knaus, W. A., D. P. Wagner, E. A. Draper, J. E. Zimmerman, M. Bergner, P. G. Bastos, C. A. Sirio, D. J. Murphy, T. Lotring, A. Damiano, and F. E. Harrell, Jr. 1991. "The APACHE III Prognostic System. Risk Prediction of Hospital Mortality for Critically Ill Hospitalized Adults." *Chest* 100 (6): 1619–36.

Krakauer, H., R. C. Bailey, K. J. Skellan, J. D. Stewart, A. J. Hartz, E. M. Kuhn, and A. A. Rimm. 1992. "Evaluation of the HCFA Model for the Analysis of Mortality Following Hospitalization." *HSR: Health Services Research* 27 (3): 317–35.

Landon, B., L. I. Iezzoni, A. S. Ash, M. Shwartz, J. Daley, J. S. Hughes, and Y. D. Mackiernan. 1996. "Judging Hospitals by Severity-Adjusted Mortality Rates: The Case of CABG Surgery." *Inquiry* 33 (2): 155–66.

Lee, K. L., D. B. Pryor, F. E. Harrell, Jr., R. M. Califf, V. S. Behar, W. L. Floyd, J. J. Morris, R. A. Waugh, R. E. Whalen, and R. A. Rosati. 1986. "Predicting Outcome in Coronary Disease. Statistical Models versus Expert Clinicians." *American Journal of Medicine* 80 (4): 553–60.

Lemeshow, S., and D. W. Hosmer, Jr. 1982. "A Review of Goodness of Fit Statistics for Use in the Development of Logistic Regression Models." *American Journal of Epidemiology* 115 (1): 92–106.

Lemeshow, S., D. Teres, J. S. Avrunin, and R. W. Gage. 1988. "Refining Intensive Care Unit Outcome Prediction by Using Changing Probabilities of Mortality." *Critical Care Medicine* 16 (5): 470–77.

McClish, D. K., and S. H. Powell. 1989. "How Well Can Physicians Estimate Mortality in a Medical Intensive Care Unit?" *Medical Decision Making* 9 (2): 125–32.

Miller, M. E., C. D. Langefeld, W. M. Tierney, S. L. Hui, and C. J. McDonald. 1993. "Validation of Probabilistic Predictions." *Medical Decision Making* 13 (1): 49–58.

Nagelkerke, N. J. D. 1991. "A Note on a General Definition of the Coefficient of Determination." *Biometrika* 78 (3): 691–92.

Poses, R. M., R. D. Cebul, and R. M. Centor. 1988. "Evaluating Physicians' Probabilistic Judgments." *Medical Decision Making* 8 (4): 233–40.

Selker H. P., J. L. Griffith, S. Patil, W. J. Long, and R. B. D'Agostino. 1995. "A Comparison of Performance of Mathematical Predictive Methods for Medical Diagnosis: Identifying Acute Cardiac Ischemia Among Emergency Department Patients." *Journal of Investigative Medicine* 43 (5): 468–76.

Smith, D. W., M. Pine, R. C. Bailey, B. Jones, A. Brewster, and H. Krakauer. 1991. "Using Clinical Variables to Estimate the Risk of Patient Mortality." *Medical Care* 29 (11): 1108–29.

Steen, P. M., A. C. Brewster, R. C. Bradbury, E. Estabrook, and J. A. Young. 1993. "Predicted Probabilities of Hospital Death as a Measure of Admission Severity of Illness." *Inquiry* 30 (2): 128–41.

Van Ruiswyk, J., A. Hartz, E. Kuhn, H. Krakauer, M. Young, and A. Rimm. 1993. "A Measure of Mortality Risk for Elderly Patients with Acute Myocardial Infarction." *Medical Decision Making* 13 (2): 152–60.

Wagner, D. P., W. A. Knaus, F. E. Harrell, J. E. Zimmerman, and C. Watts. 1994. "Daily Prognostic Estimates for Critically Ill Adults in the Intensive Care Units: Results from a Prospective, Multicenter, Inception Cohort Analysis." *Critical Care Medicine* 22 (9): 1359–72.

Wilson, P., S. R. Smoley, and D. Werdegar. 1996. *Second Report of the California Hospital Outcomes Project. Acute Myocardial Infarction. Volume Two: Technical Appendix.* Sacramento, CA: Office of Statewide Health Planning and Development.

Yates, J. F. 1982. "External Correspondence: Decompositions of the Mean Probability Score." *Organizational Behavior and Human Performance* 30: 132–56.

Chapter 10

Comparing Outcomes Across Providers

Michael Shwartz, Arlene S. Ash, and Lisa I. Iezzoni

Risk adjustment is only a tool to facilitate meaningful comparisons of outcomes across groups of patients. The purpose of risk adjustment is to account for one potential cause of observed differences in outcomes—intrinsic patient characteristics that increase risk. However, even comparisons of risk-adjusted outcomes are themselves just a means to an end: Florence Nightingale and E. A. Codman, for example, viewed outcomes comparisons as a powerful way to motivate improvement of quality of care (see Chapter 1). As Nightingale wrote in 1863 (175–76):

> In attempting to arrive at the truth, I have applied everywhere for information, but in scarcely an instance have I been able to obtain hospital records fit for any purposes of comparison . . . I am fain to sum up with an urgent appeal for adopting . . . some *uniform* system of publishing the statistical records of hospitals. There is a growing conviction that in all hospitals, even in those which are best conducted, there is a great and unnecessary waste of life. . . .

Nightingale and William Farr argued that simply comparing rates of events was insufficient, claiming instead that one must discover why differences in patient outcomes occurred and correct identified problems.

Jumping to the end of the twentieth century, comparing outcomes is now central to changing the American healthcare delivery system and responding to competitive market forces. Patients' outcomes are compared across hospitals, groups of doctors (e.g., group practices, multispecialty clinics), individual doctors, or health plans (e.g., health maintenance organizations, managed care companies). The comparisons are variously called performance or practice profiles, report cards, scorecards, and outcomes reports. In some contexts, these profiles receive daunting assignments. In 1996, for example, when investors lost confidence in the ability of HMOs to control costs, United HealthCare, one of the nation's largest investor-owned HMOs, lost 2.8 billion dollars in value in one day (Johnsson 1996, 1). To recoup that value, United HealthCare launched "aggressive medical management," including "increasing physician profiling to identify and improve performance of cost outliers" (Johnsson 1996, 27). Some HMOs view the key to maximizing efficiency as "the ability to profile care—utilization and quality issues for a population—and take that information to physicians" (Kreier 1996, 27).

Despite these vaunted expectations, methods for producing profiles generate considerable controversy and raise numerous challenging conceptual and statistical questions (Goldfield and Boland 1996). In addition to concerns about risk adjustment, profiling efforts generally must contend with small sample sizes—individual providers frequently treat too few patients of a given type each year to generate accurate and stable estimates of their long-term average performance with such patients. These simultaneous concerns about risk adjustment and small sample sizes strand profiling efforts somewhere "between the devil and the deep blue sea." The main strategy for increasing the accuracy of estimates is including more cases, but this generally increases population heterogeneity and makes risk adjustment more problematic. In addition, summary measures across diverse patient groups, such as the death rate for all hospital admissions combined, provide little insight to motivate change. In general, such statistics are most useful when they pertain to identifiable management units, such as the cardiac surgery department.

This chapter explores considerations raised in comparing outcomes across groups of patients, focusing on the specific context of profiling provider performance. In this chapter:

- We briefly mention practical considerations in producing practice profiles.
- We illustrate the effect of random error on the reliability of estimates of performance in a simple but artificial situation with no differences in patient risk.
- We next introduce differences in patient risk factors, leading to the need to determine "expected" outcomes for a group of patients.
- We then discuss the two most widely used alternatives for comparing observed (O) outcomes to expected (E) outcomes—the ratio (O/E) and the difference ($O-E$). We show that standard risk-adjustment methods do not necessarily lead to the same O to E comparison for two providers with similar performance and dissimilar patient mix.
- We consider how to incorporate the effect of random variation when examining O to E ratios.

- We then discuss methods for displaying outcomes comparisons when publishing report cards for public use.
- We close by considering two ways of improving estimates of performance—empirical Bayes estimation and a generalization called hierarchical modeling.

Practical Considerations

Before confronting these methodological challenges, efforts to compare patient outcomes across providers must first make numerous conceptual and practical decisions (Table 10.1). The words "profiles," "scorecards," and "report cards" mean different things to different people, and "profiling" alone acquires slightly different meaning and emphasis depending on who is asked. For example, leaders from United HealthCare asserted:

> Medical practice profiling may be defined as the analysis of rates of events pertaining to the process or outcomes of medical care provided by health care practitioners to defined populations . . . The overall objective of profiling is to use epidemiologic methods to describe medical practices, monitor health outcomes, and assess the efficiency and quality of care. (Brand, Quam, and Leatherman 1995, 224)

A healthcare consultant, interested in helping physician groups control "volume and intensity growth," stated:

Table 10.1   Practical Decisions for Comparing Patient Outcomes Across Providers

What data will be used?
    Can information be linked at the person-level?
    Can numerators and denominators be determined?
    What are the accuracy and reliability of the data?
    Which patient risk factors are captured in the data?
    What is the time frame encompassed by the data?
What outcomes can be measured from the data?
Which providers will be included?
    Are there reasons to exclude any providers?
      • Small sample sizes
      • Incomplete data
      • Known patient risks unable to measure with the data (e.g., public hospitals)
      • Policy considerations (e.g., small hospitals, rural hospitals)
Which patients will be included?
    What are the specific inclusion criteria (e.g., disease, surgery)?
    Are there reasons to exclude any patients?

We refer to "profiling" as the statistical analysis and monitoring of claims and encounter data to gain more information on the appropriateness of patient care. Profiling results should help clinical leaders of the groups better understand the resources used in managing specific medical conditions. (Cave 1995, 464)

Academics at a university business school observed:

Profiling involves the preparation and selective dissemination of reports that compare the practice patterns of different providers on such dimensions as resource consumption, charges, and outcomes. Thus, profiling provides relative performance measures among providers and can be used to identify potential quality problems . . . and improve utilization review. (Evans, Hwang, and Nagarajan 1995, 1107)

Therefore, before comparing outcomes across providers, clarifying one's purpose is essential. Analyses and consequent interpretations should be tailored to the stated goal. For example, in some instances, detailed information comparing individual physicians within a single institution may satisfy a hospital's goal of informing internal quality improvements. In other instances, external benchmarking information is crucial, letting that hospital know if it is doing as well as it could compared to other hospitals. In benchmarking, some hospitals may want to be profiled only against similar facilities, such as tertiary teaching hospitals.

Generally, several categories of questions motivate report card and profiling initiatives (see Chapter 11), such as:

- Do any providers (e.g., physicians, groups of physicians, hospitals, health plans) stand out as either much better or worse than average on a particular outcome of interest?

- Based on past performance, will certain providers do better or worse than others next year?

- How strong is the evidence that Provider A's performance has been (or, perhaps more importantly, will be) substandard?

Intelligent answers to such questions require both an informed methodological approach and a conceptual framework for interpreting results. As suggested below, numerous questions remain about the most appropriate approaches for answering these types of questions.

In addition, as suggested above, comparisons frequently focus on *processes of care*, for which risk adjustment may be unnecessary. For example, the Health Plan Employer Data and Information Set (HEDIS) created by the National Committee for Quality Assurance, a leading accreditor of managed care plans, focuses primarily on process measures—that is, what was done to patients. Version 3.0 of HEDIS, released first in July 1996, includes such indicators as rates of infant and adolescent immunizations, mammography, and cervical cancer screening rates for at-risk women (Iglehart 1996). Because these processes of care relate to well-defined populations and are viewed as universally applicable, risk adjustment may be unnecessary. However, motivating preventive health behaviors in certain populations (e.g., poorly educated persons, the poor) is more difficult than in other populations; interpretation of different screening rates must therefore consider population characteristics. One HEDIS indicator—influenza immunizations for "high risk" adults—builds risk stratification into its definition. Questions of risk adjustment aside, however, "we do not know whether plans that perform well on the basis of these preventive measures are likely to perform well in the diagnosis and treatment of serious acute and chronic illnesses" (Brook, McGlynn, and Cleary 1996, 969).

Therefore, evaluations of the implications of practice profiles or report cards require understanding of their clinical content. As Angell and Kassirer (1996, 884) observed:

> It is very much easier to report on the rate of mammography or childhood immunizations in a large population than to determine the success of efforts to palliate congestive heart failure . . . And it is simple enough for plans to ensure that their doctors perform such procedures so that plans can score well on quality reports. In contrast, treating congestive heart failure or urosepsis in a patient with diabetes mellitus, who may have other medical problems as well, involves . . . the nearly imponderable element of individual variation. It is for this reason that quality measures so far have focused almost exclusively on preventive care, despite the fact that the management of complex illness is arguably where high-quality care matters most. Efforts to evaluate the outcomes of care in complex illnesses are under way, but they are still in their infancy and are likely to be frustrated by variations in case mix. As yet, we have no reliable measures of quality that can deal with variations in the severity of illness and individual complications.

Finally, the single most important decision involves choosing the data source. The data delimit the outcomes, providers, patients, time frame, and risk factors that can be considered—as well as the validity and reliability of the information and the cost of generating the profile. The implications of various data choices are detailed in Chapters 3 through 7.

The Effect of Random Fluctuations on Comparisons of Patient Outcomes

Random fluctuations affect estimates of provider performance and thus limit the conclusions that can be drawn safely from performance profiles comparing patient outcomes. To illustrate the role of random effects, we will examine a simple but contrived example in which no differences in patient risks exist. We will also examine hospital costs, assuming patients with identical disease and severity, treated with the same protocol at several hospitals. Costs might be approximated from charges by cost-to-charge ratios (Shwartz et al. 1995).

Our simplest model views the costs of the n_A cases admitted to Hospital A this year as a sample from a theoretically infinite population of cases that might be treated at Hospital A. This year's observed average cost at Hospital A, $\bar{Y}_A$, is an estimate of an underlying average cost, μ_A, for all cases that might be treated there.

The distribution of observed costs of this year's patients provides information about the variability of costs among potential patients at Hospital A. Examining this distribution is always advisable. For example, one should look at standard summary statistics: the mean, median, and standard deviation; minimum and maximum values; and values associated with different percentage points of the distribution (e.g., the value demarcating the upper five percent of the cases). For facilities in Hospital A's comparison group, side-by-side box-and-whiskers plots will help to identify individual values that are probably errors (e.g., hospital stays with negative costs) or correct but extreme values. For instance, a hospital with high average costs, due to every case being expensive, would be viewed differently than an institution where one very expensive case raised the average by nearly $10,000 (e.g., one "million-dollar baby" among 100 average-cost newborns).

The standard deviation is the most common summary measure of variation for a variable Y and is estimated, for a sample of observations $Y_1, Y_2, \ldots, Y_n$ as

$$s = \sqrt{\sum_i (Y_i - \bar{Y})^2 / (n - 1)}.$$

Just as $\bar{Y}_A$ is viewed as an estimate of an unobserved mean, μ_A, of a larger theoretical population, the standard deviation in Hospital A, s_A, is viewed as an estimate of σ_A, the standard deviation of the larger theoretical population. Standard deviations have the same units as the Y's (here, dollars). Regardless of the shape of the distribution of Y, most costs are likely to lie within two or three standard deviations of the average.

A common model hypothesized when comparing hospitals (or any other provider unit) assumes that:

- Each case at Hospital A has expected value μ_A, which may differ by facility; but

- The Y's at each facility are equally variable (i.e., there is a single, common value σ of the σ_A's).

Within each facility, s_A (computed by applying the above formula to the cases at Hospital A) is an estimate of σ. The "pooled" estimate of σ, called s, is computed from a weighted average of the estimated facility-level variances, as:

$$s = \sqrt{\sum_A (w_A * s_A^2)}$$

where the Ath facility has n_A cases, all k facilities contribute to a total of $n = \sum_A n_A$ cases, and $w_A = (n_A - 1)/(n - k)$.

Our goal is both to estimate the μ_A's and to measure the accuracy of these estimates, based on what we observe, namely $\bar{Y}_A$, n_A, and s_A.

Whatever the distribution of Y, the observed average cost at Hospital A, $\bar{Y}_A$, will generally fall within two standard errors (se) of the true average μ_A—within the range $\mu_A \pm 2 * se_A$, where se_A, the standard error of the mean at Hospital A, is calculated as

$$se_A = s/\sqrt{n_A}.$$

Thus, each interval $\bar{Y}_A \pm 2 * se_A$ is likely to contain its true hospital mean value, μ_A.

For a given Hospital A, μ_A (the value around which individual Y values are centered) and σ_A (a measure of how much the individual values are dispersed around μ_A) are properties of the population and do not depend on n_A, the number of cases at Hospital A. In contrast, the standard error describes an estimator; specifically, it measures how accurately $\bar{Y}_A$ estimates μ_A. As the number of observations at Hospital A increases, se_A decreases, thus increasing the accuracy of $\bar{Y}_A$ as an estimate of μ_A. For example, suppose that we observe mean costs of $5,000 with a standard deviation of $5,000 (with hospital cost data, the standard deviations and means often have the same general magnitude). With 100 observations, we are reasonably sure that μ_A will fall into the interval $5,000 ± 2*500, that is from $4,000 to $6,000. With $n = 400$, μ_A would likely be between $4,500 and $5,500.

Even with the highly skewed distributions typical of healthcare cost data, the observed mean will be approximately normally distributed if n_A is not very small. An interval centered at $\bar{Y}_A$ and extending for two or three standard error–sized units above and below will likely include μ_A. For many purposes, 30 cases is an adequate n_A. However, when the outcome variable is extremely skewed (i.e., when extreme values have a major effect on the mean), it may require hundreds of cases before the distribution of $\bar{Y}_A$ is nearly normal. When the underlying variable (cost in the population from which the n_A cases were sampled) is distributed normally, $\bar{Y}_A$ has a 95 percent chance of falling in the interval $\mu_A \pm$

$1.96 * se_A$, which we call an "acceptance" interval. Similarly, the interval $\bar{Y}_A \pm 1.96 * se_A$ has a 95 percent chance of containing the true value, μ_A. This latter interval is called a "95 percent confidence interval." A confidence interval specifies plausible boundaries for a parameter (here, μ_A), while an acceptance interval establishes boundaries such that if $\bar{Y}_A$ falls within them, we "accept" the hypothesis that Hospital A is performing as expected.

The coefficient of variation (CV) is the ratio of the standard deviation to the mean: $s/\bar{Y}_A$. Thus:

$$1.96 * se = 1.96 * \bar{Y}_A * CV/\sqrt{n_A}.$$

Table 10.2 shows $1.96 * CV/\sqrt{n_A}$, the factor by which $\bar{Y}_A$ is multiplied to determine the half-width of the confidence interval, for different values of CV and sample size. Table 10.2 thus demonstrates the joint effect of sample size and inherent variability in the data on the range within which μ_A is likely to be contained. For example, with $CV = 1$ and a sample size of 100, the 95 percent confidence interval for μ_A is approximately

$$\bar{Y}_A \pm 0.2 * \bar{Y}_A.$$

That is, we can estimate mean cost with about 20 percent error. Achieving estimates with 10 percent error would require 400 observations.

From a different perspective, assume that average costs are $1,000 across patients from all hospitals. Because estimating across all hospitals combined yields a large n, this $\bar{Y}$ is a good estimate of μ, the true mean cost for all patients. If μ_A equals μ, then $\bar{Y}_A$ should fall in the acceptance

Table 10.2   Effect of Sample Size and Coefficient of Variation on the Half-Width of 95 Percent Acceptance/Confidence Intervals*

Sample Size (n)	Coefficient of Variation					
	0.5	1.0	1.5	2.0	2.5	3.0
10	0.32	0.63	0.95	1.26	1.58	1.90
25	0.20	0.40	0.60	0.80	1.00	1.20
50	0.14	0.28	0.42	0.57	0.71	0.85
100	0.10	0.20	0.30	0.40	0.50	0.60
150	0.08	0.16	0.24	0.33	0.41	0.49
200	0.07	0.14	0.21	0.28	0.35	0.42
300	0.06	0.12	0.17	0.23	0.29	0.35
400	0.05	0.10	0.15	0.20	0.25	0.30
500	0.04	0.09	0.13	0.18	0.22	0.27
1000	0.03	0.06	0.09	0.13	0.16	0.19

*Cells of the table are $1.96 * CV/\sqrt{n}$.

interval $1000 \pm 1.96 * s/\sqrt{n_A}$ about 95 percent of the time. Suppose $\bar{Y}_A$ falls outside the interval. Adopting a traditional hypothesis-testing framework, we conclude that Hospital A's costs differ from average. Furthermore, suppose that we are judging 100 facilities, and we flag any hospital as an "outlier" when $\bar{Y}_A$ does not fall in the interval $1000 \pm 1.96 * s/\sqrt{n_A}$. In this situation, the label "outlier" is equivalent to saying that costs at such hospitals are statistically significantly different than average at the $P = 0.05$ level.

However, even for a hospital with average mean costs (i.e., $\mu_A = \mu$), $\bar{Y}_A$ will fall outside the acceptance interval about 5 percent of the time. Thus, if 100 facilities had the same average costs (i.e., $\mu_A = \mu$ for all hospitals), the standard hypothesis testing approach will flag incorrectly about 5 of the 100 hospitals as outliers. Such errors are called Type I errors. Interpreting results of individual hypothesis tests when multiple tests are performed is called the "multiple comparisons" problem (Snedecor and Cochran 1980).

On the other hand, hospitals whose costs actually do differ substantially from the average μ have a good chance of not being flagged as outliers—a Type II error. To illustrate Type II errors, assume inefficient hospitals have "true" mean costs of $1,200, 20 percent above an average of $1,000; efficient hospitals have "true" mean costs of $800, 20 percent below average. This difference appears big: Inefficient hospitals' costs are 50 percent higher ($1,200/$800) than those of efficient hospitals. Suppose we only flag hospitals whose observed means differ from $1,000 by at least 40 percent (roughly the cutoff for distinguishing statistically significant differences on the high side when $n = 100$ and the $CV = 2$). We label a hospital as inefficient if its average costs exceed $1,400 (in this case, the 95 percent confidence interval for μ_A would not include $1,000$). Now consider an inefficient hospital, with true average costs of $1,200. There is only about a 20 percent chance that its observed mean will fall above $1,400 and that it will be flagged as abnormal.

The same considerations apply when examining a dichotomous outcome, such as death. Assume p is the death rate in a large population of patients, and $\hat{p}$ is the observed rate in a smaller population of size n (e.g., patients at Hospital A). The standard error is $\sqrt{p * (1 - p)/n}$. For different values of n and p, Table 10.3 shows the half-width of the acceptance interval around p that is likely to contain the average death rate from a sample of n cases. For example, if p were 10 percent, 95 percent of the time the observed death rate in a sample of 100 patients would be between 4 and 16 percent due to random variation alone. This interval is wide compared to reasonable differences between poor- and high-quality providers (Hofer and Hayward 1996; Ash 1996).

Thus, depending on the unknown distribution of true outcomes among providers, some substantial fraction of nonproblematic providers

Table 10.3   Effect of Sample Size and Probability of Death on the Half-Width of 95 Percent Acceptance/Confidence Intervals for a Dichotomous Outcome*

Sample Size (n)	Probability of Death (p)**							
	0.01	0.02	0.05	0.10	0.15	0.20	0.25	0.50
25	—	—	—	0.12	0.14	0.16	0.17	0.20
50	—	—	—	0.08	0.10	0.11	0.12	0.14
100	—	—	0.04	0.06	0.07	0.08	0.09	0.10
150	—	—	0.04	0.05	0.06	0.07	0.07	0.08
200	—	0.02	0.03	0.04	0.05	0.06	0.06	0.07
300	—	0.02	0.03	0.03	0.04	0.05	0.05	0.06
400	—	0.01	0.02	0.03	0.04	0.04	0.04	0.05
500	0.01	0.01	0.02	0.03	0.03	0.04	0.04	0.04
1000	0.01	0.01	0.01	0.02	0.02	0.03	0.03	0.03

*Cells of the table are $1.96\sqrt{p*(1-p)/n}$.
**When the expected number of deaths $(n*p) < 5$, the normal approximation, the basis for determining the acceptance interval, is unreliable. This is identified by a "—".

will erroneously be flagged as outliers, just as some problematic providers will not be flagged. Using data on cardiac catheterization, Luft and Hunt (1986) illustrated that small numbers of patients and relatively low rates of poor outcomes make it difficult to "be confident in the identification of individual performers" (p. 2780). For example, suppose the death rate is 1 percent, but a hospital treating 200 patients experiences no deaths. Even so, it would be impossible (using a lenient 0.10 significance level) to identify the hospital as having statistically significantly better outcomes. If the expected death rate is 15 percent and 5 deaths occurred out of 20 patients (an observed rate of 25 percent), the difference would not be sufficient to label the hospital as performing poorly, again at the lenient 0.10 significance level. When interpreting comparisons across providers, one must remember the role of random chance alone in determining outlier status.

Calculating Expected Rates of Events

The first step in considering differences in patients' risk across providers is calculating expected rates of outcomes. In the simple example above, we ignored the need for risk adjustment by concentrating on patients with identical disease and severity. In most situations, one must adjust for differences in patient risk (Salem-Schatz et al. 1994), although many profiling efforts fail to do so (Kerr et al. 1995).

As discussed in Chapter 8, linear regression modeling is the most commonly used method for risk adjusting continuous outcomes. Thus, for example, we might build a model as follows:

$$\hat{Y}_i = \hat{a} + \sum_j \hat{b}_j X_{ij},$$

where $\hat{Y}_i$ estimates the expected outcome for patient i, who has characteristics $X_{ij}, j = 1, \ldots, J$ for the J predictors in the model. Models are usually built from databases representing many patients (e.g., all patients in a given state). For patients treated by a specific provider, we calculate their expected outcome (E) as the average value of $\hat{Y}_i$'s for their cases.

As discussed in Chapter 9, the most widely used model to predict a dichotomous outcome (e.g., death, complications, readmissions) is logistic regression, in which the log of the "odds" of the event is modeled as a linear function of the predictor variables. Odds—the ratio of the probability of an event to the probability that it will not happen—are familiar to the gambling world. For example, an event has 3 to 1 odds (i.e., an odds ratio of 3) when it has a $p = 0.75$ likelihood of happening and $p = 0.25$ chance of not happening.

After fitting a logistic regression model, the predicted probability of, for example, death for the ith case ($\hat{p}_i$) can be calculated from the relationship

$$\widehat{\ln(odds_i)} = \ln(\hat{p}_i/(1 - \hat{p}_i)) = \hat{a} + \sum_j \hat{b}_j * X_{ij}$$

by solving for $\hat{p}_i$

$$\hat{p}_i = e^{\widehat{\ln(odds_i)}}/1 + e^{\widehat{\ln(odds_i)}}.$$

To determine the expected number of deaths in a group of n cases, we sum the $\hat{p}_i$'s; to determine the expected death rate, we divide this sum by n.

Comparing Observed and Expected Outcomes

Comparing observed to expected outcomes is central to drawing inferences about the quality or efficiency of care. Various approaches have been used for comparing O and E. Neither ($O - E$) nor O/E is clearly superior. For example, suppose that Hospital A treats cases with expected costs of $5,000 (the sum of the $\hat{Y}_i$'s for the patients treated at Hospital A), but costs actually average $6,000. In contrast, Hospital B treats cases that should cost $10,000 but actually average $11,500. Thus, both Hospitals A and B cost more than expected, but how do they compare with each other? On an additive or "difference" scale ($O - E$), Hospital B looks worse, because A's excess is only $1,000 per case, while B's excess is $1,500. However, on a multiplicative or "ratio" scale (O/E), Hospital A looks worse, because its cases are 20 percent higher than expected, as compared to only 15 percent for B.

As another example, suppose that the outcome of interest is a complication rate. Which is worse: 2 percent complications when only 1 percent was expected (a doubling of risk), or 50 percent complications when only 40 percent was expected (10 excess problems per hundred, but only a 25 percent increase in the problem rate)? This question has no simple answer. One can use the data to explore which model is more realistic—an additive model (where adding the same amount to each predicted probability represents the provider effect) or a multiplicative model (where provider-associated increases are proportionate to the expected outcome). Even if a multiplicative model is used, however, observers are still likely to want to know additive information (e.g., how many extra dollars are attributable to a provider or how many extra complications will occur).

Ratios, such as O/E, are "centered" at 1 but range from 0 to infinity. To put comparable distances between ratios that are less than 1 with those greater than 1, methodologists sometimes display $\log(O/E)$ values rather than O/E values (Roos, Wennberg, and McPherson 1988). A "broken" x-axis can indicate the gap between the smallest $\log(O/E)$ associated with a positive observed (O) and "negative infinity" (the value of log(0)). On an untransformed scale, substantial differences among O/E's less than 1 are hard to see and thus may appear unimportant; on a log scale, the distances between points representing O/E values of 0.25, 0.50, 1.00, 2.00, and 4.00 are equally spaced because each value doubles the one below it.

The ratio O/E has an additional drawback—its value changes dramatically with a small change in O if E is small. For example, if we observe 30 cases with a 1 percent complication rate, the expected number of complications is 0.3. If 0, 1, or 2 complications are observed, O/E is 0, 3.3, or 6.6 respectively. A good rule of thumb is to avoid examining such ratios when the expected number of events is less than 1.0. Some researchers advise against O to E comparisons unless there are five expected cases.

Fortunately, when comparing O to E, findings as extreme as these examples are unlikely. If expected costs at two hospitals are $5,000 versus $10,000, or if expected complications rates are 1 versus 40 percent, these hospitals should probably not be compared—their patient populations or other characteristics may be too different. If distributions of expected outcomes are roughly similar across hospitals, difference and ratio measures of performance are likely to produce comparable results. Examining expected outcomes across providers is therefore important, to ensure that patients' risks do not differ radically across providers (see below). Reviewing common descriptive statistics (e.g., mean and median, standard deviation, and percentage cutoffs of the distribution) is a useful first cut at comparing expected outcomes across providers. As shown in Figure 10.1, a valuable but less-familiar technique for portraying distributions of expected values is box plots (sometimes called box-and-whisker plots) (Tukey 1977).

Figure 10.1   Box Plots of Expected Lengths of Stay at Six Hospitals

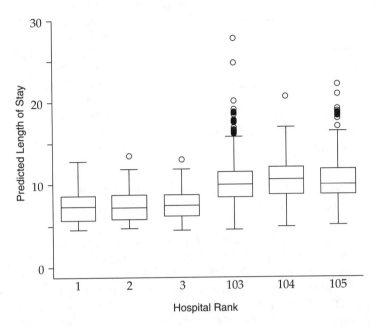

Box plots from three hospitals with the lowest and three with the highest expected lengths of stay using Disease Staging's Relative Resource Scale to determine expected values.

In our AHCPR-funded severity study, we examined the extent to which severity explained differences in hospital length of stay (LOS) for pneumonia patients (Iezzoni et al. 1996a). To illustrate the relationship between predicted and actual LOS, we examined these values for six hospitals (number of cases per hospital ranged from 73 to 316): three hospitals among those with the highest LOS and three in the lowest range. Figure 10.1 shows side-by-side box plots of the expected LOS values at these six hospitals, using Disease Staging Relative Resource Scale as the severity measure; outliers were removed, using HCFA's definition (i.e., cases more than three standard deviations above the mean on a log scale; see Chapter 8).

In Figure 10.1, the box shows the range encompassing the middle 50 percent of cases. Thus, the lower end of the box demarcates the value below which 25 percent of cases fall and the upper end the value above which 25 percent of cases fall. The horizontal line within the box is the median.

The length of the box is the interquartile range (IQR), sometimes called the "H-spread." The top of the box plus 1.5∗IQR and the bottom of the box minus 1.5∗IQR define the inner fences; the top of the box plus 3∗IQR and the bottom of the box minus 3∗IQR define the outer fences. The ends of the lines extending above and below the box indicate the highest and lowest values within the inner fences; circles indicate individual values between the inner and outer fences. Different computerized statistical packages may use different symbols for different values. From the box plots, one can see that the three hospitals with the shortest LOS had a much less "severe" patient mix: The expected LOSs of approximately 75 percent of their patients fell *below* a certain point, while 75 percent of cases at hospitals with the longest LOSs were *above* the same point.

Failure of Observed-to-Expected Comparisons to Adjust Fully for Patients' Risks

When examining death rates, epidemiologists often use standardized mortality ratios (SMRs), which are O/E ratios arising from the process of indirect standardization. To illustrate indirect standardization, consider a hypothetical situation involving two types of patients: low risk, with a 1 percent mortality rate; and high risk, with a 5 percent mortality rate (Table 10.4). Suppose further that half of all patients in a large population are low risk and half are high risk, yielding an overall mortality rate of 3 percent. Now consider Hospital A, which treats 1,000 patients, 800 at low risk and 200 at high risk. Hospital A's experience with its low-risk patients is similar to the overall experience—a 1 percent mortality rate (8 deaths among the 800 patients). However, Hospital A does poorly with high-risk patients: it has a 10 percent mortality rate, double the population average, leading to 20 deaths among the 200 high-risk patients. Despite this, due to its favorable case mix, Hospital A's mortality rate is 2.8 percent (28/1000), somewhat better than the 3 percent population average.

Indirect standardization determines a hospital's expected number of deaths by applying stratum-specific rates determined from all patients to the number of cases in each stratum in the hospital. In this case, a stratum is a risk category. Based on the overall data, we expect 8 deaths among the 800 low-risk patients (with a 1 percent mortality rate) and 10 deaths among the 200 high-risk patients (with a 5 percent mortality rate), for an expected rate of 1.8 percent. This expected rate is identical to that from a model that predicts probability of death from the whole population using the single predictor of high versus low risk. The standardized mortality ratio for Hospital A is 1.56 (28/18) because it has 56 percent more deaths than expected, based on its patient mix.

Table 10.4 Mortality Measures in Hypothetical Hospitals with Different Patient Mixes or Death Rates

Risk Category	All Patients in Population		Hospital A		Hospital B		Hospital C	
	Patient Mix %	*Death %*	*n*	*Death %*	*n*	*Death %*	*n*	*Death %*
Low	50	1	800	1	200	1	800	1.25
High	50	5	200	10	800	10	200	12.50
Performance								
Death rate	3%		28/1000 = 2.8%		82/1000 = 8.2%		28/1000 = 2.8%	
SMR[a] (O/E)			28/18 = 1.56		82/42 = 1.95		35/18 = 1.94	
Risk-adjusted mortality			3 * 1.56 = 4.68%		3 * 1.95 = 5.85%		3 * 1.94 = 5.83%	
Difference (O−E)			2.8 − 1.8 = 1%		8.2 − 4.2 = 4%		3.5 − 1.8 = 1.7%	

[a] SMR = standardized mortality ratio.

One can report this discrepancy in other ways. Some prefer to express the hospital's performance on the same scale as the population average, giving a "risk-adjusted average," achieved by multiplying the SMR by the population average rate (e.g., $1.56 \times 3 = 4.68$ percent). Another choice is to report the difference between the observed rate (2.8 percent) and the expected rate (1.8 percent); thus, Hospital A has 1 percent more deaths than expected. All these summary measures suggest that, after adjusting for its patient mix, Hospital A has more deaths than expected.

Indirect standardization and its generalization via multivariable risk-adjustment modeling are powerful tools for making fairer comparisons among providers with different types of patients. Nevertheless, comparing outcomes across providers is complicated when patient mix has a strong effect on outcome and differs widely across providers. In epidemiological terms, patient mix is a confounding factor.

As an illustration, consider Hospital B with exactly the same within-strata mortality experience as Hospital A but with an unfavorable case mix. Hospital B treats 200 low-risk patients with 2 deaths and 800 high risk patients with 80 deaths (see Table 10.4). Due solely to differences in patient mix, Hospital B's unadjusted death rate is 8.2 percent, much higher than Hospital A's 2.8 percent rate. Such differences in patient mix as observed between Hospitals A and B underscore the need for risk adjustment.

However, an indirect adjustment approach fails to make the two hospitals look equally good. To perform indirect adjustment for Hospital B, we first compute its expected number of deaths as 42 ($0.01*200 + 0.05*800$). Hospital B's SMR ratio is thus 1.95, its risk-adjusted death rate is 5.85 percent, and its excess mortality rate is 4 percent (as opposed to 1.56, 4.68, and 1 percent, respectively at Hospital A). However reported, Hospital B looks worse than A, although the same type of patient had the same outcome at either hospital. Results could be even more misleading. Imagine that Hospital C is seriously deficient: It has the same favorable patient mix as Hospital A but with 25 percent higher death rates for both patient types (1.25 and 12.5 percent mortality respectively among low- and high-risk patients). Hospital C's SMR, risk-adjusted death rate, and excess mortality rate (1.94, 5.83, and 1.7 percent respectively) look marginally better than Hospital B's, though its performance is clearly worse.

Direct standardization, an alternative adjustment approach, produces results that "feel" more correct, but it has conceptual and practical problems. In this method, provider-specific rates are computed in each risk stratum and applied to a "standard" population case mix, producing an estimate of what might be expected if the provider were to treat this standard patient mix. For example, suppose that the standard population has half-and-half low- and high-risk patients. Under this assumption, Hospital A and B have stratum-specific death rates that are estimated to yield 5.5

percent mortality in the standard population (0.5∗0.01 + 0.5∗0.10), as compared to Hospital C's estimated 6.9 percent rate (0.5∗0.0125 + 0.5∗0.125).

In epidemiological studies, the strata are generally large, such as populations in different states broken into five-year age categories. Relatively reliable estimates of stratum-specific rates can be obtained from such large populations. However, in profiling individual providers for patients stratified by disease or other risk factors, stratum-specific rates are generally based on too few cases to provide reliable estimates. Furthermore, questions arise about whether a provider should be judged harshly for doing poorly with a patient type seen very rarely. For example, suppose Hospital D treats 999 low-risk patients with only 5 deaths and 1 high-risk patient who dies. Although its death rate is only half as large as the population average for nearly all its 1,000 patients, its projected death rate for the above standard population is over 50 percent (0.5∗0.005 + 0.5∗1.00). Thus, as this example demonstrates, which of several providers looks best can change depending on the standard population's patient mix. Direct standardization has rarely been used when profiling practitioners or hospitals.

In most profiles, expected values are determined from more complex multivariable models. However, the fundamental approach is the same as indirect standardization in which each provider's "expected" is based on the risk characteristics of its patients, and its observed experience is compared to this expectation. It is not surprising that risk adjustment fails to answer definitively the question of "which provider is better" when the providers treat very different populations. In reality, some providers do better with certain types of patients and worse with others. In a rational world, providers will concentrate on their most successful types of cases. The main protection against being misled is to compare only providers with generally similar patient mixes. When providers are compared, examining patient outcomes separately within each risk stratum helps guard against misinterpretation.

Considering Random Variation in Comparing Observed and Expected Outcomes

As discussed at the start of this chapter, the standard error (*se*) captures the effect of random variation on the reliability of estimates from data. However, properly estimating the standard error becomes complex when multivariable models are used to determine expected values. Most computerized statistical regression packages produce an estimate of the variability associated with the observed outcome *for each patient*. Regression packages refer to this quantity with idiosyncratic names: For example, STATA calls it the standard error of the "forecast" (*stdf*) as distinguished from the standard error of the "prediction" (*stdp*). The *stdp* decreases to 0 as *n* increases, while the *stdf* does not. The SAS program PROC REG calls the desired quantity *stdi* for "standard error of the individual predicted value." Care is required to ensure that the right standard error is used.

If s_i is the standard error for the ith observation, then the standard error for the average of a group of *n* cases is

$$\frac{\sqrt{\sum_i s_i^2}}{n}.$$

A 95 percent confidence interval for the average cost of *n* patients at Hospital A is

$$\bar{Y}_A \pm 1.96 * \frac{\sqrt{\sum_i s_i^2}}{n}.$$

The distributions of LOS, charges, and costs often have "long right tails," including some cases with very high values. As noted in Chapter 8, the logarithm of LOS (usually the natural logarithm) is often used in modeling because its distribution is more symmetrical than that of the untransformed (or "raw") data. In this situation, although confidence intervals can be computed on the log scale, achieving estimates on the original scale requires that the point estimate of the mean and the endpoints of the confidence interval be retransformed by exponentiation. Resulting confidence intervals will not be centered around the estimated mean.

The standard deviation associated with an individual's predicted probability of death $\hat{p}_i$ (corresponding to s_i for a continuous dependent variable) is

$$\sqrt{\hat{p}_i * (1 - \hat{p}_i)}$$

and the standard deviation of the mean death rate of *n* persons, used to estimate the "real" death rate *p* that we cannot observe, is

$$\frac{\sqrt{\sum_i \hat{p}_i * (1 - \hat{p}_i)}}{n}.$$

When each provider's expected outcome (*E*) comes from a model fit to many cases, it is reasonable to calculate 95 percent confidence intervals for *O/E* ratios by treating *E* (a sum of $\hat{p}$'s) as a constant. Then, one can calculate the confidence interval around the observed number of deaths as

$$O \pm 1.96 * \sqrt{\sum_i \hat{p}_i * (1 - \hat{p}_i)}$$

and divide the resulting lower-, midpoint-, and upper-interval values by E. Multiplying each end of the confidence interval by the areawide rate yields a confidence interval for risk-adjusted outcomes. The same approach can be used when the observed outcome is a continuous variable. In this setting, the lower, midpoint, and upper values of the confidence interval are divided by the average of the expecteds. Hosmer and Lemeshow (1995) found that in the case of a dichotomous outcome this approach is reasonable based on preliminary simulation studies, including the situation in which the observed cases were not part of the data set used to build the model generating the expected findings.

The above discussion focuses on a single source of variation—that arising at the level of the individual patient. This is the approach used in most major profiling efforts around the country (see Chapter 11). An important exception involves HCFA's hospital mortality reports. In analyzing hospital mortality rates for Medicare beneficiaries, HCFA recognized four components that contributed to the variation of individual observations (Sullivan and Wilensky 1991). Their approach corresponds to the statistical technique of "decomposing" a difference between an observed outcome Y_{ik} (for individual i, with patient characteristics $X_{ij}, j = 1, \ldots, J$ treated at hospital H_k) and a population average μ into components, as follows:

1. The difference between the observed outcome and the predicted outcome from a model that contains the X_{ij}'s and dummy variables for hospital:

$$Y_{ik} - (\hat{Y}_{ik} \mid X_{ij}\text{'s}, H_k);$$

2. The difference between the predicted outcome from a model that contains the X_{ij}'s and dummy variables for hospital and a model that contains only the X_{ij}'s:

$$(\hat{Y}_{ik} \mid X_{ij}\text{'s}, H_k) - (\hat{Y}_{ik} \mid X_{ij}\text{'s});$$

3. The difference between the predicted outcome from a model that contains the X_{ij}'s and the overall mean calculated from all observations in all hospitals $(\hat{Y})$:

$$(\hat{Y}_{ik} \mid X_{ij}\text{'s}) - \bar{Y};$$

4. The difference between the overall mean $\bar{Y}$ and μ.

The squared difference $(Y_{ik} - \mu)^2$ equals the sum of the squares of the above four terms.

A standard deviation incorporating all four components is larger than an estimate using only the first component—the formula $\hat{p}_i * (1 - \hat{p}_i)$.

HCFA showed that it can be nearly 30 percent larger. Using their four-components method for an illustrative example (a hospital with 75 cases and 13.0 percent deaths), HCFA estimated a standard deviation of 5.0 percent (Sullivan and Wilensky 1991, A-5); for the same example, we calculated a standard deviation of 3.9 percent *using only their first component of variation.*

Using all four components creates wider confidence intervals and results in fewer hospitals being flagged as outliers. Thus, using the HCFA four-components approach versus the more standard method of only one source of variation has important implications. The standard approach essentially assumes that the model adjusts for all important differences among patients. Thus, unexplained hospital variation, beyond that stemming from random variation and measured differences in patient mix, are viewed as likely caused by differences in factors such as hospital quality or efficiency. If this interpretation is false, the burden falls on the flagged hospital to suggest alternative explanations. HCFA's four-components approach acknowledges that significant important unmeasured risk factors contribute to residual hospital variation. Thus, the HCFA approach is more conservative about flagging hospitals.

A more comprehensive strategy for explicitly incorporating multiple sources of variation involves hierarchical modeling, discussed at the end of this chapter.

Presenting Comparisons of Observed and Expected Outcomes

Performing the statistical analysis is only the first step in creating profiles, which are explicitly intended to be used by nontechnical audiences—purchasers, payors, and consumers. Most in this target audience do not understand the statistical underpinnings of the computations. Some creators of report cards aim for the simplest presentation, even if it obscures a full appreciation of the issues. For example, the 1996 profile of health plan performance produced by the Massachusetts Healthcare Purchaser Group initially arrayed its ratings on a scale of one to five stars, establishing cutpoints to determine the numbers of stars. Some health plans objected, noting that a single star, for the lowest-rated plan, would send a negative message. The final version of the rating used only the center part of the five-star scale, with the lowest-rated plan having two stars and the highest having four. The *Boston Globe* published this rating with the stars printed in red (Pham 1996a, C1). The numerical rankings were in small print to the right of the stars. The lowest three-star plan had 89.8 percent overall satisfaction, while the sole two-star plan, Massachusetts Blue Cross and

Blue Shield, had 87.3 percent—hardly a striking difference. Blue Cross withdrew from the voluntary rating program, noting that its low rating by the star method obscured the fact that its performance was numerically only slightly below its competitors' (Pham 1996b, C3).

Nonetheless, many appreciate that summary numbers contain an element of uncertainty. We are used to seeing political polls or public opinion surveys presented along with their "margin of error," plus or minus some number of percentage points. As noted above, comparisons of observed to expected outcomes also have uncertainty, resulting from the effects of random error. How should this uncertainty be portrayed on the printed page? The two major strategies for depicting differences between observed and expected outcomes while capturing the effect of random variation are first, by showing the observed value in relationship to an acceptance interval of the form $\mu \pm 1.96 * se$; or second, by measuring the difference between observed and expected values in units of standard error.

Acceptance Intervals

A report card on heart attack outcomes produced by the Pennsylvania Health Care Cost Containment Council (PHC4, 1996) illustrates the first approach. Separate models were developed for "direct admits" (patients in their initial period of care for a heart attack) and for "transfer-ins." Figure 10.2, reproduced from the PHC4 report, illustrates an acceptance interval generated from a multivariable model that adjusts for risk factors and a particular hospital's rate relative to the interval. Figure 10.3, also from the PHC4 report, shows an example of the results. The acceptance intervals were wide, many spanning a range of 10 percent (e.g., from 5 to 15 percent). The interval for Aliquippa Hospital is typical; based on 87 cases, the interval ranged from about 3 percent to 13 percent. Butler Hospital, with 259 cases, had a narrower interval (from about 6 to 12 percent), while Corry Memorial Hospital's interval, based on only 46 cases, went from about 2 to 15 percent. Hospitals with observed rates that were higher or lower than expected (i.e., outside the interval) are obvious and were flagged with a small symbol to the left of the hospital.

Furthermore, for all hospitals depicted on the same page, one can compare the relative widths of the acceptance intervals, which are primarily a function of the number of cases treated. Hospitals with wider intervals treat fewer cases. Despite cluttering the presentation, showing the number of cases treated at each hospital would have been useful, although detailed tables later in the Council's report list the number of cases, the percent transferred out, and actual values with 95 percent confidence intervals for mortality and LOS (PHC4 1996, 23–25).

Figure 10.2   Instructions for Reading Pennsylvania Health Care Cost
Containment Council's Hospital Performance Reports

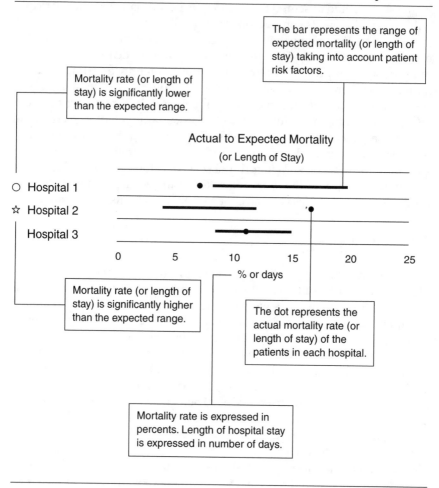

Source: Pennsylvania Health Care Cost Containment Council 1996.

In Figure 10.3, 4 of the 39 hospitals had rates outside the 95 percent
acceptance intervals, one with a higher rate than expected. The display
invites the conclusion that the three below-interval hospitals had high-
quality care and the one above-interval hospital had low-quality care.
But five percent of ordinary hospitals are expected to fall outside the 95
percent acceptance interval due to random chance alone. Thus, among 39
similar hospitals, about two would be spuriously flagged. Of the four that

Figure 10.3   Mortality Rates and Acceptance Intervals for a Sample of
Pennsylvania Hospitals

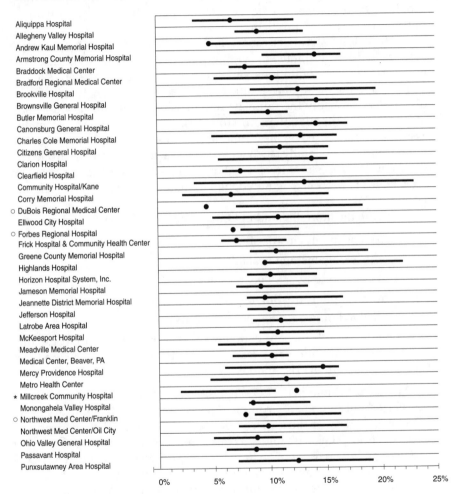

fell outside the interval, we have no way of knowing which, if any, are quality outliers. The traditional approach for adjusting for this "multiple comparisons" problem essentially expands the width of the interval. This decreases the power of tests to identify hospitals that really do differ from expected, and this approach has been rarely used when presenting profile data. As discussed later, hierarchical modeling deals better with the multiple comparisons problem.

The PHC4 heart attack report showed the same findings for physician practices within hospitals, providing they treat more than 30 cases. As noted earlier, if a continuous variable does not have a widely skewed distribution, the mean of a sample of 30 cases is approximately normally distributed, probably the rationale for choosing a minimum sample size of 30. However, in this situation, a 0/1 variable was examined. Normality assumptions are based on the normal approximation to the binomial distribution, which is generally reasonable when the problem rate multiplied by the number of cases is at least five. For 30 cases to be sufficient, a problem rate of over 15 percent is required, higher than what occurred (Landis and Localio 1996).

In both the mortality and LOS analyses, the PHC4 excluded patients:

- from hospitals closing since 1993;
- who left against medical advice;
- under 30 and over 99 years of age;
- from hospitals treating fewer than 30 cases;
- involved in two or more transfers; and
- who were "clinically complex" with a preexisting or coexisting clinical condition not related to heart attack treatment and not included in the risk model.

Additional exclusions in the LOS analyses were patients who died, patients transferred out (who had "truncated" LOS), and patients with "atypical" LOS (over 40 days or those discharged on the same day they were admitted). While hospitals with under 30 cases were excluded from the mortality analysis, all hospitals were included in the LOS analysis. The PHC4 LOS analyses used a log transform; ln(*LOS*) was the dependent variable. Upper and lower endpoints for confidence intervals were calculated in the log scale and then retransformed by exponentiation. As illustrated in Figure 10.4, presentation of LOS data was the same as for mortality data. More hospitals fell outside the acceptance intervals for LOS than for mortality.

Obviously, the number of cases treated is crucial in interpreting such data. For example, if a provider's expected problem rate is 10 percent, an observed rate of 15 percent based on 400 cases *should* be more worrisome than either an observed rate of 15 percent based on 100 cases or an observed

Figure 10.4   Average Lengths of Stay and Acceptance Intervals for a Sample of Pennsylvania Hospitals

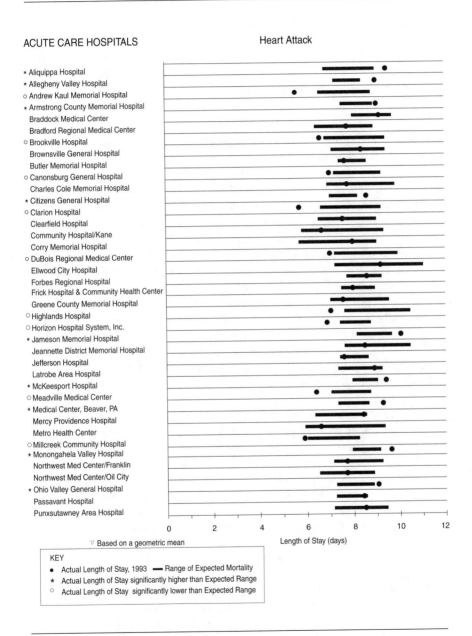

ACUTE CARE HOSPITALS   Heart Attack

▽ Based on a geometric mean   Length of Stay (days)

KEY
- ●   Actual Length of Stay, 1993   ▬ Range of Expected Mortality
- ✳   Actual Length of Stay significantly higher than Expected Range
- ○   Actual Length of Stay significantly lower than Expected Range

Source: Pennsylvania Health Care Cost Containment Council 1996.

rate of 20 percent based on 10 cases. Figures 10.3 and 10.4 appropriately remind us to pay less attention to deviations based on fewer cases.

Standardizing Using Standard Error

Standardizing is a common statistical technique for converting a deviation (that is, $O - E$) into a measure that suggests whether the deviation is statistically meaningful. We consider

$$z = (O - E)/se$$

where se, the standard error, is calculated as described above. If the observed rate pertains to a process whose expected value really is E, and if n is sufficiently large, this quantity has approximately a standard normal distribution. This is called a "z-score," because "z" is used in statistics for the standard normal random variable. The standard normal is centered at 0; 68 percent of z-scores are in the interval from -1 to $+1$; and slightly more than 95 percent are in the interval from -2 to $+2$. Widely available "standard normal" tables are used to convert z-scores into P values.

The P value measures how likely it is for observed and expected rates to differ at least as much as they do, assuming that the observations reflect the hypothesized model. For example, a standard normal variate falls outside the interval -1 to $+1$ only 32 percent of the time. Thus, a z-score of either $+1$ or -1 (i.e., O and E differ by one standard deviation) has $P = 0.32$. A z-score greater than 1.96 or less than -1.96 has P value smaller than 0.05. If a provider's $O - E$ value leads to $z = 1.96$ ($P = 0.05$), its true rate may nonetheless be E. However, random deviations this large occur only one time in 20.

We used z-scores in our AHCPR-funded severity project. Table 10.5 shows z-scores at five hospitals when different severity measures were used to determine expected rates of death for pneumonia patients (Iezzoni et al. 1996b). These 5 hospitals were selected for illustrative purposes from the 30 out of 105 hospitals in the study at which observed mortality rates differed significantly from expected ($P < 0.05$) when judged by one or more but not all 14 severity methods analyzed. For example, at Hospital B, observed mortality was significantly lower than expected when using Disease Staging's probability of mortality model ($z = -3.07, P < 0.01$), APR-DRGs ($z = -2.30, P = 0.02$), or PMC-RIS ($z = -2.16, P = 0.03$). In contrast, observed rates were less than two standard errors from expected, consistent with the null hypothesis of no difference, when using the original version of MedisGroups ($z = -1.33, P = 0.18$), physiology score 1 ($z = -1.53, P = 0.13$), or R-DRGs ($z = -0.84, P = 0.40$), as well as other severity measures. Thus, whether Hospital B was identified as a high-quality hospital—and

Table 10.5 Examples of Relative Mortality Rate Performance from Five Hospitals: Pneumonia Patients

Hospital Performance Measure and Severity Method	A	B	C	D	E
Number of cases	200	317	88	267	132
Number (percent) died	17 (8.5)	32 (10.1)	10 (11.4)	36 (13.5)	25 (18.9)
z-score (decile rank) from unadjusted model[a]	−0.53 (4)	0.29 (7)	0.56 (8)	2.14 (10)	3.63 (10)
z-score (decile rank) from severity-adjusted model[b]					
MedisGroups					
Original version	−2.30 (1)	−1.33 (2)	1.56 (9)	2.70 (10)	1.99 (10)
Empirical version	−2.73 (1)	−1.73 (1)	2.03 (10)	1.33 (9)	1.17 (9)
Physiology Score 1	−2.25 (1)	−1.53 (1)	1.64 (9)	2.24 (10)	2.79 (10)
Physiology Score 2	−3.12 (1)	−1.84 (1)	1.49 (9)	1.95 (10)	2.02 (10)
Body Systems Count	−1.74 (1)	−1.23 (3)	1.95 (9)	2.29 (10)	3.07 (10)
Comorbidity Index	−1.28 (2)	−1.13 (3)	1.32 (9)	2.11 (10)	3.16 (10)
Disease Staging					
Mortality Probability	−2.51 (1)	−3.07 (1)	1.51 (9)	3.51 (10)	2.14 (9)
Stage	−2.05 (1)	−0.95 (3)	1.87 (9)	2.12 (10)	2.88 (10)
Comorbidities	−1.15 (2)	−1.66 (1)	1.45 (8)	2.05 (10)	2.57 (10)
PMCs: Severity Score	−1.99 (1)	−1.88 (1)	2.23 (10)	1.04 (9)	2.78 (10)
AIM	−1.54 (1)	−1.97 (1)	1.99 (9)	2.17 (10)	3.20 (10)
APR-DRGs	−2.25 (1)	−2.30 (1)	2.32 (10)	1.73 (9)	2.50 (10)
PMC-RIS	−2.05 (1)	−2.16 (1)	2.60 (10)	1.48 (9)	3.41 (10)
R-DRGs	−2.08 (1)	−0.84 (3)	0.60 (8)	3.04 (10)	1.79 (10)

Source: Iezzoni et al. 1996b.

[a] Unadjusted model assumed 0.096 probability of death for all patients.

[b] Severity-adjusted model included age-sex, DRG, and severity score.

perhaps used to benchmark performance at other institutions—depended on which severity measure was used to adjust risk.

California's hospital report card initiative (see Chapter 11) used a similar approach to portray outlier hospitals (Wilson, Smoley, and Werdegar 1996). However, rather than using the normal approximation to convert a z-score into a P value, an exact P value was calculated, as described in Luft and Brown (1993). Figure 10.5, taken from the California report, shows how they portrayed their analyses.

Critics complain that z-scores and P values are not intuitive: Many consumers of report cards would rather receive their information in such familiar terms as rates of excess problems or "risk-adjusted" problem rates.

Other Approaches for Presenting Data

Pictures often convey messages more powerfully than words or numerical tables. The graphic displays shown in Figures 10.3 and 10.4, for example, do not simply provide point estimates and acceptance intervals for each hospital but also present these quantities in a way that facilitates and encourages comparison. One subtle but important feature of such displays involves the order for listing data from different hospitals. Notice that the Pennsylvania report used alphabetical order, a method that makes it easier to locate information for a particular hospital of interest but harder to find the best and worst performers.

A format that displays hospitals from highest to lowest performance draws attention to ranking. As described below, this may be unwise given the unreliability of rank determinations. Furthermore, if observed rates, O/E ratios, or risk-adjusted rates are used to establish the rank ordering, one must remember that the most extreme high and low rates are commonly those for providers with the fewest cases. These extremes thus often reflect random noise and are unlikely to remain extreme in subsequent periods.

Reordering the same data may prompt new insights. For example, hospitals listed by risk-adjusted performance may be most useful for choosing a hospital. Displaying hospitals by important characteristics (e.g., by teaching intensity, ownership, payor mix, patients' socioeconomic status) encourages comparisons among similar facilities. Such displays also highlight differences by type of hospital.

The art and science of good visual displays has advanced rapidly in recent years (Tufte 1983). Software programs for producing graphics are increasingly available, such as the many powerful display formats that have been implemented in the S or S+ computer languages (Cleveland 1993). As examples of innovative ideas, we present three interesting profiling graphics that have appeared recently.

Figure 10.5   Portraying "Outlier Status" for a Sample of California Hospitals

FACILITY	Model A	Model B
Beverly Hills Medical Center	☐	☐
Beverly Hospital	☐	☐
Brotman Medical Center	☐	☐
California Hospital Medical Center ▣	☐	☐
Cedars-Sinai Medical Center	✪	✪
Centinela Hospital Medical Center	☐	☐
Century City Hospital ▣	☐	☐
Charter Community Hospital	☐	☐
Charter Suburban Hospital	☐	☐
Cigna Hospital of Los Angeles, Inc.	☐	☐
City of Hope National Medical Center	☑	☑
Coast Plaza Doctors Hospital	☐	☐
Comm & Mission Hospital-Huntington Park	☐	☐
Community Hospital of Gardena	☐	☐
Covina Valley Community Hospital	☐	☐
Daniel Freeman Marina Hospital ▣	☐	☐
Daniel Freeman Memorial Hospital ▣	☐	☐
Doctors Hospital of West Covina	☐	☐
Dominguez Medical Center	☐	☐
Downey Community Hospital	☐	☐
Encino/Tarzana Regional Medical Center	☐	☐
Foothill Presbyterian Hospital	☐	☐
Garfield Medical Center ▣	●	☐
Glendale Adventist Medical Center	☐	☐
Glendale Memorial Hospital & Health Center	☐	☐
Glendora Community Hospital	●	●
Good Samaritan Hospital ▣	●	☐
Granada Hills Community Hospital	☐	☐
Greater El Monte Community Hospital	☐	☐
Hawthorne Hospital	☑	☑
Henry Mayo Newhall Memorial Hospital ▣	☐	☐
Hollywood Community Hospital ▣	☐	☐
Holy Cross Medical Center	✪	✪
Huntington Memorial Hospital ▣	☐	☐
Inter-Community Medical Center	☐	☐
Kaiser Foundation Hospital-LA ▣	☐	☐
Kaiser Foundation Hospital-Bellflower ▣	✪	☐
Kaiser Foundation Hospital-Harbor City ▣	☐	☐
Kaiser Foundation Hospital-Panorama City ▣	✪	☐

✪ Significantly better than expected	● Significantly worse than expected
☑ Not significantly different than expected, no patients with adverse outcomes.	▣ Comment letter received from hospital or hospital system
☐ Not significantly different than expected, one or more patients with adverse outcomes	

Source: California Office of Statewide Health Planning and Development 1996.

Figure 10.6 portrays four facts about each of several orthopedic surgeons' practices on a single graph (Bennett, McKee, and Kilberg 1994). Each practice is represented by a "bubble" whose size is proportional to the number of cases in the practice. Each bubble is colored or cross-hatched in one of several patterns, which serves only to differentiate individual "bubbles" but could also be used to distinguish physicians along another dimensions (e.g., whether the orthopedic surgeon practices at a teaching hospital). The horizontal and vertical placements of the center of the bubble indicate average values of two resource-related outcomes: charges and length of stay. Thus, this type of display can depict two outcomes, which could be a quality dimension (e.g., mortality) and a resource consumption dimension (e.g., charges), in addition to sample size and a categorical variable (e.g., teaching status).

This intricate layout can highlight whether certain providers are among the best because they simultaneously have, for example, low costs and low death rates. However, such displays become hard to read when numerous providers are profiled. Another problem involves the potential for misleading an observer when portraying a one-dimensional quantity

Figure 10.6   Portraying Multiple Dimensions of Providers' Practices on the Same Graph

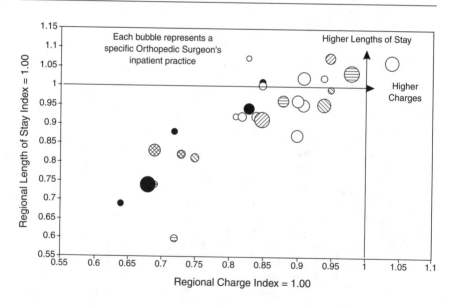

Source: Bennett, McKee, and Kilberg 1994. © 1994 Aspen Publishers, Inc.

(sample size) using a two-dimensional quantity (an area within a circle). This problem is so tricky that Tufte advises against the attempt (1983, 71). Instead, sample sizes on a graphic such as Figure 10.6 could be conveyed by the lengths of equally wide vertical bars, centered where the bubbles now are.

Figure 10.7 also conveys multidimensional information (Nathanson et al. 1994), in this case about the practices of three internists along seven dimensions. However, this display format is quite cluttered, perhaps more than necessary. For example, the thickness of the displays conveys no information, and it could be reworked, possibly by laying each practice's profile out flat in side-by-side tables. This would enable more practices to be compared.

Figure 10.8 shows how one might depict provider performance for very different patients by portraying results separately within risk cate-

Figure 10.7   Portraying Multiple Dimensions of Providers' Practices on the Same Figure

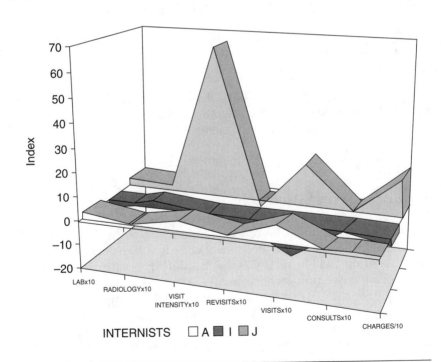

Source: Nathanson et al. 1994. © 1994 Aspen Publishers, Inc.

Figure 10.8   Portraying Outcomes by Risk Strata

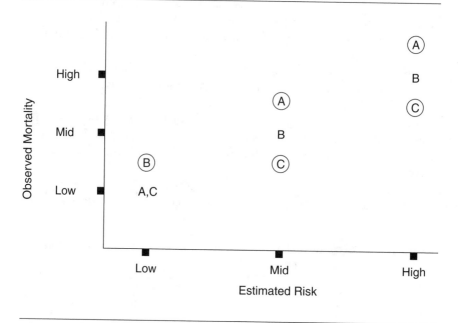

Source: Teres and Lemeshow 1993.

gories (Teres and Lemeshow 1993). Observing a multidimensional "signature" for a hospital might highlight areas that require explanation and reveal potential strategies for improvement (e.g., Hospital A may do well with low-risk patients and poorly with others). This approach demands enough patients of each type to estimate reliably rates within risk strata.

Empirical Bayes Estimation

The basis of what might be called "modern" empirical Bayes analysis (Casella 1985) has been attributed to work by Efron and Morris (1972, 1973, 1975). As Efron and Morris (1977) discussed in an excellent, nontechnical paper, parametric empirical Bayes analysis derives from a theorem initially proven by Stein (1955) that challenged traditional estimation theory. It had long been established that, for most distributions, the average of a set of data provides the best estimate of the mean of the population from which the data were drawn. However, Stein proved that there are better ways to estimate jointly the means of three or more normal populations than by using the three averages computed separately within each population.

The thinking inspired by Stein's theorem (originally called Stein's paradox because it seems paradoxical) evolved into better ways to estimate a group of means, which are now called empirical Bayes techniques.

The Bayesian Approach

Before describing empirical Bayes estimation, it is useful to understand the overall Bayesian approach to data analysis. The Bayesian approach views newly observed data within the context of prior observations. For example, suppose we observe one head out of ten coin tosses. Because experience and our understanding of coin tosses suggests that p (the true probability that the coin comes up heads) is 0.5, we do not view the observed rate of 0.1 heads as a reasonable estimate of p—although we might start to question our assumption that the coin is fair. However, as we toss the coin more and the proportion of heads remains much less than 0.5, we grow more suspicious that the coin is not fair. We will place increasing weight on our observed proportion of heads as a best estimate of the true probability of heads for this coin.

The same thought process is reasonable for evaluating providers, such as hospitals. Thus, at the outset, we assume that Hospital A is ordinary—that its outcomes are the same as outcomes at other hospitals. Based on a little evidence, we might adjust slightly our "prior" estimate that Hospital A is average. However, as evidence accumulates, we will place increasing weight on the new evidence and less weight on our prior beliefs. At some point, we may become sufficiently convinced by the data to support an investigation of Hospital A's performance.

Bayesian analysis thus interprets new data within the context of prior beliefs. For example, if we are uncertain about the safety of an operation but we observe one complication in ten operations, we may accept $\hat{p} = 0.1$ as our best guess for the true complication rate p. Nonetheless, if we observed no complications in ten operations, we would feel uncomfortable with $\hat{p} = 0$, because we know that all surgery presents risks. Implicit in this last observation is our belief that this operation is somewhat like other surgeries, whose outcomes have been observed before.

Classical statistical methods capture the level of uncertainty in estimating p by putting confidence intervals around $\hat{p}$, as described above. This approach has two major limitations: First, only current observations are used in computing $\hat{p}$ and its confidence intervals; and second, they lead to "all or nothing" decision rules. Thus, if the difference between observed and expected values is statistically significant (usually with a p value ≤ 0.05), then the observed mean is taken as the best guess for the true mean; otherwise, we assume the true mean equals the expected value. Using the tossing of a coin ten times, $\hat{p}$ equals 10 percent if one head is observed.

However, if from two to eight heads are observed, we might conclude that the coin cannot be judged unfair—implicitly, $\hat{p}$ is 0.5.

A Bayesian framework uses prior knowledge about a situation (e.g., a fair coin's p is virtually always in the range 0.49 to 0.51) to produce $\hat{p}$ values that lie somewhere between observed and expected means. The resulting $\hat{p}$ will be close to the expected mean when observed means are based on little data and when prior knowledge is strong. The $\hat{p}$ will be closer to the observed mean to the extent that either outside knowledge is less certain (e.g., surgery with an unknown complication rate) or when more data are available (e.g., when the observed mean derives from 1,000 cases, rather than just 10).

Empirical Bayes Techniques

Empirical Bayesian estimation extracts information from an entire current data set to function as the "prior knowledge" required for making Bayesian estimates. For instance, assume a database yields a 13 percent death rate among 10,000 acute myocardial infarction patients seen in 100 hospitals. This supplies a context for interpreting 10 deaths out of 100 cases seen, for example, in Hospital A. The empirical Bayes estimate for the death rate at Hospital A will fall between 10 and 13 percent. Exactly where the estimate lies depends on the relative size of two estimates: first, of random variation in the observed death rate (10 percent); and second, of the amount by which true hospital death rates tend to differ from their mean (of 13 percent).

To illustrate the empirical Bayes approach, consider comparing costs at four hospitals. A classical analysis presents two alternatives:

- to accept the null hypothesis—the true mean cost at each hospital is estimated as the common mean from the pooled sample of cases; or

- to reject the null hypothesis—the mean of each hospital is estimated from the experience of cases in that hospital.

The empirical Bayes estimator strikes a compromise between these two approaches, estimating the mean for each hospital by giving some weight to the mean from the pooled data and some weight to the mean from the hospital-specific data. Thus, the empirical Bayes estimate of the average cost in each hospital is produced by "shrinking" the hospital-specific cost toward the overall average. Figure 10.9 illustrates the principle. The term "shrinkage" reflects the fact that the resulting set of empirical Bayes estimates is more closely clustered around the overall mean than the set of individual averages.

Figure 10.9   An Illustration of the Principle of Empirical Bayes
Estimation

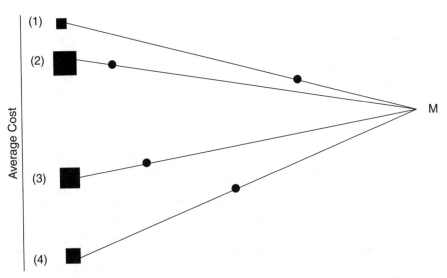

Schematic illustration of empirical Bayes (EB) estimates of average costs for
four hospitals (indicated by numbers 1–4) of varying sizes. Vertical placement of
the boxes shows observed average costs in each hospital: Hospitals 1–4 have
successively lower average costs. M shows the overall average cost. EB estimates
of each hospital's underlying cost (indicated by vertical placement of dots on lines
joining hospitals' boxes to M) is calculated as a weighted average of the observed
cost and M. In hospitals treating fewer patients (indicated by smaller boxes for 1
and 4), where observed average costs are less reliable, less weight is given to
the observed cost and more to the overall average cost. In larger hospitals (2 and
3, indicated by the larger boxes), the reverse occurs. Here, after EB shrinkage,
hospital 1 no longer has the highest estimated costs.

Source: Shwartz et al. 1994.

As noted, empirical Bayes estimates explicitly recognize two sources
of variation in the data:

- random variation within each unit examined (e.g., within each
  hospital, variation of individual patients' observed costs from the
  hospital's "true" average cost); and

- variation across hospitals in their "true" average costs.

In making empirical Bayes estimates, the weight given to the observed mean in each unit is a function of these two sources of variation:

weight = variance across units/(variance across units + variance within units).

As variation within units (e.g., hospitals) increases, less weight is placed on the unit-specific average (i.e., estimates are shrunk closer to the overall average). As described at the beginning of this chapter, variation in the average is $s/\sqrt{n}$ or

$$\sqrt{\frac{p(1-p)}{n}} \, .$$

Thus, with smaller sample sizes, within-unit variation is larger and the unit-specific observed average receives less weight. As Figure 10.9 shows, the unit with the highest observed mean may not have the highest empirical Bayes estimated mean, especially when the most extreme means come from units (e.g., hospitals) with relatively small sample sizes.

We used empirical Bayes techniques to profile small geographic areas for hospitalization rates among people 65 and over in Massachusetts (Shwartz et al. 1994). Specifically, we examined so-called "relative hospitalization rates" (RHR) in each geographic area, defined as the observed number of hospitalizations minus the expected, divided by the expected:

$$RHR = (O - E)/E.$$

Expected numbers of hospitalizations were determined using indirect standardization to adjust for differences in the age and sex distribution of the population in each area. To illustrate the effect of empirical Bayes shrinkage, consider hospitalizations for cardiac catheterization. The highest RHR for cardiac catheterization, 0.90 (observed is 90 percent above expected), occurred in a very small area with only 4,955 residents over age 64. The second-highest cardiac catheterization RHR, 0.84, was from a much larger area, with 40,390 residents over age 64. The empirical Bayes estimates for the two areas were 0.65 and 0.80, respectively. Because the first area had a small population, less weight was given to its observed rate and more weight was given the overall mean (in this case 0): The empirical Bayes estimated rate was "shrunk" much closer to the overall mean, from .90 to .65. Because the second area had a much larger population, less shrinkage occurred. Thus, empirical Bayes techniques adjust "point" estimates to reflect uncertainty. These empirical Bayes estimates guard against drawing conclusions from extreme estimates based on a few cases.

Our study also showed that empirical Bayes estimates of small geographic area rates were overall better predictors of next year's rate than making predictions based on each area's observed rate (Shwartz et al. 1994). For example, in 62 out of 68 conditions studied, empirical Bayes estimates yielded smaller weighted average errors (weighting by the size of the areas) when predicting next year's hospitalization rates.

Hierarchical Models

Hierarchical models generalize the idea of shrinkage to a population mean and provide a comprehensive framework for explicitly incorporating variation at different levels of analysis (Bryk and Raudenbush 1992). The "hierarchy" derives from "nesting." For example, patients are nested within provider (a group of patients are all treated by the same provider); in turn, providers, such as hospitals, may be nested within groups (e.g., public, private nonprofit, and private for-profit ownership). The influence of independent variables may differ within each nested subgroup. Explicit modeling of the hierarchical structure recognizes that nested observations may be correlated and that different sources of variation can occur at each level.

The basic hierarchical model that applies in provider profiling has the form:

$$Y_{ij} = \mu_i + v_j + \varepsilon_{ij},$$
$$var(v_j) = \sigma_v^2, \text{ and}$$
$$var(\varepsilon_{ij}) = \sigma_\varepsilon^2 .$$

Here Y_{ij} is the observed value for person i with characteristics X_i, seen by provider j; X may be a single variable (e.g., severity) or a collection of variables (i.e., a vector of independent variables) for the ith person; μ_i is the expected outcome for a person with characteristics X_i; v_j is the effect of provider j; and ε_{ij} is the residual for the ith case at the jth provider after accounting for individual characteristics and provider effect. The provider effect and residual terms are centered at 0, with variances σ_v^2 and σ_ε^2, respectively. These variances are estimated from the data.

The key features of hierarchical models are:

- Differences among providers (over and above what is explained by differences in patient mix) are explicitly modeled.

- Provider effects are viewed as "random variation," and their typical size, σ_v, is estimated as part of the model-fitting procedure.

- The point estimate for provider j's outcome is "shrunk" from the observed provider average toward a case mix-adjusted expected average for provider j, by an amount that depends on σ_v^2 as well as n_j, the provider's sample size.

- Narrower intervals conveying uncertainty in point estimation are often produced, which have better coverage properties than the intervals produced with traditional methods.

- The problem of multiple comparisons is avoided (Thomas, Longford, and Rolph 1994).

Hierarchical modeling was used to examine variations across states in the use of coronary angiography for over 218,000 elderly heart attack patients (Gatsonis et al. 1995). Patients were nested within state; states were nested within region. Within each state, logistic regression was used to model the probability that a patient received angiography as a function of patient age, sex, race, and comorbidities. Independent variables were coded so that the intercept was the log odds that a baseline case (a 65-year-old nonblack man with no comorbidities) received angiography in each state. These were the Stage I (or Level 1) models.

In Stage II, the intercepts from the Stage I models were modeled as a function of region and a measure of the availability of angiography in the state. Stage II models were developed using this approach for each coefficient in the Stage I models. Thus, for example, the log odds of angiography for black versus nonblack persons in each state was also modeled as a function of region and angiography availability.

This type of modeling recognizes several sources of variation: Within state, for a given set of patient characteristics, each patient's outcome is affected by random variation; within the same region, for a given level of angiography availability, states differed due to random variation; and finally, random error persists after accounting for patient and state characteristics. Variations in observed rates across states reflect all three sources of variation. The approach is similar to the empirical Bayes method, which recognizes two sources of variation—within units and across units—and which, in fact, is a special case of hierarchical modeling. Not surprisingly, the same types of shrunk estimates result. For example, the log odds of angiography in a particular state is a weighted combination of the intercept from the model that only includes patients from that state (Stage I model) and the predicted value from the Stage II model based on the region and availability of angiography in the state. The coefficient associated with the effect of race on outcome is a weighted combination of the coefficient from the Stage I model and the predicted value from the Stage II model. As in empirical Bayes estimation, the degree of shrinkage is a function of the reliability of the within-unit estimate (here, within state) and the estimate of variation across states.

We have emphasized the value of empirical Bayes estimation and hierarchical models for obtaining improved point estimates, but intervals for the shrunk estimates can also be determined. These intervals are like confidence intervals in that they quantify the uncertainty associated with point estimates. Goldstein and Spiegelhalter (1996) present strong arguments for reporting such intervals. They have illustrated the approach by reexamining mortality data published by New York state on deaths associated with coronary artery bypass graft (CABG) surgery (see Chapter 11). Figure 10.10a shows ranked, risk-adjusted, CABG mortality rates with 95 percent intervals for 17 of the 87 surgeons named individually in the report. The solid circles are the observed risk-adjusted mortality rates, and the solid lines represent traditional 95 percent confidence intervals. As in the state's report, two surgeons are identified as significantly above, and one below, the statewide average. Open circles show the "shrunk" rates and the 95 percent intervals within which observed rates are expected to fall. Based on these intervals, in only one of the 17 cases (Dr. Lajos) can we conclude that the surgeon's true rate is different from the statewide average.

Figure 10.10b shows observed ranks and confidence intervals for the ranks calculated using traditional methods (solid circles and lines) and shrunk ranks and intervals from hierarchical modeling (open circles and dashed lines) (Goldstein and Spiegelhalter 1996). Using both approaches, the intervals on ranks are quite wide. Based just on the observed data, for only five surgeons can one feel confident about estimating into which half of the rankings they would fall. The shrunk intervals are even more conservative, leading to the conclusion that only one surgeon is in the bottom half. Previously, Green and Wintfeld (1995, 1230) had criticized New York's CABG report because "in one year 46 percent of the surgeons had moved from one half of the ranked list to the other." Goldstein and Spiegelhalter (1996) note that "such variability in rankings appears to be an inevitable consequence of attempting to rank individuals with broadly similar performances." Furthermore, "an overinterpretation of a set of rankings where there are large uncertainty intervals, as in the examples we have given, can lead both to unfairness and to inefficiency and unwarranted conclusions about changes in ranks. In particular, apparent improvements for low ranking institutions may simply be a reflection of 'regression to the mean' " (Goldstein and Spiegelhalter 1996).

Hierarchical models rapidly become complex, requiring computer-intensive simulations to solve for parameter estimates, although there are computationally efficient approaches for performing the simulations (Gelfand and Smith 1990). However, an advantage of simulation-based estimates of outcomes is that more policy-relevant measures can be considered than mean outcomes. Normand and colleagues (1996) illustrate

Figure 10.10　Comparison of Classical Statistical Point and Interval Estimates to Estimates from Hierarchical Models for a Sample of New York Surgeons Performing Coronary Artery Bypass Graft

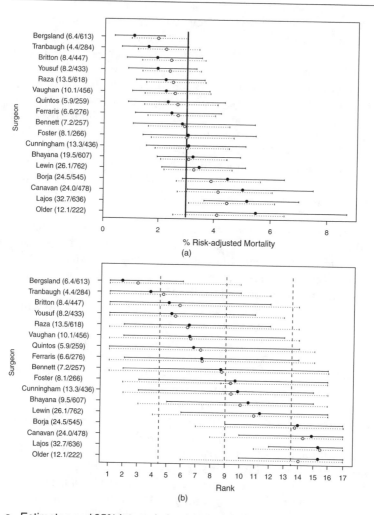

a. Estimates and 95% intervals for risk-adjusted mortality rates, classical approach (–●–) and estimates from hierarchical models (–○–) (the state average of 2.99% is shown).

b. Mean and 95% intervals for rank of surgeon, classical approach (–●–) and estimates from hierarchical models (–○–).

Source: Goldstein and Spiegelhalter 1996.

this in a study profiling hospitals in the HCFA Cooperative Cardiovascular Project. Outcome measures included the probability that hospital-specific mortality for average patients was at least 50 percent greater than median mortality and the probability that the difference between risk-adjusted mortality (calculated at each hospital based on a logistic regression model fit to the hospital's patients) and standardized mortality (predicted mortality based on a model developed from all patients) was large. Estimating such measures without simulations would be difficult.

Hierarchical modeling is an attractive framework for capturing the complexity of risk-adjusted comparisons of outcomes. Two current impediments to widespread adoption of these models are the absence of the necessary large data sets and the lack of readily available, easy-to-implement software.

While waiting for hierarchical models to "arrive," a more traditional approach has involved including dummy variables for hospitals in the model, in addition to the specific patient-level variables. Gatsonis et al. (1995) identify three conceptual problems with this approach: First, it ignores clustering of patients and thus requires adjustment of standard errors; second, when using logistic regression, the models can fail to converge if certain cells of the model do not contain any cases (e.g., Gatsonis and colleagues could fit models to only 40 of the 50 states; we could not fit certain models in our AHCPR-funded severity project); and third, it does not allow examination of the effect of factors associated with the included dummy variables (e.g., region, hospital ownership).

Nevertheless, the dummy variable approach is widely used and seems to work reasonably well for many purposes. For example, Hartz and colleagues (1992) estimated the risk-adjusted effect of each hospital on complication rates, compared to the average excluding the hospital, by including a dummy variable for that hospital in a logistic regression equation that included a variety of patient-level variables. Standard errors were not adjusted to take into account the clustering of patients in hospitals, and it is unclear if such adjustment would have produced a qualitatively different result.

Comparing Outcomes over Time

Chapter 10 thus far has concentrated on cross-sectional comparisons—information relating to a single time period. However, a powerful profiling tool involves examining changes over time—so-called "longitudinal" analysis. Berwick (1996, 4), a leading expert on quality improvement techniques for healthcare institutions, observed, "Pick a measurement you care about, and begin to plot it regularly over time. Much good will follow."

Plotting measures over time calls attention to changes. For simplicity, suppose that all patients have the same "intrinsic" level of risk. Suppose that we examine the problem rate in two hospitals in year 1. Hospital A has a problem rate of 3 percent with a 95 percent confidence interval from 2 to 4 percent, while Hospital B's rate is 5 percent, with confidence interval 4 to 6 percent. From the classical "hypothesis testing" perspective, we can reject the hypothesis that the underlying problem rates at the two hospitals (p_A and p_B) were the same in year 1, in favor of the alternative that Hospital B's rate was higher. This conclusion does not mean that next year Hospital B's problem rate will be higher than A's. Conversely, if in year 2, Hospital A's problem rate is statistically significantly higher than B's, that does not mean that the assessment of which facility did better in year 1 was wrong. Hospital B could have improved.

However, implicit in the value accorded provider profiles is the belief that the numbers reflect an underlying reality that persists over time. As noted earlier, Green and Wintfeld (1995, 1230) criticized New York state's Cardiac Surgery Reporting System, saying "The usefulness of the risk-adjusted data was also limited in that surgeons' rankings during two years of the study offered few clues about their position in the subsequent year ($R^2 = 4.9$ percent) . . . The fact that surgeons' performance ratings fluctuate so much from year to year means that by the time the data are published, users of the report can have little confidence that the ratings are still applicable." Green and Wintfeld thus are concerned that real differences in comparative performance are outdated by the time they become publicly available. As discussed above, Goldstein and Spiegelhalter (1996) demonstrate that such large changes in rank are anticipated when true differences in provider performance are small compared to random "noise."

When providers' performance appears to vary from year to year, we do not know how much variability is due to some providers improving more than others (i.e., last year's data are outdated) and how much to randomness (i.e., "noise" overwhelms the "signal"). Although analyses can help disentangle these issues, in many cases it will remain unclear. Nevertheless, longitudinal plots can show when providers' ranks change dramatically from one year to the next. When big yearly changes are common, both public reporting and decision making should be restrained. In particular, providers should generally not be ranked in order of their measured performance, because this reinforces the impression that a reliable quantity is being reported. Managers should think twice before disrupting provider-patient and network-provider relationships over findings that may be transitory, even when real.

Given the various methodological concerns and resulting questions about interpretation, profiles should be employed only in the arenas where they are likely to be useful. For example, if last year's findings differ from this year's because relative quality can change rapidly among providers, then profiling data will be most valuable for quality improvement and less useful to large purchasers and individual consumers of healthcare services attempting to select providers for the future. Even when longitudinal analyses show stability over time, legitimate concerns remain over whether consistently poor performers are the victims of inadequate risk adjustment. For example, HCFA suspended production of its hospital mortality reports, largely because of concerns about risk adjustment—public, inner-city hospitals did poorly year after year, but HCFA's method could not adjust for the health consequences of medical indigence and poverty.

Future research must identify profiling information that is relatively stable over time and distinguish it from information that fluctuates without obvious explanation. With current profiling techniques, random noise is a major consideration, as are unmeasured differences in patient risk. These factors limit the inferences that can be drawn from current practice profiles. Examining longitudinal plots often provides a sobering reality check to the evaluation process.

Conclusions

A variety of methodological issues are raised when developing or interpreting provider profiles that compare patient outcomes. In most instances, conclusions must be drawn tentatively due to small sample sizes and the difficulty of adjusting adequately for patient risk. Despite these challenges, however, profiles are increasingly generated around the country and are used as an important tool in ensuring healthcare "value"—a melding of cost and quality.

We believe that comparing patient outcomes across providers is valuable, but much depends on how the profiles are used. Given the state of the art, it is inappropriate to use such profiles alone to make "all or nothing" business decisions: for example, telling an "outlier" provider that unless their profile rating improves, business will be withdrawn. In this context, profiles are likely to generate criticism—often based on well-founded methodological concerns—and heighten adversarial relationships among providers, payors, and policymakers. Similarly, if such profiles are disseminated to a public unaware of the need to draw conclusions tentatively, further controversy will likely follow, impeding opportunities for productive dialogue and improvements. If profiles are released to providers without appropriate education about how to use them to identify areas for improvement, they are likely to be ignored.

Profiles comparing patient outcomes are most valuable in an environment of cooperation and collaboration, with incentives for learning and improvement. With increasing competitive pressures, however, this ideal environment may be more fantasy than reality. Chapter 11 describes several initiatives from around the country where risk-adjusted comparisons of patient outcomes are used to shape the healthcare marketplace and influence provider performance.

References

Angell, M., and J. P. Kassirer. 1996. "Quality and the Medical Marketplace—Following Elephants." *New England Journal of Medicine* 335 (12): 883–85.

Ash, A. 1996. "Identifying Poor-Quality Hospitals with Mortality Rates. Often There's More Noise than Signal." *Medical Care* 34 (8): 735–36.

Bennett, G., W. McKee, and L. Kilberg. 1994. "Case Study in Physician Profiling." *Managed Care Quarterly* 2 (4): 60–70.

Berwick, D. 1996. "The Year of 'How': New Systems for Delivering Health Care." *Quality Connection* 5 (1): 1–4.

Brand, D. A., L. Quam, and S. Leatherman. 1995. "Medical Practice Profiling: Concepts and Caveats." *Medical Care Research and Review* 52 (2): 223–51.

Brook, R. H., E. A. McGlynn, and P. D. Cleary. 1996. "Part 2: Measuring Quality of Care." *New England Journal of Medicine* 335 (13): 966–70.

Bryk, A.S., and S.W. Raudenbush. 1992. *Hierarchical Linear Models: Applications and Data Analysis Methods*. Newbury Park, CA: Sage Publications.

Casella, G. 1985. "An Introduction to Empirical Bayes Data Analysis." *American Statistician* 39 (2): 83–7.

Cave, D. G. 1995. "Profiling Physician Practice Patterns Using Diagnostic Episode Clusters." *Medical Care* 33 (5): 463–86.

Cleveland, W. S. 1993. *Visualizing Data*. Summit, NJ: Hobart Press.

Efron, B., and C. Morris. 1972. "Limiting the Risk of Bayes and Empirical Bayes Estimators—Part II: The Empirical Bayes Case." *Journal of the American Statistical Association* 67 (337): 130–9.

———. 1973. "Stein's Estimation Rule and Its Competitors—An Empirical Bayes Approach." *Journal of the American Statistical Association* 68 (341): 117–30.

———. 1975. "Data Analysis Using Stein's Estimator and Its Generalizations." *Journal of the American Statistical Association* 70 (350): 311–9.

———. 1977. "Stein's Paradox in Statistics." *Scientific American* 236 (5): 119–27.

Evans, J. H. III, Y. Hwang, and N. Nagarajan. 1995. "Physicians' Response to Length-of-Stay Profiling." *Medical Care* 33 (11): 1106–19.

Gatsonis, C. A., A. M. Epstein, J. P. Newhouse, S. L. Normand, and B. J. McNeil. 1995. "Variations in the Utilization of Coronary Angiography for Elderly Patients with an Acute Myocardial Infarction. An Analysis Using Hierarchical Logistic Regression." *Medical Care* 33 (6): 625–42.

Gelfand, A., and A. F. M. Smith. 1990. "Sampling-Based Approaches to Calculating Marginal Densities." *Journal of the American Statistical Association* 85 (410): 398.

Goldfield, N., and P. Boland, eds. 1996. *Physician Profiling and Risk Adjustment*. Gaithersburg, MD: Aspen Publishers, Inc.

Goldstein, H., and D. J. Spiegelhalter. 1996. "League Tables and Their Limitations: Statistical Issues in Comparisons of Institutional Performance." *Journal of the Royal Statistical Society A*, 159, part 3: 385–443.

Green, J., and N. Wintfeld. 1995. "Report Cards on Cardiac Surgeons. Assessing New York State's Approach." *New England Journal of Medicine* 332 (18): 1229–32.

Hartz, A. J., E. M. Kuhn, R. Green, and A. A. Rimm. 1992. "The Use of Risk-Adjusted Complication Rates to Compare Hospitals Performing Coronary Artery Bypass Surgery or Angioplasty." *International Journal of Technology Assessment in Health Care* 8 (3): 524–38.

Hofer, T. P., and R. A. Hayward. 1996. "Identifying Poor-Quality Hospitals. Can Hospital Mortality Rates Detect Quality Problems for Medical Diagnoses?" *Medical Care* 34 (8): 737–53.

Hosmer, D. W., and S. Lemeshow. 1995. "Confidence Interval Estimates of an Index of Quality Performance Based on Logistic Regression Models." *Statistics in Medicine* 14 (19): 2161–72.

Iezzoni, L. I., M. Shwartz, A. S. Ash, and Y. D. Mackiernan. 1996a. "Does Severity Explain Differences in Hospital Length of Stay for Pneumonia Patients?" *Journal of Health Services Research and Policy* 1 (2): 65–76.

Iezzoni, L. I., M. Shwartz, A. S. Ash, J. S. Hughes, J. Daley, and Y. D. Mackiernan. 1996b. "Severity Measurement Methods and Judging Hospital Death Rates for Pneumonia." *Medical Care* 34 (1): 11–28.

Iglehart, J. K. 1996. "The National Committee for Quality Assurance." *New England Journal of Medicine* 335 (13): 995–99.

Johnsson, J. 1996. "HMO Market Drop Could Land on Physicians." *American Medical News* 39 (28): 1, 27.

Kerr, E. A., B. S. Mittman, R. D. Hays, A. L. Siu, B. Leake, and R. H. Brook. 1995. "Managed Care and Capitation in California: How Do Physicians at Financial Risk Control Their Own Utilization?" *Annals of Internal Medicine* 123 (7): 500–4.

Kreier, R. 1996. "HMOs Without Gatekeepers." *American Medical News* 39 (29): 1, 27.

Landis J. R. and Localio, A. R. 1996. "Managed Care and Data Management. Making Comparisons Across Groups and Systems: Analytical Considerations." In *American Statistical Association 1996 Proceedings of the Section on Teaching of Statistics in the Health Sciences*. Alexandria, VA: American Statistical Association, in press.

Luft, H. S., and B. W. Brown Jr. 1993. "Calculating the Probability of Rare Events: Why Settle for an Approximation." *HSR: Health Services Research* 28 (4): 419–39.

Luft, H. S., and S. S. Hunt. 1986. "Evaluating Individual Hospital Quality Through Outcome Statistics." *Journal of the American Medical Association* 255 (20): 2780–4.

Nathanson P., M. Noether, R. J. Ozminkowski, K. M. Smith, B. E. Raney, D. Mickey, and P. M. Hawley, Jr. 1994. "Using Claims Data to Select Primary Care Physicians for a Managed Care Network." *Managed Care Quarterly* 2 (4): 50–59.

Nightingale, F. 1863. *Notes on Hospitals*, 3rd ed. London: Longman, Green, Longman, Roberts, and Green.

Normand, S. L. T., M. E. Glickman, and T. J. Ryan. 1996. "Modeling Mortality

Rates for Elderly Heart Attack Patients: Profiling Hospitals in the Cooperative Cardiovascular Project." In *Case Studies in Bayesian Statistics, Volume 3.* New York: Springer-Verlag.

Office of Statewide Health Planning and Development. 1996. *Acute Myocardial Infarction, Volume One: Study of Overview and Results Summary.* Sacramento, CA: Office of Statewide Health Planning and Development.

Pennsylvania Health Care Cost Containment Council (PHC4). 1996. *Focus on Heart Attack in Western Pennsylvania.* Harrisburg, PA: The Council.

Pham, A. "3 HMOs Win Top Marks in Survey," *Boston Globe,* October 22, 1996a, C1, C5.

———. "Insurer Rejects Ratings." *Boston Globe,* October 18, 1996b, C1, C3.

Roos, N. P., J. E. Wennberg, and K. McPherson. 1988. "Using Diagnosis-Related Groups for Studying Variations in Hospital Admissions." *Health Care Financing Review* 9 (4): 53–62.

Salem-Schatz, S., G. Moore, M. Rucker, and S. D. Pearson. 1994. "The Case for Case-Mix Adjustment in Practice Profiling. When Good Apples Look Bad." *Journal of the American Medical Association* 272 (11): 871–74.

Shwartz, M., A. S. Ash, J. Anderson, L. I. Iezzoni, S. M. C. Payne, and J. D. Restuccia. 1994. "Small Area Variations in Hospitalization Rates: How Much You See Depends on How You Look." *Medical Care* 32 (3): 189–201.

Shwartz, M., D. W. Young, and R. Siegrist. 1995. "The Ratio of Costs to Charges: How Good a Basis for Estimating Costs?" *Inquiry* 32 (4): 476–81.

Snedecor, G. W., and W. G. Cochran. 1980. *Statistical Methods,* 7th Ed. Ames, IA: Iowa State University Press.

Stein C. 1955. "Inadmissibility of the Usual Estimator for the Mean of a Multivariate Normal Distribution." In *Proceedings of the 3rd Berkeley Symposium on Mathematical Statistics and Probability, Volume 1,* p. 197. Berkeley, CA: University of California Press.

Sullivan, L. W., and G. R. Wilensky. 1991. *Medicare Hospital Mortality Information. 1987, 1988, 1989.* Washington, D.C.: U.S. Department of Health and Human Services, Health Care Financing Administration.

Teres, D., and S. Lemeshow. 1993. "Using Severity Measures to Describe High Performance Intensive Care Units." *Critical Care Clinics* 9 (3): 543–54.

Thomas, N., N. T. Longford, and J. E. Rolph. 1994. "Empirical Bayes Methods for Estimating Hospital-Specific Mortality Rates." *Statistics in Medicine* 13 (9): 889–903.

Tufte, E. R. 1983. *The Visual Display of Quantitative Information.* Cheshire, CT: Graphics Press.

Tukey, J. W. 1977. *Exploratory Data Analysis.* Reading, MA: Addison-Wesley.

Wilson, P., S. R. Smoley, and D. Werdegar. 1996. *Second Report of the California Hospital Outcomes Project. Acute Myocardial Infarction. Volume Two: Technical Appendix.* Sacramento, CA: Office of Statewide Health Planning and Development.

Chapter 11

Risk Adjustment and Current Health Policy Initiatives

Lisa I. Iezzoni

Report card day is coming in the health care world.

Dennis S. O'Leary, M.D.
President, Joint Commission on
Accreditation of Health Care Organizations, 1993

Although an arcane activity, risk adjustment has assumed center stage in many health policy initiatives around the country, ranging from business coalition report cards on local providers to determining proper payment levels for capitated health plans. Monitoring risk-adjusted outcomes is often the linchpin of efforts to ensure and promote healthcare quality in a time of cost constraints. Managed care plans explicitly use risk-adjusted report cards or practice profiles to make contracting decisions and target individual physicians for in-depth review (Goldfield and Boland 1996). Thus, measures derived using risk adjustment are increasingly affecting providers' bottom lines and, in some settings, patients' access to certain doctors and hospitals.

To date, most uses have emphasized one major dimension of risk, severity of illness, while focusing on outcomes of acute care hospitalizations (Iezzoni, Shwartz, and Restuccia 1991; Iezzoni and Greenberg 1994). As in many policy settings, this debate is neither uniformly refined nor scholarly—a luxury accorded to researchers but rarely to those on the front lines of healthcare delivery. According to the federal General Accounting Office (GAO), "Since the mid-1980s, corporate purchasers have been the driving force behind efforts to obtain information from hospitals and health plans about the quality of care they furnish" (USGAO 1994a, 13). Disagreements about severity measurement methods have polarized business and provider communities in some regions, while in others, these groups work together to develop approaches acceptable to both. Thus far, healthcare consumers have not actively participated in debates over severity methodologies, although advocates for persons with chronic illness and disabilities are voicing concerns about the implications of risk adjustment for access to capitated health plans (Giacomini, Luft, and Robinson 1995; Swartz 1995).

This chapter identifies broad themes in the public policy debate concerning risk-adjusted outcome comparisons and puts them into the context of the issues raised in previous chapters. New local and state initiatives arise almost weekly, and the managed care industry continues to hone its profiling approaches. I will not attempt, therefore, to provide a comprehensive and up-to-date picture of specific initiatives nationwide. Instead, I will describe several of the leading report card efforts and will outline common goals, approaches, and attitudes of the major stakeholders in this arena. Much of the information for this chapter comes from federal and state reports and proposals, stories appearing in the national and regional press identified through the computerized LEXIS/NEXIS on-line information service, and discussions with selected individuals around the country. Because most efforts have focused on severity of illness measures, I will also concentrate on this dimension of risk.

Overview

Two trends have led to increased use of severity measures such as those listed in Table 1.3. The first is individual hospitals' internal decisions to institute severity measurement. Individual hospitals use severity information to assist with in-house quality improvement activities, to aid strategic planning, to inform negotiations with third party payors, and to assess practice patterns with an eye to improving competitive position within the local marketplace. For example, understanding trends of patient severity over time may help individual hospitals project nursing staff requirements or need for intensive care beds; hospitals with higher per-patient costs than other local facilities may need to convince insurers that their patients are more severely ill and thus more resource intensive. Hospitals frequently send their data, such as computerized hospital discharge abstract files (see Chapter 3), to health information companies, who then score the data using a severity measure and compare individual hospital's outcomes with those of other facilities in their database. Such comparisons inform benchmarking and help individual hospitals target areas for improvement.

Often hospitals need severity information to promote a productive dialogue with their medical staffs. Even reasonable physicians may hesitate to change or even examine critically their practice patterns because of information that they believe is not medically meaningful (see Chapter 2). When told that their patients have worse outcomes than others, physicians typically respond, "But my patients are sicker. . . ." Risk adjustment enhances the clinical credibility of outcome comparisons, moving the dialogue in a more productive direction.

Few argue with individual hospitals' decisions to invest in severity measures to meet their internal needs. Concern and controversy arise when severity data are requested "voluntarily" by businesses commanding a large marketshare or are mandated by some external entity, especially for comparing hospitals with each other or some outside standard. Governmental organizations, managed care companies, and local employer coalitions are increasingly examining risk-adjusted outcome reports for providers with whom they do business. In this setting, severity information is used for two primary purposes:

- to improve the fairness of reimbursement; and
- to provide risk adjustment for monitoring the outcomes of care.

As the GAO observed in a study of the potential role of report cards in federal healthcare reform, "Unless outcomes are adjusted to determine whether patient characteristics or quality of care affected the results, conclusions about quality based on an evaluation of outcomes might be erroneous (USGAO 1994a, 14).

In general, cost and quality purposes are debated separately, and few have suggested using the same method for provider reimbursement *and* monitoring more clinical outcomes of care (e.g., mortality rates). For example, although HCFA bases Medicare's hospital reimbursement on DRGs, HCFA did not use the DRGs for risk adjusting hospital mortality rates (see below). This separation is appropriate: DRGs were designed to predict resource consumption, not imminent death (Fetter et al. 1980), while the mortality prediction models are empirically derived specifically to predict deaths (Sullivan and Wilensky 1991). Nevertheless, comparisons of aggregate costs or charges across hospitals often employ DRGs or scores derived from DRGs, such as the case-mix index (Prospective Payment Assessment Commission 1993). Here, however, I concentrate on comparisons of patient outcomes, not reimbursement considerations.

Both external data collection mandates and the use of severity information for comparisons frequently spark heated debates, generally pitting providers (e.g., hospitals or physicians) against those requiring the data (e.g., government, business coalitions). Although not shared by everyone within these two communities, frequent concerns of providers and purchasers are listed in Table 11.1. The rhetoric of today's healthcare debates evokes the memory of E. A. Codman from earlier in the century. As noted in Chapter 1, Codman observed, "Comparisons are odious, but comparison is necessary in science. Until we freely make therapeutic comparisons, we cannot claim that a given hospital is efficient, for efficiency implies that the results have been looked into" (Codman 1934, xxiii).

The difference today is perhaps the huge size of the stakes: In present-day rhetorical terms, this battle has sometimes assumed mythic propor-

Table 11.1   Common Concerns of Providers and Purchasers

Common Concerns of Providers

- The severity measure is not sufficiently clinically meaningful (e.g., capturing all pertinent risk factors) and free of bias to permit credible comparisons across providers.
- Collecting the data is logistically burdensome and expensive, adding yet another administrative expense to an already stressed system.
- Those requesting the comparisons do not understand the limitations of the data or analytic techniques and therefore draw inappropriate conclusions.
- The data do not provide useful information about how exactly to change care to improve outcomes.
- These imperfect data may be used inappropriately to threaten providers or make punitive decisions (e.g., withdrawing health plan contracts), thus reducing patient access to targeted providers.
- The data typically have a limited focus (e.g., they are only pertinent for monitoring mortality) and do not identify quality of care concerns most relevant either to patients or doctors.

Common Concerns of Purchasers

- Given the enormous healthcare cost escalation of the last three decades, providers finally need to be accountable for what they produce.
- Other industries must justify their outputs and quality of their products—healthcare is no different.
- The dollars spent on severity data are trivial compared to the total bill for healthcare services.
- Purchasers and consumers require information to make informed decisions about where to obtain their healthcare.
- Providers must be held accountable for the care they administer and the resources they expend.
- Given the dearth of information currently available about the relative performance of healthcare providers, we need to start somewhere, even if the data are not perfect.

---

tions. In his address to the joint session of Congress on September 22, 1993, introducing his ill-fated healthcare reform proposal, President Clinton said, "Our competitiveness, our whole economy, the integrity of the way the government works and, ultimately, our living standards depend upon our ability to achieve savings . . . [in] healthcare" (White House Domestic Policy Council 1993, 96). He emphasized that quality of care must be maintained and promoted: "If we reformed everything else in health care, but failed to preserve and enhance the high quality of our medical care, we will have taken a step backward, not forward. Quality is something that we simply can't leave to chance" (White House Domestic Policy Council 1993, 100).

Ironically, given the political rhetoric accompanying the demise of Clinton's plan, healthcare quality is now under constant assault within the ensuing "free market" system that is *de facto* "reforming" healthcare. Nightly news programs run series on anecdotal managed care atrocities; the president signs a bill limiting "drive-through deliveries," albeit without much evidence about the true effect of length of obstetrical stays; states around the nation ponder outlawing the "gag" rules that limit what physicians can say to patients enrolled in managed care plans. Consumers and purchasers still complain that they do not have adequate information to choose among the competitors in the healthcare marketplace. The balkanization of healthcare "reform" (Iglehart 1994) has lead to countless, disparate local and regional efforts to evaluate care, frustrating some observers. " . . . We are creating a mishmash of incomparable data," observed the head of a local business coalition in Missouri. "What we really need are national definitions that allow us to say, 'This is the quality of care in the United States' " (Harris 1994).

Risk-adjusted outcome measures have been wedged in the center of some of these debates, especially on a local level. Although concerns about fairness of reimbursement remain, this area is often treated as a purely technical concern that can be patched by adjusting payment policies (e.g., by special payments for "outliers"). The more heated exchanges in the last few years have involved using severity-adjusted data to compare outcomes across hospitals.

Monitoring Outcomes of Care

In recent years, the competing forces driving the U.S. healthcare system have raised significant concerns about the quality of care. An early worry haunting Medicare's per-case, DRG-based hospital payment system was that patients would be discharged "quicker and sicker." The key words of Clinton's failed healthcare reform proposals were "cost containment" and "access for all," but achieving these competing goals would have required curtailing ready, unquestioned access to *all* health services (Iezzoni 1993). In the current managed care environment, limiting financial access to healthcare services inevitably raises fears about compromising quality. Americans increasingly need to be reassured that their previously unquestioned quality of care is being maintained. Doing so, however, raises a complex but essential question: What do we need to know to monitor quality of care?

Any answer must start with a definition of "quality," and although a single definition may never achieve consensus, most now agree that "quality" *can* be defined (Blumenthal 1996). The Institute of Medicine's (IOM) Committee to Design a Strategy for Quality Review and Assurance in Medicare defined "quality" as:

> Quality of care is the degree to which health services for individuals and populations increase the likelihood of desired health outcomes and are consistent with current professional knowledge . . . How care is provided should reflect appropriate use of the most current knowledge about scientific, clinical, technical, interpersonal, manual, cognitive, and organizational and management elements of health care. (Lohr 1990, 4–5)

This definition carefully melds the "two camps" of quality observers that have been sparring for years—"the one that has pledged allegiance to process," or "the other that accepts no master other than outcome" (Donabedian 1980, 100–1). While acknowledging the obvious conceptual merit of this inclusive definition, the wide range of perspectives presents a daunting challenge for designing an operational quality monitoring system. Another competing perspective is an appropriate concern of payors— how much does high-quality care cost? Might there be some point at which the costs of "quality care" outweigh the benefits, or at least payors' willingness to pay? Costs are not limited to the care alone. The burden of collecting information on quality could be significant, furthering concerns about escalating administrative expenses (Woolhandler, Himmelstein, and Lewontin 1993). Given these realities, the question posed above therefore modulates somewhat: What is the *minimum* information needed to monitor quality of care in a feasible and cost-effective manner across a range of populations and types of services?

Many have not waited for a single answer to this question. Numerous initiatives at all levels of government are beginning to compare risk-adjusted outcomes across providers. Due primarily to data constraints, most of these initiatives have started with hospitalizations and are focusing on three readily available, albeit limited, outcomes—mortality, length of stay (LOS), and charges. The following sections describe several leading initiatives to monitor quality through risk-adjusted outcomes.

Federal Performance Measurement

In the last few years, state and regional initiatives examining risk-adjusted outcomes have received the greatest press coverage and public attention. However, the federal government has also contributed to developing methods for examining risk-adjusted outcomes, such as the Department of Veterans Affairs' National Veterans Affairs Surgical Risk Study (Khuri et al. 1995), described in Chapters 5 and 6. However, the most public federal effort was HCFA's release of hospital-specific mortality rates for Medicare beneficiaries.

Hospital Mortality Reports

Through its administrative data files (see Chapter 3), HCFA has maintained figures on mortality rates of Medicare beneficiaries for years. In the mid-1980s, because of reporters' demands under the federal Freedom of Information Act (5 U.S.C. 552), HCFA was finally compelled to release these data publicly (USGAO 1995, 8–9). The risks of failing to standardize adequately for severity were exemplified by the furor accompanying HCFA's initial release of hospital-level mortality figures in March 1986 (Brinkley 1986). According to governmental predictions, 142 hospitals had significantly higher death rates than predicted, while 127 had significantly lower rates. The facility with the most aberrant death rate (with 87.6 percent of Medicare patients dying compared to a predicted 22.5 percent) was a hospice caring for terminally ill patients. This early HCFA model did not adequately capture severity of illness and had several other serious methodological flaws (Blumberg 1987; Dubois 1989).

HCFA's methods improved in the intervening years, although they remain constrained by the immutable limitations of administrative data (see Chapter 3). One advantage of HCFA's data, however, is the ability to link information longitudinally at the patient level. Therefore, the Medicare risk-adjustment model used information on patients' prior hospitalization experiences. The 1991 release employed data for discharges during fiscal years 1987, 1988, and 1989 (Sullivan and Wilensky 1991). Mortality was examined as a function of time, such as within 30, 90, and 180 days of admission. Factors included in the prediction model were age, sex, major chronic comorbid illness, prior admissions within six months of the index admission, admission type (e.g., emergent, elective), and admission source. Models were developed for all cases and separately for patients admitted for one of eight conditions or nine procedures. The information was published in multiple volumes, grouping hospitals within states. Observed death rates were arrayed parallel to predicted rates as well as the standard deviation around the predicted rate (see Chapter 10). A copy of the hospital's letter of response to the HCFA findings, if sent, was published following the figures for each facility.

Despite these methodological advances, it remained unclear whether the Medicare hospital mortality reports provided useful insight into quality of hospital care. Although initial data releases received avid press interest and front-page newspaper coverage, later publications generated minimal attention and were often buried deep in local papers. The public did not appear to use this information to choose among hospitals (Vladeck et al. 1988; Dubois 1989).

In June 1993, newly appointed HCFA administrator Bruce Vladeck discontinued publication of the Medicare hospital mortality reports, stating that HCFA's risk-adjustment methodology was inadequate (USGAO 1995). Vladeck appeared most concerned that the data unfairly penalized inner-city public facilities, which were constantly flagged as egregious outliers. Vladeck observed that because the mortality figures appeared to be quality "scores," the information "has had more importance attached to it than I think was justified" (Podolsky and Beddingfield 1993). When asked if he believed the data were valid for large tertiary institutions, Vladeck responded, "My answer is quite literally that we don't know."

Medicare's Peer Review Program

The federal government also sponsors the largest single program to monitor quality of care, Medicare's Utilization and Quality Control Peer Review Organizations (the PROs) (HCFA 1992; Jencks and Wilensky 1992). In the early 1990s, HCFA fundamentally redesigned the PRO program, embarking on widespread quality improvement projects in collaboration with providers—the Health Care Quality Improvement Program (HCQIP). HCFA's Fourth Scope of Work for the PROs, released in October 1992, introduced the PRO Health Care Quality Improvement Initiative "to develop and share with the healthcare community information on patterns of care and patterns of outcomes that will lead to measurable improvements in care and outcomes for Medicare beneficiaries" (HCFA 1992).

According to Stephen F. Jencks, M.D., senior clinical advisor within the HCFA Health Standards and Quality Bureau,

> To promote improvement, both PROs and hospitals must learn to view each other as partners; each PRO must come to appear as a valuable and trustworthy partner to physician and non-physician hospital staff. Winning trust means overcoming history and ongoing PRO responsibilities that require occasional enforcement action . . . Both HCFA and the PROs must become quality-improving organizations themselves if they are to become effective agents for improvement—they must walk the walk as well as talk the talk. (Jencks 1995, 343–44)

Comparing process and outcomes of care in a benchmarking framework is a central technique of the HCQIP program. Thus far, HCQIP has primarily emphasized process measures, drawn from evidence-based clinical practice guidelines (Jencks 1995). By the end of 1995, reviewing randomly selected cases—until 1993 the PROs' core strategy—was replaced completely by cooperative PRO-provider projects (USGAO 1996). While individual case review will continue for seven mandatory categories (e.g., allegations of transferring unstable emergency patients to other facilities, potential cases of "grossly poor care," beneficiary complaints of poor care), this technique was abandoned in April 1996, the initiation date of the Fifth PRO Scope of Work (USGAO 1996, 27). Finally, HCFA is also joining various private efforts to monitor quality, as described below.

State Performance Measurement Initiatives

In 1986, Pennsylvania became the first state to enact a major new data mandate for comparing risk-adjusted outcomes. Spurred largely by concerns of its business community, Pennsylvania required all hospitals to implement the MedisGroups severity measurement system, which requires detailed abstraction of clinical information from medical records (see Chapter 1). The massive scope of this data-gathering mandate and subsequent plans to release publicly comparative information on providers were viewed as visionary by some, and by others as sheer folly that would never last. Nevertheless, as healthcare costs around the country continued to soar, frustrating those who were paying the bill, other states contemplated similar initiatives. Some states chose to start with less ambitious approaches using their existing administrative data, but a few others followed Pennsylvania's lead with new data-gathering mandates.

About 36 states across the country now have some legislative mandate to examine hospitalization outcomes, primarily mortality, LOS, and charges (Rubin 1993). What is done with these data varies from state to state. Sometimes taking the leap from analyzing data to publicizing it has required a major change in attitudes. For example, the Texas Department of Health collects some information on costs and outcomes of care, but it is prohibited from releasing information identifying individual hospitals or physicians; new laws are needed to permit this disclosure (Sorelle 1993). Until healthcare costs are controlled, it is likely that external pressures will force the healthcare delivery industry to accept and even participate in more public investigation of how they do. This section briefly describes several of the most significant state initiatives.

Pennsylvania

As described above, powerful Pennsylvania business leaders, such as Westinghouse Electric Corporation and Aluminum Company of America (ALCOA), were the motivating force behind the nation's first statewide initiative to gather and report severity-adjusted outcomes information. The Commonwealth's General Assembly created the Pennsylvania Health Care Cost Containment Council (so-called PHC4) through Act 89 in 1986. Pennsylvania required every hospital to adopt a proprietary severity measure, MedisGroups, which scores patient risk using up to approximately 250 key clinical findings abstracted from medical records. Sparking some controversy when MedisGroups was chosen, its vendor, MediQual Systems, Inc., was not required to make the logic of the method publicly available, although it has subsequently done so. The legislation incorporated many specific requirements, pertaining to such areas as the form and frequency of public data releases.

Pennsylvania's releases of MedisGroups risk-adjusted outcomes depict hospitals' "quality" side by side with average charges. The head of PHC4, which produces these reports, believes that they will help stabilize healthcare costs by assisting consumers to avoid high-price, low-quality hospitals (Hawkes 1989) and by stimulating competition (Gaul 1990). However, early experience in Pennsylvania was mixed. One problem was prolonged delays in the production and release of the hospital reports and a requirement of the original mandate that reports be issued quarterly. Timing of processing and publication of the data was staggered across regions throughout the state. The initial Philadelphia release occurred in December 1990, over four years after the legislation was enacted (Gaul 1990; Simmons 1990).

The first "Hospital Effectiveness Report," released June 28, 1989, by PHC4, reflected hospitalizations between April and June 1988 for 55 conditions at 15 hospitals in the state's south central region. Results were rated on a five-point scale, ranging from $--$ (significantly worse outcome than expected) to $++$ (significantly better outcome). The difference between actual and expected outcomes was judged at a $P = 0.25$ significance level. The small numbers of cases and resultant statistical limitations alarmed many hospitals. For example, the Hershey Medical Center received a "$-$" rating in gallbladder removal (based on only 12 cases) and hip and thigh fractures (based on only 9 cases). PHC4's director Ernest Sessa conceded that these numbers were too small to draw any conclusions, but he noted, "We have launched a dialogue that never existed before between the patient and the hospital. What we're intending to do is to promote competition" (Rounds 1989, A1). However, Judith Lave, Ph.D., a respected Pittsburgh health economist, cautioned, "The quarterly release is sufficiently unstable that it could torpedo the whole effort to publicize information" (Twedt and Flaherty 1990, A6). Adjustments were made in PHC4's methodologies to counter these concerns.

Despite these criticisms, PHC4 data have received national attention, especially the November 1992 release of statewide outcomes for coronary artery bypass graft (CABG) surgery. Findings of this study were even cited by President Clinton in his September 22, 1993, healthcare reform address:

> We have evidence that more efficient delivery of healthcare doesn't decrease quality. In fact, it may enhance it. Let me just give you one example of one commonly performed procedure, the coronary bypass operation. Pennsylvania discovered that patients who were charged $21,000 for this surgery received as good or better care as patients who were charged $84,000 for the same procedure in the same state. High prices simply don't always equal good quality. (White House Domestic Policy Council 1993, 100)

PHC4's 1992 "A Consumer Guide to Coronary Artery Bypass Graft Surgery" contained not only findings at the individual hospital level but also, for the first time, ratings for specific surgeons, each identified by name (the first physician-specific data release in the country occurred in New York). The report listed, for each hospital and cardiothoracic surgeon, the number of CABG patients, the number of in-hospital deaths, and the expected number of in-hospital deaths based on a model derived from MedisGroups data. For hospitals, average charges were also presented.

PHC4 has continued to publish "A Consumer Guide to Coronary Artery Bypass Graft Surgery." The June 1995 release pertained to 1993 data, and it indicated that three hospitals had fewer deaths than expected, while five had more (PHC4 1995, 15). Average charges per CABG across all hospitals were $54,569, ranging from $26,000 at a facility in Sayre, Pennsylvania, to $102,637 at a Philadelphia teaching hospital. For cardiothoracic surgeons operating on at least 30 patients, results were also presented by name. In addition, the report compared CABG results by hospital and individual surgeon for 1991, 1992, and 1993, allowing readers to track trends over time.

In 1996, Pennsylvania became the first state to publish report cards for heart attack treatment—by hospital, physician practices, and individual physician by name—within specific regions of the state (PHC4 1996). In addition, it examined results by payor. The report examined in-hospital mortality, total hospital charges, and length of hospital stays (see Chapter 10). Results were presented separately for hospitals with and without advanced cardiac services; total charges were uniformly higher at hospitals with advanced cardiac services than for other acute care hospitals. Numbers of cases transferred out of the hospital were also noted. The payor data was especially provocative in some regions. For example, in southeastern

Pennsylvania, patients enrolled in HMOs had higher-than-expected death rates. Philadelphia newspapers grasped this finding, with one headline warning, "Belong to an HMO? Your chances of surviving a heart attack are lower" (Prager 1996a, 27).

Pennsylvania was also the first state to confront the cost implications of this type of initiative. For example, PHC4 sought a $4.7 million budget for fiscal year 1990–1991, excluding one estimate of $28 million per year required of hospitals to collect the data. While PHC4 placed the per-case MedisGroups data collection cost at $10, some hospitals in the Pittsburgh area cited figures between $20 and $30—a cost passed on to patients (Twedt and Flaherty 1990). A study by Pennsylvania State University estimated an average per case cost of $17.43, with total costs per hospital ranging from $70,000 at small rural facilities to $134,000 at a large urban hospital (USGAO 1994a, 21).

Cost considerations prompted some in Pennsylvania to reexamine the entire effort. PHC4 members and business leaders insisted that savings greater than these costs will be achieved once businesses and consumers start shopping for hospitals based on the data (Twedt and Flaherty 1990). In 1991 and 1992, PHC4 sustained severe budget cuts and was scheduled (by the original Act 89 mandate) to "sunset" out of existence on June 30, 1993. However, PHC4 was saved by several factors. There was evidence that it was beginning to save costs and increase competition. For example, in 1992, St. Vincent's Medical Center in Erie announced a $5 million annual price reduction on open-heart surgery and other cardiac procedures. Competitive initiatives were also arising. Hahnemann University Hospital indicated that it would reduce its prices for open-heart surgery and other cardiac procedures to 70 percent of average costs for similar services at other Delaware Valley facilities. Hershey Foods, ALCOA, Capital Blue Cross, and Pennsylvania Blue Shield announced plans to contract with providers based on the PHC4 findings.

Hershey Foods has been particularly aggressive in using PHC4's reports. Hershey chose hospitals and physicians for its own network using the PHC4 data and then offered employees the option of continuing with their own providers with "full indemnity cost-sharing or using Hershey network providers with little or no cost-sharing" (Angel 1995). This approach helped Hershey Foods to discontinue indemnity plans in 1995 for most employees. Hershey estimated it gained 10 percent on its profit margin by using the PHC4 data (USGAO 1994a, 48). Nonetheless, Hershey claimed that employee satisfaction with their healthcare is higher than ever. Hershey managers believe that, by using PHC4 data to help select providers, they increased "the sensitivity of providers to price and quality differences—creating a more competitive market for medical care in their area" (Angel 1995).

There was also anecdotal evidence that hospitals were using the information to improve care. For example, Forbes Metro Hospital in Pittsburgh had a higher-than-expected death rate for pneumonia patients. The hospital set up a committee to investigate this and found several problematic procedures. Nurses, for instance, sometimes incorrectly performed microbiology cultures using patients' saliva rather than sputum. New procedures were instituted requiring respiratory therapists to perform almost all sputum tests. Following this change, the pneumonia death rate fell 6.5 percent (Riley 1993).

Sustaining legislation for PHC4 was signed on June 28, 1993, with a ten-year sunset provision. PHC4 also got a $3 million appropriation, a substantial increase over the previous year.

Iowa

Iowa provides an example of the sometimes uneasy relationship between the business and provider communities in producing and releasing risk-adjusted outcomes information. The use of MedisGroups was mandated by the Iowa General Assembly in 1989 and required in the state's 28 large hospitals (those with more than 100 beds). Final plans required data to be collected on 66 high-volume or high-cost DRGs, with information given only to hospitals during the first 18 months. Thereafter, comparative information would be released to the public.

The decision to adopt MedisGroups over other severity measures was highly controversial. The business community first introduced the notion after direct marketing by the method's vendor and other advocates of the MedisGroups approach. Many providers believed that business leaders were insensitive to their reservations about MedisGroups. However, the choice of a specific method was eventually delayed as a compromise with providers. The goal of this delay was to permit physicians at St. Luke's Hospital in Cedar Rapids to conduct a comparative evaluation of the Computerized Severity Index (CSI)—the measure preferred by some providers—and MedisGroups. In this study, both methods were used to score over 900 admissions. The investigators examined the relationships of the severity scores to LOS, hospitalization charges, and in-hospital mortality; they also studied the logic of the measures and their reporting capabilities.

The physician committee concluded that neither method was clearly superior nor inferior, but if forced to choose, the committee advocated the CSI, noting its "less mysterious" logic and that it was easier to learn to use than MedisGroups. They suggested that providers ought to be allowed to use the severity measure with which they felt more comfortable (Vanourny 1989). However, at testimony before the Iowa Health Data Commission on June 16, 1989, several observers noted a fractious polarization between some providers and business leaders on choice of the specific severity measure. Given the strong preference of the business community and the support of a number of hospitals, Iowa chose MedisGroups. After the decision was made, the different groups endeavored to work constructively and productively together, although the truce was somewhat uneasy.

The initial public release of MedisGroups data showed "that Iowa hospitals seem to be doing a pretty good job" (Gardner 1993a). Some, however, questioned whether this information was worth the cost. On March 1, 1993, the Iowa Hospital Association asked the state's General Assembly to repeal the MedisGroups mandate, primarily because of the cost of the data, which the hospitals placed at $2.5 million per year; the purchasers said the figure was $1.6 million (Resnick 1993, 51), while another figure placed the cost at $3.5 million (Gardner 1993a). The hospital association also claimed that neither purchasers nor providers were using the MedisGroups data, a view disputed by Iowa's Health Policy Corporation. On March 11, 1993, the Iowa House voted 50–47 against the hospitals, but on March 29, 1993 the Senate voted 49–0 to end the Iowa Health Data Commission, the agency administering the MedisGroups data collection, on July 1, 1994 (Resnick 1993, 52). The decision to eliminate the commission was delayed while it conducted a cost-benefit study of the MedisGroups data.

Iowa, however, never completed this cost-benefit analysis. Instead, interest focused on Iowa's Community Health Management Information System (CHMIS) initiative, sponsored by The John A. Hartford Foundation. The focus of the CHMIS program was to implement, by July 1, 1996, a uniform, electronic data transmission procedure for all bills submitted by all healthcare providers (see Chapter 3). These billing data would be aggregated in a central data repository controlled by a private, nonprofit organization. The board overseeing this organization is composed of representatives of all the important stakeholders in the healthcare delivery system, including payors, employers, and providers. This electronic transmission of bills in a uniform format attempted to facilitate not only payment but also efforts to monitor provider performance.

Given this context, the state hospital association argued that, under CHMIS, uniform data would become available across all hospitals—not just the 28 facilities with more than 100 beds targeted by the MedisGroups mandate. Readily available, UB 92 data could be used to severity adjust mortality and charge information, at a much lower cost than the Medis-Groups method. In addition, given the relatively good performance of the 28 Iowa hospitals contrasted with the MedisGroups Comparative Database benchmarks, few employers appeared interested in the data.

Through CHMIS auspices, a request for proposal was issued to solicit bids from proprietary, UB 92–based information companies for producing comparative risk-adjusted charge and mortality figures for all Iowa hospitals. The 3M Health Information Systems method, the All-Patient Refined Diagnosis-Related Groups (APR-DRG), was selected. As a result of these activities, the state halted the MedisGroups initiative on July 1, 1994. However, the Iowa CHMIS did not make its July 1996 implementation date. As described in Chapter 3, delays were caused by "overzealousness and poor planning . . . [and] trying to lead in a field fraught with conflicting agendas, increasing competition and rapidly developing technologies at a time when healthcare faces pressing demands to contain costs" (Borzo 1996, 4).

Colorado

Colorado was the third state to require collection of MedisGroups information, but unlike Pennsylvania and Iowa, however, decision makers in Colorado reacted skeptically to some vendors' claims about the utility of their severity measures. This led to a compromise strategy, using the vendor-based methods mainly to guide primary data collection from the medical record. Then, using these abstracted data elements, severity measures would be developed empirically.

Colorado issued a request for proposal, stipulating criteria to be met by a prospective severity data collection instrument. Several of the more prominent methods met these criteria, but MediQual Systems was the only major vendor to submit a proposal. Although MedisGroups was selected, its name did not appear specifically in the authorizing legislation: The state was not allowed to require hospitals to buy a particular product. Rather, the legislation specified that the clinical variables included in MedisGroups be collected by hospitals, *de facto* leading to the adoption of MedisGroups. Prompted by concerns about overburdening small hospitals, Colorado's data-reporting requirement excluded hospitals with fewer than 100 beds.

Although the Colorado mandate began in the late 1980s, numerous methodological controversies arose, and the first report did not appear until August 1994 (Colorado Health Data Commission 1994). The report compared observed-to-expected mortality rates, LOSs, and hospital charges for patients hospitalized for cardiovascular diseases and other selected conditions in 24 large Colorado hospitals in 1992. The data were severity adjusted using the empirical version of MedisGroups released in 1993. The report cautioned that the MedisGroups risk-adjustment approach had limitations, such as the absence of "do not resuscitate" status and its dependence on varying physician documentation practices. More troubling were the age of the data. As noted by the medical director of one hospital that fared poorly, " . . . We have to accept the fact that the data was [*sic*] real for 1992 . . . We are a different institution in 1994, and we're going to be a vastly different institution as things evolve this year" (Scott 1994).

On July 1, 1995, Colorado's Health Data Commission was dissolved after a stormy legislative session failed to pass its reauthorization bill ("Demise of Two State-run Commissions" 1995). Apparently, the Commission was caught in a political struggle over health plan performance-reporting requirements. Its reauthorization bill, which passed the Colorado senate, called for voluntary reporting of HEDIS-type measures by health plans. The Colorado house amended the bill to make health plan reporting mandatory. After intense lobbying, the bill was defeated and the Commission was "sunset" after a rocky ten-year existence. The Colorado Hospital Association plans to continue its reporting on inpatient outcomes. Eschewing medical record abstraction, the hospital association chose APR-DRGs as its risk adjustment approach.

California

California's first major foray into the severity measurement debate occurred when representatives of Pennsylvania's Hershey Foods brought the MedisGroups initiative to the attention of the California business community. A bill prompted by business representatives and submitted to the California Assembly on March 1, 1990, (AB 3810) stated that if the Office of Statewide Health Planning and Development did not select a method for evaluating provider quality by a certain date, "the office shall adopt and furnish to all providers the methodology employed . . . by the Pennsylvania Health Care Cost Containment Council" (Section 433.311.(e)). This default position supporting MedisGroups was viewed with consternation by many throughout the state, especially given the lack of prior investigation and the projected $61.2 million annual cost estimated by the California Association of Hospitals and Health Systems (Mullen 1990). The Assembly adjourned before the debate over this bill was completed. Consequently, the 1991 California severity initiative did not explicitly refer to Pennsylvania's approach.

Based largely on that experience, the final form of California's mandate reflected two major concerns: First, that collecting primary data directly from medical records would be prohibitively expensive and inadequately justified; and second, that no existing risk-adjustment method sold by a vendor was sufficiently clinically and statistically rigorous. Assembly Bill 524, enacted in 1991, required California state officials to create their own "home grown" risk-adjusted outcome measures, using the state's existing administrative database and developed by leading university researchers with guidance from panels of local experts.

Investigators from the University of California led initial development of the statistical model, assisted by state coding experts, epidemiologists, and teams of local physicians and health services researchers

(Romano et al. 1995). The modeling employed the state's computerized hospital discharge abstract data set, containing standard information on each discharge from California's acute care hospitals (see Chapter 3). California's data had the advantage of containing space for up to 25 diagnosis codes and 25 procedure codes, compared to the 5 diagnosis and 3 procedure slots typical of many other state data sets. In addition, California sponsored an ongoing, aggressive program to monitor and improve hospital coding, and a recently instituted unique patient identifier (encrypted social security numbers) permitted tracking of patients over time. Disease-specific models were developed because they were viewed as more clinically meaningful than generic approaches.

The first release of data occurred in December 1993 (Wilson, Smoley, and Werdegar 1993), focusing on acute myocardial infarction (AMI) and back surgery (cervical and lumbar disk excisions). These conditions were chosen because they are common, generate high costs and significant morbidity, and are clearly defined. In addition, clinical research had shown that the process of care could affect outcomes. For AMI, one outcome was examined—death within 30 days of hospital admission. The model explicitly tried to address concerns about acute hospital transfers. Two outcomes were assessed for diskectomies: first, postoperative complications, including death, unplanned reoperations before discharge, surgical complications, postoperative infections, and medical complications; and second, unusually prolonged postoperative hospital stays. Risk adjustment considered demographic characteristics (e.g., age, sex) and clinical risk factors (e.g., chronic illnesses, complications of the principal diagnosis). Because the administrative data did not indicate whether secondary diagnoses were present prior to admission (see Chapter 3), two models were developed—a conservative model including only conditions that should have been preexisting and a comprehensive model containing all potential risk factors (see Chapter 10).

California's initiative concentrated on existing administrative data because of their ready availability and consequent low cost. However, during the course of model development, numerous questions arose concerning the accuracy and completeness of the data, especially coding of postoperative complications for diskectomy cases (Romano et al. 1995). Because of these questions, the first public release did not identify hospitals that appeared to have higher-than-expected rates of poor outcomes. The state's report was explicitly concerned about inappropriately harming hospitals due to biases or inaccuracies in the data.

Hospitals were therefore lumped into two groups according to a comparison of their actual outcomes with outcomes predicted by the two models: "significantly better than expected" or "not significantly better than expected." The report was statistically conservative in making these assignments (Wilson, Smoley, and Werdegar 1993, 15–16). As Romano and colleagues (1995, 675) observed:

> . . . The choice of a *p*-value cutoff was not straightforward . . . A conventional *p*-value cutoff of 0.10 or 0.05 would have produced nearly the same number of outliers that would have been expected by chance. Balancing the risk of mislabeling a non-outlier hospital (type I error) against the risk of failing to identify a true outlier (type II error), we selected *p*-value cutoffs of 0.005 for diskectomy complications and 0.01 for AMI mortality. The numbers of hospitals beyond these cutoffs were significantly greater that the expected numbers based on chance.

Some of California's most prestigious hospitals fared poorly in the initial assessment. One reason was that these hospitals had aggressively coded complications of surgery to boost their DRG-based payments (Jost 1994)—complications sometimes direct patients to the higher-weighted of DRG pairs. Other concerns about data quality prompted the state to pursue a novel approach—a public examination of data quality.

The second California report was released in May 1996 and contained information by hospital on risk-adjusted in-hospital death rates within 30 days of admission for AMI (Wilson, Smoley, and Werdegar 1996). Deaths after 30 days in-hospital were excluded because they might have reflected social problems or unrelated conditions. Hospitals were classed into three categories, including "significantly better" and "worse than expected." This report is unique among performance measurement initiatives because it explicitly describes efforts to validate the data. As described in Chapter 3, the state sponsored a reabstraction study of 974 AMI patients admitted to California hospitals in 1990–1991. It found variation in the validity and reliability of coding of certain risk factors—even some important acute conditions were poorly coded. California no longer uses these conditions, which are poorly or questionably coded, in its risk-adjustment model. The report presents in a single volume the hospital-specific results, a readable technical description, and hospitals' letters of response (Wilson, Smoley, and Werdegar 1996).

California's effort to validate findings represents a responsible and thoughtful response to concerns about data quality. Viewed as reflecting the state's commitment to provide the most meaningful information on quality of care possible, this comprehensive and publicly released validation is unique among the various initiatives nationwide. New California initiatives, however, are finding a different mix of participants. University investigators are no longer directing the state's report card activities, and a "voluntary" CABG reporting program, using clinical data, is being developed in collaboration with the Pacific Business Group on Health (an employer coalition representing 34 large purchasers). The CABG report will be based on preoperative risk factors using data variables and definitions from the Society of Thoracic Surgery's reporting system. In addition to comparing in-hospital mortality from CABG within participating California hospitals, the Pacific Business Group on Health also plans to look at comparisons with out-of-state facilities.

New York

New York has collected and released risk-adjusted outcomes information that has had a considerable effect, both on the state's providers and policymakers and in the national debate about the merit of this approach. To date, however, New York's activities have focused specifically on one narrowly defined, albeit important, clinical area—cardiac revascularization procedures. This effort has involved considerable research to hone a "home grown" risk-adjustment methodology based on detailed clinical information obtained directly from providers.

The first effort targeted outcomes of CABG surgery, an operation that annually costs the state millions of dollars. In 1988, the Subcommittee of Statistics of the state's Cardiac Surgery Advisory Committee (composed of cardiac surgeons, cardiologists, and epidemiologists) created a patient-specific cardiac surgical report form to be completed at discharge for each CABG operation in New York (Hannan et al. 1990). The Cardiac Surgery Reporting System (CSRS) tried to avoid risk factors used in research studies that might be difficult to collect or quantify, such as ventricular dysfunction and extent of coronary atherosclerosis. Included among the final set of variables are ventricular ejection fraction, > 90 percent narrowing of the left main coronary artery, diabetes mellitus requiring medication, and whether the CABG was a reoperation.

The risk factors included in the CSRS were pilot-tested at three hospitals to evaluate whether they could be collected by cardiac surgery departments in an internally consistent fashion. Using information on common data errors detected during this pilot study, a personal computer program was developed for hospital data entry and to assist hospitals in preparing diskettes for transmission to the state. Logistic regression techniques were used to develop mortality prediction models (Hannan et al. 1990).

Even prior to its public release, New York used these data to compare observed-to-predicted mortality rates, prompting investigations of open-heart surgery practices at some facilities. For example, cardiac surgery was suspended at a hospital with an observed CABG mortality rate of 14.3 percent compared to an expected 3.9 percent following a site visit of the Cardiac Advisory Committee (Hannan et al. 1990, 2772). Interestingly, the first widespread publication of these hospital mortality rates was in a scholarly medical journal, the December 5, 1990, issue of the *Journal of the American Medical Association,* where each of the state's 28 facilities performing CABGs was indicated by a number, not by name (Hannan et al. 1990). This work gained acceptance in the broader scientific community due largely to the apparent rigor of its methods and the unique nature of its clinically detailed database. However, the local response involved cries for identifying these 28 facilities by name, not by number—especially the three that were high-mortality outliers.

Once the existence of these data became public, New York's news media clamored for additional detail, particularly information about mortality rates for individual surgeons—by name. This was a heretical request. Physician-specific mortality rates had never been released in any prior data-gathering initiative around the country, and New York state had not planned to break that precedent. Apart from resistance from the medical profession, there were reasonable statistical arguments that physician-level data might not be stable enough to support sound inferences, due to small numbers of patients. In 1991 the New York state Supreme Court, in reaction to a Freedom of Information Act lawsuit by *Newsday,* forced the state to release physician-specific information on CABG mortality rates collected by the Department of Health (DOH). In court, the DOH had tried to prevent release of the data, claiming that it could be misinterpreted by the public and that it violated physician privacy (Koska 1992). The court ruled that release of the data was in the public's best interest and that physicians' expectations of privacy were unrealistic. Physician-specific mortality rates for 140 CABG surgeons were first published in *Newsday* on December 18, 1991 (Zinman 1991), prompting a stormy response from physicians.

On January 1, 1991, New York established a new registry for patients undergoing percutaneous transluminal coronary angioplasty (PTCA). The data elements representing preprocedural risk factors were again suggested by a subcommittee of the Cardiac Advisory Committee of New York (Hannan et al. 1992a). The cardiac catheterization laboratories at the hospital where the PTCA is performed must complete a two-page form documenting patient, hospital, and physician identifiers, preprocedural risk factors, and in-hospital outcomes of the PTCA. The person performing the PTCA and the cardiac catheterization laboratory are responsible for the accuracy and completeness of this information, which is transmitted on diskette to the state DOH for analysis.

At first, these New York statistics provoked an uproar, but they have since gained widespread acceptance, even within the provider community. One compelling reason for this recognition is that CABG mortality has fallen in New York state despite increases in patient severity (Hannan et al. 1994a, 1994b, 1995). The risk-adjusted mortality rate for isolated CABG surgery fell from 4.17 percent in 1989 to 2.45 percent in 1992, a decline of 41 percent (Hannan et al. 1994a, 765). Mortality rates dropped between

1989 and 1992 at 27 of the 30 New York hospitals performing CABGs. One partial explanation for this drop was the exodus of low-volume surgeons with very high mortality profiles; some hospitals restricted the privileges of such surgeons after the *Newsday* surgeon-specific publication (Hannan et al. 1995). Quality improvement efforts within hospitals also probably contributed to the mortality rate decline (Hannan et al. 1994b).

A 1996 law supported by the New York Public Interest Research Group will expand the state's reporting requirement beyond CABGs and PTCAs to a range of conditions. The measure, part of a law establishing a new competitive financing structure for New York hospitals, requires the state to publish hospital report cards by 1998, including outcomes and cost information across various medical and surgical conditions. The Medical Society of New York State successfully lobbied against releasing figures by individual physicians, arguing that small numbers would compromise making inferences about doctor-specific performance. At this time, it is unclear how the state will accomplish this mandate ("New York Requires" 1996).

Florida

Florida has tried to balance the costs of data collection against the information to be gained. In the mid-1980s, Florida became interested in comparing performance of providers, but concerns about the expense of data argued against an ambitious undertaking, such as Pennsylvania's approach. As in California, Florida therefore concentrated on using existing data. For example, in 1991, the Florida Health Care Cost Containment Board released "Hospital Costs Got You Puzzled? A Guide to Average Hospital Charges," a booklet derived from administrative data routinely submitted by hospitals. The Board used refined DRGs to lump cases into four severity classes (uncomplicated, moderately complicated, severely complicated, and catastrophically complicated), looking at 12 common conditions.

Questions about the cost of data followed Florida into its healthcare reform effort, one of the most significant in the United States. Florida's Health Care and Insurance Reform Act of 1993, signed by Governor Lawton Chiles, grouped employers and Medicaid recipients into community health purchasing alliances to stimulate competition among providers based on cost and quality. Severity measurement became a central concern in implementing this ambitious scheme: Competition must be fed by data.

One proposed administrative rule pertained to data-reporting requirements. According to the Florida Hospital Association (FHA), the language of the proposed rule favored MedisGroups over rival systems. The FHA reportedly threatened to file a court challenge to halt the adoption of a MedisGroups mandate, warning that MedisGroups was too expensive and would "burden hospitals with unreasonable costs" (Greene 1993b). An FHA representative cited both the high initial capital investment required for MedisGroups and the need for increased staff, estimating that large hospitals might have to hire up to four employees to abstract data. The FHA estimated total costs for MedisGroups at $10 million to $50 million per year. An official of the state's Agency for Health Care Administration (AHCA) acknowledged that the rules were written to support MedisGroups because of the success some Orlando hospitals had with the system (see below).

Meanwhile, in contrast to providers in many other states, the Florida hospital community had been proactive in efforts to produce data for healthcare consumers. Anticipating the desire for outcomes information, the FHA had earlier pursued its own initiative to release risk-adjusted outcome data. According to an FHA vice president, "We hope this effort will assist the Health Care Board. If they adopt a comparative system, it would be good if they used the same one" (Gardner 1993b). The APR-DRGs method was selected for risk adjustment. In its 1993 challenge to a MedisGroups mandate, the FHA touted its approach as less expensive.

Florida's Center for Health Statistics pursued its own approach based on UB-82 data, creating a draft consumer guide to hospital performance that was unveiled to hospitals in January 1994 (Associated Press 1994). The two-year-old data precipitated a ruckus in the hospital community: Orlando hospitals in particular had closely monitored their own performance, and the state's numbers did not match the hospitals' own statistics. Hospital representatives were concerned because the state was unable to provide details about the source of the numbers.

Because of this furor and preoccupation with the 1994 gubernatorial campaign (won ultimately by Chiles), the AHCA delayed release of its first consumer report. The hospital community thus appeared effective in challenging the state's numbers, and the state agency was put on the defensive. A spokesperson for the AHCA admitted that evaluating hospital performance was complicated and methods were evolving, and indicated that the state was trying to take advantage of the latest techniques ("Hospital Report Cards" 1995).

In early 1996, AHCA finally released its report card listing mortality, LOS, and hospital charges for 15 categories of care in institutions statewide. AHCA had postponed publication of its report for over a year to include the latest version of APR-DRGs, as well as format modifications requested by hospitals ("Florida Report Card" 1996). Nevertheless, the procedures for releasing the report generated controversy—many hospitals had just 24 hours to review the data. A FHA spokesperson noted, "You can talk about the methodology all you want, but until you see the data you can't say anything" ("Florida Report Card" 1996).

It remains unclear whether Florida's hospital report card will inform purchasing the way originally intended.

Local Performance Measurement Initiatives

Regardless of activities at the state level, numerous local initiatives have sprung up—from Muskegon, Michigan, to St. Louis, Missouri, to Houston, Texas—to compare risk-adjusted outcomes across regional providers. With few exceptions, these efforts have been stimulated by businesses frustrated over mounting costs and the lack of comparative information about providers. An interesting phenomenon has been the aggressive marketing of some vendors of severity measures directly to large companies, bypassing providers altogether. In contrast, businesses and providers in other communities are working together to develop outcome measurement approaches acceptable and useful to both. This section describes only a few of these many initiatives.

Cleveland, Ohio

Cleveland's experience offers an example of businesses and providers collaborating productively to develop their own strategy for meaningful monitoring of outcomes. The Cleveland Health Quality Choice (CHQC) program was formed in 1989, representing a voluntary coalition of hospitals, physicians, and businesses—including Cleveland Tomorrow (chief executive officers from 50 major businesses in the city), the Greater Cleveland Hospital Association, the Health Action Council (an association of healthcare purchasers), the Academy of Medicine, and the Council of Smaller Enterprises. The coalition was created to address concerns about healthcare costs that continued to rise without objective means to measure the quality of care provided. The initial challenge of the CHQC program was to find fair and reliable measures with which business leaders and healthcare providers would feel comfortable and would find useful. After much discussion, the decision was made to focus on three broad areas:

- ICU outcomes;
- outcomes of general medical and surgical care and obstetrics; and
- patient satisfaction.

Outcome measures focused primarily on severity-adjusted in-hospital deaths and lengths of stay. To examine ICU outcomes, CHQC contracted with APACHE Medical Systems. Using the APACHE III risk-adjustment methodology, predicted numbers of ICU deaths were compared to expected numbers of deaths. Outcomes were also assessed for several medical conditions (heart attack, congestive heart failure, stroke, pneumonia, and chronic obstructive pulmonary disease), obstetrics, and eight surgical procedures. To perform the risk adjustment for these medical, surgical, and obstetrical analyses, CHQC representatives first considered existing severity measures (such as MedisGroups) before deciding to develop their own. Working with Dr. Michael Pine, a Chicago-based physician consultant, medical and business advisory groups developed severity measures for each condition under study. Cleveland officials believed that this local input, especially from the medical community, was critical to ensuring the acceptance of the CHQC findings as clinically credible. This risk-adjustment method is known Cleveland Hospital Outcomes Indicators of Care Evaluations (CHOICE). They concede, however, that pursuing intensive collaboration has taken time. "We've made decisions based on consensus," said Dr. Dwain L. Harper, CHQC executive director. "That takes longer" (Kenkel 1993).

Early data from the CHQC initiative were released to hospitals, many of which used the data to identify areas needing improvement. Anecdotal information suggests that this introspection was helpful to some hospitals in improving patient care procedures. The first CHQC report, "The Cleveland-Area Hospital Quality Measurement and Patient Satisfaction Report," was publicly released on April 28, 1993, and contained 261 measurements from 29 Cleveland hospitals. Observed ICU mortality was 11.0 percent compared to a predicted 12.5 percent across the city (PR Newswire Association 1993a). The amount of cost savings from Cleveland's initiative was unclear.

In January 1995, the fourth Cleveland hospital outcomes report was released, the first such report including three-year trend data. It showed that mortality for selected medical diagnoses at the 29 participating hospitals fell from 7.85 patients per 100 in 1991 to 7.04 patients in 1993 (Strickland 1995). Dr. Harper noted, "We'd like to take a small part of the credit (for the continued drop in mortality) but there are so many forces and factors involved that it's hard to sort out who's responsible" (Strickland 1995). Michael Pine & Associates is developing six severity-adjusted complication measures to add to CHQC's reports. In addition, after studying functional status measures, CHQC decided to use disease-specific measures rather than the SF-36, a generic approach (Strickland 1995). Initial functional status assessments will target laminectomy, hysterectomy, and AMI.

Throughout most of 1996, however, much of the public debate about Cleveland's program involved addressing public assertions by the Cleveland Clinic that the methods were hopelessly flawed. Since the outset, Cleveland Clinic officials had protested that their patient population had special characteristics that were not captured by the CHQC risk adjustment. The debate flared in a variety of public forums. For example, in a published interview, a Cleveland Clinic Foundation cardiologist argued:

At one point, the Cleveland Clinic received poor ratings in heart failure, even though we have very sick patients who receive left ventricular assist devices and heart transplants, and most of the other hospitals did not even determine the patients' ejection fraction. With the garbage that goes into the model for risk adjustment, how can outcomes be compared in a meaningful fashion? (Vogel and Topol 1996, 127)

The Cleveland Clinic moved to suspend CHQC until it could be substantially revised. However, several important representatives of other major academic institutions in Cleveland backed CHQC. In addition, the *Plain Dealer*, Cleveland's major newspaper, was instrumental in supporting the report card initiative. As of October 1996, the Cleveland Clinic was still participating in the program but continued to raise concerns about the inadequacy of the risk adjustment for their patients.

The Health Action Council of Northeast Ohio, comprised of 140 large businesses, announced in 1996 that there had been enough longitudinal information on hospital performance to guide contracting decisions (Mazzolini 1996). The Health Action Council plans to establish a limited purchasing program that will contract directly with "centers of excellence," such as heart surgery or joint replacements programs, at selected hospitals. Invitations to apply for direct contracting were sent to only a handful of the hospitals participating in CHQC. Council members are expected to choose hospitals for certain procedures, such as CABG surgery and hip replacement, and increase cost-sharing for employees who go to other facilities (Mazzolini 1996). To continue to qualify for the contracts, hospitals must remain in the CHQC program—to ensure that, as costs are cut, quality does not slip.

Cincinnati, Ohio

Cincinnati provides an example of a powerful business community imposing its own specific severity measurement approach on questioning providers. As one local provider noted, "Health care in Cincinnati has been driven by business" (Ashbrook 1995). There was little appearance of collaboration between purchasers and providers: The business leaders clearly had the advantage and used it. Four large, self-insured employers (Cincinnati Bell Telephone, General Electric Aircraft Engines, the Kroger Company, and Procter and Gamble) encompassed about 13 percent of the population in the city (USGAO 1994b, 7). These employers wielded their combined purchasing power to get 14 local hospitals to submit their data for analysis using Iaméter's Acuity Index Method (AIM) (Woolsey 1993c). As described in Chapter 1, AIM is a system based on administrative data, developed empirically to predict length of hospital stays. Cincinnati hospitals clearly were put into a position of competing with each other, and the four large firms used these data to negotiate lower rates for health coverage.

The first year of data (1991) showed wide variations across Cincinnati hospitals in costs and lengths of stays. For example, across the 14 Cincinnati hospitals, average AIM-adjusted charges varied by about $900 for obstetrical cases, $3,300 for circulatory cases, and $4,600 for musculoskeletal cases (USGAO 1994b, 7). This information stimulated changes in practice patterns that some observers claim saved $75 million in 1992 (Woolsey 1993c). The employers were thrilled with the results. For example, Cincinnati Bell claimed to have 5 percent lower healthcare costs in 1992 without changes in employee demographics or the healthcare package. In contrast, the hospitals appeared resigned to the inevitability of this scrutiny and tried to respond productively to maintain their competitive position and even viability. For example, a physician at Jewish Hospitals of Cincinnati observed that hospitals are committed to cost controls, despite being put in direct competition. However, he predicted that several hospitals would close due to the initiative (Woolsey 1993b). In 1995, to bolster their competitive position, Jewish Hospitals challenged other Cincinnati institutions to produce *public* report cards. The Iaméter data had not yet been made public, and Jewish Hospitals—struggling for business while other hospitals were merging—felt that releasing their data publicly was the only way to be recognized (Bonfield 1995).

One interesting by-product of Cincinnati's Iaméter initiative was the development of a highly competitive home health services market in Cincinnati. As hospitals shortened length of stay, patients moved to home healthcare. "It goes back to the Iaméter study in early '90s," said one home healthcare leader. "That study was a big impetus for healthcare change here" (Ashbrook 1995). Another home health provider concurred: "It's stemming from changes being made in hospitals . . . Patients are being sent home earlier" (Ashbrook 1995). Hospitals are now setting up their own home care programs. Thus, the impact on aggregate healthcare costs in Cincinnati remains unclear.

Orlando, Florida

Central Florida employers began monitoring healthcare data relatively early. In 1983, the Central Florida Healthcare Coalition established a nonprofit clearinghouse for information on cost and quality of healthcare services, which evolved into a vehicle for linking employers to purchase better healthcare coverage, comprising 60 companies with 120,000 employees (Clements 1993). The Orlando group joined with Tampa's Florida Gulf Coast Coalition to create the Employers Purchasing Alliance (EPA) a nationally prominent local business initiative, touted as a model of the managed competition brand of health reform (Greene 1993a). The EPA encompassed 355 companies of all sizes (including Walt Disney; General Mills Restaurants; GTE Corporation; Tampa Electric Company; and various government entities, such as the city of Orlando), representing 2 million beneficiaries in 32 of Florida's 67 counties.

Significant savings were achieved by negotiating with providers for volume discounts. But according to Frank Brocato, director of the Tampa Gulf Coast Health Coalition and a founder of EPA, half of the savings are attributable to encouraging local hospitals to adopt MedisGroups voluntarily (Greene 1993a). As of August 1993, 15 hospitals used MedisGroups in Orlando, some claiming significant savings as a result. Brocato claimed that the alliance's MedisGroups initiative was unique. "Hospitals and physicians who normally consider themselves competitors are working together with us, because this is a consumer-driven product, designed by the consumers and the providers and the payers" (Clements 1993).

Unlike in Pennsylvania, where MedisGroups data are used primarily for public comparisons rather than internal hospital self-examination, the Orlando effort started by using MedisGroups in much the same way individual facilities would—to determine areas that could be improved, thus saving money while maintaining quality. For example, the Orlando Regional Medical Center, one of the first to implement MedisGroups, observed a 2 percent decrease in the average cost per patient discharge in 1992, compared to an increase of 9 percent in 1991. Roy Wright, associated with this Orlando facility, claimed that MedisGroups helped the hospital target where improvements could occur, and he credits the EPA's approach for facilitating this cost-saving introspection. "The coalition took a non-threatening approach," he said. "They said they weren't as concerned about the numbers as much as what we were doing about improving them" (Greene 1993a). Nevertheless, Wright conceded, "We are working under the assumption that, at some point in time, purchasers will use this information to decide who is in their [healthcare] delivery network—and who isn't" (Yasuda 1992).

Recently, cracks have begun to show, and purchasers clearly appear ready to compare hospitals. Columbia Park Healthcare System, central Florida's network of Columbia/HCA Healthcare Corporation (the nation's largest hospital chain), refused to install MedisGroups and was removed from the Central Florida Healthcare Coalition's "provider council" (Oliver 1995). Columbia Park claimed it would have cost $2.5 million over three years to implement MedisGroups, and they argued that their own internal quality management system was as good. MedisGroups "quite frankly was redundant and not value-added," asserted a Columbia spokesperson (Oliver 1995). The head of the Coalition argued that employers want to make "apples-to-apples" comparisons across hospitals and that, without a consistent measurement approach, purchasers would now be "in the dark" about Columbia's relative performance (Oliver 1995).

Rochester, New York

In the late 1980s, five members of the Rochester Area Hospitals Corporation (RAHC), a consortium of hospitals in upstate New York, initiated a bold experiment that was to use MedisGroups risk-adjusted outcome information to tie reimbursement to hospital quality. The program had three major components: efforts to improve quality at RAHC members through sharing information, educational activities to enhance quality improvement, and a financial incentive to prompt behavior changes. It was "designed as a system to improve overall system performance through cooperative analysis in a positive, educational environment, with awards for high quality performance . . . not used to penalize hospitals but rather to provide both the incentive and the analytic tools required to improve quality of care" (Hartman, Mukamel, and Panzer 1990, 253). Hospital staff received information comparing their facility's performance both to other RAHC hospitals and to the MedisGroups national database.

This program, however, had a rocky course. One major problem was delays in obtaining the MedisGroups data from hospitals, attributable largely to difficulties recruiting, training, and retaining MedisGroups abstractors. "The MedisGroups system is very labor intensive and can average upwards of 30 minutes per chart in a tertiary hospital" (Hartman, Mukamel, and Panzer 1990, 255). Training abstractors to meet the Medis-Groups accuracy targets required three months. Given that 47,000 chart reviews were needed per year citywide, 15 to 20 qualified MedisGroups abstractors were necessary. In Rochester, with about 1 million residents, hospitals had difficulty recruiting adequate numbers of appropriate persons to perform the reviews. In addition, hospitals had trouble retaining these reviewers once recruited and trained. Some abstractors resigned, citing frustration with the structured and detailed nature of the MedisGroups reviews (Hartman, Mukamel, and Panzer 1990, 256).

Another problem involved the meaning of the MedisGroups morbidity score—a second measure of patient severity about one week into the hospital stay. MedisGroups morbidity ratings were to be used as an important outcome measure in assessing hospital quality (Hartman, Mukamel, and Panzer 1990). However, Rochester physicians were concerned that the morbidity rating did not adequately account for clinical derangements that were present on admission. This could unfairly penalize hospitals treating patients with serious illnesses resulting in prolonged derangement of physiologic findings (such as renal failure patients with chronically elevated creatinine and blood urea nitrogen levels). Because of these concerns, RAHC eliminated the morbidity score from plans for assessing quality, leaving MedisGroups severity-adjusted mortality rates as the quality measure.

In 1992, the RAHC discontinued this experiment. "The quality was pretty even among the institutions," reported a RAHC spokesperson. "Also, they didn't feel the [quality] assessment technology was really advanced and updated enough to warrant a transfer of funds" (Gardner 1992b). Some individual hospitals retained MedisGroups for their own internal activities, but hospitals stopped collecting MedisGroups data for the payment experiment.

St. Louis, Missouri

The Greater St. Louis Healthcare Alliance was founded in July 1992 in response to growing concerns of purchasers and providers about escalating costs and the need to improve the efficiency and effectiveness of the St. Louis healthcare delivery system. The alliance was voluntary, involving 29 hospitals, the Metropolitan St. Louis Hospital Council, the St. Louis Metropolitan Medical Society, managed care organizations, and a number of other groups.

After studying different quality measurement options and other programs around the country (especially Cleveland's initiative), the St. Louis Alliance decided that it could not rely solely on administrative or billing data for its hospital performance measures, as these sources were not viewed as clinically meaningful. Therefore, in addition to administrative sources, they decided to collect clinical data elements from medical records and to conduct telephone interviews with patients to evaluate satisfaction.

The performance measures included LOS, cost, mortality rates, patient satisfaction, and Cesarean section rates. Clinical data were abstracted from medical records by St. Anthony's Consulting, Inc., and Dun & Bradstreet Healthcare Information developed the severity adjustment models and calculated the clinical performance measures. The clinical data abstraction protocol was similar to that developed for Cleveland. The clinical conditions included in the first round of evaluations were AMI, congestive heart failure, pneumonia, CABG surgery, PTCA, hysterectomy, Cesarean section, and vaginal delivery. The initial evaluation was produced in 1995 and included patients discharged from St. Louis hospitals from October 1992 through September 1993.

Telephone surveys were conducted by Datastat, Inc., with over 12,700 patients between January 1994 and January 1995. Patients were randomly sampled from participating hospitals. The interview used a patient satisfaction instrument from the Boston-based Picker Institute, a survey that asked not only global satisfaction questions but also sought patient reports about specific areas of care (e.g., whether patients were told about medication side effects, whether their preferences for care were respected, whether their pain was controlled adequately). The Picker Institute risk adjusted its survey outcomes based on patients' self-reported global health status.

Other Performance Measurement Initiatives

A number of nongovernmental groups have also required severity information for monitoring risk-adjusted outcomes. For example, Minnesota Blue Cross/Blue Shield requires severity information produced using MedisGroups. The Minnesota program sets hospital payment rates based on differences in patient risks and resource needs and rewards good outcomes (Oszustowics 1992). According to a Minnesota Blue Cross spokesperson, this approach "has saved us money . . . it has more appropriately distributed our resources" (Anderson 1994). The 1989 Participating Hospital Agreement with Michigan Blue Cross and Blue Shield stipulated adoption of hospital-level quality measures, with the ultimate goal that "high quality" hospitals receive a 1 percent bonus, whereas "low quality" hospitals receive 1 percent or 2 percent less than requested. Risk-adjusted outcomes measurement was a cornerstone of their quality assessment, with risk assessed by Disease Staging using administrative data.

The Northern New England Cardiovascular Disease Study Group is a cooperative project of all five hospitals performing CABG surgery in Maine, New Hampshire, and Vermont (O'Connor et al. 1991, 1992, 1996). As described in Chapter 6, after developing a risk-adjustment model and clinical prediction rule, observed and predicted in-hospital mortality rates were compared among the five medical centers and among surgeons. After adjusting for clinical risk, significant variability persisted among both medical centers. To understand these differences further, the group compared processes of care and conducted site visits at the five medical centers. Considerable variation was observed in many dimensions of process of care across the five sites, initiating a dialogue among practitioners and internal quality improvement projects. Subsequent measures of adverse outcome, including risk-adjusted mortality rates, have been reported to decrease after process improvement (O'Connor et al. 1996).

A few prominent performance measurement initiatives are described below.

Joint Commission on Accreditation of Healthcare Organizations

The Joint Commission on Accreditation of Healthcare Organizations (JCAHO), which accredits 5,200 hospitals and 3,000 other organizations around the country, shifted from its traditional emphasis on structural characteristics of facilities to outcomes and measures of clinical care. Ten quality indicators were initially created for anesthesia and obstetrics, and others became available for cardiovascular disease, oncology, and trauma care (Oberman 1993). The Indicator Measurement System incorporates risk adjustment into some of its performance measures. For example, comparisons of hospital Cesarean section rates control for a variety of factors, such as fetal distress and premature rupture of the membranes.

Late in 1994, JCAHO began making reports on individual hospitals available to the public for $30 per report. The report provide scores in 28 performance areas, including staff training, infection control, and emergency services. Initial reviews by some in the hospital community were cautious. The major concern involved how to interpret causes of less-than-perfect scores: For example, they could be due to problems with actual patient care or with documentation practices—two causes with disparate implications for patients. "At best, these reports will not be helpful," stated a vice president at the FHA. "At worst, they may very well be misleading" (Landry 1994). Others scoff at the hospitals' concerns. As Dr. Sidney Wolfe, director of Public Citizen's Health Research Group, observed, "Remember the accreditation process is such that rarely do hospitals flunk" (Kong 1994a). Over 99 percent of hospitals are accredited by JCAHO; less than 50 hospitals lost accreditation in 1993 (Boodman 1994).

Private Organizations

A number of private companies also produce comparative hospital performance data, some at their own initiative. These data are then sold along with consulting services to individual hospitals, payors, or other groups, or distributed within locales targeted by the data, as in these two examples.

A list of 100 top hospitals was identified in the "Benchmarks for Success" project by the Chicago-based William M. Mercer, Inc., Health Care Consulting and the Baltimore-based HCIA, Inc., a healthcare information company. The study used routinely available discharge abstract and other administrative data from HCFA and encompassed 5,600 hospitals nationwide ("Two Local Hospitals Among Top Performers" 1994). It evaluated mortality, infection rates, and financial stability. A Mercer spokesperson noted, "If all hospitals were able to perform at the level of these benchmark facilities, the results for the healthcare industry would be dramatic; hospital charges would decline by $40 billion; mortality rates would drop 12%, and morbidity rates would drop 13%" ("2 Local Hospitals on Nation's Top 100" 1994).

Dun & Bradstreet publishes guides to selected medical procedures for hospitals within localities and distributes them through shops, such as grocery stores, and on "Good Neighbor" display boards (Oliver 1994a). For example, a guide for metropolitan Orlando looked at nine local hospitals, and such conditions as AMI, hip replacement, and coronary bypass surgery (Bellandi 1994). It was based on hospital discharge abstract data obtained from the state. When these guides first appeared in Orlando, hospital officials reportedly had not yet reviewed them and refused to comment on them publicly. However, a spokesperson for Dun & Bradstreet indicated that his company was trying to sell hospitals computer software to help them analyze such records (Oliver 1994a).

These private initiatives are also scrutinized by providers. For instance, Dun & Bradstreet produced comparable reports for Tampa Bay, Miami–Fort Lauderdale, Jacksonville, and Sarasota–Fort Myers at the company's expense, according to a company vice president (Bellandi 1994). The reports carried a disclaimer indicating that the data were two years old, and individual hospital performance might have changed. Nevertheless, a company spokesperson stated, "We'd be happy to walk through the actual numbers with anyone who's interested in it. The numbers are correct" (Bellandi 1994). Certain hospitals, however, reported errors in the reports' data. The FHA apparently "hit the roof" over these reports furnished in grocery stores ("Florida Report Card" 1996).

More consumer-oriented organizations also disseminate comparative reports (USGAO 1994a). For example, for 15 years, *Consumers' Checkbook* has published information on health plans targeting consumers, although its effect is unclear—health plans typically do not cooperate with it. *Health Pages* publishes information on physicians' board certification and charges.

Measuring Performance of Health Plans

As noted above, most of the initial programs to compare provider performance focused on hospitalizations, examining mortality, LOS, and charges. While these are clearly important outcomes, they are fairly limited, especially from many consumers' perspectives—death is not an immediate prospect for most persons, and the public may be more interested in functional outcomes or quality of life. In addition, most persons, particularly those of working age, are not hospitalized during a given year. Outcomes relating to outpatient and preventive services are therefore more applicable to their concerns. Especially as managed care increasingly constricts the reimbursable services available to consumers, the burden of proof about quality shifts somewhat from the provider alone to encompass the health plan as well.

Some organizations are beginning to address these issues. Some health plans, such as United HealthCare Corporation, Kaiser Permanente

Northern California Region, and U.S. Healthcare have published their own report cards. (USGAO 1994a). Most have started with processes of care, which are easier to measure than risk-adjusted outcomes. HEDIS is a standardized report on health plan performance developed and disseminated through the National Committee for Quality Assurance (NCQA), an independent organization whose board is composed of purchaser, health plan, and consumer representatives (Iglehart 1996). HCFA also works closely with NCQA to develop HEDIS measures explicitly for Medicare and Medicaid enrollees (USGAO 1995).

HEDIS 2.5, a recent version, examined 60 health plan performance indicators, although most pertained to administrative issues and utilization. NCQA took the unusual step of contracting with an independent organization to verify HEDIS data collected during a nationwide report card project involving 21 health plans (USGAO 1994a, 47). The new HEDIS version 3.0, released in draft form in July 1996, included new, primarily process-driven, performance measures such as immunization rates for childhood infections, influenza vaccinations for high-risk adults, screening for cervical cancer, eye exams for persons with diabetes mellitus, and appropriate treatment of otitis media in children. One outcome measure—the fraction of elderly enrollees reporting a change in their health status—would apparently "be adjusted using accepted mathematical models" controlling for "demographics and chronic conditions" (National Committee for Quality Assurance 1996, 155).

In 1995, consumer and business groups, as well as HCFA, created the Foundation for Accountability (FACCT) (USGAO 1996). According to one FACCT board member, "Its philosophy puts the consumer at the center of things. The potential of FACCT is enormous" (Cunningham 1996, 1). The first set of FACCT performance measures, released in late 1996, contained measure sets for breast cancer, major depressive disorder, diabetes, health risk behavior, and health plan satisfaction. The central measure for breast cancer will be five-year, disease-free survival, stratified by stage at diagnosis ("FACCT Proposes Stratified Reporting" 1996). For some of its outcome-based quality indicators, however, FACCT advocates releasing "raw" data, without risk adjustment, pending derivation of appropriate measures of risk.

Exactly how NCQA and FACCT will interrelate on measuring health plan performance is unclear. The rhetoric surrounding FACCT clearly advocates outcome measures over the focus of NCQA on process indicators. Although employers are attracted by FACCT's focus on concerns that they believe matter to their employees, others note methodological concerns. For example, the executive vice president of the Kaiser Family Foundation raised questions about small sample sizes and the inability to adjust adequately for patient risk (Prager 1996b). Others worry that NCQA and FACCT will place dueling data reporting demands on health plans. NCQA's vice president for performance measurement articulated these concerns: "We made the effort to communicate unequivocally to FACCT that we wanted them to be part of our process and not go off on their own creating confusion and excess burden on plans . . . There might be some anger if plans perceive there is not standardization out there" (Prager 1996b, 30). Dr. David Eddy, who works with NCQA, reportedly observed that FACCT's measures "are not ready for prime time" (Freudenheim 1996, D5). Risk adjustment appears central to the public methodological debates between NCQA and FACCT.

Views of Stakeholders

Whether at the federal, state, or local levels, much of the debate about severity information has encompassed similar themes. This section outlines the perspectives of the different stakeholders in this field and to sketch common goals, approaches, and concerns.

Providers' Perspectives

Having their clinical results publicly displayed is a new experience for healthcare providers—hospitals and doctors alike—but one that is likely to persist. As Blumenthal and Epstein (1996, 1329) observed:

> . . . It seems fair to say that in the area of quality measurement and reporting, physicians can expect little relief from the feeling that they increasingly work in a fishbowl and are being judged by groups and measures with which they have little familiarity. Managing this reality is one of the greatest challenges confronting the profession at the current time.

Not surprisingly, this public scrutiny and its sometimes very tangible results (e.g., on insurance contracts, access to patients) have aroused concern in the provider community. At the outset, however, it is important to note that some provider groups have proactively monitored and publicized their outcomes, believing that this will give them the competitive edge. An example involves a network of high-volume cardiac surgeons in 40 cities who market, directly to big companies, standardized services at lower costs but equal quality. These surgeons believe that, by assessing their results and standardizing their services, they can improve their position in a highly competitive but lucrative cardiac surgery marketplace. "Physicians have been slow to react, but we are the major drivers of costs and quality in the healthcare system," observed an Atlanta physician who heads the network. "Physicians must be brought into the process" (Winslow 1993b). In addition, there is a belief that physicians will respond productively to clinically credible information constructively presented. "I don't know any doctors that won't respond to hard data and change their practice patterns as long as it's part of a good-faith effort to improve average performance," stated the head of Fairview Hospital and Healthcare Services in Minneapolis.

The dynamics are different, however, when the driving force comes from outside the provider community and there is a sense (or presumption) that the data could be used punitively. As described above, a number of these outcomes measurement initiatives have involved close collaboration between the purchasers and providers, but others have engendered a less collegial tone. Again, a problem in this debate is that the stakes are so high: Providers feel that their livelihoods are at risk, while purchasers also assert that their financial viability is compromised by escalating healthcare costs. A sense of resignation pervades some provider comments. As an Indiana hospital executive observed, "There really are no direct measures of quality. I try to supply whatever is asked for, but I warn employers that mortality rates, readmission rates, and such things are not direct measures of quality" (Leavenworth 1995).

While providers are increasingly coming to terms with these data, several common themes typify their concerns.

Concerns about the risk-adjustment methodology

Many providers feel that the risk-adjustment measures are inadequate. A typical criticism was articulated by a retired cardiac surgeon from a teaching hospital in Rochester, New York: "When you walk the floor and see patients who are being operated on, you realize that their condition is not always something that can be quantified on paper" (Zinman 1992). Physicians are often concerned about how individual patients may differ from the group and whether the severity measure is sensitive to these individual instances. As a physician from an Orlando hospital observed, "Practicing medicine is not a science; it's an art. You cannot practice by numbers; you cannot use an average approach to treat all patients because every patient is different" (Yasuda 1992). Physicians, in particular, are often uncomfortable with summarizing a patient's clinical presentation in a single score.

In its study of report card initiatives in Cleveland, Cincinnati, and Orlando, the GAO observed, "Hospitals we visited were wary that the severity adjustment methodology is often a 'black box' because little independent validation occurs" (USGAO 1994b, 14). This concern motivated Cleveland providers to work with Michael Pine & Associates to develop their own severity measures. Nonetheless, some Cleveland providers still raise concerns about their home-grown approach—for example, that it fails to control properly for characteristics of acute hospital transfers.

The Cleveland Clinic, in particular, has protested publicly that its patient population is special and cannot be quantified using standard techniques. In California, the major response of hospitals thus far to the state's report card involves bolstering documentation and coding practices rather than examining their quality of care (Romano et al. 1995). Florida hospitals also seemed to concentrate on scrutinizing coding, claiming that undercoding caused some facilities to appear to have higher death rates than expected (Greene 1996). A mail survey in Pennsylvania found that 77 percent of cardiologists and 85 percent of cardiothoracic surgeons felt that the state's CABG "risk-adjustment methods are inadequate to compare surgeons fairly" (Schneider and Epstein 1996, 254).

Some providers raise very specific concerns about the particular severity measure. For example, certain tertiary teaching hospitals in Minnesota were concerned that, as applied by Blue Cross/Blue Shield, the MedisGroups-generated data did not control adequately for severity of patients who were stabilized prior to transfer from other acute care facilities. These hospitals accepted patients from outlying facilities whose physiologic parameters (e.g., pulse, blood pressure, arterial oxygenation) were stabilized prior to transfer, therefore resulting in low MedisGroups admission scores. Nevertheless, these high-risk patients often did poorly, an outcome contrary to expectations suggested by their low initial admission severity scores. Hospitals in Pennsylvania were particularly concerned that the PHC4 reports did not adjust for "do not resuscitate" orders—a practice that varies across hospitals (Burling 1994).

Specific criticisms are contained in letters of response from individual providers that accompany public release of the data. For example, Pennsylvania's PHC4 hospital- and physician-specific report on CABG mortality and average charges includes three slender volumes: the "Consumer Guide"; a technical report detailing the methodology; and a volume containing letters written by doctors and hospitals. Providing the technical details and hospital responses in separate volumes makes it less likely that consumers would obtain and read this information.

The 1995 "Consumer Guide" volume indicated that the Hospital of the University of Pennsylvania (HUP) treated 227 patients in 1993 and had a higher mortality rate than expected (12 deaths compared to an expected 2 to 11 deaths), with average charges of $86,509 (PHC4 1995, 15). A letter of response from HUP's executive director criticized the PHC4 CABG risk model for failing to recognize that 52.4 percent of HUP's CABG patients were transferred from other hospitals, 5 percent coming from hospitals with their own open-heart surgery programs. He noted that 11.4 percent of HUP's CABG patients had severity ratings of 3 or 4, compared to a statewide average of 7.1 percent. The CEO of Graduate Hospital, which had average CABG charges of $102,637, argued that charges give a false and misleading image of what hospitals actually received for performing CABG operations. In concurrence, the GAO noted in its study of three report card initiatives that charges do not indicate what was actually paid—"several employers participating in the coalitions [they] visited had managed care plans receiving 20- to 40-percent discounts on hospital charges" (USGAO 1994b, 13).

In Pennsylvania and Iowa (both states that have released Medis-Groups-based data), hospitals with lower-than-expected mortality and low costs are typically not academic institutions (Rubin 1993), which has led community hospitals to challenge the position of tertiary teaching institutions as the "high quality" provider. For example, Bryn Mawr Hospital, a 393-bed facility in suburban Philadelphia, noted that its CABG mortality was within the expected range but that its average 1990 charges, at $49,000, were much lower than those of HUP, then $79,000 (Rubin 1993). Representatives from academic facilities generally responded that the risk adjustment was inadequate.

Some providers raise concerns that risk measures pick up differences in local documentation practices, rather than true differences in patient severity. They also recognize that "surgeons might 'game' (alter) the system by entering more high-risk data about their patients" (Topol and Califf 1994, 67). Green and Wintfeld (1995) argued that this happened in New York, although officials there attributed apparent changes in prevalence of reported risk factors to refinements of data definitions over time (Chassin, Hannan, and DeBuono 1996). New York has periodically audited the quality of risk-factor reporting and has occasionally required hospitals to recode data (Hannan 1994a). California's retrospective coding validation project found that coding differences, including coding of risk factors not justified by the clinical evidence, accounted for some of the variability across hospitals in their risk-adjusted AMI mortality rates (Wilson, Smoley, and Werdegar 1996).

Some initiatives have tried to develop methodologically rigorous risk-adjustment approaches, believing that increasing the credibility of methods will enhance their ability to motivate improvement. An example is New York's CABG and PTCA risk-adjustment methodologies that were published separately in the *Journal of the American Medical Association* (Hannan et al. 1990, 1992a). Data for New York's models come directly from surgeons or providers (e.g., cardiac catheterization laboratories). According to Dr. Mark Chassin, New York's former health commissioner, the risk adjustment is so "scientifically sound" that providers stopped criticizing it and started using the information to direct improvements (Oberman 1992, 24). However, as suggested above, anecdotal evidence hints that documentation of some patient risk factors can be manipulated by surgeons (e.g., New York Heart Association functional class assignments) (Green and

Wintfeld 1995). Unfortunately, the reliability of some of these risk factors cannot be assessed by re-reviewing medical records. Unlike abstracting laboratory values, for example, it is impossible to tell whether a narrative description of a patient's function is truly accurate without independently examining the patient (see Chapter 4).

Using the data as a screen

Largely because of concerns about the risk adjustment, providers often view severity-adjusted information as a screening tool, highlighting areas that should be examined in greater detail, generally by the providers themselves. For example, following the first public release of the MedisGroups-based "Hospital Effectiveness Report" in Pennsylvania in June 1989, the Hospital Association of Pennsylvania cautioned:

> The council has required all hospitals to install a computerized screening program known as MedisGroups and to use this program to supply data the council reports as a measure of quality. MedisGroups was never designed to be used in this way. Rather, it is an internal screening device to be used by hospitals as part of their physician peer review program. MedisGroups flags cases which require further review by a hospital's peer review committee. The committee reviews the complete chart and determines if high quality care was provided. The system does not make such a determination and never was expected to make such a determination. (Hospital Association of Pennsylvania 1989)

Even the JCAHO's initiative to monitor outcomes is using the measurements primarily as screens to direct further analysis (Abramowitz 1991).

Anecdotal evidence from Orlando suggests that when the data are used internally to screen for areas to be investigated in greater depth, provider acceptance increases. For example, a general internist at the Orlando Regional Health System observed that when MedisGroups was first implemented, he and his colleagues were unhappy that their facility had high costs. "We could no longer blame it on having sicker patients, because the figures were all severity-adjusted. So we had to do something, and we wanted it driven by doctors" (Clemens 1993). He credited the data with motivating changes that cut costs while maintaining quality, such as modifications in antibiotic prescribing. Some physicians had been "leery and paranoid and said 'This is none of your business,'" he recalled. "But most of them are now coming to us, asking about their six-month analysis. It's like a report card—they like to see how they're doing" (Clemens 1993).

In some instances, however, conflicts arise: Viewing these data only as a screen is distinctly different from the intentions of purchasers (see below). "My main concern with any system is people in the business environment may be tempted to pick a system and use it as the gold standard or final statement on the quality of care in a particular setting," observed a professor of health administration at the University of Iowa. "These systems should be used only to suggest areas of strengths and weaknesses. They are the first stage, not the final word" (Woolsey 1993c).

Reporting of results

Given their reservations about the quality and purpose of the data, many providers are concerned by what they perceive as sensational reporting of the results, without appropriate emphasis on their limitations (Topol and Califf 1994). Some differences across hospitals are striking, making for exciting news copy in what otherwise might be viewed as a tedious story. For example, the lead paragraph of a *Wall Street Journal* article accompanying the first release of three months' worth of MedisGroups-generated data for the Pittsburgh area stated, "Allegheny General Hospital in Pittsburgh charged an average of $95,185 to repair or replace a heart valve during a recent quarter. Across town, Mercy Hospital did the same procedure for $48,559" (Winslow 1990, B1). These charge figures were described as "average charges." The president of the Hospital Council of Western Pennsylvania argued that these average charge data had "very little use" because they were not adjusted for patient severity. Only in the second-to-last paragraph of a fairly lengthy article did a response appear from an Allegheny General Hospital spokesperson. He claimed that the $95,185 average charge figure included some exceedingly ill patients, such as one who died following 144 days in the hospital (Winslow 1990, B8).

Some report card producers chide doctors for being concerned about publicizing results; producers couch their rationale in the desire for improving quality. Providers are "reluctant to have information published on how they're doing because they're afraid of how it will be used," said Dr. Barbara DeBuono, New York's Commissioner of Health. "Of course, this is the same reason my seventh grader's school mails its report cards, rather than having them delivered by the students . . . We don't want to punish or embarrass anyone. We just want to see where improvements can be made" (Montague 1996).

J. William Thomas, a leading investigator of severity measures, shared concerns about publicizing report cards, observing, "The unfortunate thing is that after these figures are published in the newspaper, all of the cautions that may be incorporated in the original document are usually cast aside and the numbers are taken as facts" (Koska 1989). In California, the first release of comparative hospital outcomes data specifically advised readers to review the entire document, including the discussion of methodological limitations and the responses of individual hospitals. Of particular concern was whether the administrative data employed in the California study were sufficient for valid risk adjustment—obviously an arcane argument unlikely to capture public interest. With a society that receives its news largely as sound bites, it is unlikely that methodological complexities will be explored fully in most press reports.

Concerns of providers about reporting of outcomes may not be limited to the press. As described above, Pennsylvania's highly publicized consumers' guide for CABG surgery is published in three slender volumes, with hospitals' and physicians' comments relegated to a separate volume that is not routinely distributed. Under the tables summarizing the provider-specific results in the main volume is a note in small print: "Hospitals and Physicians may have commented on this report. Copies are available upon request." It is unclear whether people take the comments of providers seriously, especially those with worse outcomes than expected. For example, as described above, HUP's executive director attempted to highlight problems with the PHC4 methodology that could explain why his facility had more deaths than expected. Were his comments just "sour grapes"? Some take the PHC4 HUP at face value. "It explodes the notion that you have to go to the highest-cost places to get top-notch care," observed a PHC4 spokesperson. "It shows that high cost and quality don't necessarily correlate" (Priest 1992).

Some providers' first negative reactions to publicity are not sustained after the implications of the data are explored. For example, after initial release of surgeon-specific data prompted by the *Newsday* lawsuit, New York's Cardiac Advisory Committee advocated encrypting physician identifiers so that individual physicians' names would no longer be available. One year later, following compelling evidence of improvement in CABG outcomes statewide, the committee reversed this position and voted to support release of these data. Surgeons conceded that the publicity surrounding the data forced them to conduct a useful, albeit painful, introspection that sometimes improved practices. For example, at Winthrop University Hospital, the cardiac surgery service is "totally different than it was two years ago. And it all started with the state . . . The state system helped us intensify our own peer review process" (Oberman 1992, 1).

The rhetoric surrounding release of data worries some providers, especially if the claims do not appear supported by appropriate methodological rigor. For instance, in 1993, a New Jersey business-union coalition looked at 1990 Medicare mortality rates and announced that 48 New Jersey hospitals combined quality with low costs. The head of the Health Care Payers Coalition of New Jersey said he viewed the data "as a first step of comparing price and quality for hospitals" (United Press International 1993). However, few of the methodological limitations of this approach were addressed by the business group. Of concern was that no hospital in Newark, the state's largest city, were listed, neither were several other facilities known for high-technology, high-mortality care (such as burn care)—especially of younger patients (i.e., not Medicare beneficiaries). A representative of major academic institutions in New Jersey accused the group of inadequate adjustment for severity.

A related concern involves the timeliness of data publication. Data collection initiatives requiring primary data from medical records may be more clinically credible, but they also take longer than approaches using readily available administrative data (see Chapters 3 and 4). For example, the first publication of Pennsylvania data was much later than original deadlines. The initial public release of outcomes data in Cleveland occurred in April 1993 but reflected experiences from 1991 and 1992. Privately, local hospitals had preliminary numbers for some time, allowing some institutions to improve practices—an improvement not evident until the next report. "Our numbers have completely flipped around," noted a representative of one hospital that had a higher-than-expected ICU mortality rate. "The project did just what it is supposed to do: It helped us improve our patient service." Following retraining of ICU staff, the figures apparently improved, but this improvement was not publicly apparent until the next report (Mazzolini 1993).

Distinguishing individual problems from "systems" problems

One concern, especially about releasing physician-specific ratings, is that perceived problems will be attributed to individual physicians rather than to the systems of care within which they practice. From the consumer's point of view, this distinction may be spurious—consumers may argue that bad outcomes are bad outcomes, regardless of the culprit. But from the individual physician's perspective, pinpointing the source of the problem also identifies solutions. An example that exemplifies these arguments comes from New York.

On September 6, 1995, a front-page article in the *New York Times* published the names, photographs, and stories of the best- and worst-ranked cardiothoracic surgeons in the state (Bumiller 1995). Commenting on the state's report card, the best-ranked surgeon realistically observed, "I'm concerned about the predictability of it," and went on to credit his surgical team and hospital for his good results (Bumiller 1995, B2). The worst-ranked surgeon, in contrast, described his personal devastation. He reported leaving the operating room in terror after another critically ill patient had died before he could even start the surgery. " 'We've got to do something!' he recalls shouting in his anger at the system. 'They're going to pull my license if this continues' " (Bumiller 1995, A1). That year his risk-adjusted mortality rate was 7.4 percent compared to the state average of 2.99 percent.

However, St. Peter's Hospital in Albany—where he worked—was itself fearing imminent release of a report card that showed it to have the third-highest risk-adjusted mortality rate in the state (Dziuban et al. 1994). Despite doubts about the state's methodology and "initial polarization and resistance among the staff," an interdisciplinary team began to look at its data (Dziuban et al. 1994, 1872). After several false starts and dead ends, it finally honed in on the problem—gravely ill, unstable patients (such as the one who had died before surgery even began) were not being adequately stabilized preoperatively. The death rate at St. Peter's for gravely ill patients (those with AMI, shock, or unstable hemodynamics) was 30.9 percent, much above the state's average for such patients. The clinical teams changed preoperative care of these patients, such as instituting use of intraaortic balloon pumps. As a result, mortality rates fell dramatically.

And the St. Peter's surgeon with the worst rating in the state? Among his 245 bypasses tallied by New York state for 1994 and 1995, he had no deaths (Bumiller 1995, B2). "I want to tell the next poor guy at the bottom of the list not to panic," he observed.

External motivations and decisions

Business leaders are increasingly explicit about intentions to network with providers based on their risk-adjusted outcomes. Cincinnati exemplifies this strategy, where four large businesses basically dictated the measurement approach. According to one local business leader, "This is just the beginning. It will be a long-term process and the real savings will occur when we use the data to pick out the most efficient hospitals and add them to our existing networks or directly contract with them" (Woolsey 1993b). This intention obviously motivates provider responses. As the business leader further observed, "We are courted by hospitals and third parties like I've never experienced before" (Neus 1993). Business leaders are not the only ones who feel this way. As noted earlier, New York's former health commissioner Dr. Mark Chassin reportedly suggested linking reimbursement to results of the state's CABG and PTCA monitoring, rewarding hospitals with lower risk-adjusted mortality than the state average (Zinman 1993).

This linking may help purchasers and government save money, but some providers want the different parties to be honest about their motivations. Many providers feel that cost containment is the primary goal of businesses. As the chair of the Minnesota Medical Association's committee on quality assessment observed, "The primary motive behind the quality effort is cost containment. So the primary movers are the insurers, government, and the employers. I think they're giving a lot of lip service to quality, when its actually cost containment they're after" (Regan 1993). Providers are especially unhappy when business leaders imply that producing meaningful, risk-adjusted outcome information is simple. According to ethicist

Dr. Arthur Caplan, "I'm for it, and it's good, but it will take some effort. Let's not delude ourselves it will be like buying a car . . . It will be much more complicated" (Day 1993).

Providers are frustrated when they feel excluded from decisions regarding the externally imposed risk-adjustment methodology. An example is Iowa, where the preference of the business community for Medis-Groups was accepted over the alternative (the CSI) advocated by some providers. Several years later, this situation continued to rankle certain Iowa providers, prompting public displays of anger and frustration. "We're madder than hell that we had this crammed down our throats," the president of Iowa Methodist Medical Center was quoted as saying of the MedisGroups initiative (Resnick 1993, 51). The Iowa Hospital Association president reportedly viewed the MedisGroups information coming out of the state's initiative to be of "minimal" utility, calling it "gibberish" (Resnick 1993, 51). In Cincinnati, some providers hesitated to criticize the clinical merit of AIM for fear of alienating powerful business interests.

For risk-adjusted outcome data to be accepted, they must be perceived as fair and nonpunitive—or at least providing "due process" for those contesting findings. For example, Berwick and Wald (1990, 248) surveyed the opinions of leaders at 195 hospitals across the country about the HCFA mortality releases: 80 percent viewed the data as a fair to poor indicator of hospital performance, and 95 percent rated their usefulness to hospitals in improving quality as fair to poor. The researchers concluded:

> These survey results likely reflect the degree of fear abroad in the hospital community today—fear that overwhelms more constructive possible responses to these mortality data. This is a tough time to run a hospital; the executives facing the HCFA data may be thinking first of the fragility of their organizations and not of their long-range improvement. Their concerns about public reaction forestall the more subtle enterprise of using the data. (Berwick and Wald 1990, 249)

Many providers believe that the limitations of the data must be fully accepted by these external forces. "This is all first-generation stuff," noted a San Francisco physician. "It's like the first car built: You have to ask, 'Is this a good means of transportation given where I want to go?' " (Woolsey 1993c).

The "lamp post" effect

In "The Adventure of the Six Napoleons," Sherlock Holmes noticed that the criminal had daringly examined his booty several doors down from the burgled house rather than in front of a darkened, deserted structure closer to his crime. Inspector Lestrade was baffled, and when asked by Holmes for his explanation confessed "I give it up."

Holmes pointed to the street lamp above our heads.

"He could see what he was doing here, and he could not there. That was his reason."

Some are concerned that the consuming focus on report card measures will produce a "lamp post" effect. As the GAO described, "administrators will place all their organizations' resources in areas that are being measured. Areas that are not highlighted in report cards will be ignored" (1994a, 55). "If additional indicators of quality were assessed, hospitals would have less of an incentive to unduly focus on improving a single performance indicator, such as length of stay, to the potential neglect of other indicators" (GAO 1994b, 13). As one physician observed:

> Physicians are responsive to data because data allow them to judge whether they are doing a good job . . . Physicians are conditioned from early in their academic careers to respond to grades. Profiles and norms tap into that psychological framework. But, just as attention to achieving a good grade may distract the student from the real work of learning, attending to easily measured phenomena may divert physicians attention from things to which they should pay greater attention. (Povar 1995, JS67)

Another strategy for dealing with this is to rotate a battery of measures, so that different issues would be examined in different years. But this could be cumbersome and costly (Jost 1994), especially if it involves changing data collection protocols and retraining reviewers.

Fairness

The wide range of provider concerns boils down to questions of fairness—whether it is fair to judge provider performance, and act on those judgments, based on data that are as yet poorly understood.

> Physicians may be forgiven if they are dubious. They have heard it before. In the 1970s, peer review was supposed to improve the quality of care. In the 1980s, it was quality assurance. Quality improvement is the chosen phrase of this decade . . . In the 1990s we hear that marketplace competition will improve quality and that public "report cards" are the answer. (Chassin 1996, 1060)

The fairness of report cards containing average *charge* information has particularly concerned some providers in Pennsylvania, especially given the increasing use of negotiated prices. For example, hospital officials criticized a 1994 PHC4 report, saying that charge data are almost meaningless, given that insurance companies (and consumers) rarely pay actual charges. A spokesperson for the Hospital Association of Pennsylvania said that less than 10 percent of insurance companies pay full charges (Burling 1994). PHC4, however, views hospital charges as reflective of costs.

Many hospital performance reporting initiatives rely on severity adjustment using proprietary severity measures. Many are concerned about rhetoric that mixes the concepts of "severity" and "quality" (Kaple 1987; Aquilina, McLaughlin, and Levy 1988; Koska 1989). "It's important to note that what comes out of these systems are not absolute measures of quality," observed Dr. John T. Kelly, former director of the American Medical Association's office on quality measurement methods (Woolsey 1993c).

Many in the research community agree. "Measures of severity are in no way measures of quality," stated University of Michigan researcher J. William Thomas. He noted that scientific evidence is not yet available linking severity information to quality of care. He continued, "The data provided by severity of illness systems are useful internally for hospital management purposes. Used externally for viewing relative performance requires that the limitations of the data be kept in mind and interpreted cautiously" (Koska 1989). Despite these caveats, many providers understand that the handwriting is on the wall—there is no turning back from release of provider-specific risk-adjusted outcome information. They remain unconvinced, however, that this approach will save money while maintaining quality.

Purchasers' Perspectives

Purchasers—businesses and government—are universally motivated by concerns about what is being obtained for the ever-expanding healthcare dollar. Despite this unifying motivation, they do not speak with one voice when it comes to strategies for capturing and using risk-adjusted outcome information. As suggested by the preceding descriptions of different initiatives in this area, purchasers have adopted numerous stances on this issue. Nevertheless, the themes they address are often shared.

Need for data

Most purchasers agree that comparative data across providers are absolutely essential (Iglehart 1988). They echo the sentiments expressed by the president of the *Des Moines Register*. He claimed that, while not tied to a particular measurement approach, he was committed to holding hospitals accountable for what they do. "I have more information on the quality and cost of newsprint than I do on the quality and cost of the healthcare I buy," he stated. "Only when employers and consumers have this information can we start to make healthcare decisions based on something other than what the providers are inclined to tell us" (Resnick 1993, 52).

Other purchasers also view healthcare as yet another business that can be motivated (e.g., to improve, to cut costs) just as can other industries.

This is the position of the head of the Employers Association Buyers' Coalition, a group of 363 Minnesota companies. "Health care is just another product or service," he said. "Whatever quality measures you would like to see in other sectors, you need to see in healthcare. Once the information is out there, you will see that most providers will take steps to assure that they are viewed as a quality healthcare system" (Regan 1993).

In Florida, comparative performance data are viewed as central to market-based reform. After hospitals objected to the form and content of a draft performance report produced by the state, purchasers were concerned Florida's entire reform program could be jeopardized. "Many hospitals are afraid of public scrutiny—they are afraid of being held accountable in public," observed the former head of the Central Florida Health Care Coalition, an Orlando business alliance. "The data is [*sic*] the heart of this whole reform" (Oliver 1994b).

Risk-adjusted outcomes information could be used even more broadly than making purchasing agreements with hospitals. These data may drive hospital bond ratings and overall perceptions of financial health, as measured, for example, by Standard & Poor's Corporation and Moody's Investor Service (Oszustowics 1992). "This is the beginning of a very long term trend," observed the vice president for healthcare at Standard & Poor's (Winslow 1990). He justified using these data to assess hospitals' financial viability by noting that third party payors "are going to direct their subscribers to those facilities that provide the best outcome for the least cost."

Some data are better than none

Purchasers rarely argue with providers about the specifics of particular risk-adjustment strategies. They generally concede the data have flaws but argue that some data are better than none. "The data aren't perfect," said the executive director of the Pennsylvania Business Roundtable. "But you've got to start someplace" (Winslow 1990, B8). The manager of health benefits at Westinghouse Corporation in Pittsburgh concurred: "We've really got to start someplace. Most of the business leaders I talk to say they would rather have crude information than no information" (Twedt and Flaherty 1990, A7). The *Des Moines Register* president agreed, saying "While the MedisGroups information still isn't as specific and useful as we would like, it is certainly a step in the right direction" (Resnick 1993, 52).

Despite this, some business leaders have expressed caution in interpreting results, especially if they are based upon a short time period. For example, the first data release in the Pittsburgh area covered only three months as mandated by law, and PHC4 claimed that three months was long enough to spot the beginning of trends (Winslow 1990). But some business leaders demurred, saying more time was clearly needed before drawing conclusions. "I don't think anybody should make any significant decisions off this first report," said a Westinghouse health benefits manager (Winslow 1990, B8). Longer-term information, however, would be helpful for Westinghouse's purchasing decisions. Looking at changes in outcomes over time was advocated by Hershey Foods. "What the data indicates is there is a substantial difference in the marketplace with regard to outcomes," noted Hershey's director of employee benefits. "As it grows over time, the data will have more credibility and will be an even more valuable tool" (Zinman 1992).

Some business leaders advocate waiting to see how providers respond to the data, echoing a concern articulated by providers who wanted to make good-faith efforts to improve based on the information. For example, employers are only now beginning to use the data produced in Cleveland to determine hospital contracts. The question is when purchasers should make their move. "Some companies are ready to react fairly quickly," noted the executive director of the Health Action Council of Northeastern Ohio, a local business group. "But there is some worry that if they contract on the basis of this first report, they'll be surprised by data in the second report" (Mazzolini 1993).

Approach toward providers

Initiatives have varied in the approach of the purchasers toward providers. Contrary to the past, when healthcare delivery was viewed as a sacrosanct and untouchable, the tremendous costs and increasing number of providers demystified this system. Purchasers often now have the advantage. Some wield it toward providers in an explicitly directive fashion, while others have chosen a more collaborative route.

For example, the Cleveland program initially progressed fairly smoothly because business, hospital, and medical leaders were willing to get down "in the trenches" together, according to a professor of health policy at the University of Colorado (Kenkel 1991). The cooperative nature of the Cleveland activity and its effort to elicit local clinical input were notable, resulting in public praise by leaders representing a variety of perspectives. For instance, the chair of the Executive Council of the Greater Cleveland Hospital Association observed, "Cleveland is to be applauded for its leadership role in creating a cooperative community-based process to produce meaningful outcome data . . . The program provides hospitals with focused and very useful measurements against which to develop and implement total quality management improvement" (PR Newswire Association 1993a). The executive director of the Health Action Council of Northeast Ohio concurred, stating, "We have demonstrated to the community, and most importantly to ourselves, purchasers and providers, that we can work together in an atmosphere of candor, honesty and mutual respect" (PR Newswire Association 1993a).

Much of the decision about taking a collaborative approach may depend on the perceived urgency of the business community's need for information. Working together takes more time than imposing an approach. According to some observers, Cleveland's activities took longer than hoped because of the local desire for discussion and agreement. Other regions have agreed with this general need for collaboration. For example, a leader of the Houston business initiative conceded, "It has to be a partnership between business and hospitals. You can't just do it overnight" (Beachy 1992).

Some acknowledge that working together may be the best way to achieve a longer-term goal of better healthcare, which may require business concessions to providers in the way that data are displayed and released. According to the director of a coalition of 14 Minnesota companies, "You can generate a lot of fear if you start ranking physicians . . . It's hard to improve quality in an atmosphere of fear" (Regan 1993).

What purchasers want

Purchasers clearly want healthcare providers to measure their performance. Companies such as GTE and Xerox live by the credo "If you can't measure it, you can't manage it" (Freudenheim 1996, D5). Nonetheless, questions remain about whether this first generation of risk-adjustment tools will get purchasers where they really need to go. "Although the systems offer improved comparisons of mortality rates and length of hospital stays, many of the most meaningful patient outcomes for employers, such as functional status and time needed to return to work, are not documented by the systems" (USGAO 1994b, 6). As stated earlier, for most employed populations, hospitalizations are uncommon and deaths rare. Therefore, some business organizations advocate moving beyond this approach.

"Four years ago, we took a look at severity adjustment systems and made the decision that it would be too costly and too much of a burden on our employer members given what these systems yield," noted the executive director of the Health Care Purchasers Association (a coalition of 100 large Washington State employers). "Clearly we are interested in quality measures, but the systems measured organ failure," not such areas as immunization rates or other preventive services. She observed, "The bulk of our employees receive treatment in the outpatient area, so we wanted a system that measured outcomes in both arenas" (Woolsey 1993c).

Even if severity-adjusted outcomes are measured, many recognize that this is insufficient to contain costs—the goal of many purchasers. "The system itself won't lower healthcare costs," noted the manager of institutional contracting and payment at Minnesota Blue Cross/Blue Shield. "Clinical data is nothing more than data. It's of no use in a vacuum. Creative use of the data to change provider behavior is what leads to saving money" (Woolsey 1993c).

However, some already claim to be saving large sums. For example, 1994 data from Cleveland suggested that nearly $100 million has been saved in healthcare costs, without any decrease in quality (Mazzolini 1994). The report showed that death rates for certain conditions had dropped over the previous two years, while LOS had dropped by an average of almost a day. Purchasers were pleased. The director of the Health Action Council of Northeast Ohio, a business group of 90 companies, observed, "When you talk about what community market reform is supposed to do, this is it" (Mazzolini 1994).

Some providers use risk-adjusted outcomes information to attract purchasers or direct contracting arrangements. For example, the Park Nicollet Medical Center had 375 multispecialty physicians scattered around Minneapolis. To develop a direct-contracting provider network for self-insured employers, Park Nicollet first had to prove itself. It used MedisGroups data to compare outcomes of its physicians with those of doctors in Minnesota and nationwide, and, in both comparisons, Park Nicollet appeared very good (Clemens 1995). These comparative outcomes reports helped Park Nicollet get business.

News Media

The news media have become central players, both in forcing public release of comparative outcomes information and in commenting on provider performance demonstrated by the data. For example, HCFA's hospital mortality data were initially produced to help Medicare's PROs identify areas for improvement; they were released publicly only after a Freedom of Information Act request from the *New York Times* (Jencks 1996).

In some settings, the news media have assumed varying guises—ranging from investigative sleuth, to nagging irritant, to aggressive whistle-blower, to relentless consumer advocate. Nowhere has the media's role been so pivotal as in New York.

As described above, *Newsday* challenged New York's DOH to release surgeon-specific CABG mortality data under their state's Freedom of Information Act request. In granting *Newsday*'s request, state Supreme Court Justice H. Hughes reportedly rejected the state's argument that "the state must protect its citizens from their intellectual shortcomings by keeping from them information beyond their ability to comprehend. Following the department's position to its logical end, it appears that if members of the public were more intelligent it would be in the public's interest to disclose this information" (Zinman 1991, 37).

On June 4, 1992, the broadcast media joined the clamor when the American Broadcasting Company presented a segment entitled "Surgical Scorecards" on its *Primetime Live* news magazine. Host Diane Sawyer introduced the piece: "It's one of the quirks of human nature that most of us spend more time shopping for a car or VCR than choosing our doctors." The reporters interviewed several patients who had suffered poor outcomes from surgeons with bad ratings on the New York report card, eliciting the anticipated sentiment, "If only we had known. . . ." Then, a reporter posing as a prospective patient—but wired with a hidden camera and microphone—interviewed a poorly rated surgeon, asking him about his CABG volume and mortality rates. The surgeon's statements were inaccurate. The reporters then showed the surgeon's chief this videotaped interview, forcing the chief to admit the misrepresentations.

However, the concern is legitimate that reporters do not understand fully the underlying context and source—and thus inherent limitations—of the data. According to New York state officials:

> The initial press accounts disclosing the 1989 data were superficial and misleading, emphasizing numerical ranking of hospital performance. These news stories made differences between hospitals of a few 10ths of a percentage point appear important when the differences were not meaningful either statistically or clinically. The media failed to present the reason for the program's existence—namely, the need to provide comparative data on the performance of cardiac-surgery programs in order to spur efforts to improve the quality of care.
>
> Beginning in 1992, we made a major effort to educate members of the media. This effort was continuous and persistent . . . The majority of journalists responded positively. In the past several years, news stories have stressed how hospitals and surgeons have used the data to improve outcomes for their patients (Chassin, Hannan, and DeBuono 1996, 395).

For example, an editorial in the *New York Times* on September 7, 1995, observed, "New York State's annual report card for cardiac surgeons is clearly having beneficial effects . . . Such report cards are needed everywhere if . . . healthcare is to be driven by market forces" ("Rating the Surgeons" 1995, A26).

Educating the media has been central to the public dissemination strategy in the CHQC program and is credited with raising the level of the dialogue citywide about hospital quality. Two days before publishing their first hospital report card, California officials held a two-hour press briefing in Sacramento, attracting only 15 media representatives (Romano et al. 1995, 680). While most California newspapers printed stories based on the state's report, few appeared on the front page. Most were either neutral articles noting the report's publication or stories about a local hospital that did well.

One media commentator, however, questioned the value of media education, observing:

> Education may work in markets like Cleveland, but the press corps in Washington, New York, Chicago, and Los Angeles—places that set the national agenda—are different. I remember when the Health Care Financing Administration tried to precede the release of its mortality data with a day of media education. Most of the influential television types skipped the education . . . They then attended the press conference, did not listen to the caveats presented there, and asked questions that had already been answered. In any event, the persons who need educating the most may be the editors who decide the story's tone and where it is placed.
>
> [If you think that you] can even use the term *case mix* with the news media, [you've] been talking too much to the trade press . . . As a group, general reporters think they are math whizzes if they can figure out that "66.66 percent" is the same as "two thirds." (Millenson 1996, 28)

Sometimes, however, reporters become data analysts. In 1994, re-porters for the *Boston Globe*'s Spotlight Team acquired three years' worth of publicly available, computerized hospital discharge abstract data tapes from the state's Rate Setting Commission (Kong 1994b). They used the Refined-DRGs (R-DRGs) to perform risk stratification (see Chapter 1), but they did not adjust for patient age or other patient characteristics. They then published the names and death rates of ten hospitals that had death rates at least 30 percent over the state average. Given that their goal was examining mortality, the reporters' choice of R-DRGs was questionable: R-DRGs, designed to predict resource consumption, group all medical patients who died within two days of admission into their own category because of their relatively low costs. Therefore, using R-DRGs to predict death results in a virtual tautology. The reporters finessed this point by eliminating from their analysis all deaths within two days of hospitalization, stating that such patients "may have been so sick they would have died any-way" (Kong 1994b). Despite its flaws, the *Boston Globe* report card did prod a rather reluctant provider community to begin self-examination. A coalition of providers, insurers, and purchasers formed the Massachusetts Health Quality Partnership and explored various measurement options. The Partnership is starting with a study of patients' experiences with their hospital care using the Picker Institute survey; hospital participation is voluntary.

In the end, the media repeatedly reinforce the position that con-sumers' legitimate interest in full disclosure of comparative performance reports should outweigh providers' reservations. As one media analyst noted:

Unfortunately, almost all the discussion by providers about public data release has one element in common: whining. Report cards violate one of W. Edwards Deming's key principles of continuous quality improvement (CQI), providers invariably protest: you are supposed to "drive out fear." How can we expect innocent providers to join in CQI activities when they worry about being pilloried by the release of inaccurate, misleading, or confusing data to the untutored masses?

Drive out fear? How about driving out *my* fear each time I seek treatment from my profit-driven health maintenance organization, which has just signed up a joint venture consisting of a panic-stricken community hospital and a pampered group of physicians. . . . (Millenson 1996, 26–27)

Consumers

Empowering consumers to shop for value in healthcare is a driving—albeit untested—tenet of market-based reform (Jost 1994). Consumers are slowly but increasingly using report cards to guide their choices of providers. For example, the GAO interviewed consumers in Pennsylvania, California, and Minnesota who had explicitly requested provider report cards and found that the consumers valued the information in making purchasing decisions. These consumers reported that they preferred outcome to process information, and that they wanted standardized information that permits meaningful comparisons across providers (USGAO 1995). Nonetheless, apart from their media advocates, the consumer's voice is curiously absent from many of the public debates about monitoring risk-adjusted outcomes.

Often the rhetoric of purchasers conveys a sense that they are representing consumer's views. But if cost containment is a major goal of this activity, purchasers' first responsibility is to their pocketbook, not necessarily to consumers' interests. These concerns are reinforced by results of employer surveys such as the one by actuarial consultants William M. Mercer, which found that employers rate ease of access and cost before quality in choosing health plans for their employees (Moskowitz 1996). Some employers interviewed by the GAO asserted that their employees would neither understand nor use comparative data. As one manufacturing executive said,

I've been in healthcare benefits for 15 years. I don't know how to make the choice. What happens to poor Harry the Huffer working on the shop floor when you give him . . . the morbidity in this hospital is here, and you know the readmission rate is this, and the reinfection rate is this, and the guy says, "I don't know what I should do." Because what they do to our counselors is say, "I don't want to make choices." (USGAO 1995, 18)

Nonetheless, purchasers' and employees' views are not necessarily incompatible. One might argue that healthy employees are also more likely to be productive.

Exactly how and when consumers should use the report cards is sometimes unclear. For example, PHC4's report card comparing heart attack death rates is the only one in the country to include doctor-specific information. Is this information of interest to consumers? One study used focus groups and surveys to evaluate interest in 17 quality indicators. Hospital death rates after a heart attack were chosen as an important indicator by 39.4 percent of respondents; they gave them a mean (standard deviation) rating of 3.4 (1.3) on a 1 (least important) to 5 (most important) scale (Hibbard and Jewett 1996, 38). In contrast, mammography rates were chosen by 71.2 percent of respondents, and given a rating of 3.78. Comments about why "undesirable events" such as heart attack deaths were not rated as highly as others revealed consumer recognition of the need for risk adjustment. As one person said, "Maybe the patients who have complications after surgery are in bad shape before the surgery" (Hibbard and Jewett 1996, 43).

PHC4 recognizes that consumers would need to plan ahead to use information on heart attack death rates effectively. Even if hospitals vary in their risk-adjusted death rates, "if you're having a heart attack, the best decision is to get to the nearest hospital as soon as possible," said a PHC4 spokesperson. "That is not the time to start examining our report" (Twedt 1996). However, expecting the public to anticipate such events—and plan accordingly—seems unrealistic. Whether report cards are really intended for public consumption is sometimes unclear. One University of Florida researcher who worked with state officials on their 1996 hospital report card noted that it should not be the sole information used by consumers to choose hospitals. He acknowledged that "the way it is fashioned it is of use mainly to hospitals" (Galewitz 1996).

Data from New York state do not suggest that consumers are avoiding hospitals or surgeons with high risk-adjusted mortality, despite the prominent publicity afforded the CABG report cards. In 1989, the percentage of CABG surgeries performed at low and high outlier hospitals was 15.7 and 8.7 percent respectively; in 1992, comparable percentages were 16.3 and 9.1—barely a change (Hannan et al. 1994b, 1855). Findings by individual surgeon were similar. Therefore, no major shifts of patient volume from high to low outlier providers occurred from 1989 to 1992.

A few consumer-specific concerns have been raised, such as qualms about patient confidentiality when outcomes and severity data are released outside of the hospital (Koska 1992). Nevertheless, few groups specifically representing consumers have been involved in the methodological particulars of report card efforts. The spokesperson for the Consumer Coalition for Quality Health Care downplayed methodological reservations, observing, "We must not let the perfect get in the way of the good. Certainly consumers must understand the limitations of quality measures. But the complexities of outcome measurement, risk adjustment, data validation, and a dynamic and evolving medical knowledge base must not be used as an excuse to keep quality-based information and data in the closet" (Moskowitz 1996, 4).

States producing data also appear to be consumer advocates, but generally in the context of trying to change the healthcare delivery system. For example, Florida officials see comparative provider performance data as crucial to their reforms. The state delayed initial publication of its initial hospital consumer guide after hospitals challenged the numbers during a preview of the document in January 1994. But a state official observed, "If we are going to go ahead with the competitive, free-market approach, we need to empower consumers . . . We are going to move ahead with the consumer guides" (Oliver 1994c). The CHQC program makes its reports easily accessible to consumers. The 1994 report, for example, was available at local Rite Aid Pharmacies for $6 plus tax (Mazzolini 1994). Nonetheless, whether consumers can use report cards effectively to choose high-quality healthcare remains hotly debated (Jost 1994).

Where managed care heavily penetrates the market, a sense of irony emerges. This is especially true in California. One California professor of health policy and ethics observed, "I clearly believe people should have the information. But we're in a funny stage now where people will have less choice of the providers than they used to, but may have a chance to make better-informed decisions about those providers" (Olmos and Kristof 1994).

Avoiding high-risk patients

One of the most troubling consequences of publishing report cards—especially by individual doctor—is the possibility that providers will avoid high-risk patients. These patients are, by definition, more likely to suffer bad outcomes, thereby potentially decreasing their provider's performance. A mail survey of cardiologists (64 percent response rate) and cardiothoracic surgeons (74 percent response rate) in Pennsylvania contained worrisome warning signs (Schneider and Epstein 1996, 252). Most cardiologists said that it was "much more difficult" (18 percent) or "more difficult" (41 percent) to find a surgeon willing to operate than before PHC4's CABG report card. Similarly, 35 percent of cardiothoracic surgeons reported being "much less willing" and 28 percent were "less willing" to operate than before (Schneider and Epstein 1996, 255). California apparently decided to release data on CABG mortality by hospital but not by individual surgeon (Blumenthal and Epstein 1996).

Anecdotal information in New York suggested that certain high-risk patients were avoided by cardiothoracic surgeons. For example, several months after *Newsday*'s publication of surgeon-specific mortality rates, a plaintive op-ed piece appeared in the *New York Times* by a woman whose mother had had a heart attack and who apparently needed a CABG. The essay documented a five-day struggle to find a cardiothoracic surgeon willing to accept a high-risk case.

> We learned that in New York State the Department of Health scrutinizes a cardiac surgeon's rate of failure and success. A high incidence of mortality produces poor records. This information is then shared with the public. The state rating takes into account the degree of risk of patients going into surgery. But the public disclosure of a surgeon's record seems to have created skittishness to downright paranoia among doctors.
>
> "Don't you think that the chief of surgery would love to do this operation?" one doctor said. "He's a great surgeon but he's taken too many high-risk cases lately and has too many black marks on his name." Black mark is the doctor's code phrase for death. While the surgeons worried about black marks, my mother lay dying 20 feet down the hall in need of an operation that no one would perform. (Byer 1992, 23)

The mother eventually did receive a CABG and survived.

At least one New York hospital admitted rejecting high-risk patients, turning away 23 such patients specifically to improve its CABG outcomes (Oberman 1992). The institution's risk-adjusted mortality did fall, from 5.15 percent in 1989–1990 to 3.25 percent in 1991. "Previously we didn't want to shut the door on these patients who were willing to take the risk of surgery," a hospital representative stated. Although refusing to operate on high-risk patients may be medically appropriate, he observed, "What this really may be is a form of health care rationing."

However, this logic fails to grasp the purpose of risk adjustment: If appropriate risk adjustment is performed, it should control for higher numbers of deaths related specifically to treating sicker patients. Dr. Sidney Wolfe chided surgeons who criticized New York's risk-adjustment approach: "It shows they fail to believe or understand the whole process of risk adjustment . . . there is no advantage in taking low-risk patients because their condition is taken into consideration when a doctor's mortality rate is risk adjusted . . . It is also unethical for physicians to say they won't care for sick patients because they are worried about their mortality rates" (Zinman 1991, 35).

Another spokesperson for the hospital that turned patients away repeated concerns about the adequacy of the risk-adjustment methodology, saying, "We still think that there are many flaws in the methodology and that as a result the conclusions are often skewed . . . there is not sufficient weight given to certain kinds of high-risk conditions" (Lyall 1992). Nonetheless, state officials demonstrated that their risk-prediction model is well-calibrated, including at the upper end: For the group of patients at highest risk, 43.2 percent died compared to a predicted 48.1 percent (Chassin, Hannan, and DeBuono 1996, 396).

Quantifying whether high-risk patients are shunned by New York surgeons is hard. Omoigui and colleagues (1996) argued that patients from western New York were increasingly migrating out of state to the Cleveland Clinic for their CABG surgery. They bolstered this argument by observing that Cleveland Clinic bypass patients from New York had a higher prevalence of some cardiac risk factors and higher death rates than Ohio residents, and that referrals from New York had increased over time. However, the time frame used by Omoigui and collaborators as the post–report card period actually extended two years before a report card effect could have materialized, compromising one's ability to draw firm conclusions from this study (Chassin, Hannan, and DeBuono 1996).

A related concern involves avoiding uninsured patients. Hospitals admitting large numbers of uninsured patients often charge insured persons more to compensate for the loss, resulting in higher average charges and thus bad "cost" ratings on report cards. Ability to pay is not considered in risk adjusting charges. "Because performance measurement programs give hospitals an incentive to reduce their charges to compare more favorably on the systems' indicators, the programs also could create an unintended incentive to reduce services to patients without private insurance" (USGAO 1994b, 15).

More information is required about how patients and providers make individual care decisions using the risk-adjusted outcomes information. It is not even clear that this type of information (i.e., short-term mortality, LOS, hospitalization charges) reflects the primary concern of persons choosing healthcare providers. According to Dr. Robert Brook, one of the leading researchers of quality measures in the United States, three things matter to patients about healthcare services: "First, if you need it, you want it, but if it will hurt you without improving your health, you don't want it; second, you want it done well; and third, you want to be treated like a human being" (Freudenheim 1990). Jacqueline Kosecoff, another well-respected expert on quality measures, observed, "The important questions after a treatment are: Is the quality of your life better? Do you have more symptom-free days? Is your physical, mental and social functioning what it should be?" (Freudenheim 1990). It is unclear that the major initiatives described above are addressing these specific concerns.

Other Issues Raised by Performance Measurement

Choosing a Risk-Adjustment Methodology

One impediment to selecting a specific risk-adjustment approach is the relative dearth of independent, objective, comparative information about existing severity measures. Decision makers therefore often rely on the claims of the severity method's vendors or on data that they produce. Some severity vendors craft a carefully honed message, targeting the explicit needs of the business community. Sales are made less on the clinical content of the measure than on its perceived ability to address purchasers' concerns. In many instances, the single most important decision involves a choice between a measure based on available administrative data or one requiring new data collection from medical records. These two alternatives have very different implications for the cost of implementing the severity measure (see below) and for its clinical meaningfulness (see Chapters 3 and 4).

Questions about clinical content have played a critical role in some initiatives. Concern about the clinical validity has led to explicit trade-offs of time and expense versus acceptability to local providers. This was a particular issue in Cleveland and Colorado, where measures based on primary data were viewed as the only clinically credible option for quality assessment. In New York, much of the information came directly from the providers being evaluated, such as cardiothoracic surgeons or cardiac catheterization laboratories. Data elements were determined by a panel including physicians from several specialties.

Sometimes specific measures are enthusiastically endorsed by users in other regions. As described earlier, representatives of Hershey Foods were instrumental in bringing MedisGroups to the attention of the California business community. The bill submitted initially to the California Assembly stipulated adoption of PHC4's methodology if the state did not act by a specified date. This position supporting MedisGroups was viewed with great concern by many as being anticompetitive and as reflecting specific views of Hershey Foods, an entity from outside the state.

Many regions invite severity developers and vendors to speak or ask them to respond in writing to a series of questions. Some regions establish special commissions or panels to consider the severity issue. Representatives of these panels often express concern that the claims of the developers and vendors cannot be substantiated by an independent source. They are also discouraged by the lack of published literature on the performance of severity data for quality assessment.

In Washington, for example, the Foundation for Health Care Quality sponsored a comparative study of severity measures by conducting a literature review, contacting experts in the field, surveying vendors, and involving three expert panels (physicians, hospital managers, and purchasers). Each panel was given a series of prototype reports using severity information and then asked whether the reports would supply useful information concerning quality of care. "The Foundation Pilot Study findings cast grave doubt on the ability of any one system to be useful across a broad array of disease categories . . . None offer a comprehensive or proven system for quality assessment" (Jones, Schreiner, and LoGerfo 1989). Washington consequently deferred active consideration of a severity method for quality measurement.

One troubling issue involves vendors' reluctance to provide complete information concerning their method's logic, typically due to proprietary considerations. According to Dr. Robert Brook, "If I were a purchaser, I would look for a system that is in the public domain . . . Purchasers should have an absolute right to know what is in a severity adjustment model—that shouldn't be kept proprietary. It would be like saying, 'Take this drug to get better, but I'm not going to tell you its name or chemical compound' " (Woolsey 1993a). For example, when Pennsylvania first mandated Medis-Groups in 1986, its vendor, MediQual Systems, Inc., withheld the logic as a proprietary trade secret. The company later changed this policy, and the explicit logic of the new empirically derived version is available to purchasers of the measure.

Nevertheless, reservations about sweeping claims made by certain vendors and the lack of corroborating evidence have heightened skepticism about the utility of severity information among decision makers in some states.

Costs of Data

Collecting severity data adds to the administrative costs of the healthcare system. For several years, administrative expenses have been a lightning rod for concerns about how healthcare is administered in the United States. "We now spend in excess of 20 percent of our health-care costs, in excess of $150 to $180 billion a year, on administration of health care," observed the vice president of corporate personnel at General Motors. "Small employers are paying almost 40 percent of their premium in administrative costs. Our system is somewhat like a Dr. Seuss novel, where we've got people watching people who are watching the people who are watching the people" (Raphael and Goodaker 1993). Dr. Robert Brook reportedly projected that collecting comprehensive provider performance data could cost $1 to $5 billion annually (Connell 1993).

Few argue that the costs of reviewing an individual case using a severity measure represent a significant fraction of the hospital bill. For example, the percent of total hospital expenditures spent collecting MedisGroups data in Pennsylvania ranged from 0.36 percent at small rural hospitals to 0.27 percent at large urban institutions (USGAO 1994a, 21). Pennsylvania hospitals found MedisGroups "very costly and burdensome" at first, noted a Pennsylvania State University health administration professor. "But they really did recognize early on that it was to their benefit. If the state were to have discontinued the requirement, they probably would have kept it on because of the opportunity to do internal assessment" ("Pennsylvania: Business as Usual" 1995).

Obtaining more comprehensive data is undoubtedly more costly but perhaps necessary to capture important health concerns. For example, "A new version of HEDIS that assesses the quality of care for chronic conditions will be much more expensive to use than is HEDIS 2.5 [the older version]. We need to educate the public and other purchasers about the value of using more sophisticated and clinically meaningful measurement techniques" (Brook, McGlynn, and Cleary 1996, 969).

Nonetheless, the aggregate costs and the logistical demands of implementing severity measurement raise concerns, particularly among hospitals in areas requiring new data from the medical record. For example, noting that MedisGroups data cost Iowa hospitals $2.5 million annually, the state abandoned this mandate, arguing that neither consumers nor purchasers used the data anyway ("Iowa: Classic Test of a Future Concept" 1995). Kentucky hospitals supported their state's notion of a health data commission but were concerned about the practical implications of data requirements. "I'm clearly concerned we don't end up with an administrative nightmare," said the director of Suburban Medical Center (Benmour 1993). Feasibility and cost issues have even dogged the JCAHO's effort to derive a more meaningful system for assessing hospitals. A 1991 report noted that, four years after announcing its Agenda for Change, the JCAHO was only starting to test its new outcome measures (Abramowitz 1991). One of the limiting factors had been the tremendous cost of collecting the required information, especially in hospitals that had rudimentary computerized information systems. Medicare's peer review program retreated from requiring widespread use of the Uniform Clinical Data Set, with its 1,800 data elements, because it was viewed as overly burdensome (Gardner 1993a).

Concerns about data costs are the major impetus for choosing severity measures based on existing administrative data, as in Illinois. "We had intended to do a lot of quality measurement, but our budget got whacked 55 percent," stated the executive director of the Illinois Health Care Cost Containment Board. "Our problems are probably typical of other health data organizations. As you achieve maturity and begin to do things that annoy power groups, you risk getting your budget cut. We need to establish a revenue base for our organization that doesn't depend on the general revenue fund, because that pot's not going to grow and the type of thing we do is one of the first things cut when the state runs into budget problems" (Gardner 1993a).

Areas considering severity for analyzing cost information, such as California, Florida, Illinois, Ohio, and Utah, have generally focused on methods using secondary data, largely because of cost and potential burden on hospitals. Such states increasingly ask vendors of severity methods to analyze a test data set from the state using their severity software to allow state decision makers to evaluate relative performance of the different systems. An exception was a New Jersey study of the CSI (Averill et al. 1992), where extensive chart-based information was abstracted specifically to analyze resource consumption. However, cost of data was a major impediment to widespread implementation of the CSI.

Even in areas where primary data gathering is legislated, cost considerations can guide implementation of the mandate. Prompted by concerns about overburdening small hospitals, the Iowa and Colorado MedisGroups mandates required severity information only from hospitals with over 100 beds.

"Time and money are the major issues to discuss when you are deciding to buy a developed system or create one yourself with local providers and researchers," commented Dr. William Mohlenbrock, a developer of AIM (Woolsey 1993a). Florida's APR-DRG software cost from $2,500 to $13,800 per year depending on the hospital's volume (Gardner 1993b). However, others believe that the costs of data must be viewed against their benefits. A representative of the Orlando Regional Medical Center noted that its data collection cost about $600,000 per year (Greene 1993a), although he credited the data with helping the hospital save millions of dollars per year.

Nevertheless, the Iowa Hospital Association cited expense as one of the reasons for its request that the state abolish the MedisGroups mandate. The president of the Iowa Methodist Medical Center in Des Moines reported that the annual cost of MedisGroups to his facility was $400,000 more than the software previously used (Resnick 1993). Four new employees were hired to enter the MedisGroups data, and the hospital was required to pay whenever a customized report was requested. A purchaser group noted, however, that the cost of collecting MedisGroups data statewide (which they placed at $1.6 million) was 0.1 percent of the state's $1.9 billion annual hospital operating budget.

In Cleveland, an effort was made to convince hospitals that they would potentially benefit by paying for data collection. The annual cost of Cleveland's CHQC data was $3 million—$2.4 million incurred by hospitals and about $600,000 paid by businesses and foundation grants (PR Newswire Association 1993a)—an amount that was approximately on target with the planned $7 to $8 per discharge. According to the executive director of the Health Action Council of Northeast Ohio, "The glue that holds this project together and that has driven it from the beginning has been the commitment from businesses as represented by the CEOs to use the data. Their message to hospitals was, 'We're going to reward you for collecting this data.' That makes it all the more meaningful" (Kenkel 1991).

The unknown in this discussion of data costs is how soon electronic transmittal of severity data will become a reality. Computerized medical records and diagnostic test reports should streamline data flows and minimize the costs of this information. President Clinton's failed healthcare reform proposal specifically advocated eventual electronic transmission of data. Although electronic transmission would make it easier and less costly to monitor outcomes (Jones 1993), it is not clear when such a system will be implemented widely.

Even if hospitals can provide costly severity and outcomes information, a lingering question is whether they will have the resources to initiate the improvements based on the data. Quality improvements may cost rather than save money—not a reason to avoid improvements, but a potential expense that must be factored into the cost-quality equation. This concern has been raised in the context of JCAHO's initiative. "The hospitals are wary," commented a former leader of the American Hospital Association, about JCAHO activity. "They are understandably edgy about how well they are going to measure up. Will they have the resources to meet the standards?" (Abramowitz 1991). Dr. Brent James of Intermountain Health Care in Utah attempted to change physicians' behavior based on outcomes data concerning postoperative infection. He found that long-term savings could only be achieved after initial increases in costs. "I would go to an administrator and say, 'We have hard data on how to deal with deep postoperative wound infections. You'll save $750,000 a year, but only one fourth of that is immediate savings. You need to hire extra people, and it's going to reduce revenues.'" Administrators met James' requests less than enthusiastically. "We had a right good fight on our hands," James observed (Gardner 1992a).

Analytic Issues

As described in Chapter 10, to compare risk-adjusted outcomes one must use a variety of methodological techniques, many based on explicit statistical assumptions (e.g., concerning distribution of specific values within the patient sample). Despite increasing experience with such efforts, it is not always clear what statistical methods should be employed, but methodological choices could have an important effect on perceptions about whether a hospital is doing well or poorly. For example, as described earlier, the initial data releases by PHC4 judged the difference between actual and expected outcomes using a $P = 0.25$ significance level. Therefore, one-quarter of hospitals having outcomes similar to their expected range would be identified as outliers only by chance—not because their outcomes were truly different from what was expected. Remembering the cautions highlighted in Chapter 10 is therefore crucial when evaluating risk-adjusted outcomes comparisons.

Even if statistical methods are state-of-the-art, it is not always obvious what the risk-adjusted outcomes data mean about quality and efficiency of providers—the ultimate motivation behind producing these data (see Chapter 6). These questions about what the data mean are unlikely to be answered soon.

Conclusions

Common Themes

Several common threads emerge in attitudes of participants toward severity measurement. Purchasers in areas that are already examining risk-adjusted outcomes are often excited about the potential of this information to inform better decisions and generate significant cost savings. They believe that even if the data have drawbacks, some information is more useful than none. Others still struggle over the cost of the information and what it all means. Even in Pennsylvania, the first state to mandate large-scale outcomes monitoring, it is too soon to tell whether consumers value the information and whether it will lead not only to maintaining but actually improving quality of care.

Another recurring theme involves the different specific goals of the various constituencies within a region or state. Business coalitions are commonly arrayed against providers, with business representatives believing that it is possible to use risk-adjusted outcome data to quantify provider performance. In contrast, providers view the information as a screen to suggest areas that should be examined in greater detail for quality problems. These different perspectives sometimes lead to overt conflict between the two groups. This fundamental divergence in viewpoints about the utility of the information is difficult to resolve because it is founded on basic differences in understanding about healthcare quality measurement. In addition, little objective evidence exists about the actual practical usefulness of risk-adjusted outcomes information—its attributional validity (see Chapter 6).

The final common theme is that decisions, especially about a risk-adjustment method, are often made with little information. Therefore, many decisions are based on the hope and expectation, but not the certainty, that this information will address specific local needs. In some places, expectations are founded on the assertions of severity method vendors, raising concerns about objectivity of seemingly sweeping claims. This situation can result in decisions driven by subjective considerations, such as the general tenor of a vendor's marketing approach and claims, or fear of legal challenge to a decision. Some regions, such as California, Cleveland, and New York, circumvented this difficulty by developing their own "home grown" risk adjustors. While this approach enhances local acceptance, these activities are time consuming and expensive.

Policy Implications

As observed in Chapter 1, change in our healthcare system is increasingly fragmented into diverse regional marketplaces. Locally, competition is fierce among health plans and providers, with constant jockeying to achieve the market edge. This balkanization extends to quality measurement efforts, including comparisons of outcomes using various risk-adjustment methodologies. A bewildering array of reports are produced, even in neighboring cities. For example, in Ohio alone, Cleveland uses its own, home-grown risk adjustment (developed by Michael Pine & Associates); Cincinnati uses Iaméter's AIM; and the Dayton employer coalition chose MedStat's Disease Staging (Verna 1996). It is sobering to remember that our AHCPR-funded research study showed that perceptions of hospital performance may vary, depending on which severity measure is used for risk adjustment (see Table 6.6).

Without common methods, comparisons are meaningless. Calls are therefore increasing for national standards to enhance the consistency of quality measures and permit comparisons across regions. As a representative of a midsized manufacturing firm asserted, "The government should prescribe some standards and force providers to adhere to these standards in the publishing of information. The government should say, 'You're going to code this disease this way, and you do it consistently and uniformly' " (USGAO 1995, 17). Efforts such as HEDIS are beginning to standardize ratings nationwide, at least for health plans, but even the HEDIS initiative has its competitors (Iglehart 1996). For example, some observers are worried about both NCQA's HEDIS and FACCT placing dual data demands on health plans (Prager 1996b).

Nonetheless, experience suggests that local stakeholders in different marketplaces do differ in their interests and emphasis. As Dr. Arnold Epstein (1995, 60) observed, "A single national report card is not necessary and may be a mistake." Quality concerns in San Francisco, for example, may include a focus on AIDS care, while in Florida, targets of interest may include operations common among the elderly, such as cataract surgery (Epstein 1995). Achieving a balance between standardizing measures to facilitate widespread comparisons and customizing measures to address local needs is the current challenge.

However, even in regions with longer experience in this endeavor, two questions remain unanswered: What do risk-adjusted outcomes (mostly mortality rates) mean about the quality of care; and What is the aggregate effect of these initiatives on total healthcare costs? As the GAO observed, the staples of most hospital reports (mortality and length of stay) "are considered too narrow to truly reflect quality" (USGAO 1994b, 12); "some of the cost savings employers attribute to efficiency improvements in inpatient hospital care are partially offset by higher expenditures for ambulatory care" (USGAO 1994b, 9). This situation has not stopped purchasers from using report card findings. Nonetheless, it heightens concerns about balancing reservations about methodological limitations and data costs versus the need of purchasers to act. The dearth of objective independent information about the actual implications of most risk-adjusted outcome information suggests several factors that must be addressed.

First, the participants in this activity should understand that they are jointly entering a large, applied experiment. In an experiment—as opposed to an endeavor using well-accepted, rigorous methods with clearly understood benefits—evaluation is critical. Some initiatives have recognized this concern. For example, New York state officials made site visits to providers whose risk-adjusted mortality rates raised questions; California validated its data source. If providers and business coalitions jointly recognize the experimental nature of their undertaking, tensions between the two groups may lessen. It also would allow them to unify around the common objective of learning the value of severity-derived data for interpreting hospital cost and quality figures.

Second, as in all controversies, the participants in the discourse about severity-derived information must understand better the goals and concerns of the other sides. American business is often interested in quality from the standpoint of a competitive edge (Berwick and Knapp 1987). Providers, in turn, have spent decades debating what constitutes appropriate quality measures and continually return to difficulties capturing the complexities surrounding individual patients. This focus on the idiosyncracies of individual cases has led to a long history of rejecting any efforts at standardization in the patient care context—physicians typically do not believe that presentations of complex patients can be summarized in a single numeric score or category. In addition, limiting the outcomes to short-term mortality, LOS, and hospital charges neglects many outcomes (such as functional status and quality of life) that not only reflect the objectives of providers but also the goals of patients.

Providers could learn more about the desire of local businesses to quantify hospital quality, permitting more prudent, better-informed decisions—purchasers reasonably no longer accept vague promises about quality monitoring, without concrete evidence of its results. In turn, business leaders could explore the legitimate reservations of providers about the limitations of severity data and the outcomes that are being studied. Providers need to be intimately involved in selecting the risk adjustors, to ensure—at a minimum—face validity (see Chapter 6). This involvement is happening in some regions, such as Cleveland and New York, but not in others. Collecting severity-adjusted outcome information is one approach toward measuring quality, but there are others. Is focusing on severity the best method available, given local constraints and concerns? By working in concert, the common goal of improving quality and efficiency may be achieved, albeit perhaps not as quickly.

Third, given the uncertainty surrounding interpretation of much of these data, it is important to weigh what actions may reasonably be founded on this information. Purchasers' need to act aggressively to control costs must be balanced against what inferences about comparative provider performance the data realistically support. At a minimum, even if the breadth and quality of the severity data itself cannot be enhanced, it is appropriate to adopt statistically rigorous techniques to analyze it (see Chapter 10). For example, given concerns about the quality of its administrative data, California's first report card used conservative significance levels to avoid overcalling outlier providers; HCFA also used a cautious methodological approach in computing its hospital mortality statistics (see Chapter 10). Using the data to direct punitive actions against providers may not be indicated until it is clearer what the data mean. Even if the information appears methodologically sound, publicity surrounding release of provider-specific findings can have unfortunate consequences that must be monitored (e.g., cardiothoracic surgeons avoiding high-risk patients).

Fourth, in times of increasingly constrained resources, concerns about costs and trade-offs inevitably arise. Questions about spending large sums on severity measurement are increasingly debated across the country. This concern is particularly acute when hospitals do not even have resources to support operational quality assurance programs—or staff that can translate the risk-adjusted outcome information into actual improvements in care. Business leaders in particular, however, note that the cost of severity information is small compared to the total healthcare dollar. Plus, purchasers anticipate saving money by using these data to network or negotiate with providers. As funds become tighter, however, the debate about the appropriate level of expenditures for measuring hospital quality will escalate. The participants in this debate should understand clearly the costs and potential benefits of these specific data, relative to other needs and goals of the healthcare system.

Finally, the Institute of Medicine observed:

> The public interest is materially served when society is given as much information on costs, quality, and value for healthcare dollar expended as can be given accurately and provided with educational materials that aid interpretation of that information . . . Public disclosure is acceptable *only* when it: (1) involves information and analytic results that come from studies that have been well conducted, (2) is based on data that can be shown to be reliable and valid for the purposes intended, and (3) is accompanied by appropriate educational material. (Donaldson and Lohr 1994, 95)

While this proposal has a cool, scholarly tone, little in the current healthcare marketplace remains this detached. The use of report cards to direct purchasing decisions is likely to grow despite lingering questions about the methodological underpinnings and consequences of these efforts.

As suggested in Chapter 1, we are not the first to confront such issues and make these observations. Historical precedents anticipate precisely the controversies of our times about measuring provider performance and promoting change. Therefore, in conclusion to this chapter and book, the story about Florence Nightingale, William Farr, and hospital mortality statistics resumes (excerpted from Iezzoni 1996).

Epilogue: Nightingale, Farr, and Hospital Death Rates

As described in Chapter 1, Florence Nightingale published the third edition of her *Notes on Hospitals* in 1863, proposing reforms that she believed would improve the quality of hospitals and patient outcomes. To bolster her arguments about the direction of reforms, she included a table listing death rates at 106 hospitals in England from 1861 (Table 1.2). Nightingale drew attention to the startling mortality rates at 24 London hospitals:

> We have 24 London hospitals, affording a mortality of no less than 90.84 per cent., very nearly every bed yielding a death in the course of the year . . . Here we have at once a hospital problem demanding solution. . . .
>
> Facts such as these (and it is not the first time that they have been placed before the public) have sometimes raised grave doubts as to the advantages to be derived from hospitals at all, and have led many an one to think that in all probability a poor sufferer would have a much better chance of recovery if treated at home. (Nightingale 1863, 4)

Subtly embedded within Nightingale's commentary, although obvious from the table itself, is the method employed for calculating these death rates—a method that raises serious questions about interpreting these figures. Taken verbatim from William Farr's *24th Annual Report of the Registrar-General*, death rates were calculated as (total number of deaths at the hospital in 1861)/(number of patients at the hospital on April 8, 1861). Thus, the numerator reflected figures from an entire year, while the denominator encompassed a single day. Farr had calculated death rates per occupied hospital bed—or deaths per person year in-hospital—not death rates per total number of hospitalized patients. Not surprisingly, ostensible hospital death rates fell considerably when calculated as the annual number of deaths divided by the total number of inpatients treated during the year. Using this method, mortality rates for 1861 in the "general wards" at 14 London hospitals averaged 9.7% (Statistical Society 1865).

Cynical modern observers might think Farr and Nightingale intentionally skewed statistics to bolster political arguments. In the 1860s, however, little consensus existed on statistical techniques, let alone how to calculate hospital death rates. Victorian statisticians emphasized subject content rather than methods, accepting "men of little mathematical ability" into their field (Eyler 1979, 19). Modern standard statistical techniques and ways of thinking about error and uncertainty (see Chapters 8 through 10) were decades away.

Hospitals calculated death rates in different ways to suit their particular goals (Woodward 1974; Bristowe and Holmes 1864). The most effective way to modulate death rates involved changing specification of the numerators. As the 1863 Privy Council report noted:

William Farr

Courtesy of the Francis A. Countway Library of Medicine, Harvard University, Boston, Massachusetts.

> In the majority of hospitals, it is . . . the custom to reckon among their deaths those who have been brought dead to the institution; but there are many hospitals where such cases are not reckoned, and there are some indeed where even those who die within 24 hours are, on the ground that they were moribund at the time of admission, excluded from computation. (Bristowe and Holmes 1864, 527)

In addition, admission practices affected death rate comparisons between urban and provincial hospitals. Many provincial hospitals explicitly refused patients with phthisis (consumption), fevers, and the "dead or dying," whereas urban facilities accepted everyone. Urban facilities objected to comparisons with outlying hospitals that excluded such patients. As the 1846 Glasgow Royal Infirmary report stated, "The reception of moribund cases greatly swells the number of deaths recorded in the Hospital, and very materially increases the proportionate mortality thereby producing misconceptions in the public mind . . ." (Woodward 1974, 135).

Farr and Nightingale were criticized primarily because of their denominator. Nonetheless, in the mid-nineteenth century, some viewed the number of "deaths per bed" as a useful indicator of a hospital's productivity—another way of showing charitable donors that they were getting their money's worth.

Hospital mortality rates over 90 percent would prompt swift and vigorous outcries from today's newspapers and television. Review of indices to *The Times* from 1861 through 1865, however, found few articles about hospitals and none about controversies over Nightingale's book and hospital mortality statistics. Nevertheless, a raucous debate immediately erupted in the London *Medical Times and Gazette* and the *Lancet*, with men practicing at urban hospitals as the major critics (Eyler 1979).

An anonymous reviewer of *Notes on Hospitals* began, "It is sad to see a work of so much value—full of such useful information—disfigured by a few serious and elementary mistakes. Much as all Medical men must appreciate the philanthropic labour of its authoress, it is a false kindness to pass erroneous views without protest" (Anonymous 1864a, 129). The reviewer observed that, because the mortality rate table came from the Registrar-General, "perhaps Miss Nightingale can hardly be held responsible for it," but he nonetheless excoriated the methodology:

> The inmates of a single day are balanced with the deaths of a whole year, and no wonder the results are "striking enough." It is to be hoped there are valid reasons for giving to the world what seems to us a simple piece of arithmetical legerdemain. Surely it is the very essence of percentages and of averages (both, we believe, fruitful sources of error), that the figures dealt with should stand on one and the same bottom, and that deaths for one year should be compared with admissions or discharges for that period, and no other. There is something audacious in the last column of this table, where twenty-four London Hospitals are accredited with a "mortality per cent. on inmates" of

90.84. No doubt it will be said this is the quotient of the figures employed; but we entirely deny their validity and the accuracy of the impression thus conveyed. The problem as here put is exactly that so often asked of forward schoolboys—What is the quotient of a hundred apples divided by fifteen red herrings. (Anonymous 1864a, 129)

John Bristowe, a prominent London physician, slyly caricatured Farr's arithmetic choices, showing that hospital "recovery" rates calculated using Farr's methods would range from 899.5 to 953 percent (1864, 492). Timothy Holmes, a London surgeon, indicated that, by Farr's method, one hospital had a mortality rate of 130 percent (1864, 365)!

Another anonymous critic objected to the absence of risk adjustment, viewing comparisons between inner-city and rural hospitals as hopelessly flawed. "Any comparison which ignores the difference between the apple-cheeked farm-laborers who seek relief at Stoke Pogis (probably for rheumatism and sore legs), and the wizzened [*sic*], red-herring-like mechanics of Soho or Southwark, who comes from a London Hospital, is fallacious" (Anonymous 1864b, 187). Bristowe concurred, "Has Dr. Farr . . . really overlooked the differences in relative severity of cases admitted into his different classes of Hospitals, the different relative length of stay of their inmates, the different numbers of patients treated in them in relation to the numbers of constantly-occupied beds? Has he no suspicion that his death-rate is determined almost wholly by these causes?" (1864, 492).

Bristowe also questioned how the public would interpret Farr's death rates. "That Dr. Farr understands the mathematical meaning of his figures no one will doubt; but that the majority of his readers understand them neither in this sense nor in any other, and are utterly mislead by them, is certain" (1864, 491). Bristowe directly challenged the motivations of Farr and Nightingale, stating that when they "try to mislead others into the belief that the unhealthiness of Hospitals is in proportion to Dr. Farr's death-rates of Hospitals, we are bound to protest against the whole matter as an unfounded and mischievous delusion" (1864, 492).

Two weeks after the first review of *Notes on Hospitals*, the *Medical Times and Gazette* published Farr's response. He took exception to an anonymous reviewer "who could treat a lady roughly" (1864a, 186)—although he later accurately acknowledged that Nightingale was "well able to defend herself" (1864b, 421). Farr argued that, if hospitals would provide accurate figures concerning cases treated and died, few disputes would arise. In several back-and-forth rebuttals of his critiques over two months, Farr did not refute specific attacks on his calculation. Instead, he emphasized fundamental reservations about most death-rate calculations:

This [Farr's approach] is one method; there is another which is less correct, but more common. The deaths are divided by the mean number of cases admitted and discharged . . . The defect of this method lies in this: it does not take the element of time into account, which is important, as it so happens that cases are scarcely ever admitted as in-patients of Hospitals at their origin, and that many cases are discharged from Hospital before they have terminated. (1864a, 186)

Farr wanted to hold constant the window of observation, saying, for example, that it was unfair to compare death rates at St. Thomas's in London with an average inpatient stay of 39 days with rates at two Dublin hospitals with average stays of 27 days (1864a, 186). At least, Farr argued, his calculation was clear in exactly what it was observing.

At the end of the heated letter exchange between Farr and his critics, however, Bristowe made perhaps the key point: "If Dr. Farr had made his calculations about Hospitals in a tentative spirit, with the object of ascertaining whether they were likely to lead to any useful results, he would have acted in a way to which no exception could have been taken" (Bristowe 1864, 492).

One year later, when the Statistical Society, with Farr as treasurer, published hospital death rates for 1863, death rates were calculated as: annual deaths/(annual admissions + [patients at the beginning − those at the end of the year]) (Statistical Society 1865). The publication noted that hospital stays were very long, averaging 30 days for 14 London hospitals. Despite this methodological shift, Farr continued using statistics to urge reform, writing to Nightingale in 1864, "What are figures worth if they do no good to men's bodies or souls?" (Diamond and Stone 1981, 70).

References

Abramowitz, M. "Judging the Quality of Care: It's Not Easy for Consumers to Know How Good Their Hospitals Are," *Washington Post*, August 27, 1991, Health Section, Z10.

Anderson, J. 1994. "Report from the Field: Minnesota Blues' Program Ties Reimbursement to Outcomes." *Medical Outcomes & Guidelines Alert* 2 (16).

Angel, K. 1995. "Prepared Testimony of Kathleen Angel, Worldwide Manager, Corporate Benefits Digital Equipment Corporation on Behalf of the Corporate Health Care Reform Coalition on Effective Health Care Reform in a Changing Marketplace before the Labor and Human Resources Committee, United States Senate." *Federal News Service* (March 14).

Anonymous. "Reviews. Notes on Hospitals. By Florence Nightingale," *Medical Times and Gazette*, January 30, 1864a, 129–30.

———. "Untitled. Response to Letter by William Farr." *Medical Times and Gazette*, February 13, 1864b, 187–88.

Aquilina, D., B. McLaughlin, and S. Levy. 1988. "Using Severity Data to Measure Quality." *Business and Health* 5 (8): 40–42.

Ashbrook, P. 1995. "Cost Concerns, Rise in Elderly Population Fuels Home Care Boom." *Greater Cincinnati Business Record* 8 (11): 30.

Associated Press. "Health Care Report Card Raises Questions," *Sun Sentinel*, January 31, 1994, 21A.

Averill, R. F., T. E. McGuire, B. E. Manning, D. A. Fowler, S. D. Horn, P. S. Dickson, M. J. Coye, D. L. Knowlton, and J. A. Bender. 1992. "A Study of the Relationship Between Severity of Illness and Hospital Cost in New Jersey Hospitals." *HSR: Health Services Research* 27 (5): 587–606.

Beachy, D. "Easier Said Than Done: Cost-conscious Employer Coalitions Want Hospital Data on Cost and Quality of Care," *Houston Chronicle*, July 5, 1992, Business Section, 1.

Bellandi, D. "Guide Rates Suncoast Hospitals," *St. Petersburg Times*, June 8, 1994, 1B.

Benmour, E. 1993. "Commission to Collect Data on Health Costs." *Business Dateline* 9 (46): 1.

Berwick, D. M., and M. G. Knapp. 1987. "Theory and Practice for Measuring Health Care Quality." *Health Care Financing Review* Annual Supplement: 49–55.

Berwick, D. M., and D. L. Wald. 1990. "Hospital Leaders' Opinions of the HCFA Mortality Data." *Journal of the American Medical Association* 263 (2): 247–49.

Blumberg, M. S. 1987. "Comments on HCFA Hospital Death Rate Statistical Outliers." *HSR: Health Services Research* 21 (6): 715–39.

Blumenthal, D. 1996. "Quality of Health Care. Part 1: Quality of Care—What Is It?" *New England Journal of Medicine* 335 (12): 891–94.

Blumenthal, D., and A. M. Epstein. 1996. "Quality of Health Care. Part 6: The Role of Physicians in the Future of Quality Management." *New England Journal of Medicine* 335 (17): 1328–31.

Boodman, S. G. "Report Cards for Hospitals: Soon the Public Will Get a Peek at Them," *Washington Post*, December 6, 1994, Z7.

Bonfield, T. "Jewish Wants Public To Know the ABC's of Local Hospitals 'Report Card' a Bid to be More Attractive for Managed Care," *Cincinnati Enquirer*, April 13, 1995, AO1.

Borzo, G. 1996. "Iowa Delays, Scales Back Electronic Billing Plan." *American Medical News* 39 (28): 4–5.

Brinkley, J. "U.S. Releasing Lists of Hospitals with Abnormal Mortality Rates," *New York Times*, March 12, 1986, 1.

Bristowe, J. S., and T. Holmes. 1864. Report on the Hospitals of the United Kingdom. *Sixth Report of the Medical Officer of the Privy Council. 1863.* London: George E. Eyre and William Spottiswoode for Her Majesty's Stationery Office.

Bristowe, J. S. "Hospital Mortality," *Medical Times and Gazette*, April 30, 1864, 491–92.

Brook, R. H., E. A. McGlynn, and P. D. Cleary. 1996. "Quality of Health Care. Part 2: Measuring Quality of Care." *New England Journal of Medicine* 335 (13): 966–70.

Bumiller, E. "Death-Rate Rankings Shake New York Cardiac Surgeons," *New York Times*, September 6, 1995, A1.

Burling, S. "Hospital Fees Vary Widely, Study Finds an Analysis Was 'Mixed' on Quality of Care and Charges. It Evaluated Suburban Facilities in 1992," *Philadelphia Inquirer*, September 29, 1994, B02.

Byer, M. J. "Faint Hearts," *New York Times*, March 21, 1992, 23.

Chassin, M. R. 1996. "Quality of Health Care. Part 3: Improving the Quality of Care." *New England Journal of Medicine* 335 (14): 1060–63.

Chassin, M. R., E. L. Hannan, and B. A. DeBuono. 1996. "Benefits and Hazards of Reporting Medical Outcomes Publicly." *New England Journal of Medicine* 334 (6): 394–98.

Clemens, B. 1995. "Becoming the Middleman: Direct Contracting Can Be Done, but It Means Taking on Burdens Your Insurer Once Shouldered." *American Medical News* 38 (30): 15.

———. 1993. "Physicians, Hospitals Unite to Meet Reform Head-On." *American Medical News* 36 (22): 1, 7.

Codman, E. A. 1934. *The Shoulder: Rupture of the Supraspinatus Tendon and Other Lesions in or about the Subacromial Bursa.* Boston, MA: Thomas Todd Company.

Colorado Health Data Commission, Office of Public and Private Initiatives, Department of Health Care Policy and Financing. 1994. *Colorado Hospital Outcomes: Mortality, Length of Stay and Charges for Cardiovascular and Other Diseases, 1992. Main Report.* Denver, CO: Colorado Health Data Commission.

Connell, C. 1993. "Health Reformers Push for Report Cards on Care." *Associated Press* (July 29).

Cunningham, R. 1996. "Consumers Gaining Leverage in Quality Assessment Arena." *Medicine & Health Perspectives* 50 (25): 1–4.

Day, K. "Hastening Health Care's Consumer Era: An Industry Emerges to Collect, Compare Price and Quality Data," *Washington Post*, June 8, 1993, H1.

"Demise of Two State-run Commissions Signals Shift to Voluntary Initiatives in Data Collection." 1995. *State Health Watch* 2 (8): 4, 10.

Diamond, M., and M. Stone. 1981. "Nightingale on Quetelet. Part I. The Passionate Statistician." *Journal of the Royal Statistical Society* A. 144, Part 1: 66–79.

Donabedian, A. 1980. *Explorations in Quality Assessment and Monitoring. Volume 1. The Definition of Quality and Approaches to Its Assessment.* Ann Arbor, MI: Health Administration Press.

Donaldson, M. S., and K. N. Lohr. 1994. *Health Data in the Information Age. Use, Disclosure, and Privacy.* Washington, D.C.: National Academy Press.

Dubois, R. W. 1989. "Hospital Mortality as an Indicator of Quality." In *Providing Quality Care: The Challenge to Clinicians*, edited by N. Goldfield and D. B. Nash. Philadelphia, PA: American College of Physicians.

Dziuban, S. W., Jr., J. B. McIlduff, S. J. Miller, and R. H. DalCol. 1994. "How a New York Cardiac Surgery Program Uses Outcomes Data." *Annals of Thoracic Surgery* 58 (6): 1871–76.

Epstein, A. M. 1995. "Performance Reports on Quality—Prototypes, Problems, and Prospects." *New England Journal of Medicine* 333 (1): 57–61.

Eyler, J. M. 1979. *Victorian Social Medicine. The Ideas and Methods of William Farr.* Baltimore, MD: The Johns Hopkins University Press.

Farr, W. "Miss Nightingale's 'Notes on Hospitals'," *Medical Times and Gazette, Volume 1*, February 13, 1864a, 186–87.

———. 1864b. "Mortality in Hospitals." *Lancet* 1 (April 9): 420–22.

Fetter, R. B., Y. Shin, J. L. Freeman, R. F. Averill, and J. D. Thompson. 1980. "Case Mix Definition by Diagnosis Related Groups." *Medical Care* 18 (2): 1–53.

Freudenheim, M. "Quality of Care Being Measured," *New York Times*, June 5, 1990, D2.

———. "The Grading Becomes Stricter on H.M.O.s," *New York Times*, July 16, 1996, D1, D5.

Galewitz, P. "Long-Awaited Hospital 'Report Cards' Won't Satisfy All." *Palm Beach Post*, February 25, 1996, 1E.

Gardner, E. 1992a. "Putting Guidelines into Practice." *Modern Healthcare* 22 (36): 24–26.

———. 1992b. "Rochester, New York, Consortium Ends Outcomes Data Experiment." *Modern Healthcare* 22 (26): 30.

Gaul, G. M. "The Costs of Surgery Vary Greatly at Hospitals in Philadelphia, Study Shows," *Philadelphia Inquirer*, December 13, 1990, 1-A.

Giacomini, M., H. S. Luft, and J. C. Robinson. 1995. "Risk Adjusting Community Rated Health Plan Premiums: A Survey of Risk Assessment Literature and Policy Applications." *Annual Review of Public Health* 16: 401–30.

Goldfield, N. and P. Boland, eds. 1996. *Physician Profiling and Risk Adjustment.* Gaithersburg, MD: Aspen Publishers, Inc.

Green, J. and N. Wintfeld. 1995. "Report Cards on Cardiac Surgeons. Assessing New York State's Approach." *New England Journal of Medicine* 332 (18): 1229–32.

Greene, J. 1993a. "Employers Purchasing Alliance the Model for New Fla. System." *Modern Healthcare* 23 (31): 30.

———. 1993b. "Fla. Hospitals to Fight Plan's Rules." *Modern Healthcare* 23 (35): 6.

———. 1996. "Hospital Ratings Cause Uproar." *Modern Healthcare* 26 (14): 20.

Hannan, E. L., H. Kilburn, Jr., M. Racz, E. Shields, and M. R. Chassin. 1994a. "Improving the Outcomes of Coronary Artery Bypass Surgery in New York State." *Journal of the American Medical Association* 271 (10): 761–66.

Hannan, E. L., D. Kumar, M. Racz, A. L. Siu, and M. R. Chassin. 1994b. "New York State's Cardiac Surgery Reporting System: Four Years Later." *Annals of Thoracic Surgery* 58 (6): 1852–57.

Hannan, E. L., A. L. Siu, D. Kumar, H. Kilburn, Jr., and M. R. Chassin. 1995. "The Decline in Coronary Artery Bypass Graft Surgery Mortality in New York State. The Role of Surgeon Volume." *Journal of the American Medical Association* 273 (3): 209–13.

Hannan, E. L., D. T. Arani, L. W. Johnson, H. G. Kemp, Jr., and G. Lukacik. 1992a. "Percutaneous Transluminal Coronary Angioplasty in New York State: Risk Factors and Outcomes." *Journal of the American Medical Association* 268 (21): 3092–97.

Hannan, E. L., H. Kilburn, Jr., M. L. Lindsey, and R. Lewis. 1992b. "Clinical Versus Administrative Data Bases for CABG Surgery: Does It Matter?" *Medical Care* 30 (10): 892–907.

Hannan, E. L., H. Kilburn, Jr., J. F. O'Donnell, G. Lukacik, and E. P. Shields. 1990. "Adult Open Heart Surgery in New York State: An Analysis of Risk Factors and Hospital Mortality Rates." *Journal of the American Medical Association* 264 (21): 2768–74.

Harris, N. 1994. "How Hospitals Measure Up: Focusing on Ways to Evaluate Performance, Hospitals Are Following the Lead of Managed Care by Issuing Report Cards." *Business & Health* 12 (8): 20.

Hartman, S. E., D. B. Mukamel, and R. J. Panzer. 1990. "A Hospital Payment System with Incentives for Improvement in Quality of Care: First Lessons." *Quality Review Bulletin* 16 (7): 252–56.

Hawkes, J. "1st Consumer Guide to Hospitals Compares Costs, Results in Region," *Intelligencer Journal*, Lancaster, PA, June 1, 1989, 1.

Health Care Financing Administration (HCFA), Health Standards and Quality Bureau. "Request for Proposal: Cycle 4.0." (October 1, 1992).

Health Care Financing Administration (HCFA), Office of Research and Demonstrations. 1987. *Report to Congress: DRG Refinement: Outliers, Severity of Illness, and Intensity of Care.* Baltimore, MD: U.S. Department of Health and Human Services, HCFA Pub. No. 03254.

Hibbard, J. H., and J. J. Jewett. 1996. "What Type of Quality Information Do Consumers Want in a Health Care Report Card?" *Medical Care Research and Review* 53 (1): 28–47.

Holmes T. 1864. "Mortality in Hospitals." *Lancet* 1 (March 26): 365–66.

Hospital Association of Pennsylvania. 1989. *Statement of the Hospital Association of Pennsylvania on the Hospital Effectiveness Report Issued by the Pennsylvania Health Care Cost Containment Council.* Camp Hill, PA: Hospital Association of Pennsylvania.

"Hospital Report Cards." *Orlando Sentinel*, January 22, 1995, B3.

Iezzoni, L. I. 1996. "100 Apples Divided by 15 Red Herrings: A Cautionary Tale from the Mid-19th Century on Comparing Hospital Mortality Rates." *Annals of Internal Medicine* 124 (12): 1079–85.

———. 1993. "Monitoring Quality of Care: What Do We Need to Know?" *Inquiry* 30 (2): 112–14.

Iezzoni, L. I., and L. G. Greenberg. 1994. "Widespread Assessment of Risk-Adjusted Outcomes: Lessons from Local Initiatives." *Joint Commission Journal on Quality Improvement* 20 (6): 305–16.

Iezzoni, L. I., M. Shwartz, and J. Restuccia. 1991. "The Role of Severity Information in Health Policy Debates: A Survey of State and Regional Concerns." *Inquiry* 28 (2): 117–28.

Iglehart, J. K. 1994. "Health Care Reform: The States."*New England Journal of Medicine* 330 (1): 75–79.

———. 1996. "The National Committee for Quality Assurance." *New England Journal of Medicine* 335 (13): 995–99.

———. 1988. "Competition and the Pursuit of Quality: A Conversation with Walter McClure." *Health Affairs* 7 (1): 79–90.

"Iowa: Classic Test of a Future Concept." 1995. *Medical Outcomes & Guidelines Alert* 3 (8).

Jencks, S. F. 1995. "Changing Health Care Practices in Medicare's Health Care Quality Improvement Program." *Joint Commission Journal on Quality Improvement* 21 (7): 343–47.

———. 1996. "Public Disclosure: A Response from a HCFA Experience." In *Physician Profiling and Risk Adjustment*, edited by N. Goldfield and P. Boland. Gaithersburg, MD: Aspen Publishers, Inc.

Jencks, S. F., and G. R. Wilensky. 1992. "The Health Care Quality Improvement

Initiative. A New Approach to Quality Assurance in Medicare." *Journal of the American Medical Association* 268 (7): 900–3.

Jones, D. "EDI to Play Key Role in Clinton Health Reforms," *National Underwriter*, June 21, 1993, Life & Health/Financial Services edition, 26.

Jones, L., S. Schreiner, and J. LoGerfo. "Interpreting Severity Adjusted Quality Indicators." A report for the Foundation for Health Care Quality, Seattle, WA, (May 1989): 52.

Jost, T. S. 1994. "Health System Reform. Forward or Backward With Quality Oversight?" *Journal of the American Medical Association* 271 (19): 1508–11.

Kaple, J. G. 1987. "Using Severity Indices to Assess Quality of Care." *Business and Health* 4 (10): 23–25, 28.

Kenkel, P. 1991. "6 New Orleans-Area Hospitals to Take Part in Study." *Modern Healthcare* 21 (33): 12.

———. 1993. "Projects Serving Up a Data Smorgasbord." *Modern Healthcare* 23 (15): 43, 48–51.

Khuri, S. F., J. Daley, W. G. Henderson, G. Barbour, P. Lowry, G. Irvin, J. Gibbs, F. Grover, K. E. Hammermeister, J. F. Stremple, J. B. Aust, J. Demakis, D. Deykin, and G. McDonald, and the Participants in the National Veterans Administration Surgical Risk Study. 1995. "The National Veterans Administration Surgical Risk Study: Risk Adjustment for the Comparative Assessment of the Quality of Surgical Care." *Journal of the American College of Surgeons* 180 (5): 519–31.

Kong, D. "Public Gets Access to Hospital Reviews; Plan Lifts Accreditation Secrecy," *Boston Globe*, November 10, 1994a, 1.

———. "High Hospital Death Rates." *Boston Globe*, October 3, 1994b, 1, 6, 7.

Koska, M. 1989. "Are Severity Data an Effective Consumer Tool?" *Journal of the American Hospital Association* 63 (16): 24.

———. 1992. "Outcomes Research: Hospitals Face Confidentiality Concerns." *Journal of the American Hospital Association* 1 (1): 32.

Landry, S. "Hospital Report Cards May Prove Confusing," *St. Petersburg Times*, December 10, 1994, 1B.

Leavenworth, G. 1995. "Direct Contracting; Employers and Hospitals." *Business & Health* 13 (2): 31.

Lohr, K. N., ed. 1990. *Medicare: A Strategy for Quality Assurance.* Volume I. Washington, D.C.: National Academy Press.

Lyall, S. "Heart-Bypass Survival Rates Up in New York, Study Says," *New York Times*, December 9, 1992.

Mazzolini, J. "Hospitals Cut Costs; Quality is Stable," *Plain Dealer*, December 8, 1994, 1A.

———. "Area Businesses to Give Hospital Contracts Based on Performance," *Plain Dealer*, May 17, 1996, 1A.

———. "Report Grades Cleveland Hospitals: Businesses Hope Innovative Plan Will Keep Costs Down, Improve Quality," *Plain Dealer*, April 29, 1993, 1A.

Millenson, M. L. 1996. "Public Disclosure: A Media Perspective." In *Physician Profiling and Risk Adjustment*, edited by N. Goldfield and P. Boland. Gaithersburg, MD: Aspen Publishers, Inc.

Montague, J. 1996. "Report Card Daze: Published Ratings of Physician Performance." *Hospitals and Health Networks* 70 (1): 33.

Moskowitz, D. 1996. "NCQA: Setting the Standard in Setting the Standards." *Medicine & Health Perspectives* 50 (35): 1–4.

Mullen, P. 1990. "Hospitals, Payers Grapple on Data Bill." *Healthweek* 4 (11): 1.

National Committee for Quality Assurance, Committee on Performance Measurement. 1996. *HEDIS 3.0: Health Plan Employer Data and Information Set.* Washington, D.C.: National Committee for Quality Assurance.

Neus, E. 1993. "In Cincinnati: Big Firms Set Health Care Rules." *Gannett News Service* (September 8).

"New York Requires Public Hospital Report Cards by 1998." 1996. *American Medical News* 39 (38): 12.

Nightingale, F. *Notes on Hospitals*, 3rd Ed. London: Longman, Green, Longman, Roberts, and Green, 1863.

Oberman, L. 1992. "Valuable Input? Risk-Adjusted Data Credited for Better Outcomes." *American Medical News* 35 (48): 1, 24.

———. 1993. "Dishing the Data: Joint Commission to Detail Performance of Health Facilities." *American Medical News* 36 (22): 2.

O'Connor, G. T., S. K. Plume, E. M. Olmstead, L. H. Coffin, J. R. Morton, C. T. Maloney, E. R. Nowicki, J. F. Tryzelaar, F. Hernandez, L. Adrian, K. J. Casey, D. N. Soule, C. A. S. Marrin, W. C. Nugent, D. C. Charlesworth, R. Clough, S. Katz, B. J. Leavitt, and J. E. Wennberg for the Northern New England Cardiovascular Disease Study Group. 1991. "A Regional Prospective Study of In-Hospital Mortality Associated with Coronary Artery Bypass Grafting." *Journal of the American Medical Association* 266 (6): 803–9.

O'Connor, G. T., S. K. Plume, E. M. Olmstead, L. H. Coffin, J. R. Morton, C. T. Maloney, E. R. Nowicki, D. G. Levy, J. F. Tryzelaar, F. Hernandez, Jr., L. Adrian, K. J. Casey, D. Bundy, D. N. Soule, C. A. S. Marrin, W. C. Nugent, D. C. Charlesworth, R. Clough, S. Katz, B. J. Leavitt, and J. E. Wennberg for the Northern New England Cardiovascular Disease Study Group. 1992. "Multivariate Prediction of In-Hospital Mortality Associated with Coronary Artery Bypass Graft Surgery." *Circulation* 85 (6): 2110–18.

O'Connor, G. T., S. K. Plume, E. M. Olmstead, J. R. Morton, C. T. Maloney, W. C. Nugent, F. Hernandez, Jr., R. Clough, B. J. Leavitt, L. H. Coffin, C. A. S. Marrin, D. Wennberg, J. D. Birkmeyer, D. C. Charlesworth, D. J. Malenka, H. B. Quinton, and J. F. Kasper for the Northern New England Cardiovascular Disease Study Group. 1996. "A Regional Intervention to Improve the Hospital Mortality Associated with Coronary Artery Bypass Graft Surgery." *Journal of the American Medical Association* 275 (11): 841–46.

O'Leary, D. S. 1993. "The Measurement Mandate: Report Card Day is Coming." *Joint Commission Journal on Quality Improvement* 19 (11): 487–91.

Oliver, M. "Hospital Guide Lets Shoppers Shop Around. The Comparison of Costs for Medical Procedures is One Step Toward Health-Care Reform in Florida," *Orlando Sentinel*, June 9, 1994a, C1.

———. "Florida Hospitals Check Grades on 1st Report Cards." *Orlando Sentinel*, January 25, 1994b, A1.

————. "1st Version of Hospital Report Card Booed. Hospital Administrators Criticize the Attempt Up and Down the Line. State Officials Said They Will Press On," *Orlando Sentinel*, January 27, 1994c, B1.

————. "Columbia Park Won't Install Quality Monitor; the Hospital Company Says It Would Duplicate an Assessment System Already in Place," *Orlando Sentinel*, February 17, 1995, B1.

Olmos, D. R., and K. M. Kristof. "Informed Consent: Business, Consumers Are Getting Savvier About Choosing Health Plans," *Los Angeles Times*, October 16, 1994, D1.

Omoigui, N. A., D. P. Miller, K. J. Brown, K. Annan, D. Cosgrove, III, B. Lytle, F. Lop, and E. J. Topol. 1996. "Outmigration for Coronary Bypass Surgery in an Era of Public Dissemination of Clinical Outcomes." *Circulation* 93 (1): 27–33.

Oszustowics, R. 1992. "Quality of Care Emerges as a Determinant of Credit Worthiness." *Healthcare Financial* 46 (3): 48.

"Pennsylvania: Business As Usual." 1995. *Medical Outcomes & Guidelines Alert* 3 (8).

Pennsylvania Health Care Cost Containment Council. 1995. *A Consumer Guide to Coronary Artery Bypass Graft Surgery. Volume IV. 1993 Data*. Harrisburg, PA: Pennsylvania Health Care Cost Containment Council.

————. 1996. *Focus on Heart Attack in Western Pennsylvania. A 1993 Summary Report for Health Benefits Purchasers, Health Care Providers, Policy-makers, and Consumers*. Harrisburg, PA: Pennsylvania Health Care Cost Containment Council.

Podolsky, D., and K. T. Beddingfield. 1993. "America's Best Hospitals." *U.S. News and World Report* 115 (2): 66.

Povar, G. 1995. "Profiling and Performance Measures. What Are the Ethical Issues?" *Medical Care* 33 (1): JS60-JS68.

PR Newswire Association, Inc. 1993a. "Cleveland Health Quality Choice Releases First Hospital Quality Assessment Report." (April 28).

————. 1993b. "What About Quality of Care? National Survey Finds Americans Concerned about Health Care Quality." (September 14).

Prager, L. O. 1996a. "Quality Data Target Providers, Payers." *American Medical News* 39 (28): 1, 27.

————. 1996b. "As Pressure Grows, Plan Performance Measures Move Toward Outcomes." *American Medical News* 39 (25): 3, 30.

Priest, D. "Pennsylvania Rates Hospitals Surgeons on Heart Bypass Patient Deaths," *Washington Post*, November 20, 1992.

Prospective Payment Assessment Commission. 1993. *Report and Recommendations to the Congress, March 1, 1993*. Washington, D.C.: The Commission.

Raphael, S., and C. Goodaker. 1993. "The Health-Care Dilemma: How to Cut Costs While Keeping Quality." *Crain's Detroit Business* 9 (26): 17.

"Rating the Surgeons." *New York Times*, September 7, 1995, A26.

Regan, S. 1993. "Does the Quality of Health Care Justify Its Cost?" *Minneapolis–St. Paul City Business* 10 (51): 16.

Resnick, R. 1993. "Iowa Employers Defend Data Effort." *Business and Health* (July): 51–52.

Riley, K. "Quality Care Runs Off the Chart." *Washington Times*, March 14, 1993, C13.

Romano, P. S., A. Zach, H. S. Luft, J. Rainwater, L. L. Remy, and D. Campa. 1995. "The

California Hospital Outcomes Project: Using Administrative Data to Compare Hospital Performance." *Joint Commission Journal on Quality Improvement* 21 (12): 668–82.

Rounds, J. 1989. "Report Rates Medical Center." *Hershey Chronicle* 6 (3): 1.

Rubin, R. 1993. "The Local Alternative." *U.S. News and World Report* 115 (2): 76.

Schneider, E. C., and A. M. Epstein. 1996. "Influence of Cardiac-Surgery Performance Reports on Referral Practices and Access to Care. A Survey of Cardiovascular Specialists." *New England Journal of Medicine* 335 (4): 251–56.

Scott, L. 1994. "High Charges, Mortality Linked." *Modern Healthcare* 24 (32): 26.

Simmons, S. "A 'Snapshot' of City Hospital Services," *Philadelphia Daily News,* December 13, 1990, 47–48.

Sorelle, R. "Texas Firms Pledge $2 Billion to Support Health Care Measure: Bill Would Collect Price, Quality Data," *Houston Chronicle,* April 10, 1993, 24.

Statistical Society. 1865. "Statistics of Metropolitan and Provincial General Hospitals for 1863." *Journal of the Statistical Society of London* 28 (Part 4): 527–35.

Strickland, D. 1995. "Report from the Field: Cleveland Outcome Report Shows Steady Decline in Hospital Mortality." *Medical Outcomes & Guidelines Alert* 3 (2).

Sullivan, L. W., and G. R. Wilensky. 1991. *Medicare Hospital Mortality Information. 1987, 1988, 1989.* Washington, D.C.: U.S. Department of Health and Human Services, Health Care Financing Administration.

Swartz, K. 1995. "Reducing Risk Selection Requires More than Risk Adjustments." *Inquiry* 32 (1): 6–10.

Topol, E. J. and R. M. Califf. 1994. "Scorecard Cardiovascular Medicine. Its Impact and Future Directions." *Annals of Internal Medicine* 120 (1): 65–70.

Twedt, S. "Heart Report Hails AGH Success," *Pittsburgh Post-Gazette,* June 19, 1996, 1.

Twedt, S., and M. P. Flaherty. 1990. "Agency Formed to Contain Hospital Costs Is Big Spender," *Pittsburgh Press* 106 (285): A1, 6, 7.

"Two Local Hospitals Among Top Performers." *Cincinnati Post,* January 13, 1994, 13A.

"2 Local Hospitals on Nation's Top 100." *Los Angeles Times,* February 3, 1994, J6.

United Press International. 1993. "Coalition Recommends Forty-Eight New Jersey Hospitals for Value." (May 4).

United States General Accounting Office; Health, Education, and Human Services Division (USGAO). 1996. *Medicare. Federal Efforts to Enhance Patient Quality of Care.* (GAO/HEHS-96–20) Washington, D.C.: United States General Accounting Office.

———. 1995. *Employers and Individual Consumers Want Additional Information on Quality.* (GAO/HEHS-95–201) Washington, D.C.: United States General Accounting Office.

———. 1994a. *"Report Cards" Are Useful but Significant Issues Need to be Addressed.* (GAO/HEHS-94–219) Washington, D.C.: United States General Accounting Office.

———. 1994b. *Employers Urge Hospitals to Battle Costs Using Performance Data Sys-*

tems. (GAO/HEHS-95-1) Washington, D.C.: United States General Accounting Office.

Vanourny, S. E. 1989. "Comparison of MedisGroups and Computerized Severity Index at St. Luke's Hospital." Testimony before the Iowa Health Data Commission, June 16, Cedar Rapids, IA: St. Luke's Hospital.

Verna, G. 1996. "Dayton Hospitals Link to Perform Cost Study." *Cincinnati Business Courier* 13 (4): 8C.

Vladeck, B. C., E. J. Goodwin, L. P. Myers, and M. Sinisi. 1988. "Consumers and Hospital Use the HCFA 'Death List'." *Health Affairs* 7 (1): 122–25.

Vogel, R. A., and E. J. Topol. 1996. "Practice Guidelines and Physician Scorecards: Grading the Graders." *Cleveland Clinic Journal of Medicine* 63 (2): 124–28.

White House Domestic Policy Council. 1993. *Health Security: The President's Report to the American People.* Washington, D.C.: The Council.

Wilson, P., S. R. Smoley, and D. Werdegar. 1993. *Annual Report of the California Hospital Outcomes Project.* Sacramento, CA: Office of Statewide Health Planning and Development.

———. 1996. *Second Report of the California Hospital Outcomes Project. Acute Myocardial Infarction. Volume One: Study Overview and Results Summary.* Sacramento, CA: Office of Statewide Health Planning and Development.

Winslow, R. "Data Spur Debate on Hospital Quality," *Wall Street Journal,* May 24, 1990, B1, 8.

———. "Big Health Concerns Agree to Develop Data System to Gauge Quality of Care," *Wall Street Journal,* January 15, 1993a, B7.

———. "Network of Doctors to Market Heart Care for Set Fee, " *Wall Street Journal,* March 2, 1993b, B1.

Woodward, J. H. 1974. *To Do the Sick No Harm. A Study of the British Voluntary Hospital System to 1875.* London: Routledge & Kegan Paul.

Woolhandler, S., D. U. Himmelstein, and J. P. Lewontin. 1993. "Administrative Costs in U.S. Hospitals." *New England Journal of Medicine* 329 (6): 400–3.

Woolsey, C. "Buyer's Guide to Outcome Management Systems," *Business Insurance,* June 28, 1993a, 23.

———. "Cincinnati Employers Attain Goal of More Cost-Effective Health Care," *Business Insurance,* April 12, 1993b, 3.

———. "Outcome Measurements Raise Doubts," *Business Insurance,* June 28, 1993c, 1.

Yasuda, G. "Computing Health-Care Efficiency: Use of 'Practice Patterns' Divides Medical Community on Cost Issues," *Orlando Sentinel Tribune,* January 6, 1992, Business Section, 12.

Zinman, D. "Heart Surgeons Rated," *Newsday,* December 18, 1991, 3.

———. "A New Statistical Tool Called 'Outcome Analysis' Measures the Performance of Doctors and the Treatment They Prescribe," *Newsday,* January 21, 1992, 51.

———. "Standards Set for Heart Procedures: Outcomes Analysis Used to Assess Quality of Care by Hospitals, Surgeons," *Newsday,* January 19, 1993, 55.

Index

ACGs. *See* Ambulatory Care Groups

Activities of daily living (ADLs). *See* Functional status

Acuity Index Method (AIM): implementation in cities, 541–42; objectives of, 19; predicting cost with, 402, 403–04; scoring system, 25, 30, 394. *See also* Severity measurement systems

Acute clinical stability: as dimension of risk, 45, 46, 60–63, 291; measures of, 61

Acute myocardial infarction (AMI), 32; age/sex and, 52, 338; comorbidities and, 210, 211; cost prediction, 290, 398; under CSI, 119–24; under Disease Staging, 140–43; under Medicare, 17; under MedisGroups, 153–57; mortality prediction, 290, 308, 336, 347–51, 440; outcomes monitoring, 282, 357; outcomes prediction, 49, 62, 214, 262, 338–39; under PMCs, 165; severity of, 67, 68–69; time frame for risk adjustment, 291

Acute Physiology and Chronic Health Evaluation (APACHE): and acute clinical stability, 60, 61; age in, 47, 62, 311; Brier score, 459; comorbidities in, 62; cost prediction, 402; evolution of, 303; functional status and, 82; implementation in cities, 539–40; model building for, 289, 394; mortality prediction, 286–87, 347–51; outcomes prediction, 63, 262, 263, 338, 340; race/ethnicity and, 58; reliability of, 373–74, 383–85; risk factor selection, 53, 292–93, 300;

scoring system, 25, 29, 32, 288; treatment of missing values, 306–08; unit of analysis for, 25; validity of, 343–44, 345–46. *See also* Severity measurement systems

Acute Physiology Score, Simplified (SAPS II): outcomes prediction, 60-61

Administrative data, 169–234; diagnosis coding in, 193–220; procedure coding in, 220–23; reliability of, 366; research utility of, 184, 261, 262, 263, 265; structural attributes of, 223–26. *See also* Data; Discharge abstract data

Administrative data, sources of: federal government, 171–76, 180–82; hospital records, 171, 179–80, 226; private insurance, 182–83, 226, 230

Age: as dimension of risk, 45, 46, 47–52, 289; "oldest old", 51; as variable, 25, 52, 62, 262, 311

AHCPR: funding for research, 32, 169, 214; use of databases, 184

AIM. *See* Acuity Index Method

Algebra of effectiveness, 46

All Patient Refined Diagnosis-Related Groups (APR-DRGs): complexity classes, 25, 30; outcomes monitoring, 347–51, 530–31, 532, 538. *See also* Severity measurement systems

Ambulatory Care Groups (ACGs): age/sex in, 25; assignment to, 78, 395; measures of resource use, 282, 395. *See also* Severity measurement systems

American Hospital Association (AHA): annual survey, 28; coding guidelines, 194